Dictionary of Probation and Offender Management

Edited by

Rob Canton and David Hancock

WILLAN
PUBLISHING

Published by

Willan Publishing
Culmcott House
Mill Street, Uffculme
Cullompton, Devon
EX15 3AT, UK
Tel: +44(0)1884 840337
Fax: +44(0)1884 840251
e-mail: info@willanpublishing.co.uk
website: www.willanpublishing.co.uk

Published simultaneously in the USA and Canada by

Willan Publishing
c/o ISBS, 920 NE 58th Ave, Suite 300,
Portland, Oregon 97213-3786, USA
Tel: +001(0)503 287 3093
Fax: +001(0)503 280 8832
e-mail: info@isbs.com
website: www.isbs.com

First published 2007

Paperback
ISBN 978-1-84392-289-6

Hardback
ISBN 978-1-84392-290-2

British Library Cataloguing-in-Publication Data

A catalogue record for this book is available from the British Library

Project managed by Deer Park Productions, Tavistock, Devon
Typeset by Pantek Arts Ltd, Maidstone, Kent
Printed and bound by T.J. International Ltd, Padstow, Cornwall

Dictionary of Probation and Offender Management

To the memory of Bryan Taylor who, as probation officer, trainer and manager, minded about probation

Contents

List of entries ix
List of contributors xiii
About this book xvii
Acknowledgements xxi
Introduction and overview xxiii

Dictionary of Probation and Offender Management **1–335**

Appendix I: Abbreviations 337
Appendix II: Timeline 349
Appendix III: Concept maps 353
List of references 359
Index 381

List of entries

Accountability
Accredited programmes
Accredited programmes in common use
Actuarialism
Alcohol
Anti-discriminatory practice
Anti-social behaviour
Approved premises
ASPIRE
Assessment
Assessment instruments and systems
Association of Black Probation Officers (ABPO)
Association of Chief Officers of Probation (ACOP)
Asylum
Attendance centres
Attrition
Autism and Asperger syndrome

Bifurcation
Black and minority ethnic (BME) offenders
Borstal
Butler Trust

Carter Report
Case management
Case records
Central Council of Probation Committees (CCPC)
Chief officers
Child protection
Children and families of offenders
Children and Family Court Advisory Support Service (CAFCASS)
Citizenship
C-NOMIS
Cognitive-behavioural

Community
Community justice
Community order
Community penalties
Community safety
Complaints
Compliance
Conciliation
Conférence permanente européenne de la Probation (CEP)
Contestability
Correctional Services Accreditation Panel
Council of Europe
Court work
Crime and Disorder Reduction Partnerships
Crime prevention
Criminal careers
Criminal Justice Act 1991
Criminal Justice Act 2003
Criminal justice boards
Criminal justice system
Criminogenic needs
Criminology
Crown Prosecution Service (CPS)
Curfews
Custody Plus, Intermittent Custody and Custody Minus
Cycle of change

Dangerousness
Data Protection Act 1998
Day centres
Deportation
Desistance
Desistance studies vs. cognitive-behavioural therapies: which offers most hope for the long term?

Discretion
Diversity
Domestic violence
Drug action teams
Drug rehabilitation requirement
Drug treatment and testing orders
   (DTTOs)
Drugs
Drugs Intervention Programme
Dual diagnosis
Dyslexia

Education, Skills for Life
Effective practice
Electronic monitoring
Employment, Training and Education
   (ETE)
Enforcement
Estates strategy
Evaluation
Extended sentencing
External audit

Financial penalties
Freedom of Information Act 2000

Gender
Groupwork

Halliday Report
Hate crime
Heterosexism
HM Inspectorate of Probation
Home visits
Human rights

Information strategy
Information technology developments
   in areas
Inter-agency work
Internal audit
Interpreting and translation
Interventions

Judges

Learning disabilities
Learning styles

Legitimacy
Lesbians and Gay Men in Probation
   (LAGIP)
Licence
Lifers
Local authorities

Macpherson Report
Magistrates
Managerialism
Masculinity and offending
Mediation
Mentally disordered offenders
Ministry of Justice
Motivation
Motivational interviewing
Mubarek Inquiry
Multi-agency public protection
   arrangements (MAPPAs)

Napo
National Association of Asian Probation
   Staff (Naaps)
National Offender Management Service
   (NOMS)
National Probation Research and
   Information Exchange (NPRIE)
National Probation Service for England
   and Wales
National Standards

OASys Data Evaluation and Analysis
   Team (O-DEAT)
Offender Assessment System (OASys)
Offender management
Offender management as seen by other
   agencies
Offender perceptions
Older offenders

Parole Board
Partnerships
Penal policy
Performance management
Persistent and serious offenders
Personality disorder
Police
Populist punitiveness

Poverty
Practice development assessors
Pre-sentence report (PSR)
Prison
Prison probation teams
Prisons and Probation Ombudsman
Privatization
Probation
Probation Board for Northern Ireland
Probation board secretaries
Probation board treasurers
Probation boards
Probation Boards' Association (PBA)
Probation in Africa
Probation in Europe
Probation in the USA and Canada
Probation officers
Probation service officers
Probation training
Probation trusts
Probation values
Prolific and other priority offenders
Prosocial modelling
Psychopathy/psychopathic disorder
Public attitudes to probation
Public protection
Punishment (aims and justifications)
Punishment as communication
Punishment in the community

Race and racism
Racially motivated offenders
Reconviction
Regional offender managers (ROMs)
Regional training consortia
Rehabilitation
Reintegration
Remand services
Reparation
Research
Resettlement
Responsivity
Restorative justice
Risk assessment and risk management
Risk of harm
Risk principle
Risk society

Scotland: criminal justice social work
Scotland: youth justice
Scottish courts and sanctions
Section 90 and 91 offenders
Self-harm
Senior probation officers
Sentence plan
Sentencing Guidelines Council
Serious further offences
Sex offender treatment programmes
  (SOTPs)
Sex offenders
Social capital
Social exclusion
Social work
Solution-focused work
Staff supervision
Suicide
Supervision of offenders
Supporting People

Teamwork
Therapeutic community
Tracking
Transgender
Treatment manager
Triangle of offender needs

United Nations
Unpaid work

Victim awareness
Victim contact
Victims
Violent offenders
Volunteers

Welsh
Women offenders

Young offenders
Youth Justice Board (for England and
  Wales)
Youth offending teams

List of contributors

At this time of unprecedented change in the Probation Service and NOMS, a number of contributors have moved to different roles. This list shows the position they held at the time they composed their contribution.

Dr Jill Annison, University of Plymouth.
Judi Apiafi, Manager, Positive Action for Learning, Nottinghamshire Probation Area.
Anton Ashcroft, Chartered Consultant Forensic Psychologist.
Dr Roy Bailey, De Montfort University.
Lucy Baldwin, De Montfort University.
Bob Bearne, Leicestershire and Rutland Probation Area.
Hindpal Singh Bhui, HM Inspectorate of Prisons and University of Hertfordshire.
Dr Thilo Boeck, De Montfort University.
Professor Gwyneth Boswell, University of East Anglia.
Professor Anthony Bottoms, University of Cambridge.
Dr Denis Bracken, University of Manitoba.
Patricia Bradbury JP, Chair, West Mercia Probation Board.
Andrew Bridges, HM Chief Inspector of Probation.
Imogen Brown, Assistant Chief Officer, Information Services, West Yorkshire
    Probation Area.
Dr Ros Burnett, University of Oxford.
Professor Rob Canton, De Montfort University.
Sally Cherry, Midlands Consortium.
Alan Clark, Midlands Consortium and De Montfort University.
Ann Corsellis JP, Vice-chairman of Council, Chartered Institute of Linguists.
Francis Cowe, University of Wales, Newport.
Helen Dale, Co-chair, LAGIP.
Bill Daly, ACO Business Support, West Midlands Probation Area.
Dr Mia Debidin, Head of O-DEAT.
Professor James Dignan, University of Sheffield.
Jane Dominey, De Montfort University.
Professor Mark Drakeford, Cardiff University.
Professor Anthony Duff, University of Stirling.
Eunice Dunkley, General Secretary, National Association of Probation and Bail
    Hostels.
Pauline Durrance, Senior Research Officer, London Probation Area.
Tina Eadie, De Montfort University.
Louise Ehlers, Criminal Justice Initiative, Open Society Foundation for South Africa.
Dr Stephen Farrall, University of Keele.
Professor David Farrington, University of Cambridge.

David Faulkner, University of Oxford.

Kathy Ferguson, Senior Probation Officer, London Probation Area.

Kevin Fisher, Manager, Dyfed-Powys Drug Intervention Programme.

Harry Fletcher, Assistant General Secretary, Napo.

Ann Flintham JP, Communications Manager, Magistrates' Association.

Dr Loraine Gelsthorpe, University of Cambridge.

Ann Gerty, Victim Contact Co-ordinator, Nottinghamshire Probation Area.

Andy Gill, West Midlands Probation Area.

Alan Goode, Deputy Director of Offender Management, Nottinghamshire Probation Area.

Dr Steve Goode, Regional Offender Manager, West Midlands Region.

Dr Anthony Goodman, Middlesex University.

Hannah Goodman, De Montfort University.

Sarah Gore Langton, Business Manager, Probation Boards' Association.

Tony Grapes, Offender Management Unit, NOMS.

Nick Hammond, Diversity Implementation Officer, London Probation Area.

David Hancock, former Chief Officer, Nottinghamshire Probation Area.

Professor John Harding, former Chief Probation Officer, Inner London, Visiting Professor, Hertfordshire University.

Gill Henson, Chief Executive, SOVA.

Sarah Hilder, De Montfort University.

Andy Hill, De Montfort University.

Roger Hill, Director General, National Probation Service.

Jean Hine, De Montfort University.

Victoria Hodgett, Manager and Co-ordinator, Nottinghamshire MAPPA.

Liz Holden, Enforcement Implementation Manager, Performance and Improvement Directorate, NOMS.

Tony Holden, Holden McAllister Ltd.

Paul Holt, Assistant Chief Officer, Merseyside Probation Area.

Professor Mike Hough, King's College London.

Judy Hudson, De Montfort University.

Heather Jasper, Senior Probation Officer, Staffordshire Probation Area.

John Kay, former Assistant Chief Probation Officer, Nottinghamshire Probation Area.

Professor Hazel Kemshall, De Montfort University.

Brian Kerslake, Treasurer, South Yorkshire Probation Board.

Charlotte Knight, De Montfort University.

Christine Knott, National Offender Manager, NOMS.

Michael Lloyd, Training Consultant, former Senior Probation Officer, London Probation Area.

Professor Gill Mackenzie, former Chief Probation Officer, Gloucestershire, Visiting Professor, De Montfort University.

Karen MacLeod, Assistant Chief Officer, Nottinghamshire, currently on secondment to NOMS.

Ian Macnair, Midlands Consortium.

Professor George Mair, Liverpool John Moores University.

Shehzad Malik, Freelance Psychotherapist and Trainer (www.neuro-dynamics.co.uk).

Sarah Mann, Head of Interventions, National Probation Directorate.

Dr Greg Mantle, Anglia Ruskin University.

David Marley, Communications Manager, Crown Prosecution Service, Nottinghamshire.

Alan Martin, British Institute of Learning Disabilities.

Roger McGarva, Head of Regions and Performance Management Unit, National Probation Directorate.

Professor James McGuire, University of Liverpool.

Professor Gill McIvor, Lancaster University.

Judy McKnight, General Secretary, Napo.

Fergus McNeill, Universities of Glasgow and Strathclyde.

Jo Mead, Community Commissioning Manager, East Midlands ROM Office.

Professor David Middleton, Visiting Professor, De Montfort University.

Dr John Milton, Consultant Forensic Psychiatrist, Rampton Hospital.

Valari Mitchell-Clark, Chair, ABPO.

Dr Robin Moore, Senior Research Officer, NOMS.

Tim Morris, Head of Communications, Parole Board.

Una Mulrenan, Accommodation and Benefits Advice Service, Nottinghamshire Probation Area.

Steve Murphy, Regional Offender Manager, London Region.

National Autistic Society.

Professor Mike Nellis, University of Strathclyde.

Graham Nicholls, Chief Officer, Lincolnshire Probation Area.

Mike Octigan, West Midlands Probation Area and De Montfort University.

Dr Mark Oldfield, University of Kent.

Kaushika Patel, De Montfort University.

David Phillips, Sheffield Hallam University.

Professor Herschel Prins, Visiting Professor, University of Loughborough.

John Raine, Chair, Probation Boards' Association.

Professor John W. Raine, Institute of Local Government Studies, University of Birmingham.

Peter Ramell, Assistant Chief Inspector, HM Inspectorate of Probation.

Professor Peter Raynor, University of Wales, Swansea.

Dr Colin Roberts, University of Oxford.

Jenny Roberts, former Chief Probation Officer, Hereford and Worcester Probation Service.

Dr Gwen Robinson, University of Sheffield.

Mike Rose, Communications Manager, C-NOMIS team, NOMS.

Dr Judith Rumgay, London School of Economics.

Frances Rutter, Assistant Chief Probation Officer, Dyfed-Powys Probation Area.

James Sandham, Director, JP Partners, Oxford.

Ralph Sandland, University of Nottingham.

Katherine Savage, Publications Manager, Youth Justice Board for England and Wales.

Stephen Shaw, Prisons and Probation Ombudsman.

Gurdev Singh, Senior Probation Officer, Nottinghamshire Probation Area.

David Skidmore, Regional Manager for West Midlands, National Treatment Agency.

Michael Slade, Chair, NPRIE, and Information Manager, Derbyshire Probation Area.

Professor David Smith, University of Lancaster.

Graham Smith, Assurance and Audit Unit, Home Office.

Professor Roger Smith, De Montfort University.

Ann Snowden, Senior Probation Officer, HMP Whatton.

Jon Spencer, University of Manchester.

Stephen Stanley, Independent Consultant, former Head of Research, London Probation Area.

Richard Steer, Secretary, West Midlands Probation Board.

Nigel Stone, University of East Anglia.

Wendy Storer, Delivery Manager, Nottinghamshire Criminal Justice Board.

Dr Brian Stout, De Montfort University.

Carole Sutton, De Montfort University.

Justice Tankebe, University of Cambridge.

His Honour Judge Jonathan Teare, Nottingham Crown Court.

Jill Thomas, former Administrative Officer and Assistant General Secretary, ACOP.

Jo Thompson, Head of Pre and Post Release, Public Protection and Licensed Release Unit, NOMS.

Andrew Underdown, Probation Regional Manager, North West of England.

Dr Ira Unell, Senior Lecturer in Substance Misuse, Leicestershire Community Drug and Alcohol Services.

Dr Maurice Vanstone, University of Wales, Swansea.

Dr Azrini Wahidin, University of Central England.

John Walters, former Secretary General, CEP.

Michelle Walters, Midlands Consortium.

David Walton, former Chief Officer, Staffordshire Probation Area.

Dr Stuart Ware, Visiting Scholar at Sarum College, Salisbury.

Martin Wargent, Chief Executive, Probation Boards' Association.

Beth Weaver, University of Strathclyde.

Professor Peter Wedge, Emeritus, University of East Anglia.

Dr Sally Wentworth-James, Regional Resettlement Manager and National Lead – Older Offenders, NACRO.

Bill Weston, former Honorary and General Secretary, ACOP.

Carole Wham, Secretary to the Correctional Services Accreditation Panel.

Dick Whitfield, former Chief Probation Officer, Kent.

Bill Whyte, Criminal Justice Social Work Development Centre for Scotland.

Professor Brian Williams, late Professor in Community Justice and Victimology, De Montfort University.

Patrick Williams, Research and Evaluation Officer, Greater Manchester Probation Area.

Juliet Woodin, former Chair, Nottingham Drug Action Team.

Professor Anne Worrall, University of Keele.

Dr Joe Yates, De Montfort University.

About this book

This Dictionary has been compiled mainly for people already working – or perhaps contemplating a career – in the community justice sector, especially those with an interest in working constructively with offenders in the community to protect the public and to support rehabilitation. This includes current or future probation service staff, itself an increasingly diverse group, Probation Board members and staff in partner agencies. Those who might benefit from the information in this Dictionary are not confined to them: the not-for-profit sector and, nowadays, some organizations in the commercial sector need a sophisticated understanding of the terms discussed in this volume. It is also intended for further education and higher education students on community justice programmes and on criminology, applied criminology and criminal justice studies courses.

This Dictionary attempts to offer accessible and reliable definitions of key terms – concepts, ideas, institutions, legal and organizational arrangements – as well as challenges, methods and practices involved in working with offenders in the community.

It is a *Dictionary of Probation* because the Probation Service remains the principal agency with responsibility for this work. The volume accordingly includes accounts of the system of governance of the Probation Service and its constituent areas. With the creation of the National Service in 2001 – and as it is now subsumed into the National Offender Management Service – there have been many changes in organization, authority and responsibility – and no doubt there are many more to come.

The book is also a *Dictionary of Offender Management* because, with the emergence of the National Offender Management Service, integrating the Prison and Probation Services, new practice arrangements and working concepts are being introduced. Neither contemporary probation nor offender management can be understood without reference to the other, and this is the rationale for the volume.

As well as major organizational and structural change, in the past decade there have been many changes and innovations in how practitioners understand and undertake their work. The prominence of 'what works' introduced a set of new concepts and terms for describing offending behaviour and responding to it. Offender management – itself a new term and concept – has already begun to introduce new ideas and new ways of referring to established ones.

The sentences of the court, too, have changed in name and in substance. While the contemporary terminology is mostly used in this book (e.g. unpaid work, community order), sometimes the older – and indeed, more familiar – expressions may be found (community service/community punishment order, probation order). Sometimes these differences have been allowed to stand: while there is a risk of inconsistency, it is instructive for readers to be conversant with the whole lexicon and to ponder the significance of the terminological changes. Such changes, after all, often represent different and contested understandings of practice. The contributors are distinguished and knowledgeable practitioners, managers and scholars. All were asked to think first about what a member of probation staff or student might most need to know about his or her topic. The contributions are intended to be reliable but also to stimulate further research, and each entry includes some 'Key texts and sources' to which reference can next be made.

Within this remit, we have encouraged contributors to express their own views in their own way. This approach can lead to inconsistency, but we see this diversity as a strength – and indeed as a reflection of probation's own rich diversity. In some areas, we have deliberately invited people with different points of view to write on similar topics to enable readers to form their own opinions and to recognize the complexity of some of these themes. Part of the discipline of working in an organization is to advance its policies, but practitioners will do this better – and, furthermore, contribute to the enhancement of these policies – if they have a critical and reflective understanding of their work.

Our contributors have been encouraged to express their opinions. Their opinions are, of course, theirs alone and no one here should be taken to be setting out the formal views of an organization. We have been concerned to find that some people who were invited to contribute were diffident, feeling constrained by their role in their organization. If it is indeed the case that some experienced, thoughtful and responsible managers feel worried about setting out a reliable and thought-provoking account of their work for fear that it may not be quite 'on message', then that would be very worrying. Politicians let us all down if they pretend that the many complex challenges with which criminal justice policy must engage are straightforward. Plainly they are not. All policy has drawbacks as well as strengths and, in a domain where policy has so often brought failure and disappointment, it is wasteful and perverse to suppress considered debate or discourage responsible and informed commentators from open discussion about future developments.

At the same time, many of our contributors work in the organizations they describe and, while their views remain theirs alone, their accounts sometimes reflect their belief in their work and their commitment to their organization. Our intention as editors has been to balance contributions as necessary with others expressing another point of view. Readers should therefore find information in the volume that will equip them to make their own judgements and to question the views of contributors.

It was a risk in preparing this book that the speed of new developments in probation and offender management would outpace our work. The division of the Home Office and the creation of a Ministry of Justice in May 2007 occurred too late in the publication process for all the references to the Home Office to be amended and replaced with an account of the new departmental arrangements. For that matter, some of these arrangements are themselves in transition. Readers will need to be aware, then, that Probation and NOMS are the responsibility of the new Ministry of Justice (which has an entry here) and to bear this in mind especially when there is a reference to the role of the Home Office.

The volume covers probation and offender management in England and Wales. There are entries about other UK jurisdictions and also contributions about practice in other parts of the world – partly to enable readers to understand that other countries and cultures approach things quite differently (though sometimes not so very differently) and partly for their intrinsic interest. International comparison enhances understanding of our own jurisdiction. Nevertheless there is no attempt here to claim that probation and offender management in other countries are adequately considered.

The 'Key texts and sources' point to the next destination for a reader interested to know more. The entries also often include 'Related entries' in the Dictionary itself. We have tried to choose (literally and figuratively) *accessible* sources and to avoid (say) too many papers in hard-to-obtain periodicals. We have in particular tried to make a great deal of use of the Internet. Sometimes a full web address has been provided, but it is recognized that it is tiresome to type long addresses into a browser, and readers will no doubt want to make use of a good search engine.

Generally, it may be helpful to state here that Acts of the UK Parliament can be accessed from **http://www.opsi.gov.uk/acts.htm**. The National Probation Service website (**http://www.probation. homeoffice.gov.uk/**) gives access to an enormous amount of policy and practice documents, including many probation circulars, as does the site of the National Offender Management Service (**http://www.noms. homeoffice.gov.uk/**). **http://www.probation2000.com/** is generally a useful resource and, in particular, can help to track down elusive circulars and documents. The Prison Service website is at **http://www.hmprisonservice.gov.uk** and is also valuable.

Other useful resources include **http://www.direct.gov.uk/CrimeJusticeAnd TheLaw/fs/en**, **www.crimeinfo.org.uk** and **http://www.homeoffice.gov.uk/rds/ pubsintro1.html** – where many of the publications of the Home Office Research Development and Statistics Directorate (RDS) are to be found. We understand that the Ministry of Justice website will in time accommodate the online resources of Probation and NOMS, but that the Home Office site will continue to run in parallel for the time being.

As probation reaches its centenary, rather than a telegram from the Queen, the service nervously awaits what may be less welcome and certainly less congratulatory correspondence from Her Majesty's government. The entries in this Dictionary will help staff and students of probation to make sense of the contemporary debates, to participate in them and perhaps even to contribute to shaping probation's future.

Rob Canton
David Hancock

Acknowledgements

The editors would like offer their thanks to all the contributors who were unfailingly good natured and professional in their response to requests to cover large subjects in unreasonably short compass. Very busy people made time to meet deadlines (well, mostly!). Books have been written (in not a few cases, by our contributors themselves) on some topics that are covered here in no more than a few hundred words. A number of referees commented on the original proposal and their advice was extremely helpful. Referees and contributors, as well as several friends and colleagues, made suggestions about which entries to include, and their ideas, even when not accepted, were always appreciated. Some contributors kindly introduced us to others.

Brian Willan has steered the project wisely and patiently from the beginning. Rob Canton would especially like to thank Brian Stout, Charlotte Knight, Tina Eadie, Sarah Hilder, Judy Hudson and Jean Hine for the very many ways in which they supported this project. Mike Nellis and Fergus McNeill also contributed sound advice and gave their time generously. He would also like to thank Liz, Matt, Phil and Rich for their patience and good humour. David Hancock is indebted to Gill Francis, Kirsty Lewis, Karen MacLeod, Tony Raban, Martin Ryder, David Skidmore, Liz Stafford and Jo Thompson for their willingness to give their time and advice generously.

One of our contributors, Brian Williams, Professor in Community Justice at De Montfort University, died while book was in production. His contribution to the study of victims' concerns, reparation and restorative justice was very considerable and he is a sad loss to the academic and probation communities as well as to his many friends, his colleagues and his family.

We dedicate this volume to the memory of our late friend and colleague, Bryan Taylor, who worked, as we both did, for the Nottinghamshire Probation Service for many years and then for the Midlands Consortium. As a practitioner, manager and trainer, Bryan made a huge contribution to probation in so many ways. We hope that he would have enjoyed a volume that tries to enhance the understanding and practice of work to which he was so committed.

Introduction and overview

A dictionary is (at least) a compendium of definitions. Is it possible to define 'probation' itself? Throughout its history, the Probation Service has undergone changes in organization and governance, changes in its tasks and responsibilities, in its methods of practice, in its stated objectives. But are there some characteristics that are fundamental and persistent and that *define* probation? This introductory essay explores this question and also attempts an overview to show how many of the key terms and concepts that are defined and discussed in the specific entries in this volume relate to one another.

Some account of probation's history is an instructive beginning.[1] Institutional arrangements and practices sometimes only make sense in historical perspective. An historical appreciation, moreover, is a reminder of *change* – that what now seems established and self-evident was not always so and will not necessarily be so in future. Again, as Nellis (2007) points out, we must understand – or construct – an understanding of probation's traditions, whether our intention is to reaffirm or to repudiate them. So inquiry into probation's history is an illuminating and instructive endeavour, not only for its own sake but also in the attempt to understand the dynamics of change; to appreciate (or to criticize) probation's contemporary position and significance; and to anticipate (and even, perhaps, to influence) its future.

PROBATION'S HISTORY: A CONVENTIONAL ACCOUNT

The year 2007 – one hundred years after the Probation of Offenders Act 1907 – is being widely celebrated as probation's centenary. Probation, however, like many other social institutions, has no determinable date of birth and, well before 1907, in different courts in the UK and elsewhere, offenders, instead of being fined or imprisoned, were being released on their promise of good behaviour or under the supervision of a responsible person (Bochel 1976; Raynor and Vanstone 2002). The 1907 Act, however, consolidated, reshaped and formalized these practices and, even though implementation was uneven and gradual, the Act, which famously enjoined probation officers to 'advise, assist and befriend' those under their supervision, merits the commemoration of its centenary.

Again, like almost all social institutions, probation has no simple origin but was shaped by complex social, moral, economic and political influences working sometimes together, but sometimes against each other (Garland 1985, 1990). A conventional and useful way of recounting its origins and subsequent developments is to distinguish a number of *phases*. A recent book offers this framework:

- saving offenders' souls by divine grace
- casework, diagnosis, rehabilitation and positivism

- collapse of the rehabilitative ideal
- alternatives to custody
- punishment in the community; penal pessimism
- punishment; renaissance of rehabilitation; evidence-based practice (Whitehead and Statham 2006).

A conventional account, then, is that, in its beginnings, probation was a moral enterprise, originating in the work of the Church of England Temperance Society's missionaries to the Police Court, with their strong Christian convictions and opposition to alcohol. While the need to defend the social order against the perceived threats of crime, indolence and intemperance was quite as influential in the origins of probation as the motivation to help or redeem offenders (Vanstone 2004), probation articulated its mission as helping the deserving to find redemption.

Whitehead and Statham (2006) quote extensively from a Police Court Mission report book, recounting the experiences of two probation officers in Sunderland (1918–1923), and draw attention to their explicit profession of their Christian faith. At the same time, they are sensitive to the economic hardships in their community, and their account testifies to very practical endeavours: providing clothing, for example, and finding employment for probationers. Theirs is a hard-headed Christianity that recognizes that, to walk the path to salvation, you need a pair of stout boots.

The instrument of change was principally the character of the probation officers – 'specially chosen men and women of strong character who could exercise good influence' (Home Office 1910) – through their *relationship* with the probationer. If probationers failed to take advantage of the opportunities afforded during this period of testing, this time 'on probation', they could be taken back to court for punishment.

In the next phase, religious accounts progressively gave way to an avowedly scientific understanding of human behaviour: 'The probation system in England was transformed from a service devoted to the saving of souls through divine grace to an agency concerned with the scientific assessment and treatment of offenders' (McWilliams 1986: 241). Human conduct has its causes, and the probation officer's task was to identify and address them. Psychological understandings of the mainsprings of human behaviour now informed the officer's work, and skilled method, more than the influence of personal character, came to be seen as the principal means of effecting change. The predominant technique was social casework, often with Freudian undertones, involving investigation, diagnosis and treatment.

In the conventional account, this 'treatment model' was the dominant paradigm for most of the middle years of the twentieth century and its abandonment precipitated probation's next 'phase'. The model came under attack:

- from the political left for its denial of the role of social injustice in the causes of crime through seeking explanation in terms of personal shortcoming;
- from the political right for its erosion of individual responsibility by claiming to find reasons for misbehaviour that were too readily seen as excuses;
- and, fatally it is said, from research that seemed to show that probation interventions did not 'work'.

This lead to a collapse of the rehabilitative ideal. The best probation could affirm was that it was no less effective than prison, that it was more humane and that it was cheaper. Its primary objective became the provision of alternatives to custody.

The expanding prison population continued to dominate policy. By the mid-1980s, the dilemma for the Conservative government was how to limit this expansion without compromising its claims to be the party of law and order. Punishment in the community was the preferred solution: punishment should be demanding, but could take place outside prison so long as community penalties were demanding and rigorously enforced. Probation was the agency to give this effect.

The aspiration that intervention could lead to change and reduce offending was reinvigorated, however, by research findings from Canada and the USA. These appeared to show that, if programmes were implemented as designed and targeted at the right offenders, a measurable reduction in reconvictions could be demonstrated. Effective practice should be 'evidence led' and responsive to the findings of research. Many new concepts and terms entered the probation vocabulary at that time, including the risk principle, the criminogenic needs principle and responsivity.

Some would propose another phase – public protection. The assessment and management of risk are contemporary probation's first priority. In this phase, too, emerges the concept of offender management. The offender manager is to co-ordinate and oversee a coherent set of interventions, provided by a range of specialized organizations and services to reduce offending.

PHASES: SOME CAUTIONS

The conventional account, then, is of a journey from 'advise, assist and befriend' to 'enforcement, rehabilitation and public protection' (Worrall and Hoy 2005) – a journey with discernible steps and identifiable milestones and turning points.

This schematic account provides a serviceable framework within which to locate developments in probation, but it has its limitations. A new phase never completely displaces its predecessor. Features of the earlier phases remain, often exerting a continuing influence on practice. Thus, probation's original overtly moral mission, more usually framed nowadays in secular language, has an abiding importance and an identifiable contemporary echo in the profession's affirmation of 'probation values'. Again, the recognition of the value of consistency, reliability and encouragement by the first officers is close to what is now called 'prosocial modelling', while the importance of the relationship in enabling change has been reaffirmed by contemporary research (Dowden and Andrews 2004).

Less obviously, phases sometimes *anticipate* their successors. For example, psychology, alongside eugenics and other 'social sciences', was an influence on probation's development well before the 'phase' of treatment (Garland 1985; Vanstone 2004). Again, the attempt to establish probation as an 'alternative to prison' is not something that can sensibly be confined to a single phase, but has been a near constant theme throughout probation's history.

Just as the steps are not so clearly demarcated, the turning points may not be as decisive as claimed. For example, the IMPACT studies of 1974 and 1978 and, above all, the 1974 findings of Martinson (crudely summarized as 'nothing works') are sometimes said to have presaged the end of the treatment phase (see Raynor and Vanstone 2002 for a summary of this research) and ushered in a period of penal pessimism. The case, however, can be overstated: it is to be noted that, in his major work, David Haxby makes no mention of Martinson and concludes his discussion of contemporary research: 'Certainly there is nothing in the IMPACT results which should deter probation officers from trying to develop a more varied range of methods of intervention' (1978: 220). Here the conventional narrative exaggerates the influence of research on penal policy – and, indeed, oversimplifies the relationship between research, policy and practice.

In practice, at a time when the conventional account would have it that the service was largely confining itself to providing alternatives to custody, probation officers were bringing energy and imagination to the development of creative ways of working with people. Particularly influential were Philip Priestley, James McGuire and their colleagues, whose work on social skills and personal problem-solving was widely adopted and applied to many types of offending. In a survey of contemporary practice, Despicht (1987) found that almost every service in the country was running one or more programmes that drew inspiration from this approach. Though the expression was less familiar at the time, these methods were unmistakably cognitive-behavioural: to this extent, the practice of the mid-1980s anticipated the 'what works' findings in the late 1990s (compare Vanstone 2000).

LIMITATIONS OF THE HISTORIES

An episodic history, then, calls attention to change and risks suppressing continuities that may be quite as significant. The changes in legislation, policy and research which the conventional history recounts are variably and contingently related to the realities of practice. A policy history, after all, is a history of aspiration, but some (perhaps many) of probation's aspirations have, notoriously, been confounded. Some historians (notably, McWilliams and Vanstone) have therefore tried to get closer to the practitioner experience – through court reports, case records and personal accounts. Raynor and Vanstone (2002) accordingly augment the history of policy and ideas with a set of 'practice paradigms'. Yet there are still other stories to be told.

The received history is assuredly never a history from the point of view of the probationer/ client/service user/offender. To a significant extent, these experiences are lost and unrecoverable, but they are a central part of probation's history even so and a reminder that the histories told by policymakers, researchers or even practitioners are not the only possible accounts. Appreciation of this limitation can reframe reflections on probation's past – and present. For example, practitioners and scholars long debated whether probation's purpose was 'care' or 'control', but (with the important exception of Willis 1986) this debate took place almost entirely at the level of intention and aspiration. Few people asked service users: when probation strove to 'care', was it experienced as caring? When it tried to 'control', was it felt to be controlling?

The desistance literature in particular recognizes that it is not just life events and opportunities that conduce to (or delay) desistance, but the meaning and significance that (ex-)offenders attach to such experiences – on which they have a privileged insight. Again, as punishment gives messages, in its pronouncement and in the manner of its implementation, then whether and how this message is 'received' and interpreted must be critically important. So while offenders' perceptions may be hard to get, their absence is a serious gap in probation's history, and recent attempts to address this are greatly to be welcomed (Bailey 1995; Rex 1999, 2005; Maruna 2000; Farrall and Calverley 2006).

It is possible to think of probation's activities as marginal, encountered by few and to which the great majority of people are indifferent, if aware at all. Yet the number of people who have direct experience of probation must be very considerable. We know from 'cohort studies' (for example, Prime *et al.* 2001) that some 33 per cent of men and 9 per cent of women are convicted of at least one 'standard list' offence by their mid-forties. Many of this very large number of people will have encountered probation staff, have had pre-sentence reports prepared upon them, for example, and varying involvement thereafter depending on sentence. Yet precisely because it may be remembered as a time of anxiety, distress and shame, people may be uncomfortable in recalling their experience, and the probation officer who served them well or poorly is part of this unhappy memory. Recollection may evoke complex and ambivalent emotions that mould their current view of probation.

There are other accounts to be told besides. Families and friends of defendants and of probation staff have their experience of the service. There are other professionals; victims of crime – often overlooked (which in itself may lead to a particular impression), but also often given supportive counsel and advice; the beneficiaries of communities service/unpaid work; the communities with which probation engaged (or failed to).

All these experiences of probation, however multifarious and elusive, are quite as much a part of its history as the more formal accounts, and a sensitivity to these dimensions and possibilities suggests much about probation's past – and indeed its contemporary significance.

SOME THEMES IN PROBATION'S HISTORY

Although the history of probation is usually narrated episodically, it is also possible to explore it thematically. One way of doing this is through an account of a number of tensions that have characterized its history and indeed its present. While managerialism sometimes assumes clear aims and objectives, the character of social institutions is typically *contested*: 'Having developed as a means of managing tensions, arbitrating between conflicting forces, and getting certain necessary things done, social institutions typically contain within themselves traces of the contradictions and pluralities of interest which they seek to regulate' (Garland 1990: 282).

These tensions are, therefore, inevitable and irreconcilable. But they are also *constructive*. These dynamic tensions are the torque in the engine that provides probation's motive power, the impetus for its developments.

Local or national

For most of the past hundred years, policy and direction were formally determined by local probation committees (probation boards) – independent bodies corporate, constituted mainly by justices of the peace. Local influences – social, demographic and geographical characteristics, local custom and practice, the preferences and personalities of committee members and probation staff – are likely to have tended to diversity in different areas.

At the same time, there have always been influences towards uniformity – a common statutory framework and system of governance, the 'Probation Rules', Home Office circulars and memoranda, Her Majesty's Inspectorate of Probation. The Home Office, from the beginning exercising its influences through exhortation, authoritative advice, regulation and inspection, progressively became first more assertive and then more directive. The first Statement of National Objectives and Priorities in 1984, tighter financial control at national level, the dissemination of National Standards, the requirement to plan and report to prescribed formats, the setting of targets, the linking of funding to achievement of targets and many other disciplines of managerialism have all pushed towards a uniformity directed by central government.

There have been other (non-governmental) influences towards uniformity too. National organizations like the National Association of Probation Officers (now Napo), the Association of Chief Officers of Probation and the Central Council of Probation Committees promulgated their ideas of good practice and sound governance. There were handbooks (Le Mesurier, King) and manuals (Jarvis) that set out models of good practice and procedure. Unevenly but progressively, professional training contributed to a common set of theoretical understandings which began to mould practice.

The Probation Boards' Association identifies 'localism' as one of its central principles. The locus of crime – and, many think, the place where ex-offenders must find their pathway out of offending – is the local community, and the provision of service should be sensitive to local characteristics. Perhaps communities, no less than individuals, have their 'responsivity' which must be respected and which can be better appreciated by local agencies, locally controlled. Not all variation in practice is inconsistency. But whatever opinion is held on the proper apportioning of authority and policy between local and national levels, the tension between them has been a persistent and dynamic feature of probation's history.

Judicial or executive

Overlapping (but not co-extensive) with the first dynamic is the tension between probation as 'officers of the court' or as an instrument of the executive. Originally, as we have seen, probation officers were seen as officers of the court but, as crime and justice have become increasingly politicized, government has had to try to direct probation practice to deliver its policies of law and order.

The Home Office was originally anxious to avoid creating a new central government bureaucracy (Nellis 2007) – partly because of the burden and cost, but partly too for constitutional reasons: it was inappropriate for the authority of magistrates over their officers to be unduly influenced by the executive. So light was the touch that the Morison Report many years later (1962) found that some services felt neglected by the Home Office.

The extent to which sentencing and the institutions of punishment 'belong' to courts or to the legislative is a debate with constitutional implications. Should probation's primary accountability be to the court as it gives effect to its orders? Or to central government to implement penal policy? This tension has been a significant feature of probation's history, its present and its future.

'Inside' or 'outside'

Much of probation's work throughout its history has been with serving former prisoners. (Indeed, for a significant part of its history, the correct title was 'Probation and After-care Service'.) One of probation's 'phases', as we have seen, was as a provider of alternatives to custody. Setting aside questions about whether or not this is a helpful way of characterizing practice, the aspiration that providing 'alternatives to custody' is the way to reduce the prison population yokes probation firmly to prison, its challenges and its volatile politics. At the level of practice, many probation officers work (or have worked) as seconded officers in prison; all work with former prisoners at some time or another. Probation officers, as offender managers, are increasingly influencing the lived experiences of imprisonment.

The recognition that after-care should build upon the experience in custody in a 'seamless sentence' consolidates the bond, and the inference was drawn that the services should amalgamate in a National Offender Management Service. But quite other conclusions might have been reached. No doubt probation ought to work closely with prisons, but so too must it work closely with police and with local authorities. Indeed, the priority of public protection through community practices seems to call for at least as close an alignment with local community-based organizations as with prisons. Since 1998, probation has located itself in a sector known as community justice, and the Crime and Disorder Act 1998 anticipated a future in which probation would be a local agency in primary partnership with local authorities and police. This pointed in an exciting direction and offered an entirely feasible means of promoting public protection and indeed enhanced rehabilitation and resettlement. Instead the link with prison was affirmed.

Structural ties to prison in pursuit of the seamless sentence risk distancing probation from its local community. As Nellis (2007) says, probation officers have sometimes seen themselves as advocates of offenders to the community: after all, principles like integration and inclusion call not only for individual change but also for the community to accept responsibility towards those of its members who have offended. Yet this aspiration will at best be incompletely realized unless probation is (and is seen to be) connected to and involved in the community.

A related point is probation's role in crime prevention and community safety where, arguably, probation has yet to realize its complete contribution. Probation officers come to know an enormous amount about the circumstances in which offending takes place and, while this is put to good use in individual cases, it is rarely conceptualized or compiled in the aggregate and deployed to inform local crime reduction strategies. O-DEAT, collecting and collating OASys information, could begin to redress this if areas are given the opportunity and latitude to respond intelligently to what this information shows about characteristic local criminogenic factors and the services required (compare Smith and Vanstone 2002).

Certainly probation needs a working understanding of prisons, its effects, possibilities and limitations. It also needs a strong grounding in its local community and must never allow its practices to be evaluated solely in terms of the impact of its work on the prison population (always limited) or its capacity to be 'prison-like' (always a claim that struggles to command political credibility). Community engagement can be in tension with the priorities of prison and this too has been a dynamic in the service's history.

Social or psychological

The contemporary prominence of 'what works' tends to an individualized understanding of the origins of offending. In fact, sophisticated expositions of cognitive-behavioural methods do justice to the social context of offending and desistance, but a conventional critique is that undue attention to 'cognitive deficits' can obscure or suppress an awareness of the significance of the social, economic and political context of offending.

Yet probation officers have always been sensitive to social context, recognizing the common predicaments of so many of their service users, often based in poverty, deprivation and locally depressed economic and social conditions. This is the origin of community development work, and a revived interest in concepts like social capital, with its identifiable connection with desistance, is now apparent.

Many offenders have biographies of neglect, trauma and distress, leading sometimes to a blunted sensitivity to the effects of their behaviour on others – a limited victim awareness – as well as to insufficiently developed abilities to manage their problems effectively. Yet behaviour is a function not only of personal motivation and abilities but also of opportunities – including opportunities that are presented or constrained by economic and structural factors. In reality, both social and psychological factors influence offending behaviour and usually both must be addressed in response. At different times and in different places, probation has given more or less prominence to these considerations in its work.

Offenders or clients

For much of its history, probation practice walked in step with social work. One aspect of this was its use of the term 'clients' to refer to those under supervision. This characterization was vehemently repudiated in the late 1980s and displaced in official discourse by the term 'offender'. People were under supervision, after all, because they had committed crimes and in any case lacked many of the formal characteristics of being a client.

In fact, that debate was always more about connotation than denotation. To refer to someone as an offender is to take (and invite others to take) a particular attitude towards him or her – for example, an attitude of punishment or discipline – and the conceit that offenders were 'clients' undermined the idea of punishment in the community. It remained important to many probation officers precisely because 'client' connotes respect, dignity and entitlement to service.

There is some irony in the fact that, in the decade following the emphatic rejection of social work, probation began to rediscover many of its principles and practices. Nor was this just a matter of a conceptualizing of the role – as 'case manager' rather than unique provider – or of sharing core practice models like ASPIRE. Probation (re)discovered the critical importance of motivation, its volatility (as recognized, for example, in the cycle of change) and the value of developing methods, like motivational interviewing, to enhance and sustain it. Prosocial modelling and solution-focused work recognized that encouragement and support are much more effective in inducing change than censoriousness or scolding.

Compliance – a principal challenge of community supervision – is centrally related to legitimacy and calls for courtesy and individual respect – even towards those whose behaviour and dispositions make such attitudes extremely difficult to adopt. Evidence-led practice, then, pointed in a quite different direction from the agenda of punishment and reintroduced, in a different vocabulary, many of the ideas and approaches that government had thought it had jettisoned when social work was rejected. Social work research, meanwhile, continues to inform our understanding of what works and, as Raynor wryly remarks, 'the search for effective practice cannot afford to ignore relevant research just because it goes under a currently disparaged label' (2003: 84).

As Smith puts it:

> *for all the rhetoric of punishment and public protection, risk management and enforcement, when practitioners decide what they are actually going to do to engage and motivate clients, help them access resources and convey a sense of hope in the possibility of constructive change, they will find themselves using ideas and skills that have emerged from social work theory and research*
>
> (2005: 634).

Individuals and families

Until the creation of the Children and Family Court Advisory Support Service (CAFCASS) in 2001, when separating parents unable to agree about residence or contact took their dispute to court, the agency with the responsibility to offer impartial advice was the Family Court Welfare Service, a part of the Probation Service. While this eventually became a specialist unit within the service, most probation officers undertook at least some family court work. Whether or not insights from 'civil work' were *sufficiently* applied to criminal work, the participation of probation officers in these activities enriched their understanding and broadened their repertoire of skills – for example, in conciliation and mediation that could be applied to other aspects of 'conflict resolution'.

Most obviously, civil work enabled officers to acquire an appreciation of the significance of family and upbringing in children's development. Contemporary probation is very much an adult service, but probation officers often used to attempt family work, recognizing that a young person's well-being is often decisively influenced by experiences at home. Home visits are mostly undertaken nowadays to verify an address, but used to be a way of involving the family in supervision. The desistance literature reclaims this recognition that people typically come to refrain from offending in a context of a life made meaningful in and through personal relationships.

Contemporary probation is mostly office based and individualized, but at other times in its history probation has recognized that, whether considering offenders as 'children' or as parents, the family is a critical influence on people's behaviour and potentially a decisive resource in achieving and sustaining desistance. This perspective also offers a holistic appreciation of people in their personal lives, rather than seeing them solely in terms of their offending – a counter to the actuarialist tendency to assess offenders as carriers of risks and needs.

Sameness or difference

The disciplines of working in an organization call for consistent and systematic practice in the implementation of policy. Managerialism, accordingly, is inherently wary of claims for professional discretion, fearing that, if practitioners assume too much latitude, the organization's achievement of its objectives will be jeopardized. Unfettered discretion can also result in unfairness and discrimination (Fitzgerald 1993). Part of the rationale for National Standards was to eliminate prejudice by ensuring consistency.

At the same time, people and circumstances differ in so many ways that there will always be a need for complex decisions to be taken, calling for sound professional judgement. Several contributions in this Dictionary attest to *diversity* – the many ways in which people differ from one another – and explore the implications of these differences for ethical and effective practice. Gelsthorpe (2001) has rightly insisted that respect and due regard for difference are a requirement of probation's *legitimacy*.

The tension here lies in probation's struggle to do justice to relevant differences among people without this collapsing into arbitrariness or capriciousness. Organizations must be sufficiently predictable so that service users and others can be confident about what to expect; individual circumstances, however, differ in many ways. Both these propositions express something important, but they often point practitioners in different directions and this, too, is a dynamic tension in probation's story.

Inclusion or exclusion

Discussion so far has offered a fairly benign account of probation but, as an agency of the state, it has always exercised a function of discipline and control. The first officers, in making a case for the deserving defendant, either explicitly or by implication rejected or abandoned the undeserving. In this sense, probation from the beginning was 'contributing to the exclusion and severe treatment of the undeserving' (Vanstone 2004: 37). Social diagnosis tried to differentiate the treatable from the intractable; alternatives to custody urged community sentences for some – in contrast to those for whom custody was 'inevitable'; and risk assessment assigns people to categories which determine the character of their dealings with probation.

The language changes – redeemable or damned, treatable or recalcitrant, safe or risky, motivated or unmotivated – but it is at least possible that all the time it is much the same people who find themselves on the wrong side of this divide. Probation affirms its belief in the possibility of change but, in practice, has to qualify this optimism with other considerations. This too constitutes another dynamic in probation's history.

Other tensions could be elaborated: care and control; consent and compulsion; relationship and professional method. The point is that these tensions are the very stuff of probation and it is neither possible nor in any case desirable to seek to reconcile them. At times, having tried to reject one 'pull' in each of these tensions, probation has soon had to rediscover it in the realities of practice.

PROBATION, POLICY AND PRACTICE

A neglected consideration is the extent to which the realities of probation work circumscribe the capacity of policy initiatives to change things. Dick Whitfield puts it

clearly: 'Some things do not change. The world in which the probation service operates is the real world of social change and conflict, crime and human frailty.
Structures, laws, expectations and organisational requirements do change at often
bewildering speed but people ... are the threads which are constant' (2001: 8).

These realities continue to insist themselves upon probation practice and constitute another mediating factor when the attempt is made to implement policy.

Enforcement...

Prominent among these realities is the challenge of compliance. Community penalties
involve requirements – to keep appointments, to participate in or refrain from activities – which people might choose not to do. This creates the possibility of default and
entails that probation officers have to engage with all the complexities of motivation.
Legitimacy captures the idea that treating people fairly and well commands their consent and is critical to securing compliance (Bottoms 2001).

Rehabilitation...

A recent meta-analysis identifies the core components of 'correctional practice'
(Dowden and Andrews 2004). These include a 'firm but fair' approach to interacting
with offenders and the appropriate modelling and reinforcing of anti-criminal attitudes. Of the fifth component, the authors state:

> The fifth and final component ..., relationship factors, is also arguably the most
> important. Essentially, this approach argues that the interpersonal influence exerted
> by the correctional staff member is maximized under conditions characterized by
> open, warm, and enthusiastic communication. An equally important consideration is
> the development of mutual respect and liking between the offender and correctional
> staff member. This approach asserts that correctional interventions will be most effec-
> tive when these types of relationships exist within the treatment program.
>
> (2004: 205).

The offender management model puts the relationship at the centre of the management process. But if the conceptual distinction between management and
interventions were to lead to a fragmentation in the service user's experience, it
could undermine much of what is known to be effective and make it harder for staff
to realize the 'core components of correctional practice' (compare Robinson 2005).

... and public protection

If risk management is to go beyond surveillance, immobilization and, external
checks, it must involve an attempt to engage the offender and, where possible, command consent. In any case, no risk management strategy can afford to be indifferent
to the offender's own attitudes and response to that strategy, which can range – even
in a single case over time – between extremes of resistance and compliance. Risk
management and compliance need to be considered side by side: a state of affairs
where the offender avoids all contact is especially dangerous. So approaches that
maximize compliance at the same time contribute to good risk management.

The history of probation has, then, as we have seen, been characterized as a journey from 'advise, assist and befriend' to 'enforcement, rehabilitation and public

protection' . It has been suggested here, however, that there is now a weight of evidence and argument to show that the way to get the best from people is to treat them well – with fairness, respect, encouragement and personal interest. This is not only ethically valuable but also conduces to probation's objectives. In each of its phases, probation has sooner or later made this discovery. Perhaps the best way to enforce, rehabilitate and protect the public is by *advising, assisting* and *befriending*.

The essence of probation is to be found, perhaps, not so much in its tasks or organization as in its values. The practices of probation *express values* as well as trying to achieve objectives. The manner in which it goes about its work is eloquent about what the organization stands for and represents. An excessive preoccupation with instrumental objectives (not all of which can be assumed to be achievable anyway) risks losing Garland's essential insight that 'the pursuit of values such as justice, tolerance, decency, humanity and civility should be part of any penal institution's self-consciousness – an intrinsic and constitutive aspect of its role – rather than a diversion from its 'real' goals or an inhibition on its capacity to be "effective"' (1990: 292).

Among the principles that probation distinctively stands for are social inclusion and belief in the possibility of change. If imprisonment vividly represents (at least temporary) exile, social exclusion and suspension from citizenship, probation betokens a determination to work with offenders in their communities – where they live their lives, have their relationships, have committed their offences and where one day they will accomplish desistance.

What probation represents often jars with the emotions that we are called upon to feel towards offenders, bringing political vulnerability. To insist that the community has responsibilities towards offenders as well as claims against them is unfashionable and requires political courage to affirm. Yet social exclusion – blocking pathways to desistance – creates disaffected and sometimes dangerous people. For all its shortcomings and limitations, probation strives for a social inclusion that constitutes the strongest form of public protection.

The probation ideal, articulated (and criticized) in many different ways by the contributors to this volume, recognizes the many influences on offending behaviour and the challenges of sustaining motivation and supporting offenders in the process of desistance. It calls for an appreciation of the social as well as the psychological; of the community as well as the prison; of the many ways in which people are alike and are different; and of the need to *do justice* in practice by responding not only to people as offenders but also with a clear view of their qualities, potential and worth.

Rob Canton

NOTE

1. Serious students of probation's history should refer to Bochel (1976), McWilliams (1983, 1985, 1986, 1987), Garland (1985), Radzinowicz and Hood (1990), Brownlee (1998), Oldfield (2002), Raynor and Vanstone (2002), Vanstone (2004), Whitehead and Statham (2006), Nellis (2007), Raynor and Vanstone (2007).

ACCOUNTABILITY

> Arrangements for ensuring that probation boards, managers and practitioners are able to explain their actions.

Probation is a public service financed by the taxpayer, and it is therefore essential that effective procedures are in place to account for the actions of staff. Open and clear accountability safeguards the credibility of the service.

It is sometimes said that there was a time in the mid-twentieth century when probation officers regarded themselves as quasi-independent practitioners accountable to a set of professional values. This was always a partial view, but it did represent something of the sense of professional confidence that existed at that time. Later critics saw this as arrogance. Whatever the merits of those arguments, probation staff have always recognized that they are accountable to a wide range of individual and community interests, including service users, victims and the community at large.

Until 2001, probation officers were specifically assigned to one of the petty sessional divisions in their area. This reinforced the view that a probation officer was 'an officer of the court'. Until the 1980s each court had a 'case committee' where supervising officers informed the magistrates of the progress or otherwise of each offender.

The Probation Service has generally had a strong culture of staff supervision. The primary task of senior probation officers has always been to ask for an account of the work being carried out, to advise on difficulties, support and appraise. This accountability to the line manager was then extended to the top of the organization. This was formalized through the committee's annual report and accounts. The government sets its requirements on staff through legislation and the distribution of instructions (circulars) from the Home Office. HM Inspectorate of Probation has the right to see records and reports regularly on the work in each probation area.

In the National Probation Service, formed in 2001, operational staff are accountable to their employing body, the area probation board. However, the chief officers are appointed by the Home Secretary and are 'accountable officers' within the meaning of civil service accounting.

The need to meet government targets has impacted on the culture of accountability. The system of 'performance bonus' means that budgets and staffing levels can only be maintained if targets are met. Managers bear down on 'poor performers'.

The National Probation Service embraces 'strong centre and strong local'. This is a strength. The boards provide the strong local, and the strong centre certainly makes itself felt in the areas. The direct accountability of chief officers and board members to officials and ministers means the service has to be very responsive to the needs of Parliament (MPs' questions in particular) and to the questions posed by the media. The vulnerability of ministers to adverse comment in the tabloid press means that policy can be amended rapidly in the light of media interest. This makes for an unstable and incrementally more cautious and defensive policy position.

David Hancock

Related entries

HM Inspectorate of Probation; Probation boards; Staff supervision.

Key texts and sources

Faulkner, D. (2006) *Crime, State and Citizen* (2nd edn). Winchester: Waterside Press.
Morgan, R. (2007) 'Probation, governance and accountability' in L. Gelsthorpe and R. Morgan (eds) *Handbook of Probation*. Cullompton: Willan Publishing.

ACCREDITED PROGRAMMES

'Programmes' represent a structured approach to helping offenders to acquire the skills and knowledge which can help them to stay out of trouble. Mostly (but not always) delivered to groups of offenders, programmes have their origins in attempts to help offenders to acquire problem-solving, thinking and self-management skills, and in combining a range of learning opportunities into a structured sequence.

Origins and development

A major influence on the development of programmes was work undertaken particularly in Canada during the 1980s, which was strongly influenced by studies of the psychology of criminal conduct and of the role of social learning in both starting and ceasing to offend. A number of research reviews helped to identify promising methods, encouraging a broadly cognitive-behavioural approach. These approaches, challenging the scepticism of 'nothing works', were introduced into Britain through a series of 'What Works' conferences, the persuasive advocacy of experts (such as James McGuire and Philip Priestley) and pilot studies such as the 'Straight Thinking On Probation' (STOP) project in South Wales. (STOP was a variant of one of the best known Canadian programmes, 'Reasoning and Rehabilitation', developed by Robert Ross.)

By the mid-1990s there was substantial interest in the development and delivery of programmes as a significant part of the evidence-based approach that was being advocated as a strategy to improve the standing and impact of the service. However, the early developments were somewhat haphazard and variable in quality: an inspection carried out in 1996 (published in 1998) found 267 projects which chief probation officers claimed were effective, of which only four turned out to have both methodologically sound evaluation and positive results. The resulting report proposed a form of national expert review of the quality and design of programmes to make the best knowledge available to all areas. This was described as a form of 'accreditation'.

Accredited programmes had existed in prisons in England and Wales since 1996, for both 'general' offenders and sex offenders, but their development as a high-volume activity in the community dates from 1999 when the Joint Prison/Probation Services Accreditation Panel was established (later renamed the Correctional Services Accreditation Panel). The Home Office had already launched an Effective Practice Initiative for the Probation Service ('What Works') and had identified some promising programmes as 'Pathfinders', but in 1999 the scale and ambition of these developments were greatly increased by the availability of central funding under the Crime Reduction Programme. The panel's report for 2004–5 lists 32 programmes fully or partly accredited: some for prisons only, but with a majority available in the community or in both settings. They include six 'general offending' programmes, six targeting violent behaviour (including programmes to reduce domestic violence), one for women who have committed acquisitive offences, thirteen for various kinds of substance misuse, five for sex offenders and one therapeutic community regime (contrary to widespread belief, not all accredited programmes are primarily cognitive behavioural). The programmes originate from various sources, including Home Office psychologists, voluntary organizations and independent developers or consultancies. The Prison and Probation Services have developed systems for the selection and training of programme staff, for the maintenance and development of the quality of delivery through the use of treatment managers and for regular audits to help to maintain programme integrity (i.e. to ensure that programmes are being delivered as intended).

Accredited programmes in probation: achievements and problems

The latest of the National Probation Directorate Interventions Unit's annual reports on the implementation of accredited programmes (for 2004–5) shows 15,596 programme completions in the year. The greatest volume of completions is found in the 'General Offending' programmes, particularly the 'Think First' group programme (developed by James McGuire) and the individually delivered 'One-to-One' programme (developed by Philip Priestley). There is also substantial activity in violence programmes, substance misuse programmes (including those for drink-impaired drivers) and sex offender treatment programmes. The aim of making a suite of programmes available in every probation area has largely been met. This represents a major achievement and a significant step towards the development of an evidence-based culture in the Probation Service, which now does far more programme-based work than the prisons. However, the roll-out of accredited programmes in probation has also revealed a number of problems which have tended to limit its impact and effectiveness. Many of these problems can be traced back to the speed and context of the roll-out.

The targets originally agreed with the Treasury in 1999 for the level of programme completions to be achieved under the Crime Reduction Programme were not based on any systematic study of the risk levels and criminogenic needs of the population under supervision, and were set unfeasibly high, at 30,000 programme completions plus another 30,000 Enhanced Community Punishment completions per year. Subsequent necessary reductions in the targets would not have looked like failure if the original targets had been realistic. The rush to implement programmes and

to achieve these targets antagonized many practitioners (including some who had to discontinue their earlier non-accredited programmes). The targets also encouraged recruitment of offenders who fell outside (often below) the intended risk range, or whose needs or problems did not fit the programme. Other aspects of supervision, such as individual supportive or motivational case management, were often neglected, leading the Chief Inspector of Probation to warn against 'programme fetishism'. At one stage, fewer than a third of those required to undertake programmes actually completed them, and still less than half do so. This high rate of attrition, associated at least partly with problems in case management, means that research on the effectiveness of community-based general offending programmes in Britain has been inconclusive: programme completers offend less than offenders in comparison groups, but non-completers often offend more, so we cannot tell whether the results show the effect of the programme or simply that those who completed it were better prospects anyway.

Although international research continues to point to the effectiveness of programmes, research in Britain has shown only modest positive results, which have been found mainly in some (not all) prison-based studies where attrition is much lower. Programmes need to be well supported by sound assessment and by skilled case management: the programme is part of the supervision process, not a substitute for it. Attrition could also be reduced by a return to more flexible and discretionary enforcement. Problems of resources and political 'toughness' may make such improvements difficult to achieve but, if such progress can be made, programmes will be more likely to achieve their potential.

The future of accredited programmes

The Criminal Justice Act 2003 provides a continuing legal basis for accreditation, with attendance on an accredited programme among the requirements available for inclusion in a community order. Programmes will probably continue to be the main intervention for many offenders; however, figures for 2004–5 suggest that referrals may have reached a plateau at just under 44,000 per year. The regional strategies for reducing reoffending, prepared by regional offender managers, are designed around seven 'pathways' out of offending, or areas of criminogenic need, on which services should be targeted: accommodation; education, training and employment; mental and physical health; drugs and alcohol; finance, benefits and debt; children and families of offenders; and attitudes, thinking and behaviour. Only two of these are covered by the current range of programmes. It seems likely that programmes will retain their place as one of a range of approaches, which should also include a consistently supportive, pro-social and problem-solving approach to personal supervision. If programmes are no longer overemphasized as the main or even only driver of evidence-based practice, the prospects of addressing problems of targeting and attrition may be better.

The other major determinant of the future of programmes will be the precise form taken by the restructuring of the Probation Service to fit the National Offender Management Service (NOMS), and the intention to commission a substantial proportion of 'interventions', including programmes, from the private and voluntary sectors. The details of these arrangements remain unclear. However, some private and voluntary sector representatives have suggested that existing accreditation arrangements are too complex and burdensome. The Home Office has also announced that the Correctional Services Accreditation Panel will lose its independent status as soon as the legislative timetable allows, and accreditation will now be a decision made within NOMS. It remains to be seen whether these developments will have any impact on the design and quality of accredited programmes.

Peter Raynor

Related entries

Accredited programmes in common use; Cognitive-behavioural; Correctional Services Accreditation Panel; Effective Practice; Groupwork.

Key texts and sources

Burnett, R., Baker, K. and Roberts, C. (2007) 'Assessment, supervision and intervention: fundamental practice in probation' in L. Gelsthorpe and R. Morgan (eds) *Handbook of Probation.* Cullompton: Willan Publishing.

Correctional Services Accreditation Panel (2005) *Annual Report 2004–5.* London: CSAP.

Hollin, C., Palmer, E., McGuire, J., Hounsome, J., Hatcher, R., Bilby, C. and Clark, C. (2004) *Pathfinder Programmes in the Probation Service: A Retrospective Analysis, Home Office Online Report 66/04.* London: Home Office.

Raynor, P. (2003) 'Evidence-based probation and its critics', *Probation Journal,* 50: 334–45.

Raynor, P. (2004) 'Rehabilitative and reintegrative approaches', in A. Bottoms *et al.* (eds) *Alternatives to Prison.* Cullompton: Willan Publishing.

Underdown, A. (1998) *Strategies for Effective Offender Supervision: Report of the HMIP What Works Project.* London: Home Office.

Vanstone, M. (2000) 'Cognitive-behavioural work with offenders in the UK: a history of influential endeavour', *Howard Journal,* 39: 171–183.

ACCREDITED PROGRAMMES IN COMMON USE

The following programmes have been approved by the Correctional Services Accreditation Panel and are widely used throughout probation areas in England and Wales. (The sex offender treatment programmes are detailed in a separate entry.)

Enhanced thinking skills

This is a sequenced series of structured exercises designed to teach interpersonal problem-solving skills. It comprises 20 groupwork sessions of two and a half hours and, like all programmes, uses cognitive-behavioural methods.

Think first

This involves four pre-programme sessions followed by 22 group sessions of between two and two and a half hours. These focus on skills to change behaviour, such as problem-solving, antisocial attitudes, tackling pressures to offend, victim awareness, moral reasoning, self-management and social interaction. The course is followed by seven post-programme sessions on an individual basis.

One to one

This is a programme designed to be delivered on an individual basis. It covers much the same curriculum as Think First and comprises one pre-programme session of motivational interviewing followed by 21 one-to-one programme sessions of between an hour and an hour and a half.

Women's acquisitive crime programme

This is designed for women offenders whose crime is for financial gain, who have poor problem-solving skills and who do not think through the consequences of their actions. It is run over 31 two-hour sessions, with additional work needed for those with a high risk of reoffending or with a high level of need. The programme is based on motivational interviewing techniques with an emphasis on emotional management and building healthy relationships.

Aggression replacement training (ART)

This aims to reduce aggressive behaviour and involves five structured individual sessions on risk assessment and management, and group preparation. This is followed by 18 groupwork sessions focusing on reducing violent behaviour through teaching social skills, anger management techniques and improved moral reasoning. There are five post-programme individual, evaluation and relapse prevention sessions.

Controlling anger and learning to manage it (CALM)

This aims to reduce aggressive and offending behaviour related to poor emotional management through teaching social skills, emotional management and cognitive techniques. It comprises 24 groupwork sessions of between two and two and a half hours. Offenders learn to control their emotional arousal, learn the skills they need to resolve conflict and learn how to deal with relapse.

Drink impaired drivers (DIDs)

This aims to reduce the risk of drink-driving offences and is for men and women who have up to four previous convictions for excess alcohol. The programme involves four risk assessment and preparation sessions followed by 14 weekly groupwork sessions and then six post-programme and relapse prevention sessions. The content focuses on structured learning to develop pro-social skills, effective decision-making and knowledge about the effects of drinking and driving.

Addressing substance related offending (ASRO)

This programme is designed to teach offenders the skills required to reduce or stop substance misuse. Like almost all programmes it is for offenders who pose a medium or high risk of reoffending. The programme has three optional pre-programme sessions and 20 sessions of two and a half hours generally delivered twice a week over ten weeks.

Offender substance abuse programme (OSAP)

The programme aims to raise awareness of the link between drugs and/or alcohol misuse and offending and to teach the skills to enable offenders to reduce or stop substance misuse. There are three pre-programme sessions followed by 26 groupwork sessions with a modular structure, delivered up to four times a week. The groupwork is followed by at least four maintenance sessions with an offender manager.

Personal reduction in substance misuse (PRISM)

This is a programme designed to be delivered on an individual basis. It teaches skills to reduce or stop substance misuse. There is one pre-programme motivational interview followed by 20 programme sessions, each lasting between 45 minutes and two hours.

Community domestic violence programme

The programme aims to reduce the risk of domestic violence, violent crime and abusive behaviour towards women in relationships by helping perpetrators change their attitudes and behaviour. The programme is for men who are assessed as medium to high risk for relationship violence using the Spousal Abuse Risk Assessment (SARA). The programme involves contact with the victim or current partner by a women's safety worker and risk management through continual assessment and information sharing with other agencies, including the police. There are three pre-programme sessions to increase motivation, 26 two-hour groupwork sessions, usually delivered twice a week, and at least four relapse prevention sessions on an individual basis.

Integrated domestic abuse programme (IDAP)

This has similar aims to the Community Domestic Violence Programme above, and it is also for men who are assessed as medium to high risk on SARA. The programme involves contact with the victim or current partner and risk management through continual assessment and information sharing with other agencies, including the police. There are four individual pre-programme sessions, followed by 27 two-hour groupwork sessions and six individual sessions. These are followed by at least four relapse prevention sessions with the offender manager.

David Hancock

Related entries

Accredited programmes; Cognitive-behavioural; Correctional Services Accreditation Panel; Criminogenic needs; Effective practice; Groupwork.

Key texts and sources

See 'Accredited programmes', above.

ACTUARIALISM

> Actuarialism is an approach to crime prevention and control using statistical practices of risk assessment and management, basing penal decisions and interventions on generalized predictions of future offending rather than individualized evidence of past behaviour.

Actuarialism has come to prominence in the field of criminal justice because it encapsulates an approach to crime control that dispenses with deeper concerns about the origins and meaning of offences in favour of an approach based on 'risk minimization' and the elimination of potential threats to the social order. This development reflects broader social movements, captured in the notion of the 'risk society' and operationalized through emergent 'technologies' of control. In the context of crime and justice, there has been a notable shift from concerns about the motivation and well-being of offenders, to forms of intervention based on the measurement and prediction of *future* risk, and the commitment to take action to avert this. Thus, there have been attempts to develop scientific means of quantifying the potential for future offending (notably assessment instruments), and disposals are often predicated on surveillance and control (electronic monitoring and tracking, for example).

The government has also instigated other measures to identify at an early stage those whose behaviour may become problematic. The 'Every Child Matters' policy has at its centre a scheme to provide comprehensive information on all children, with the capacity to provide an 'early warning' of potential problems, including anticipated offending. The Youth Inclusion Programme and youth inclusion and support panels have incorporated into their 'preventive' approaches a process of selection based on those most 'at risk', while the courts have been given a range of powers to impose orders proactively, ostensibly to prevent offending, including antisocial behaviour orders, child safety orders and parenting orders.

However, the use of predictive tools to justify such measures has a number of crucial limitations. First, they are crude, applying *generalized* probabilities to *individual* children and young people. The selection process is accordingly arbitrary, so that interventions incorporate inherent unfairness and 'label' individuals without substantive justification. Secondly, these predictive tools are based on subjective judgements and prone to significant inaccuracies, inevitably identifying numbers of 'false positives' – individuals wrongly identified as potential (re)offenders. Thirdly, the process of identifying and acting against individuals on the basis of their putative future behaviour is itself divisive and exclusive, posing a threat to the rights of those concerned, who do not have to be proven offenders to incur intrusive interventions.

Two major concerns therefore arise about the increasing influence of actuarial practices: actuarial justice is based on speculative and often unsupportable assumptions about the nature of risk and the capacity to control it, while the increasing dominance of this approach distorts other more inclusive approaches to early intervention and social inclusion.

Roger Smith

Related entries

Assessment instruments and systems; OASys; Risk society.

Key texts and sources

Beck, U. (1992) *Risk Society*. London: Sage.
Feeley, M. and Simon, J. (1994) 'Actuarial justice: the emerging new criminal law', in D. Nelken (ed.) *The Futures of Criminology*. London: Sage.
France, A., Hine, J., Armstrong, D. and Camina, M. (2004) *The On Track Early Intervention and Prevention Programme: From Theory to Action*. London: Home Office.

ALCOHOL

Alcohol is the most common psychoactive drug in the world, consumed by most people in varying quantities with little or no ill effect. If used in large quantities or at inappropriate times, it can cause health, personal and social problems. Much offending is associated with the misuse of alcohol.

All civilizations have tried to control the production and consumption of alcohol. The Babylonians worshipped a goddess of alcohol, Ninkasi, and used alcohol as a reward. Hammurabi, the Babylonian king, decreed a daily beer ration of two litres for a worker, three for civil servants and five for high priests. He also passed strict laws to control the distribution and sale of alcohol. Tavern owners, usually women, could be sentenced to trial by ordeal by being thrown into the Euphrates if they failed to sell beer at the agreed price.

The consequences of drinking have been recognized since ancient times. Plato (around 400 BCE) commented in his *Symposium*:

When a man drinks wine he begins to be better pleased with himself and the more he is filled full of brave hopes, and conceit of his powers, and at least the string of his tongue is loosened and fancying himself wise, he is brimming over with lawlessness and has no fear or respect to do or say anything.

Prohibition was attempted in the USA (Volstead Act 1920). There is disagreement about the effectiveness of prohibition: no doubt some people stopped drinking as a result of the Act, but many more continued. The increase in crime, however, is not disputed as organized crime stepped in to supply a ready-made market. This increase in crime, public misgiving about the effectiveness of prohibition and growing economic depression led to the Act's repeal in 1933.

Alcohol as a drug

Alcohol is a depressant drug, inhibiting the activity of the central nervous system. Differing in its effects from one individual to another, it will often enhance mood – for example, if we are already happy and relaxed, alcohol (in small amounts) will usually enhance those feelings; however, if we are depressed and anxious, it will enhance those moods. Consumed in excess it can lead to poor co-ordination and reflexes, and aggression, violence, nausea, vomiting, increased risk behaviour, confusion, loss of inhibitions and unconsciousness. In extreme cases, death can result.

The chronic use of large quantities can, over time, lead to the development of withdrawal symptoms, including headache, nausea or vomiting, tremor, anxiety, sleep problems and, in extreme cases, hallucinations and epileptic-type fits. Severe alcohol withdrawal is physically dangerous and requires medical supervision. Longer-term damage from excessive drinking over time includes increased tolerance, liver damage, higher risk of many diseases (including various types of cancer and cardiovascular disease), sexual dysfunction, weight gain, mental health problems, brain damage, higher risk of accidents, foetal damage and an increased propensity to commit crime. Alcohol causes an estimated 22,000 early deaths a year from accidents and disease, many more than illicit drugs.

Prevalence

Over 90 per cent of adults in the UK drink alcohol, with about one third of men and one fifth of women drinking more than the Department of Health's recommendations. While annual alcohol consumption in the UK is about the European average, most European countries have reduced or maintained levels of drinking over the last 15 years, whereas the UK has steadily increased consumption. Binge drinking accounts for about two fifths of all drinking sessions for men and one fifth for women. (This is defined as six units in a day for women and eight units for men, though some object to this definition because adverse behavioural consequences usually begin at a higher level of consumption.)

Assessing alcohol problems

As most people drink alcohol, what constitutes an alcohol problem or alcoholism? Alcohol problems are defined by the consequences of drinking. A good assessment will consider physical and mental health, financial implications, work, relationships and offending, as well as taking a careful and detailed note of the quantities consumed. Several questionnaires have been developed to indicate alcohol problems, such as CAGE or AUDIT.

Alcohol and crime

A 1990 Home Office study estimated that over one third of offenders had a current alcohol problem. Alcohol has been associated with three quarters (73 per cent) of domestic violence incidences, 60–70 per cent of all homicides, 75 per cent of stabbings and 48 per cent of all offences. Concern about the criminogenic effects of alcohol was among the first inspirations of probation work. While there is strong evidence of a relationship between excessive drinking and crime – especially violence – statistics need to be carefully interpreted because they point to only one of many factors associated with offending. Alcohol is rarely the sole cause of crime.

Treating alcohol problems

Most people, even very heavy drinkers, reduce their consumption as they grow older. Professional help from an alcohol treatment agency will probably include counselling of some kind, with the philosophy of the agency the key determinant of the approach. A twelve-step model (similar to Alcoholics Anonymous) suggests that 'alcoholism' is a lifelong disease that can only be controlled by total abstinence. Most alcohol treatment agencies, both within the NHS and the voluntary sector, advocate a learning model which suggests that 'alcoholism' is not a disease but, rather, a learnt set of behaviours that can be replaced by new learning. This model can work towards total abstinence or 'controlled' drinking, using cognitive and/or behavioural techniques to achieve a negotiated goal with the client. Severe withdrawals are usually treated by a brief (and reducing) prescription of tranquillizers to help with most of the symptoms and to prevent some of the more dangerous aspects of withdrawal (such as convulsions). Success rates are difficult to measure because goals – abstinence, reduced consumption, reduced offending – differ between agencies. Usually between one third and a half of those who go for help to a treatment agency report reduced consumption (or abstinence), improved health and decreased problems. Many relapse but can be helped to regain their previous abstinence or controlled status. However, many people learn to reduce or stop drinking with no professional help, sometimes with the help of self-help groups such as Alcoholics Anonymous. Those who go for help have often tried to reduce their consumption or to stop themselves and can link their motivation to specific reasons (offending, relationship or work problems, poor health, etc.).

Ira Unell

Related entries

Assessment; Criminogenic needs; Motivation.

Key texts and sources

Plant, M. and Cameron, D. (eds) (2000) *The Alcohol Report*. London: Free Association Press.
The Institute of Alcohol Studies (**www.ias.org.uk**) and Alcohol Concern (**www.alcoholconcern.org.uk**) have well documented fact sheets, links to other websites and access to specialist information.

ANTI-DISCRIMINATORY PRACTICE

Anti-discriminatory practice recognizes the significance of discrimination and oppression in people's lives and seeks to reduce or eradicate practices and structures which create or reinforce disadvantage.

Anti-discriminatory practice is practice which is 'against' discrimination. Negative discrimination is the detrimental combination of prejudice and power, which results in particular individuals or groups being treated less favourably than others. Systematic disadvantages, denial of equal rights and lack of equal access to opportunities, resources and services can occur on the basis of race, ethnicity, religion, gender, sexuality, disability, age, class, mental health, educational attainment and/or many other diverse factors of personal and social identity. The various manifestations of discrimination are multifarious and complex, can take direct or indirect forms and can be intentional or unwitting. The impact of a dominant group's discriminatory power over another group results in the denial of equal rights and citizenship.

Thompson's (2006) model identifies three different levels of discrimination. *Personal* discrimination pertains to beliefs, attitudes and prejudices held by individuals which demean others while enhancing a personal sense of worth and superiority. *Cultural* discrimination refers to patterns of prejudicial behaviour shared by particular groups. Group norms and negative assumptions and stereotypes about others provide cohesion for dominant groups. On a *structural* level, various social and political forces and divisions enable certain groups to have power over others and to operate in a manner which maintains inequalities. Again, stereotypical assumptions may be widely endorsed to sustain negativity and maintain dominance and power. The three levels – personal, cultural and structural – do not operate in isolation but have elaborate patterns of interdependency.

Anti-discriminatory probation practice recognizes the impact of individual prejudice and the wider process of social exclusion and disadvantage. It also acknowledges the inherent power imbalances within professional relationships and the various sources of organizational, professional, coercive and personal power that can be used to promote or deny equality. It strives to eradicate discrimination and oppression by challenging it in the practice of others and within the wider organizational context. Anti-discriminatory practice is characterized by a positive use of power, openness to new ideas and information, and a proactive approach to a diverse range of backgrounds, needs and experience. The principles therefore apply just as significantly to the treatment of staff within an organization as to the practices, organizational systems and processes which impact differentially upon service users.

The Probation Service has a long-established commitment to equal opportunity and social justice. Probation practice in the 1980s and early 1990s, in particular, emphasized the socio-economic structures that create discrimination and unequal access to resources. This included concerns regarding unjust actions and decision-making in relation to certain groups who were disproportionately represented within the criminal justice system, such as minority ethnic groups, people with mental health problems, etc. Civil rights campaigns, feminist, black political perspectives and social models of disability have all been influential. Legislation (such as the Sex Discrimination, Disability and Race Relations Acts) has had a significant impact, but anti-discriminatory practice stretches far beyond legalities into principles of morality, ethics and rights. Some writers distinguish between *anti-discriminatory* practice – a legalistic approach to equality – and *anti-oppressive* practice, which entails a wider social analysis. What is essential is an understanding of the relationship between the two, in terms of the accumulative effects of discrimination resulting in the subjugation of marginalized groups.

There are criticisms that anti-discriminatory practice within probation has been too opposi-tional and concentrated primarily on issues of gender and race. The latter probably remains the case. Within the National Probation Service, the term has been displaced by the diversity agenda, which places a rather different emphasis on the embracement and celebration of difference that may be perceived as less threatening to the mainstream. National policy documents, such as the *Heart of the Dance*, highlight 'a commitment to equal service and opportunities for all NPS members, offenders, victims of crime and communities', but the terminology used is perhaps more neutral and less impassioned. This move to 'non-discriminatory practice' and 'valuing diversity' risks obscuring the realities of discrimination and power imbalances. Building on positives should also require the jettisoning of negatives, and it remains debatable whether the relatively new discourse of diversity actively encourages such an approach.

To treat people equally, practitioners need to understand and respond to differences, not just to avoid discrimination, but to engage with the politics of difference. To work effectively with offenders, victims and communities it is also vital that practitioners acknowledge and understand the impact of inequality and oppressive forces on people's lives and behaviour.

Anti-discriminatory practice retains a high profile in new staff training, but the service's attention to it has been variable. The Macpherson Inquiry placed institutionalized racism firmly on the agenda, but inspection reports have found that, although there are many excellent examples of progress, developments in areas of work (such as interventions with racially motivated offenders) have been piecemeal.

Recognition of other issues, such as homophobia and discrimination on grounds of disability, is also less well developed. The National Offender Management Service brings the further challenge of reconciling the managerial and professional priorities of the Prison and Probation Services, with their very different histories of race relations, approaches to discrimination and humanitarian concerns. While anti-discriminatory practice continues as the core integral element of good practice, these ideals are frequently undermined, pressurized and compromised by other managerial and organizational preoccupations.

Sarah Hilder

Related entries

ABPO; Diversity; Hate crime; Heterosexism; LAGIP; Naaps; Racially motivated offenders.

Key texts and sources

Bhui, H. (2006) 'Anti-racist practice in NOMS: reconciling managerialist and professional realities', *Howard Journal*, 45: 171–90.

Chouhan, K. (2002) 'Race issues in probation' in D. Ward *et al.* (eds) *Probation: Working for Justice.* Oxford: Oxford University Press.

Gelsthorpe, L. and McIvor, G. (2007) 'Difference and diversity in probation' in L. and R. Morgan (eds) *Handbook of Probation.* Cullompton: Willan Publishing.

Her Majesty's Inspectorate of Probation (2005) *Effective Supervision Thematic Element.* London: HMIP.

NPD (2003) *The Heart of the Dance.* London: Home Office.

Smith, D. and Vanstone, M. (2002) 'Probation and social justice', *British Journal of Social Work*, 32: 815–30.

Thompson, N. (2006) *Anti-Discriminatory Practice* (4th edition). Basingstoke: Palgrave Macmillan.

ANTI-SOCIAL BEHAVIOUR

Behaviour which causes, or is likely to cause, harassment, alarm or distress to one or more persons not in the same household as the perpetrator.

The expression 'anti-social behaviour' (ASB) entered legal usage in the Crime and Disorder Act (CDA) 1998 and has quickly become common parlance. The CDA defined it in the rather general terms shown above, which has not always made for ease of interpretation. ASB is a concept very much dependent on the eye of the beholder. A common media image is of male teenage 'hoodies' gathering on street corners, causing low-level nuisance such as noise and graffiti. The Anti-social Behaviour Act 2003, however, extends the powers of social landlords, in particular, to take action against ASB.

The main sanction is the anti-social behaviour order (ASBO), the Youth Justice Service having usually attempted work with juveniles before the order is imposed. This ASBO, introduced by the CDA, is usually made in civil proceedings, on application by the local authority or the police, but can be imposed alongside a criminal court sentence (a CRASBO). The court must be satisfied that the person has behaved in an anti-social manner and that the order is necessary to protect the community. An ASBO includes prohibitions, the most prevalent (and frequently breached) tending to be against entering 'exclusion zones', congregating in groups and associating with named others in a public place. The 'naming and shaming' of its subjects has been one of the measure's more controversial features.

ASB is not itself a crime, but breach *is* a criminal offence for which custody may, and frequently has been, imposed. Research has found that young people often cannot remember the detail of all their prohibitions, are sometimes counterproductively prevented from entering normal transport routes to go to school, college or work, and are further disaffected by being prevented from engaging in what might be regarded as normal group behaviour for their age. Some prohibitions have been quashed by higher courts.

The role of probation professionals who find themselves supervising an adult with an ASBO is likely to be one of helping them find realistic ways of managing their prohibitions and reminding them that they are entitled to apply to the court for variation or discharge of their ASBO. At worst, this may represent yet a further dimension of fire-fighting work with the 'parade of local youths, alcoholics and drug addicts to be labelled, shamed and expelled' (Burney 2005: 169). At best, however, it may constitute a genuine opportunity to contribute to an inter-agency problem-solving process along the path to community justice.

Gwyneth Boswell

Key texts and sources

Burney, E. (2005) *Making People Behave: Anti-social Behaviour, Politics and Policy.* Cullompton: Willan Publishing.

Greatorex, P. and Falkowski, D. (2006) *Anti-social Behaviour Law.* Bristol: Jordan Publishing.

Solanki, A., Bateman, T., Boswell, G. and Hill, E. (2006) *Research into the Use of Anti-social Behaviour Orders for Young People.* London: Youth Justice Board

For information on the government's approach, **www.homeoffice.gov.uk/antisocialbehaviour/** and **www.respect.gov.uk**. The resource website for practitioners is at **www.together.gov.uk**.

APPROVED PREMISES

Approved premises (formerly known as probation and bail hostels) are those premises approved under s. 9 of the Criminal Justice and Court Services Act 2000.

Currently the term applies to 101 hostels for offenders managed by area probation boards or by voluntary organizations that provide over 2,000 bed-spaces. There are also up to five approved premises (also known as 'prospect hostels') being developed for use by short-term prisoners to address their drug problems following their release from custody.

The purpose of approved premises is to protect the public from offenders or bailees who pose a high or very high risk of harm. Residence is therefore restricted to those:

- on bail in criminal proceedings (remand services);
- serving a community sentence;
- on post-custody licence or supervision;

- for whom residence at approved premises is considered to be necessary for the protection of the public; and
- for whom supervision or treatment is required, and residence at approved premises is necessary in order to enable them to receive it.

Approved premises cater for men and women offenders in mixed or single-sex accommodation. There are a small number of 'women only' approved premises.

All approved premises work to National Standards and Approved Premises Regulations. They are required to have an admissions policy that must comply with the requirements of the Secretary of State and be made known to local courts. Admission of residents is based on an assessment of the offender's risk of harm to the public, victims and staff. There should be no blanket exclusions of offenders convicted of specific types of offence except as directed by the Secretary of State (e.g. changes to admissions regarding child sex offenders in 2006).

Context

The history of approved premises dates back more than a century, when probation homes were founded by voluntary organizations long before the Probation Service was established in 1907. The Criminal Justice Act 1948 provided for the public funding of probation homes and hostels, but it was not until the Powers of the Criminal Courts Act 1973 that probation committees were invited to establish approved probation and bail hostels. During that time, the role of approved hostels has reflected the changing preoccupations of the criminal justice system, including housing homeless boys convicted of petty offences, providing substitute families for adolescents, training unemployed offenders for work, groupwork, counselling in a therapeutic community, offering alternatives to custody and more recently, providing enhanced supervision in the community.

Today, approved premises are at the forefront of efforts to protect the public by reducing offending and by risk assessment and management. Approved premises are a facility that offers an enhanced level of supervision to those offenders and defendants who present a significant risk to the public. They play a key role in the Probation Service's delivery of public protection.

Regime

Approved premises carry out their risk management and crime reduction function with offenders by providing supervision and support to residents in three ways: adherence to rules; oversight and monitoring; and a regime that encourages positive behaviour (prosocial modelling) and that challenges attitudes, thinking and behaviour that can lead to offending.

There is rigorous enforcement of the rules. These include a curfew; the prohibition of the use of non-prescribed drugs and alcohol; and a requirement of good conduct towards staff, other residents and members of the public. Many residents will have additional conditions as part of their licence or bail conditions, and staff will monitor compliance with these as far as they can as part of their routine oversight of residents.

Oversight is ensured by the requirement that there should, as a minimum, be two members of supervisory staff on duty at all times, including a more recent requirement that there are two staff awake and on duty during the night. Staff are empowered to carry out searches of residents' rooms and any possessions kept on the premises. They may also subject residents to drug and/or alcohol testing in appropriate cases.

All new residents are interviewed when they arrive by approved premises staff, who will make sure the rules are explained and understood and that the implications of the risk management plan are understood by the resident. A key worker will be assigned to oversee and co-ordinate the interventions undertaken while at the approved premises which will deal with issues related to the seven pathways for preventing reoffending: accommodation; education, training and employment; mental and physical health; drugs and alcohol; finance, benefit and debt; children and families; and attitude, thinking and behaviour.

All staff are expected to behave in a prosocial way in their interactions with residents and to encourage residents to do likewise. Approved premises will require residents to attend a range of residents' meetings and other group activities, covering shared living, domestic issues, life skills, social skills, thinking skills, offending behaviour, constructive use of time and leisure, education, employment and accommodation opportunities. Residents may also be required to attend accredited programmes.

While the focus is on public protection, it is very important to recognize that this encompasses working towards the most appropriate, safest and successful long-term resettlement and rehabilitation of residents.

Debates and issues

As the Probation Service became increasingly concerned with the management of risk in the community, the proportion of residents who were bailees or those serving community sentences fell steadily, and these were replaced by those on post-custody licences, usually for more serious offences. Because approved premises are primarily used for offenders who are unable to return to previous accommodation, often by virtue of the offence and the need to protect victims, the proportion of sex offenders has increased, as has public awareness and hostility.

The Home Office Approved Premises and Offender Housing Strategy for Higher Risk Offenders recognized the problem, and argued that the regimes and resourcing should be enhanced to reflect the need for increased security. The implementation of several recent developmental initiatives is, however, in abeyance, and evaluation reports remain unpublished, mainly due to the wider structural changes towards a National Offender Management Service.

Eunice Dunkley

Related entries

Groupwork; Remand services; Therapeutic community.

Key texts and sources

Home Office (2000) *Approved Premises Handbook.* London: Home Office (available online at **http://www.probation.justice.gov.uk/files/pdf/ Approved%20Prem.pdf**)

Home Office (2001) *Approved Premises Regulations* 2001 (Statutory Instrument 2001 no. 850). London: HMSO.

Home Office (2002) *Approved Premises Handbook.* London: Home Office.

National Association of Probation and Bail Hostels (2005) *Issues for Women Offenders in Approved Premises.*

National Probation Directorate (2004a) *Approved Premises – Resource Review.* London: Home Office.

National Probation Directorate (2004) *Approved Premises and Offender Housing Strategy for Higher Rish Offenders.* London: Home Office.

National Probation Service (2005) *National Standards* 2005 (p. 25) (available online at **http:// www.probation.homeoffice.gov.uk/files/pdf/NPS %20National%20Standard%202005.pdf**).

National Probation Service (2006) *Probation Circular 26/2006: Changes to Admissions Policy for Approved Premises* (available online at **www.probation. homeoffice.gov.uk/output/page31.asp**).

ASPIRE

ASPIRE is a mnemonic and an acronym of Assessment, Planning, Implementing the plan, Review and Evaluation.

ASPIRE provides a process for practice. Originally set out in linear format by Sutton and Herbert in 1992, it was subsequently set out in cyclical format, since this better represents reality. Practitioners are constantly having to take account of fresh information, new developments and unexpected events, which can all be accommodated within the cyclical form of the ASPIRE process (see Figure 1).

Assessment

This stage will be conducted in accordance with professional requirements and will be under-pinned by counselling or active listening skills. Probation officers will typically employ the OASys documentation, while a range of assessment instruments are frequently used in youth offending teams and by other practitioners. Figure 1 shows how this stage leads to the clarification by client and practitioner of key concerns, issues or needs, together with priorities for action.

Planning

This stage takes place in the light of the assessment and the information (or lack of it) which the assessments have elicited. Often practitioners at this stage are planning on a number of 'fronts', which may include the following:

- A written contract with the court (for example, concerning accommodation or bail arrangements).
- An agreement among client, practitioner and a range of others, including, for example, bail hostel staff.
- An agreement between practitioner and client.

Such agreements are typically written down on a pro forma and should at least contain a statement of the objectives of working together – who has agreed to do what, which data will be collected and by whom, and when and how progress towards the objectives will be monitored.

Implementation

If the details of the plan have been set out explicitly and in sufficiently small increments for some progress to be achievable by both client and practitioner, then this stage, while demanding, should be clear. What seems to be essential here is that the practitioner, using principles of social learning theory, is available and able to commend, appreciate and give positive feedback to the client as progress is made towards the attainment of each objective. In addition, the practitioner should also be able to use such skills as motivational interviewing to encourage clients to persist in their efforts.

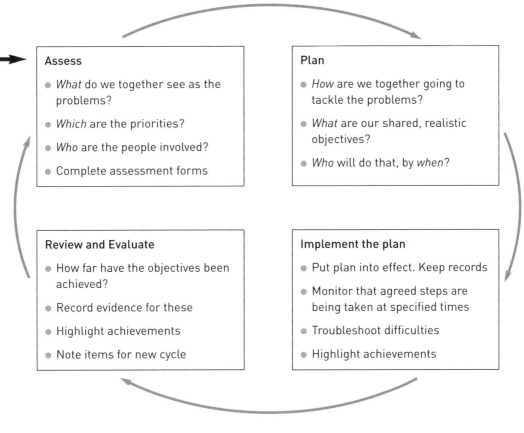

Figure 1 The ASPIRE process

Review and evaluate

Reviewing is a general term typically used when the client and practitioner consider their progress towards agreed objectives. It can take place at any point in a series of meetings and it is likely to depend mainly upon qualitative data. By contrast, the term 'evaluating' is more likely to be used for considering progress right at the end of the series of meetings or, perhaps, at the end of the first cycle, and may depend mainly upon quantitative data.

Carole Sutton

Related entries

Assessment; Evaluation; Interventions; Offender management.

Key texts and sources

Prochaska, J. O. and DiClemente, C.C. (1982) 'Transtheoretical therapy: toward a more integrative model of change', *Psychotherapy: Theory, Research and Practice*, 19, 276–88.

Sutton, C. (1999) *Social Work, Community Work and Psychology*. Leicester: British Psychological Society.

Sutton, C. and Herbert, M. (1992) *Mental Health: A Client Support Resource Pack*. NFER/Nelson.

The NOMS offender management model uses a recognizable variant of ASPIRE.

ASSESSMENT

> The process of determining or estimating the risks posed by an offender as the basis for providing advice to courts or others. Assessment also seeks to identify the causes of offending, and whether anything can be done to reduce the likelihood of repetition. It is the starting point for working out sentence plans.

OASys is the instrument now used by practitioners for the assessment of adult offenders in England and Wales. It is a structured interview instrument and it generates information about the probability of reoffending and the level of risk posed by the offender. It also highlights areas of criminogenic need that can be taken into account in drawing up a sentence plan. There are now about 500,000 assessments on the OASys Data Evaluation and Analysis Team (ODEAT) database, and this information is used to refine the assessment process and to plan the provision of services to meet the needs of offenders.

Assessment is needed to prepare pre-sentence reports, to advise the parole board and to assist decisions such as home leave. Assessment information is shared where appropriate in multi-agency meetings to do with risk assessment and management, and child protection.

Until the development of assessment instruments and systems, assessment was based almost entirely on practitioner judgement. Both experienced judgement and intuitive reactions have a place in these clinical assessments but, unless the work is scrutinized and validated, this approach can be subjective, inaccurate and culture bound, introducing a source of discrimination.

Actuarial assessment assigns a probability to future reoffending or to the risk of the person causing serious harm. This method relates the data about the person being assessed to a large database. Actuarial assessment is less useful in identifying causes of offending or in pointing towards what might be done about it.

Anamnestic assessment (from the Greek, meaning 'remembering') involves an analysis of the circumstances in which an individual has offended in the past, with a view to anticipating and managing these circumstances in the future.

Assessment depends on establishing a positive relationship with the person to be assessed. The disclosure of personal information in the context of impending court procedures can be an uncomfortable experience. The assessor will need to examine past case records, interview the person at length, observe any discrepancies between information that emerge and recognize repeated patterns of behaviour. In many cases standardized pro formas will have to be completed to find the probability scores. Information may have to be sought from relatives and from social, medical and criminal justice agencies. All these tasks have been brought together in the OASys process.

Good practice in assessment depends on attending to dynamic factors, as well as the static facts of the past. Understanding how the offender reacts to the current circumstances and his or her motivation to change are examples of these dynamic factors. The term ASPIRE has been developed to show how assessment is part of a reinforcing, cyclical process.

David Hancock

Related entries

ASPIRE; Assessment instruments and systems; OASys; Risk assessment and risk management.

Key texts and sources

Burnett, R., Baker, K. and Roberts, C. (2007) 'Assessment, supervision and intervention: fundamental practice in probation' in, L. Gelsthorpe and R. Morgan (eds) *Handbook of Probation*. Cullompton: Willan Publishing.

See also the key texts and sources listed under the related entries.

ASSESSMENT INSTRUMENTS AND SYSTEMS

Structured methods of assessing offenders at different stages of the criminal justice process.

The use and development of 'assessment instruments' has a long and distinguished history in criminology and probation practice. The origins of predictive inventories and scales can be traced to three distinctive elements in the growth of criminological research and in improvements in probation practice and penal decision-making:

1. The desire to improve empirical research methods, particularly the measurement of expected and actual rates of reoffending. This would enable evaluative research to be undertaken without having to run random controlled trials in every aspect of penal practice and innovation.

2. The aim of early identification of young people at risk of offending and most likely to persist in offending. Prediction scales and classificatory systems were produced to try to establish links between patterns of 'maladjusted' behaviour and certain child-rearing practices.

3. The desire by prison administrators, parole boards and policy advisers to have 'risk' predictors to apply to offenders individually or collectively to indicate the probability of reoffending on release. An early risk predictor was devised to guide Borstal allocation and release decisions. The introduction of parole in 1968 led directly to the development of a parole prediction score, the first actuarial instrument to be used routinely in the UK.

From these original instruments two main approaches to 'risk' assessment have developed: the clinical model and the static or actuarial model, referred to respectively as 'first' and 'second generation' tools. The clinical model may contain structured elements but is fundamentally diagnostic, relying on the completer's professional judgement. Much research evidence questions the accuracy and reliability of clinical-only instruments. The principal sources of error include personal factors in the raters (such as age, ethnicity, sex, social class and lifestyle), along with professional style, experience and knowledge, beliefs and attitudes, which can contribute to unintentional bias and variability in judgements.

The static or actuarial approach is based on statistical data about the characteristics of offenders, usually derived from large sample groups which are collected consistently over fixed time periods and in widely but randomly different locations. These multiple characteristics are statistically analysed, either individually or in combination, to predict increased or decreased probabilities of future events or behaviours occurring (e.g. future offending or non-compliant behaviour). The OGRS (Offender Group Reconviction Scale), developed by John Copas and soon to reach its third edition, is proving to be resilient and consistently accurate, achieving reconviction predictions at an almost 75 per cent level of accuracy, across widely different populations, including a large sample of violent offenders. Like other scales, OGRS contains mainly static items relating to criminal history, age at first offending, gender, current age, type of current offence(s) and penal history. These factors are statistically weighted to a predetermined formula to predict the probability of reconviction during a fixed time period (usually two years). Actuarial scales are not usually accurate in predicting rare events, such as serious violent or sexual attacks, and, because they are based largely on previous events, they do not identify what in future could be modified to reduce or change dynamic risk factors.

Recent emphasis on evidence-based practice and the promotion of provenly effective forms of intervention and assistance have encouraged the growth of a 'third generation' of instruments. These attempt to combine the best of static and clinical methods by emphasizing dynamic factors, in combination with static factors and limited elements of professional judgement. These 'risk and need assessment tools' combine:

- an estimate a risk of reconviction based on static and dynamic risk factors;
- pointers to target interventions to achieve the greatest impact;
- measures of change in risk and need during supervision.

The best known and most widely used third-generation instruments are ACE (Assessment and Case Evaluation system) and the LSI-R (Level of Service Inventory-Revised). LSI-R was found in the 1990s to be the most useful assessment tool for predicting recidivism. ACE was developed jointly by Colin Roberts and colleagues and the Warwickshire Probation Service. It is still being used by the Probation Board in Northern Ireland, in Swedish prisons and in several other countries. ACE was designed to be both a prediction and case management inventory with a built-in offender self-assessment schedule.

Comparing the respective merits and accuracy of ACE and LSI-R, Raynor *et al.* (2000) found that both could be effectively used by probation staff – for preparing pre-sentence reports, supervision plans, home circumstances reports for the parole board, in single-case evaluations and for measuring change in reconvictions. Both instruments demonstrated their potential to support staff to deliver more effective practice with widely different risk profiles and different clusters of needs. While there is evidence of initial reservations and 'teething problems' for practitioners and middle managers over the imposition of structured assessment systems, the use of the longer versions of both tools was positively associated with improved overall standards of pre-sentence report writing, and with significantly fewer reports for courts that were rated as poor.

In 1999 the Home Office began three pilot studies of an in-house designed assessment tool called OASys. The first evaluation of the original pilots up to 2001 was eventually published in 2006, but there has yet to be an independent study to validate OASys scoring and reliability.

In 1998 the new Youth Justice Board commissioned the design of a risk and needs assessment instrument for use with young offenders (aged 10–17 years). This was intended to provide a common framework for assessment within the new multidisciplinary youth offending teams and to demonstrate that tools for young people should accurately reflect their risks (including risks to the young person) and needs and the possible differences between adults and young people. The Probation Studies Unit at the University of Oxford, drawing on their experience of developing ACE, designed and developed a system called ASSET. ASSET has 12 main sections which focus on dynamic and static factors: living arrangements; family and personal relationships; education, training and employment; neighbourhood; lifestyle; substance use; thinking and behaviour; and attitudes to offending. As with OASys, it has sections covering risks of serious harm, but also a section on self-harm and vulnerability to abuse, neglect and injury.

An important and unique element of ASSET is the young person's self-assessment – 'What do you think?' A voice-activated computer version enables young people with poor reading skills to complete this by touching the screen, and it includes games and small rewards for successful completion. Responses can be represented for ongoing work with the young person.

Conclusion

While assessment tools have a real value in promoting consistency and structuring judgement, their uncritical application could be unjust and counterproductive. It is therefore essential that assessment tools are used appropriately and creatively within a practice framework that promotes high-quality assessment, values professional skills and, above all, engages offenders to understand better why they have offended and how they can change. Robinson found that many probation staff fear that such systems erode discretion and deprofessionalize probation work. New tools like OASys and ASSET demand much time and work, even as caseloads and the demand for court reports continue to grow. Tools should be ways of structuring judgement and discretion – not simple tick boxes – so design, length and user-friendliness are important. If practitioners believe such systems remove their discretion in order to achieve centrally set targets, they may well become cynical and fail to take the assessment process seriously. As electronic versions become more widespread, some practitioners are believed to be simply copying old assessments instead of completing new ones during periods of supervision or for court reports.

If, on the other hand, practitioners feel the system improves their own assessment, enhances their reports, makes supervision plans more understandable and precise and gives meaningful and accurate feedback on effectiveness, these instruments are likely to succeed and contribute to more effective collective outcomes. These tools can provide comprehensive coverage of key risk and protective factors and point to areas for intervention, individually or in aggregate. Offenders can also benefit from high-quality assessments and intervention plans, especially if their own views captured in a self-assessment can be properly considered and incorporated into the planning and delivery processes.

Colin Roberts

Related entries

Actuarialism; Assessment; OASys.

Key texts and sources

Baker, K. (2004) 'Is ASSET really an asset? Assessment of young offenders in practice' in R. Burnett and C. Roberts (eds) *What Works in Probation and Youth Justice: Developing Evidence-based Practice.* Cullompton: Willan Publishing.

Burnett, R., Baker, K. and Roberts, C. (2007) 'Assessment, supervision and intervention: fundamental practice in probation' in L. Gelsthorpe and R. Morgan (eds) *Handbook of Probation.* Cullompton: Willan Publishing.

Merrington, S. (2002) 'Assessment tools in probation' in R. Burnett, and C. Roberts (eds) *What works in Probation and Youth Justice: Developing Evidence-based Practice.* Cullompton: Willan Publishing.

Raynor, P., Roberts, C., Kynch, K. and Merrington, S. (2000) *Risk and Need Assessment in Probation Services: An Evaluation. Home Office Research Study* 211. London: Home Office.

Robinson, G. (2003) 'Implementing OASys: lessons from research into LSI-R and ACE', *Probation Journal,* 50: 30–40.

ASSOCIATION OF BLACK PROBATION OFFICERS (ABPO)

ABPO is a national, professional, black staff association within the National Probation Service (NPS) and the National Offender Management Service (NOMS).

ABPO was established in 1982, having intially been formed in 1981 as the Black Social Workers and Probation Officers (BSWPO) Association. In Febrary 1984, the association held its first annual general meeting, where it adopted its first constitution. It currently has over 300 members nationally, representing all grades and disciplines within the National Probation Service, Youth Justice Service and a range of voluntary sector organizations.

Although a national association, it is organized into three regions and has a managers group. There is also a portfolio for trainee probation officers (TPOs). Meeting monthly in each region and bimonthly for the managers group, its primary role as a national staff association is to provide support for its members in relation to recruitment, development and retention. It supports its members by providing representation in formal grievance and disciplinary matters. Often working with the recognized probation unions – Napo and Unison – ABPO tries to ensure that black perspectives are aired and understood by all parties concerned.

ABPO has also played a significant role in legislative, policy and practice developments in relation to black and minority ethnic (BME) staff and offenders. Since its inception, ABPO has been involved in the following areas:

- National Standards.
- Criminal justice Acts.
- Pre-sentence report training materials.
- Race and ethnic monitoring.
- Middle managers training.
- Good practice guidelines.
- TPO recruitment and selection.

As a probation staff association, ABPO recognizes the need to:

- tackle discrimination, disadvantage, harassment and intimidation;
- promote good relations between all staff within NOMS and the NPS;
- provide equality of opportunity;
- make the NOMS/NPS workforce more representative of the diverse communities it serves;
- support other organizations, partners, service providers, and the private and voluntary sectors to adopt similar policies on equality and diversity; and
- enable the paticipation of all these diverse communities so that they can benefit from the agenda of citizenship within a framework of inclusiveness.

ABPO has links with probation officer associations around the world (including America, the Caribbean and Asia), which have enabled it to develop collaborative working relationships with other statutory bodies and voluntary/community agencies. The publication recently of several key strategic documents has required ABPO to perform on a number of platforms, both strategically and operationally, in order to represent the needs of its members and to contribute to the diversity agenda. It is also being increasingly called upon by local probation areas to assist in the delivery of race equality action plans, to provide mediation and mentoring, and to develop consultation on service delivery, policy and practice.

Valari Mitchell-Clark

Relation entries

Anti-discriminatory practice; Black and minority ethnic offenders; Diversity; Napo.

Key texts and sources

National Probation Directorate (2002) *The Heart of the Dance.* London: Home Office.

ASSOCIATION OF CHIEF OFFICERS OF PROBATION (ACOP)

The professional organization of chief officers of probation in England and Wales, 1982–2001.

The Association of Chief Officers of Probation (and its predecessor organization, the Conference of Chief Probation Officers) provided a nationally co-ordinated approach for the management of the Probation Service at a time when it was organized under 54 independent local probation committees and when the Home Office's probation department was staffed by career civil servants. ACOP's role, carried out through a structure of subject-related committees, working groups and lead officers, included the development of policy and practice across the spectrum of probation work; the dissemination of good practice; negotiating for resources at national level; and representing the Probation Service to a wide range of statutory and voluntary organizations. It also provided an invaluable support and information network for its members. These were all the chief, deputy and assistant chief probation officers of the local services (including Northern Ireland, the Isle of Man and the Channel Islands) and, later, legal, finance, administrative and other officers employed on similar grades.

Established in 1982, with only two full-time staff supporting an honorary secretary, ACOP's role rapidly grew in importance, and a chief probation officer was appointed as full-time General Secretary in 1986. It was funded by local services on a per capita basis, and directed by honorary elected officers and an executive committee. Local services expected their chief officers to be involved in ACOP's work, and it benefited from a high level of active participation by members, their mature experience and the exclusive purpose to 'promote, develop and co-ordinate' the work of the service (ACOP had no 'union' functions). As the potential of this was realized, increasing use was made of secondments to ACOP for specific aspects of work, often in partnership with other public sector organizations, especially in new areas of development. ACOP also appointed specialist PR staff to promote the service's national profile. Joint work with the Central Council of Probation Committees (CCPC), particularly conferences held at the Queen Elizabeth II Conference Centre, were notable statements of the growing confidence of local probation services in their contribution to the criminal justice system.

ACOP was at the heart of the major debates, issues and changes which affected probation and criminal justice policy throughout the 1980s and 1990s, and worked closely with related organizations in the criminal justice system, social services and local government. It was in the front line in addressing a continuous flow of government green papers, white papers and legislation, contributing to inquiries and working groups, and formulating new initiatives.

The establishment of the National Probation Service in 2001 changed the employment status of chief probation officers, and ACOP ceased to exist.

Jill Thomas and Bill Weston

Related entries

Central Council of Probation Committees; Chief officers.

***

Key texts and sources

The political and social environment of the probation service, in which ACOP worked, and some reference to that work, are well described in Whitehead, P. and Statham, R. (2006) *The History of Probation.* Crayford: Shaw and Sons.

ASYLUM

Asylum is the leave (permission) to enter or remain given to a person recognized as a refugee under the 1951 United Nations Convention on Refugees. The rights that go with it also stem mostly from the convention.

An asylum seeker is someone who has applied to the Home Office for asylum as a refugee but has not yet received a decision. A refugee is someone who has been recognized by the Home Office as a refugee within the terms of the 1951 United Nations Convention related to the status of refugees. A refugee is a person who is unable to return to his or her country of origin due to 'a well-founded fear of being persecuted for reasons of race, religion, nationality, political opinion or membership of a particular social group'.

While there has been a 40 per cent reduction in asylum seekers in the UK since 2001, a situation mirrored throughout Western Europe, there were still 34,000 asylum applications into the UK in 2004 and 25,000 applications in 2005. It was also estimated that there were 283,000 failed asylum seekers in the UK in 2004. During 2003–5, about 17 per cent of those deported following criminal convictions were failed asylum seekers.

Asylum applicants receive various immigration statuses, which are increasingly time limited, with the government stating its intention to undertake 'active reviews' after a set period to assess whether the asylum claimant can return to his or her country of origin. It remains to be seen how this policy of time-limited permission to remain in the UK affects the integration and settlement of asylum applicants and migrants in general.

There is no evidence that asylum seekers are over- or, indeed, under-represented in offending since criminal justice agencies do not at present monitor consistently for immigration status. However, anecdotally, probation staff, particularly in metropolitan areas, regularly work with foreign nationals who hold a variety of immigration statuses, including those given following asylum applications. Probation staff should therefore possess a basic knowledge of immigration status, and how it affects rehabilitation and resettlement issues, as well as of how offending may place their continued residence in the UK in jeopardy.

The National Asylum Support Service (NASS) manages new asylum seekers' accommodation and support needs. New asylum seekers are usually initially dispersed outside the south east and may face difficulties in settling in areas with few members of their ethnic and cultural group. Some asylum seekers move back from their dispersal area and can therefore disbar themselves from NASS support, becoming destitute, dependent on others and vulnerable to health and other problems.

Asylum benefits are a complex and rapidly changing area of public policy. It is important that probation areas establish access to good welfare and benefits advice for staff and for the asylum seekers with whom they work. Probation staff should not give advice or opinions, however 'well intended', on immigration or nationality law. Offenders needing such advice should be directed to agencies who can assist, such as citizens' advice services, local authority 'one-stop shops', legal centres and specialist immigration advice services.

Nick Hammond

Related entries

Deportation; Interpreting and translation; United Nations.

Key texts and sources

Nationality, Immigration and Asylum Act 2002.
Immigration, Asylum and Nationality Act 2005.
Joint Council for the Welfare of Immigrants (2006) *Immigration, Nationality and Refugee Law Handbook.* London: Joint Council for the Welfare of Immigrants.
The Refugee Council is the largest refugee organization in the UK providing advice to asylum seekers and other organizations supporting refugees and asylum seekers (**www.refugeecouncil.org.uk**). The National Asylum Support Service website is also useful (**www.asylumsupport.info/nass.htm**).

ATTENDANCE CENTRES

An attendance centre order sentences a young person (10–25 years old) to attend an attendance centre for a minimum of 12 hours and a maximum of 36 hours, dependent on the seriousness of the offence.

There are 112 centres in England and Wales, catering for both male and female offenders aged from 10–25 years old. They are expected to attend up to 2–3 hours per week on a Saturday morning or afternoon in either junior or senior centres. The main purpose of the attendance centre is to restrict a young person's leisure time.

Programmes at the centres focus on two distinct areas. First, they offer the opportunity to engage in physical education, usually football, basketball or circuit training. Secondly, groupwork sessions focus on basic skills, such as literacy, numeracy, life skills, cookery, first aid and money management. Programmes also address issues of victim awareness, drug and alcohol awareness, and sexual health matters.

Attendance centres are provided by the Home Office under s. 62 of the Powers of Criminal Courts (Sentencing) Act 2000. Originally established by statute in 1948, their original purpose was to 'deprive a young offender of a half day holiday, to prevent their going to a football match or a cinema'.

The centres themselves were originally established to cater for attendance centre orders but, since the establishment of youth offending teams and since the range of new sentences for young people has been extended, they have evolved to deliver programmes which support community sentences, including intensive supervision and surveillance programmes, reparation orders, action plan orders and referral orders.

Attendance centres have the following objectives. To:

- prevent reoffending;
- punish by imposing a loss of leisure time;
- allow the offender to acquire or develop personal responsibility, self-discipline, new practical skills and interests; and

- enable the offender to develop social skills and to make better use of leisure time.

The following are the main circumstances in which offenders can be made subject to an attendance centre order:

- When a person under 21 is convicted of an offence punishable with imprisonment.
- Non-payment of fines or compensation by offenders aged under 25.
- On breach of the following orders:
  - supervision order;
  - action plan order;
  - reparation order;
  - community rehabilitation order (16–17 years old);
  - community punishment and rehabilitation order (under 18 year olds);
  - curfew order (under 16 years old).
- Breach of anti-social behaviour orders.
- Attendance centre orders can also be made as an element of a referral order contract (under 17 year olds).

Both junior and senior centres are currently accountable to the Youth Justice and Children Unit within the Home Office.

Kaushika Patel

Related entries

Community order; Community penalties; Youth Justice Board.

Key texts and sources

Mair, G. and Canton, R. (2007) 'Sentencing, community penalties and the role of the Probation Service', in L. Gelsthorpe and R. Morgan (eds) *Handbook of Probation*. Cullompton: Willan Publishing.

Muncie, J. Hughes, G. and McLaughlin, E. (eds) (2002) *Youth Justice: Critical Readings*. London: Sage.

Stone, N. (2001) *A Companion Guide to Sentencing*. Crayford: Shaw & Sons.

Youth Justice Board (1999) *National Standards for Youth Justice*. London: Youth Justice Board.

www.yjb.gov.uk
www.homeoffice.gov.uk

ATTRITION

> The progressive reduction in size of a group or population as it proceeds through a series of stages.

This term is relevant to this dictionary in two distinct senses.

Attrition in the criminal justice process

Criminologists have always known that the number of offences leading to a criminal conviction is probably a small proportion of all crimes committed. The British Crime Survey (BCS) began to give an idea of the size of the 'iceberg' of which convictions are the tip. Between crime and punishment stand a number of processes – reporting the crime, recording it, 'clear up', prosecution, conviction – and, at each stage, the population reduces, sometimes substantially (many crimes are not reported, not recorded, not cleared up, etc.). Although there is variation among offences, for a set of BCS crimes it is thought that no more than 2 or 3 per cent of crimes lead to conviction and punishment. The significance of this finding is considerable. It means that any studies of convicted offenders will only give information about offenders in general on the very doubtful assumption that those convicted are *representative*. Generalizations about the characteristics of offenders based on a study of those convicted are vulnerable to this criticism. Secondly, this level of attrition exposes the limited potential of the penal system to influence crime: although deterrence, denunciation and the communications of punishment may reach a wider audience (see Punishment (aims and justifications); Punishment as communication), only a small proportion of offences lead to punishment.

Attrition from accredited programmes

The target number of offenders to go through accredited programmes was very challenging. It soon became clear that the 'what works' project was threatened by poor rates of completion: many offenders failed to complete and indeed many failed even to commence. It is known that 'completers' are less likely to be reconvicted than a matched group of non-participants, but those who start and fail to complete do worst of all. While the causal connections here are unclear (see accredited programmes), this high attrition rate became a cause of concern. Addressing the problem raises discussion about motivation, enforcement and compliance. A long interval between court and commencement, for instance, was believed not only to prolong an at-risk period but also in itself to be demotivating. Some areas have significantly improved their performance and have been imaginative in deploying incentives and removing disincentives to participation. These include the provision of transport in appropriate cases, appointment cards, phoning and texting as reminders, breakfast clubs and access to a gym and leisure facilities for those attending centres for programmes. Successful completion is sometimes acknowledged through the presentation of a reward or a certificate – which might be highly prized by those who are unfamiliar with achievement and still less with praise.

Rob Canton

Related entries

Attrition in the criminal justice process
Criminal justice system; Punishment (aims and justifications).

Attrition from accredited programmes
Accredited programmes; Compliance; Enforcement; Motivation.

Key texts and sources

Attrition in the criminal justice process
Garside, R. and McMahon, W. (eds) (2006) *Does Criminal Justice Work? The 'Right for the Wrong Reasons' debate* (available at http://www.crimeandsociety. org.uk/briefings/dcjw.html).
Home Office (1999) *Information on the Criminal Justice System. Digest 4* (available online at http://www.homeoffice.gov.uk/rds/digest41.html).

Attrition from accredited programmes
Kemshall, H. and Canton, R. (2002) *The Effective Management of Programme Attrition* (available online at http://www.dmu.ac.uk/faculties/hls/research/commcrimjustice/commcrimjus.jsp).

AUTISM AND ASPERGER SYNDROME

> Autism, including Asperger syndrome, is a lifelong developmental condition. It is a 'hidden' disability characterized by a 'triad of impairments': difficulties forming social relationships, problems with verbal and non-verbal communication and difficulties with social imagination.

Autism and Asperger syndrome (often referred to by the term 'autistic spectrum disorders' or ASDs) affects an estimated 587,900 people in the UK. In addition to the characteristic difficulties, there may be sensory issues (for example, heightened or acute sensitivity to noise and touch) and co-ordination problems. Some people with autism may also have severe learning disabilities, and some may never speak. People with Asperger syndrome, on the other hand, usually have an average or above average IQ and fewer problems with language, though their words can sometimes sound stilted or pedantic.

There is no evidence that people with autism are any more likely to commit crimes than others. Those who do come into contact with the criminal justice system are typically from the more 'high-functioning' end of the autistic spectrum. However, their command of spoken language is not necessarily indicative of their level of understanding or social awareness; they often don't understand the implications of their actions (they do not instinctively link cause and effect) or the motivations of others, and they may not be able to learn from past experience.

Lack of understanding of autism can sometimes lead to behaviour being misconstrued. For example, difficulties with making eye contact can be misconstrued as dishonesty or disrespect. Social naivety (such as making inappropriate social approaches or being duped into acting as unwitting accomplices due to an inability to read others' motives), unusual behaviour (such as aggression or elated outbursts in response to unexpected change) or obsessional interests can lead – inadvertently – to offending. Unexpected situations can provoke high levels of anxiety which can result in alarming and, sometimes, (unintentional) criminal or challenging behaviour.

If the behaviour and response of an individual under probation supervision are unusual, the possibility of an autistic spectrum disorder should be considered in order to access appropriate support. It is good practice to seek advice (where possible) from the individual's parents, carers or professionals involved, and the advice of a psychologist or specialist social worker may also be necessary. The support of an 'appropriate adult', especially one who has knowledge of autism, is often essential, and the services of an advocate can sometimes be valuable.

The reactions that people with autism display are different in every individual, and professionals involved in their care and support while in contact with the criminal justice system should be as prepared and able to assist as possible.

National Autistic Society

Related entries

Diversity; Learning disabilities.

Key texts and sources

The National Autistic Society (2005) *Autism: A Guide for Criminal Justice Professionals*. London: National Autistic Society. (available online at **www.autism. org.uk/cjp**).

A web-based learning resource for criminal justice professionals is available online at **www.autism. org.uk/cjp**).

The National Autistic Society's Autism Helpline, 0845 070 4004 (Monday-Friday, 10am–4pm), has a list of specialists able to offer support.

B

BIFURCATION

> A type of penal policy in which punishments are simultaneously increased for serious offenders and decreased for less serious offenders.

Bifurcation is sometimes referred to as 'the twin-track approach'; the two terms are synonymous. The term 'bifurcation', in relation to penal policy, was first utilized in an essay by Anthony Bottoms (1977).

The definition given above can be regarded as the ideal-typical version of the concept of bifurcation. The term is also, however, sometimes used to refer to policies whereby punishments for serious offenders are increased, but other punishments are held constant.

A classic example of a policy embodying bifurcation may be seen in an initiative on parole policy in England and Wales in 1983–4. The new policy, announced by the then Home Secretary (Leon Brittan) at the Conservative Party conference in 1983, made the possibility of obtaining parole much more remote for offenders sentenced to lengthy terms of imprisonment for violent, sexual or drug offences. Simultaneously, however, parole eligibility was significantly widened for short-term prisoners.

The contrast between the immediate and the delayed results of this initiative is noteworthy. On announcing the policy, the Home Secretary gained significant political credit (with his party and with the wider public) for the first part of the initiative, but the second part (on short-term prisoners) attracted very little attention. However, this was a time of pressure on the available stock of prison places, and the immediate effect of the second leg of the policy was to reduce the prison population by about 2,000. Thus, a government minister simultaneously obtained political kudos *and* significantly relieved the pressure on the prison system – a very successful result, from his point of view. In the longer term, however, the second part of the policy led to significant structural difficulties with the whole parole system, and the restrictive policy for more serious offenders was considered by some to be unfair because it applied only to specified offences and not to prisoners serving the same terms for other offences (e.g. serious fraud). Both parts of the bifurcatory parole policy were therefore criticized by an independent committee (the Carlisle Committee) in 1990, resulting in a major reform of the parole system in the Criminal Justice Act 1991 (see, generally, Maguire 1992).

This example provides an excellent illustration of the reason why bifurcatory policies are sometimes introduced. The policy for serious offenders was fairly clearly promulgated for reasons of populist punitiveness, while the policy for less serious offenders was introduced because of resource constraints on the prison system. Both these factors can weigh powerfully with politicians in contemporary societies. But the value of the illustration does not stop there, for the short-term pragmatism of the reasons underpinning Leon Brittan's policy left it, instructively, very vulnerable to longer-term criticism.

While bifurcation policies are usually developed by politicians, it is not unknown for such a strategy to appeal also to non-political actors, such as judges. A good illustration of this is to be found in some guideline sentencing judgments handed down by the English Court of Appeal in the 1980s. The court first encouraged sentencers to impose significantly shorter terms of imprisonment than hitherto for those property offenders thought to deserve a custodial sentence; then, a few years later, it gave guidance to Crown Court judges that many sentences then being passed for rape offences were too short. In this example, the non-political appeal of bifurcation seems to depend upon 1) an attempt to reinforce the moral consensus in society against certain kinds of seriously anti-social activity, in a contemporary social context of moral uncertainty (see Boutellier 2000, 2) a wish to be as accommodating as possible to politicians faced with resource constraints on the prison system; and 3) perhaps a diffused ideological effect whereby the concept of bifurcation, originally adopted in a given country for political reasons, can become in effect a kind of 'received common sense', and therefore easily capable of being adopted by non-political actors. Of these factors, the first is of the greatest general significance, and, of course, it has links with the concept of populist punitiveness, though these links are not straightforward.

Anthony Bottoms

Related entries

Penal policy; Populist punitiveness.

Key texts and sources

Bottoms, A.E. (1977) 'Reflections on the renaissance of dangerousness', *Howard Journal*, 16: 70–96.
Boutellier, H. (2000) *Crime and Morality: The Significance of Criminal Justice in Post-modern Culture*. Dordrecht: Kluwer Academic.
Maguire, M. (1992) 'Parole', in E. Stockdale and S. Casale (eds) *Criminal Justice Under Stress*. London: Blackstone Press.

BLACK AND MINORITY ETHNIC (BME) OFFENDERS

Black and minority ethnic offender refers to people of African, African Caribbean and Asian descent who have come into contact with the criminal justice system and specifically the National Offender Management Service (NOMS).

The history of the study of BME offenders suggests a history of differential treatment and variable practice as a result of the interplay among the agencies of the criminal justice system. The complexity of this 'system' has made it difficult for research to isolate and explain empirically the cause for this differential. What is not contentious is that, in relation to their numbers within the overall population (currently 8.7 per cent), BME people are more likely to be 'stopped and searched', arrested and charged by the police. A study by Hood (1992) provided clear evidence of racial disparities in the sentencing process, with an increased likelihood of BME people being sentenced to imprisonment. Moreover, BME prisoners are heavily over-represented at 24.6 per cent of the prison population, with differences between men and women offenders in the profile of this population. From the outset, it is important to highlight that, overall, patterns of BME offending behaviour are similar to those of their white counterparts although there are ethnic variances, with some groups offending at a lower level than the white majority. Addressing the complex picture of the causes of these differences provides a demanding challenge to both research and criminal justice agencies.

In ascertaining the impact of practice on BME offenders it is necessary to look at the assessment process (pre-sentence reports, OASys and supervision planning), which is crucial for correct targeting and implementation, and at subsequent interventions – some of which (for example, accredited programmes) have been designed principally for white offenders.

In 2000, a thematic inspection entitled *Towards Race Equality* concluded that an 'examination [of pre-sentence reports] revealed a significantly higher quality of reports overall written on white compared to minority ethnic offenders'. Although a subsequent follow-up inspection noted marked improvements in the overall quality of pre-sentence reports, stubborn differences persist between reports written on BME and white offenders (HMIP 2004). Hudson and Bramhall (2005) suggested that officers may have problems in establishing the sort of dialogue with BME offenders necessary to produce effective reports. They describe reports on Asian offenders as tending to be 'thinner' than those written on white offenders and being less likely to reflect 'remorsefulness'. Report writers were more likely to employ 'distancing language' which, in turn, reduced the credibility of any mitigating factors. These findings reflected earlier research which suggested that differences in assessment and pre-sentence reports may impact on disposals given, with BME more likely than white offenders to be sentenced to punitive rather than rehabilitative interventions.

Over the last few years the tendency has been to explain offending behaviour in terms of the cognitive deficits of individuals rather than in relation to issues concerning class or social exclusion. Alternative explanations for offending focus on the variations in life chances that result from being located in certain parts of the social structure. These approaches see the over-representation of BME offenders in the criminal justice system as related to their greater likelihood of living in poor areas with high unemployment and social problems, areas which, in turn, are often more heavily policed, thereby increasing the chances of arrest. This has been referred to as institutional 'classism'. Whereas this could apply to both BME and the poor white offenders who live alongside them, it has also been argued that BME offenders have an added disadvantage in that they often have to endure the results of racism, 'the double burden of prejudice and exclusion' (Mooney and Young 2000: 83), where young black men respond to their perceptions of rejection by society by seeking recognition on the streets. Furthermore, it seems important not to underestimate the impact that the possible internalization of prejudiced attitudes may have upon the identity of people in BME groups. These more socially based explanations of offending suggest that, to work effectively with offenders, it will be necessary to adopt a more holistic approach that acknowledges the individual's lived experience, including poverty and prejudice and how these interact (Durrance and Williams 2003).

Given the increasing heterogeneity and diversification of European countries and specifically the UK, there have to be questions asked as to whether the definition provided above is adequate. One danger of the term has always been that the considerable variation between the different ethnic and cultural groups subsumed under the definition of BME will be underplayed. Moreover, within the BME 'group' there are other dimensions of diversity: most obviously BME women and men have different experiences. If exclusion from the mainstream is a criterion for inclusion … in the definition … then, increasingly, some groups from, for example, Ireland and more recently eastern Europe should be included on the grounds of their similar experience. But this approach will minimize or even mask the effects of discrimination and racism on the grounds of skin colour. Furthermore poor, young white males may often feel a similar sense of exclusion from the mainstream. In order to ensure that NOMS can continue to explore the impact of its work with members of all groups within society, perhaps its best response would be to collect information relating to race, country of origin and religion on all offenders. Without this type of detail it would be a complex task to establish whether or not individuals from different backgrounds are treated fairly, let alone how NOMS can effectively engage with minority groups.

Patrick Williams and Pauline Durrance

Related entries

Anti-discriminatory practice; Diversity.

Key texts and sources

Bowling, B. and Phillips, C. (2002) *Racism, Crime and Justice*. London: Longman.

Durrance, P and Williams, P. (2003) 'Broadening the agenda around what works for black and Asian offenders', *Probation Journal*, 50: 211–24.

HMIP (2000) *Towards Race Equality: A Thematic Inspection*. London: Home Office.

HMIP (2004) *Towards Race Equality: Follow-up Inspection Report*. London: Home Office.

Hood, R. (1992) *Race and Sentencing*. Oxford: Clarendon Press.

Hudson, B. and Bramhall, G. (2005) 'Assessing the "other": constructions of "Asianness" in risk assessments by probation officers', *British Journal of Criminology*, 45: 721–40.

Lewis, S., Raynor, P., Smith, D. and Wardak, A. (eds) (2006) *Race and Probation*. Cullompton: Willan Publishing.

Mooney, J. and Young, J. (2000) 'Policing ethnic minorities: stop and search in north London. in A. Marlow and B. Loveday (eds) *After Macpherson: Policing after the Stephen Lawrence Inquiry*. London: Russell House Press.

http://www.homeoffice.gov.uk/rds/pubsstatistical. html gives links to statistical reports produced under Criminal Justice Act 1991, s. 95.

BORSTAL

A semi-indeterminate custodial sentence for young offenders that, like probation, represented a belief in reform through education and guidance. Borstal was abolished in 1982.

For most of the twentieth century Borstal was, in the public consciousness, the archetypal custodial institution for young offenders. Originally established by the Prevention of Crime Act 1908 following an experiment in the prison at Borstal near Rochester in Kent, detention in Borstal was to be imposed where this seemed 'most conducive to [his] reformation and the repression of crime'. Reform, more than punishment or deterrence (although these were by no means disavowed), was its guiding rationale: the term 'Borstal training' was later adopted.

Sir Alexander Paterson influentially developed the Borstal system, abandoning the military discipline that had characterized its earliest years and adopting instead the model of a public school with its 'conception of building discipline from within, by encouraging the boys' social instincts of loyalty and esprit de corps, and stimulating their latent capacity for leadership'. Governors and 'housemasters' were appointed for their qualities of character and leadership, which Paterson saw as decisive influences of reform. Classifications leading to appropriate allocation, education and progress through personal endeavour were the guiding precepts of the system.

The sentence of Borstal training was semi-indeterminate. Trainees were liable to be detained for between six months and two years, the duration determined not by the court but by executive decision based on judgements about progress. Formal supervision followed release, administered by the Borstal Association for boys and the Aylesbury Association for girls. (Both associations, later subsumed into the Central After-care Association, employed probation officers as their agents.) Further wrong-doing could lead to recall, but supervision was mainly intended to consolidate and develop the learning achieved in the institution. The principle of the 'seamless sentence' (if not the expression) is emphasized in many of the relevant policy statements.

The histories of Borstal and probation are closely connected. The key legislation was enacted in consecutive years, and Herbert Gladstone, who as Home Secretary was architect of both measures, saw them as different aspects of a single coherent philosophy. Both were inspired by the belief in the possibility of change, to be achieved through education, encouragement and guidance – especially by the example of the staff. Borstal was a victim of the collapse of faith in the rehabilitative ideal and was abolished when the Criminal Justice Act 1982 introduced youth custody, setting other penal priorities.

Depictions in literature (Brendan Behan's *Borstal Boy*, Alan Sillitoe's *The Loneliness of the Long Distance Runner*) and cinema (*Scum*) show Borstal as violent and oppressive, its staff callous and cruel. Yet the Borstal ideal, whatever its subsequent developments or corruptions, represents a rare instance in penal history when, in defiance of *less eligibility* arguments, the ambition was to offer young offenders an education modelled on a form of schooling normally available only to the most privileged young people.

Rob Canton

Key texts and sources

Garland, D. (1985) *Punishment and Welfare: A History of Penal Strategies.* Aldershot: Gower.

Hood, R. (1965) *Borstal Re-Assessed.* London: Heinemann.

http://www.borstal.skinheads.co.uk/

BUTLER TRUST

The annual award scheme for work with offenders in the UK.

The Butler Trust was set up as a registerd charity in 1985 in memory of 'Rab' Butler to promote and encourage positive regimes in UK prisons. 'Rab' Butler was Home Secretary from 1957 to 1962. During this time he brought in the enlightened 'Penal Policy in a Changing Society', seen by many as a major step forward. He is also remembered for the Education Act 1944.

The trust runs an independent annual award scheme to recognize exceptionally dedicated, and often creative, work undertaken by prison staff and volunteers. In 2005 the award scheme was extended to probation staff in England and Wales. Criminal justice social work staff in

Scotland and probation staff in Northern Ireland joined the scheme the following year.

The trust develops effective care for offenders by:

- identifying and promoting excellence and innovation by staff;
- developing and disseminating best practice; and
- providing development opportunities through the award scheme.

Nominations for awards are invited annually during the spring and summer months. Nominations can be for an individual, for two colleagues working together or for a team of staff. During the autumn the trust's Awarding Panel draws up a shortlist of nominees who are interviewed at the end of November. The panel's recommendations are endorsed by the trustees at their December meeting, and the award winners are announced at the end of the year. The award ceremony takes place in March each year.

The trust gives several 'Development' and 'Achievement' awards. In addition there are 20 other major awards, given for particular areas of work. Winners of major awards have the opportunity to develop their work in collaboration with their employer and the trust. Development plans are drawn up with the aim of developing the work of the award winner, evaluating it and disseminating the development more widely. Development plans also attend to the professional and personal developmental needs of award winners. The trust provides expert support and some resource towards the implementation of the development plan, and the employer gives some special leave for the person concerned to develop his or her work.

The extension of the Butler Trust award scheme to the community setting was a response to the government's integration of prison and probation, as expressed through the adoption of the Carter Report recommendations and the creation of the National Offender Management Service in England and Wales. The award scheme not only values routine work that is exceptionally well done but also recognizes creative and innovative intiatives that go beyond prescribed practice. The trust has instituted new awards for offender management and public protection work that reflect the community setting. In 2007 six major awards were given to probation staff in England and Wales, and two to criminal justice social work teams in Scotland.

David Hancock

Related entries

Carter Report; Drug rehabilitiation requirement; NOMS.

Key texts and sources

Full information about the work of the trust and the process of making a nomination for an award can be found at **www.thebutlertrust.org.uk**.

C

CARTER REPORT

An independent review of the correctional services led by Patrick Carter, and published in 2004.

Interest in amalgamating the Prison and Probation Services into an American-style 'corrections' service was signalled when the Labour government was elected in 1997. Talk of a merger subsided when the National Probation Service was formed in 2001. However, in 2003 Patrick Carter was commissioned to carry out a review. This mainly took place inside government, and there was little consultation.

The product of the review, the Carter Report, was published in January 2004. It was not easy to interpret. It signalled a radical overhaul of prison and probation, putting offender management at the centre. Each offender would have an identified offender manager who would be responsible for protecting the public from that offender and reducing the risk of reoffending. In order to do this the offender manager would commission the services necessary from other providers. The model was seen as a penal equivalent to the National Health Service system of primary care staff purchasing the necessary services for patients from other health trusts. The model embraced the government's cherished values of choice and plurality of providers.

Carter recommended the creation of the National Offender Management Service (NOMS) which would foster 'end-to-end offender management' and bring together the Prison and Probation Services to ensure that progress made in prison is followed through in the community, and that cutting reoffending is a top priority for all.

The report recommended demanding community penalties, extensive use of electronic monitoring and the unit fine (see Financial penalties). The Sentencing Guidelines Council was to regulate sentencing to fit the capacity available. This proposal envisioned the fashioning of periodic agreements between sentencers and government about the size of the prison and probation capacity to be financed by government.

Carter put a strong emphasis on private and 'not for profit' sectors competing to run prisons and manage offenders in the community. It was said that, as a market develops, offender managers would be able to buy custodial places or community interventions from whatever sector, based only on their cost effectiveness. The term contestability was coined to define the operation of the market in correctional services.

The Carter analysis and recommendations had two major flaws. First, because of its size and political weight, the Prison Service is unlikely to be corralled within a model where their provision might be subject to the unpredictability of choice by offender managers. Secondly, and more fundamentally, there was a failure to recognize that the principal resources needed to protect the public and to stop reoffending are not products to be purchased. They are the public services of police, health, employment, education, housing, etc. The skills and culture needed to develop partnerships with these services so they can be useful to offenders are worlds away from the consumerist market culture signalled by Carter's view of contestability.

David Hancock

Related entries
Contestability; Interventions; NOMS; Offender management

Key texts and sources

Bailey, R., Knight, C. and Williams, B. (2007) 'The Probation Service as part of NOMS in England and Wales: fit for purpose?' in L. Gelsthorpe and R. Morgan (eds) *Handbook of Probation.* Cullompton: Willan Publishing.

Carter, P. (2004) *Managing Offenders, Reducing Crime: A New Approach.* London: Strategy Unit.

Home Office (2004) *Reducing Crime – Changing Lives: The Government's Plans for Transforming the Management of Offenders.* London: Home Office.

CASE MANAGEMENT

Originating in social work and healthcare and introduced subsequently into probation, case management is a method of combining a range of interventions into a process experienced as coherent by the offender.

Case management evolved in social work and community healthcare. A recognition that services to those with multiple (and inter-related) needs were often unco-ordinated and inaccessible suggested a role for the 'generalist worker' to co-ordinate services. Case management is not a discrete homogeneous activity. Different models have developed, relative to service user need and to the specific contribution of case management to the agency's overall objectives.

The effective practice initiative brought the concept to prominence in probation. A form of modularized supervision with more than one provider with a *case manager* overseeing delivery was envisaged. Generic case management had to be 'translated' into the specifics of probation, clarifying its purpose to guide implementation and evaluation. Holt (2000) found two complementary faces of case management: one a series of events in the timeline of a case; the other a process within which these events were embedded. It was also necessary to distinguish between the case manager and case management, as the one did not simply exercise a bureaucratic function over the other.

Several core functions are common across all models of case management, in particular Assessment, Planning, Intervention, Review and Evaluation (ASPIRE). The case manager 'form[s] the key relationship with the supervised offender. In this way they come to represent the probation service to the individual' (Chapman and Hough 1998: 44), providing the 'human link' between the service user and the system. Holt (2000) suggested that the case manager's role was to embed the delivery of case events in a qualitative process designed to 'make it work' from the offender perspective. Thus the offender's experience of involvement with probation should be characterized by *continuity, consistency*, provision of opportunities for *consolidation* and *commitment* (from staff) – the 'four Cs' (Holt 2000).

Work to implement case management in probation services was wide and varied and, while the phrase rapidly appeared in official accounts, it was less clear what case management should look like 'on the ground'. There was considerable variety of quality and coherence. In 2003, the National Probation Directorate appointed a case management implementation manager to give central drive and direction. However, the Carter Report and the identified need for 'end-to-end offender management' partly overtook this work. A wholesale rebranding of case management as offender management has subsequently taken place, although the key components described above remain.

While case management has been a prominent policy objective, it is less clear how far practice has changed on the ground. Despite the involvement of multiple providers, most probation supervision still takes place on an individual basis and is rarely the subject of scrutiny beyond entries in case records. However, case management has undeniably introduced two key changes to delivery: the systematic involvement of other providers in addressing offender need, and a reformulation of the role of the relationship between probation worker and offender as a means of effecting change.

The ascendancy of case management must be understood in the context of the emergence of public protection and risk assessment and management (rather than 'welfare') as the service's first priority. Probation supervision was originally predicated on an individualistic understanding of the offender and a championing of rehabilitation. By contrast, case management emerged at a time when crime control was increasingly being seen in 'partnership' terms – no longer the sole preserve of state institutions (Garland 2001).

The Crime and Disorder Act 1998 enacted these new 'joined up' arrangements, which required a revised form of supervision to co-ordinate resources from many providers and to synthesize them into a coherent delivery plan. Although technique has largely replaced personal influence as the engine of change in offender rehabilitation, the research literature continues to emphasize the importance of the relationship between case manager and offender.

Case management has also gained prominence at a time when more traditional 'public sector' administrative forms of activity (characterized by workers with specialist knowledge and professional judgement) have been replaced by routinized, highly bureaucratic and standardized work. Indeed, case management provides a potent example of the ascendancy of managerialism. Nevertheless, while National Standards and other practice requirements have squeezed the space occupied by probation workers' traditional autonomy, the content of supervision remains largely unprescribed. The view of case management as a complementary arrangement of two faces, events and context, provides space for the more traditional forms of personal interaction directed towards specific achievements by the offender. It has thus provided a new focus for some familiar tools.

Paul Holt

Related entries

ASPIRE; Effective practice; Offender management; Offender management as seen by other agencies.

Key texts and sources

Chapman, T. and Hough, M. (1998) *Evidence Based Practice: A Guide to Effective Practice.* London: Home Office.

Garland, D. (2001) *The Culture of Control.* Oxford: Oxford University Press.

Holt, P. (2000) *Case Management: Context for Supervision.* Leicester: De Montfort University (available online at **http://www.dmu.ac.uk/ Images/Monograph%202_tcm2-35042.pdf**).

CASE RECORDS

Formal records kept by an organization to structure and account for assessment, planning, intervention and evaluation, typically including personal details of the individual concerned, a record of his or her contact with the agency and work undertaken in relation to him or her.

Keeping case records is a significant part of the work of the Probation Service. Accurate, complete and up-to-date records – showing when, how and why certain events or activities occurred and decisions were made – are a precondition of effective accountability. Case records convey information within the organization and between the organization and other interested parties. In the absence of the supervising officer, for example, a sound and up-to-date case record is an indispensable resource to anyone working with the offender. The record ensures that work remains purposeful: setting out the basis of the assessment, supervision plans, interventions and an evaluation of their effect.

Historically, the Probation Service sometimes compiled and retained information of uncertain value. Forms held information – number of rooms in the offender's accommodation, amount of rent and so on – the relevance of which may well have been no plainer then than now, but with an unspoken assumption that the more information gained, the more complete and rounded might be the understanding of the offender. Generally, it is interesting to speculate how the structure and content of records may reflect particular conceptions of the character and purpose of supervision.

Records typically include personal information – name, date of birth, address, education, employment; a record of assessment and planning, reviewed regularly, setting out objectives and evaluating the effect of the work undertaken; and a record of contact, recording attendance (or non-attendance) at the office, home visits and other significant activities. The file also retains information about an offender's previous convictions and earlier experiences of supervision or imprisonment.

Increasingly, the service has tried to integrate the different components of its case records through electronic systems (see C-NOMIS; OASys). Records are now used more systematically to inform other documents, like formal reports. Electronic systems offer considerable scope for collation, integration and sharing, although development has been uneven and often troubled.

Records are scrutinized by line managers to provide management information, including monitoring of adherence to policy and National Standards. They are an important source of information to HM Inspectorate of Probation.

Offenders have a right of access to their records, although part of the record – 'third party' information (which might compromise the safety or well-being of another person) – would not be available. Records used to be considered confidential to the agency, but this principle has been largely superseded by an expectation that information should be shared among responsible agencies, particularly in cases of high-risk management. Ethical dilemmas around data protection remain, however, not least concerning the extent to which a risk management strategy may or should be shared with the offender.

Rob Canton

Related entries

Accountability; C-NOMIS; Data Protection Act; Freedom of Information Act; HM Inspectorate of Probation; National Standards; OASys.

Key texts and sources

Kemshall, H., Mackenzie, G., Wood, J., Bailey, R. and Yates, J. (2005) *Strengthening Multi-Agency Public Protection Arrangements (MAPPAs)* (available online at **http://www.homeoffice.gov.uk/rds/pdfs05/dpr45.pdf**).

CENTRAL COUNCIL OF PROBATION COMMITTEES (CCPC)

The Central Council of Probation Committees in England and Wales was founded in 1959 to 'speak with one voice' for the 108 probation committees which had been established in 1926.

In 1952 the Home Office had approved the establishment of a national Joint Negotiating Committee for the Probation Service. However, it was the Magistrates' Association rather than the employing probation committees that was invited to take up three of the thirteen employer seats (the rest being held by local authority members, reflecting the funding system of the time and the links with social services). In 1958 a group of probation committees asked the Magistrates' Association to convene a meeting of committee representatives from England and Wales to consider the formation of a separate organization that would represent and support them in their duties as employers. This initiative was given impetus by the appointment of a departmental committee to inquire into the Probation Service (the Morison Committee appointed in 1959 – report published 1962). The inaugural meeting of the Central Council held in November 1959 was attended by the Home Secretary, R.A. ('Rab') Butler, who said: 'I wish you well. I think that your service is perhaps the most devoted in the country.'

The CCPC thus became the main channel of communication between the Home Office and local committees, being consulted over policy and resource issues in addition to its core role as the national organization for the employers of probation staff. Its members were invited to sit on government advisory committees, regional planning groups and a royal commission. CCPC representatives formed part of the national negotiating forum for the salaries and conditions of service of probation staff, sitting alongside local authority members.

All area probation committees (which had reduced to 54 by the 1990s) were members of the council. It was funded by annual subscription. Work was carried out in a series of subcommittees dealing with salaries and conditions of service, recruitment and training of probation staff, custody and through-care, probation hostels, resources, policy and governance. Training events for committee members were provided. Professional advisers were drawn from the Magistrates' Association, the Justices' Clerks' Society, the judiciary, chief (probation) officers and others, as required. A close working relationship was maintained with the Local Government Management Board which provided industrial relations services to the council.

In 1990 the council proposed smaller, more business-like boards to manage an expanding service, retaining its all-important links with the courts and local authorities, but including a wider variety of members of the local community. A firmer performance agenda was proposed, together with grant-aiding powers for local committees and some voluntary amalgamations. These proposals gained Home Office approval and formed the basis of draft legislation at a time when the government was promoting a role for probation 'at centre stage'.

Concurrently, discussions were taking place about amalgamating the Association of Chief Officers of Probation (ACOP) with the CCPC. In readiness for the new structure, the council changed its name to the Central Probation Council, and then changed into the Probation Boards' Association.

Sarah Gore Langton

Related entries

Association of Chief Officers of Probation; Probation Boards' Association.

Key texts and sources

Probation Boards Association website (www. probationboards.co.uk).

CHIEF OFFICERS

The accountable officer of a probation area, responsible for the strategic management of staff.

It is instructive to consider that it took some 30 years following the establishment of the Probation Service for principal probation officers (as they were first known) to be seen as necessary. The first few decades of probation's existence are characterized by a complete lack of any organizational or bureaucratic structure – and, therefore, a consequent lack of any formal supervision of the work of probation officers. The relatively small number of officers (by 1933 there were still only around 300 full-time probation officers), the allegiance of some to the Church of England Temperance Society (CETS), the essentially local nature of probation work and the authority of the sentencers with whom they worked meant that supervisors were deemed to be unnecessary. As the number of staff grew, however, and the power of CETS diminished, the Home Office saw a need for supervision. The 1926 Probation Rules provided for higher salaries to be paid to a principal probation officer (PPO) and a few areas subsequently made such appointments (a chief probation officer had been appointed in Liverpool as early as 1920). Ten years later, the Departmental Committee on the Social Services in Courts of Summary Jurisdiction recommended the appointment of principal probation officers partly in acknowledgement of the growth in the service and consequent organizational problems. The 1937 Probation Rules permitted such appointments, and the Home Office moved to appoint a PPO for the Metropolitan Police Court District. While probation committees were responsible for appointing PPOs, appointments required the approval of the Home Secretary. By 1966, there were 70 PPOs in post.

Reorganization reduced further the number of probation services and, in 1974, when the name was changed, there were 54 chief probation officers (CPOs) in post. CPOs were accountable to their committees for the leadership, organization, supervision and control of the service. They therefore had considerable freedom and could – to a large degree – run their areas with minimal intervention from their committee or the Home Office. While CPO autonomy had undoubted advantages, these were increasingly viewed as out of step with government moves, beginning under the Conservative administration of 1979, to exert greater control over state spending. The *Statement of National Objectives and Priorities* (1984), the introduction of National Standards and the imposition of cash limits on probation funding in 1992 all constrained – indirectly, if not directly – the power of CPOs. When the National Probation Service came into being in April 2001, CPO numbers dropped to 42 and their power was diminished. The newly named chief officers now became managers, with accountability to the Home Secretary (selection is under National Probation Directorate control but appointment remains subject to ministerial approval), but also having to respond to the requirements of their boards and the increasing expectations of regional directors.

Assuming that current moves towards a fully fledged National Offender Management Service proceed, including increased contestability, the introduction of trusts to replace Boards and the amalgamation of areas, the role of chief officer is likely to change again soon.

George Mair

Related entries

National Offender Management Service; National Probation Service for England and Wales.

Key texts and sources

Haxby, D. (1978) *Probation: A Changing Service.* London: Constable.

Mair, G. (2004) 'What Works – a view from the chiefs', in G. Mair (ed) *What Matters in Probation.* Cullompton: Willan Publishing.

CHILD PROTECTION

The key functions of the National Probation Service are to protect the public and reduce reoffending. Section 11 of the Children Act 2004 provides direction to ensure that probation staff also operate in the wider context of safeguarding and promoting the welfare of children. In doing this, the legislation does not compromise probation boards' ability to execute properly their key functions.

The Children Act 2004 has changed the structures and arrangements for multi-agency work for the protection of children. Section 11 of the Act came into force on 1 October 2005 and was implemented in Wales on 1 October 2006. The Act provides for local safeguarding children boards (LSCBs), which replace the area child protection committees (ACPCs), and revises the 'Working Together to Safeguard Children' arrangements.

The Act places a duty on probation boards and chief officers to provide senior management membership of the LSCBs. This means that probation has a responsibility, along with the local authority, police, NHS health authority and trusts, youth offending teams (YOTs) and governors of prisons, etc., for safeguarding and promoting the well-being of children. Section 10 (2) of the Children Act 2004 strengthens the provisions of the Children Act 1989, to extend the protection of children from maltreatment to encompass:

- physical and mental health and emotional well-being;
- protection from harm and neglect;

- education, training and recreation;
- making a positive contribution to society; and
- social and economic well-being.

The LCSBs' responsibilities do not differ greatly from the ACPCs'. However, the Act 'requires them to carry out their functions in a way that takes into account the need to safeguard and promote the welfare of children'. This widens the responsibility of the LSCBs and that of probation areas to all children under the age of 18.

Probation Circular 63/2005 (Statutory Guidance on Implementing Section 11 of the Children Act 2004) identifies the contribution of the Probation Service in safeguarding and promoting the welfare of children as follows:

- The management of adult offenders in ways that will reduce the risk of harm they may present to children through skilful assessments, the delivery of well targeted and high-quality interventions and risk management plans.
- The delivery of services to adult offenders, who may be parents or carers, that address the factors that influence their reasons to offend.
- The recognition of factors which pose a risk to children's safety and welfare, and the implementation of agency procedures to protect children from harm. This will include appropriate information sharing and collaborative multi-agency risk management planning – i.e. multi-agency public protection arrangements (MAPPAs), child protection and domestic violence forums.
- Seconding staff to work in YOTs.
- Providing a service to child victims of serious sexual or violent offences.
- Providing a service to the women victims of male perpetrators of domestic abuse participating in accredited programmes for domestic violence. In particular, having regard to the needs of any dependent children if there is domestic abuse within the home.

Within this context, probation staff have a key role in working with adult offenders who may pose a risk of serious harm to children and their carers. In these cases, probation staff have a

responsibility to undertake a comprehensive assessment using all the available information (through OASys). These offenders will normally be subject to regular multi-agency meetings which focus on developing plans to reduce the risk the offender poses. Appropriate information should be shared with other relevant agencies via MAPPA or LSCBs arrangements. This will support the multi-agency management of these offenders, with the aim of promoting the safety and welfare of children and of protecting the public.

In risk assessment and management work, staff should ensure that the risk management and sentence plans contain specific strategies and objectives to reduce the risk posed by the offender. These plans will then provide the focus of the work with the offender. The offender may also have to comply with additional requirements, as part of a community order or specific licence conditions, following a custodial sentence. Both these can strengthen the ability of offender managers to intervene, change and monitor the behaviour of offenders.

Probation staff have a responsibility to be mindful of the safety and welfare of children when they construct sentence plans for all offenders. They need to consider how any planned interventions might impact on an offender's parental responsibilities or contribute to an improvement in the well-being or welfare of the children in the family (see Children and families of offenders). The aims of the plan must be shared with the other members of the offender management team and the other agencies involved.

Probation staff come into contact with children within their normal working environment. This could be when a child is brought to the probation office or when they undertake home visits. If a member of staff becomes aware of a child who appears to be at risk or he or she has concerns about the welfare of a child, he or she must inform his or her line manager and share the information with the local suthority children's services. The local 'Working Together to Safeguard Children' arrangements will provide guidance on whom to contact, including 'out of hours' arrangements.

Individual probation areas will have local information-sharing protocols to support the sharing of this type of information, but the MAPPA guidance (PC52/2004) also outlines the duty to share information across agencies to promote public protection. The focus of probation intervention is on the ability of offenders to change their behaviour. Therefore, sharing information on child protection issues can be a sensitive task, especially if the offender is making progress and the offender manager has developed a productive working relationship. However, the primary responsibility of probation staff must be to the child or children: to safeguard their welfare and protect the public.

Frances Rutter

Related entries

Inter-agency work; Partnerships; Public protection; Risk assessment and risk management; Risk of harm.

***

Key texts and sources

Children Act 2004.
Home Office (2005) *Statutory Guidance on Implementing Section 11 of the Children Act 2004.*
Probation Circular 63/2005. London: Home Office (this circular provides a list of useful references).
Home Office (2005) *Implementing Section 10 of the Children Act 2004. Probation Circular* 22/2005. London: Home Office.
Good material and links are on the website **www.everychildmatters.gov.uk/.**

***

CHILDREN AND FAMILIES OF OFFENDERS

Relatives can be part of an offender's problem and/or part of the solution; there is also the possibility of trauma for any children, and of 'learned behaviour' replicating offending in the next generation. Rehabilitation and prevention are key aims.

The nature of close relationships is likely to influence behaviour, for better or worse. An 'at-risk' person could be tipped into offending or reoffending by numerous family factors – for example, demands of partner and family, the frustrations of uneasy relationships or the reduction in an offender's self-esteem within the family. The locus of failure or success for the offender as a person can lie in his or her functioning as partner and/or parent.

Only limited research has been undertaken about the children and families of prisoners, and even less about the children and families of offenders serving community sentences. Doubtless, many of the same crucial issues will be relevant to both groups, and early intervention could reduce the difficulties. Promoting and maintaining good family relationships while an offender is in prison help to reduce subsequent reoffending. Prison sentences are known to damage family relationships. Additionally, when an offender returns from prison, readjustment can prove problematic: the family has had to learn to cope without the offender, and prison can have institutionalized the returnee.

For parents in prison, preserving a meaningful relationship with their children can be difficult. Yet contact during imprisonment and the nurturing of the parental role do influence future relationships. An absent parent is likely to return home (or, if not, will want to keep in touch), and contact matters, not only in terms of children's rights and access to their parent but also in terms of the prisoner's reoffending and the child's role modelling. Murray and Farrington show that parental imprisonment during childhood is 'a clear marker of a number of risk factors for children's own anti-social behaviour and delinquency' (2005: 1274): intervention should seek to minimize deleterious factors, including separation, stigma, loss of family income, a reduced quality of care, a poor explanation given to children and children's modelling of their parents' behaviour.

'Children and families of offenders' is one of the seven pathways to reducing reoffending in the 'Reducing re-offending delivery' plan. Regional pathways are typically led by the voluntary sector in partnership with criminal justice agencies, health, education, youth justice and children's services, to provide a 'joined up' approach to resolving family difficulties, and the probation officer/offender manager usually participates in this network. Families of offenders should not, however, automatically be problematized. They can be well placed to offer positive solutions and should be afforded the opportunity to contribute to pre-sentence reports and sentence plans to improve the accuracy and efficacy of interventions.

Peter Wedge

Key texts and sources

Boswell, G. and Wedge, P. (2002) *Imprisoned Fathers and their Children.* London: Jessica Kingsley.

Ditchfield, J. (1994) *Family Ties and Recidivism: Main Findings of the Literature. Home Office Research Bulletin* 36. London: HMSO.

Home Office (2005) *Reducing Re-offending Delivery Plan.* London: Home Office.

Murray, J. and Farrington, D. (2005) 'Parental imprisonment: effect on boys' anti-social behaviour and delinquency through the life course', *Journal of Child Psychology and Psychiatry*, 46: 1269–78

Action for Prisoners' Families: (www.prisonersfamilies.org.uk).

Ormiston 'Time for Families' (www.ormiston.org).

CHILDREN AND FAMILY COURT ADVISORY SUPPORT SERVICE (CAFCASS)

CAFCASS is an independent public body working with children and families involved in family court proceedings. Through their reports, CAFCASS officers provide advice to the courts so that their decisions will be in the child's best interests.

Since CAFCASS officers practise in the family courts, it might be thought that their contact with the criminal justice system would be minimal. However, this is far from true: if you are working with 'offenders', you can expect a number of encounters with CAFCASS. Supervising offenders may well involve liaison with CAFCASS personnel – most likely where the person is a par-

ent who is divorcing or separating or where he or she is connected in some way with an application for care proceedings by the local authority.

CAFCASS is an independent, public agency and was launched in England in 2001. In Wales, the service is CAFCASS Cymru, while different arrangements pertain in Scotland and Northern Ireland. Section 12 of the Criminal Justice and Court Services Act 2000 sets out four key functions for CAFCASS's work in proceedings where the child's welfare may be in question:

1. Safeguard and promote the welfare of the child.
2. Give advice to the court about any application made to it in such proceedings.
3. Make provision for children to be represented in such proceedings.
4. Provide information, advice and support for children and their families.

The last of these is perhaps the least well developed. There is a growing recognition of the needs of children whose parents are separating or divorcing, but many children in such circumstances still have little option but to 'suffer in silence' given the lack of support available to them. CAFCASS do undertake some longer-term social work with families experiencing difficulties after separation or divorce, but the number of such 'family assistance orders' is very small. Similarly, CAFCASS could play an important role in partnership with schools, giving information to children and ensuring that they know about access to services, including helplines.

The creation of CAFCASS brought together the Family Court Welfare Service (FCWS), guardian *ad litem* services and the Children's Division of the Official Solicitor, and the initial job of gaining a coherent identity for the new agency was especially difficult given the three different groups of staff. FCWS was a part of the Probation Service: its staff were probation officers, specializing in an area of interest, and most became CAFCASS employees in 2001, bringing with them a wealth of knowledge and experience about offenders and child protection issues. A CAFCASS officer who contacts the Probation Service – in the course of welfare report inquiries, wanting to check out arrangements for someone's release from prison – may well have a good grounding in work with offenders.

CAFCASS officers were involved in more than 12,000 public law cases in 2004–5, including applications for local authority care orders and applications for adoption. In private law cases, when parents or carers are unable to agree on where a child will live and/or how contact with the non-resident parent will be managed, CAFCASS staff have two main tasks:

1. Undertaking court-directed dispute resolution/mediation.
2. Preparing welfare reports in accordance with s. 7 of the Children Act 1989.

In 2004–5, approaching 35,000 dispute resolution sessions were provided and more than 28,000 reports requested. In both public and private law work, CAFCASS officers seek to promote the child's best interests through collecting relevant information and views from all other agencies involved, including the child's school, and by keeping fellow professionals aware of developments. Establishing whether or not a case is known to child protection services, police or probation is standard practice in welfare report inquiries, although the precise arrangements for this vary from area to area. Criminal justice personnel are therefore most likely to encounter CAFCASS colleagues engaged in public or private law report inquiries. As parents, many offenders undergo separation or divorce and some struggle to reach an agreement with their ex-partner about their children. Imprisonment is often a key precipitating factor but, more generally, socio-economic deprivation has a similar effect on the likelihood of parental discord, as it does on the propensity to become embroiled in the criminal justice system.

CAFCASS is one of a range of organizations with a duty to safeguard children and it participates in local and national collaborative arrangements. CAFCASS is one of the statutory members of local safeguarding children boards and is also represented on family justice councils.

Although it is not one of the core members for multi-agency public protection arrangements, co-operation does take place in relation to cases where a potentially dangerous individual is involved. CAFCASS officers are also alert to the possibility of domestic violence, and the agency is involved, in some areas, in multi-agency risk assessment conference (MARAC) meetings, managing risk in domestic violence cases.

CAFCASS continues to be at the centre of a great deal of controversy, with a widespread agreement that change is needed, especially in private law cases. Various groups, seeking to represent the rights of fathers, have been vociferous in their criticisms of CAFCASS's role in private law cases and have taken various forms of direct action. At the extreme end of this, CAFCASS staff have been threatened and offices vandalized – in Ipswich, CAFCASS premises were 'fire-bombed' – leading to a number of prosecutions. This sets an unfortunate context for the criminal justice practitioner's work with offenders, some of whom will be fathers with estranged children.

Greg Mantle

Related entries

Children and families of offenders; Domestic violence; Mediation.

Key texts and sources

Children and Family Court Advisory Support Service (2005) *Delivering Quality Services for Children: Transforming Services – Transforming the Organisation, Business Plan 2005/07*. London: CAFCASS.

James, A.L., James, A. and McNamee, S. (2003) 'Constructing children's welfare in family proceedings', *Family Law*, 33, 889–95.

Mantle, G., Moules, T. and Johnson, K. (2006) 'Whose wishes and feelings? Children's autonomy and parental influence in family court enquiries', *British Journal of Social Work*.

http//www.cafcass.gov.uk

CITIZENSHIP

The concept of citizenship has been used with various meanings at various times, in the context of different implied social and political values, and in pursuit of various objectives. The dictionary definition is a native or inhabitant of a state or a city, and the term is often used in a narrow and technical sense related to immigration or nationality law. In classical times, the concept implied a privileged status above that of slaves or other inhabitants. In revolutionary France or the USA, or among radicals such as Levellers and Chartists, it was used to imply a sense of freedom and independence, often in contrast to the situation of those who were still 'subjects' of a hereditary sovereign. It can thus be used 'exclusively' or 'inclusively', with very different implications and connotations.

In the period after the Second World War, citizenship began to be associated with social justice, with ideas of public service and of social obligation, and with rights such as those expressed in the United Nations' Universal Declaration of Human Rights, the United Nations' Covenant on Civil and Political Rights and the European Convention on Human Rights (see Council of Europe). The concept also came to be extended to the economic and social rights associated with the welfare state. It began to recede from political debate when the idealism of the immediate postwar period gave way to scepticism and disappointment or, it might be said, political realism, during the 1960s and 1970s.

The Conservative government of 1979–97 revived the concept in the 'Citizen's Charter'. There it was associated with a person's 'rights' in relation to services provided by the state. The revival was in the context of that government's distinctive social and economic policies – there was a narrow, individualistic focus on a person's rights as a consumer (essentially to choose between competing providers, or to complain) and no suggestion of any wider sense of social or civic duty or responsibility.

In other debates, citizenship began to be used to counter the individualism that had become pervasive in politics and in working and social relationships during the period. It was again associated with the ideas of public duty and social responsibility, and it was used to emphasize shared interests and responsibilities, often among people from different ethnic and religious backgrounds. In the report of the Power Inquiry it was associated with a revival of political activism and democratic engagement.

For the Labour government which took office in 1997, citizenship was similarly connected with duties and obligations. The focus was now on duties to obey the law, to be of good behaviour, to care for and control one's children, to work and pay taxes. Observing those duties was seen as a counterpart to the human rights which Parliament had incorporated into domestic law in the Human Rights Act 1998. In a return to the older idea of 'lesser eligibility', people were sometimes portrayed as having forfeited their status as citizens if they committed a criminal offence, especially if they received a prison sentence. Citizenship was reserved for the 'law-abiding' and 'hard-working' majority.

In the programme for 'civil renewal', introduced by David Blunkett during his time as Home Secretary (2001–4), the government gave encouragement to a concept of 'active citizenship'. The idea was essentially that people should give some of their time to voluntary work for the benefit of their community and, by implication, in support of the government's own policies. 'Active citizenship' would not, for example, include taking part in demonstrations. Responsibility for the programme was transferred from the Home Office to the Department for Communities and Local Government in 2006, where it became part of a wider range of policies concerned with the teaching of citizenship in schools and with subjects such as community cohesion, urban regeneration and neighbourhood renewal. A common aim was to enable people to engage with public bodies and influence the decisions that affect their communities. Most of the programme was outside the area of criminal justice, but it included, for example, the development of community justice and 'community courts', together with various forms of engagement between local communities and the National Offender Management Service to help reduce reoffending.

There has been less emphasis on offenders' own rights and responsibilities as citizens, and the notion of 'lesser eligibility' has always had some influence. Unpaid work has usually been seen more as a punishment than an act of citizenship. There is a long tradition of prisoners doing work that benefits local communities, but it has rarely been seen in a theoretical framework and it has always been marginal to the main tasks of the Prison and Probation Services and vulnerable to political and operational pressures. The concept of citizenship was implicit in Lord Wilberforce's well-known judgment in *Raymond v. Honey* (1983) that 'in spite of his imprisonment, a convicted prisoner retains all civil rights that are not taken away expressly or by necessary implication', but that judgment has not had much practical effect. The concept is also implicit in restorative justice and in approaches to the treatment of offenders, especially prisoners, which emphasize their equal status as human beings, their entitlement to dignity and respect, their own obligation to take responsibility for what they have done and for rebuilding their own lives. That obligation includes playing a part in their communities, and a duty of society as a whole to give them the opportunities to do so. The right to vote in parliamentary elections is a symbolic but important example.

Approaches such as those are still very much on the margins of penal policy. But they may still have some potential as a driving force for penal reform, in a favourable political climate and if they could be given some credible content. One necessary condition would be the capacity of local communities, including minority communities, to respond to the opportunities which could be made available, and the power and responsibility to do so constructively and in a spirit of public duty and service. Building local capacity – and with it responsibility – will be as important as the provision of actual services or interventions. Another condition is that civil renewal and active citizenship should not be seen as a matter that is only for people outside the system or for offenders. Staff should be enabled and encouraged to play their own part as members of their own communities, with the authority and opportunity to act as innovators, as many probation officers were able to do in the early days of victim support and restorative justice.

David Faulkner

Related entries

Community; Community justice; Penal policy; Reintegration; Social exclusion.

Key texts and sources

Farrant, F. and Levenson, J. (2002) *Barred Citizens*. London: Prison Reform Trust.
Faulkner, D. (2006) *Crime, State and Citizen: A Field Full of Folk* (2nd edn). Winchester: Waterside Press.
Power Inquiry (2006) *Power to the People* (the report of the Power Inquiry) (available online at **www.powerinquiry.org/report**).

C-NOMIS

Managing offenders in real time, whether in custody or in the community, with a unique record on a single, shared database.

C-NOMIS is an IT system that has been designed to support end-to-end offender management by providing the Prisons and Probation Services with a single case record of an offender that can be accessed and updated in real time.

The need to target offenders more effectively across organizational boundaries, and the development of a system that places the offender at the centre of a range of interventions, was identified in the Carter Report as key to reducing reoffending and increasing public protection. This was the starting point for the creation of C-NOMIS.

Work on C-NOMIS was initiated the following year using an existing case management system whose capability has been proved in North America and Australia but which needed to be adapted to domestic needs – a process whereby it will eventually become the largest joined-up corrections case management system in the world.

The present situation is that each of the 42 probation areas in England and Wales has a separate local IT system, none of which are connected. The Prison Service has a national but outmoded system. C-NOMIS will replace all the existing legacy systems within both organizations and create, for the first time, a national database for the management of offenders within the National Offender Management System (NOMS). Contracted-out prisons will also be part of the new system.

The aim is to match the functionality of existing systems used within probation, such as Delius, ICMS, etc. It is recognized that these have great strengths but not the national, strategic benefit of a single shared view of the individual offender that C-NOMIS will confer across the National Probation Service, the Prison Service and the contracted-out sector.

As well as information on offenders being shared between the Prison and Probation Services, the risk that they pose will be more clearly highlighted. A feature of C-NOMIS is a prominent header block, on screen, containing accessible information of the type and degree of risk the offender poses to him or herself and others. This information will be derived from OASys assessments and managed through the case notes updates that the system generates. In the early phases of introduction of the system, a two-way interface will exist between OASys and C-NOMIS but after roll-out there are plans to embed the OASys function fully within C-NOMIS.

Intervention measures, such as drug rehabilitation and accredited programmes, can be initiated and monitored more effectively using the C-NOMIS integrated national database of interventions. This comprehensive online services catalogue will provide information on courses and other interventions both locally and nationally.

As well as strengthening the offender management process, C-NOMIS is a system that will underpin and support the working routine of all probation and prison officers. Because there will only be one shared record per offender, offenders will be entered on the system once only and will be allocated a unique national number that will stay with them forever. Pointless duplication and endless rekeying of information will, in time, disappear.

C-NOMIS will speed up such processes as the granting of a home detention curfew, which requires the combined input of the Prison and Probation Services and which will be undertaken electronically. Sharing information among virtual teams and across organizational boundaries will be a key benefit of the system and one that was welcomed by the Mubarek Inquiry.

Users will also be able to pull off both local and national data, profiling offender behaviour and outcomes. There will be a national library of key management information reports, and users will also have a local *ad hoc* report-writing facility to enable them to obtain performance information on specific local criteria.

The introduction of C-NOMIS into probation areas and the 139 prisons (including privately run establishments) will take place over two years. The process started in December 2006, with the go-live of Albany Prison on the Isle of Wight.

Implementation will involve not just the building of a single IT infrastructure but significant business change and new ways of working. C-NOMIS will necessitate the national standardization of forms, documents and processes. It will introduce new concepts into working life, such as role-based access, virtual teams and electronic workflow, all of which will require probation areas and prison establishments to adapt their current ways of working. The central business-change team in the project will work with local areas to prepare them for these changes as part of the implementation approach. Other major projects to be undertaken will be the training of over 78,000 staff and the merging and migration of 200,000 records of offenders from existing systems. In the process, existing offender records will be checked and upgraded where data are incomplete or inaccurate.

On the completion of roll-out to prisons and probation areas and the replacement of all legacy systems by 2009, it will be time to join C-NOMIS with the police, courts, Crown

Prosecution Service and other criminal justice agencies that will benefit from access.

C-NOMIS is a major element in the transformation of criminal justice IT, but it will also be a valuable professional tool for prison and probation staff, improving ways of working (including the assessment and management of risk), increasing job satisfaction and saving money that can be reinvested locally.

Mike Rose

Related entries

Case records; Information technology developments in areas; NOMS; OASys; O-DEAT; Offender management.

Key texts and sources

C-NOMIS implementation toolkit (available on Epic – the NPS staff intranet).

COGNITIVE-BEHAVIOURAL

The term refers respectively to (1) a specific theoretically driven approach to human action; and (2) a collection of intervention methods applied to a variety of individual problems. Some of these methods have been extensively used with offenders and have recently become highly influential in probation practice.

Historical context

The phrase 'cognitive-behavioural' emerged during the 1970s as a result of the convergence of two previously separate approaches or 'schools' in psychology. The theory on which they are based represents a synthesis of concepts from behavioural and cognitive psychology, entitled 'cognitive social learning theory'.

The basic tenets of behaviourism, initially stated in 1913 by American psychologist, John B. Watson (1878–1958), rejected the pervasive mentalism of that period and its core method, introspection. Watson asserted that, in order to become properly scientific, psychology should focus on external events that could be directly observed, with data corroborated by independent observers. Watson also emphasized learning as a pre-eminent factor in human development, proposing that the phenomenon of conditioning, discovered by the Russian physiologist, Ivan Pavlov (1849–1936), provided a mechanism capable of explaining the acquisition and establishment of complex behaviour patterns. Subsequently behaviourism, in its progressive transformations, became a dominant force in psychology. Discussion of internal, unobservable 'states of mind' or experience was regarded as suspect; in its most radical form, behaviourism avoids the use of any hypothetical entities or constructs. The application of learning-based models and procedures led later to the advent of behaviour modification, in which behavioural change is accomplished by altering the environment and the consequences of actions; and behaviour therapy, a set of procedures in which conditioning principles are applied to the reduction or eradication of behavioural and emotional difficulties.

Cognitive psychology evolved independently as the study of hypothesized internal sequences of activity through which the central nervous system processes information from external and internal environments and initiates action based upon it. Hence it focuses on studying attention, perception, memory, reasoning, problem-solving, decision-making and creativity. This investigation makes extensive use of hypothetical constructs and the development of theoretical accounts of events not directly observable. From 1960 onwards cognitive psychology was significantly influenced by the growing field of artificial intelligence and the application of information-processing concepts to gain an understanding of human cognition.

The work of Albert Bandura (b. 1925) was a significant influence on the synthesis of behavioural and cognitive concepts. Bandura discovered the possibility that animals could learn indirectly, through observation and contact with others, rather than solely through the direct experience of reinforcement. His work played a major part in initiating the detailed study of modelling and other processes in socialization and development. This afforded a bridge between behavioural and cognitive perspectives and, alongside other discoveries, led to the articulation of new models that drew on research findings and theoretical constructs from both traditions.

Concepts

A cognitive-social-learning approach seeks to understand offending behaviour as a function of learning – of the cumulative experiences to which an individual has been exposed and the environment in which that has taken place. Socialization and other interpersonal processes within families play the most powerful role in individual development, but similar processes also help to explain the profound influence of neighbourhoods and peers (differential association). Alongside behavioural development, cognitive learning occurs in parallel and influences the formation of attitudes, beliefs and habitual patterns of thought. Variability in learning opportunities will affect the pattern of acquisition of skills for effective living, engaging in relationships and solving personal problems. Different permutations of these variables interact with environmental factors (including crime opportunities) and influence the pathways along which individuals travel through successive maturational stages.

It can be useful to consider events within three interdependent domains of activity – *cognition* (thoughts), *emotion* (feelings) and *behaviour* (see Figure 2). Cause–effect relationships are thought to operate in multiple pathways.

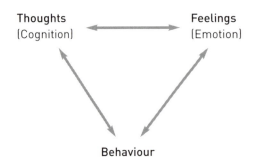

Figure 2 The domains of activity

Methods

The assessment of thoughts, feelings and behaviour, and of their mutual interactions, generates information that can enable individuals to enact change in their lives. Applying this to entrenched problems (such as persistent offending) entails combining knowledge of underlying processes with a systematic exploration of the personal meanings individuals ascribe to situations and events. Such meanings include individuals' explanations of their own experience, their constructions of the world and of the self, and awareness of the skills they possess for identifying problems, generating solutions, anticipating consequences and comprehending the perspectives of others.

Cognitive-behavioural therapy (CBT) is a family of methods used in mental health settings to address a wide variety of different forms of individual distress and dysfunction. These include interpersonal problem-solving, social skills training, assertiveness training, cognitive therapy, self-management, anger control training, relapse prevention, prosocial modelling, moral reasoning education and motivational enhancement, among others. Together these methods can be described as a constructional approach to the development of new repertoires of skill, as contrasted with the eliminative approach used in some forms of behaviour modification (e.g. aversion therapy) and in criminal deterrence.

While all these methods were originally used on an individual basis, it has proved possible to assemble them into structured sequences that can be specified in prepared manuals and so made reproducible. This is the essence of accredited programmes for offending behaviour.

Outcomes

Large-scale reviews of the outcomes of intervention in mental health settings have yielded positive and consistent findings concerning the efficacy of CBT. In the UK this has led to its endorsement by the Department of Health as a 'treatment of choice' for many clinical problems. Similarly in criminal justice, numerous literature reviews employing the integrative technique of meta-analysis firmly support the value of cognitive-behavioural interventions for reducing reoffending. This is not to say that these are the *only* effective approach to achieving that goal.

The movement towards the identification of 'empirically supported treatments' has not been uniformly welcomed by all researchers and practitioners, and claims that, in some instances, CBT and its variants can be indicated as 'methods of choice' are vigorously disputed. These issues continue to be controversial in both mental health and criminal justice.

James McGuire

Related entries

Accredited programmes; Desistance studies vs. cognitive-behavioural therapies: which offers most hope for the long-term?

Key texts and sources

Andrews, D.A. and Bonta, J. (2003) *The Psychology of Criminal Conduct* (3rd edn). Cincinnati, OH: Anderson Publishing.

Department of Health (2001) *Treatment Choice in Psychological Therapies and Counselling: Evidence Based Clinical Practice Guidelines.* London: Department of Health.

Hollin, C.R. and Palmer, E.J. (eds) (2006) *Offending Behaviour Programmes: Development, Application, and Controversies.* Chichester: Wiley.

McGuire, J. (2004) *Understanding Psychology and Crime: Perspectives on Theory and Action.* Maidenhead: Open University Press/McGraw-Hill Education.

McGuire, J. (2000) *Cognitive-behavioural Approaches – an Introduction to Theory and Research* (available at http://inspectorates.homeoffice.gov.uk/hmiprobation/docs/cogbeh1.pdf).

COMMUNITY

Community is a commonly used word in the criminal justice context and yet it is difficult to define. It usually refers to a geographical area or a 'community of interests'. Community is viewed by policymakers as a key element in the strategy to reduce crime.

Criminal justice policies utilize the notion of community extensively: a community order locates treatment and punishment in the community; offenders released from prison are resettled and reintegrated into the community. The Crime and Disorder Act 1998 introduced community safety units and Crime Reduction Partnerships that rely on community involvement. Community representatives are included in a range of criminal justice tasks, from independent monitoring boards (IMBs) in prisons to lay community members of multi-agency public protection arrangements (MAPPAs). So, 'community' is a concept integrated into the language of criminal justice.

The perceived loss of community is often cited as evidence of the decline of social relationships and social control and a reason for the increase in anti-social behaviour and disorder and increases in crime. A romanticized ideal of community, when there was no crime, people could leave their houses unsecured in the knowledge that they would be safe and where everybody knew everybody, is often presented as the lost 'golden age', a time when things were more secure and society safer. However, there is little evidence to support this romantic ideal of the cohesive, supportive, safe and crime-free community of the past. Communities are also described in less positive terms: as hostile, anti-social, crime ridden, deprived and disadvantaged. All these images conjure up another view of community that is a place of threat rather than one of safety. So, community is an ambiguous term: on the one hand community is presented as safe, secure and supportive; on the other, as a place of conflict, tension, hostility and insecurity.

Among the many ways of defining community is as *a geographical area that has definite borders.* These areas can vary from large areas to relatively small ones (for example, a city or town as a community to one or two streets being defined as a community). The architect Oscar Newman viewed community as a geographical area that provided protection and social interaction through shared space. The important element for Newman was that, through proper design, 'defensible space' could be created that would allow people to control their immediate surroundings. This social concept of community through the shared control of space is one way of understanding community. However, geographic definitions are not unproblematic (for example, there can be conflict between different groups in the same geographical locations). The definition of a community by geography or spatial relationships relies upon there being an agreed geographical definition, and this may vary between areas with some areas not recognizing that they are part of a geographical area.

A community can be defined as a *community of interests*. In this respect community does not have defined geographical borders but is defined by common and shared interests or experience (for example, the gay community). A community may be defined by shared beliefs, such as faith and religion. These are all different and yet all are defined as being 'communities'.

Community is viewed by policymakers as a key element in the strategy to reduce crime. The Home Office published *Confident Communities* in 2004, which set out the government's vision as to the role of community in 'tackling social problems'. The main focus of the strategy is to create, build and sustain 'social capital'. The concept of social capital is debated by sociologists. However, it is the core of the government's policy in relation to communities, and law enforcement and crime reduction. Social capital is concerned with shared norms and effective forms of social control and processes that assist different groups within communities to work together and access resources. Communities comprise different social networks. These social networks in communities that are stable provide networks that include kinship and friendship structures, and some of these networks will be inter-generational. These networks will provide many individuals with contact with a broad spectrum of people across their community. This is the foundation of the means of informal social control – those contacts that result in anti-social behaviour are not tolerated. Such communities are described as having a high level of social capital. However, what is considered to be anti-social can be dependent on what such communities define as

anti-social or unacceptable behaviour. It might be that crime is viewed as being unacceptable, but gay relationships are also viewed as unacceptable. Therefore social capital has a negative as well as a positive aspect.

Communities with a high degree of informal social control can be defined as offence intolerant. However, there are also communities that have a high level of social capital – that is, shared values and norms, strong bonds between individuals and groups, and a series of informal social controls that are, in particular communities, offence tolerant. For example, a community that experiences high levels of deprivation and social exclusion may have an economic structure where acquisitive criminal activity is an important element of how the community functions economically. Therefore property offences are not viewed as being anti-social or to contravene community norms. This highlights another issue of complexity: communities possess different levels of tolerance in relation to different types of offences. For some communities, all types of offending are not tolerated; in others, some offences are tolerated and others are not acceptable. It is also important to note that what is considered acceptable and unacceptable can be dependent upon age and gender.

What appears to be the most effective type of community at preventing crime are those communities where its members have a broad range of social relationships. These communities can exercise a broad spectrum of informal social control – that is, where community members share the values and norms and conform in order to maintain their membership and status within the community. These communities are also effective in managing conflict and resolving issues of offending through restorative approaches to crime and offending. Therefore, criminal justice approaches are utilized sparingly and usually when it is perceived as being in the community's collective interest to do so. Consequently, such communities are more able to resolve conflict and to provide positive forms of intervention with offenders. However, in many post-industrialized societies such communities are uncommon, and governments (through interventions such as Crime and Disorder Reduction Partnerships and community safety units) attempt to stimulate or recreate those more tightly bound communities with a high level of social capital. At the same time governments put in place strategies to manage anti-social behaviour and disorder. These strategies are in many respects exclusionary inasmuch as the person identified as being anti-social is excluded from geographical areas or is not allowed contact with certain individuals. Such a strategy is counter to the ideal of an inclusive community that has a high degree of informal social control.

Community is, then, an ambiguous term. It is, however, viewed as a positive element in ensuring offenders desist from further offending. Establishing effective community relationships with offenders is also viewed as a key part of the strategy of reintegrating offenders into the community after sentence. However, it is apparent from an analysis of the term community that the process of reintegration is not a straightforward task – the process of reintegration may take place in a crime-tolerant community. It may be that a period of imprisonment is so damaging to positive community networks that, on release, the ex-offender experiences difficulty in maintaining crime-intolerant networks that form the basis of social control and, consequently, establish and sustain crime-tolerant networks. Communities with high levels of informal social control that are crime-intolerant are a significant component in ensuring desistance from offending. However, many communities where residents do not have integrated social networks across the community, where offending is tolerated and where there is little investment by residents in their locality suggest that the elements of social capital that encourage desistance are missing.

Communities are an important part of criminal justice strategy as they provide the environment in which the reintegration of offenders as full members of the community takes place. However, the fractured nature of many communities that experience disadvantage, poverty and social exclusion demonstrates the crucial link between social policy and criminal justice policy.

Jon Spencer

Related entries

Citizenship; Community justice; Community safety; Punishment in the community; Reintegration; Social capital; Social exclusion.

Key texts and sources

Home Office (2004) *Confident Communities* (available online at http://www.crimereduction.gov.uk/publications10htm).

Maguire, M. and Raynor, P. (2006) 'How the resettlement of prisoners promotes desistance from crime – or does it?', *Criminology and Criminal Justice*, 6: 19–38.

Prior, D. (2005) 'Civil renewal and community safety: virtuous policy spiral or dynamic of exclusion?', *Social Policy and Society*, 4 : 357–67.

Spencer, J. and Deakin, J. (2004) 'Community reintegration: for whom?', in G. Mair (ed.) *What Matters in Probation*. Cullompton: Willan Publishing.

COMMUNITY JUSTICE

'Four core elements distinguish the new "Community Justice" from past policies and practices. Community Justice operates at the neighbourhood level, is problem solving, has decentralised authority and accountability and, finally, involves local citizens in the justice process' (Clear 1999).

In England and Wales, over 225,000 offenders are supervised in the community each year, either under some form of supervision or under parole licence. Despite experimentation and innovation within the case worker paradigm, the approach has come under much criticism on the grounds that even intensive supervision or cognitive behavioural methods do not necessarily achieve significantly better outcomes in terms of offence reduction than the use of custody. New control technologies, too, may have increased the distance between the offender in the community and the probation officer. Community supervision staff are frequently characterized as suffering from burnout and low morale and subject to a range of increasing performance management routines. Public confidence in community supervision is not very high, with attention drawn to failures rather than successes (see Public attitudes to probation).

Out of the disillusionment with current correctional practices that seem to give little attention to the impact of crime on neighbourhoods, victims and the quality of life, we can observe over the last two decades in the USA, the UK and further afield the development of a community justice approach. This new approach to crime prevention explicitly includes the community in the criminal justice process: 'It is expressly concerned with improving the quality of community life, and the capacity of local communities to prevent crime and to respond to criminal incidents when they occur' (Karp and Clear 2002). Much of the thrust of community justice innovation stems from the USA, but community-oriented models can also be discerned in other countries.

Family group conferences for juvenile offenders are a prominent method in New Zealand and Australia. In the UK, in 2005, the then Home Secretary, David Blunkett, following a visit to the Red Hook Community Justice Center in New York, piloted a similar model in north Liverpool. Part of the Liverpool experience, again following an American initiative of the mid-1990s in the creation of community reparation boards in Vermont, has seen the recruitment of a panel of community members who will help to identify priorities for unpaid work to be performed by offenders subject to community orders. A more formal pilot to do this, funded by the Esme Fairbairn Foundation, is taking place in the Thames Valley partnership area (Clarke 2006).

The sense of neighbourhood is central to community justice. In addressing elements of crime and disorder, officials and participants draw on local responses and initiatives, supplementing their work with extra help from outside the area to sustain a particular programme if necessary. The Red Hook Community Court in Brooklyn, New York, is now 10 years old. It has been tackling crime and anti-social behaviour in two novel ways. First, it has engaged the direct help of local people, both in crime prevention

and in tailoring punishments to what they want done – clearing up graffiti, removing rubbish and so on. Secondly, it has treated the underlying causes of offending, whether housing, debt, alcohol, drug abuse or domestic violence.

Under community justice, crime is seen as a social problem affecting the lives of offenders, victims, and their families and neighbours. Problem-solving approaches rely on the sharing of information, deliberation and mutual interest. When crime is approached as a problem, solutions can take various forms, from addressing kerb-crawling behaviour by men in search of prostitutes to providing oversight of troublesome youth. In north Liverpool, the resident judge, David Fletcher, meets with a panel of local residents to address their concerns. Within the court itself, the judge can call upon an array of expertise from local agencies, who can provide timely assessments and services for offenders with substance misuse problems, accommodation problems or debts. The court, apart from administering justice, can be seen, as well, as a one-stop service to a range of consumers who also happen to be offenders.

The third strand of community justice requires traditional criminal justice agencies, police, probation and prosecutors to rethink the way they work together, to share information and lines of accountability and, most importantly, to recruit and mobilize the informal resources of local neighbourhoods, self-help groups and faith communities. Faced with a rise in youth homicides in a Boston suburb in the early 1990s, the local police and probation services abandoned isolated practices to create Operation Night Light – in effect, police/probation patrols involving intensive home and street contacts with high-risk offenders during the evening hours. Night Light was also concerned to use local citizens as part of the outreach activity. The project recruited local people to set up recreational facilities for the young, including drug treatment centres, detached street workers, schools initiatives, employment and education advice centres, and intensive follow-ups with the families of at-risk juveniles.

In the UK schemes focusing on prolific and other priority offenders, where the police and probation services work intensively with serious and persistent offenders on a daily basis, have developed from the Night Light model. The essence of such programmes is rooted in shared risk assessments, information exchange, mutual trust and a developing sense of accountability that lies beyond the organizational hierarchy to the local citizenry, who have the biggest investment in improving the quality of neighbourhood life.

Finally, citizen participation is central to the development of community justice. Not only do citizens participate to ensure that local concerns are addressed but also citizens' participation is strategic for building community capacity so that informal mechanisms of crime control can gradually share the burden with the more formal processes of criminal justice services.

John Harding

Related entries

Citizenship; Community; Community Safety; Punishment in the community; Reintegration; Social capital; Social exclusion.

Key texts and sources

Clarke, D. (2006) 'Communities engaging with community service', *Criminal Justice Matters*, 34–5.

Clear, T. (1999) *The Community Justice Ideal* Boulder: CO: Westview Press.

Karp, D. and Clear, T. (eds) (2002) *What is Community Justice?* London: Sage.

Nellis, M. (2000) 'Creating community justice', in S. Ballintyne *et al.* (eds) *Secure Foundations: Key Issues in Crime Reduction and Community Safety.* London: Institute for Public Policy Research.

COMMUNITY ORDER

The name of the sentence used to place an adult offender under some form of supervision in the community.

The Criminal Justice Act 2003 reformed the sentencing framework and established the nature of the contemporary community sentence. These changes, which also reformed custodial sentences, had been recommended in the Halliday Report. In the place of a variety of different types of community sentences, the new generic community order was implemented in April 2005.

The community order comes with a 'menu' of 12 possible requirements that can be included in the sentence. Courts are able to choose from the different requirements to make up a bespoke community order. Each order must contain at least one of the 12 requirements. The order can run for up to three years. There is no minimum duration, but some of the requirements have a minimum number of hours that must be imposed.

Requirements in a community order may be combined subject to their being compatible, suitable for the offender, not compromising the offender's religious beliefs or times of work and education, and subject to the overall package being commensurate with the seriousness of the offending. The Sentencing Guidelines Council has advised that, in most cases of low seriousness, 'only one requirement will be appropriate, and the length may be curtailed if additional requirements are necessary'.

The 12 possible requirements are:

- unpaid work;
- activity;
- programme;
- prohibited activity;
- curfew;
- exclusion;
- residence;
- mental health treatment;
- drug rehabilitation;
- alcohol treatment;
- supervision; and
- attendance centre.

This list contains all the familiar work streams that had been well established by the Probation Service at the time of the change. Community punishment orders became 'unpaid work requirements', drug treatment and testing orders became 'drug rehabilitation requirement', and the 'programme requirement' was introduced for those cases where an accredited programme was recommended. The 'residence requirement' is for situations where residence in approved premises is appropriate. There is provision for activity, attendance centre, prohibited activity, curfew and exclusion as specified requirements of the order. The provision of requirements for mental health treatment and alcohol treatment was welcomed as giving additional recognition to significant issues that had previously been somewhat neglected in terms of services provided.

The supervision requirement became the successor to the previous community rehabilitation order (probation). This obliges the offender to attend regular appointments with the responsible offender manager to promote rehabilitation. Work will be undertaken to change attitudes and behaviour, and this may include, for example, monitoring and reviewing patterns of behaviour, increasing motivation to achieve law-abiding goals, practical support, etc.

At the time of implementation, there were considerable concerns that the new sentence would have unpredictable outcomes in terms of the workload of the Probation Service. Whereas in the past the high-volume orders had been community punishment and community rehabilitation with a small proportion of combined orders, the new order held out the prospect that many more of the generic bespoke orders would comprise several requirements. In practice, the transition has been accomplished fairly smoothly, with the greatest area of concern about the new sentencing framework focusing on the increase in the prison population, rather than on the delivery of the community order.

Another unpredictable aspect at the time of implementation was that the 2005 sentencing framework also reintroduced suspended sentences. These can incorporate the same conditions, and it remains to be seen whether the community order and the suspended sentence have to compete for the same market and what is the overall effect on the use of custodial sentences.

David Hancock

Related entries

Criminal Justice Act 2003; Custody Plus, Intermittent Custody and Custody Minus; Halliday Report; Offender management; Supervision of offenders.

Key texts and sources

Mair, G. and Canton, R. (2007) 'Sentencing, community penalties and the role of the probation service', in L. Gelsthorpe and R. Morgan (eds) *Handbook of Probation.* Cullompton: Willan.
See also key texts and sources of the related entries.

COMMUNITY PENALTIES

Those sentences of the court which involved the offender serving a sentence in the community under the direct or indirect supervision of a penal agent (usually a probation officer).

In the second half of the 1980s, pressure was slowly building up on the Probation Service. A *Statement of National Objectives and Priorities* had appeared in 1984, and the Conservative government was turning its attention to sentencing. Serious questions were being formulated about the contribution of the Probation Service – was it 'tough' enough on offenders? Was it effective in terms of its outcomes? How much did it cost? While the term 'community penalties' may appear to be relatively innocuous, it carries a considerable amount of baggage as its appearance signalled a key change for the Probation Service. Prior to the activity leading up to the Criminal Justice Act 1991, the probation order and the community service order (also the attendance centre order and the supervision order) tended to be referred to collectively as non-custodial disposals, or alternatives to custody. The limitations of such terms lie within them: 'disposals' is used as the probation order had never been a sentence of the court (in other words, not a *proper* punishment); and 'non-custodial' and 'alternatives to custody' gave the message that such disposals were lighter sentence than imprisonment. Probation and community service were, therefore, seen as weak, not particularly punitive court orders and, with the Conservative government lining up the Probation Service in its sights, it was not a good time to be seen as soft on crime.

As a term, 'community penalties' is used in the 1988 green paper *Punishment, Custody and the Community*, but only in passing. In the 1990 white paper, *Crime, Justice and Protecting the Public*, however, Chapter 4 bears the title 'Community penalties', signifying the importance of the new term for the government's plans – and the language of the chapter was robust. Community penalties were to be one part of a sentencing framework based around the concept of 'just deserts'. Three levels of sentences were introduced by the 1991 Act: Level 1 included financial penalties and discharges; Level 2 was community penalties; and Level 3 was custody. The level would be determined by the seriousness of the offence, with *community penalties* used for offences that were 'serious enough' to warrant such a sentence but not so serious that custody could be justified. Restriction of liberty was to become the way in which the punitiveness of a sentence was to be measured – and, while the aims of probation and community service had always been relatively elastic, restricting liberty was not an idea normally associated with these disposals. Indeed, it remains difficult to see how such penalties could possibly be seen to compete with a custodial sentence in such terms.

The 1991 Act introduced two new *community penalties* to add to the four in existence (probation, community service, supervision and the attendance centre order), and both of these led to anxieties on the part of probation officers. The combination order was the lesser worry, combining as it did probation and community service. There was some unease about how the two rather different staff groups involved in the two sentences would work together, and rather more unease about the place of the new order – indeed, the Association of Chief Officers of Probation tried to restrict its use to the Crown Court as it was considered to be so demanding. Curfew orders, enforced through electronic monitoring, however, were seen as much more of a threat to Probation Service integrity. Probation staff had been distinctly unco-operative with the 1989 trials of electronically monitored curfews for bailees, losing the chance of becoming the responsible officers for 'tagging'. Accusations of tagging being demeaning, an attack on civil liberties and simply a punitive form of surveillance with no rehabilitative purpose followed. Whatever probation's doubts about the new orders, there is no doubt that both clearly constituted more rigorous and more punitive sentences.

The Act went even further and made the probation order a sentence of the court, whereas previously it had been used instead of sentencing. While this was in one sense a purely symbolic gesture, for many probation officers it held considerable significance. Although the Probation Service remained responsible for divorce court work, the change in the status of the probation order was a crucial step in the development of the service as a purely criminal justice agency.

The term 'community penalties' is, therefore, associated with a major effort to construct a coherent, rational sentencing framework in which all sentences have a specific place. In addition, the term is also closely tied to the idea of 'toughening up' probation and community service – a process that began with the green paper and has continued to the present day with little sign of stopping. And it can be seen, too, as a critical early step in beginning the deliberate blurring of the boundary between prison and community sentence – again, a process that has gathered pace with the advent of the National Offender Management Service, suspended sentence and the possibility of Custody Plus.

It is interesting to note the vagueness of the term. Precisely what should count as a community penalty? The suspended sentence is served in the community, but is officially a custodial sentence. What is the meaning of 'community' – is it simply the location where the sentence is served? Are community penalties synonymous with community orders and/or community sentences? Ironically, while this brief discussion about community penalties has emphasized its significance, it is important to note that the term is time bound and is now out of date. Since the Criminal Justice Act 2003, the Probation Service runs only one sentence (the community order), so to talk of community penalties in the plural is obsolete, although various penalties run by youth offending teams can be so defined.

George Mair

Related entries

Community; Community order; Custody Plus Intermittent Custody and Custody Minus; Punishment in the community; Supervision of offenders; Unpaid work.

Key texts and sources

Brownlee, I. (1998) *Community Punishment: A Critical Introduction.* London: Longman.
Home Office (1988) *Punishment, Custody and the Community* (Cm 424). London: HMSO.
Home Office (1990) *Crime, Justice and Protecting the Public* (Cm 965). London: HMSO.
Mair, G. and Canton, R. (2007) 'Sentencing, community penalties and the role of the Probation Service', in L. Gelsthorpe and R. Morgan (eds) *Handbook of Probation.* Cullompton: Willan Publishing.

COMMUNITY SAFETY

Community safety focuses on measures to reduce crime and anti-social behaviour, as well as the fear of crime and environmental crime in high-crime, disadvantaged neighbourhoods. The role of the Probation Service in promoting safer communities focuses on its role in public protection and the management of risk, the identification of the needs of the offender and assisting the rehabilitation of offenders in the community.

The term 'community safety' used in the context of social and criminal justice in England and Wales is wide ranging, encompassing measures to reduce crime and anti-social behaviour, as well as the fear of crime and the so-called 'environmental crimes' of graffiti, abandoned vehicles and vandalism. Statutory local Crime and Disorder Reduction Partnerships have often retitled themselves 'Community Safety Partnerships' to indicate to the public that they embrace this wider public safety agenda. The equivalent Community Safety Partnerships in Scotland are even broader ranging, embracing fire safety, road safety and water safety.

Several commentators have argued that the Home Office crime reduction policy has moved from its early reliance on situational crime prevention in the 1970s and 1980s to a recognition of the need to stimulate social crime prevention through programmes (such as On Track and the Crime Reduction in Schools programme), to its current focus on crime reduction measures and neighbourhood policing focused in the highest crime areas. From the point of view of the Department of Communities and Local Government (formerly the Office of the Deputy Prime Minister), action to promote community safety also has a strong neighbourhood focus. This is seen particularly in the 88 most disadvantaged neighbourhood renewal areas where specific targets have been set for reducing crime, environmental crime and fear of crime.

From the point of view of local government, concerns about crime and anti-social behaviour, fear of crime and environmental crime are most frequently expressed in disadvantaged communities. Community safety thus has the advantage from the point of view of central and local government of helping to create a single agenda for action to promote safer communities in high-crime, disadvantaged neighbourhoods.

Community safety forms an important part of the context in which offender management takes place. The role of probation in promoting safer communities is focused on public protection and risk assessment and management, the identification of the needs of the offender and assisting the rehabilitation of offenders in the community. These elements can be seen in the Probation Service's contribution to delivering the national strategy for prolific and other priority offenders, which is co-ordinated by local Community Safety Partnerships.

The national strategy has three strands:

1. *Prevent and deter:* to prevent and deter young people who are at risk of becoming serious and persistent adult offenders or those who are at risk of becoming offenders. Under this

strand, probation is expected to work with the police and other agencies in the local Community Safety Partnership to identify the most persistent adult offenders and to put in place robust measures to manage their offending behaviour.

2. *Catch and convict*: to ensure that agencies prioritize resources in order to target the most prolific and persistent offenders with the aim of putting an end to the harm they are causing the community. Under the 'catch and convict' strand, probation is expected to have carried out an OASys assessment to identify the risk factors that relate to that particular offender's offending behaviour and to work with other agencies in the partnership to put in place the resources (e.g. accommodation, drug treatment and education, training or employment opportunities) that are required to address the needs of that offender.

3. *Rehabilitate and resettle*: to rehabilitate and resettle those offenders who have returned to the community and those who are serving sentences in the community and to encourage them to live offence-free lives. Under this strand, probation is expected to work with the Prison Service to carry out further risk assessments and then ensure that programmes are in place to rehabilitate offenders in the community.

The principles of social exclusion and community cohesion are central to the delivery of the safer communities agenda. Sometimes these core principles can be presented as being at odds with a perceived need to be seen to be taking strong enforcement action, particularly with regard to anti-social behaviour. The Probation Service has a key role to play in ensuring that decisions taken about enforcement action are proportionate and that other options have been considered, including, for example, the availability of support packages where they are needed to support an anti-social behaviour order. By sharing the findings of an OASys assessment a probation officer may be able to demonstrate that low-level interventions may be feasible, particularly when risk factors have been shown to be low.

The Probation Service's knowledge of offending behaviour can be of value when preventive programmes are being developed. Probation officers have played a valuable role in the development of burglary reduction and the recent street crime initiatives. More broadly at a neighbourhood level the service has a role to play in sharing aggregated data about patterns of offending in an area and in supporting the development of neighbourhood safety strategies by helping to analyse the factors that may have led to observed increases in offending. This can contribute to the social capital of a community. For example, a failure to develop supported housing for offenders may have led to their clustering in low-rent, private sector accommodation that is not best suited to their rehabilitation or their family's housing needs. The part that the service plays in commissioning arrangements for 'Supporting People' is also a vital part of the broader community safety agenda.

Tony Holden

Related entries

Community; Crime and Disorder Reduction Partnerships; Crime prevention; Inter-agency work; Prolific and other priority offenders; Social capital; Social exclusion.

Key texts and sources

Matthews, R. and Pitts, J. (2001) *Crime, Disorder and Community Safety*. London: Routledge.
Tilley, N. (ed.) (2005) *Handbook of Crime Prevention and Community Safety*. Cullompton: Willan Publishing.
Tonry, T. and Farrington, D. (1995) *Building a Safer Society*. Chicago, IL: University of Chicago Press.
Useful material and links can be found on http://homeoffice.gov.uk/crime-victims/reducing-crime/community-safety/.

COMPLAINTS

A mechanism for raising concerns when services have not been delivered properly.

Each probation board has a complaints procedure in line with a national model. Leaflets should be available at the reception desk of each probation office giving information about how to complain and how the procedure works.

It is good practice to be as responsive as possible when complaints are raised informally, since a speedy resolution by the person concerned will benefit all parties. Once a complaint has been made formally, a person of a higher grade than the person complained about will investigate the matter. The investigator reports back to the complainant, either upholding or not upholding the complaint. If the complaint is upheld, an apology and/or some redress may be offered.

If the complainant wants to take it further, the matter will then be reinvestigated by a senior manager, usually at assistant chief officer level, and the details will be reported to members of the probation board. If the complainant is aggrieved after the outcome of the second stage, the matter can be referred to the Prisons and Probation Ombudsman, whose office will undertake an independent external investigation.

Serious complaints are sometimes accelerated to the second tier for investigation, and allegations of criminal behaviour by staff may be referred directly to the police for investigation.

Generally, probation areas do not receive a large number of complaints. In a large area there are usually fewer than 100 complaints a year, and perhaps a third of them will progress to the second stage. Most complaints are about some aspect of the way supervision is carried out. The second most common reason for complaint is about information placed in pre-sentence reports or parole board reports.

Despite relatively low numbers, complaints are a touchstone as to the nature of an organization. It is no accident that organizational quality standards, such as Investors in People and Charter Mark, place emphasis on the availability of complaints procedures and the objectivity with which they are implemented. A healthy organization can use complaints to spot areas for improvement and staff in need of additional supervision. There are parallels here with the scheme for investigating serious further offences.

There is a natural tendency in organizations to stick together in the face of an external threat, and the investigation of complaints sometimes raises issues of whether the supervisor has been sufficiently objective in approaching the investigation. Equally, senior managers and board members who ask searching questions can be seen as embracing unreasonable demands and expectations. These tensions are inevitable and are a manifestation of a healthy organizational culture.

When staff feel aggrieved about the way they are dealt with at work, the complaints procedure is not appropriate. Supervision, grievance and harassment procedures are available for staff to raise issues. Unions can advise, and 'whistle blowing' procedures, including 'anti-corruption' direct access to external audit, may also be used in appropriate cases.

David Hancock

Related entries

Accountability; Prisons and Probation Ombudsman; Probation boards.

Key texts and sources

Every area provides details of its complaints procedure on request and publishes aggregate data of complaints received and outcomes in the area annual report.

COMPLIANCE

Observing the legal requirements of the order of the court or the terms of a licence or, more broadly, conforming with the purpose and expectations of supervision.

In the quest for punitive credibility, government policy has usually tried to emphasize the demanding *content* of community punishment. But, of course, this all comes to nothing unless the punishment is given effect. This is the challenge of compliance: ensuring that offenders fulfil their obligations in accordance with the law and the order of the court. This challenge of compliance is peculiar to community sanctions and measures: community penalties require people to do things – to keep appointments as instructed, to participate in (or refrain from) activities, to work – which they might otherwise choose not to do. This creates the possibility of default. At its most ambitious, imprisonment seeks to engage the participation of prisoners in an active and purposeful rehabilitative endeavour, but a passive or recalcitrant prisoner is still being punished; an unenforced community penalty, by contrast, is indistinguishable from 'getting away with it'. Nor is this only a requirement of just punishment: rehabilitation calls for intervention, reparation calls for involvement, and these can only take place with the offender's attendance and participation.

Increased levels of punishment entail ever weightier impositions, and some community penalties make considerable demands on people's time, resources and personal organization. While this may constitute appropriate punishment and/or be needed to deliver the most effective programme, the more that is asked, the greater the opportunities for default, and the proportion of orders breached has been increasing in recent years.

This challenge has usually been approached in the language of enforcement – a term that has a reassuringly 'tough' tone – and policy has been ever more prescriptive about how probation officers must respond to default. Yet much of this instruction, set out explicitly in National Standards, has been about sanctioning failure, with a reliance on the threat of breach and return to court. Courts and the public need to know that non-compliance meets a firm response, but the principal objective must be to give effect to that penalty which the court has judged appropriate. It may be more productive, therefore, to consider carefully what makes offenders most likely to comply, and not just to be preoccupied with response to default.

The debate has been given a valuable change of emphasis and direction by Anthony Bottoms. He identifies several dimensions to compliance: most people in most circumstances certainly take account of the anticipated costs and benefits of their actions, but other considerations are influential too. Bottoms distinguishes 'constraint-based' compliance (for example, the extent to which conduct is guided or circumscribed by physical restrictions) and 'compliance based on habit and routine' (typically unreflective patterns of conduct).

Most important for the present purposes is what Bottoms terms 'normative compliance', a concept which itself has a number of aspects. Among these is the idea of attachment – for example, 'attachment' to a member of staff who demonstrates concern for and personal interest in the offender may promote compliance. So might the supportive involvement of someone to whom the offender is attached, like a friend or family member. The concept of legitimacy is also significant here: people are more likely to comply with expectations on them and to accept decisions – *even decisions that go against their own preferences* – when they are persuaded that these are fair (have been fairly arrived at) and are reasonable. Arguably, this implies a degree of individualization and associated discretion which may jar against managerial conceptions of consistency; it certainly implies personal concern, explanation, dialogue and even negotiation with the offender about the manner in which the order is to be fulfilled.

The key point is that these different aspects of compliance are all significant and must be made to work together. Enforcement policy has arguably limited itself by concentrating on a single dimension – the instrumental/prudential dimension. And even here it has often been unimaginative, with more punishments than positive incentives at the supervisor's disposal. A preoccupation with punishment for non-compliance may have jeopardized the chances of enhancing compliance through paying insufficient attention to normative influences such as legitimacy.

At the same time, whatever the character of national policy, at local and at practice level there are several imaginative and successful initiatives to engage with offenders – creative attempts to identify and overcome practical obstacles to compliance and to enhance motivation. These initiatives, introduced to minimize attrition, represent an attempt to make the several dimensions of compliance work together.

With its (sometimes tacit) assumption that non-compliance is a result of recalcitrance or backsliding to which threat of breach is the proper response, policy has paid insufficient attention to the complexity and ambivalence of motivation. Indeed, it is remarkable how policy has disregarded the subtle and nuanced understandings of motivation that have been developed in probation practice in recent years. The cycle of change, for instance, recognizes that motivation is variable and shifting, while the insights of motivational interviewing appreciate that resistance must be worked with and cannot just be suppressed. (This is perhaps especially true in the case of substance users, but is not unique to them.) None of this seems to have had its influence on enforcement policy, which retains its faith in the efficacy of threat of breach – despite the fact that many offenders on supervision have a substantial history of being unresponsive to threats of this kind. At the same time, however, the political imperative for rigorous enforcement must be acknowledged to be compelling. This may be an example of circumstances in which retribution and rehabilitation point in different directions or where evidence-led practice is subordinate to the demands of punishment.

There are no doubt many reasons why offenders fail to comply or comply variably with the legal requirements of supervision. 'Can't comply' and 'Won't comply' are probably better seen as ends of a spectrum on which an instance of non-compliance can be plotted. Unless supervisors consider the reasons behind non-compliance, it is possible that their response will simply miss the point or make matters worse: their duty may be met by returning the offender to the court, but not enough will have been done to effect the required changes in the offender. The criminogenic problems on which work was to be done may be brought back to the court unresolved. For example, nothing is more demotivating than helplessness – a sense that change is impossible – and this despondency is likely only to be aggravated if it is met by nothing much more than the threat of breach.

What counts as compliance? Minimally, it seems to require a respect for the formal requirements of the order of the court or the terms of post-custodial supervision, but supervisors usually endeavour to bring about compliance with the spirit as well as the letter. Compare, for example, an offender who unfailingly keeps appointments and, just as unfailingly, resists or avoids attempts to 'address offending behaviour' and, on the other hand, one whose attendance is unreliable but seems genuinely if variably intent on changing his or her ways. Perhaps it is because it is so readily *auditable* that the keeping of appointments is the favoured index of compliance. But if the purpose of the exercise is to effect change – a continuing compliance, as it were, with the requirements of the law – then formal compliance may not be enough.

Successful completion of an order often constitutes a genuine accomplishment by the individual under supervision and this sense of completing successfully something worthwhile has been shown to be associated with reduced reoffending, as well as chiming with research findings that desistance is often sustained through achievement. Supervisors accordingly have a very practical reason to focus on compliance more than enforcement.

Compliance is a critical and fascinating topic because it goes to the heart of so many questions about probation practice – the credibility, even the feasibility, of punishment in the community, the purposes of supervision, the character of the supervisory relationship, the proper boundaries of discretion and the balancing of the demands of consistency with the more individualized considerations which legitimacy and respect for diversity seem to require.

Rob Canton

Related entries

Community penalties; Enforcement; Legitimacy; Motivation; National Standards.

Key texts and sources

Bottoms, A. (2001) 'Compliance and Community Penalties', in A. Bottoms *et al.* (eds) *Community Penalties: Changes and Challenges.* Cullompton: Willan Publishing.

Canton, R. and Eadie, T. (2005) 'From enforcement to compliance: implications for supervising officers', *Vista,* 9: 152–8.

Hearnden, I. and Millie, A. (2004) 'Does tougher enforcement lead to lower conviction ?', *Probation Journal,* 51: 48–59.

Hedderman, C. and Hough, M. (2004) 'Getting tough or being effective: what matters?', in G. Mair (ed.) *What Matters in Probation.* Cullompton: Willan Publishing.

Rex, S. (1999) 'Desistance from offending: experiences of probation', *Howard Journal,* 38: 366–83.

CONCILIATION

Conciliation involves a third party helping people in a dispute to resolve their problem. The conciliator should be impartial and should not take one party's side.

All conciliation has the following elements:

- It is voluntary – the parties choose to conciliate or not.
- It is private and confidential.
- The parties are free to agree to the resolution or not.

Conciliated agreements are usually non-binding, although they can be made into binding contracts. In employment disputes, however, a signed conciliated agreement is binding.

For such a simple concept, the word conciliation has suffered from a considerable complexity of definitions in the context of the law. In the probation context, however, conciliation is *contrasted* with 'reconciliation' – it is an alternative approach.

In family law, therefore, the word provided a transitional articulation of the probation officers' role as they moved away from 'saving marriages' and into saving children from irresolvable parental conflict. The task became one of seeking to provide a context in which parents could safely argue out their differences, rather than one of making an effort to reconcile couples. The word 'mediation' then seemed less ambiguous and tended to replace 'conciliation'.

For offender management, the word conciliation provides a link, therefore, with that legacy of skills and experience from within family law. Offender managers will still find themselves in the midst of family conflicts – patterns of domestic violence, marital strain in the face of a partner's imprisonment, young people in conflict with parental authority and so on. They will also find in many cases that inclusion of a wider family in their work is essential if an offender's steps to desistance from offending are to be supported and maintained. While the offender manager can rarely adopt the classic neutral role of the conciliator – he or she is likely to have a statutory responsibility for the supervision of one party to a relationship conflict – the skills and understanding that went with conciliation work remain relevant:

- A focus on the process and quality of an argument, not its outcome.
- Ensuring that any resolution of differences *belongs* to the parties who have been in dispute, rather than being a solution provided or imposed by the worker.
- Encouraging negotiation by providing clarifications, and reframing of arguments.
- Remaining hopeful and sustaining discussion.
- Setting boundaries to protect the safety of all concerned.

This last element of conciliation is of particular importance in the context of domestic violence. In family law work, the word conciliation was often used as a shorthand for face-to-face meetings between parties in dispute. This, of course, was often inappropriate where one party was at risk from the other's violence. The conciliation approach does not have to be used only in face-to-face negotiation, however.

These skills and understandings can be useful in circumstances beyond family arguments. Work with employers, supported accommodation providers or other helping agencies may call on the offender manager to seek resolution of conflict. Judgements have to be made about whether to adopt an 'advocacy' role on behalf of the offender under supervision, or whether a more neutral conciliating role would be more effective. The latter has less danger of disguising the offender's responsibility for his or her own behaviour.

David Skidmore

Related entries

Mediation; Restorative justice; Victims.

Key texts and sources

Howard J. and Shepherd G. (1987) *Conciliation, Children and Divorce: A Family Systems Approach.* London: Batsford.

CONFÉRENCE PERMANENTE EUROPÉENNE DE LA PROBATION (CEP)

The Conférence permanente européenne de la Probation (CEP) is a network of probation organizations in Europe whose declared aim is to promote the social inclusion of offenders through community sanctions and measures such as probation, community service, mediation and conciliation.

The CEP organizes seminars, conferences and workshops which bring together managers and practitioners from probation and similar services across Europe, together with academics and others working in criminal justice. A bulletin, *Probation in Europe*, is circulated to members, and information about the organization, reports of past events and notices of forthcoming events are posted on the CEP's website.

The CEP has observer status at the Council of Europe and works with other international organizations. The CEP provides advice to governments and those working for them on developing their own criminal justice systems.

The CEP commissioned the production of *Probation and Probation Services: A European Perspective*, a source book on the organization and working methods of probation services in 19 European countries.

Members of the CEP are statutory and voluntary organizations working in the field of probation in Europe, and a number of interested individuals. In most countries the member is the ministry of justice or that part of the ministry concerned with community sanctions, either a penitentiary department dealing with both prison and probation or a department concerned exclusively with community measures and sanctions. In two federal countries, Germany and Switzerland, where there is no centralized responsibility for probation, the member is a probation association. In two countries, the Netherlands and Austria, probation work remains the responsibility of a private organization largely funded by government, an arrangement which was once more widespread in Europe. UK members are the Home Office, the Scottish Executive Justice Department and the Probation Board for Northern Ireland.

Members of the CEP meet in general assembly every three years and elect a board, comprising a president, two vice-presidents, six further members and a secretary general, who are responsible for the business of the CEP until the next general assembly. The CEP is financed by the subscriptions of its members, fixed according to a formula contained in its statute and at levels approved by the general assembly.

The Secretariat of the CEP is accommodated by the Dutch probation service, the Reclassering Nederland, in the service's head office in Utrecht. The working languages of the CEP are French, English and German. The CEP is a private association subject to Dutch law.

John Walters

Related entries

Council of Europe; Probation in Europe; United Nations.

Key texts and sources

van Kalmthout, A. and Derks, J. (eds) (2000) *Probation and Probation Services – A European Perspective.* Nijmegen: Wolf Legal Publishers.

van Kalmthout, A., Roberts, J. and Vinding, S. (eds) (2003) *Probation and Probation Services in the EU Accession Countries.* Nijmegen: Wolf Legal Publishers.

The CEP website (www.cep-probation.org) describes what the CEP does, lists CEP members and current board members, contains copies of the bulletin and reports of workshops and conferences, lists forthcoming events and has a shortlist of useful links.

CONTESTABILITY

A term that denotes the use of competition and market economics in the provision of public services.

The origins of this word are unclear. It is generally accepted, however, that contestability theory was first developed in the early 1980s by the American economist, Baumol. He contended that monopoly providers do not need to be exposed to actual competition in order to act competitively, but only to the threat of competition.

In relation to criminal justice, the term was probably first used in the Carter Report. Here the word is used interchangeably with competition:

The introduction of competition has provided a strong incentive for improvements in public sector prisons. There is a danger that the full benefits of contestability will not be realised if the involvement of the private sector is linked to new and failing prisons. Private providers need to be given an incentive to invest if they are to continue to be a credible alternative to public sector prisons ... Currently, there is minimal contestability in front line provision of probation services. However, internationally (especially in the United States) there is strong evidence of potential providers especially from the voluntary sector.

In essence, Carter sought 'market development' in correctional services. A view less polarized into the 'public versus private', and for a phased introduction of competition, was indicated in the recent Home Office publication, *Public Value Partnerships* (2006).

Competition does not necessarily mean only the private sector can compete, but also consortia of public, private and independent bodies. Such an approach may mean that the risks of service delivery can be shared between parties. Mixed consortia may also give greater scope for innovations and specialist services, since different aspects of offender need for both containment and rehabilitation can be addressed.

In broad consortia the private sector might contribute technology, logistics and access to investment funds, with the voluntary sector co-ordinating elements such as specialist services with a strong local approach to resettlement, in-depth knowledge of communities and their diversity, and a range of mentors and volunteers. This approach to 'market development' is probably one of the most exciting responses to the creation of the National Offender Management Service. Such consortia could develop more sophisticated approaches to market entry both in relation to traditional ways of dealing with offenders and more innovative integrated 'through the gate' services that combine both incarceration and resettlement provision.

'Contestability' can be seen as a mechanism to unfreeze the public sector's view of itself as a monopolistic provider of correctional services. Carter believed that market forces were a central part of the new landscape and hence he also proposed the establishment of ten regional commissioners of correctional services or regional offender managers. Their initial focus has been on the establishment of more joined-up approaches to offender management, and on more integrated services between prisons and probation areas based on assessment of offender need. They have also been building the capacity and potential of the voluntary sector to deliver an increased range of correctional services.

The absence of a significant increase in public expenditure, and a ministerial concern not to destabilize the main public sector providers, has meant that there has not been a major redistribution of resources that would allow full-scale 'contestability' exercises. Carter recognized the importance of sentencing practice, but the absence of a more balanced use of community as opposed to custodial sentences has meant that the 'headroom' to introduce new forms of delivery has been limited, as the priority for additional expenditure has been to purchase more prison places.

Theory argues that a contestable market has no entry barriers, and firms or providers of services can enter or leave an industry costlessly. This position may not yet exist in correctional services as new providers may still be considering the costs and risk of market entry, and whether there are significant incentives for their initial outlay.

The Home Office document *Public Value Partnerships* (2006) refers to an existing investment with non-public sector providers of £800 million and a future commitment of £250 million. The extent of franchising of services has varied. In transport, for instance, doubts about short-term franchises have deterred long-term investments as firms feared future loss of franchise and experienced sunk costs – that is, costs associated with leaving the industry that cannot be recovered. However, it requires an authoritative commissioner to drive change, innovation and flexibility in long-term franchises (beyond 15 years).

The Audit Commission in a recent research proposal (2006), agreed that promoting a mixed market in the delivery of public services was a key component of the government's service reform agenda. This is also reflected in the new requirement for probation boards to spend 10 per cent of their budgets on purchasing partnership services. The process to ensure commissioners, users and funders of public services get the best value for money from a mixed pool of providers is crucial to service improvement and sustainability. The study does not aim to add to the 'public good, private bad' debate but highlights the mechanisms by which competition and contestability can drive improvement. The authors contend that it is behaviours and cultures, not structures or sectors, which account for different outcomes, and identifying those behaviours and cultural characteristics is essential to advancing the debate and spreading improved practice.

The debate needs to move beyond 'threat' and the unfreezing of current providers to improve performance and lower costs, to a more wide-ranging discussion of the marketplace. The crucial question is what partnerships and consortium developments will better reduce reoffending and protect the public? To what extent could more flexible and responsive arrangements replace the polarized 'public or private' choice? This is a potential scenario for developing the proper balance of commissioning, competition and contestability and improving the performance of all providers in correctional services.

Steve Goode

Related entries

Carter Report; NOMS; Partnerships; Privatization; Probation boards; Probation trusts; Regional offender managers.

Key texts and sources

Audit Commission (2006) *Competition and Contestability in Local Public Services: Research Proposal and Interim Report.* London: Audit Commission.

Bailey, R., Knight, C. and Williams, B. (2007) 'The Probation Service as part of NOMS in England and Wales: fit for purpose?', in L. Gelsthorpe and R. Morgan (eds) *Handbook of Probation.* Cullompton: Willan Publishing.

Baumol, W. and Willig, R. (1986). *Contestability: Developments since the Book. Oxford Economic Paper.* Oxford University Press 38: 9–36.

Carter, P. (2004) *Managing Offenders, Reducing Crime: A New Approach.* London: Strategy Unit.

Home Office (2006) *Public Value Partnerships.* London: Home Office.

Home Office (2006) *Five Year Plan: Protecting the Public and Reducing Re-offending* (Cm 6717). London: HMSO.

CORRECTIONAL SERVICES ACCREDITATION PANEL

A body appointed by the government to advise on programmes of effective treatment for use in prisons and probation areas in England and Wales.

The Correctional Services Accreditation Panel (CSAP), formerly known as the Joint Prison/Probation Services Accreditation Panel, was set up in 1999 by the Home Office and the Prison Service as part of the government's Crime Reduction Programme. It replaced the Prison Service's earlier general and sex offender treatment programme accreditation panels, which were established in 1996.

The panel is an advisory non-departmental public body (NDPB) with an independent chair. Appointments to the panel were made in 1999 and 2002 in accordance with the Code of Practice on Ministerial Appointments. In addition to the chair, the panel currently consists of 11 appointed members, who are independent experts, and one nominated member. Members are mostly either psychologists or criminologists who have experience of developing programmes or researching into their effectiveness. Appointed members have specific expertise in:

- cognitive-behavioural treatment;
- sex offending;
- substance misuse-related offending;
- programme audit;
- therapeutic communities;
- inter-agency service delivery.

The CSAP's main remit is to accredit offender treatment programmes to reduce reoffending, against criteria based on 'what works' principles (derived from international research on the kinds of interventions that appear effective in reducing reoffending). The panel has assisted the Prison and Probation Services in embracing 'what works' and has implemented high-quality programmes for offenders to improve their reasoning, address sexual and violent offending and tackle drugs misuse. The principal criteria in deciding whether or not to accredit are as follows:

- Evidence that the approach will work with the offenders selected.
- Identifying the characteristics of the offenders selected, including the offences being tackled, risk, motivation, learning style, gender and race.
- Targeting the dynamic (i.e. capable of being changed) risk factors.

- Demonstrating how risks are interlinked and how the programme will bring about change.
- Using methods proven to work.
- Teaching skills for offence-free living (for example, literacy, numeracy, how to find work, making and keeping relationships, problem-solving).
- Matching frequency and number of sessions to learning styles, abilities and risk.
- Combining with other services in the offender management model.
- Monitoring staff selection, training and supervision to ensure the programme is run as intended.
- Continuous evaluation for improvements.

In addition to accrediting programmes, the panel's remit has included agreeing audit and quality assurance procedures for such programmes and – since 2002 – advising on training and the implications of evidence of impact and effectiveness.

The panel's focus has been largely cognitive-behavioural, although it has accredited some programmes based on other models, such as therapeutic communities and the 12-steps approach for drug treatment. The accreditation function was extended in 2002 to 'integrated systems', such as community punishment (see Unpaid work), offender management and other 'rehabilitative services'. One integrated system, Enhanced Community Punishment, has been provisionally accredited, and the Probation Service has brought applications for advice within this framework on approved premises and employment.

Following the publication of the Carter Report and the creation of the National Offender Management Service, the panel moved to new ways of working to enhance its effectiveness. A significant change was the move away from fixed twice-yearly plenary meetings where, in addition to panel business, programmes were submitted for accreditation. Currently, sub-panels are convened to consider programmes for advice and accreditation and the panel meets once a year to discuss business in plenary.

Carole Wham

Related entries

Accredited programmes, Accredited programmes in common use; Cognitive-behavioural; Effective practice; Sex offender treatment programmes.

Key texts and sources

The panel's reports and publications are available from the NOMS website (**www.noms.homeoffice. gov.uk**).

COUNCIL OF EUROPE

Based in Strasbourg, the council is Europe's oldest political organization. It was established to defend human rights, parliamentary democracy and the rule of law.

In 1946 Winston Churchill proclaimed:

> *Our constant aim must be to build and fortify the strength of the United Nations organisation. Under and within that world concept we must recreate the European family in a regional structure called – it may be – the United States of Europe and the first practical step will be to form a Council of Europe.*

The Council stood for Europe's determination to guard against any recurrence of the atrocities witnessed during the war. The Convention for the Protection of Human Rights and Fundamental Freedoms (adopted in 1950) affirmed that there were some human rights that people possessed in virtue of their humanity – some rights that the state may not take away in any circumstances and others that may only be denied or compromised in specifically defined circumstances. Individuals who have not found satisfaction through domestic legal processes may have recourse to the European Court of Human Rights and may be awarded compensation for a violation of their rights. The Human Rights Act 1998 incorporated the convention into the law of the UK.

The Council therefore has a quite different origin, significance and purpose from the European Union. Apart from Belarus and Montenegro (who are applying for membership), every country in Europe is a member. The decision-making body is the Committee of Ministers (foreign ministers or their deputies), giving the Council's formal 'recommendations' considerable authority.

The Council advances its work through the following methods:

- *Setting standards*: the European Prison Rules, for example, apply the (often necessarily quite general) principles of the convention to the specific circumstances of imprisonment. There are also European rules on community sanctions and measures (CSM), which include the practices of probation and offender management, although they are obsolescent and in need of revision.
- *Inspection*: the Council inspects the practices of member states to check their conformity with the convention. The Committee for the Prevention of Torture (CPT), notably, undertakes visits to examine the treatment of those detained to protect them from torture and inhuman treatment.
- *Co-operation*: as well as calling states to account, the Council supports them in developing good practice. In penal affairs, this is achieved through the work of committees of experts, twinning projects and advisory groups.

In the realm of criminal justice and punishment, the Council gives expression to the principle that states must have regard to the rights, dignity and human worth of all concerned (offenders, victims of crime and others), even in the practice of law enforcement and punishment. Perhaps it should be said *especially* in such circumstances, because it is here that people's rights are most vulnerable to abuse.

Rob Canton

Related entries

CEP; Human rights; Probation in Europe; United Nations.

Key texs and sources

The Council's website is full of useful information (http://www.coe.int/). The European Committee on Crime Problems contains links to many important documents (http://www.coe.int/t/e/legal_affairs/legal_co-operation/steering_committees/CDPC/). See also Committee for the Prevention of Torture (http://www.cpt.coe.int/en/) and the European Court of Human Rights (http://www.echr.coe.int/echr).

COURT WORK

Probation court work is the activity at the interface of the Probation Service and the courts, involving the gathering and exchange of information relating to remand, sentencing, review and enforcement decisions.

The Probation Service's relationship with the courts is long-standing, dating back to the nineteenth century when missionaries were first appointed to the London police courts to supervise those whose heavy drinking was thought to have led to their offending. Over time, court work also extended to include mediation responsibilities within the family courts. This is now the remit of the Children and Family Court Advisory Support Service (CAFCASS), and a contemporary definition of court work must concentrate on the services provided in the criminal courts.

The remand service function involves making inquiries pertaining to any defendants who have been arrested, charged and denied police bail overnight to appear in court the following day. The court officer or bail information officer will seek to gather and verify relevant information that may influence the court's decision about bail. This may include making a referral to an approved premises hostel.

Probation staff also assist the courts in the sentencing of an offender, by providing an objective assessment of the individual's offending behaviour, the likelihood of reoffending and the risk of harm posed to the public, making a proposal to the court as to how the case might best be dealt with. Information is presented in a standard delivery report, formally known as a pre-sentence report, a fast delivery report or an oral report. The OASys 'risk of harm' screening tool has been widely adopted to assist in providing this information.

Some sentences (such as supervision with a drug rehabilitation requirement) also require a regular court review process. At each court review hearing, a report will be provided and presented by probation staff commenting on progress made.

A further core probation task in court relates to the enforcement of community orders. Where non-compliance with an order supervised by the service has occurred resulting in breach proceedings, the Probation Service will make arrangements to lay information before the court to that effect. At a magistrates' court, probation staff will take on the role of the prosecutor in the case; at a Crown Court breach hearing a barrister will be instructed to act on the service's behalf.

Other court staff duties include interviewing offenders post-sentence, arranging the commencement of a new community order and assessing the risk of self-harm for those who have received custodial sentences. The court officer is often the offender's first point of contact with the service, and it is essential that he or she behaves in a prosocial manner, consistent with effective practice.

How the Probation Service should resource court work has been the subject of much debate, with many varying staffing models. Probation areas engage with their criminal justice partners in the courts, mostly at a senior management level, to explore best practice protocols.

The use of Probation service officers in court has increased considerably and it is essential that staff are appropriately trained and supported. However, court work has sometimes struggled to maintain a high profile within the service. This perhaps reflects a very narrow view of court work that has not appreciated the increasing complexities of the role, which are influenced by the rising profiles of risk assessment, public protection and enforcement agendas that have permeated throughout the service as a whole.

Sarah Hilder

Related entries

Approved premises; CAFCASS; Crown Prosecution Service; Enforcement; Judges; Magistrates; Presentence report; Remand services.

Key texts and sources

Haines, K. and Morgan, R. (2007) 'Services before trial and sentence: achievement, decline and potential', in L. Gelsthorpe and R. Morgan (eds) *Handbook of Probation.* Cullompton: Willan.

Hill, L. (2002) 'Working in the courts', in D. Ward *et al.* (eds) *Probation: Working for Justice* (2nd edn). Oxford: Oxford University Press.

Nash, M. (2003) 'Pre-trial investigation', in W.H. Chui and M. Nellis (eds) *Moving Probation Forward: Evidence, Arguments and Practice.* Harlow: Pearson Education.

National Probation Service (2005) *Role Boundary Issues in the NPS Probation Circular 90/2005.* London: Home Office.

CRIME AND DISORDER REDUCTION PARTNERSHIPS

Statutory arrangements to bring about a multi-agency approach in the work to reduce crime and disorder.

The Crime and Disorder Act 1998 brought in a range of innovative developments that were seen as the hallmarks of an incoming government. 'Tough on crime, and tough on the causes of crime' and 'joined-up government' were two phrases that captured the legislative intention.

The Act established the Crime and Disorder Reduction Partnerships (CDRPs) in England, and the equivalent Community Safety Partnerships in Wales. The police and the local authorities are the principal partners. The CDRP has to carry out an audit of crime, disorder and misuse of drugs every three years. Based on the audit, and in consultation with the local community and other agencies, the CDRP has a duty to formulate and implement a strategy for combating crime, disorder and the misuse of drugs.

The partnerships are based on local authority areas, either unitary or district authority. This structure means that it is often difficult for the Probation Service to send an appropriate senior manager to each of the district CDRP meetings in their area. One of the unique contributions of probation data to the audit is the provision of data about the geographical distribution of the homes of offenders. This can be done on an aggregated basis and by offence type. Police data are strong on where offences are committed and, when these are combined with data about where the offenders live, it becomes easier to plan appropriate actions.

CDRPs work closely with other partnership arrangements, especially the drug action teams. In unitary authority areas the two bodies have sometimes chosen to merge.

CDRPs have the effect of enabling staff in a wide variety of public services to see how their work contributes to crime prevention and community safety. It is fascinating to see that the priorities of a wide range of staff from diverse disciplines such as economic regeneration, health, schools, housing, fire prevention, police and probation are often focused on a small number of neighbourhoods in their district. Indeed, many apparently unconnected agencies often concentrate their efforts on the same small number of individuals and families who present particular challenges for service providers. The CDRP enables agencies and workers to see the 'bigger picture' and to form alliances that make their particular work more effective.

The probation contribution to CDPR action plans usually focuses on their work with multi-agency public protection arrangement high risk of harm offenders and on their contribution to prolific and other priority offenders schemes. Frequently, Probation Service work with offenders in specific offence categories, especially burglars and the perpetrators of domestic violence, is recognized in CDRP plans.

A recent government review called for reform in five areas:

1. National Standards;
2. clarification of roles and structures;
3. improved delivery ;
4. changed governance and accountability; and
5. mainstreaming services.

Work is progressing on these issues.

David Hancock

Related entries

Community safety; Inter-agency work; Partnerships.

Key texts and sources

Rumgay, J. (2007) 'Partnerships in probation', in L. Gelsthorpe and R. Morgan (eds) *Handbook of Probation*. Cullompton: Willan.

The website **www.crimereduction.gov.uk/regions/ regions00.htm** provides a wide range of information and sources.

CRIME PREVENTION

Policy and practice to prevent (or, more plausibly, reduce) crime by a range of strategies that recognize the limits of the contribution that can be made by the formal agencies of criminal justice.

Most people most of the time have always taken sensible measures to protect themselves, to protect those for whom they are responsible and to protect their own property against potential offenders. Modern crime prevention policy, however, has its origins in the late 1970s and early 1980s at a time when it was becoming increasingly apparent that the criminal justice system could make no more than a limited contribution to reducing crime. (This is not only because a relatively small number of offences lead to the perpetrator's arrest and conviction – see Attrition – but also because the most important influences in socialization and the shaping of attitudes that dispose people to offend or refrain are largely beyond the reach of criminal justice agencies.) A further stimulus to this policy was the recognition that criminal justice involvement could not be shown to lead reliably to reduced reoffending.

At the Home Office, Ronald Clarke influentially suggested that the reasons why people become offenders are largely unknown and, in any case, are unlikely to be amenable to much influence. Much better, then, to look at the particular circumstances in which crimes take place and to see how the environment might be manipulated to prevent them or, if they do take place, increase the chances of the offender's apprehension. Among the ways in which this might be achieved were 'target-hardening' (barriers, locks, immobilization devices) and surveillance ('natural' – where the sites of offending were more visible – or through devices like CCTV). Empowering potential victims by alerting them to the ways in which people might try to take advantage of them is another strand in this approach. This came to be known as 'situational' crime prevention. 'Social' crime prevention recognizes that educational and social provision, especially for those most likely to offend, can make an important difference.

Crime prevention assumes that most offenders reason in the same way as other people, taking (though sometimes creating) opportunities and weighing costs and benefits. The opportunities arise from ordinary, routine activities and it is through careful scrutiny of these activities that it becomes possible to see how opportunities might be blocked. Crime and its prevention are therefore the business of everyone: how we design our living space, our transport routes, our shopping areas, the design of the products we buy, all make a difference to criminal opportunities. Crime prevention strategies, however, have tended to focus on the 'crimes of the streets' and have had relatively less to say about the crimes of the powerful or (notably) domestic violence.

A useful framework involves distinguishing

- *primary* prevention – through various forms of environmental design or manipulation;
- *secondary* prevention – identifying and working with those considered most likely to offend ('at risk of offending'); and
- *tertiary* prevention – working with known offenders to reduce the incidence of their offending.

The Probation Service is, most obviously, engaged in tertiary crime prevention, but it is arguable that it has important – and largely unrealized – contributions to make at other levels besides. For example, probation staff come to know a great deal about the circumstances in which offences take place, but this information is rarely collated and deployed to contribute to a primary prevention strategy. Again, secondary prevention could be enhanced through work in the community to try to enhance social capital, but contemporary probation's commitment to this seems uncertain.

In recent years, the language of crime prevention has been largely superseded by the terminology of community safety. In its interagency working and partnerships, probation makes its contribution to crime reduction, although largely at the tertiary level.

Rob Canton

Related entries

Community safety; Inter-agency work; Partnerships.

Key texts and sources

Garland, D. (2001) *The Culture of Control.* Oxford: Oxford University Press.

Please, K. (2002) 'Crime Reduction', in M. Maguire *et al.* (eds) *The Oxford Handbook of Criminology.* Oxford: Oxford University Press.

Tilley, N. (ed.) (2006) *Handbook of Crime Prevention and Community Safety.* Cullompton: Willan Publishing.

http://www.crimereduction.gov.uk/

CRIMINAL CAREERS

A criminal career is basically a sequence of offences committed at different ages. Much is known about the development of criminal careers and about the extent to which they are predictable.

A criminal career has a beginning (onset), an end (desistance) and a career length in between (duration). Only a certain proportion of each birth cohort (prevalence) commits offences and has a criminal career. During their careers, offenders commit crimes at a certain rate (frequency) while they are at risk of offending in the community (e.g. not incarcerated, abroad or incapacitated by illness). For offenders who

commit several offences, it is possible to investigate how far they specialize in certain types of crimes and to what extent the seriousness of their offending escalates over time.

Offending is typically measured using either official records or self-reports. Most is known about crimes committed by lower-class males living in urban areas. In order to study the development of offending and criminal careers, longitudinal (follow-up) research is needed in which persons are interviewed repeatedly from childhood to adulthood. For example, in the Cambridge Study in Delinquent Development (Farrington *et al.* 2006), about 400 south London males were followed up from the age of 8 to the age of 48.

The prevalence of offending by males is surprisingly high. In the Cambridge study, 40 per cent of males were convicted up to the age of 40, and 96 per cent self-reported an offence up to the age of 32. The peak age of offending was at the age of 17, although it was higher for some types of crimes (e.g. violence and fraud). The peak age of onset was at 14, and the peak age of desistance was at 23. The average duration of criminal careers between the first and last convictions was nine years. There was little evidence of specialization or escalation; most offenders were versatile and committed a variety of different types of offences.

Criminal behaviour does not generally appear without warning. It is commonly preceded by childhood anti-social behaviour (e.g. bullying, lying, truanting and cruelty to animals) and followed by adult anti-social behaviour (e.g. spouse assault, child abuse and neglect, excessive drinking and sexual promiscuity). Similarly, there are developmental sequences in types of crimes, with shoplifting typically occurring before burglary, and burglary typically occurring before robbery. There is considerable persistence and continuity in anti-social behaviour over time. For example, in the Cambridge study, 60 per cent of the most anti-social males at the age of 18 persisted to be among the most anti-social males at the age of 32, despite the dramatic changes in life circumstances between these ages.

An early onset of offending typically predicts a long criminal career and many offences. A small fraction of each birth cohort (e.g. 5 per cent of males) typically commits at least half of all offences. In the criminal career literature, these are often termed 'chronic offenders', although Terrie Moffitt's theory distinguishes between 'life-course-persistent' and 'adolescence-limited' offenders. Most crimes up to the teenage years are committed with others, whereas most crimes from the age of 20 onwards are committed alone. Some persistent offenders are 'recruiters' who constantly commit crimes with less experienced offenders, thus dragging more and more people into the net of offending. The reasons given for offending up to the teenage years are quite variable, including both utilitarian or rational reasons and more emotional reasons (e.g. for excitement or enjoyment, because the person got angry). In contrast, from the age of 20 onwards, utilitarian motives become increasingly dominant.

The main childhood risk factors for the early onset of offending before the age of 20 are well known: individual factors (e.g. low intelligence, low school attainment, hyperactivity, impulsiveness, risk-taking, low empathy, anti-social and aggressive behaviour); family factors (e.g. poor parental supervision, harsh discipline, child physical abuse, inconsistent discipline, a cold parental attitude and child neglect, low involvement of parents with children, parental conflict, broken families, criminal parents, delinquent siblings); socio-economic factors (e.g. low family income, large family size, poor housing); peer factors (e.g. delinquent peers, peer rejection, low popularity); school factors (e.g. attending a high delinquency-rate school); and neighbourhood factors (e.g. living in a deprived, high-crime neighbourhood). The main life events that encourage desistance after the age of 20 are getting married, getting a satisfying job and moving to a better area, while getting convicted tends to prolong rather than curtail criminal careers.

Criminal career research has many policy implications. First, offending can be prevented by targeting key risk factors. Parent training and general parent education can improve parenting skills, cognitive-behavioural skills training can reduce impulsiveness and increase empathy, and preschool intellectual enrichment programmes can improve school success. Secondly, it is important to identify chronic offenders (and recruiters) at an early stage and devise special programmes for them. Thirdly, it is important to take account of residual career length in setting the length of prison sentences, because it is futile to incarcerate people after they would have stopped offending anyway. Fourthly, the versatility of offenders means that it does not make much sense to have specific programmes for violent offenders. Since criminal career research shows that violent offenders are essentially frequent offenders, programmes to prevent violent offending should target frequent or chronic offenders. Fifthly, desistance can be fostered by programmes that help offenders to settle down with a steady job and a steady partner.

In recent years, many developmental and life-course theories have been proposed to explain the development of offending and criminal careers and the effect of early risk factors and later life events on the course of development. Future criminal career research needs to be based on self-reports as well as official records, needs to focus on females and middle-class people, and needs to study protective factors as well as risk factors. Protective factors that prevent the development of offending can have important policy implications, but little is known about them.

David Farrington

Related entries

Children and families of offenders; Criminology; Desistance.

Key texts and sources

Farrington, D.P. (ed.) (2005) *Integrated Developmental and Life-Course Theories of Offending*. New Brunswick, NJ: Transaction Books.

Farrington, D.P. *et al.* (2006) *Criminal Careers up to Age 50 and Life Success up to Age 48: New Findings from the Cambridge Study in Delinquent Development*. Home Office Research Study 299. London: Home Office (available online at http://www.homeoffice.gov.uk/rdsd/pdfs06/hors299.pdf).

Farrington, D.P. and Welsh, B.C. (2007) *Saving Children from a Life of Crime: Early Risk Factors and Effective Interventions*. Oxford: Oxford University Press.

Moffitt, T. (1993) 'Adolescence-Limited and Life-Course-Persistent Antisocial Behaviour: A Developmental Taxonomy, *Psychological Review*. 100(4): 674–701.

Piquero, A.R., Farrington, D.P. and Blumstein, A. (2007) *Key Issues in Criminal Career Research: New Analyses of the Cambridge Study in Delinquent Development*. Cambridge: Cambridge University Press.

CRIMINAL JUSTICE ACT 1991

A major initiative to provide a comprehensive statutory framework for sentencing, based primarily on the seriousness of the offence, while providing some scope for longer custodial sentences for public protection.

Providing the broad statutory architecture for sentencing (and also early release) that prevailed until the Criminal Justice Act 2003, this Act sought to identify *proportionality* as the principal sentencing rationale. It aimed to introduce greater consistency in sentencing which had previously been characterized by unduly wide discretion, allowing sentencers to subscribe freely to other aims, particularly deterrence and rehabilitation. It did not embrace newly emerging concepts of reparation or restorative justice. It gave greater prominence to the information provided to courts by the Probation Service in newly styled pre-sentence reports that now had to be considered prior to key decision-making.

In furtherance of the principle of 'just deserts', identified in the 1990 white paper,

Crime, Justice and Protecting the Public, the Act specified upper and intermediate sentencing bands, and custodial and community sentencing, with two accompanying threshold tests, requiring courts to determine whether the offence was 'so serious' that only a custodial sentence could be justified for it or, less onerously, was 'serious enough' to warrant a community sentence. The Act thus aimed, first, to curb the unwarranted use of custody which the white paper had identified as often an expensive, counterproductive way of making bad persons worse; and secondly, to create a distinctive zone of community punishment in which restrictions on liberty in the community could gain a credible penal identity in their own right. Below the community sentencing tier, courts should impose other measures, principally financial penalties and discharge without punishment.

To emphasize that the court should focus principally upon the offence for which the defendant was then facing sentence, the Act specified that the sentencer should not weigh the seriousness of all the offences being dealt with in aggregate, but only the offence under consideration viewed in tandem with one other offence. This was to ensure that offenders did not attract disproportionate sentences based on the sum of matters that individually might be quite petty. Further, to guard against the possibility that offenders could be dealt on past record, with the obvious prospect of over-punishing petty persistent offenders, the Act also indicated that an offence should not be regarded as more serious on the basis of previous convictions or failure to respond to previous sentences. These provisions were subject to early, diluting amendment, largely at the behest of the judiciary.

Though the Act sought to direct the attention of courts primarily to the offence, its circumstances and its aggravating or mitigating factors, rather than to the offender, it nevertheless allowed sentencers to take into account any mitigating factors, thus affording scope for a wide range of offender-centred considerations to shape the sentencing decision, including the possibility of imposing sentence at a *lower* band level than indicated by the relevant threshold test.

The most prominent exception to proportionality applied to those sex offenders or violent offenders where a longer-than-commensurate determinate custodial sentence could be imposed where this was considered necessary to protect the public from serious harm. Critics argued that this served simply to delay somewhat the exposure of the public to risk rather than as an effective measure to address dangerousness.

Nigel Stone

Related entries

Punishment (aims and justifications).

Key texts and sources

Ashworth A. (1992) *Sentencing and Criminal Justice.* London: Weidenfeld & Nicolson.
Home Office (1990) *Crime, Justice and Protecting the Public.* London: HMSO.

CRIMINAL JUSTICE ACT 2003

A wide-ranging, labyrinthine and controversial initiative to win public confidence in criminal justice, attempting to embrace crime prevention and public protection in sentencing in tandem with proportionate punishment. It revises 'early release' and expands the use of confinement and extended regulation of violent and sexual offenders.

This gargantuan Act introduced changes across a wide spectrum, ranging from conditional cautioning of adults to a new scheme of sentences for murder, now divided into categories of homicidal seriousness. Measures include changes to police and bail powers, relaxation of rules of evidence, (including scope for wider use of hearsay), tighter restrictions on the right to jury trial and relaxation of the 'double jeopardy' rule, thus permitting retrial in the light of further evidence.

The Act requires courts to 'have regard to' a raft of sentencing purposes ranging from 'punishment' to 'reparation' and specifically refers to 'deterrence' and 'reform'. No ranking of priority or other guidance is given to sentencers in resolving tensions between these objectives or in weighing the merits of competing values. This provision thus weakens the pre-eminence of *proportionality* in the Criminal Justice Act 1991 that had been criticized in the Halliday Report for taking insufficient account of offenders' propensity to reoffend and for underemphasizing public protection. The return of the 'smorgasbord' approach begs questions about the capacity of sentencing to prevent crime and suggests that consistency will be undermined as sentencers seek to give dubious simultaneous effect to deterrence, incapacitation and rehabilitation.

Offence seriousness remains prominent: courts must consider *culpability* and any harm which the offence caused, was intended to cause or might foreseeably have caused. The threshold seriousness tests for custodial and community sentences introduced by the 1991 Act are retained in adapted form, notwithstanding the slackness with which these had been reinforced by parsimony provisions such as that requiring a custodial sentence to be for the shortest commensurate term. It is open to doubt whether courts now required to embrace a variety of aims will apply proportionality more rigorously. Further, the Act requires sentencers to treat each previous conviction as an aggravating factor (provided that 'it can reasonably be so treated', having regard to its relevance and the time that has since elapsed). Application of this 'recidivist premium' has the potential to allow significant uplift in the level of sanction.

With regard to imprisonment, for shorter terms the Act seeks to counter the risk that brief incarceration will simply serve as temporary and unproductive warehousing by seeking to bridge the prison–community divide through the renaissance of the suspended sentence, now with community demands attached as standard and with the obvious potential for boosting the prison population following non-compliance, and the introduction of both intermittent custody (part-time prison) and 'Custody Plus', though the challenges of servicing the community element of the latter have to date caused implementation to be deferred. At the deep end, the Act increases incapacitative powers to respond to 'dangerous' offenders, deemed to pose a substantial risk of serious harm, by semi-automatic use of either indeterminate sentencing ('life' by another name) or the reinvented extended sentence. Community penalties are merged into a single, menu-style generic community order with obvious inflationary potential. The Act introduces the Sentencing Guidelines Council to set the compass for the interpretation of the new provisions, and the effect of this complex and often confusing Act will depend heavily on the extent to which the council rises to the challenge.

Nigel Stone

Related entries

Community order; Criminal Justice Act 1991; Custody Plus, Intermittent Custody and Custody Minus; Halliday Report; Sentencing Guidelines Council.

Key texts and sources

Home Office (2002) *Justice for All* (Cm. 5563). London: HMSO.

von Hirsch, A. and Roberts, J. (2004) 'Legislating sentencing principles: the provisions of the Criminal Justice Act 2003 relating to sentencing purposes and the role of previous convictions', *Criminal Law Review*, 639–52.

For a good account of the principles and provisions of the Act, see Taylor, R. *et al.* (2004) *Blackstone's Guide to the Criminal Justice Act 2003*. Oxford: Blackstone Press.

CRIMINAL JUSTICE BOARDS

A non-statutory alliance of the managers of the criminal justice agencies in an area. The purpose is to improve the criminal justice system through collaborative work.

In the 1990s the criminal justice co-ordinating committees were established. They ironed out problems in the boundaries between agencies. Some overall issues (such as the treatment of mentally disordered offenders and concern about racial discrimination) were also addressed. The work progressed by consensus and had a low profile. The outcomes were modest.

From 2000 onwards, the government sought stronger direction and focused 'delivery systems'. Central government became co-ordinated through interdepartmental bodies involving the Home Office, the Lord Chancellor's Department and the Attorney General's Office. A National Criminal Justice Board was established to set priorities, targets and a performance management system. Regrettably it took several years before priorities for the individual agencies were brought into line with this national framework.

In each of the 42 criminal justice areas of England and Wales an area criminal justice board was established. Each is made up of the leaders of HM Courts Service, the Crown Prosecution Service, the police, HM Prison Service, the Probation Service and the youth offending teams. Co-opted members may be appointed, and these, for example, may represent victims, race issues and the legal profession.

Although these boards have never been placed on a statutory footing, funds were made available to appoint 'performance managers' and a small support team. The government monitors the work of the boards very closely. A national performance reporting system, with league tables, is in place, and a routine of ministerial and official visits focuses on performance.

From the outset the main job of the boards has been to address the problem that, although the crime rate has been falling, the fear of crime remains high. The essential difficulty, of course, is that only a minority of offenders are detected, convicted and punished (see Attrition). This is not compatible with 'tough on crime'. Rather than recognizing the limits of the criminal justice system in reducing the fear of crime, and investing heavily in victim support and crime prevention as an alternative strategy, the government has placed an emphasis on 'narrowing the justice gap'. This means increasing the proportion of offences reported, detected and prosecuted successfully. Action plans to improve practice in this regard are devised, implemented and monitored. The number of 'offences brought to justice', and the level of public confidence in the system as measured by opinion polling, are now two of the key performance indicators.

Other government initiatives were incorporated into the work of the criminal justice boards. The Street Crime Initiative was a well funded programme to reduce robbery in ten metropolitan and urban centres. The Persistent Young Offender Pledge is a promise to reduce the time from arrest to sentence in the youth court. This recognizes that, for young people, the immediacy of consequence is a significant issue.

David Hancock

Related entries

Community safety; Criminal justice system; Inter-agency work.

Key texts and sources

Information about the composition and work of the national (and each area) criminal justice board can be accessed via **www.lcjb.cjsonline.gov.uk.**

CRIMINAL JUSTICE SYSTEM

A collective term encompassing the various agencies that are responsible for determining how offences should be dealt with and for the administration of criminal justice, including the police, prosecuting authorities, criminal courts and 'correctional agencies', such as the Probation Service and Prison Service. The term also encompasses the personnel who work within these agencies and the procedures they employ.

The main agencies comprising the criminal justice system include the police, the Crown Prosecution Service, courts (magistrates' court, Crown Court and Appeal Court), the Probation Service and Prison Service though, since 2004, these two main 'correctional agencies' have been jointly administered by the National Offender Management Service (NOMS). In addition, there are also various more specialist agencies, including the Criminal Defence Service, the Serious Fraud Office, parole boards, the Criminal Injuries Compensation Authority, Victim Support and youth offending teams.

The basic operation of the criminal justice system is relatively uncontentious though the detailed procedures themselves are somewhat complicated. The police have a wide range of investigative powers for dealing with offences that come to their attention. They also have considerable discretion when deciding how suspected offenders should be dealt with. For example, they may decide to take no further action (NFA), to caution or warn formally an adult offender (or, in the case of juveniles, to issue a 'reprimand' or 'final warning') or to refer a suspect for prosecution.

Prosecutions may commence either by means of a summons that is granted by a magistrate on application by the police, or by means of a charge against the suspect that is again brought by the police. In both instances, the suspect is obliged to appear in court, but an alleged offender who receives a summons remains at liberty in the meantime, whereas an offender who is charged is remanded either on bail or in custody prior to the hearing.

The conduct of the prosecution is the responsibility of the independent Crown Prosecution Service. Depending on the seriousness of the alleged offence, a defendant may be tried either in the magistrates' court or the Crown Court. Certain very serious offences (known as 'indictable only'), such as murder, rape and robbery, can only be tried in the Crown Court by a judge and jury. The least serious (known as 'summary') offences are invariably tried in magistrates' courts either by a panel of (normally three) lay magistrates or by a single professional magistrate, known as a 'district judge'. Certain offences, such as theft, arson and most burglaries, fall into an intermediate category known as 'triable either way', which means that both sets of courts are competent to deal with them. In practice, such cases are liable to be dealt with in the magistrates' court if the defendant pleads guilty. In the event of a not-guilty plea, however, a defendant may be tried in the Crown Court if the magistrates think it appropriate or because the defendant insists on this method of trial.

Although defendants are at liberty to plead 'not guilty', thereby forcing the prosecution to prove the case against them, the great majority plead guilty. In the event of a conviction, the court then sentences the defendant. The penalties that are available may vary, however, depending on the age of the offender, the seriousness of the offence and also the level of court in which the case was heard, since there are statutory limits on the sentencing powers of magistrates. The court may be assisted in its choice of sentence by a pre-sentence report containing information relating to the offender's offending behaviour, social and family background and, often, a recommended penalty. Pre-sentence reports are prepared by probation officers in the case of adult offenders and by members of youth offending teams in the case of juveniles. Depending on the type of penalty that is imposed, probation officers and youth offending team workers may continue to be involved in the execution and enforcement of a sentence (particularly in the case of community penalties, but also following the release of prisoners on licence).

Moving beyond such bland operational accounts, however, the criminal justice system is the focus of considerable controversy relating to each of its constituent terms. First, the term 'criminal' arguably glosses over a significant extension in the ambit of the criminal justice system in recent years to encompass a wide range of anti-social behaviour and relatively minor 'incivilities'. Whether it is appropriate and sensible to resort to formal punitive interventions that do little to address the factors that give rise to such behaviour, however, is open to question.

Secondly, the ability of the criminal justice system to deliver 'just' outcomes has long been questioned. For many years critics pointed to a succession of high-profile 'miscarriages of justice' involving the wrongful conviction of innocent suspects. More recently the government has sought to reframe the debate by arguing that the system needs to be 'rebalanced' if it is to deliver justice to victims. Whether this can be rectified by dismantling the procedural safeguards that have traditionally been accorded to suspects, however, is again seriously open to question.

Thirdly, many have queried the appositeness of the term 'system' when applied to a collection of disparate agencies with wide and unaccountable discretionary powers working in relative isolation from each other, and subject to no overall co-ordination or strategic control. Recent attempts have been made to develop a more integrated system, for example, by redefining the role of the Probation Service, bringing it under central control and then effectively merging it with the Prison Service under the auspices of the National Offender Management Service. Somewhat ironically, however, the insistence on promoting competition under the auspices of the 'contestability' mantra seems destined to result in greater fragmentation and insularity among a greater plurality of service providers rather than closer integration and co-operation between agencies.

James Dignan

Related entries

Criminal justice boards; Crown Prosecution Service; Magistrates; NOMS; National Probation Service for England and Wales; Police; Prison.

Key Texts and Sources

Cavadino, M. and Dignan, J. (2007) *The Penal System: An Introduction* (4th edn). London: Sage (see the 'Introduction').

Home Office (2000) *A Guide to the Criminal Justice System in England and Wales.* London: Home Office (available online at: **http://www.homeoffice.gov.uk/rds/pdfs/cjs2000.pdf**).

CRIMINOGENIC NEEDS

Criminogenic needs are attributes and/or dynamic risk factors of offenders which, if changed, are very likely to influence the probability of reoffending.

Criminogenic needs are critical elements in the rehabilitation process for offenders. They are the reason a rehabilitation programme has been initiated, as well as the key elements in deciding what the programme should address. If criminogenic needs are correctly assessed and then positively changed, the risk of reoffending for that individual will be reduced. It should be recognized that all offenders have many and varied needs, some related to offending and some not (often called *non-criminogenic needs*). However, it could be argued that any need may well be a factor in an offender committing a criminal act and, to this extent, *all* such needs are criminogenic.

Currently the National Offender Management Service is aiming to reduce reoffending by changing offenders' behaviour and addressing the issues that may lead them to reoffend. This work is delivered under seven pathways: accommodation; education, training and employment; health; drugs and alcohol; finance, benefits and debt; children and families; and attitudes, thinking and behaviour. These pathways link very closely to the criminogenic needs identified by research over the last few years.

Andrews and Bonta (1998) proposed that theories of criminal behaviour can be largely grouped into three broad perspectives: sociological, psychopathological and general personality/social psychological (PSP). Under the sociological perspective are needs such as poverty, unemployment, poor educational opportunities and systematic bias against minority groups. The psychopathological perspective supposes that people commit crime because there is something psychologically or emotionally wrong with them. Finally, the general PSP perspective emphasizes the learning of emotions, behaviours and attitudes as the main factors in offending.

However, the concept of criminogenic needs as used today originated in the theoretical background of effective practice. The principle of criminogenic need combines with the risk principle and responsivity to suggest that any reduction in reoffending will be at its greatest when appropriate offenders are targeted, the factors directly related to their offending are identified correctly and any intervention to target these factors is delivered in ways that facilitate learning and positive change. These understandings of criminal behaviour have been used to develop offender assessment instruments, such as

OASys (probation/prison) or ASSET (youth justice), which prompt an exploration into the many areas of an offender's life.

Chapman and Hough (1998: 27) lists criminogenic needs under two headings:
Individual offending-related needs:

- Anti-social attitudes and feelings.
- Ties to anti-social models (anti-social associates).
- Lack of ties/identification with prosocial models.
- Poor decision-making; poor problem-solving skills.
- Lack of prosocial interpersonal skills; lack of self-control and self-management skills; lack of rehearsed plan to deal with risk situations.
- Dependence on alcohol/drugs.
- Lack of contingencies/rewards that favour prosocial behaviour.
- Lack of belief in legitimacy of relevant areas of law or criminal justice.

Relevant social circumstances:

- Unemployment.
- Accommodation if relevant to persistence of offending (e.g. homelessness).
- No income.
- Social isolation.
- Family factors (poor communication, relationships, supervision where linked to offending and amenable to change).
- Mental health problems which require community support.

In practice, once the criminogenic needs have been assessed, the next step is to identify which is the highest priority to address first and, clearly, at present this must relate to addressing any risk of harm issues. Review of these needs in regards to priority and effectiveness should then occur throughout the period of supervision.

Diversity is a crucial aspect of criminogenic needs. One of the major criticisms regarding the 'what works' agenda has been that the research was based primarily on young, white male offenders. As criminogenic needs are strongly linked to the 'what works' agenda, are there any differences for offenders who do not fit into this profile?

While there are many complex and inter-related variables here, the process for either discrimination or anti-discriminatory practice in identifying criminogenic needs is the same for any offender. As an example, black people living in British society are a heterogeneous group, but do have the common experience of racism. Durrance and Williams (2003) argue that the effects of racism can add to the other criminogenic needs that might be present in the black offender's life. Caverley *et al.* (2004) found that only 30 per cent of the black and Asian offenders interviewed had had a discussion with their main supervisor about needs and feelings as a black or Asian offender. If practitioners are not asking the right questions or addressing all the relevant issues, an accurate assessment of criminogenic needs will not be gained. Conversely, by being aware of the possible diversity issues for each offender, a much more complete picture of his or her criminogenic needs will be identified.

In conclusion, for the majority of offenders the only consensus about the causes of their offending behaviour is that it is the product of more than one criminogenic need and the inter-relation between these. It is perhaps this which makes assessment not only a complex piece of work but also one of the most interesting areas of work staff in the criminal justice system can undertake. The importance of understanding criminogenic needs has always been part of the rehabilitation of offenders. How these needs are to be met in the future is still, however, open to debate and political change.

Alan Clark

Related entries

Anti-discriminatory practice; Criminology; Desistance; Diversity; Effective practice; Responsivity; Risk principle; Triangle of offender needs.

Key texts and sources

Andrews D.A. and Bonta, J. (1998) *The Psychology of Criminal Conduct* (2nd edn). Cincinnati, OH: Anderson Publishing.

Caverley, A. *et al.* (2004) *Black and Asian Offenders on Probation. HORS 277*. London: Home Office Research, Development and Statistics Directorate, (available online at **http://www.homeoffice.gov.uk/rds/pdfs04/hors277.pdf**).

Chapman, T. and Hough, M. (1998) *Evidence Based Practice: A Guide to Effective Practice*. London: HM Inspectorate of Probation.

Durrance, P. and Williams, P. (2003) 'Broadening the agenda around what works for black and Asian offenders', *Probation Journal*, 50: 211–24.

CRIMINOLOGY

The study of crime, criminals and criminal justice systems, informed by theories and perspectives from sociology, psychology and social policy.

The origins of criminology are often traced back to the Italian philosopher and reformer, Cesare Beccaria, whose 1764 book, *On Crimes and Punishments*, was a major influence on thinking about criminal justice in Europe and later in the USA. Beccaria argued for consistency and pro-portionality in sentencing, and inaugurated what has remained an important theme in crim-inology – the nature and purpose of criminal laws and the criminal justice system. In 1876 another Italian, the psychiatrist, Cesare Lombroso, published *The Criminal Man*, focus-ing on the characteristics of criminals and their differences from law-abiding people. Lombroso's work appealed to many as a successful applica-tion of contemporary scientific discoveries to the study of criminality. Although Lombroso's claim to have identified the roots of criminality in the primitive biological make-up of criminals is now regarded as discredited, his basic approach, with its interest in biological or psychological peculiarities, has survived, and was given new impetus at the beginning of the twenty-first century when new discoveries in genetics led to claims that a 'gene for crime' would soon be found.

The earliest versions of criminology were therefore based in legal philosophy and psychiatry. In the first quarter of the twentieth century, these perspectives were joined by a more sociological approach, deriving originally from the work of sociologists of the Chicago School. Their focus was not specifically on crime but on social problems, especially the problems of a rapidly growing and culturally diverse city; like their predecessors in law and psychiatry, the Chicago criminologists saw their work as socially relevant and potentially helpful in dealing with crime problems. Criminology was thus conceived as essentially an *applied* discipline, and the early sociologists of crime were just as 'positivist' – committed to scientific methods of investigation – as their colleagues in psychiatry and psychology.

The 1960s and early 1970s saw a new kind of criminology. In 1963 Howard Becker's *Outsiders* argued for a change of focus from deviant individuals to the processes of labelling that defined them and their actions as deviant, and this 'labelling perspective' was hugely influential in the sociology of deviance over the next 20 years. It was not to be assumed that people who committed offences were in some way pathological, and legal definitions of certain acts as criminal should be challenged rather than taken for granted. Instead of seeing the criminal as requiring to be cured or punished, and crime as a social evil, sociologists in this new form of criminology argued that deviance should be sympathetically appreciated rather than automatically condemned. The study of crime and deviance should break with the 'correctional' assumptions of conventional criminology, and sociologists should not concern themselves with finding answers to social problems (which were, in any case, only defined as such by powerful interest groups).

This radical and sceptical approach had a strong intellectual influence, but if criminology ceases to be an applied discipline with a policy-oriented, problem-solving focus, it is not clear why anyone outside academia should be interested in it. In fact, as Downes and Rock (2003) argue, all criminological theories have implications for social policy, and this turned out to be the case for the labelling perspective. Its focus on processes of social control enabled youth justice workers in the 1980s to develop a sophisticated approach to 'system management', to divert young offenders from the formal system when possible, and thereafter slow their progress up the penal tariff. More recently, ideas from the labelling perspective were used to argue against Tony Blair's proposals (in September 2006) for state intervention in the lives of infants born into 'at risk' families.

The labelling perspective had its origins in sociology and has taken its place alongside more traditional sociological theories as one of the key influences on criminological thought. The main strands of theory are often categorized as strain theories, control theories and cultural deviance (or subcultural) theories.

Strain theories assume that, in general, people are disposed to conform to social norms; some powerful strain or pressure is therefore required to push them into breaking the law. Robert Merton argued in 1938 that crime arose when legitimate aspirations were thwarted by inequalities in the social and economic structure: those who lacked legal means of advancement might resort to illegal means. Strain theories have been criticized for being concerned only with the crimes of the disadvantaged, for predicting more deviance than actually occurs, for failing to explain desistance from crime and, importantly, for failing to explain why most crimes are committed by males, when it is females who experience the greater economic disadvantage. But strain theories continue to provide an important reminder of the importance of inequality and injustice for an understanding of crime and the experiences of victims, and there is good evidence that the more unequal a society is, the higher its rates of crime, and especially of violent crime, will tend to be (see, for example, Hagan and Peterson 1995).

Instead of asking, 'Why do they do it?', control theories start with the question, 'Why *don't* they (or we) do it?' They assume that, without some social or internal control, people will be disposed to break the rules when they see some advantage. In his original, very influential statement of control theory, Hirschi (1969) emphasized social controls and the importance of having a bond to conventional society. He identified the elements of the bond as attachment to others, commitment to conventional lines of behaviour, involvement in conventional activities and belief in the importance of law-abiding and conforming behaviour. He later argued that variations in self-control rather than social control explained differences in individuals' propensity to crime. Control theories have been criticized for suggesting that we refrain from crime solely out of fear – of losing the good opinion of others, or of punishment – rather than because we have an internal system of values that makes serious crime unthinkable. But they do better than strain theories in explaining why many people 'grow out' of crime as their bonds to conventional society become stronger, and why males are much more criminally inclined than females, who are socialized differently and tend to be more closely involved in networks of caring relationships.

Cultural deviance theories developed to explain why some neighbourhoods have high levels of criminal activity that persist over time and, in extreme versions, propose that it is cultures, not individuals, that are deviant: people who are defined as deviant are in fact conforming, but to the wrong values and codes of behaviour. The first cultural deviance theories suggested that variations in crime rates could be explained by the presence in some areas of widely shared cultural values that were radically at odds with those of the dominant culture. It is probably more fruitful, however, to think in terms of a variety of subcultures to which people may become affiliated at some stage of their lives, often briefly and superficially. Youth subcultures, in particular, attracted much scholarly attention from the 1970s, and the study of subcultures came to be linked with the labelling

perspective, a classic example being Cohen's work on the 'mods and rockers' violence of the early 1960s. Cultural deviance theories have been criticized for lending support to discriminatory and racist definitions of whole social groups as deviant, and for an unhelpfully circular style of reasoning: to say that people behave as they do because it is part of their culture is not very illuminating. On the other hand, criminology can hardly do without some conception of subculture (for example, to explain how markets for illegal drugs are maintained).

Criminology has sometimes come under criticism for its neglect of diversity. Feminist criminology challenged research undertaken by and for men that rendered women's experiences irrelevant or even invisible. Recognizing gender as a critical criminological variable illuminates the study not only of women offenders but also of masculinity. Similarly it may not be assumed that criminological theories apply in quite the same way to all groups – for example, black and minority ethnic offenders.

It is in the nature of theories in criminology, as in the social sciences generally, that no single theory will explain everything or produce invariably accurate predictions. Although some criminologists have argued that the different types of theory are mutually exclusive and that if you accept (say) control theory you must reject the others, it seems preferable to view any theory not as a statement of final truth but as a source of potentially useful and complementary ideas. Thus choices among theories should not be either/or but based on what is useful for a particular problem in a particular context. You do not even have to decide between psychological and sociological explanations: cognitive-behavioural psychology has been hugely influential on probation practice, but it would be strange to argue that practitioners using this approach should not also be aware of local patterns of unemployment or drug use. Criminology loses its point if it ceases to be a helping, problem-solving discipline, and this is the way practitioners should approach it.

David Smith

Related entries

Black and minority ethnic offenders; Cognitive-behavioural; Criminal careers; Desistance; Diversity; Masculinity and offending; Women offenders.

Key texts and sources

Cohen, S. (1980) *Folk Devils and Moral Panics* (2nd edn). London: Martin Robertson.

Downes, D. and Rock, P. (2003) *Understanding Deviance* (4th edn). Oxford: Oxford University Press.

Hagan, J, and Peterson, R.D. (eds) (1995) *Crime and Inequality*. Stanford, CA: Stanford University Press.

Hirschi, T. (1969) *Causes of Delinquency*. Berkeley, CA: University of California Press.

Maguire, M., Morgan, R. and Reiner, R. (eds) (2002) *The Oxford Handbook of Criminology* (3rd edn). Oxford: Oxford University Press.

Soothill, K., Peelo, M. and Taylor, C. (2002) *Making Sense of Criminology*. Cambridge: Polity Press.

CROWN PROSECUTION SERVICE (CPS)

The national statutory organization responsible for prosecuting the criminal cases investigated by the police in England and Wales.

The Crown Prosecution Service (CPS) works closely with its partners in the criminal justice system on all aspects of the prosecution process. Before progressing a prosecution, the CPS has to be satisfied that the evidence is likely to produce a conviction and that it is in the public interest to prosecute. Some years ago there were experimental schemes where the Probation Service provided information relevant to the decision about whether it was in the public interest to prosecute, but these never became widely established. The CPS partners include the police, HM Courts Service, the Prison Service, youth offending teams, Victim Support and the Probation Service. In addition to liaising with these partners, the CPS also works closely with groups within the community on issues such as domestic violence, rape and hate crime.

Pre-sentence reports (PSRs)

Courts are required to obtain PSRs or a specific sentence report (SSR) prepared by the Probation Service or the youth offending team before imposing a custodial or community sentence. The PSR includes an assessment of the nature and seriousness of the offence.

The CPS provides information to the Probation Service to enable them to make this assessment. The current agreement is set out in a national standard which came into effect on 1 April 1998. The prosecution should see the probation report in order to guard against unfairly critical comments about prosecution witnesses in mitigation or any other inaccuracies the prosecuting lawyer ought to correct.

There are four categories of cases where information will be supplied:

1. Imprisonable summary-only cases.
2. Either-way offences dealt with in the magistrates' courts and youth courts.
3. Either-way cases dealt with in the Crown court.
4. Indictable-only offences where proceeding in the Crown court or in the youth court.

Unduly lenient sentences (ULS's)

The CPS has arrangements in place for considering cases where a sentence may be unduly lenient. Sentences are first considered by a lawyer from the original CPS area. If the area considers that the sentence could be unduly lenient, it refers the papers to the ULS Unit, Special Crime Division, where they are reviewed by a different lawyer.

The Special Crime Division lawyer has to decide if the sentence can be said to fall outside the range of sentences which the judge could reasonably consider appropriate, taking into account all relevant factors and sentencing guidelines given by the Court of Appeal.

If the lawyer decides that the sentence does not fall into that category, that is the end of the matter. If the lawyer takes the view that the sentence may be unduly lenient, the papers are sent to Treasury Counsel for advice. Once the CPS receives Treasury's Counsel's advice, it is for the Special Crime Division lawyer to decide whether or not to refer the case to the Attorney General for consideration.

If, after contact from an interested party, the CPS does not consider the sentence to be unduly lenient, the party will be told immediately that he or she can complain direct to the Attorney General's office. Victims, their families and members of the public sometimes complain to the CPS area, which may refer the sentence to the attorney if the above tests are met.

David Marley

Related entries

Pre-sentence reports; Victim contact; Victims.

Key texts and sources

Full information about the CPS is available at their website (**www.cps.gov.uk/**).

CURFEWS

A restriction on liberty by being obliged to stay at home during specified periods. The use of curfews has expanded rapidly because of electronic monitoring and because more child curfews are being employed as part of anti-social behaviour legislation.

A curfew is a restriction on movement, obliging people to be indoors at certain times, usually during the night. It has a long history in terms of dealing with crime and disorder but, in modern times, was first used only as a condition of bail.

All this changed once the technology to monitor curfews electronically became available. The first British experiment with electronic tagging, in 1989, was concerned with enforcing curfews for offenders on bail. With the rapid expansion of electronic monitoring, nearly 300,000 people had been made subject to curfews between 1999 and 2006. The September 2006 caseload of electronically monitored curfews was 13,000, of which 15 per cent were pre-trial bail cases, 64 per cent were court orders and 21 per cent were short-term post-release cases.

Why use the curfew? The period of restriction may be between 2 and 12 hours per day and it can apply for up to six months, or three months for offenders under 16. The hope is that curfews will reduce the likelihood of reoffending by restricting freedom of movement and, in particular, that they may break a pattern of offending (e.g. night-time burglaries or night-time taking and driving offences). Curfew orders have been used to prohibit attendance at football matches, to keep offenders at a specific address during school opening and closing hours or to reduce the time available for drinking. The starting point is to analyse patterns of offending, then assess whether a curfew could, realistically, disrupt them.

Child curfews have been a much more controversial area. The government's first attempt to launch child curfew schemes, in 1998, failed because local authorities did not support them as they thought they would be almost impossible to enforce. The scheme was extended in 2001, however, with the police also given powers to apply for curfew orders. It was said that experience in Scotland had shown them to be effective in reducing juvenile crime and vandalism.

Orders can cover a 'known trouble spot' such as a town centre or part of a housing estate and can last from 9 p.m. to 6 a.m. for up to 90 days. Such orders are not intended to be used in isolation but as part of wider attempts to reduce neighbourhood crime and anti-social behaviour. Children breaking the curfew are returned to their parents, but there are no criminal sanctions for refusing to obey the order.

Powers were again extended by the Anti-social Behaviour Act 2003 and, by 2006, 80 per cent of police forces had made use of them. A successful challenge to the Act by a child who had been doing nothing wrong but who had nevertheless been removed from a curfew zone by force has subsequently limited the draconian powers that such indiscriminate curfew orders provide.

Dick Whitfield

Related entries

Anti-social behaviour; Electronic monitoring; Tracking.

Key texts and sources

Mair, G. and Canton, R. (2007) 'Sentencing, community penalties and the role of the Probation Service', in L. Gelsthorpe and R. Morgan (eds) *Handbook of Probation*. Cullompton: Willan Publishing.

CUSTODY PLUS, INTERMITTENT CUSTODY AND CUSTODY MINUS

The Criminal Justice Act 2003 provides for the replacement of short prison terms with three new provisions: Custody Plus, Custody Minus and the Intermittent Custody order. However, in June 2006, the planned implementation of Custody Plus and Custody Minus was deferred on the grounds that they could not yet be adequately resourced.

The Criminal Justice Act 2003 purported to create an entirely new sentencing framework. The various community penalties are replaced by a single 'community order' with a range of conditions; short custodial sentences were to be replaced by three new provisions:

1. *Custody Plus*: a custodial sentence of less than 12 months (expressed in weeks with a minimum of 28 weeks and a maximum of 51 weeks) consisting of a short 'custodial period' of between two weeks and three months followed by a 'licence period' of at least six months. The court may order a similar range of conditions to be attached to the licence as is available under the community order.

2. *Intermittent Custody*: a custodial sentence of 14–90 days that is served in blocks of a few days at a time, enabling offenders to maintain community ties (such as work, education or childcare) while serving a custodial sentence. Conditions may be attached to the licence period that follows the custodial period. A

similar proposal in the 1970s for 'weekend imprisonment' was criticized as impractical and was never introduced. Pilot schemes for intermittent custody were introduced at two prisons (Kirkham for male prisoners and Morton Hall for female prisoners) in January 2004. In a report of an inspection of Morton Hall in March 2006, the Chief Inspector of Prisons warned that the pilot had failed to attract sufficient prisoners to enable a worthwhile regime and had serious doubts that it could ever do so in a location well away from the main conurbations from which the majority of women come. These were precisely the concerns that had led to the abandonment of the idea of weekend imprisonment 30 years earlier.

3. *Custody Minus*: a new suspended sentence order under which an offender will have requirements to fulfil in the community, as in a community sentence. If an offender breaches the requirements the presumption is that the suspended prison sentence is activated. However, during the passage of the bill, courts dealing with breaches of an order were given discretion to vary the term to be served in custody, or to enhance the conditions to be served in the community without implementing the custodial element. If the custodial element was invoked, the offender would subsequently be subject to a licence period to which, once again, conditions could be added (and could once again be returned to prison for breaching those conditions).

These new provisions were based on the Halliday Report, which decried the 'lack of utility' in short prison terms (Home Office 2001: iv) because they 'literally mean half what they say' – after the first half is served in prison, nothing is required of the offender, nor is anything done to change the offender or his or her circumstances in ways that might avert new offences, rendering the second half 'meaningless and ineffective' (2001: 3). Some 60 per cent of offenders sentenced to prison for 12 months or less who were discharged in 1996 were reconvicted within two years, with virtually the same rate of reconviction, after two years at risk, among those who had been sentenced to community penalties

(2001: 126). The white paper, *Justice for All*, similarly maintained that short prison sentences do not afford enough time for effective work to be done on offending behaviours before release on licence, and offer no support or supervision after release for any meaningful behavioural or rehabilitation work. Effectively, the Act prohibits sentences that imprison for more than 13 weeks but less than six months. Under its provisions, courts can still keep an offender behind bars for six months or longer by imposing prison sentences of 12 months or more, half of which is served under licence in the community. For shorter prison sentences, the Act requires sentencers to specify a number of weeks between 2 and 13 to be served in custody before release on licence. This narrowing of the range of permissible short prison sentences is a more modest reform than at first appears: in 2001, only 8 per cent of adult offenders received into prison arrived on prison sentences that would be eliminated by these provisions (Home Office 2003: 91, Table 4.8).

In effect, these provisions make any prison sentence of less than a year an additional requirement of a community order. The new Custody Plus sentence is in effect a community order commenced by up to three months' imprisonment. Similarly, Custody Minus is a community order for which the consequence of an offender's failure to comply with its community requirements – a short prison stay – is fixed by the court at the time the order is imposed.

Wrapping shorter periods of custody in community orders tailored to the needs and circumstances of individual offenders might render short prison sentences less destructive, but making them (or making them appear to be) more 'effective' seems very likely to encourage their use, enabling courts to 'have it both ways' by combining the perceived benefits of a community sentence with the punishment of custody. In the great majority of criminal cases, sentencing courts would no longer need to choose between a prison sentence and a community penalty, or between one community

penalty and another. The difficulty of resourcing these new sentences at a time when the prison population was reaching record levels in 2006 strongly suggests that the measures were withheld because of fears that they would further inflate prison numbers, as well as inflating the workload of the Probation Service.

Custody Minus (or suspended sentence order) can be seen as an attempt to give meaning to the original provision introduced in the Criminal Justice Act 1967, and it is regularly criticized either in the media in individual cases as a let-off or, in academic circles, as having replaced community sentences rather than custodial sentences (see Bottoms 1979) or, more fundamentally, as not fitting easily in a just-deserts sentencing framework because there was no effective punishment element unless breached. The suspended sentence order would overcome that last defect, but is very likely to be liable to the other two. The distinction between the suspended sentence order and a community sentence that can attract a custodial sentence for a breach of conditions is also a fine one, but the risk is that the suspended sentence order will be seen as a more credible way of sentencing an offender than a community order.

Jenny Roberts

Related entries

Criminal Justice Act 2003; Halliday Report; Licence.

Key texts and sources

Bottoms, A.E. (1979) 'The Advisory Council and the Suspended Sentence', *Criminal Law Review*, 437–46.
Home Office (2001) *Making Punishments Work: Report of a Review of the Sentencing Framework for England and Wales.* London: Home Office.
Home Office (2002) *Justice for All* (Cm 5563). London: Home Office.
Roberts, J. and Smith, M. (2004) 'Custody Plus, Custody Minus', in M. Tonry (ed.) *Confronting Crime: Crime Control Policy under New Labour.* Cullompton: Willan Publishing.

CYCLE OF CHANGE

A transtheoretical model of change first proposed by Prochaska and DiClemente that highlights five main active stages within a behavioural change process, with differential methods of intervention likely to facilitate change at each stage of the cycle.

Prochaska and DiClemente initially undertook research in the area of patterns of substance abuse and concluded that individuals appeared to go through five stages of change when actively addressing their substance abuse. (The passive precontemplative stage was initially taken out of the cycle, but was later incorporated.) This they put forward in the circular model shown in Figure 3.

Although circular, suggesting that individuals must go through each stage in sequence before entering the next, it is now generally accepted that the process of change in reality is somewhat more complex, often involving being in different stages for different types of substance and moving from one stage to any one of the others (and back) according to a variety of internal and external factors (Prochaska and DiClemente 1992). Prochaska and DiClemente (1992) thus highlighted a new spiral model of change, replacing the 'decision' stage with the 'preparation' stage.

Miller and Rollnick (1994) have proposed that facilitating change then becomes more likely when the intervention approach matches directly the needs of the individual in relation to the stage of change he or she is inhabiting at the time (see Table 1).

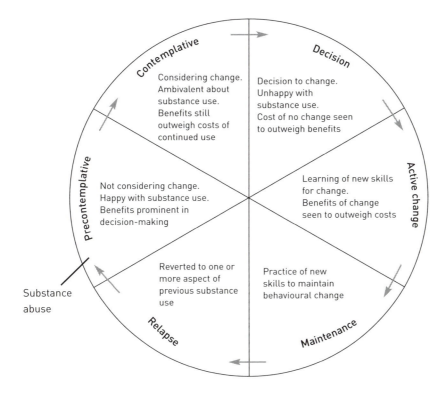

Figure 3 Cycle of change

Table 1 Stage of change and intervention

Stage of change	Matched intervention
Precontemplative	Rapport building Problem-free talk
Contemplative	Identifying the positives and not so positives of no change Building upon concerns
Preparation	Building optimism that change is possible Enhancing commitment to change
Action	Identifying practical strategies to begin change
Maintenance	Relapse prevention training
Relapse	Identifying the learning experience of lapse Rebuilding commitment to change

In addition, Prochaska and DiClemente (1994) have suggested there are five hierarchically organized factors that are involved in symptom maintenance, with earlier factors being more responsive to change than later factors. They suggest these factors to be:

● situational symptom-maintaining factors;
● maladaptive cognitions;
● interpersonal conflicts;
● family conflicts; and
● intrapsychic conflicts.

While originally devised as a framework from which to address substance use, Prochaska and DiClemente (1994) have more recently proposed this to be a model that can be useful when considering any behavioural change processes, including offending. It has widely been found to be useful to practitioners in helping them to make sense of fluctuations in people's motivation and to adapt their interventions accordingly.

Similarly, it is a model that clients themselves find illuminating and easy to understand.

Anton Ashcroft

Related entries

Motivation; Motivational interviewing.

Key texts and sources

Miller, W.R. and Rollnick, S. (1994) 'Variations in the effectiveness in the treatment of patients with substance use disorders: An empirical review', *Addiction*, 89: 688–97.
Prochaska, J.O. and DiClemente, C.C. (1992) 'In search of how people change: Applications to addictive behaviours', *American Psychologist*, September: 1102–14.
Prochaska, J.O. and DiClemente, C.C. (1994) *The Transtheoretical Approach: Crossing Traditional Boundaries of Therapy*. Malabar, FL: Krieger Publishing.

D

DANGEROUSNESS

A term used to describe an offender's potential for committing acts that would cause serious harm to others. The term was previously used in relation to parole decisions, but it has now taken on a specific meaning in relation to new sentences.

The terms 'potentially dangerous offender' and 'dangerousness' were commonly used in the 1970s and 1980s when the lifer and parole systems were evolving. Dangerousness is a concept that hints at an inherent and immutable individual characteristic and, during recent years it has been replaced by the term 'risk of serious harm'. The implementation of assessment frameworks such as OASys (in particular, the 'Risk of serious harm analysis' section) and the introduction of levels of risk of serious harm have sealed this change in terminology.

The assessment analyses two variables: likelihood and impact. It defines the individual's 'potential for committing further acts that will cause serious harm'.

The terms 'dangerousness' and 'dangerous offenders' remain, however, in the parlance of the Home Office as a result of the Criminal Justice Act 2003, which has had an unprecedented effect on the sentencing of sexual and violent offenders. Public protection (i.e. protecting the public from sexual and violent offending that causes serious harm), is high on the Home Office agenda.

The new legislation has introduced preventative sentences, based on risk of harm. Sections 224–229 allow for the imposition of an indeterminate sentence of imprisonment for public protection for offenders who have committed a serious sexual or violent offence specified in Schedule 15 to the Act. Offenders convicted of lesser offences in the schedule are eligible for an extended sentence.

These public protection sentences are imposed only after an 'assessment of dangerousness'. This is defined as 'whether there is a significant risk to members of the public of serious harm occasioned by the commission by him of further such offences'. If the court decides that the offender has passed this 'significant risk' test, there is no alternative but that the court imposes one of the public protection sentences.

The pre-sentence report is obviously the prime vehicle for informing the court's judgment of the offender's level of risk of serious harm. The National Probation Service guide to the new sentences advises that, if the OASys risk of serious harm assessment is rigorously applied, the assessment of dangerousness required under the Act would be completed through this exercise. It generates a well evidenced conclusion on the level of risk of serious harm posed by the offender.

In the judgment on the first cases of appeal against these sentences this view was upheld. Thus the assessment of dangerousness and the assessment of risk of serious harm are compatible exercises, and 'dangerous' and 'high/very high risk of serious harm' are compatible concepts. Or perhaps they are one and the same thing after all?

Jo Thompson

Related entries

Domestic violence; Extended sentencing; Multi-agency public protection arrangements (MAPPAs); Public protection; Risk assessment and risk management; Risk of harm; Sex offenders; Violent offenders.

Key texts and sources

Judgement in the Court of Appeal Criminal Division [2005] EWCA Crim 2864.

Kemshall, H. and Wood, J. (2007) 'High-risk offenders and public protection', in L. Gelsthorpe and R. Morgan (eds) *Handbook of Probation*. Cullompton: Willan Publishing.

National Probation Service (2005) *National Guide for the New Criminal Justice Act 2003 Sentences for Public Protection*. (edition 1, version 1). London: Home Office.

Walker, N. (ed.) (1996) *Dangerous People*. Oxford: Blackstone Press.

DATA PROTECTION ACT 1998

Legislation designed to prevent the misuse of personal data by any organization.

The Data Protection Act 1998 regulates the use of personal data processed by any organization. Personal data are defined as any information that can identify any living individual. Processing means recording, storing or destroying personal data and sensitive personal data.

The Probation Service will process sensitive personal data of all its employees and all offenders it works with. The Data Protection Act provides a legal framework on how to process this information, based on eight principles. These principles are as follows:

1. That personal data shall be processed fairly and lawfully.
2. The purpose for processing personal data should be specified.
3. Personal data shall be adequate, relevant and not excessive.
4. Personal data shall be accurate and kept up to date.
5. Personal data shall not be kept for longer than required.
6. Personal data shall be processed within the rights of the data subject.
7. Appropriate measures shall be taken to ensure personal data are secure.
8. Personal data shall not be transferred outside the European Union.

Each probation area must register its use of personal data with the Information Commissioner's Office and, as such, is accountable to the Information Commissioner in the event of a data subject wishing to place a complaint.

The principles outlined above and underlying the Act have led to the development of strict guidance on the use of personal data, specifically around the security of personal data. This has led to a raft of policies which have to be complied with for personal data held in manual files and those held on IT systems. The 'clear desk' policy is the most obvious example, requiring staff to leave desks clear of any personal data. Probation staff are responsible for ensuring they comply with these policies to protect the information they are working with.

Data subjects have a right of access to information being processed about them by any organization. Offenders have a right to request access to their information. This has to be done in a structured, managed way, to ensure they are not given access to any information other than that which directly relates to them. Most case records will contain information about third parties (i.e. information that may have been passed to the organization in confidence). Each area should have an expert member of staff who can support colleagues and ensure the rights of offenders are met when a subject access request comes into the organization.

The Information Commissioner can impose fines on any organization when there are breaches of the Data Protection Act.

Sometimes requests for the disclosure of personal information are made using the Freedom of Information Act 2000. The Data Protection Act gives protection to personal data being processed and, in such cases, the Data Protection Act would be referenced, if applicable, to explain why disclosure cannot be made under the Freedom of Information Act.

Wendy Storer

Related entries

Case records; Freedom of Information Act 2000.

Key texts and sources

The Information Commissioner's Office's website is at http://www.ico.gov.uk/.

DAY CENTRES

> Premises attended by Probation Service users, on a voluntary or statutory basis, in which they might be involved in various activities.

Within the context of current Probation Service concerns, day centres may seem a relic of doubtful relevance to present policy and practice. However, many states in the USA have drawn on the British experience and currently include day reporting centres in their range of criminal justice provision, so perhaps closer examination might reveal some useful lessons for the future direction of practice in the UK.

Day centres evolved during the early 1970s. Voluntary centres such as the Barbican Centre in Gloucester, Sherbourne House in London and the Pontefract Activity Centre were organized around the notion of voluntary commitment to change and rehabilitation, and had programmes of activities (for instance, art, pottery and woodwork) alongside groupwork based on contracts. In some, ex-offenders were used as link people to work with probationers and ex-prisoners. They were unusual for involving a wide range of people, not all necessarily currently in trouble with the courts. In contrast, the four 'day training centres', which were an experiment designed to divert people from custody and offer the opportunity of rehabilitation, required probationers to attend for a fixed period (usually 60 days). While this distinguished them from voluntary centres, there were some marked similarities: they, too, provided programmes of practical activities combined with groupwork which encompassed, for example, the social skills and problem-solving, and therapeutic models. Ultimately the compulsory principle prevailed, and voluntary centres were incorporated into the statutory model.

The Criminal Justice Act 2003 redefines day centres as community rehabilitation centres. Section 201 allows the court to require someone to attend a centre approved by the local probation board and 'participate in activities specified in the order' for no more than 60 days. Rather than use special probation premises, some areas (but not many) use this specified activity provision to provide employment, training and education opportunities (ETE); debt counselling; and mediation between an offender and the victim(s) of his or her offending. Areas are using elements of the day centre idea while making it more consistent with the process of community reintegration and the principle that people who offend have the opportunity of rehabilitating themselves as citizens with associated rights and responsibilities.

Although a relatively brief and transitory part in probation's probation history, day centres are a significant element of the service's engagement with control and enforcement (the opening of the Kent Control Unit in the late 1970s sparked considerable controversy), and the centres themselves made an enduring contribution to probation theory and practice. They played a significant part in the pioneering of information systems and monitoring; developed experience in intensive work with high-risk offenders; modelled the involvement of different grades of staff in co-working (thereby contributing to the idea of case management); experimented with methods (thus providing an alternative template to the current one-track approach); exposed staff to evaluative scrutiny; and, although part of a diversionary strategy, contributed to the preservation of the concept of rehabilitation.

Maurice Vanstone

Related entries

Enforcement; Groupwork.

Key texts and sources

Mair, G. (1988) *Probation Day Centres. HORS* 100. London: HMSO.

Vanstone, M. (1985) 'Moving away from help? Policy and practice in probation day centres', *Howard Journal*, 24: 20–28.

Vanstone, M. (1993) 'A "missed opportunity" reassessed: the influence of the day training centre experiment on the criminal justice system and probation practice', *British Journal of Social Work*, 23: 213–29.

DEPORTATION

Deportation is sending a person out of the UK under an order signed by the Home Secretary. In criminal cases for which the maximum sentence is a prison term, a court has the power to recommend deportation as part of the criminal sentence for people aged 17 or over (s. 3(6) of the Immigration Act 1971). Even if the court made no recommendation, s. 3(5) of the Act permits the Home Office to deport a person on the grounds that 'their presence in the UK is not conducive to the public good'.

Deportation is the power used by the government to remove foreign nationals from the UK whom it does not want to remain here. The Home Office can use deportation powers to remove a range of people. This includes those who are convicted of either immigration or non-immigration criminal offences who are recommended for deportation by the criminal court as part of their sentence for the offence. People can also be deported on the grounds that their presence is not 'conducive to the public good'. They may or may not have committed criminal offences in order to be liable for deportation on these grounds. Family members of people being deported from the above two categories can also be deported.

Legislation

Section 5 of the Immigration Act 1971 provides for the Home Secretary to make or revoke a deportation order. This requires a person to leave the UK and prohibits him or her from re-entering the UK unless it is revoked. Any leave to enter or remain which a person gains is invalid while a deportation order is outstanding against him or her. There is no expiry date to a deportation order. A person who enters the UK in breach of a deportation order is an illegal entrant and may be removed as such. Family members of deportees can also be deported.

Persons liable to deportation are described in ss. 3(5) and 3(6) of the 1971 Act. Section 3(5)(a) refers to deportations on what is called non-conducive grounds, which can include political views, terrorism or ideology or because of criminal cases. Section 3(6) allows a court that convicts a person aged 17 or older (who is subject to immigration control), of an offence punishable with imprisonment to recommend to the Home Secretary that the person concerned should be deported.

Probation practice

Court practice

A criminal court can only recommend deportation as part of the sentence if the defendant has been notified of his or her liability for deportation seven days prior to making a recommendation. This notification is sometimes known as form 'IM3'. If it has not been served, sometimes a court will adjourn for the form to be served. Probation practitioners should therefore be aware whether an offender, on whom they are preparing a pre-sentence report, is liable to a court recommendation for deportation if an IM3 has been served. It is important, therefore, that court probation staff include in the report request whether an IM3 has been served. The Crown Prosecution Service (CPS) and the arresting officer may also be contacted to confirm whether an IM3 has been served should there be doubt or confusion. The Immigration Services Evidence and Enquiry Unit, to which probation staff have access rights, can also be contacted to verify immigration status and the intentions of the Immigration Service with regards to deportation.

If a court requests a sentencing report on a defendant on whom an IM3 has been served, it should be assumed that it is considering both deportation and community sentence options. It should not be assumed that a court will inevitably recommend deportation if an IM3 has been served, and the report writer should explore sentencing options and the impact of deportation on the defendant.

If a foreign national defendant receives a prison sentence, the CPS and Prison Service have various duties to inform the Criminal Casework Directorate (CCD) of the Immigration and Nationality Directorate (IND) of their sentence. It is the duty of the CCD to consider whether to ask the Home Secretary to approve a court deportation recommendation. In practice, the Home Secretary approves most court deportation recommendations.

Even if a court decided not to recommend deportation or, indeed, if there was no request from the IND to recommend it, the Home Office can later use s. 3(5)(a) of their immigration powers if they consider the person's continued presence in the UK is not 'conducive to the public good'. In deciding whether to deport on these grounds, the Home Office has to consider a wider range of factors than the criminal court considers in deciding whether to recommend deportation.

There is a range of appeal processes for foreign nationals who intend to challenge deportation recommendations.

At present, probation staff are not required to contribute to the decision-making process of the CCD when they decide whether to pursue a court deportation recommendation. Neither, at present, are probation staff required to provide information for the CCD to contribute to their decision-making as to whether to pursue deportation using their s. 3(5)(a) powers. This situation may change with the current Home Office review of foreign national prisoners.

Offender management

There are, however, requirements on probation staff/offender managers when a foreign national prisoner, who has completed the custodial element of his or her sentence but continues to be held in immigration detention, applies for immigration bail. In these cases, when the foreign national would be on licence if released in the community, *Probation Circular (PC) 37/2006* instructs probation staff/offender managers on the provision of reports at the request of the CCD for the use of the Asylum and Immigration Tribunal who hear bail applications.

Probation Circular 24/2006, issued following the problems revealed in 2006 of foreign national prisoners having been released over a seven-year period without proper consideration for deportation by the CCD, places general duties on probation areas regarding foreign national prisoners. These include areas nominating offender managers to prisoners 'regardless of nationality, immigration status or perceived likelihood of deportation at the earliest stages, and undertaking risk assessments and risk management plans of a high standard'. Both PCs 24 and 37 place responsibilities on offender managers to liaise regularly with CCD caseworkers in their management of foreign national prisoners. It is to be expected that these cases will remain particularly sensitive, and it is important that offender managers maintain a high level of vigilance and are proactive in their contact with the CCD in their management.

Nick Hammond

Related entries

Asylum; Interpretation and translation.

Key texts and sources

HM Prison Service (2006) *Foreign National Prisoners Liable to Deportation. Prison Service Instruction 6000.* London: HM Prison Service.

HM Prison Service (2006) *Immigration and Foreign National in Prison. Prison Service Order 4630.* London: HM Prison Service.

Home Office (2006) *Foreign National Prisoners. Probation Circular 24/2006.* London: Home Office.

Home Office (2006) *Information Exchange between the IND, Prison Service and NPD Regarding Licenses and Bail Hearings. Probation Circular 37/2006.* London: Home Office.

DESISTANCE

The processes by which people come to cease and sustain cessation of offending behaviour, with or without intervention by criminal justice agencies.

There is no single accepted definition of desistance. Most empirical measures emphasize the state of non-offending, but defining desistance as the absence of something (offending) leaves unclear whether the term applies only to the final termination of a criminal career or to any significant crime-free gap. To focus on the end point of non-offending may neglect the *process* by which this state is reached (Bushway *et al.* 2001). Moreover, there is an important difference between someone merely not offending for a period and a person coming, through a process of change, to identify him or herself as a non-offender. Maruna and Farrall (2004) therefore propose a definition incorporating two distinguishable phases in the desistance process: *primary* desistance refers to any lull or crime-free gap in the course of a criminal career; *secondary* desistance is the assumption of the identity of a non-offender or 'changed person'.

Theories of Desistance

While sharing some commonalities, theories of desistance may be broadly categorised as *individual, structural* and *interactionist*.

Individual

Individual theories have the longest history and are based on the established links between age and certain criminal behaviours, locating explanations of desistance within age and maturation. The aggregate age–crime curve indicates a sharp increase in the arrest rate in the early teen years; a peak in the late teen or early adult years; and a decrease over the remaining age distribution. Explanations of this age–crime relationship can be located within 'ontogenic' or 'maturational reform' theories, which contend that, over time and with age, young people tend naturally to grow out of crime. Maturational reform theories attribute these changes to the physical, mental

and biological changes that accompany ageing: the effect of age on crime is natural, direct and invariant across social, temporal and economic conditions.

However, Bushway *et al.* (2001) argue that identifying desistance as a process rather than a state of termination, particularly in reference to developmental accounts, renders the idea of age as a causal explanation of desistance implausible. Age indexes a range of different variables, including biological changes, social and normative transitions (and the associated social meanings ascribed to them), life experiences, the impact of social or institutional processes, and internal factors such as motivation or attitudinal change. Age in itself is not, therefore, the explanation.

Structural

Structural theories include social bond theories which postulate an association between desistance and circumstances external to the individual, but including the individual's reaction to and interaction with those circumstances. Such theories stress the significance of family ties, employment or education, for example, in explaining changes in criminal behaviour across the life course. These ties create a stake in conformity. Social control theorists argue that 'deviance' arises from weak social bonds, and desistance is facilitated where bonds to mainstream institutions (such as a spouse or a career) are developed or strengthened. (Social bonds include significant relationships, responsibilities and 'stakes in conformity' broadly and are not confined to the formal institutions of marriage or employment.)

Most social control theorists, therefore, recognize that key life events such as marriage or employment are likely to be correlated with, although not necessarily causal of, desistance (Sampson and Laub 1993; Graham and Bowling 1995). Such findings imply that desistance cannot be attributed solely to social attachments acting as external forces; what matters, rather, is what these ties *mean* to 'offenders'; the perceived strength, quality and interdependence of these ties; and their impact in buttressing informal social controls which reduce both opportunities and motivations to offend.

Interactionist

Interactionist theories combine individual and structural explanations. These investigations of the dynamics of desistance often draw on offenders' accounts of their own experiences of desistance processes (Maruna 2001) and stress the significance of subjective changes in self and identity, reflected in changing motivations, greater concern for others and more consideration of the future.

Desistance theorists are increasingly focusing on changes of personal cognition, self-identity and self-concept which might precede or coincide with changes in social bonds. 'Turning point' events may have a different impact depending on the person's level of motivation, readiness to reform or interpretation of, or assignation of, the meanings of such events. The development of a 'coherent pro-social identity' (Maruna 2001: 7) and involvement in 'generative activities' contributing to the well-being of others are seen as critical. Agency, self-determination and societal reaction, in supporting and reinforcing the development of fledgling prosocial identities, influence the process of desistance.

Supporting Desistance in Practice

Because desistance is about the subjective meanings of age, maturation, social bonds, life events and identities for individuals, a desistance-focused perspective in practice fundamentally requires recognition of diversity and heterogeneity in people's pathways to desistance. That said, some of those authors who have directly examined 'supported desistance' (desistance among those subject to interventions) have tried to provide some general advice about how various pathways may be best supported in practice. Indeed, some have gone as far as to suggest that desistance research requires a new paradigm for the practice of offender management (McNeill 2006).

The relational aspects of supervision processes are frequently highlighted in such discussions as being key supportive factors in desistance processes. Farrall (2002) emphasized the importance of a partnership approach to the identification, negotiation and resolution of obstacles to desistance. Rex (1999) found that motivation and commitment to desist appeared to be generated or enhanced by the personal and professional commitment shown to probationers by their workers, whose reasonableness, fairness and encouragement seemed to engender a sense of loyalty, obligation and accountability. Desisters cited efforts to improve reasoning and decision-making skills, reinforcement of prosocial behaviour, practical assistance and guidance with their problems as assisting the wider process of desistance. These studies highlight the need for individualized, active and participatory approaches which encourage the discovery and exercise of agency and self-determination.

Farrall (2002) also advocates interventions directed towards the offender's community, social and personal context. Necessarily, this requires that interventions be focused not solely on individuals and their supposed 'deficits'; while such approaches can build human capital, for example in terms of enhanced cognitive skills or improved employability, they cannot generate the social capital which resides in the relationships through which participation, inclusion in society and (ultimately) desistance are facilitated. This implies a role for workers in assessing, engaging with and developing the resources within people's social networks as well as an advocacy role in seeking to engineer opportunities with and for people.

At a more personal level, desistance is also about finding redemption and working at reformation; it often involves discovering new purposes, achievements and forms of recognition which may be facilitated through involvement in generative activities. Practitioners should therefore support desisters to access opportunities to make a constructive contribution to local communities – for example, through civic participation facilitated through involvement in voluntary work. This may highlight the need for stronger partnership approaches between offender management and community development agencies.

Increased civic participation is one medium through which prosocial identity reinforcement can be facilitated, supporting the process of secondary desistance. If desistance is reinforced by someone believing in the offender and by the recognition of a reformed identity, this underlines the importance of workers sustaining an optimistic and persistent approach in supporting the desister's efforts, even when the desister struggles to recognize them for him or herself. Such optimism and persistence also link to a strengths-based approach which recognizes and exploits people's resources, capacities and possibilities, further reinforcing their efforts to change. Practice discourses should therefore be future-oriented and the necessary focus on risks and needs explicitly balanced with an emphasis on individual strengths to avoid the reinforcement of negative messages about dangerousness and/or helplessness.

Interventions which best support desistance are likely to be based on a recognition of diversity and the need for skilled assessment, individualized case planning and management; on strong, respectful and motivating relationships between those subject to supervision and their supervisors; and on the development of both human and social capital through multifaceted interventions. Crucially, supporting desistance means recognizing the need to work *with* communities to build opportunities *for* 'offenders' to reconstruct themselves, as well as *with* 'offenders' in constructing safer communities.

Beth Weaver and Fergus McNeill

Related entries

Criminal careers; Desistance studies vs. cognitive behavioural therapies: which offers most hope for the long term?; Diversity; Motivation; Social capital.

Key texts and sources

Bushway S.D., Piquero, A., Broidy, L., Cauffman, E. and Mazerole, P. (2001) 'An empirical framework for studying desistance as a process', *Criminology*, 39: 496–515.

Farrall, S. (2002) *Rethinking What Works with Offenders*. Cullompton: Willan Publishing.

Farrall, S. and Calverley, A. (2006) *Understanding Desistance from Crime*. Maidenhead: Open University Press.

Graham, J. and Bowling, B. (1995) *Young People and Crime. Home Office Research Study* 145. London: HMSO.

Maruna, S. (2001) *Making Good: How Ex-convicts Reform and Rebuild their Lives*. Washington, DC: American Psychological Association.

Maruna, S. and Farrall, S. (2004) 'Desistance-focused criminal justice policy research: introduction to a special issue on desistance from crime and public policy', *Howard Journal of Criminal Justice*, 43: 358–67.

McNeill, F. (2006) 'A desistance paradigm for offender management', *Criminology and Criminal Justice*, 6: 39–63.

Rex, S. (1999) 'Desistance from offending: experiences of probation', *Howard Journal of Criminal Justice*, 36: 366–83.

Sampson R.J and Laub J.H (1993) *Crime in the Making: Pathways and Turning Points Through Life*. London: Harvard University Press.

DESISTANCE STUDIES VS. COGNITIVE-BEHAVIOURAL THERAPIES: WHICH OFFERS MOST HOPE FOR THE LONG TERM?

The study of desistance – how and why people come to stop offending – calls into question received understandings about effective practice and the dominance of cognitive-behavioural approaches.

Debates about the role of formal agencies of criminal justice are not new, of course, having flowed back and forth for decades. In the 1980s and for much of the 1990s, psychologists laboured to design groupwork accredited programmes which would 'teach' prosocial behaviours to offenders. The aim was to encourage offenders to 'think straight' or learn new ways of behaving, putting crime behind them.

This wave of cognitive-behavioural treatment (CBT) was part of an individualized, neoconservative crime policy. The dominant approach, at least within part of the Home Office during the 1980s, was aimed not at rehabilitation but at making crime harder to commit. Situational crime prevention claimed that better security and physical design would prevent many offences. The social or economic basis of crime was downplayed (in keeping with Thatcher's claim that there was 'no such thing as society' and Major's that 'there is no excuse for crime. Society is not to blame and individuals are'; Morris 1994: 311). In the context of individual responsibility and an outright rejection of the notion of any societal-level causes of crime, CBT offered an attractive alternative to social work.

Yet CBT now seems less able to deliver the goods – recent reviews finding evidence inconclusive (Harper and Chitty 2005) or even counterproductive (Travis 2006). Studies of desistance start at a different place. Instead of asking 'what is the impact of what we do on rates of recidivism?', desistance research asks 'why do people stop offending?', prompting the further question: 'What can the criminal justice system do to assist (or at least not disrupt) these processes?' Studies of desistance score over CBT approaches in a number of important ways. By exploring why people stop offending we are better able to understand the *whole* range of reasons why people cease committing crime (rather than being limited to focusing just on what probation officers do).

This more holistic approach helps to locate desistance as not just an individual decision but as a set of processes mediated by significant social institutions, such as employment, educational institutions, the family, political engagement and peer relations, and also the role of these within the life course of individuals. A consideration of the role of social institutions and the individual offender's relationship with these at key points in their life also emphasizes the importance of understanding how these institutions operate and how they might be harnessed to assist desistance. The processes identified by those researching desistance are accordingly not at odds with more developed accounts of why people become engaged in crime over the life course.

Interviewing ex-probationers or ex-prisoners has produced some surprising results. Far from lessening, it would appear that the long-term impact of probation supervision may become *more* salient for some offenders over time (Farrall and Calverley 2006). With the work of writers such as Fergus McNeill (2004, 2006) forging ever closer and more refined connections between desistance and policy, there is real hope that we may be better able to assist more people away from crime in the future. This, however, is embedded in an understanding of the role of social institutions, not behavioural therapies.

Stephen Farrall

Related entries

Accredited programmes; Cognitive-behavioural; Desistance.

Key texts and sources

Farrall, S. and Calverley, A. (2006) *Understanding Desistance From Crime.* Maidenhead: Open University Press.

Harper, G. and Chitty, C. (2005) *The Impact of Corrections on Re-Offending: A Review of 'What Works'* Home Office Research Study 291. London: Home Office (available online at **http://www.homeoffice.gov.uk/rds04/hors291.pdf**).

Jamieson, J., McIvor, G. and Murray, C. (1999) *Understanding Offending Among Young People.* Edinburgh: HMSO (available online at **http://www.scotland.gov.uk/cru/resfinds/swr37-00.htm**).

McNeill, F. (2004) 'Desistance, rehabilitation and correctionalism', *Howard Journal of Criminal Justice*, 43: 420–36.

McNeill, F. (2006) 'A desistance paradigm for offender management', *Criminology and Criminal Justice*, 6: 37–60.

Morris, T. (1994) 'Crime and penal policy', in D. Kavanagh and A. Seldon (eds) *The Major Effect.* London: Macmillan.

Travis, A. (2006) 'Offenders' anger control classes help make some more dangerous', *Guardian*, 24 April: 4.

DISCRETION

> The freedom or authority to make a judgement about what to do (or not do) in a given situation.

Using discretion through the exercise of judgement is a key component of professional practice throughout the criminal justice process, contrasting with more rule-bound, routinized elements of work with offenders. The central conundrum around discretion is that justice requires sufficient regulation and predictability to guard against arbitrariness, while also needing to allow for exceptions to the rule. Linking this to offender management includes the question of when to return an individual to court for breach of a community sentence. While a probation officer might use his or her discretion in an arbitrary or discriminatory way, a set of rules risks achieving bureaucratic sameness at the cost of ignoring relevant differences. Is it fairer, therefore, for officers to use their discretion to individualize decision-making, or to apply standardized rules to each and every case?

Probation officers have traditionally enjoyed a considerable degree of discretion. Until the Criminal Justice Act 1991, probation orders were imposed *instead of* a sentence, officers having authority bestowed upon them by the court to supervise probationers. How this was accomplished was left largely up to individual officers – resulting in a lack of consistency (of both approach and method) and the potential for discriminatory practice. The recent shift towards cognitive-behavioural approaches and the introduction of increasingly rigid National Standards in relation to the enforcement of orders were – in part – an attempt to address these concerns.

More consistency, however, does not necessarily lead to a fairer or more just system. Attempting to treat all offenders the same ignores very real differences in their make-up and circumstances, diminishing the professional skills of probation officers. Judicious use of discretion – judging when, what and how to challenge – is part and parcel of the professional role. Officers weigh up a range of factors, including offenders' attendance, their response to any offending behaviour work being undertaken and any particular circumstances that might suggest an exception should be made. A sentencer might, for example, have imposed a community sentence in part because of someone's chaotic lifestyle and general unreliability – and few would expect changes in behaviour and lifestyle to occur overnight.

Balancing the need for consistency with the need for flexibility is more of an art than a science: if the rules are drawn too tightly, officers' lack of discretion will constrain their practice with offenders. Conversely, a lack of any guidelines can result in discretion deteriorating into caprice, resulting in inconsistent practice. In attempting (rightly) to guard against arbitrariness and to ensure more direct accountability, policymakers have tried to circumscribe or at least structure discretion, but sufficient flexibility needs to be allowed to accommodate the many ways in which individual circumstances can differ from one another.

Tina Eadie

Related entries

Accountability; Diversity; National Standards; Staff supervision.

Key texts and sources

Eadie, T. and Canton, R. (2002). 'Practising in a context of ambivalence: the challenge for youth justice workers', *Youth Justice*, 2: 14–26.

Gelsthorpe, L. and Padfield, N. (eds) (2003) *Exercising Discretion: Decision-making in the Criminal Justice System and Beyond*. Cullompton: Willan Publishing.

Hawkins, K. (ed.) (1992) *The Uses of Discretion*. Oxford: Clarendon Press.

DIVERSITY

> Diversity relates to the visible and non-visible differences between people. Valuing diversity allows differences to be celebrated and organizational goals to be met.

Valuing diversity is central to modern probation practice, and diversity has now all but replaced anti-discriminatory practice as the primary discourse within which matters of difference and equality are discussed. The National Probation Service (NPS) states that one of the values of probation officers should be to respond and learn to work positively with difference in order to value and achieve diversity.

Despite emphasizing its importance, the NPS does not define diversity. Since the use of the term is not confined to the world of probation and social work (unlike anti-discriminatory practice), it is possible to look elsewhere for assistance in defining it. The term has the potential to be defined so widely as to lose all meaning and thus provide a justification for just carrying on with business as usual. However, diversity can be defined in a positive way and linked to an intention to create an inclusive society, to bring harmony and to celebrate difference. Diversity is particularly associated with business goals: it is about harnessing visible and non-visible differences to allow organizational goals to be met.

Parekh (2000) identifies three different kinds of diversity. *Subcultural* diversity relates to members of groups who share a broad common culture but evolve relatively distinct ways of life of their own, seeking to pluralize existing culture. *Perspectival* diversity relates to society members who criticize and seek to change central principles of society. *Communal* diversity relates to self-conscious and organized communities living by their own systems of beliefs and practices. He distinguishes between a multicultural society which is one that contains two or more cultural communities, and a multiculturalist society which is one that responds to cultural diversity by welcoming it, making it central to its self-understanding and respecting the cultural demands of its constituent communities.

Although diversity has a wider meaning than 'anti-racist practice', race and racism have had most attention in discussions of diversity. The Commission on the Future of Multi-ethnic Britain (CFMEB) was set up in January 1998 by the Runnymede Trust. Its remit was to analyse the current situation in multi-ethnic Britain and to propose ways of combating racial discrimination and disadvantage. The CFMEB Report (2000) provides a vision for valuing diversity that goes beyond a mere passive acceptance of difference. The Preface to the CFMEB Report (2000: viii) sets out six guiding principles for valuing diversity. These can be summarized as follows:

1. All individuals have equal worth.
2. Britain is both a community of citizens and a community of communities.
3. Equal treatment needs to take account of difference.
4. Society needs to be both cohesive and respectful of diversity.
5. Human rights principles provide values around which society can unite.
6. Racism can have no place in a decent society.

Diversity is now a fact – the society we live in is a multi-ethnic and multicultural one. However, minority groups are becoming less clearly defined. More people are of mixed heritage or identify themselves as not having a single ethnic, national or cultural identity. It makes no sense to suggest that members of minority groups can be simply described by one-word labels, such as 'black' or 'Asian'. It is not sensible and is insulting to think of people from ethnic groups as always disadvantaged or vulnerable. Race is not the only issue – issues of race, gender, class and opportunity are often connected and sometimes confused. There is diversity between cultures but also within cultures – many young black and Asian men may find more in common with young white men than with older members of their community.

The question is what we do about this diversity and whether the old language of race relations equips us for the world we live in today. The focus of campaigning has changed from preventing discrimination and promoting integration in the 1960s to encouraging and demanding recognition and respect for diversity at the start of the twenty-first century. Perhaps there is a continuum between integration and diversity, with political and social forces causing societies to move on this continuum as circumstances change. The richness that comes from a diverse society is widely acknowledged, but this should neither lead to tokenism nor to an expectation that those from minority groups must discuss discrimination issues or that white people may not raise those issues. Difference should not be emphasized above commonality, and people should be treated as if they belong.

There needs to be a continuing and energetic commitment to the elimination of racism and improper discrimination in all forms. This should be accompanied by a long-term process of reflection and discussion with different points of focus but common understanding of principles and values.

There has been some improvement in how the criminal justice system responds to diversity issues and there are some grounds for cautious optimism, but not complacency. However, there are still disturbing examples of racism in all its forms – most prominently identified in the Macpherson Report (1999) and the Keith Report (2006). In the specific instance of probation, the key document that deals with the NPS's attitude to diversity is *The Heart of the Dance*. The NPS pledges itself to equal service for all, and states its commitment to embracing difference and gaining the advantages of a positive multicultural business environment.

The Probation Service has not always been successful in meeting these high aspirations. An inspection following the Macpherson Report found both good practice and grounds for serious concerns. It suggested that the commitment of probation services to justice and equality had declined from the 1970s and 1980s. However, a follow-up inspection in 2004 found considerable improvement, with positive leadership and examples of good practice. In 2005 HM Inspectorate of Probation published a further report on the work that the Probation Service was doing with racially motivated offenders. The inspectors found that the Probation Service was committed to working with this group of offenders and that, although there were examples of good practice, there was considerable scope for improvement.

In addition to these inspections, there has been recent research into the experiences of black and Asian offenders on probation and in prison (see Black and minority ethnic (BME) offenders). Among the findings of the research was that probation staff were generally accepted as behaving fairly, but other parts of the criminal justice system, particularly the police, were described much less favourably. Respondents in the study expected to be treated fairly, as individuals, as 'a normal person', by staff who listened to them and respected their views. Policies and practice therefore need to be informed by awareness of diversity, but not based on untested assumptions about what diversity implies.

Probation training has placed an emphasis on anti-discriminatory practice (ADP) for many years, with the move to a diversity discourse being a very recent development. The language of ADP is still used within probation but is rarely, if ever, seen in official documents. This shift in the discourse from ADP to diversity does more accurately reflect contemporary society but could lead to losses as well as gains. One of the perceived weaknesses of discussions of diversity is that it can minimize the importance of power – it is not enough merely to acknowledge that there are lots of different groups in society: some of those groups are more powerful than other groups, and this can lead to inequality and discrimination. An understanding of social construction is important to understand the power relations within society.

Nellis and Gelsthorpe (2003) question the achievements of ADP, particularly with regard to women offenders. It has long been recognized that women commit less crime than men and what crime they commit is less serious – yet the numbers of women prisoners has grown and there is a lack of adequate community provision for women (see Gender; Women offenders). They ask why the increased knowledge from feminist criminology and the increasing feminization of the probation workforce had so little impact. Their concern is that the diversity agenda might not improve these outcomes but might repeat the same mistakes of focusing on management and bureaucratic processes.

Brian Stout

Related entries

Anti-discriminatory practice; Black and minority ethnic (BME) offenders; Gender; Heterosexism; Legitimacy; Masculinity and offending; Mubarek Inquiry; Probation values; Race and racism; Women offenders.

Key texts and sources

Commission on the Future of Multi-Ethnic Britain (2000) *The Future of Multi-ethnic Britain: The Parekh Report*. London: Profile Books for the Runnymede Trust.

Faulkner, D. (2004) *Civil Renewal, Diversity and Social Capital in a Multi-ethnic Britain*. London: Runnymede Perspectives.

Gelsthorpe, L. and McIvor, G. (2007) 'Difference and diversity in probation', in L. Gelsthorpe and R. Morgan (eds) *Handbook of Probation*. Cullompton: Willan Publishing.

HM Inspector of Probation (2000) *Towards Race Equality*. London: Home Office.

HM Inspector of Probation (2004) *Towards Race Equality – Follow-Up Inspection Report*. London: Home Office.

Home Office (2001) *The British Crime Survey 2001*. London: The Home Office.

Home Office (2004) *Black and Asian Offenders on Probation. Research Study 277*. London: Home Office Research, Development and Statistics Directorate.

Hudson, B. (2007) 'Diversity, Crime and Criminal Justice' in M. Maguire, R. Morgan and R. Reiner (eds) *The Oxford Handbook of Criminology*, London: Oxford University Press.

Keith, B. (2006) *Report of the Zahid Mubarek Inquiry*. London: Home Office.

Macpherson, Sir W. (1999) *The Stephen Lawrence Inquiry: Report of an Inquiry by Sir William Macpherson of Cluny* (Cm 4262). London: HMSO.

National Probation Directorate (2002) *The Heart of the Dance*. London: Home Office.

Nellis, M. and Gelsthorpe, L. (2003) 'Human rights and the probation values debate', in W.H. Chui, and M. Nellis (eds) *Moving Probation Forward: Evidence, Arguments and Practice*. Harlow: Pearson.

Parekh, B. (2000) *Rethinking Multiculturalism – Cultural Diversity and Political Theory*. Basingstoke: Palgrave.

Sanglin-Grant, S. (2003) *Divided by the Same Language?* London: Runnymede Trust.

See the Commission for Racial Equality website (http://www.cre.gov.uk/index.html).

DOMESTIC VIOLENCE

Domestic violence is any incident of threatening behaviour, violence or abuse (psychological, physical, sexual, financial or emotional) between adults who are or who have been intimate partners or family members.

While a broad definition has no regard to gender, crime statistics and research both show that domestic violence is gender specific and that usually the perpetrator of a pattern of repeated assaults is a man, whereas women experience the most serious physical and repeated assaults. Some 42 per cent of all female homicide victims compared with 4 per cent of male homicide victims were killed by current or former partners in England and Wales in the year 2000–01. This equates to 102 women, an average of two women each week (Home Office 2001).

Most definitions of domestic violence adopted by agencies of the criminal justice system and the voluntary sector describe it as above. The Women's Aid definition goes further in recognizing that it forms a pattern of coercive and controlling behaviour. This can also include forced marriage and so-called 'honour crimes'. Domestic violence, then, may include a range of abusive behaviours, not all of which are in themselves inherently 'violent'.

Any woman can experience domestic violence regardless of race, ethnic or religious group, class, disability or lifestyle. There are still a number of myths associated with the concept of domestic violence, including the notion that women somehow 'deserve it', that it is a 'private' matter and that some women seek out abusive men. In reality, in addition to physical, emotional, sexual or financial abuse, it can also include intimidation, social isolation, humiliation and, ultimately murder.

Stanko found in her 1998 study that:

- more than one in two women had been in psychologically abusive relationships during their lives;

- one in four women had been in psychologically abusive relationships in the past year;
- one in three women had suffered physical and sexual abuse requiring medical attention in their lives;
- one in nine women had suffered physical and sexual abuse requiring medical attention in the past year;
- one in four women are abused during their lifetimes;
- one in nine are severely physically abused each year;
- two are killed each week; and
- the after-effects may include depression, trauma effects and self-harm.

Some of the reasons why women do not report include the fear that no one will believe them; of retaliation; of deportation; of what might happen to the children; of the consequences for their partner/family if they report; and a belief that they can change their partner. They also report feelings of responsibility for the violence, feeling trapped and confused, and feeling too ashamed and embarrassed to tell anyone. The 2000 British Crime Survey (BCS) found that only one in three domestic violence victims reported this to the police.

There are some clear risk factors for women in this situation of which probation officers should be aware, including previous domestic assault; minor violence predicting escalation to major violence; separation (women separating from their partners are at much greater risk than other marital statuses); poverty and social exclusion; women's employment status; ill-health and disability; violence in the family of origin/witnessing of violence/criminal career; co-occurrence of child abuse; youth; and pregnancy. In relation to the last point, over a third of domestic violence starts or gets worse when a woman is pregnant, and domestic violence is the biggest unborn-baby killer. There are also strong links between domestic violence and child abuse (see also Child protection). The risk of child abuse is between three and nine times greater in homes where the adult partners hit each other.

Domestic violence is experienced by women from all ethnic groups, but black and minority ethnic women are significantly more likely than white women to suffer substantial problems, both emotionally and materially, more than six months after separation. Specialist services are valuable in helping with complex emotional, immigration and cultural issues. South Asian women are often doubly victimized: first, by their partner and then by society, which often fails to provide them with appropriate support and interventions that would empower women from black and minority ethnic groups. In particular, the research has highlighted that indifference or hostility to these women can make them less likely to report to the police. Issues of 'honour' and 'shame', the position of women within the community, the acceptance of some level of violence (e.g. slapping), embarrassment, the unacceptability of divorce in some communities and the fact that defining themselves as victims may take time, all discourage black and minority ethnic women from reporting.

Figures on the extent of male victims vary considerably so it is difficult to state with any accuracy the true extent. However, the 2001–02 BCS found 19 per cent of domestic violence incidents were reported to be male victims, with just under half of these being committed by a female abuser. Men find it difficult to report because of the stereotypes of masculinity and a denial of vulnerability.

Partner abuse among same-sex couples (both female and male) has been found to be relatively similar in prevalence and dynamics to that among heterosexual couples. Gays and lesbians, however, face special obstacles in dealing with the issues that some researchers have labelled 'the double closet': gay and lesbian people often feel discriminated against, are dismissed by police and social services, and can also meet with a lack of support from their peers who would rather keep quiet about the problem to avert negative attention towards the gay community.

Theoretical models used to explain domestic violence range from those that focus on individual pathology and psychological explanations, to psychodynamic accounts that identify dysfunctional relationships and seek resolutions within family dynamics, to more broadly based sociological explanations that identify patriarchy and issues of power and control by men over women. Feminist models, originating with the Duluth programme in the USA, identify that 'Men's violence to known women is clearly a form of power: it arises from and is under-written by men's domination of women as a social group and persists as a form of gendered power and control in individual situations' (Hearn and Whitehead 2006).

Interventions in a probation context are increasingly delivered via groupwork on accredited programmes with a focus on a cognitive-behavioural model, combined with challenging negative gender attitudes. Some offenders are still directed towards more traditional anger management programmes that do not, of themselves, tackle the underlying cultural values that underpin and sustain the behaviour. Increasingly, interventions recognize that the safety of the partner and children is critical and employ a women's worker to liaise with the partners during the course of the intervention. There is still insufficient attention given to individual work with offenders when domestic violence is not the index offence.

Charlotte Knight

Related entries

Child protection; Gender; Masculinity and offending; Victims; Violent offenders.

Key texts and sources

Gill, A. (2004) 'Voicing the silent fear: south Asian women's experiences of domestic violence', *Howard Journal*, 43: 465–83.

Hearn, J and Whitehead, A. (2006) 'Collateral damage: men's "domestic" violence to women seen through men's relations with men', *Probation Journal*, 51: 38–56.

Home Office (2001) *The British Crime Survey 2001*. London: Home Office.

Humphreys, C. and Thiara, R. (2003) 'Mental health and domestic violence: "I call it symptoms of abuse"', *British Journal of Social Work*, 33: 209–26.

McDermitt, M.J. and Garofalo, J. (2004) 'When advocacy for domestic violence victims backfires', *Violence Against Women*, 10: 1245–66.

Stanko, E.A. (2001) 'The day to count: reflections on a methodology to raise awareness about the impact of domestic violence in the UK', *Criminal Justice*, 1: 215–26.

See **http://refuge.org.uk/page_I1-2_I2-162_I3-2338_.htm** See also the account of Integrated Domestic Abuse Programme (IDAP) in Accredited programmes in common use.

DRUG ACTION TEAMS

The partnerships charged with the local delivery of the National Drugs Strategy, which includes co-ordinating the work of agencies in each locality involved in the prevention and treatment of drug misuse, and the allocation of funds.

The prevention and treatment of drug misuse (the problematic use of illegal drugs), and the rehabilitation of former drug users, are complex issues which form a significant part of the work of many agencies but which cannot be tackled by any single agency acting alone. Drug action teams (DATs) were first established in 1995, following the publication of *Tackling Drugs Together*, the first national drugs strategy, in recognition of this need for inter-agency work. Health authorities were given the responsibility of establishing multi-agency teams to take an overview of drugs issues, co-ordinate service planning and delivery and develop local action plans. Since their establishment, the roles and responsibilities of DATs have developed further.

Most DATs do not provide services direct to clients but operate at a more strategic level as funders and service planners. They act as joint commissioners of services, working through the classic commissioning cycle of needs assessment, strategy and prioritization, service specification, purchasing, monitoring and evaluation. In many areas DATs have taken the lead in developing new programmes for drug-related offending, such as the Drug Interventions Programme (DIP). Many DATs are also involved in activities such as training front-line professionals, information provision and consultation with users and carers. Some DATs also now include alcohol within their remit.

DATs are allocated a number of specific budgets with which to commission substance misuse services and interventions, including the pooled treatment budget allocated by the National Treatment Agency (NTA) and DIP funding allocated by the Home Office. In addition, DAT partner agencies identify the relevant elements of their mainstream budgets (such as primary care trust funding of specialist drug treatment services, or funding deployed by the Police and Probation Services for drug-related activity) and co-ordinate the spending of these budgets through the DAT. The budgets under the control of DATs have increased considerably in recent years, but much of this funding is short term.

DATs normally consist of a decision-making body (usually referred to as the DAT board) and a small staff team. The DAT board consists of senior officers from the local statutory bodies involved with tackling drug misuse. One of these officers – often a chief officer of one of the agencies – takes on the role of DAT chair. DAT boards are supported by the infrastructure of other decision-making groups and networks accountable to them, such as a joint commissioning group, drug reference groups and others, depending upon local circumstances. The staff team is headed by the DAT co-ordinator (though many DATs are adopting different titles for their senior staff post) and provides support to the board and its subgroups, ensuring that they can operate effectively in setting strategy and managing performance, and that action is taken to implement decisions.

The membership of DATs is, to an extent, locally determined, but there is a core membership prescribed nationally. This was defined in 1995 as consisting of health authorities, education, social services, police, prisons and probation. Local authority housing functions were added to the core membership in 1998, and health representation is now through primary care trusts. National strategy documents encourage DATs to engage with, and involve, a wide range of other organizations, interests and partnerships in their work, including voluntary sector organizations. The mechanisms for doing this vary from locality to locality.

There are a number of important challenges facing DATs. National policy increasingly views drug treatment services as part of the strategy for reducing acquisitive crime. Significant elements of new funding are earmarked for services for offenders referred by the criminal justice system. Following the Police Reform Act 2002, many DATs in unitary local authority areas have merged with the Crime and Disorder Reduction Partnership to form a single integrated partnership covering all crime and drugs issues.

The increasingly close linkage between the criminal justice process and access to drug treatment, while bringing welcome new funding, creates a number of challenges for DATs. These include maintaining equity of access to treatment for clients referred through routes other than the criminal justice system; managing the dual requirements of maintaining confidentiality of clinical information; and providing information about compliance to the courts and enforcement agencies.

A further challenge is the complexity of accountability arrangements. As partnerships, DATs are accountable to the Home Office. Individual members of DAT boards are accountable to their own authorities, but also to their partners on the DAT for delivery of their partnership commitments. DATs are not statutory bodies nor legal entities in their own right, so the budgets which they manage are held on their behalf by one or other of the local statutory bodies, which is legally accountable for the expenditure. DATs are expected to consult widely and to engage with the public in conducting audits or needs assessments. DATs are set targets and experience performance management by both the National Treatment Agency and the Home Office. Regulation is fragmented, with the regulatory bodies for each of the partner agencies having an involvement. The complexity and workload involved in this web of accountability, while typical of modern governance, are a considerable burden for DAT partnerships and support teams.

Finally, DATs face considerable challenges in ensuring that their commissioning is evidence based and fully informed by the expertise and experience of service providers (statutory and voluntary), users, ex-users and their carers. While the evidence base for drug misuse services has increased considerably over recent years, there are still many areas of uncertainty. The views of different service providers as to the most effective approach to treatment differ, as do the opinions and experience of service users and their carers.

Despite these challenges, and the continual need to adapt to change in structures and personnel in partner agencies, many DATs have succeeded in making 'impressive progress' (Audit Commission 2004) in improving drug misuse services and interventions in their areas.

Juliet Woodin

Related entries

Crime and Disorder Reduction Partnership; Drug rehabilitation requirement; Drugs; Drugs Intervention Programme; Drug treatment and testing orders (DTTOs); Inter-agency work.

Key texts and sources

Audit Commission (2002) *Changing Habits: The Commissioning and Management of Community Drug Treatment Services for Adults.* London: Audit Commission.

Audit Commission (2004) *Drug Misuse 2004: Reducing the Local Impact.* London: Audit Commission.

Home Office (1998) *Tackling Drugs to Build a Better Britain: The Government's 10-year Strategy for Tackling Drug Misuse* (Cm 39450). Lord President of the Council. London: HMSO.

Home Office (2002) *Updated Drug Strategy, 2002.* London: Home Office.

www.drugs.gov.uk

www.nta.nhs.uk

www.crimereduction.gov.uk

DRUG REHABILITATION REQUIREMENT

One of the 12 possible requirements of the community order. It is rehabilitative in purpose, ensures treatment for drug misuse, involves regular testing and court review, and lasts at least six months.

The drug rehabilitation requirement (DRR) replaced the drug treatment and testing order (DTTO) in April 2005. It is a vehicle for providing drug treatment to reduce or eliminate dependency on or propensity to misuse drugs, and for regular drug testing.

The court can only impose this requirement if it has been specifically recommended and if the offender is willing to comply. The court must be satisfied that the person concerned is dependent on drugs or is likely to misuse them; that he or she requires and is susceptible to treatment; and that treatment is available.

The requirement is a more flexible instrument than the DTTO. Levels of contact vary depending on offence seriousness and treatment need. High seriousness offenders undertake up to 20 hours contact per week; medium seriousness offenders 8 hours minimum contact; and low seriousness offenders one appointment per week. Contact is divided between probation staff, treatment providers and a range of other activities organized by the offender manager.

The DRR usually involves twice-weekly drug testing to monitor the drug use of the offender. Oral or urine testing is utilized and can be supplemented by more accurate laboratory-based confirmatory testing when there are ambiguities or disputed results. The other special feature is monthly review at court. These are optional for DRRs up to 12 months but mandatory for longer orders. There is growing evidence that the review process is an effective motivator for a significant number of offenders. At a Butler Trust conference in Dyfed-Powys in November 2006, several offenders testified that they were greatly supported and encouraged by the interest shown by magistrates and judges: 'When I go to my review the judge really encourages me even when I have made only a small amount of progress, and it makes a big difference.'

Performance measures in relation to DRRs are the number of orders made and the proportion completed. In high-performing areas such as Dyfed-Powys, there is a very strong emphasis on retaining offenders in the programme. Confidence is enhanced by user consultation and by acting on the messages received. Partnerships are developed by a community orientation and by placing offenders with community-based groups for activities. For example, in Dyfed-Powys strong partnerships have developed with gardening, outdoor activities and community arts. This has led to some notable success, such as the winning of gold medals for gardening at the Royal Welsh Show and the exhibiting of ceramics and sculpture by offenders on DRRs at the Senedd (Welsh Assembly Building). Experiences such as these add to the cumulative process of building confidence in the scheme and strengthening individuals in their quest for rehabilitation and desistance from offending.

Kevin Fisher

Related entries

Community order; Drug action teams; Drugs; Drugs Intervention Programme; Drug treatment and testing orders (DTTOs); Inter-agency work.

Key texts and sources

Davies, G. (2006) *Service User Consultation on the Impact of Drug Treatment and Testing Orders and DRRs across Dyfed-Powys.* Available from Dyfed-Powys DIP, St David's Park, Jobswell Road, Carmarthen SA31 3HB.

Mair, G. and Canton, R. (2007) 'Sentencing, community penalties and the role of the Probation Service', in L. Gelsthorpe and R. Morgan (eds) *Handbook of Probation.* Cullompton: Willan Publishing.

DRUG TREATMENT AND TESTING ORDERS (DTTOS)

Introduced by the Crime and Disorder Act 1998, DTTOs were subsumed into the community order introduced by the Criminal Justice Act 2003. Although now superseded, DTTOs were an important innovation in dealing with drug-dependent offenders.

DTTOs were designed in response to growing evidence of links between problem drug use and persistent acquisitive offending. The order was targeted at drug-dependent offenders facing prison sentences for offences such as burglary. Those on DTTOs were required to attend a treatment programme five days a week, at least in the early stages of the order, and to undergo regular drug testing. Offenders were also required to go back to court for regular progress reviews carried out by sentencers – similar to procedures in American drug courts.

DTTOs were originally piloted at three sites – in Croydon, Gloucestershire and Liverpool. Results were less encouraging than expected, with only 30 per cent of offenders completing their orders successfully, and four out of five being reconvicted within two years. However, those who managed to complete showed greatly reduced offending and much lower levels of drug use. Sentencers, probation officers and offenders all found the court review process valuable.

While disappointing, the overall results reflected the fact that those placed on DTTOs were among the most persistent offenders passing through the criminal process. It was therefore decided to introduce DTTOs nationally. Following roll-out, completion rates failed to improve and reconviction rates actually rose. This may have been a consequence of the introduction of a system of targets for achieving a specified number of *commencements*. A more sensible form of target would have rewarded areas for successful *completions*.

DTTOs were also introduced in Scotland, where the evaluation of the pilot was more positive. A higher proportion of offenders completed the order (44 per cent), and a lower proportion ended up back in court (66 per cent). Such differences between the two countries (and between schemes) are probably attributable to different DTTO regimes. A pragmatic approach to retaining offenders on the orders is thought to be critical to success.

The Criminal Justice Act 2003 subsumed DTTOs into the new community order under which a drug rehabilitation requirement (DRR) is among the possible conditions. DRRs are expected to be used more flexibly than DTTOs and for a wider range of drug-dependent offenders. The court review process has been retained, though is mandatory only for orders lasting more than a year. (Sentencers now have the option of calling for court reviews in *any* community order they impose.)

Since the introduction of DTTOs there have been experimental trials of drug courts both in England and Wales and in Scotland, and the outcome of these may influence the development of DRRs. The results of the Scottish pilot were promising.

Mike Hough

Related entries

Drug rehabilitation requirement; Drugs

Key texts and sources

Hough, M., Clancy, A., Turnbull, P.J. and McSweeney, T. (2003) *The Impact of Drug Treatment and Testing Orders on Offending: Two-year Reconviction Results. Findings* 184. London: Home Office.

Mair, G. and Canton, R. (2007) 'Sentencing, community penalties and the role of the Probation Service', in L. Gelsthorpe and R. Morgan (eds) *Handbook of Probation*. Cullompton: Willan Publishing.

McIvor, G. (2004) *Reconviction following Drug Treatment and Testing Orders*. Edinburgh: Scottish Executive.

Turnbull, P.J., McSweeney, T., Webster, R., Edmunds, M. and Hough, M. (2000) *Drug Treatment and Testing Orders: Evaluation Report. Home Office Research Study* 212. London: HMSO.

DRUGS

In this context a drug is any substance that acts upon the nervous system in order to have a psychoactive effect – that is, altering emotions, cognitions, perceptions and behaviour in some way.

With repeated exposure the body develops physiological tolerance, becoming less responsive to the drug so that the user requires increasing quantities to obtain the same effect. Repeated use can also lead to physical and psychological dependence. Physical dependence occurs when drug use has lead to physiological changes such that, when use is discontinued, a range of physical symptoms ensue. These withdrawal symptoms tend to be typical for any drug group (see Table 2).

Psychological dependence relies upon a process of (associative and instrumental) learning, so that discontinuation leads to a desire or cravings to use again. This can involve seeking to avoid distress or to get a feeling of well-being or enjoyment.

Withdrawal symptoms interact with psychological factors, cravings, etc., often in complex ways, thus often becoming conflated in the user's mind. Subjectively the user feels that he or she requires continued use of the drug in order to function.

Routes of administration include oral, inhalation, sniffing (or other routes involving mucus membranes, e.g. mouth cavity, gums, rectal) and injecting (includes intravenous, intramuscular, subcutaneous). These will have a significant bearing on the subjective effects, as well as potential harms.

Prevalence

The British Crime Survey looks at the extent of illicit drug use and trends in drug use since 1998 (see Tables 3 and 4). For the age range 16–24, illicit use decreased and Class A use was stable. For 16–59 age range, overall illicit drug use decreased (reflecting a decline in cannabis use), while Class A use increased (mainly due to increased cocaine use).

Table 2 Drugs and their withdrawal symptoms

Type of drug	Main effects	Main withdrawal symptoms
Stimulants – e.g. amphetamines, cocaine (powder and crack), ecstasy (MDMA and analogues), caffeine, nicotine	Drugs that act upon the nervous system (central nervous system in particular) in such a way that the system is activated. Increased physical and mental energy, feelings of elation, confidence and pressure of speech. Suppression of sleep and appetite	The 'comedown or crash' involves physical and psychological symptoms more or less opposite to those experienced while under the influence. These include apathy, lethargy, increased appetite, tiredness, dysphoria, anxiety and depression

▶

Table 2 Continued

Type of drug	Main effects	Main withdrawal symptoms
Depressants – e.g. alcohol, benzodiazepines such as diazepam and temazepam, barbiturates. Other tranquillizers such as zopiclone. Depressant drugs are utilized in mainstream medicine as tranquillizers	Drugs that act as a central nervous system depressant. Prescribed widely as anxiolytics and hypnotics. Effects include sedation, increased sleep, muscle relaxation and disinhibition	Anxiety and tremors, disturbances in mood, sleep problems, headaches, increased perception of pain. In extreme cases, perceptual disturbances and epileptic fits may develop
Hallucinogens – e.g. cannabis, LSD, magic mushrooms	Drugs that alter perception in some way. Can lead to visual, auditory and other sensory hallucinations and non-consensual thoughts and beliefs	In most cases, not known to produce withdrawal although with cannabis, following heavy prolonged use, a withdrawal syndrome has been observed and users have reported cravings. Whether this is mainly psychological is subject to debate
Opiate (and opioid) analgesics – e.g. heroin, opium, morphine, methadone, codeine, buprenorphine	Drugs that impact on the perception of pain – physical as well as psychological/emotional pain. Feelings of calm, a sense of being removed from one's environment and free from distress	Pupil dilation, sweating, yawning, tremors, cramps, diarrhoea and vomiting, runny eyes and nose, anxiety, sleep difficulties, increased sensitivity to pain, emotional distress

Table 3 Extent of illicit drug use

	Lifetime	Last year	Last month
All drugs	34.9% of population 11 million people	10.5% < 3.5 million	6.3% ~ 2 million
Class A	13.9% < 4.5 million	3.4% > 1 million	1.6% > 0.5 million
Cocaine		> 0.75 million	
Ecstasy		~ 0.5 million	

Source: Data from the British Crime Survey 2006.

Table 4 Extent of drug use in past year

Drug	Per cent of people who used in the last year
Cannabis	8.7
Cocaine (powder and crack)	2.4
Ecstasy	1.6
Amphetamines	1.3
Amyl nitrate (poppers)	1.2
Hallucinogens (LSD and magic mushrooms)	1.1

Source: Data from the British Crime Survey 2006.

Historical, social and legal context

Throughout history, people have sought altered states by using psychoactive plants and fungi. In traditional societies this was often part of social and spiritual rituals and was not usually problematic: problem substance use seems a feature of modern society.

Drug use can be seen in terms of patterns – i.e. experimental, recreational, dependent and problematic. Clear and agreed definitions of 'addiction' are not easy to obtain, so a more useful concept may be that of 'problem drug use'. Thus, having identified the 'problems' we can seek to remedy them. It is also useful to contextualize drug use as:

Drug + Mindset + Setting = Consequences

This enables treatment to focus on a range of issues in a more holistic way.

The legality of a drug may to some degree be arbitrary and more to do with the context of its use. For example, heroin is seen as an illegal drug but is used in pharmaceutical form as a treatment for a number of conditions, in particular the management of pain and the treatment of dependence. The Misuse of Drugs Act 1971 provides a legal classification of drugs as Class A, B and C, which determines the severity of penalties. This classification reflects the level of risk associated with each drug, but may also be in part historical. Recently there have been proposals to review the classification, basing it on a more logical premise of 'risk of harm'. In these heated, often politicized, debates, governments (and opposition) are wary of being branded 'soft on drugs'.

While there seems a clear association between some but not all drugs and crime, especially heroin and cocaine, it is not entirely clear if there is a 'cause and effect' relationship. It is more likely that they interact in complex ways.

Similarly, while there appears to be a demonstrable correlation between drug use and mental health difficulties, the relationship is complex. The incidence of drug use among people with mental health problems is higher than the general population. In addition, drug use can exacerbate existing problems. This impact will often be quite specific, depending on the drug and the type of mental health problem.

Treatment usually consists of *bio-psycho-social interventions* aimed at reducing harm and assisting users in controlling, reducing or stopping their use. Thus treatment can have *bio*logical aspects, such as substitute prescribing, medical interventions aimed at managing detoxification, advice and treatments around physical problems, reduction of blood-borne viruses, etc. *Psycho*logical interventions include counselling, motivational interviewing, cue exposure work, etc. *Social* interventions seek to help people make positive changes to reduce social exclusion and to improve access to housing, employment and constructive interests and pursuits. Different agencies emphasize different aspects of treatment but should be expected to operate within this holistic framework as this seems to produce the best outcomes.

In the early 1980s drug treatment was revolutionized in the UK by the impact of blood-borne infections – in particular, HIV. This was later reinforced by concerns about the transmission of hepatitis B and C. 'Harm reduction' – seeking to reduce the harm to drug users and society arising from drug use – became the principal focus. Older 'abstinence'-based ('12-step' and 'Minnesota') models are still used and remain the key focus of self-help groups like Alcoholics Anonymous and Narcotics Anonymous.

In recent years there has been a greater linking of drugs and crime, which has had a dramatic impact on the structure and philosophy of treatment. Treatment and rehabilitation agencies have become linked ever more to the criminal justice system. While most would agree that there are progressive elements to this 'out of crime into treatment' approach, both the effectiveness and the ethics of the 'coercive' nature of treatment have been questioned.

The National Treatment Agency (a special health authority within the NHS) has produced the *Models of Care* document, which attempts to map out treatment and agency roles comprehensively and to improve the quality and consistency of treatment. While there are advantages to this attempt at 'standardization', there is some discussion among drug treatment practitioners about its impact on diversity in treatment modes.

Shehzad Malik

Related entries

Cycle of change; Drug action teams; Drugs rehabilitation requirement; Drug Intervention Programme; Drug treatment and testing orders (DTTOs); Motivation; Motivational interviewing.

Key texts and sources

Department of Health (1999) *Drug Misuse and Dependence: Guidelines on Clinical Management* (available online at **http://www.dh.gov.uk/ assetRoot/04/07/81/98/04078198.pdf**).

Home Office (2006) *Drug Misuse Declared: Findings from the 2005/6 British Crime Survey. Home Office Statistical Bulletin.* London: Home Office.

Tyler, A. (1995) *Street Drugs.* London: Hodder & Stoughton.

See the National Treatment Agency website (**www.nta.nhs.uk**), especially 'Models of care for the treatment of drug misusers'. See also Drugscope (**www.drugscope.org.uk**), the National Institute of Drug Abuse (**www.drugabuse.gov**) and **www.drugs.gov.uk**.

DRUGS INTERVENTION PROGRAMME

This Home Office-funded programme is designed to get offenders who misuse drugs out of crime and into drug treatment. People who misuse Class A drugs often commit crimes to fund their habit. The programme aims to enable offenders to enter treatment at every stage in the criminal justice system:

- Point of arrest and charge.
- Court.
- Community supervision.
- In prison.
- On release from prison.

The programme is also available for people who are leaving structured treatment to ensure effective after-care is provided, especially for housing, employment and training needs.

The National Drug Strategy to 2008 has overseen a massive increase in the availability of structured drug treatment across England. The Drugs Intervention Programme (DIP) is one component of that strategy, and aims to ensure that increased treatment availability results in reduced levels of offending by problematic drug users. With the clearer definition of effective treatment as a journey that includes motivational interviewing from the start of engagement with users, DIP services are increasingly integrated into local drug treatment systems.

DIP services are commissioned by local crime reduction strategic partnerships (also known variously as drug action teams or drug and alcohol action teams) through the joint commissioning groups responsible for local drug treatment systems. These groups should include probation, police, prison, local authority and primary care trusts. Partnerships are expected to make arrangements to ensure that the user voice is heard to support the planning and effectiveness of services.

Cases are registered within DIP teams and a 'single point of contact' supports the continuity of their care in each area. These ensure that cases can be referred to the appropriate service and enable their case plans to be tracked so that contact with cases, wherever possible, is not lost.

DIP services include the following:

- In designated high-crime areas, people arrested for certain trigger offences (mostly for acquisitive crime) are tested to identify potentially problematic drug use, and then required to undergo a 'required assessment'.
- Arrest–referral services operate in police custody suites and courts in all areas to conduct required assessments and to engage arrestees voluntarily in drug treatment where there is a need.
- CARAT (Counselling, Assessment, Referral, Advice and Through-care) services operate to assess and deliver care plans to drug users within prisons.
- CJITs (criminal justice interventions teams) work with cases in the community. They may signpost people (or incorporate specialist services) to tackle employability, accommodation

or other needs that are barriers to stability or to drug-free lifestyles. They will also refer cases to structured treatment when appropriate. These services are especially significant for people who are leaving structured treatment. After-care support can improve the levels of successful reintegration into a stable or drug-free life.

- Rapid prescribing facilities for those with opiate dependency should be available in each area to ensure that users engage in treatment as speedily as possible.

DIP services work with many of the same people who are on probation caseloads, and it is important that close working relationships are established between offender managers and DIP services so that, subject to appropriate information-sharing consents, case and treatment plans can be co-ordinated.

DIP services work closely with prolific and other priority offender schemes so that the most challenging individuals are engaged in and held in treatment. This requires police, probation and drug services to agree ways of working that protect the community and also command the confidence of the user.

David Skidmore

Related entries

Drug action teams; Drug rehabilitation requirement; Drugs; Drug treatment and testing orders (DTTOs); Inter-agency work; Prolific and other priority offenders.

Key texts and sources

The following Home Office publications are available from the **drugs.gov.uk** website:
An Introduction to the Drug Interventions Programme for Prisons and Probation (aimed at staff in prisons and probation staff).
Treatment: The Works (a DVD aimed at explaining DIP to users).

DUAL DIAGNOSIS

Dual diagnosis/co-morbidity are terms used to refer to the condition of people with more than one mental disorder (for instance, depression and personality disorder) and/or those who have mental disorder(s) and are using alcohol or street drugs.

Dual diagnosis – the co-incidence of more than one type of mental disorder or of a mental disorder with misuse of drugs or alcohol – is not a single clinical condition but may be implicated in a wide range of needs and behaviours. An assessment of co-morbidity should enable individuals to have access to appropriate services to meet their complex needs but, in practice, it can become the occasion for rejection, with busy mental health services suggesting initial referral to drug services and vice versa.

People who are mentally disturbed are at least as likely as anyone else to misuse substances – and often more so. For instance, people with anti-social personality disorder are significantly more likely than average to drink too much, and the combination of anti-social personality disorder and use of alcohol is associated with a high risk of harm to others. (Alcohol can depress inhibitions – internal restraints on behaviour – which are already weaker in people with this disorder.)

While there is debate about the extent to which substance use 'causes' mental disturbance, misuse of certain substances can produce signs of mental illness and, equally, mental distress can lead to substance misuse – for example, through self-medication. Conjecture about causal priority is unlikely to be profitable. Neither problem can be understood without an appreciation of the other: it is precisely the interaction that exacerbates the distress and the risk. The implication is that therapeutic intervention should address both the substance misuse and the mental disturbance in a complementary multidisciplinary endeavour.

Probation officers are likely to encounter many offenders whose behaviour is influenced by mental distress in combination with misuse of drink or drugs. This can pose notorious problems for referral. Specialists typically deal with specific disorders and may prefer to place elsewhere the responsibility for dealing with other conditions. People who span diagnostic categories are accordingly always likely to cause difficulties of referral. Under pressure of resources, this can lead to a disowning, a refusal to accept the referral. Dual diagnosis services are therefore becoming increasingly common, but they, too, have to manage their resources and referrals. As always with referral to other agencies, offender managers need a clear sense of the reason why they are making a specific referral, what can reasonably be expected of the other agency and their own continuing role in contributing to meeting complex and interrelated needs.

Rob Canton

Related entries

Alcohol; Drugs; Inter-agency work; Mentally disordered offenders; Personality disorder.

Key texts and sources

Rassool, G.H. (2001) *Dual Diagnosis: Substance Misuse and Psychiatric Disorders.* Oxford: Blackwell Science.

Watkins, T., Lewellen, A. and Barrett, M. (2001) *Dual Diagnosis: An Integrated Approach to Treatment.* London: Sage.

Mind provides a useful introduction with its booklet that is available online at http://www.mind.org.uk/Information/Booklets/Understanding/Understanding+dual+diagnosis.htm. The website http://www.rethink.org/dualdiagnosis/toolkit.html is a very full and useful resource.

DYSLEXIA

Dyslexia is a lifelong developmental condition. It is a 'hidden' disability characterized by a range of difficulties which often include literacy, short-term memory, sequencing and personal organization (including poor time management). Low confidence and low self-esteem are also frequently associated with dyslexia. These difficulties are more usually present from childhood, but dyslexia can be 'acquired' as a result of brain injury or trauma.

Dyslexia is frequently described as a specific learning difficulty. One in four of the population in the UK is believed to be dyslexic to some degree. Signs of dyslexia have sometimes been misinterpreted, with people being labelled as lazy or disruptive, a response which aggravates their own feelings of frustration and low confidence.

As with learning difficulties more generally, individuals are usually described as being mildly, moderately or severely dyslexic. Not all dyslexic people will experience the same difficulties nor will they all experience difficulties to the same extent. Dyslexic people will, through necessity, develop a range of coping or compensatory strategies both in education and in life more generally. These strategies can make the identification of dyslexia more difficult and therefore identification or 'diagnosis' should be left to psychologists or other suitably qualified persons.

The two principal methods used to identify dyslexia are screening and assessment. Screening is usually conducted by way of a one-to-one interview or through a computer program. Screening is more usually conducted by schools, colleges, universities, charities and sometimes by disability advisers at a Job Centre Plus. There are many screening packages available and these can be used with minimal training. Because of the relatively low cost of these packages, large numbers of people can be screened in a short time. Many organizations and charities offer free screenings.

Assessment is predominantly but not exclusively conducted by chartered psychologists. Assessment lengths vary. However, they often take over half a day to complete and can be very expensive. Arrangements for assessments can be made through support organizations, such as the Dyslexia Institute. Where an employee is experiencing difficulties at work, then assessment may be provided free of charge by a psychologist via the disability adviser at a Job Centre Plus. It is not uncommon for dyslexic staff – for example, trainee probation officers – to seek reasonable adjustment (RA) while undertaking training in higher education.

One significant area of controversy within social science research is the suggestion that there are a disproportionate number of dyslexic people in the prison population. The number was put as high as 50 per cent in one study in 2000 (Reid and Kirk 2001). What is clear is that dyslexia does not cause criminal or deviant behaviour. It cannot be, nor should it be, accepted as an excuse. When the characteristics of dyslexia are considered together and operationalized, it is possible that the frustrations felt by some dyslexic individuals could be a 'mitigating' factor to some degree. It should also be remembered that dyslexia can lead to educational underachievement and can compound problems of gaining

employment and of social exclusion which may be linked with offending. Initiatives to respond actively and constructively to the challenges of dyslexia are still relatively new.

Dyslexia poses a challenge to probation to ensure that their services are accessible and inclusive. Practitioners and criminal justice professionals should remember that dyslexia is primarily a difficulty with words – written and oral. These difficulties are often exacerbated or compounded by stress or time pressures. It is useful to consider these factors when conducting interviews or when the reading of reports or text is required (McLoughlin *et al.* 2002: 252).

Andy Hill

Related entries

Education, Skills for Life; Learning disabilities; Responsivity.

Key texts and sources

McLoughlin, D., Leather, C. and Stringer, P. (2002) *The Dyslexic Adult: Interventions and Outcomes.* London: Whurr.

Reid, G. and Kirk, J. (2001) *Dyslexia in Adults: Education and Employment.* Chichester: Wiley.

See also 'Dyslexia Action: Helping Probation and Prison Services', the Positive Action through Learning Support Project (PALS) partnership between Nottingham Dyslexia Action and Nottinghamshire Probation Service (available online at **http://www.dyslexiaaction.org.uk/Page.aspx?PageId=179**).

E

EDUCATION, SKILLS FOR LIFE

Recognizing the educational deficits among offenders, identifying need and linking offenders with the provision necessary to overcome educational disadvantage.

Significance and scale of educational deficits

The probation services have long had employment and training advice for offenders, as it has been recognized that an offender gaining employment is less likely to reoffend. However, Napo research in 1999 found that 'up to 60% of offenders are unable to access 96% of the available job vacancies due to their poor literacy skills'. Since 2002, all probation services have had to provide an educational element for people on a community order.

Partnerships with outside providers have been developed, and now further education colleges, training agencies and others have been engaged to screen, assess, teach and offer national adult qualifications in literacy and numeracy.

These developments have coincided with the launch of the government's Skills for Life strategy. The key goal of this is 'to reduce the number of adults in England with literacy and numeracy difficulties to the levels of our main international competition – that is from one in five adults to one in ten or better' (DfEE 2001). Prisoners and offenders are listed as a priority group.

A study in Nottinghamshire found that at least 50 per cent of offenders screened had very poor basic skills, significantly higher than the estimated 20 per cent of the general population. There is no reason to think that this sample is unrepresentative of the country as a whole.

Basic skills are defined as 'The ability to read, write and speak in English or Welsh and use mathematics at a level necessary to function and progress at work and in society in general' (Basic Skills Quality Mark for post-16 programmes).

Why do people have basic skills problems?

'The vast majority of adults with basic skills needs are of normal, "average" intelligence. They have simply not been able to develop their skills in this area' (BSA 1998). From research commissioned by Nottinghamshire Learning Skills Council, it was found that many of the offenders had experienced an incomplete statutory education and held negative recollections. Some 62 per cent were regular truants, 41 per cent were excluded and 58 per cent left school before their sixteenth birthday. Alongside this, these vulnerable learners may also have health issues (e.g. 22 per cent had had birthing difficulties, 39 per cent head injuries requiring hospital treatment, 35 per cent had been prescribed glasses but did not own a pair and 13 per cent had hearing difficulties).

John Rack's (2005) study of the prison population showed there is a significant over-representation of people with specific learning disabilities in that population (e.g. dyslexia, dyspraxia, dyscalculia, attention deficit and hyperactivity disorder). In this study, 52 per cent of the prison population had 'learning difficulties which would limit their learning and work opportunity'. Some 20 per cent had dyslexic profiles compared with the general population of 5–10 per cent. This significant incidence of specified difficulties should be recognized with specialist assessment, counselling and tuition.

Process of education

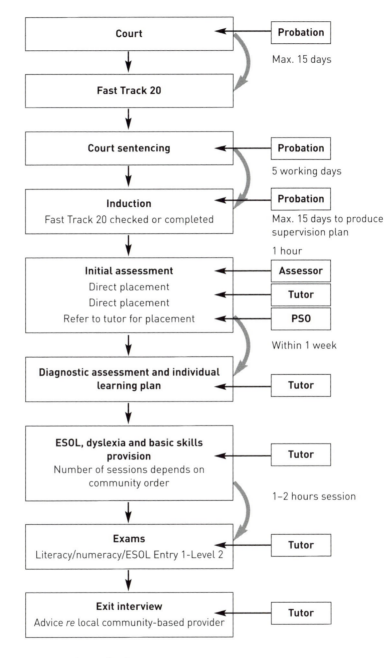

Figure 4 The education journey in probation

When a pre-sentence report is prepared, the offender is screened for literacy deficits. This is built into the OASys assessment tool, or an instrument such as the 'Fast Track 20 questions' can be used (see Figure 4).

If needs are identified, or a lack of qualifications, the offender manager will, at induction, put education as an intervention and refer to the education providers. The providers will meet with the offender and take time carefully assessing relevant background information, motivating influences and achievement to ascertain at what level the offender is performing. The levels are designated in the Adult Core Curriculum. Once the initial assessment has taken place, the offender will be placed into tuition, either one to one or in a small group.

Only qualified professional tutors will take groups. Resources, both paper and IT based, will be of adult quality. Providers will be inspected by the Adult Literacy Inspectorate to promote quality provision.

Further diagnostic, dyslexic or English for speakers of another language (ESOL) assessments can take place so that an individual learning plan can be agreed. ESOL specialists should provide ESOL tuition as with dyslexia tuition. Education will prepare the offender for national adult literacy, numeracy and ESOL qualifications. These awards not only give some their first qualification, thus increasing their employability, but also increased self-confidence or self-esteem is usual.

Throughout the learning journey the provider will communicate all contacts with the offender manager. These appointments will be recorded on the case records. At an appropriate time, the offender should be supported on to a literacy and numeracy or specialized course (e.g. painting and decorating) with his or her nearest local community provider.

Judi Apiafi

Related entries

Dyslexia; Employment, Training and Education (ETE); Learning disabilities; Partnerships; Responsivity.

Key texts and sources

Basic Skills Agency (BSA) (1998) *Influences in Adult Basic Skills.* London: BSA.

DfEE (2001) *Skills for Life: The national strategy for improving adult literacy and numeracy skills.* London: DfEE.

DFES (2004) *Raising Standards: A Contextual Guide to Support.* London: DfES (available online at http://www.dfes.gov.uk/readwriteplus/bank/LLDD.pdf.

National Probation Service (2006) *Learning and Skills for Offenders* (A1749). London: Home Office.

Rack, J. (2005) *The Incidence of Hidden Disabilities in the Prison Population.* London: The Dyslexia Institute (available online at http://www.dyslexia-inst.org.uk/pdffiles/Hidden%20Disabilities%20Prison.pdf

Details of the offender's learning journey for both adult and juvenile provision can be found on the Offender Learning and Skills Service website (www.dfes.gov.uk/offenderlearning). See also the Whole Organisation Approach for Skills for Life contextualized for offender settings (prison and probation) at www.woasfl.org.

EFFECTIVE PRACTICE

Effective practice is probation practice that produces the intended results, specifically to achieve a reduction in reoffending or, more broadly, to fulfil other sentencing aims, including public protection, rehabilitation and compliance. Effective practice seeks to be evidence-led by being informed by or consistent with research findings; in a wider view, it includes a commitment to develop further probation's evidence base.

The primary aim of probation practice has usually been to reduce further offending or to achieve the rehabilitation of the offender. These goals were present from the earliest decades of probation work, with probation officers of the period seeking to reduce reoffending by working on alcohol abuse, employment, training and education or a settled home. While these were the results probation officers were seeking to achieve, their methods and approach provide an informal description of what was considered effective. The expression and focus of these goals varied with the decades, but only rarely did probation in its accounts and theorization move away from a view that effective work involved seeking to achieve individual change in offenders.

The advocacy of 'alternatives to custody' in the late 1970s and early 1980s provides a significant exception. Influenced by the academic viewpoint that 'nothing works' in relation to probation work and reoffending, a prime importance was instead given to the probation officer's influence on sentencing decisions.

However, through most of a century of probation practice there has been a focus on the individual offender and reducing his or her future offending. Accounts of probation practice sought to evidence the effectiveness of that work by case examples or basic statistics about the absence of further offending or positive rehabilitation, such as placement in jobs or settled accommodation.

'Effective practice' came to be used as a term when discussing the implications for probation of 'what works' – the phrase used for the research reviews and related academic discussion that provided a more encouraging view of the potential for achieving reductions in reoffending. The 'what works' reviews made considerable use of meta-analysis to summarize and identify the findings from current and previous research studies. From these broad-based studies, but with a particular influence from cognitive-behavioural researchers, general principles of 'effective practice' were developed and promoted throughout the late 1980s and 1990s (McGuire 1995).

Specific cognitive-behavioural programmes were also developed that met these general principles and that drew on cognitive-behavioural methods which had been found effective in achieving changed behaviour with service users in a number of settings – the STOP programme in Mid-Glamorgan (from 1991) was a pioneer in applying these 'cognitive skills' approaches in England and Wales.

The general principles of effective practice, identified at this time and supported by later research, include the following:

- The 'risk principle': offenders with higher risks of reoffending should receive more intensive and extended supervision, and lower-risk offenders should be dealt with by lower-level sanctions.
- The 'needs principle': the supervision of offenders should target needs related to offending – 'criminogenic needs' which, if addressed, will reduce the risk of reoffending.
- The 'responsivity principle': effective work with offenders will be relevant to offenders' learning styles and requires a context and staff style and approach that engage their active participation.

These general principles and other specific research on (largely) cognitive-behavioural programmes led to the identification of accreditation criteria for structured programmes (the Correctional Services Accreditation Panel), first developed for prison-based programmes. The accreditation process gave particular emphasis to assessing critically the treatment model on which the programme was based.

Throughout the 1990s, the opportunity to develop probation work towards 'effective practice' aroused increasing interest and attention within probation and related fields. Probation policymakers' interest in 'what works' was expressed in the Effective Practice Initiative backed by the Home Office and championed by Sir Graham Smith, then Chief Inspector of Probation (Underdown 1998). That initiative was part of a wider governmental interest in evidence-based policy; the funding for the expansion of accredited programmes was just one element in a wider Crime Reduction Programme arising from interest and commitment by an incoming government for evidence-based policy.

The Effective Practice Initiative promoted a model of 'effective practice' at the level of individual practice, service design and organizational arrangements. The initiative involved funding specific developments and giving general guidance on 'evidence-based practice' to probation staff and managers (Chapman and Hough 1998). Taking account of available research, the initiative promoted a model that included the following:

- Assessment, including the use of assessment instruments and referral decisions based on dynamic risk factors.

- *Case management*, including risk assessment and management, supervision planning and review, co-ordination and sequencing of interventions, developing motivation and giving attention to prosocial modelling.
- *Structured accredited programmes*, targeting change in thinking and behaviour relevant to reoffending.
- *Community reintegration*, addressing reintegration factors closely linked to desistance from offending and broader protective factors that could support a settled lifestyle.

In practice, the implementation of this broad-based initiative moved at an uneven pace across these key elements. There was a major initial investment in accredited programmes, the later deployment of the OASys instrument and improvements in case management ('offender management'). Attention to community reintegration was emphasized less in these Home Office-led developments: not until 2004 did the Reducing Reoffending Action Plan establish a national planning framework for working with the wide range of partners involved.

Two broader issues underlie the scope and focus of 'effective practice'. First, how do practitioners, researchers or policymakers define the 'intended results' of probation work? There is a widely shared view of the primacy of a reduction in reoffending as a key test for effectiveness. Assessing outcomes in reduced reoffending or reconviction has been a challenging and complex area for research. The routine monitoring of reconviction has rarely been achieved, although advances in information systems mean such developments are currently being planned. Key issues and complexities include the differences and distinction between reoffending and reconviction rates, the basis of comparison or control groups and how to distinguish reductions in the frequency or seriousness of offending.

There is significant interest but differing views about the relevance of other criteria for effectiveness. From some perspectives, convincing evidence of effective practice would include considering how offenders contribute to or fulfil other community responsibilities; achieve a settled lifestyle; secure and maintain work and settled accommodation; meet family responsi-

bilities; desist from substance abuse or control addiction; and comply with the court order. Issues of access to services and the relevance of provision for minority groups, taking account of the range of diversity considerations, need to be considered in setting criteria for effectiveness.

Secondly, does effective practice seek to be 'evidence informed' or 'evidence led'? Research into probation work increasingly demonstrates the interplay of the factors involved – 'what works, for whom, in what circumstances?' Taking into account the scope and relevance of previous research, it is important that current practice is informed by previous evidence. To become 'evidence led', ongoing monitoring, evaluation and research are essential. Advocates of effective practice have consistently promoted a sustained commitment to the following:

- Practitioners and operational managers being involved in monitoring, small-scale evaluation and in applying research findings to individual or group practice.
- Organizational arrangements for monitoring and for large-scale evaluation.
- Basing decisions on policy, priorities and resource allocation on information from monitoring, evaluation and research.

This broader view recognizes effective practice as a continuing goal for a learning organization and emphasizes the role of research in giving direction to the continuing development of practice.

'Effective practice' had its strongest influence on Home Office policy from the launch of the national initiative in 1998 to its eclipse in the closure of the Crime Reduction Programme and the new agenda set by the Carter Report. The challenges to its ascendancy arose from several directions. Research results from the early implementation of 'accredited programmes' in England and Wales were variable and did not evidence the 'effect sizes' which had been anticipated from the 'what works' literature (Maguire 2004).

These results can be seen as 'implementation failure'. The large-scale implementation of accredited programmes ran ahead of other initiatives to develop those supporting conditions, notably initiatives on case management and community reintegration. Performance targets and funding arrangements supported major programmes of implementation but were not always consistent with careful targeting and considerations of responsivity. Research on the first phase of community programme implementation found shortfalls in effective assessment and targeting, motivational work and follow-through. Academic critics challenged the new orthodoxy with their critique revisiting the wider literature, drawing on research findings from early implementation and challenging an undue emphasis on cognitive-behavioural programmes (Mair 2004).

Judged against the aspirations of the Effective Practice Initiative, it can be argued that there have been significant improvements in probation practice but some serious shortfalls in effective monitoring, evaluation and research – the cornerstone of a sustainable evidence-led strategy.

Legislation to recast the organizational arrangements for the Probation and Prison Services (commissioning and contestability) will provide a changing organizational context. The new structures would seek to strengthen the focus on delivering intended results. However, the principles of effective practice also require an environment which gives sustained priority to staff development, practice development and practice quality, and which supports long-term investment and a commitment towards monitoring, evaluation and research. Their efficacy against these crucial tests remains to be seen.

Andrew Underdown

Related entries

Accredited programmes; Cognitive-behavioural; Criminogenic needs; Reconviction; Research; Responsivity; Risk principle.

Key texts and sources

Bailey, R., Knight, C. and Williams, B. (2007) 'The Probation Service as part of NOMS in England and Wales: fit for purpose?', in L. Gelsthorpe and R. Morgan (eds) *Handbook of Probation*. Cullompton: Willan Publishing.

Chapman, T. and Hough, M. (1998) *Evidence Based Practice*. London: Home Office.

Hedderman, C. (2007) 'Past, present and future sentences: what do we know about their effectiveness?', in L. Gelstorpe and R. Morgan (eds) *Handbook of Probation*. Cullompton: Willian Publishing.

Maguire, M. (2004) 'The Crime Reduction Programme Reflections on the vision and the reality', *Criminal Justice*. 4: 213–38.

Mair, G. (ed.) (2004) *What Matters in Probation*. Cullompton: Willan Publishing.

McGuire, J. (ed.) (1995) *What Works*. Chichester: Wiley.

Merrington, S. and Stanley, S. (2007) 'Effectiveness: who counts what?', in L. Gelsthorpe and R. Morgan (eds) *Handbook of Probation*. Cullompton: Willan Publishing.

Underdown, A. (1998) *Strategies for Effective Offender Supervision*. London: Home Office.

ELECTRONIC MONITORING

The use of remote surveillance technologies to monitor the presence, absence or movement of offenders during the community element of their sentences or orders.

The term 'electronic monitoring' (EM) refers to a range of technologies which can be used to achieve remote oversight of the locations and schedules of offenders under supervision in the community. In England and Wales and in Scotland, it is still most commonly associated with 'tagging' – the use of an electronic signalling device attached to an offender's ankle which monitors his or her presence, under curfew, in his or her home. Satellite tracking (using the Global Position System) is another form of EM which, in either real time or retrospectively (using computerized records), can monitor an offender's general whereabouts or his or her compliance with specified exclusion zones (around a former victim's home or public spaces in which crime might reasonably occur). Satellite tracking is becoming commonplace in the USA, especially with released sex offenders, but has thus far only been used experimentally in England and Wales as well as in the Netherlands and France. Voice verification technology, using telephones and a computerized voice print rather than a tag to authenticate an offender's presence at an agreed location, has been used on a small scale in England and Wales, but is not yet widespread anywhere. Remote alcohol monitoring, which combines a breathalyzer with tagging or tracking technology, can be used to ensure that offenders do not drink while under curfew. It is used in the USA and in some mainland European countries.

Tagging was first promoted in England in the early 1980s by a private individual, Tom Stacey, as a potentially more effective means of supervising offenders in the community than probation, and as a means of dramatically reducing the use of imprisonment. The Home Office initially rejected the idea but, subsequently, after visiting the early American schemes, made it integral to its 'punishment in the community' initiative in 1988. The first pilots – using EM as a bail condition to reduce custodial remand – were not, however, deemed a success and, although an EM curfew order was legislated for in the Criminal Justice Act 1991, no more pilots took place until 1995. Home Office research on these pilots found the technology reliable, compliance rates high and the measure cost-effective, despite an acknowledged element of net-widening.

The Probation Service was deeply hostile to tagging where it was first introduced, believing it to be an Orwellian development, at odds with probation values because it was a form of surveillance and failed to accord with emerging evidence on effective interventions. Its implementation was contracted out to the private sector partly to circumvent probation opposition, but in some respects this increased the service's wariness of it. In the mid-1990s, Dick Whitfield, Chief Probation Officer of Kent and lead commentator on tagging for the Association of Chief Officers of Probation, successfully encouraged probation staff to view it more positively. This was fortunate, because the New Labour government proved even more committed to EM than the Conservatives had been, rolling EM curfew orders out as a national scheme, and introducing an EM early release from prison (home detention curfew) scheme to cope with a crisis of rising prison numbers. This brought probation officers into contact with prisoners and families who appreciated the opportunity of early release and further reduced their scepticism towards EM,

although their support has never been whole-hearted. Bail, sentence and post-release schemes for juveniles were subsequently introduced and, by the autumn of 2006, just under 300,000 people had experienced tagging.

Scotland piloted tagging from 1998 and introduced a national scheme in 2001, which permitted both restrictions of liberty 'to a place' (curfews) and 'from a place' (exclusion zones), although the latter have been little used. The tagging of juveniles was considered much more controversial in the welfare-oriented youth justice system in Scotland, was not introduced until 2004 and is used very sparingly. Scotland introduced an EM early release from prison in 2006. Northern Ireland has considered EM but so far has not introduced it.

EM technology enables the tight specification of the times and places at which offenders must be present and logs their compliance or lack of it on computerized databases. It is a surveillant rather than an incapacitative measure; as with other forms of community supervision (but unlike prison or a ball and chain), it leaves offenders with a degree of choice about compliance and trusts them to act responsibly. Although compliance rates are generally high, offenders can and have reoffended while tagged (or have simply removed the tag). The more serious of such offences (including murder) have generated very critical media coverage and have significantly tarnished tagging's earlier image as a high-tariff, tougher-than-probation penalty. This backlash – which has not occurred in other countries to the same extent – will not impede EM's expansion (although it may slow it down) because in England, at least, it has behind it the immense momentum of New Labour's modernizing reforms, to which the use of new technologies is central.

There has been a tendency in England and Wales and Scotland for EM and probation to develop on parallel tracks, rather than in an integrated way. This partly reflects the fact that EM is delivered by commercial contractors – Group4Securicor and Serco in England and Wales, Serco alone in Scotland – rather than by statutory organizations. This contrasts with Sweden, where the Probation Service runs EM, and Belgium, where the Prison Service runs it, using social workers to support and assist all tagged individuals. The question of how EM is best operationalized remains open – internationally, the evaluative research is inconclusive. It is important that its future uses are shaped in dialogue with humanistic probation ideals rather than being allowed to evolve in accordance with purely commercial or technological imperatives and, since 2001, the Conférence permanente européenne de la Probation (CEP) has organized four influential conferences on EM to enable just such dialogue. It is also important that probation and social work leaders keep track of coming changes in EM technology, because the present forms of it will not necessarily to be the last.

Mike Nellis

Related entries

Curfew; Probation values; Punishment in the community; Tracking.

Key texts and sources

Mair, G. (2005) 'Electronic Monitoring in England and Wales: evidence-based or not?', *Criminal Justice*, 5: 257–78.
National Audit Office (2006) *The Electronic Monitoring of Adult Offenders*. London: National Audit Office (available online at **http://www.nao.org.uk/publications/nao_reports/05-06/0506800.pdf**).
Nellis, M. (2005) 'Electronic monitoring, satellite tracking and the new punitiveness in England and Wales', in J. Pratt *et al.* (eds) *The New Punitiveness*. Cullompton: Willan Publishing.

EMPLOYMENT, TRAINING AND EDUCATION (ETE)

Work done by or with the Probation Service to increase the employability of the offenders it supervises in order to reduce their likelihood of reoffending. (This includes the specialist work of basic skills, which is covered in 'Education, Skills for Life'.)

The National Offender Management Service (NOMS) aims to increase the employability of the offenders it manages in order to reduce their likelihood of reoffending. There is a well developed evidential basis ('business case') for pursuing this course that may be thought of as the 'working hypothesis' for ETE work.

Recent research from Britain and North America supports the view that the three most common criminogenic needs that generate repeat offending are cognitive skills, substance misuse and lack of employment (for example, May 1999). More than half the offenders who receive community or custodial sentences are unemployed at the time of conviction. Hence there is a clear case for probation and other agencies to try to increase offender employment.

The nature of the link between unemployment and offending is not completely straightforward. On the one hand, considerable research, using a range of approaches, has been undertaken to test the hypothesis that unemployment is a cause of crime, and yet the evidence is inconclusive. It is difficult to demonstrate that unemployment is a significant factor in leading a person of previous good character to become an offender. On the other hand, there is strong evidence that, once a person has become an offender, gaining employment is a significant factor in determining whether or not he or she reoffends (see also Desistance).

Hence the working hypothesis for probation is that it should improve offenders' basic skills so that they become more employable, and also increase their employability in other ways, because getting offenders into employment makes them less likely to reoffend. Indeed, the aim should be to 'maximize the employability' of each sentenced offender.

There are additional benefits from increasing offenders' basic skills, including the following:

● Improved participation and involvement in other aspects of community supervision, such as accredited programmes.
● Contributing to the government's 'Skills for Life' targets which are designed to improve the relevant skills of the working population.

'Maximizing the employability' of each offender means assessing the needs of each individual and, consequently, undertaking work which is realistic and relevant to those individual needs to develop his or her employment prospects within the local labour market. The work will vary between individuals: general education for some, vocational training for others, job-search skills and placements for yet others. The main strategy must by necessity engage with the labour market as it exists in the offender's home area – there is no point training for skills which are not required by local employers.

Hence some key principles follow concerning this work with 'current offenders' (see the 'Note on terminology' below). The aims are to:

- maximise the opportunity for offenders to obtain training opportunities, qualifications and employment on their own individual merits;
- enable offenders to find their place in the existing labour market;
- enhance integration into relevant community-based employment and training (rather than separate specialist provision);
- foster independence rather than promote dependency;
- ensure in particular that the needs of black and minority ethnic offenders and women offenders are assessed so that they gain fair access to the same ETE opportunities;
- confirm that the achievement of this and every other purpose of the sentence remains the responsibility of the offender manager;
- recognize that all involved must take into account the public protection needs of colleagues, partners, previous victims and the general public, including potential employers, when referring offenders for ETE opportunities; and
- far from 'setting people up to fail' by raising unrealistic expectations within offenders (as has sometimes been alleged), recognize the importance of working with each individual realistically and relevantly. Doing nothing is what will 'set people up to fail'.

No single organization can deliver such a strategy on its own. This approach has rightly developed in recent years through multi-agency partnerships at both local and national level. The Department for Education and Skills (DfES), the Learning and Skills Council (LSC) and the Offender Learning and Skills Service (OLASS) work with NOMS on this strategic task. One consequence of their partnership with the criminal justice world is an increase in their public protection duties. It is now periodically the responsibility of any member agency to play its part in preventing a potentially dangerous offender from accessing an unsuitable job or training opportunity (i.e. one that puts a member of the public at increased risk of serious harm).

Experience has shown that it is helpful to group the many different tasks of increasing the employability of offenders under three broad headings:

1. Assessment and planning.
2. Training and development.
3. Placement and employment.

Each of these headings involves work both with offenders themselves *and* in the wider local employment market. Hence *assessment and planning* involves an initial employability assessment of each person under probation supervision, plus a structured capability assessment in appropriate cases. This enables an individual plan of action to be made for each person at the start of a sentence. At the same time, there needs to be a constant monitoring of the local labour market to identify where there are current or future shortages. This information will inform the individual action plans since it will be important to train people for jobs that are, in reality, likely to be available locally.

Development and training accordingly has to be appropriate to the individual: basic skills for some, workplace skills for others and specific vocational skills for yet others. As indicated above, a key consideration is that training should be relevant to preparing the person for his or her local labour market. For this reason resources need to be sought to help train offenders for jobs where there are local labour shortages.

Placement partly means working with offenders to enable them to compete on their own merits as potential employees for available jobs. Bearing in mind the specific difficulties facing people with a criminal record, especially with the advent of the Criminal Records

Table 5 Assessment, development and placement

	Offender	Employment market
Assessment and planning	Basic skills screening, capability assessments	Identifying local labour market shortages
Training and development	Basic skills tuition Workplace skills Vocational skills	Resources for vocational training
Placement and employment	Interviewing and disclosure skills	Marketing with employers, customer service

Bureau, training them to disclose effectively needs to be much more comprehensive than in the past. However, placement also means working with employers, providing them with a customer service, to enable them to employ offenders with confidence.

Table 5 provides a summary of how work with both offenders and the employment market breaks into the three broad headings of assessment, development and placement.

A note on terminology re offender/ex-offender

The words 'offender' and 'ex-offender' at present have different meanings with different audiences both in Britain and in the rest of Europe. The Chief Inspector of Probation has sought to promote for several years the following standard three categories to describe people who are recorded as having committed an offence.

Current offender

Someone currently serving his or her custodial or community sentence, including supervision after release from custody. This category may gain more coherence in the future should 'Custody Plus' be implemented. In that eventuality, the term will become more useful than ever before in identifying the *c.* 250,000 people at any one time for whom special provision needs to be made by other government departments for accommodation, employment and training, and drug and other health treatments.

Unspent ex-offender

Someone who has completed all his or her sentences, but who has one or more unspent convictions on record, under the current rehabilitation of offenders legislation.

Spent ex-offender

Someone who has completed all his or her sentences and who has no unspent convictions on record. These convictions still have to be declared to exempted bodies under the legislation.

Andrew Bridges

Related entries

Criminogenic needs; Diversity; Education, Skills for Life; Partnerships.

Key texts and sources

Association of Chief Officers of Probation (1993–2001) *Offender Employment Statistics* (produced and circulated every six months).

Bridges, A. (1998) *Increasing the Employability of Offenders: An Inquiry into Probation Service Effectiveness. Probation Studies Unit Report 5.* Oxford: University of Oxford Centre for Criminological Research.

Burnett, R. (1996) *Fitting Supervision to Offenders: Assessment and Allocation Decisions in the Probation Service. Home Office Research Study* 153. London: Home Office.

HMI Prisons and HMI Probation (2001) *Through the Prison Gate: A Joint Thematic Review.* London: Home Office.

May, C. (1999) *Explaining Reconviction Following a Community Sentence: The Role of Social Factors. Home Office Research Study* 192. London: Home Office.

ENFORCEMENT

Action taken by the Probation Service in response to non-compliance, either through the courts in relation to community orders, or through executive recall to prison in the case of the vast majority of post-release licences.

Few areas of probation practice illustrate the changes in function, culture and activity that have taken place in the Probation Service during the last ten years as emblematically as enforcement.

Until the publication of the first National Standards for the Probation Service in 1987, there was comparatively little guidance to probation staff as to how they should exercise their powers of enforcement. Moreover, the significance of enforcement as an integral element of the supervisory process was under-appreciated, reflected in the relatively limited research into its effect. Broadly speaking, probation officers saw enforcement as the final, usually reluctant, action of the supervisor in 'failed' cases. This may have been consistent with the original legal concept of probation, but appeared less sustainable when the probation order became a sentence.

The development of cognitive-behavioural models of practice, emphasizing cause, effect and modelling, the emergence of risk assessment and management as major practice and organizational preoccupations, and a more critical political and social climate combined to focus greater attention on the importance of enforcement.

The National Standards for the Probation Service, published for the first time in 1992 and revised regularly thereafter, set out the expectation that enforcement should be consistent and timely, and that deviation from the standard requires managerial authority.

The development of new evidence-based models of probation practice in the mid-1990s, based on meta-analysis techniques and commonly referred to as the 'what works' approach, brought enforcement practice to the fore. In particular, effective practice in reducing reoffending was found to require consistency, clarity of communication, mutual expectation and a demonstrable connection between actions and consequences. This was all based on cognitive-behavioural theories. In this context, it was unsurprising that enforcement action became a key performance indicator and began to be seen as central to the supervisory process.

Enforcement became defined less in relation to cases which had irrevocably broken down but, rather, as a means to model consistency and improvement for the future, giving rise to the oft-quoted mantra that 'the purpose of enforcement is less to punish for past failure but rather to ensure future compliance'.

This shift in focus coincided with growing political concern about the effectiveness of community penalties and a reduction in confidence in the way they were managed by probation services. However, it was not until 2006 that the National Director of Probation was able to report that, nationally, the service had met the enforcement standard in 90 per cent of cases.

The emergence of risk assessment and risk management as core activities for the Probation Service has also led to increased focus on enforcement, mainly in relation to executive recall of prisoners. Until comparatively recently, recall of serious offenders was rare, mainly restricted to life-sentence prisoners (lifers) and those sentenced to four years' imprisonment or more in the event of further serious offending. National Standards created the responsibility for probation staff to assess the risk an offender poses to the public and to propose recall proactively where non-compliance raised the risk of reoffending or the risk of harm to others. The consequence has been a very significant increase in the numbers of prisoners returned to prison for non-compliance with licence requirements. The parole board has overall responsibility for the process, including appeals. The efficiency of the recall system is now such that an offender may be recalled and detained within an hour of the application being made by the offender manager.

In view of the cultural and practice shifts that have taken place in probation enforcement practice, it is perhaps surprising how little recent research has focused on the effectiveness of the changes that have taken place. On one hand, it appears entirely consistent with public expectations that there should be a serious consequence for those offenders who fail to comply with their sentence requirements. On the other, the impact of recall on prison numbers is significant, as is the cost of disrupted or uncompleted rehabilitative programmes. Although National Standards are clear, are they operated consistently and fairly; might some groups of offenders be breached and recalled disproportionately or at an earlier point than others? Do all those recalled or sent to prison for breaching community orders present a risk to the community that requires this penalty? Finally, is there any evidence that either the individual offender or his or her peers comply better either now or in the future if enforcement action is taken against them? Hearnden and Millie (2003) concluded, in relation to the last point, that there probably was not, because those under supervision already had a long history of insensitivity to a deterrent threat.

While the use of imprisonment as a sanction for non-compliance can be justified in relation to public confidence in sentencing and the management of high-risk offenders, it is probably less easy to find a rationale for those who pose no significant risk of causing harm. The challenge for the future must be in reducing the need for enforcement or, as Hearnden and Millie put it, placing more emphasis on *securing* compliance rather than simply *demonstrating* it.

Finally, the introduction of local criminal justice boards and the work of the Office for Criminal Justice Reform have, since 2003, created greater emphasis on the need for all criminal justice agencies to work collaboratively to improve compliance with court penalties. These measures include better enforcement of unpaid fines, swifter execution of warrants and, since 2005, shared targets to reduce the time taken to conclude court proceedings for breach of community orders.

Graham Nicholls

Related entries

Compliance; Discretion; Effective practice; National Standards; Reconviction; Risk assessment and risk management.

Key texts and sources

Hearnden, I. and Millie, A. (2003) *Investigating Links between Probation Enforcement and Reconviction.* (available at **www.homeoffice.gov.uk/rds/pdfs2/rdsolr4103.pdf**).
Stone, N. (1999) *A Companion Guide to Enforcement*, (3rd edn). Ilkley: Owen Wells.

ESTATES STRATEGY

An overall approach to the acquisition, location and development of property to provide adequate and appropriate accommodation for the delivery of probation activity now and in the future.

The Probation Service utilizes a diverse range of accommodation to enable it to deliver a wide range of services within the community, with some 1,300 properties (390,000 sq m) and 101 approved premises (55,000 sq m) accommodating 22,500 employees. Properties currently include commercial office buildings, offices within magistrates' and Crown courts, workshops, stores, garages and hostels.

The early development of estate strategies was focused in part on supporting the work of the courts, and magistrates' court committees advised by local authorities developed much of this strategy. At the same time, in some areas, there was collaboration with the local authorities to place small probation offices close to the community. These neighbourhood offices were sometimes incorporated into larger social services buildings.

Before 2001, local authorities had a duty to provide accommodation for the work of the Probation Service. Probation committees frequently sought the professional advice of local authorities to develop strategies, and to deliver estate management and facilities management services. In larger areas, probation committees appointed their own staff to manage their property.

Up to this period in time there was very little central leadership of estate strategy by the Home Office. Central leadership largely focused on major capital developments and relied on probation committees providing business cases. Centrally there was little information on the overall estate, its condition or the appropriateness of the accommodation. Home Office validation of business cases was therefore difficult.

When the National Probation Service was formed in 2001, the Secretary of State took over ownership of all property owned by the old committees, and probation boards were expressly prohibited from holding land.

As a result of this change, a central structure was created within the new National Probation Directorate (NPD) and the estate management and facilities management were outsourced. England and Wales divided into three regions for this purpose. The NPD only retained estate management of the East contract, and all other estate and facilities management was outsourced on three-year contracts. The intention was to gather information regarding the estate, to rationalize and modernize it and to put it into a better condition so that it would be attractive to a commercial body for complete outsourcing – e.g. as part of a private finance initiative (PFI) or public–private partnership.

This PFI strategy, which was part of the government's modernization agenda, has currently faded away. Existing contracts are being re-tendered. The NPD decision to re-charge boards for property on a formula, based on gross internal area rather than actual costs, had a significant impact on area boards. Some areas rewrote their property strategies and gave up properties purely because the formula increased costs by significant amounts, especially as garages and stores were being charged at the same formula as top-grade commercial offices.

Current estate strategies consider the 'offender journey' through the criminal justice system, taking into account population demographics, postcode analysis of offenders, options for sharing accommodation with the public, voluntary and private sectors and planning for increased commissioning and contestability. The design of offices now separates offender contact from secure office space to provide a safer environment for staff and to ensure sensitive information is secure.

Bill Daly

Related entries

Approved premises; National Probation Service for England and Wales; Probation boards.

Key texts and sources

Home Office (2001) *Design Standards for Probation Service and Non-hostel Buildings.* London: Home Office.

Home Office (2001) *Probation Estate: Property Management and Legal Arrangements* (PC 56/2001). London: Home Office.

Home Office (2003) *Approved Premises Planning and Development Programme Framework.* London: Home Office.

NOMS Property Service (2005) *Probation Estate Annual Report, 2004/05.* London: Home Office.

EVALUATION

The means of finding out whether a particular activity – programme, hostel regime, new process, etc. – is achieving its objectives.

As the 'what works' agenda (effective practice) gathered momentum in the second half of the 1990s, the importance of integrating evaluation within new probation initiatives was increasingly recognized. Nevertheless, when HM Inspectorate of Probation surveyed probation services in 1997 for examples of programmes potentially suitable for accreditation, of the 210 programmes submitted, only 11 were accompanied by evaluation studies which were considered to embody good evaluation practice. Although recognized today as an important component in developing practice and strategy, evaluation is still not consistently incorporated into the planning stage of new interventions.

Evaluation is commonly considered to be on the continuum between monitoring and research, but has much in common with both. The systematic collection of data, which is the essence of monitoring, is fundamental to evaluation, as are the rigorous methods and ethical considerations which are at the heart of pure research. Evaluation is best seen as a form of applied research: applied in the sense that it examines very specific methods of working, or examples of practice, and seeks to answer questions about that work.

The type of the evaluation undertaken will depend very much upon the nature of those questions which are being asked. These may be predominantly exploratory, in which the questions will commonly be phrased in terms of *what…?* (e.g. 'What methods are offender managers using to address [a specific] criminogenic need?'). A second set of questions will be of descriptive nature, answering the *how…?* questions, such as: 'How frequently are these methods used?', 'How many offenders start or finish?', 'How many are reconvicted?' Finally, an evaluation may seek to explain *why…?* (e.g. 'Why did that outcome occur in those circumstances?').

Evaluations will frequently embody elements of all question types, depending upon the precise area of work under examination. The two types of evaluation most frequently commissioned are 'outcome' evaluations and 'process' evaluations. Outcome evaluations are concerned with cause and effect: did the particular work undertaken lead to the results observed? In order to be able to answer such a question, rigorous design must be employed to ensure that the methods chosen are appropriate and capable of answering the question. Thus considerations of sample size, control groups, outcome measures and potentially confounding variables (such as other work being undertaken with the offender at the same time) need to be attended to, and the timescale for such an evaluation will generally be lengthy. At its most rigorous, such an evaluation will seek to answer not just the question 'Does this work?', but also 'What works, for whom, and in what circumstances?'

Process evaluations, on the other hand, are more concerned with the 'inputs' of a piece of work: what was done, how rigorously a manual was adhered to and whether the targeting criteria for the intervention were met. Such evaluations are key to ensuring programme integrity: whether a programme is delivered in the way it was designed to be delivered. Frequently, when an intervention fails to deliver the desired outcome, it is because it was not implemented in the way intended. One stage

back from this type of evaluation is the 'programme design' evaluation which measures the extent to which a programme meets specified design criteria. This is likely to become more common as probation areas develop a range of 'specified activities'.

One further group of evaluations comprises those concerned with cost-effectiveness, or value for money. Clearly these are relevant considerations and will become increasingly so within the context of contestability. Before such an evaluation is embarked upon, it is essential to be clear about the questions being asked, because the scope of such an evaluation is potentially extremely wide. For example, to determine whether a drug-related intervention is cost-effective, the unit cost of delivery could be balanced by the value of offences prevented, treatment costs potentially saved, policing and prosecution costs per offence prevented and the cost of imprisonment, not to mention wider social costs. Only the most sophisticated study can aim to measure all such costs and produce a comprehensive cost-benefit analysis. More modest evaluations should seek to produce unit costs and an estimate of the number of offences prevented, together with a monetary value multiplier.

Who should undertake evaluations? The traditional role of 'research and information officer' which existed in many probation areas in the 1990s has all but disappeared, with the increased emphasis upon performance monitoring. Few probation areas now have the capacity to employ staff whose primary role relates to research and evaluation. Where such capacity lies within a region, a collaborative approach may be feasible, and indeed add to the value of the evaluation by increasing the potential sample and enabling comparisons to be made. There exists a range of other possibilities: developing links with universities can lead to the identification of PhD or MA students wishing to undertake projects which coincide with the evaluation needs of areas. Alternatively, contracts may be entered into with universities or freelance researchers to undertake specific evaluations.

The quality assurance framework adopted within the Home Office has recently been extended to research and evaluation activity undertaken by probation areas. The purpose is to raise the quality of research throughout the criminal justice system, and the framework comprises an approval process and set of standards which apply to all delivery units, including the National Probation Service, HMPS (Prison Service) and the Youth Justice Board. Any research or evaluation, whether commissioned to be undertaken internally or externally, meeting certain criteria must be submitted for approval. All outcome evaluations, and others which exceed defined monetary or time values, fall within these criteria.

Regardless of whether a proposed evaluation meets the criteria, careful planning at the initial design stage will help to ensure that the study undertaken answers the questions posed. The starting point is to clarify the objectives of the intervention, programme or working method to be evaluated; these will determine how the evaluation should be conducted, what samples should be looked at, what data should be collected, how those data should be analysed and, finally, how and to whom the results should be disseminated.

Imogen Brown

Related entries

Effective practice; Interventions; Research.

Key texts and sources

Merrington, S. and Hine, J. (2001) *A Handbook for Evaluating Probation Work with Offenders* (available online at **www.inspectorates.homeoffice. gov.uk/hmiprobation/docs/whole.pdf**).

Merrington, S. and Stanley, S. (2007) 'Effectiveness: who counts what?', in L. Gelsthorpe and R. Morgan (eds) *Handbook of Probation*. Cullompton: Willan Publishing.

See also key texts and sources under NPRIE; Research.

EXTENDED SENTENCING

An enduring penal term for determinate custodial measures aimed at incapacitating and controlling higher-risk offenders, latterly concentrated on the confinement and extended regulation of violent and sexual offenders.

Perhaps a little confusingly, this term has been recycled in modern criminal justice legislation to apply to a succession of different custodial measures that centre on risk. These criminologically questionable disposals have in common subscription either to protective incapacitation, beyond the ambit of special psychiatric measures designed for mentally disordered offenders, and/or to the potential benefits of longer statutory oversight on licence of higher-risk offenders. The use of extended incarceration has also prompted a belief in the potential for prison-based treatment. There are enduring problems in determining who should be targeted for special sentencing, in assessing risk with any degree of accuracy and in developing appropriate safeguards in gate-keeping these extra-punitive measures.

First deployed by the Criminal Justice Act 1967 in place of 'preventive detention' (a form of custody that had allowed persistent but often relatively petty offenders to be confined out of harm's way), the original extended sentence allowed courts to impose a longer sentence than would otherwise have been justified on more serious offenders who met relatively wide criteria and where it was considered expedient to 'protect the public from him for a substantial time'. If paroled, the offender remained subject to licence until the expiry of the sentence. The target group included professional criminals and others regarded as 'a real menace to society'.

That relatively infrequently used measure was abolished by the Criminal Justice Act 1991, which sought to narrow protective sentencing to concentrate on higher-risk sexual and violent offenders. In addition, sexual offenders' liability to licence could be extended to the sentence expiry date, irrespective of whether a longer incapacitative term had been passed.

The extended sentence nomenclature was revived by the Crime and Disorder Act 1998. Expanding the armoury of measures for sexual and violent offenders, the Act enabled the courts to combine a custodial term with an 'extension period' through which the offender remains subject to licence beyond what would otherwise be his or her licence expiry date, where the normal licence period would not be adequate to prevent reoffending and to secure rehabilitation.

Though '1998' extended sentences will remain a current concern for some while (given delays in the disclosure and prosecution of many sexual offences), the term has acquired a new meaning in the so-called 'dangerous offenders' provisions of the Criminal Justice Act 2003, in respect of specified (but not 'serious') sexual/violent offences committed from 4 April 2005. This, too, empowers the imposition of a custodial term (minimum of 12 months), together with an extension period, where the court considers that there is a significant risk to members of the public of serious harm occasioned by the commission by the offender of further specified offences.

Probation officers have favoured the use of post-1998 extended sentences, particularly for sexual offenders, to facilitate the delivery of protracted group programmes and longer oversight in the community. However, enforcement action, recall (often for non-compliance unrelated to heightening risk) and risk aversion can result in the offender spending substantial additional time in custody, often with limited prospect of treatment intervention either in prison or outside.

Nigel Stone

Related entries

Criminal Justice Act 2003; Dangerousness; Licence; Public protection; Risk assessment and risk management; Sex offenders; Violent offenders.

Key texts and sources

Ashworth A. (2005) *Sentencing and Criminal Justice.* London: Butterworths.

For an appreciation of the Court of Appeal's approach to extended sentences under the 2003 Act, see *R* v. *Lang and Others* [2005] EWCA 2864.

EXTERNAL AUDIT

> A process for the independent checking of accounts and organizational propriety.

Role and status

The external auditor's role is to audit the annual accounts and to report whether, in his or her opinion, they express a 'true and fair view'. The external auditor must also state whether the accounts are compliant with legislation and indicate whether or not they can provide reasonable assurance that the financial statements are free from material misstatement. The external auditor's role extends beyond the statutory financial audit.

In the public sector, the National Audit Office (NAO) provides assurance that the financial reporting of government departments and agencies is sound, and it also assesses whether departments provide good value for money. The Audit Commission is responsible for appointing auditors to probation boards, along with local government, etc.

Standards

The Auditing Practices Board (APB) sets a range of prescriptive standards for statutory audit. External auditors are required to comply with the International Standards of Auditing set by the APB. A general requirement of these standards is that external audit must provide those charged with governance constructive observations arising from their audit. For probation areas this includes probation board members, the audit committee and the senior managers.

Audit process

In order to perform its work, external audit must be given access to all relevant information, and be given full explanations to its inquiries. External audit will want assurance that the organization's internal controls have been in operation throughout the period they are auditing. They will therefore test the effectiveness of these controls, to support their conclusions on the integrity of the financial statements and other aspects of their audit.

If external audit rely upon the work of internal audit to reduce the extent of their own work, they must examine and evaluate that work. However, neither the board nor internal audit has a right of access to the work of external audit. The board should encourage co-operation between the two sets of auditors. The audit committee should have a good understanding of the board's expectations of its external auditors and should monitor the relationship between internal and external audit.

Audit plan

External audit will plan their work in relation to the key business risks, and their specific remits of financial audit, governance and value for money. The external audit will often be phased in two stages, an interim audit part way through the year and a final audit of the financial accounts.

Annual report

The external auditor's report provides an opinion on the financial statements to the board. As with internal audit, they will, on occasions, make recommendations to improve the systems of internal control.

Fraud

Both sets of auditors should maintain a professional scepticism that fraud could exist, not withstanding past experience which indicates the board's honesty and integrity.

Graham Smith

Related entries

Internal audit; Probation boards.

Key texts and sources

The annual report of each probation area, available on its website, contains a summary of the external auditor's report. Full reports may be available through the papers and minutes. The National Audit Office website is at **http://www.nao.org.uk**, and the Audit Commission website is at **http://www.audit-commission.gov.uk**.

F

FINANCIAL PENALTIES

The imposition of a fine, compensation or costs by magistrates' or Crown courts.

The sentencing of offenders is an integral part of the criminal justice process, and the fine dominates as the most commonly imposed penal sanction: three quarters of all offenders sentenced at magistrates' courts in 2000 were fined. The attractions of the fine are as follows:

- It is flexible and combines elements of reparation and deterrence (see Punishment (aims and justifications)). A fine can punish the offender without impeding his or her employment opportunities or family responsibilities.
- It is economical. It involves the offender actually paying back to the community something in return for the damage done, rather than requiring society to spend more money so that the debt can be repaid.
- In terms of reconviction rates, it compares relatively well with other sentences.

The fine is the oldest of the regular non-custodial penalties available the courts, and was available for various common law offences in the late seventeenth century. By the end of the nineteenth century, further statutory provisions had been introduced for the payment of costs and compensation to those who had been defrauded or injured. Today, financial penalties can comprise fines, compensation and/or costs. Efforts at encouraging greater use of compensation orders were made in the 1980s, with new legislation enabling them to be the sole penalty, to take precedence over fines and requiring the court to give reasons for failing to make an order in any case. Compensation can now be made for any personal injury, loss or damage resulting from an offence, with the court having held that this extends to distress and anxiety.

Despite the attractions of the fine and the efforts at encouraging the use of compensation orders, there has been a recent decline in their use. Their credibility has increasingly been brought into question by ineffective enforcement and high levels of non-payment. For example, the total amount of fines and costs written off rose dramatically from £4 million in 1985–6 to £74 million in 2000–1. At some magistrates' courts, the amounts written off have exceeded the amounts collected. The fall in the use of the fine has been accompanied by an increasing use of community penalties, placing greater demands upon an already-stretched Probation Service. The Carter Report accordingly envisaged a greater use of financial penalties to enable the Probation Service to concentrate its work on more serious offenders.

When imposing a financial penalty, the court must ensure that the fine reflects both the seriousness of the offence and the offender's financial circumstances. A unit fine system was introduced through the Criminal Justice Act 1991, requiring the amount imposed to be the product of a number of units, reflecting the seriousness of the offence, and the value given to each unit, representing the offender's disposable income. However, this system was disbanded just two years later, with some magistrates having argued that the scheme was too rigid, and the press having drawn attention to people who had committed similar offences and yet received very different fines.

While there is now a relatively flexible approach towards fine impositions, the case law provides the following guidance:

- It is perfectly proper that the offender endures a degree of hardship – one of the objects of the fine is to remind the offender that what he or she has done is wrong.
- The fine is to reflect the offender's means and is not intended as a fine on the family.
- It should not be expected that a third party will make the necessary payments.
- Any fine should be capable of being paid in full within 12 months.

Turning to enforcement, there has been a significant fall in the number of imprisonments for default. The 8,600 defaulters imprisoned in 1996 were less than half the 1995 level, while the 2,480 receptions for default during the year 2000 were less than one third of the 1996 level. A wide range of methods is now available, with new provisions in both the Criminal Justice Act 2003 and the Courts Act 2003. Some methods are designed to facilitate payment, such as remitting part of the sums outstanding or allowing payments by instalments. Other methods are designed to support the process of prompt settlement, such as deductions from benefits, attachments of earnings and money payment supervision orders. There are also stronger methods available to the courts which are designed to elicit payment, including distress warrants, curfew orders or, ultimately, committal warrants.

The majority of enforcement methods are rarely used, however, and most defaulters are simply given further time to pay through set instalments. This one-dimensional approach is clearly failing to deal with those defaulters who are unable to organize their finances and those who are playing the system. Some argue that a version of the ill-treated unit fines system should be introduced. Such systems work well in other countries, and the failure of unit fines to find acceptance in the UK was largely due to the specifics of that particular system and a lack of understanding, rather than its core principles. Furthermore, bearing in mind the current deficiencies, there is a strong case for arguing that its abolition was overhasty and ill-judged.

Robin Moore

Related entries

Carter Report; Criminal Justice Act 1991; Punishment (aims and justifications); Reconviction.

Key texts and sources

Mackie, A., Raine, J., Burrows, J., Hopkins, M. and Dunstan, E. (2003) *Clearing the Debts: The Enforcement of Financial Penalties in Magistrates' Courts. Home Office Online Report* 09/03. London: Home Office.

Moore, R. (2003) 'The use of financial penalties and the amounts imposed: the need for a new approach', *Criminal Law Review*, 13–27.

National Audit Office (2002) *Collection of Fines and other Financial Penalties in the Criminal Justice System.* London: HMSO.

FREEDOM OF INFORMATION ACT 2000

Legislation enabling citizens to access information held by public bodies.

The Freedom of Information (FOI) Act 2000 came into force on 1 January 2005. The Act gives the right of access to information held by any public authority to anyone from anywhere in the world.

The FOI Act is regulated by the Information Commissioner's Office. The Act states that each public authority has to have a publication scheme. This is a method by which all information that can be released via this Act is accessible to members of the public. Guidance produced prior to the launch of the Act advised public authorities to have a web-based system to enable easy access to information. All information has to be put into 'classifications' which then have to be approved by the Information Commissioner's Office. An example of a classification would be 'financial information'. Once approval has been given by the Commissioner's Office for a classification to be included in a publication scheme, this cannot be removed without their approval; however, classes can be added in without reference to the Commissioner's Office.

Requests for information can be 'purpose blind' (i.e. no reason has to be given for wanting the information). All that is required is an address, electronic or otherwise, to provide the information to. Information requests have to be provided in writing, electronic or hard copy. Once a request has been received, the organization has 20 days to provide this information, in the format the requester has suggested. A fee may be charged.

Examples of the types of information that may be requested would be annual reports, financial statements, policy information and board-meeting minutes. Exemptions can be placed upon information being released (e.g. if the information may be business sensitive or is planned to be released at a future date, then it can be withheld). However, if the requester feels aggrieved at this decision he or she has the right to appeal to the Information Commissioner's Office, which will then investigate.

Best practice is to ensure all requests for information are logged. In the event of the same information being requested from various sources, it would be practical to place this information within the publication scheme so that future requesters can be pointed in that direction.

Year-end annual reports would be an example of information that members of the public may ask for frequently. If a request comes to an organization to access this information, a response would be that this is included in the publication scheme on the area's website, and therefore can be printed directly. However, should the person requesting this information not have access to the Internet, then the area should send a hard copy via the post.

The Data Protection Act 1998 gives protection to personal data. Therefore, if a request were made under the FOI Act for information that would be classified as personal data, then the Data Protection Act would be referenced to provide guidance in dealing with this request.

Wendy Storer

Related entries

Data Protection Act 1998.

Key texts and sources

The Information Commissioner's Office is at http://www.ico.gov.uk/.

G

GENDER

Gender is a critical variable in understanding offending, criminal justice practice, victimization and fear of crime.

Age is the single most important variable affecting offending rates, but at any age gender is the main variable. In 2004, about four times as many males as females were convicted by the courts. There are equally clear links between gender and the type, severity and frequency of offending. Although women commit more crimes than they used to, almost all serious crime is committed by men.

Female-only headed households are disproportionately found at the lower end of the socio-economic scale: but why, then, do women generally commit so little crime compared with men? And what can be learnt about women's relative conformity with the law that would help in understanding and addressing male offending? These questions cannot be answered here, but it should be noted that asking questions about gender is to problematize conformity as much as deviance. Equally, gender studies often begin with a focus on women offenders, but also raise important questions about masculinity.

Interestingly, in 2004, 46.3 women per 100,000 population received a police caution, compared with 110 per 100,000 men – a rate of only around two men to one woman. This may be partly because women tend to commit less serious crimes and fewer female offenders tend to have a criminal record. But the figures may also suggest that gender functions as a frame-work by which criminal justice personnel make sense of their work, influencing decisions at all stages of the process, from police officers to court officials, to prison and probation officers.

This much is uncontroversial these days. What remains controversial is the explanation for the discrepancies. The 'chivalry hypothesis' supposes that the criminal justice system treats women more leniently than men. There is some evidence for this but, while adherence to the gendered expectations of criminal justice personnel might elicit leniency, failure to measure up might well elicit overly harsh treatment.

Putting to one side the question of whether there is direct sex discrimination in the criminal justice and penal systems, any system which is set up to deal almost all the time with one group (male offenders) will not always respond well when charged to deal with another group (female offenders). Also raised is the question of whether the criminal justice and penal systems impact differently by gender and, if they do, whether such differences should be taken into account.

Patterns of victimization and fear of crime also show gender variables. For example, women are three times more likely than men to be victims of domestic violence. Indeed, for women, most violent crime is experienced at home. Males are more likely to be victims of assault in public places. Yet women more than men fear assault outside the home.

Ralph Sandland

Related entries

Domestic violence; Masculinity and offending; Women offenders.

Key texts and sources

Carlen, P. (1983) *Women's Imprisonment*. London: Routledge.

Gelsthorpe, L. and McIvor, G. 'Difference and diversity in probation', in L. Gelsthorpe and R. Morgan (eds) *Handbook of Probation*. Cullompton: Willan Publishing.

Heidensohn, F. (2002) 'Gender and Crime', in M. Maguire *et al.* (eds) *The Oxford Handbook of Criminology* (3rd ed). Oxford: Oxford University Press.

Walklate, S. (2004) *Gender, Crime and Criminal Justice* (2nd edn). Cullompton: Willan Publishing.

Reports under Criminal Justice Act 1991, s. 95 can be found at **http://www.homeoffice.gov.uk/rds/pubsstatistical.html**.

GROUPWORK

> The application of a prescribed set of theoretically informed activities (usually discussion based) with a group of people over a specified period of time in order to address their problems and help them change their behaviour.

The modern form of groupwork in probation, represented by accredited programmes, is ensconced in a framework of theoretical and practice integrity, formal evaluation and specifically focused staff training. It has not always been so.

Groupwork in probation has taken many forms, from exploring the great outdoors to investigating the indoor world of the personality. Usually a marginal activity, since the 1990s groupwork has become a cornerstone of probation practice. Certainly, probation officers ran groups from as early as 1915, but it was not until the late 1940s, when social psychology was first introduced in training, that it made an impact on the theoretical canon of probation practice. It became part of the treatment (or medical) model and, like most probation practice at that time, went largely unevaluated. Groupwork included family therapy, discussion groups, intermediate treatment, music

therapy, therapeutic community models and psychoanalytically based groups. Black offender groups, all-women groups and groups focused on violence and masculinity have contributed significantly to anti-discriminatory practice.

All this has left a rich legacy of experience and a professional bedrock on which current practice rests. Indeed, through the work of Priestley and McGuire and evaluations of groupwork programmes, it can be seen as an important part of the eventual promotion of evidence-based practice in the UK, more recently forming the main basis of accredited programmes.

The history is not all positive, however, and certainly the proliferation of unevaluated group programmes did little to contribute to the credibility of a service increasingly held accountable to its objective of protecting the public through the reduction of offending. Indeed, it was concern about the lack of quality controls over design and delivery that prompted the Home Office to establish in 1999 a panel of independent experts (later, the Correctional Services Accreditation Panel) to approve programmes which meet demanding published criteria in relation to design, delivery, management, staff training, monitoring and evaluation.

Some critics have branded this form of groupwork as a one-track approach which encourages the delusion that offending behaviour can be changed by simple adherence to a set formula. Nevertheless, areas offer several general programmes which focus on the thoughts, attitudes and values that contribute to offending:

- Generic offending behaviour programmes like 'Think First'.
- The Integrated Domestic Abuse Programme, in co-operation with relevant agencies for male domestic abusers.
- The Drink Impaired Drivers, which offers education about alcohol and focuses on thinking and behaviour that contribute to drink-driving.
- The Offender Substance Abuse Programme (OSAP), which addresses the link between drug misuse and offending.

- The Community Sex-offender Groupwork Programme (CSOGP), which is designed to reduce the risk posed by sex offenders.
- The Women's Programme for women convicted of acquisitive crime.
- The focus on Male Violence Programme.

Maurice Vanstone

Related entries

Accredited programmes; Anti-discriminatory practice; Therapeutic community.

Key texts and sources

Brown, A. and Caddick, B. (eds) (1993) *Groupwork with Offenders*. London: Whiting & Birch.

McGuire, J. and Priestley, P. (1985) *Offending Behaviour: Skills and Stratagems for Going Straight*. London: Batsford.

Vanstone, M. (2003) 'A history of the use of groups in probation work. Part One From "clubbing the unclubbables" to therapeutic intervention', *Howard Journal*, 42: 69–86.

Vanstone, M. (2004) 'A History of the use of groups in probation work. Part two. From negotiated treatment to evidence-based practice in an accountable service', *Howard Journal*, 43: 180–202.

H

HALLIDAY REPORT

A review of sentencing carried out in 2000–1. It led to substantial changes enacted in the Criminal Justice Act 2003 and established the current sentencing framework.

The Halliday Review considered whether the sentencing framework for England and Wales could be changed so as to improve outcomes, especially by reducing crime, at justifiable expense. The review was published in July 2001 and it proposed a wide range of changes in its 55 recommendations. The principal issues that the review team had been grappling with were how to sentence persistent offenders, how to respond to dangerousness and how to make sentences more effective by bringing prison and probation work more closely together.

The sentencing framework of the Criminal Justice Act 1991 had emphasized the seriousness of the offence as a principal determinant of sentence. The problem was how to combine seriousness and persistence. Prolific and priority offenders were seen as receiving inadequate sentences. Halliday re-established that sentence severity should increase as a consequence of previous convictions. It also established that violent offenders or sex offenders who present a risk of serious harm to the public should be eligible for a new sentence. Release in the second half of this sentence was to be dependent on a parole board decision, and courts could also extend the community supervision part of the sentence.

The Halliday Report recommended the creation of the generic community sentence. Courts would use only one 'community sentence'. In making this order, the court would specify the requirements to be placed on the offender, drawing from a menu of a dozen types of activity and restriction.

Community supervision was seen as an essential component of custodial sentences, and the recommended framework of prison sentences ensured that supervision in the community followed every period of incarceration. The notion that custodial sentences were served partly in prison and partly in the community would see a closer partnership between prison and probation and was an expression of the intention that custodial sentences would become more rehabilitative.

In order to respond to concerns about consistency in sentencing, Halliday recommended the establishment of new independent machinery to produce codified guidelines. This led to the setting up of the Sentencing Guidelines Council.

It was estimated that Halliday would have the effect of significantly increasing both the prison population and the workload of the Probation Service. Halliday called for a greater emphasis on research and cost-benefit analysis to study further the effectiveness and economic rationale of different sentences.

The publication of the report was followed by a period of consultation, including a white paper, *Justice for All*, in July 2002. The principal Halliday recommendations were enacted in the Criminal Justice Act 2003, but the postponements in implementing the 'Custody Plus' sentence highlight the resource deficits that hamper the realization of the Halliday goals.

David Hancock

Related entries

Criminal Justice Act 1991; Criminal Justice Act 2003; Custody Plus, Intermittent Custody and Custody Minus; Prolific and other priority offenders; Public protection; Punishment (aims and justifications); Sentencing Guidelines Council.

HATE CRIME

'Any incident, which constitutes a criminal offence, which is perceived by the victim or any other person as being motivated by prejudice or hate' (Home Office 2006).

In 1999 the *Admiral Duncan* public house was blown up, killing three and injuring 70. The establishment was attacked because it was known to be a gay pub. This is a stark illustration of hate crime – crime motivated by prejudice towards certain groups.

The basis of the motivation can be:

- religion;
- race, colour, ethnic origin, national origins;
- gender or gender identity;
- sexual orientation; or
- disability.

Hate crime and the attitudes it expresses often have their foundation in wider structural inequalities and methods of oppression within society. The concept of hate crime developed in the USA. In the UK, the crimes of racially motivated offenders – and particularly the murder of Stephen Lawrence and its aftermath (see Macpherson Report) – increased awareness that offending was frequently targeted against individuals because of their race, colour or ethnicity. It became increasingly recognized that offending could be aimed at members of other groups, as well as on the basis of identifiable characteristics, such as sexuality or religion.

The Crime and Disorder Act 1998 (ss. 28–32) provides that certain racially aggravated crimes constitute offences in their own right. Thus if an assault can be shown to be racially motivated, it will be dealt with as a racially aggravated assault and the liability to punishment increased. The Anti-terrorism, Crime and Security Act 2001 (s. 39) gives similar powers where the offending is targeted on the basis of religion. The Criminal Justice Act 2003 (s. 146) increases sentences for aggravation related to disability or sexual orientation while, if an offence is accompanied by hostility on racial or religious grounds, this must also be treated as an aggravating factor (s. 145).

Legislating against hate crime, however, is notoriously difficult. As well as the difficulties of proving motivation, the boundaries between hate crime and harassment can be difficult to draw; there may often be relatively low levels of seriousness, but high levels of repeat offending and victim impact; there are typically high attrition rates from incidence to reporting, arrest and conviction. Crime and Disorder Reduction Partnerships have tried to address some of these challenges – see, for example, Home Office (2006).

The development of the notion of hate crime has attracted criticism. Possibly due to the greater political influence of some groups, not all potentially vulnerable groups are equally defended by legislation. Spalek (2006) argues that those individuals who are motivated to offend against disabled people will be punished less harshly than racially motivated offenders. There is also the philosophical problem of punishing people on the basis of their motivation rather than solely on what they have done. Yet a crime motivated by prejudice needs to be dealt with differently since it impacts not just on the victim but also on those who share the same identity. Furthermore, such legal sanctions have an important symbolic function in signalling that hate-motivated offending will not be tolerated.

To fulfil their primary duty of protecting the public, practitioners must ensure that where a hate crime has been identified this is fully captured in the assessment process and effectively applied to the management of the offender. (There will also be occasions where such motivation is identified, even though it is not central to the index offence.) All such risk issues need to be taken into account when managing contact with the community in, for example, unpaid work. Hate-crime motivations need to be taken into account with regard to staff safety during supervision and with regard to contact with other offenders, such as in groupwork, approved premises or prisons. Inspection reports have found that staff often lack confidence in working with perpetrators of hate crime (see, for example, HM Inspectorate 2000, 2004), but the necessary skills must be developed and specific areas of work must be identified to challenge prejudice and reduce such offending.

Andy Gill

Related entries

Heterosexism; Racially motivated offenders.

Key texts and sources

Hall, N. (2005) *Hate Crime*. Cullompton: Willan Publishing.
HMIP (2000) *Towards Race Equality: A Thematic Inspection*. London: Home Office.
HMIP (2004) *Towards Race Equality: Follow-up Inspection Report*. London: Home Office.
Home Office (2006) *Tackling Hate Crime: Homophobic Hate Crime* (available online at http://www.crimereduction.gov.uk/sexual028.pdf).
Spalek, B. (2006) *Crime Victims: Theory, Policy and Practice*. Basingstoke: Palgrave Macmillan.

HETEROSEXISM

Heterosexism is activity based on and enforced by judgements and statements about lesbians and gay men arising from prejudice and homophobia and the assumption that heterosexuality is the only appropriate and morally acceptable way of exercising sexual choice. This process is overt and covert and is both deep seated and systemic. It operates on a personal and institutional level. The effect of such discrimination is to deprive lesbians and gay men of their rights and dignity.

The Napo definition of heterosexism appears above. However, bisexuality should have been included in it because prejudice is as high and, indeed, sometimes higher, towards bisexual people. These days the acronym 'LGBT' is used for lesbians, gay men, bisexuals and transgender people. These are now put together because the root cause of their discrimination is heterosexism. Transgender people also experience transphobia, which is about their gender reassignment, not their sexuality.

Sexual affection between people of the same gender is as old as humanity itself. It was not until the nineteenth century that scientists first defined 'homosexuality'. Prior to that, it was generally believed that people chose to be different. These people were persecuted in some cultures as they broke 'the divine law'. The level of hostility was highest from the Abrahamic religions. However, this was not universal, as many cultures either enjoyed or tolerated difference.

Scientific progress did not lead to a more positive response: it led to LGBT people being seen as mad rather than bad. The word 'homosexuality' is resented because of its link with the medical model. Biology shows that, within all creatures, there are those who form sexual relations with others of their own gender. Others change their gender or take on the role of the opposite gender.

The levels of heterosexism ebb and flow. Historically in Western Europe there were periods when love between people of the same gender was tolerated and periods when there was organized persecution. The new law, which trapped Oscar Wilde, was a reaction to the behaviour of some people in the eighteenth and nineteenth centuries. Female homosexuality was not made illegal because there was a total denial of women's sexuality. This did not stop persecution, however. Although the root of most prejudice comes from religious belief, it was in Nazi Germany and the Soviet Union under Stalin, two states designated as atheist, that the worst persecutions have taken place.

Since the second half of the twentieth century, considerable progress has been made, leading to the equalization of the age of consent, the decriminalization of gay behaviour and civil partnerships. There has been some reaction in fundamentalist groups of the major religions. As far as the workplace is concerned, legislation now protects LGBT people against harassment, isolation and discriminatory behaviour. Similar legislation covers faith. To sum up, the Advisory, Conciliation and Arbitration Service (ACAS) guidelines state that all people regardless of their sexual orientation or faith must be treated with respect.

Michael Lloyd

Related entries

Gender; LAGIP; Transgender.

Key texts and sources

ACAS guidelines and an e-learning package on sexual orientation can be found at **www.acas.co.uk**.

HM INSPECTORATE OF PROBATION

HM Inspectorate of Probation (HMI Probation) is an independent inspectorate, funded by the Home Office and reporting directly to the Home Secretary. It inspects the work of probation areas and youth offending teams in England and Wales and, in this context, is inspecting offender management as this develops.

HMI Probation was established in 1936 as an independent inspectorate within the Home Office. Until the mid-1980s its role included training and confirming the appointment of probation officers as well as the inspection of probation services but, in 1987, the training function of HMI Probation was transferred to educational establishments.

Under the Criminal Justice Act 1991, the inspectorate was given a statutory basis for the first time. The Criminal Justice and Court Services Act 2000 renamed the inspectorate 'Her Majesty's Inspectorate of the National Probation Service for England and Wales'. A further change is likely to be made to the statutory basis of the inspectorate to reflect the continuing current changes to the Probation Service, though this is unlikely to affect the nature of inspection work itself.

During the late 1990s HMI Probation took the lead in the development of the 'what works' project to identify and promote effective practice in the supervision of offenders in the community. With the establishment of the National Probation Service in 2001, this role passed mainly to the National Probation Directorate in its capacity of providing leadership to the Probation Service and its responsibility for performance management. HMI Probation's role has focused more specifically on inspection of the quality of work with offenders to reduce the likelihood of reoffending and to minimize the risk of harm they pose to others. This reflects an underlying approach that sees inspection of a public service as primarily concerned with the quality of processes aimed at delivering the right impact on service users: inspection is therefore distinct from, and complementary to, performance management. This approach to inspection also seeks to encourage continuous improvement in the work inspected.

In recent years, HMI Probation's main inspection work has comprised the following:

- Inspections of individual probation areas. These have taken the form of inspection programmes of all probation areas in England and Wales (42 since 2001), over a three-year period. From 1999 to 2002, the programmes were the Performance Improvement Programme and, from 2003 to 2006, the Effective Supervision Inspection Programme.
- In this connection, HMI Probation is currently leading, in close association with HMI Prisons, the Offender Management Inspection Programme, which started in May 2006. The programme is inspecting the management of offenders in each criminal justice area (currently probation area) from the start to the end of their custodial or community sentence under the auspices of the National Offender Management Service.
- The joint inspection programme of youth offending teams (YOTs), under which HMI Probation leads a team of eight inspectorates which are inspecting the 156 YOTs in England

and Wales over the five-year period 2003–08. The YOT inspection programme has been a major development in recent years and is currently HMI Probation's largest programme in resource terms.

- Independent reviews of serious further offences (i.e. cases where an offender under Probation Service or YOT supervision commits a serious further offence) and other similar inquiries, at the request of the Home Secretary. In particular, three independent reviews carried out in 2005–6 – of the cases of Peter Williams; Damien Hanson and Elliot White; and Anthony Rice – each indicated substantial shortcomings in the handling of the cases and attracted considerable publicity.
- A number of pieces of thematic inspection work, increasingly on a joint basis with other criminal justice and other inspectorates. Among other things, this has included joint work on enforcement, some of it led by HMI Probation.
- A contribution to inspections led by the Audit Commission of the Supporting People Programme which is aimed at delivering support services to help vulnerable people to live independently.

All inspection reports and annual reports are published and are available on the HMI Probation website.

A significant development in HMI Probation's inspection work from around 2005–6 has been an increasing focus on the need for improvement in risk assessment and the management of offenders – the public protection aspect of Probation Service and YOT work. Along with the independent reviews of serious further offence cases noted above, there has been an increased focus on risk of harm work in HMI Probation's regular inspections, reflecting concerns identified in previous inspection programmes and also the publication of the report of a joint inspection of public protection led by HMI Probation.

Another important development is an increasing focus on joint inspection work, particularly with the other criminal justice inspectorates. In this connection, there has been consideration in recent years of a merger of the five criminal justice inspectorates, including HMI Probation. Legislative plans for a merger – which HMI Probation supported – were made in 2006. It was subsequently decided not to pursue these, but the five criminal justice inspectorates agreed with the criminal justice ministers that they would work together to strengthen and broaden joint working across the inspectorates, while remaining separate organizations. HMI Probation, most of whose inspection work is joint, will work closely with the other criminal justice inspectorates to achieve improved joint working, and so contribute to the overall effectiveness of the criminal justice system.

HMI Probation aims to promote actively race equality and wider diversity issues, and to work to eliminate improper discrimination in the criminal justice system. As well as specific inspections on diversity issues, each main inspection programme includes criteria to identify whether or not offenders are being treated proportionately at each step of the processes inspected, irrespective of their diversity characteristics.

HMI Probation comprises about 50 salaried staff and also a panel of some 15 fee-paid inspectors who work for the inspectorate on a sessional basis. HMI Probation has offices in London and Manchester.

Peter Ramell

Related entries

Accountability; Effective practice; Performance management; Probation training; Risk of harm; Serious further offences.

Key text and sources

HMI Inspectorate of Probation's website is at http://inspectorates.homeoffice.gov.uk/hmiprobation.

HOME VISITS

> The practice by probation staff of visiting the home of an offender in order to confirm his or her residence at that address, or to further some aspect of assessment, supervision or safeguarding children.

Contemporary National Standards require a probation staff member to visit the home of an offender released early from prison on licence within five days of release. The purpose is to confirm that the person concerned has taken up residence at the specified address. In most cases residence at a specific address is a licence condition, and compliance needs to be confirmed.

In past times, home visiting by probation officers was a standard part of the preparation of pre-sentence reports and of the supervision of offenders in the community. The home contains messages about the lifestyle and behaviour of a person that may not emerge in an office interview. Staff in residential settings will be familiar with this phenomenon. A very experienced and compassionate field senior probation officer who had recently taken on the management of some approved premises once confided: 'I have been supervising youngsters like this for years, but I had no idea they were so deviant until I started living with them!'

It is also informative to see offenders interacting with parents, partners or children. The opportunity to speak to those with an interest in an offender's well-being is often an invaluable addition to the process of risk assessment and management. Through discussions with relatives, problems can be resolved and supervision aims re-enforced. Where there are small children at home, supervision by visiting spares the children from visits to the probation office. The parent may be more relaxed and forthcoming at home. Home visits also enable a level of child protection monitoring where this is appropriate.

Why has home visiting become so unfashionable? In part it is because of the adoption of more systematic and standardized forms of working. This work cannot accommodate the kind of random data that home visits reveal. In the 1970s court reports were based on a statutory duty 'to enquire into the circumstances or home surroundings'. Now they are focused on the offending behaviour and are generated from the data collected through the completion of OASys which, for the most part, is achieved by discussion with the offender in an office setting.

From the 1980s onwards there were increasing concerns about the safety of staff making home visits. Safety assessments led to safer practice – sometimes staff working in pairs. The increased cost of this, together with the generally increasing demands on the time of probation officers, also contributed to the decline. The reduction in home visits was mirrored in a parallel process that saw the closure of many small neighbourhood probation offices at about the same time. The move to a smaller number of larger city or town-centre offices was understandable for reasons of cost, staff safety and the development of more groupwork. However, the unintended consequence was that probation staff became more distant from the community they served.

David Hancock

Related entries

Community; Licence; National Standards; Risk assessment and risk management.

> **Key texts and sources**
>
> Harding, J. (2000) 'A community justice dimension to effective probation practice', *Howard Journal*, 39: 132–49.
> Safer working practices for home visits have been developed with the help of the Suzy Lamplugh Trust (**www.suzylamplugh.org**).

HUMAN RIGHTS

> Human rights are liberties or claims that people have or may make in virtue of their humanity and are, consequently, not at the disposal of the state.

The Human Rights Act (HRA) 1998 incorporated the European Convention on Human Rights into the law of the UK (see Council of

Europe). The procedures of criminal justice – of crime prevention, detection, prosecution and punishment – inevitably impinge upon people's rights, and the HRA imposes a legal constraint to ensure that the government does not unreasonably suppress individual rights in its pursuit of the common good. Thus the aspiration – although, as Gearty (1998) argues, in practice human rights discourse and legislation have often fallen disappointingly short.

Invoking a right is by no means always decisive. The convention distinguishes absolute rights (which may never be taken away), limited rights (which may only be compromised in explicitly identified specific circumstances) and qualified rights (where individual rights must be considered alongside broader social and community interests). Moreover, the rights of *everyone* are relevant, so judgements have to be made in cases where individuals' rights are in conflict.

Arguably, the language of human rights represents the best prospect of affirming an ethical dimension to criminal justice practice, of invoking moral considerations against (or at least alongside) the managerialist imperatives of effectiveness, efficiency and economy. Can the discourse of human rights enrich probation values? It has been argued that human rights set a bare minimum ethical standard and that probation should aspire to much more than this. Yet rights can sometimes evolve from liberties into claims or 'positive obligations' – for example, the right to life minimally means that the state may not kill people but also generates the positive obligation that the state should take steps to safeguard and protect. There is, then, a potential – albeit so far only modestly realized – for these minimum rights to develop into much stronger claims.

The government often suggests that insistence on the rights of offenders has disturbed a balance which should be redressed in favour of victims and communities. The metaphor is unhelpful: restorative justice, for example, explicitly rejects this conception and urges an approach to crime that respects and seeks to maximize the rights and interests of *all* involved. The rights of defendants (or even offenders) and victims are certainly not always in opposition – and perhaps less often than this rhetorical device implies: for example, due process rights to protect the innocent against wrongful conviction *support* the rights of victims since it is not in the victim's interests that the wrong person be convicted. Where there is indeed a conflict between individuals' rights and the common good, it is not clear that the state is an even-handed judge in its own cause, and the protection of the law is accordingly required.

Rob Canton

Related entries

Council of Europe; Probation values; United Nations.

Key texts and sources

Department for Constitutional Affairs (2006) *Making Sense of Human Rights* (available online at: http://www.dca.gov.uk/peoples-rights/human-rights/pdf/hr-handbook-introduction.pdf).

Gearty, C. (1998) 'No human rights please, we're capitalists', *Independent*, 13 December: 14.

Gelsthorpe, L. (2007) 'Probation values and human rights', in L. Gelsthorpe and R. Morgan (eds) *Handbook of Probation*. Cullompton: Willan Publishing.

Nellis, M. and Gelsthorpe, L. (2003) 'Human rights and the probation values debate', in W.H. Chui, and M. Nellis (eds) *Moving Probation Forward: Evidence, Arguments and Practice.* Harlow: Pearson.

INFORMATION STRATEGY

> An information strategy helps an organiza-
> tion to respond to change and to be more
> effective by maximizing the value of systems
> to turn data into information and information
> into knowledge.

A paper by Coopers & Lybrand (1995) on an
information strategy for the universities' Joint
Information Systems Committee made several
key points about what an information strategy
should and should not be. It should be developmental and responsive. It should help an
organization respond to change and to improve
its effectiveness. It is not just concerned with the
production of management information but
with how information is used across the organization. Key shortcomings are where information
strategies are technology driven, concentrate on
management information and are directed only
towards improving efficiency.

How information is to be used, then, should
reflect the goals of the organization. In the
Probation Service, there are long-term continuities in the goals of the enforcement of court
orders and licences and in the rehabilitation of
offenders and public protection, but the priorities and the context for these have differed
significantly over time. These differences reflect
changes in the 'knowledge base' of the service
but, more importantly, in the legislative and
political contexts in which it operates.

When the concept of information came into
probation, it tended to be associated with quantitative measurement. From the experiments of
such services as West Yorkshire and Inner London
came a strong identification of information use
with planning and measurement. Information

use development has – from PROBIS to C-
NOMIS – been driven by technology. PROBIS
used the capacities of then novel microcomputers
to record data about cases and court reports. The
National Probation Service Information Systems
Strategy (NPSISS) concentrated on the provision
of technology and software – email and the case
management system, CRAMS. The business
analysis that underpinned these was essentially
conservative and concentrated on efficiency.
Similarly, the National Offender Management
Information System (NOMIS) features only as an
aid to efficiency in the NOMS *Strategic Business
Case* (NOMS 2005).

However, alongside this there was strategic
thinking about information use, starting with a
paper by the Association of Chief Officers of
Probation's (ACOP's) Management Information
Committee. This incorporated two major concepts: that of what is now called 'end to end'
management of offenders and the tailoring of
systems to measure performance against outputs. However, the increasing use of information
in probation and the risk of incompatible and
overlapping systems led the Home Office, working with ACOP, to develop the NPSISS. While it
would be untrue to say that NPSISS lacked a
strategic dimension of information use – not
least because it built on ACOP's work – it would
be fair to say that more thought went into specifying what systems should be in place rather
than what information should go through them.
However, there is value in developing systems,
and NPSISS delivered improvements in connectivity and efficiency.

It is not surprising, then, that the only attempt
to develop an information strategy for the
Probation Service was made at a time when the
service was under scrutiny for its ability to
deliver government goals and targets. NPSISS

was commissioned by the Home Office and developed through a series of workshops which attempted to elicit key information needs and to identify the systems that supported them. This would then drive a revised information systems strategy to ensure that information would be collected and used consistently. However, there was no final strategy document – the published version was entitled *A Developing Probation Service National Information Strategy* (Heape 1999).

The observable impact of this project was small, perhaps because it was presented in the Foreword to the executive summary (Heape 1999) as being of interest only to information managers. Arguably, however, it stimulated two further developments – the National Probation Service Information Management Strategy (NPSIMS) (NPS 2002a) and a move towards knowledge management. In other words, the focus shifted again from deciding what information should be collected to how the transmission of information and knowledge should be managed.

The NPSIMS followed the establishment of the National Probation Service (NPS) in 2001. While the NPS briefing (NPS 2002b) on this document did not refer to the NPSISS, it was at least informed by similar ideas. The NPSIMS was presented as a successor to the NPSISS but was less focused on systems and hardware. In part, its approach was a response to criticisms by the National Audit Office (NAO) (House of Commons 2001) and the House of Commons Public Accounts Committee (House of Commons 2002) about the implementation of the NPSISS. These criticisms were fundamentally about the management of the project, not the concept, but the NAO report recommended an information strategy linked to the business strategy.

The view the NPSIMS took was one of incremental development in accordance with a set of principles. In doing this, it met at least some criteria for an effective information strategy. It gave priority to outputs, it tried to keep a dynamic business link and it did not concentrate just on systems. But here the trail goes cold. The Carter Report and the move to the National Offender Management Service (NOMS) (and NOMIS)

effectively stopped the NPSIMS in its tracks. There have been no further published strategies for probation.

If we look back at the Coopers & Lybrand criteria, we find that the NPS's and now the NOMS' strategic approaches to information have been characterized by a concentration on systems, management information and efficiency gains.

Stephen Stanley

Related entries

C-NOMIS; Evaluation; Research.

Key texts and sources

Coopers & Lybrand/JISC (1995) *Guidelines for Developing an Information Strategy* (available online at **www.webarchive.org.uk**).

Heape, N. (1999) *A Developing Probation Service National Information Strategy*. London: Home Office (available online at **www.nationalarchives. gov.uk/ERO/records/ho415/1/cpd/probu/ strategy.htm**).

House of Commons (2001) *The Implementation of the National Probation Service Information Systems Strategy. Report by the Comptroller and Auditor General*. London: HMSO.

House of Commons (2002) *Thirty-second Report: The Implementation of the National Probation Service Information Systems Strategy*. London: House of Commons.

National Probation Service (2002a) *The National Probation Service Information Management Strategy*. London: Home Office.

National Probation Service (2002b) *Managing Information. NPS Briefing* 05. London: Home Office.

NOMS (2005) *NOMS Change Programme: Strategic Business Case*. London: Home Office.

INFORMATION TECHNOLOGY DEVELOPMENTS IN AREAS

The development of information technology (IT) systems in local probation areas.

At the time of the formation of the National Probation Service (NPS), the slogan 'strong national; strong local' was frequently used. It conveyed the aspiration that the new organization would combine the benefits of strong national leadership in Westminster, well connected to influence and resources, with strong local organizations adapting the service to meet local community requirements. While the phrase was a fine ideal, it was also recognized that, sometimes, national and local were set in opposition to each other. Nowhere was this felt more keenly than in the area of IT developments.

The 1980s and 1990s had seen piecemeal IT developments and the emergence of several groups of services collaborating to gain economies of scale. This had produced some excellent results. A particularly good system for case recording and information management (ICMS) emerged from the east of England. However, at the time the Home Office was busy with IT procurement for all probation areas, and local area developments began to be discouraged on the grounds that central procurement and development could achieve greater efficiency and nationally transferable data systems.

The Home Office had taken responsibility for developing a standard case recording and statistics system (CRAMS), but the development was protracted and, when it did emerge, it was found to be inferior to some of the locally developed programmes. CRAMS was very laborious and provoked disputes with the unions because it was not 'ergonomically sound'. Also, it had been so delayed that many areas turned to alternatives in frustration.

For example, in Nottinghamshire, in-house programmers working in close collaboration with practitioners, information staff and managers developed a modest interim case record (ICR) in a few months. Based on Lotus Notes, it was user-friendly and an instant success with practitioners. It guided practice by embedding National Standards and enforcement requirements, so that practitioners were prompted when to make decisions or take action. A continuous dialogue between the field and the IT staff meant that ICR was amended and enhanced regularly in response to suggestions by practitioners. This was a far cry from a national system that had to meet an inflexible national specification that no group of practitioners could hope to influence.

However, area developments have much inefficiency, whereas a single central development can produce software that is usable throughout England and Wales in both prison and probation settings. A single central development also means there is neither repetition of creative effort nor duplication of cost. The roll-out of the electronic version of OASys is an example of a centrally driven application that has met many expectations in timing and functionality. New offender management software is currently in development, and structured arrangements are in place to control the risks involved. However, the track record of large public sector software developments is not good, and the risks that the project may be overtaken by policy change, technology change, delays or cost overruns are ever present.

David Hancock

Related entries

C-NOMIS; Information strategy.

Key texts and sources

See Key texts and sources at the Related entries.

INTER-AGENCY WORK

A relationship between two or more organizations intended to increase the efficiency, effectiveness and economy of effort of interventions with specific individuals or target groups of mutual interest to each agency.

The Probation Service has a long history of working relationships with other organizations in the statutory and voluntary sectors. Until relatively recently, most of these arrangements were quite informal, generally involving information exchange on areas of mutual interest and, at the practice level, referral of offenders under supervision to relevant specialist services. Greater formality emerged with the growing recognition of the value of sharing information, jointly designing intervention plans and reviewing progress in cases of high public concern, such as the development of child protection procedures.

Since the early 1990s, inter-agency work has been increasingly emphasized in government policy, leading to a growing formalization of arrangements. Where the extent, type and content of inter-agency relationships were previously highly dependent on local initiative and voluntary mutual co-operation, there is a growing shift towards central policy and legislative mandate to develop the forms of relationships and the foci of inter-agency work that are expected to produce the outcomes desired by government. An early example was the requirement in the Crime and Disorder Act 1998 to develop youth justice services by creating local youth offending teams, drawing on the experience of best practice in some areas where concerted inter-agency effort significantly reduced the level of custodial sentencing during the 1980s. This was a notable exercise in mandating multidisciplinary work because it required the contribution of staff from police, probation, health, education and social services. Volunteer community representatives are also involved in some areas of youth justice activity – notably the referral panels that determine the content of supervision. Other government requirements to create inter-agency working relationships have often been less inspired by such grass-roots exemplars, reflecting instead centrally determined priorities and the assumption that multi-agency collaboration will achieve these.

Other forms of inter-agency work have focused on strategic planning and problem-solving rather than on front-line service delivery. For example, the formation of drug action teams in 1995 explicitly required the participation of senior representatives of both statutory organizations and voluntary agencies in order to develop action plans to tackle local drug problems. Similarly, the Supporting People programme (launched in 2003) that assists independent living among vulnerable populations requires those same organizations, together with housing associations and user groups, to engage in collaborative planning for the design of relevant services.

This growth of policy interest in inter-agency work in the field of social provision has included a strong emphasis on crime prevention, community safety and public protection. The Safer Cities Programme (a major action research project) pioneered multi-agency collaboration and co-operation in crime prevention during the 1990s, with the aim of disseminating good practice examples. The Crime and Disorder Act 1998 required local authorities, the police and other relevant agencies, including the Probation Service, to develop crime reduction strategies based on local crime audits drawn from pooled agency knowledge and public consultation. The Criminal Justice and Court Services Act 2000 required police and probation services jointly, as the responsible authority (including, since 2003, the Prison Service), to make arrangements for the assessment and management of risks posed locally by known sexual, violent and other potentially dangerous offenders. Such arrangements also involve health and social services and local authority housing departments in the relevant planning and provision. These multi-agency public protection arrangements must include community representatives in their deliberations.

These examples of inter-agency work illustrate several themes. First, there is a clear expectation that inter-agency collaboration and co-operation will deliver improvements in the quality of support services for vulnerable groups, including the supervision of offenders. Secondly, government has increasingly intervened to determine both the focus and the form of inter-agency work in accordance with its own policy priorities. Thirdly, the central mandate requires not only that inter-agency activity should happen but that it should also be publicly visible in its engagement with and responsiveness to local interests and concerns. By making inter-agency work locally visible, it is presumably intended that communities will recognize and approve the activity being undertaken by professional organizations in the interests of local welfare and safety. Thus, one ambition of policy appears to be to assuage public concern about crime and disorder.

The assumption that inter-agency work will improve service quality appeals to a common-sense notion that has mixed support. It is notable that, in central policy mandates, the advantages of inter-agency collaboration have been treated as self-evident, while little has been said about the challenges of making such work effective. While it is laudable for government to take steps formally to ensure that positive inter-agency work happens, little attention has been paid to the reasons why (given its assumed benefits) it was not already highly developed at the local level. The complexities of delivering effective inter-agency work include establishing an appropriate and committed leadership; achieving clarity of aims, objectives and professional roles; and determining action plans and evaluative measures. None of these requirements is easily met, and many inter-agency working relationships have been troubled by conflicts that are often rooted in ignorance of other agencies' priorities and constraints, professional perspectives and resources.

While the Probation Service's contribution to inter-agency collaboration has frequently, though not invariably, been judged constructive in evaluations, the task of supporting the growing number of requirements for such activity represents a considerable burden on the organization. This is particularly striking when the service's capacity is compared with the number of local authorities within a probation area and the size of other key agencies, such as the police and health services.

Judith Rumgay

Related entries

Community safety; Local authorities; Multiagency public protection arrangements (MAPPAs); Partnerships; Supporting people.

Key texts and sources

Huxham, C. (ed.) (1996) *Creating Collaborative Advantage*. London: Sage.

Mattessich, P.W., Murray-Close, M. and Monsey, B.R. (2001) *Collaboration: What Makes it Work* (2nd edn). Saint Paul, MN: Amherst H. Wilder Foundation.

Rumgay, J. (2004) 'The barking dog? Partnership and effective practice', in G. Mair (ed.) *What Matters in Probation*. Cullompton: Willan Publishing.

Rumgay, J. (2007) 'Partnerships in probation', in L. Gelsthorpe and R. Morgan (eds) *Handbook of Probation*. Cullompton: Willan Publishing.

See http://www.communities.gov.uk/index.asp?id=1128634 for an evaluation of the Safer Cities initiative.

INTERNAL AUDIT

Work carried out in probation areas to assure the quality of corporate governance and business risk management, and to check that resources are being used properly.

Corporate governance is the framework that promotes effective stewardship of assets and the sound management of resources. It includes organizational structures, policies, ethical values, planning, objective setting, monitoring and reporting. In probation areas, the probation board is accountable to the Home Secretary for the provision of services, and the chief officer, a member of the board, is the government's 'accounting officer', responsible for the management, operations and finances of the department.

Internal and external audit provide a valuable contribution to good corporate governance by forming independent opinions on the effectiveness of operational controls, business risk management and the integrity of the financial statements. The board must have an audit committee, and that body is charged with seeking assurance from management and, independently, from audit, that controls, risk management and financial procedures are in place and operating effectively.

Role and status

Internal audit provides an assurance service to the board, audit committee and the 'accountable officer'. This work requires unconstrained access to all information, people and records across the organization. Internal audit is independent of the organization's routine operations.

Audit plan

At least annually, internal audit will prepare a programme of work, through consultation with the audit committee, management and external audit. The plan should have sufficient breadth of audit coverage to provide assurance of the effectiveness of controls to mitigate the main business risks, governance and risk management process.

Audit process

Each audit should be fully scoped in consultation with the auditee, agreeing the specific risks associated with each audit topic. The management systems will be reviewed, analysed and documented. Transactions will be tested to ensure that the system operates in the way it has been described. The overall effectiveness of internal control will be evaluated and conclusions drawn. Audit findings need to be communicated in a clear, concise and constructive way. This usually entails the auditee being given initial verbal feedback on the results of the audit, followed by a draft report for management comment. Where recommendations are made, management action will be agreed with the auditee. Internal audit will periodically follow up agreed management actions to ensure they have been implemented.

Annual report

Throughout the year, internal audit will report progress on its planned work to the audit committee. Shortly after the financial year end, internal audit will prepare an annual report on its preceding year's work and will provide an overall opinion on the organization's control environment. This will form an important source of assurance for those senior managers in the organization who are responsible for making a statement on internal control and governance arrangements as part of their annual report.

Graham Smith

Related entries

Accountability; Chief officers; External audit; Probation boards.

Key texts and sources

The work of internal audit should be visible through the minutes of the audit committee in each probation area and available on its website. The National Audit Office website is at **http://www.nao.org.uk**, and the Audit Commission website is at **http://www.audit-commission.gov.uk**.

INTERPRETING AND TRANSLATION

Interpreting is the transfer of meaning of what is said in one language into speech in a second language. Sign-language interpreters transfer meaning between the signed and spoken modes. Translation is the transfer of meaning of a text written in one language into the written form of a second language.

Increasingly, probation officers are required to deal with offenders and other service users who may have little or no command of English. Where there is any doubt as to the adequacy of a shared language, a qualified impartial interpreter should be called or, where necessary, a translator. Relatives, children and friends should not be used.

Legal interpreting and translating requires proven:

- graduate-equivalent (level 6) written and spoken competence in both languages;
- skills to transfer meaning accurately between those languages;
- understanding of the procedures, processes and terminology of the legal services;
- adherence to a code of conduct that includes confidentiality and impartiality and that precludes the interpreter/translator from giving his or her own advice or opinion; and
- security clearance at the appropriate levels.

The Probation Service is a signatory to the National Agreement on Arrangements for the Attendance of Interpreters in Investigations and Proceedings within the Criminal Justice System. Natural justice should require the same standards to apply in civil proceedings, such as family work. The agreement sets out standards and procedures and requires criminal justice system agencies to aim to engage only interpreters from the National Register of Public Service Interpreters (NRPSI) or the Council for Communication with Deaf People (CACDP) directory, or the equivalent.

To work successfully with interpreters, probation staff should ensure a language match; brief the interpreters in advance on the subject matter; express themselves clearly and unambiguously; and accommodate the interpreting process, including speed and audibility. Technology such as telephone and video interpreting, as opposed to face-to-face interpreting, should only be used with a full understanding of any limitations of those methods in relation to the particular task. Translators should also be briefed and given adequate time to do their job and access to a staff member to consult in case clarification is needed.

Inevitably, where interpreters and translators are needed, staff will be working across cultures. Probation staff should inform themselves of, and keep in mind, the relevant starting points of the individual service users. Staff should take care to give more information to non-English speakers about the service and procedures to enable those clients to understand their situation fully. Case records and assessments should include relevant cultural and language aspects.

Legal interpreters and translators work on a freelance, sessional basis. There are national guidelines as to engagement arrangements, including fees, expenses and subsistence, cancellation and insurance. These should be set out and confirmed in writing in advance on each occasion.

The suitable deployment of interpreters and translators, where a sequence of events can be predicted and perhaps the engagement of the same interpreter for one individual, makes matters run more smoothly.

Ann Corsellis

Related entries

Diversity; Responsivity.

Key texts and sources

http://www.cps.gov.uk/legal/section16/chapter_ c.html#_Toc44729560
http://www.iol.org.uk/nrpsi
http://www.iol.org.uk/qualifications
http://www.cacdp.org.uk.

The revised CJS National Agreement, on the arrangements for the engagement of interpreters, was published in January 2007, and is available online at http://police.homeoffice.gov.uk/news-and-publications/publication/operational-policing/national-agreement-interpret.pdf

INTERVENTIONS

Interventions are structured and planned pieces of work whose purpose may be punishment, rehabilitation or public protection. They include, for example, the delivery of accredited programmes, curfews with electronic monitoring and unpaid work. Interventions are delivered by trained, qualified staff in a way that models good behaviour and positive relationships, and that is sensitive to the way in which offenders learn.

The work done to assess offenders and plan their sentences is part of offender management. The boundary between offender management and interventions is not clear-cut, and different probation areas may draw the boundaries in different ways. The 'grey' area arises because good offender management arrangements are not purely administrative but help integrate and extend the learning of the various interventions. Some work, such as helping offenders to access housing or employment (see Employment, training and education (ETE); Supporting people), motivational work or specialist assessments, may be delivered as an intervention or as offender management.

A single intervention on its own is unlikely to bring about a reduction in reoffending: a holistic approach that integrates interventions and offender management is more likely to do so.

Interventions have been designed to meet the needs of the court for punishment (unpaid work and curfew) and in response to the range of needs displayed by offenders which, evidence suggests, are linked to offending. They are central to the overall aim of reducing reoffending and protecting the public. The current range of interventions was developed as part of the 'what works' (effective practice) initiative launched in 1998.

The portfolio of interventions is closely linked to factors identified in the offender assessment system, OASys. OASys considers a range of risk factors that research has demonstrated are closely linked to risk of reconviction (criminogenic needs). They fall into two broad groups. The first are needs associated with the wider environment, such as housing and employability, where the offender's prospects are influenced by local and national trends. The second includes aspects of the offender's personality, attitudes and behaviours, such as thoughtless or impulsive behaviour, that are linked to offending. These factors not only contribute to offending but are also often the underlying reasons for difficulties in many other areas of life.

The principles that underpin evidence-based practice

The following principles underpin evidence-based practice:

- *Risk principle*: the degree of intervention required in each case should be related to an assessment of the risk of reoffending and the risk of serious harm.
- *Needs principle*: the intervention in each case should be targeted on those personal and social factors which are assessed as being likely to cause reoffending.
- *Responsivity principle*: the intervention should be based on methods which are demonstrably effective in reducing offending, and which are responsive to the culture, gender and learning styles of individual offenders.

Rehabilitation should include work on accommodation, employment, basic skills, attitudes,

cognitive skills, mental health, and drugs and alcohol, which is intended to reintegrate the offender into the community.

Equality of opportunity requires provision of a full range of interventions designed to meet the risk/needs profile of each region throughout England and Wales, with each intervention delivered to a consistently high standard. Interventions should be accessible to all offenders regardless of factors such as gender, race, sexual orientation and disability (see Diversity) and, as a minimum, should meet legislative expectations.

Interventions should be subject to evaluation, including using data from audits and OASys assessments, to demonstrate effectiveness in relation to stated objectives; this in turn will ensure confidence in the interventions provided to protect the public (public protection), to reduce reoffending and to support the rehabilitation of offenders.

Critical success factors

The development and delivery of interventions are guided by research findings that highlight the following critical success factors:

- Strong offender management – the offender management model highlights the importance of assessment, targeting, preparation and motivation.
- The close integration of offender management and interventions and other partnerships.
- Quality assurance, especially with regard to staff, delivery and tackling attrition.
- Integrating work inside and outside prisons.
- Equity of provision.
- Review and evaluation.

The principal interventions

Enhanced community punishment (ECP as it was then known) was provisionally accredited by the Correctional Services Accreditation Panel in 2003 and rolled out nationally from 2004 onwards. The term ECP has been replaced by 'unpaid work' in line with the requirements of the Criminal Justice Act 2003. Over five million hours of unpaid work are carried out by offenders each year in close co-operation with the local community. The work may be made visible by the use of a plaque bearing the words 'Community Payback' and the restorative justice logo.

Curfews backed by electronic monitoring are commissioned centrally by the National Offender Management Service and delivered by private sector contractors. Employment interventions are often delivered in partnership with local employers and Job Centre Plus. Education interventions are now provided by the Offenders' Learning and Skills Service (OLASS), which is funded by the Learning and Skills Council, but probation is heavily involved in assessment, motivation and referral.

Approved premises are for convicted offenders or persons on bail, for whom no other type of accommodation would be suitable. They provide an enhanced level of supervision to reduce the risk of harm to the public. Intensive interventions are combinations of the requirements contained in the Criminal Justice Act 2003 community order. They are particularly appropriate for prolific and other priority offenders (PPOs) and for substance abusers who have committed more serious offences, and they frequently include a requirement for drug or alcohol treatment.

Finally, offending behaviour programmes (accredited programmes) are evidence-based, cognitive behavioural programmes that are accredited by the Correctional Services Accreditation Panel. They are designed to reduce reoffending by helping offenders to learn new skills that improve the way in which they think and solve problems. They help them to cope with pressure, to consider the consequences of their actions, to see things from the perspective of others and to act less impulsively.

Sarah Mann

Related entries

Criminogenic needs; Offender management; Rehabilitation.

Key texts and sources

Burnett, R., Baker, K. and Roberts, C. (2007) 'Assessment, supervision and intervention: fundamental practice in probation', in L. Gelsthorpe and R. Morgan (eds) *Handbook of Probation.* Cullompton: Willan Publishing.

NPD (2005) *Interventions: A Guide to Interventions in the National Probation Service* (NPD/010/2005) (available on line at **http://www.probation. homeoffice.gov.uk**).

Underdown, A. (1998) *Strategies for Effective Offender Supervision.* London: HMIP.

J

JUDGES

Persons appointed to preside over the superior courts. They are significant to probation staff because of their sentencing duties and their membership of probation boards.

All judges in the superior courts in England and Wales are appointed by the Queen on the recommendation of the Lord Chief Justice, who is advised by the Judicial Appointments Group.

Judges in the Crown court fall into three categories:

1. *High court judges*: known formally as Mr/Mrs Justice Smith, these are addressed as My Lord or My Lady and are authorized to try all categories of crime. They wear predominantly red robes.
2. *Circuit judges*: known formally as His/Her Honour Judge Smith, these are addressed as Your Honour. They wear blue robes with purple facings and a red sash.
3. *Recorders*: part-time judges known formally as Mr/Mrs Recorder Smith. They are also addressed as Your Honour. They wear black barristers' or solicitors' robes.

Both circuit judges and recorders are entitled to try all minor Crown court crime, and are individually authorized to try more serious categories, sometimes including murder. Appeals from magistrates' courts are heard by a Crown court judge accompanied by lay magistrates.

The role of Crown court judges is to conduct trials, together with a jury of 12 members of the public, and to sentence those who have been convicted or have pleaded guilty, as well as conducting administrative tasks to ensure the proper management of cases. Each court centre will have a resident judge, who will be a circuit judge appointed to be in overall charge of case management for that court centre. He or she will be subject to the overall control of the presiding judge of the circuit, who will be one of the high court judges.

Appeals from the Crown court to the Court of Appeal will be heard by three judges, presided over by a lord/lady justice of appeal, sitting in the Royal Courts of Justice in London. The other members will either be high court or circuit judges. The Court of Appeal has the power, on appeal against conviction, to allow the appeal, dismiss it or allow it and order a new trial. On appeal against sentence they may dismiss the appeal, allow it and decrease the sentence, or (in serious cases only, and on the Attorney General's reference) increase the sentence.

At the present a local circuit judge will be designated by the Lord Chief Justice to be a member of the local probation board. The role of this judge is not only to be a full-time member of the board and to participate in all its meetings and training but also to act as a liaison between local probation services and the local courts centre(s). This position is particularly useful in promoting smooth working relationships between probation and judges, in informing the courts of the availability and practicalities of available sentences, and in improving the punctuality and availability of pre-sentence reports and the onward provision of information.

His Honour Judge Teare

Related entries

Court work; Magistrates.

Key texts and sources

Pannick, D. (1987) *Judges*. Oxford: Oxford University Press.

http://www.bbc.co.uk/crime/fighters/crowncourt.shtml.

L

LEARNING DISABILITIES

The World Health Organization defines learning disability as 'a state of arrested or incomplete development of mind'. It involves significant impairment of intellectual and social functioning. These impairments are present from childhood, not acquired as a result of accident or adult illness.

Between 1.2 and 2 million people in the UK may have a learning disability. People with learning disabilities may have difficulties understanding, learning and remembering new things, and in generalizing any learning to new situations. They may therefore have difficulties with a number of social tasks (for example, communication, self-care, awareness of health and safety).

The words 'mild', 'moderate', 'severe' and 'profound' (linking to IQ test scores) are commonly used alongside learning disability, but the level of support people need to live their lives is more/as important as the label given to their level of impairment.

Terms in legislation have very specific legal meanings, which will not always correspond with 'clinical' definitions. Someone who fits the definition for one piece of legislation may not be covered by another piece of legislation. Terms like 'defective', 'mental handicap' and 'learning difficulty' are all found in law.

People with learning disabilities may become involved in offending because of the following factors:

- Inadequate/faulty socialization skills.
- Impaired self-control.
- An inability to resist temptation.
- Naivety or gullibility.

- Lack of understanding of social norms – often aggravated by the reluctance of caregivers to deal appropriately with offending behaviour.
- Immature sexuality or disinhibited sexual behaviour.
- An inability to manage finances.
- Low self-esteem/poor self-image.
- An inability adequately/appropriately to express emotions – affection, dissent, anger or frustration.

Approximately 6 per cent of the people on community orders (supervised by probation staff) have a learning disability (Mason and Murphy 2002). While realizing that many of their procedures need adapting for this particular client group, probation staff often feel unsure about which of their clients have learning disabilities, feel uncertain how to help people with learning disabilities and often do not have good contact with local community learning disability teams.

Many accredited programmes are not suitable for people with learning disabilities and few adapted programmes are available in the Probation Service (an exception is the Sex Offender Treatment Programme, which is now being adapted for men with learning disabilities).

Probation areas should:

- have a system of screening for learning disabilities (which many people cover up);
- take account of learning disabilities in pre-sentence reports, in assessment and in supervision;
- adapt their procedures – for example, make letters and information leaflets accessible;
- adapt programmes;
- have good contact with community learning disability teams to enable referrals for assessment or other help, perhaps including co-working; and

- consider developing contractual partnerships with specialist services to support them in offering equal treatment options, more suited to the specific needs of people with an intellectual impairment.

Alan Martin

Related entries

Accredited programmes; Anti-discriminatory practice; Dyslexia; Responsivity.

Key texts and sources

Mason, J. and Murphy, G. (2002) 'People with intellectual disabilities on probation: an initial study', *Journal of Community and Applied Social Psychology*, 12: 44–55

See the websites of the British Institute of Learning Disability (**www.bild.org.uk**), the Valuing People Support Team (**www.valuingpeople.gov.uk**) and the Care and Treatment of Offenders with a Learning Disability (**www.ldoffenders.co.uk**).

LEARNING STYLES

Learning styles have been characterized as the different approaches preferred by different individuals in learning environments. Staff delivering interventions in probation must have regard to the offender's learning style. This idea is closely related to the concept of responsivity.

Learning styles came into regular usage in probation as an integral part of the 'what works' agenda and were included among the criteria underpinning programme accreditation. While there was acknowledgement that offenders could have various learning styles, US and Canadian research and Home Office studies in the late 1990s indicated that most offenders displayed activist learning styles. This categorization drew on Honey and Mumford's work, activists being one of four identified learning styles (i.e. activists, reflectors, theorists and pragmatists). This classification had implications for matching learning styles to appropriate interventions: activists are considered to respond best to practical, participatory approaches. The rationale underlying such work with offenders was to integrate abstract thinking skills and prosocial values into a problem-solving process that would facilitate engagement and change offenders' behaviour.

Here, probation mirrored developments in other areas: learning style models were, for example, widely adopted in education, and these trends found political support. However, a comprehensive review of the evidence base of learning styles published by the Learning and Skills Research Centre in 2004 voiced important provisos about the research foundations and practical applications of such approaches. There were criticisms relating to the theoretical frameworks and the robustness of the research evidence of the two main models used in probation – Kolb's 'learning cycle' and Honey and Mumford's 'learning styles', particularly in connection with their use in real-life settings. These findings pose concerns in view of the lack of in-depth scrutiny of these aspects in probation. Moreover, there should be caution about the potential overextension of learning styles in work with offenders: there is a danger of labelling, together with associated problems of stereotyping, and the risk of reinforcing detrimental experiences that many offenders may have undergone in earlier learning situations.

Notwithstanding these negative aspects, learning styles can provide a framework for discussion about change and can foster a sense of constructive engagement between staff and individual offenders in structured probation interventions. Nevertheless, at this point it appears that the evidence base may be more fragile than was originally envisaged, and these concerns thus demand that rigorous, ongoing evaluation should be carried out concerning their use within probation.

Jill Annison

Related entries

Accredited programmes; Responsivity.

Key texts and sources

Annison, J. (2006) 'Style over substance: a review of the evidence base for the use of learning styles in probation', *Criminology and Criminal Justice*, 6: 239–57.

Coffield, F., Moseley, D., Hall, E. and Ecclestone, K. (2004) *Should we be Using Learning Styles? What Research has to Say to Practice*. London: Learning and Skills Research Centre (available online at http://www.lsrc.ac.uk/publications/index.asp).

LEGITIMACY

The word legitimacy comes from the Latin word *legitimare*, and its main use is to indicate whether or not people accept the validity of a law or ruling or the validity of a governing regime or other kind of authority.

In the context of criminology and criminal justice, the concept of legitimacy is often used to describe whether or not an action is perceived to be valid and acceptable. For example, in meeting their responsibilities, legal and criminal justice authorities often rely on strategies that, explicitly or implicitly, are guided by a deterrent philosophy, aiming to compel compliance via a threat, or the actual implementation, of sanctions. But deterrence alone has proven ineffective in ensuring compliance and co-operation with legal authorities. Rather, it has been observed that compliance can be explained by a number of reasons – 'moral as well as prudential, normative as well as self-interested' (Beetham 1991: 27). In this way, compliance and co-operation with legal authorities are as much based on perceptions of *moral legitimacy* as they are on rational calculations of potential risks of sanctions.

The concept of the legitimacy of an authority system has a long history. A number of theorists – among them Plato and Aristotle – implicitly touched on various aspects. Its contemporary usage in criminological discourse and in the social sciences more generally is often identified with the seminal work of Max Weber. Weber argues that 'the basis of every authority, and correspondingly of every kind of willingness to obey, is a *belief*, a belief by virtue of which persons exercising authority are lent prestige' (1968: 263). A structure of domination that is considered legitimate is therefore seen to be more stable and can be exercised more efficiently.

Attempting to map out the multifaceted structure of legitimacy, Beetham maintains that we can identify a general structure that underpins legitimacy in all societies – both past and present – though the specific content of this structure is historically and culturally variable. This structure, he argues, has three qualitatively distinct elements, each operating at different levels. The first element is legal validity. This is rule derived and requires power to be acquired and exercised in conformity with the established rules of the society in question. Power acquired in this way bestows on the holder the right to exercise it and obliges subordinates to acknowledge and respect it. Thus, within the context of the police, Reiss observes that any legitimate claim to intervene in the affairs of individuals is beyond question only when this is done legally – legality that 'rests in the constitutional law and in substantive and procedural law' (1971: 2). The acquisition and exercise of power in accordance with rules, however, constitute provisional and therefore insufficient grounds for legitimacy. There is the need for further justification by looking beyond legality. This brings us to the second element – the justifiability of power in terms of the shared beliefs of the society in which it is exercised.

This element requires that rules are themselves rooted in the moral consensus or a society's 'common framework of beliefs' (Beetham 1991: 69). It is important for those who wield power to have moral authority and to be able to justify it by moral considerations that transcend the power itself. This requires that power be recognized as furtherance of the collective good of society rather than the interests of the powerful. Issues of fairness, respect and probity in the exercise of authority are all obvious normative expectations here, the absence of which may affect the legitimacy of authority and power. For example, if the police are seen as capricious and biased in the exercise of their authority through, for instance, discriminating against particular minority ethnic groups, their legitimacy would be impugned. It also involves the exercise of authority within limits prescribed by the moral consensus. These limits, argues Beetham, impose obligations on the public and define the reciprocal duties, obligations and behaviour of those who wield power (what they can and cannot legitimately demand from the public) and public expectations of them. So, if 'legitimate power is limited power' (Beetham 1991: 35), it is crucial that, in maintaining authority, the powerful respect these limits and do not breach them with impunity by making new or additional demands and obligations on the public without their consent. Police corruption and prison officer brutality would be clear examples of violation of those limits.

The third element of the structure of legitimacy involves demonstrable expression of public consent to the power relationship in which they are involved. To give consent is 'to recognize the government's right to issue commands and to assume a duty to obey them' (Alagappa 1995: 23). The grounds for believing that there is consent vary from apathy, coercion and self-interest, of course. A legitimacy-based model of compliance thus involves securing long-term public subjective commitments and it is important to understand the socio-political circumstances under which such consent to authority is given.

These three elements together constitute necessary conditions which every authority or power must meet to be deemed fully legitimate. When fully met, they provide not only 'a set of general criteria for legitimacy' (Beetham 1991: 21) but also moral grounds for obligation to comply and co-operate with the powerful.

By the very nature of their work, legal and criminal justice authorities (such as the police, Crown Prosecution Service, probation and prison authorities) are deemed to be authority structures which, while in constant need of legitimacy, equally risk squandering it. There are concerns about the quality of police–public relations, for example, and the implication of the latter's subjective evaluations of the legitimacy of the former for co-operative and compliant

behaviour. The police thus aim to gain the trust and confidence of the public to make their work less difficult. This is especially critical in the light of the evidence that the police alone are ineffective and that they require public co-operation as much as a multi-agency approach. Roberts and Hough suggest that, without legitimacy, 'the police wield power but command no authority; without authority they must police by force rather than by *consent*' (2005: 53).

Equally, strategies to ensure order in prisons might work best where actions are seen as legitimate. Sparks and Bottoms (1995) have convincingly argued for issues of legitimacy to be taken seriously in accounting for the outbreak of disorder in prisons. They suggest that prisoners' perceptions of the fairness of procedures, of the consistency of outcomes and of the quality of the behaviour of staff are important. When prisoners perceive the institutional structure of the prison and the authority of prison officers as legitimate in this sense, then they would be more inclined towards law-abiding behaviour. In probation and offender management, too, fairness is likely to be an important element of the perceived legitimacy of attempts to engage offenders.

Tyler's work on procedural fairness represents an important contribution to the legitimacy renaissance in criminology. Tyler's argument, supported by robust empirical evidence, is that people are concerned much more about the quality of the treatment and decision-making they receive from authorities than they are about a favourable outcome. He argues that this independently shapes people's law-abiding behaviour.

Research by McIvor (1992) on community service orders in Scotland linked meaningfulness, legitimacy and effectiveness by suggesting that there was an association between the degree to which offenders saw the unpaid work as worthwhile and lower rates of reconviction. Generally, the legitimacy of probation officers derives not only from legal authority but also from the manner in which they undertake their work – not least the capacity of the officer to form a good relationship and represent the requirements placed on the offender as just, relevant and valuable. Gelsthorpe (2001) has argued that, in this context, accommodation of diversity is a critical aspect of legitimacy, which not only promotes the effectiveness of intervention through attention to responsivity but also ultimately enhances the prospects for compliance and citizenship since it reflects ethicality and respect for offenders.

Justice Tankebe and Loraine Gelsthorpe

Related entries

Compliance; Diversity.

Key texts and sources

Alagappa, M. (1995) 'Anatomy of legitimacy', in M. Alagappa (ed.) *Political Legitimacy in South East Asia: The Quest for Moral Authority.* Stanford, CA: Stanford University Press.

Beetham, D. (1991) *The Legitimation of Power.* London: Macmillan.

Gelsthorpe, L. (2001) 'Accountability: difference and diversity in the delivery of community penalties', in A.E. Bottoms *et al.* (eds) *Community Penalties: Change and Challenges.* Cullompton: Willan Publishing.

Gelsthorpe, L. (2007) 'Probation values and human rights', in L. Gelsthorpe and R. Morgan (eds) *Handbook of Probation.* Cullompton: Willan Publishing.

McIvor, G. (1992) *Sentenced to Serve.* Aldershot: Gower.

Reiss, A.J. (1971) *The Police and the Public.* New Haven, CT: Yale University Press.

Roberts, J. and Hough, J.M. (2005) *Understanding Public Attitudes to Criminal Justice.* Maidenhead: Open University Press.

Sparks, J.R. and Bottoms, A.E. (1995) 'Legitimacy and order in prisons', *British Journal of Sociology*, 46: 45–62.

Tyler, T. (2003) 'Procedural justice, legitimacy and the effective rule of law', in M. Tonry (ed.) *Crime and Justice: A Review of Research. Volume 30.* Chicago, IL: University of Chicago Press.

Weber, M. (1968) *Economy and Society: An Outline of Interpretative Sociology* (ed. G. Roth and C. Wittich). New York, NY: Bedminster Press.

LESBIANS AND GAY MEN IN PROBATION (LAGIP)

LAGIP is the National Probation Service LGBT (lesbian, gay, bisexual and transgendered) staff association.

LAGIP was originally set up for lesbian and gay men. Hence the name: Lesbians and Gay men in probation. It extended its membership to include transgendered and bisexual individuals at the 2002 annual general meeting in Manchester.

Full membership is open to all LGBT employees in probation, the National Offender Management Service (NOMS) and the Children and Family Court Advisory Support Service (CAFCASS). Retired/former members can remain as associates, and others who support the aims and objectives but do not qualify for full membership can be honorary members.

Its objectives are to:

- ensure that LGBT issues are addressed at national and local levels;
- ensure that no LGBT staff or service users are disadvantaged owing to their sexual orientation or gender identity;
- provide an effective formal and informal support network for LGBT staff;
- increase awareness of LGBT issues; and
- work with the National Probation Service, the National Probation Directorate and the NOMS to take forward diversity policies and strategies.

As well as informal support at meetings, conferences, annual general meetings, etc., and from contacts and friendships established at those events, LAGIP is able to provide more formal support for members who may be encountering difficulties. This can include meetings with senior managers in areas and briefings for colleagues. In extreme cases, LAGIP can support members and help to brief union representatives in the event of grievances.

Helen Dale

Related entries

Diversity; Heterosexism; Transgender.

Key texts and sources

The LAGIP website (**www.lagip.com**) provides contact details and more information about its activities, including the annual conference.

LICENCE

A document authorizing the early release of a prisoner and setting out the requirements to be followed by the offender in the community.

Release on licence forms the community supervision part of custodial sentences. The Criminal Justice Act 2003 and the Carter Report set out to create a situation where all custodial sentences had both custodial and community supervision components. They were to be experienced as 'seamless sentences' with 'end to end' offender management. Some aspects of this vision are unlikely to be implemented for resource reasons.

Young prisoners (up to the age of 21 when sentenced) are released on a three-month notice of supervision, regardless of the length of the custodial sentence. Those sentenced to 12 months and over, and all indeterminate sentence prisoners, are released on a form of licence until the end of the sentence. They are on a licence which requires them to keep to very specific conditions until the three-quarter point of their sentence, and then on an 'at risk' notice until the full term has expired, reminding them of the penalty if they reoffend. In the case of sex offenders and violent offenders, the court can extend the period of licence for public protection reasons.

Normally, offenders are automatically released on licence halfway through the sentence. Where the sentence is over four years or indeterminate, the parole board and the Home Secretary can authorize release on licence.

Six standard conditions are applied to all licences. Further licence conditions can be individualized to meet the needs of the case. Almost all licences require the offender to report to the probation office on the day of release, and then as instructed afterwards. The licensee may be required to live at a specific address, and to observe a curfew and be subject to electronic monitoring. The offender may have to attend an accredited programme or undertake specific activities. The licence may identify prohibited activities, such as contacting victims or visiting certain areas.

The offender manager will use OASys to assess the risks and needs of the situation, and develop a supervision plan identifying the counselling, interventions and monitoring that will be carried out in the licence period.

If there is a breach of conditions, a warning will be given. After two warnings or earlier if the situation is serious, enforcement action will be taken on breach. In cases where there is a serious risk to the public, the recall process can be very swift and, with good police collaboration, a dangerous person can be rearrested and recalled within an hour of the matter first being reported.

Licence supervision can provide significant support at a time of vulnerability and assist with resettlement and rehabilitation. Often initial reluctance ('I've done my bird') has to be dealt with. However, once expectations have been clarified and accepted, the sense of progress can be incremental as the offender begins to gain confidence in his or her ability to achieve his or her aims in the community through a law-abiding lifestyle.

David Hancock

Related entries

Enforcement; Parole board; Public protection; Reintegration; Resettlement; Victim contact.

Key texts and sources

Prison Service Order 4400 (available online at **www.hmprisonservice.gov.uk/resourcecentre/ psispsos/listpsos/index.asp?startrow=51**).

LIFERS

Prisoners who are sentenced to life imprisonment – a liability to be detained for life though, in practice, almost all prisoners so sentenced are released on licence. In February 2006, there were 6,088 prisoners serving life in England and Wales – more than in the all the other member countries of the European Union combined.

The sentence of life imprisonment entails a liability to be detained for life. Since the abolition of the death penalty, life is the only sentence available to the court for the offence of murder; successive home secretaries have resisted proposals to allow courts more discretion in these circumstances, insisting that the unique gravity of this offence must be marked. Other grave offences can also attract a life sentence. Life is also commonly used not so much as a retributive punishment but to maximize public protection by detention until release is thought not to pose undue risk to public safety. (The legal provisions for indeterminate sentencing for public protection have been amended by the Criminal Justice Act 2003, ss. 224 and following.) (See also Extended sentencing.)

How long a time is actually served before release on licence depends on a number of considerations. At the time of sentence, a 'tariff date' is set – a judicial decision which specifies how long must be served to meet the requirements of justice and deterrence. The tariff date, however, is a *minimum* term, and lifers are commonly released considerably over this tariff.

Lifers are subject to a specific form of sentence planning called the 'life sentence plan' (LSP), which is reviewed annually. Probation officers from inside and outside the prison may attend the LSP board. Depending on the level of assessed risk, lifers will pass through 'stages' of their sentence and progress through less secure prisons until deemed suitable for 'escorted absences' in preparation for release. Within this LSP structure every lifer's experience of prison and sentence planning is as individual as they are.

It is important not to overlook the distinct position of women offenders here: though just a small minority in the overall lifer population, women experience the prison system, and partic-

ularly a life sentence, differently from males, not least often because of separation from children or the loss of 'child bearing' years. Self-harm, attempted suicide and mental health issues are more commonplace in the female estate, and this has implication for the management, care and supervision of female life-sentenced prisoners.

Lifers are over-represented among older prisoners and, on eventual release, may return into a very different world from the one they left. Currency, scenery and fashion are likely to be different. They may have lost contact with family and friends because of time or even through death. Children will have grown up and moved away.

All lifers are released under probation supervision and will always be subject to life licence. Active supervision may eventually be suspended, but in all cases the possibility of recall to prison remains.

Being sentenced to life imprisonment brings with it unique feelings and experiences. Prisoners serving even long determinate sentences (despite many uncertainties) know, as do their families, that there is a date when they must be released. A life sentence brings no such certainty. Prisoners facing this prospect react in complex ways and commonly go through stages – from denial (of the offence and its consequences), withdrawal, frustration, rage and disappointment. Accepting responsibility for a grave crime inevitably occasions overwhelming guilt and distress. These emotions make unusual demands on those working with them throughout their sentence.

Lucy Baldwin and Rob Canton

Related entries

Extended sentencing; Licence; Older offenders; Public protection.

Key texts and sources

Parker, T. (1991) *Life after Life.* London: Pan.
Prison Reform Trust (2004) *England and Wales: Europe's Lifer Capital* (available online at http://www.prisonreformtrust.org.uk/subsection.asp?id=352).
Go to http://www.hmprisonservice.gov.uk/adviceandsupport/prison_life/ and follow the link to 'Life sentenced prisoners'. See also http://noms.homeoffice.gov.uk/managing-offenders/sentences/3727962/Life-sentences/.

LOCAL AUTHORITIES

> Elected bodies at parish, district, unitary authority or county level responsible for the provision of certain public services.

With the inception of the National Probation Service, the need for a close relationship between probation and the local authorities based on support services ceased. Probation boards reflected the importance of good links with local authority services by having councillor members.

The Crime and Disorder Act 1998 put the local authorities at the centre of the alliances needed for community safety and crime prevention. Further legislation has strengthened this position, especially the drive against anti-social behaviour. The management of the youth offending team is the responsibility of the chief executive of the local authority and, in practice, a multi-agency team of managers carries out the detailed work. The Crime and Disorder Reduction Partnerships, the drug action teams and the child protection and supporting people systems are structures where probation and local authority staff work together on common agendas.

Probation staff rely on good relationships with local authority services for the access offenders need to services valuable in diminishing the risk of reoffending. Housing, education and social services are where the main links lie. In many cases there are formalized arrangements for the regulation of work between probation staff and local authority services.

Until the formation of the National Probation Service in 2001, the local authorities were significant partners for probation services in other ways. County councils and unitary authorities were required to act as the 'paying authority' for the probation committees, and in this role they had to fund the approved expenditure. The county councils generally provided support services, including the secretary and treasurer to the committees. Experience of this varied. In some counties the Probation Service prospered and grew. Some county councils saw the Probation Service as a good community investment and, with an 80 per cent rebate, it was seen as an affordable and cost-effective investment. In other areas there was a reluctance to finance developments.

In a few significant urban areas the local authority used the probation committee as a vehicle for managing new investments under urban renewal schemes. Probation was seen as politically neutral in sensitive communities, and it was thought that projects run by probation would be owned and used by the local residents. Consequently, in the West Midlands, for example, ground-breaking schemes such as the Motor Sports Park in Bordesley, the Cultural Centre in Handsworth and the Black Arts Centre in Moseley were established and run by the Probation Service. Such tasks would not be seen as within the remit of probation today.

David Hancock

Related entries

Community safety; Crime and Disorder Reduction Partnerships.

Key texts and sources

Each local authority publishes an annual report, which is usually available on its website. The Local Government Association publishes a wide range of relevant books and publications (**www.lga.gov.uk**).

M

MACPHERSON REPORT

A public inquiry led by Sir William Macpherson into the police investigation of the murder of Stephen Lawrence. It highlighted police racism and identified and defined 'institutional racism'.

In 1993 a black teenager, Stephen Lawrence, was murdered in London by a group of five young white men. In spite of the fact that these young men are all known, none has been convicted. Stephen's parents mounted a campaign of criticism about the police investigation of their son's death. A number of internal police investigations of these complaints, culminating in a report by the Police Complaints Authority, identified faults in the investigation. However, none satisfied the fundamental complaint that the offence was racially motivated and that the investigation was flawed by racism on the part of the Metropolitan Police.

The incoming Labour government in 1997 immediately commissioned an independent public inquiry under the chairmanship of Sir William Macpherson. The inquiry sat in two phases, the first looking at the murder and its investigation, the second at the general issues. Phase one was conducted in a judicial style with formal hearings, legal representation, examination and cross-examination. It achieved significant publicity, particularly when police witnesses and the five men suspected of Stephen's murder appeared.

The second phase was more informal and travelled around the country inviting written and oral evidence from any interested bodies and individuals. The Association of Chief Officers of Probation was one of the bodies making written submission and attending one of the inquiry's open meetings.

The report was published early in 1999 and made an immediate impact. The most significant of the report's findings was that the conduct of the Metropolitan Police in the investigation of the murder amounted to 'institutional racism'. This was defined as:

the collective failure of an organization to provide an appropriate and professional service to people because of their colour, culture or ethnic origin. It can be seen or detected in the processes, attitudes and behaviour which amount to discrimination through unwitting prejudice, ignorance, thoughtlessness and racist stereotyping which disadvantage minority ethnic people.

This complex concept had the immediate effect of enabling the Metropolitan Police to accept and work with a criticism of racism. Other public organizations, including probation, quickly followed suit. Central government began to promote or impose this definition on its own departments and other public sector organizations. Clearly Macpherson had shifted the ground from racism as an individual to an organizational issue.

Alongside the definition of 'institutional racism', Macpherson also produced a definition of a 'racist incident', clarifying previous definitions. This immediately became prescribed for use in all public sector organizations and has meant that all data are now comparable.

The report contained more than 70 other recommendations addressed primarily to the police and local authorities. These were all accepted by central government and have been required practice since. The lasting impact of Macpherson is not in these details but in the shift in understanding of institutional racism and in opening the door to specific offences of racially aggravated crime.

John Kay

Related entries

Hate crime; Race and racism; Racially motivated offenders.

Key texts and sources

Macpherson, Sir W. (1999) *Report of an Inquiry by Sir William Macpherson of Cluny Advised by Tom Cook, the Right Reverend Dr John Sentamu, Dr Richard Stone, Presented to Parliament by the Secretary of State for the Home Department by Command of Her Majesty* (the Stephen Lawrence Inquiry) (Cm 4262-I). London: HMSO (especially Chapter 6). www.archive.official-documents.co.uk/document/cm42/4262/4262.htm.

MAGISTRATES

Persons appointed to preside over lower courts. They are significant to probation staff because of sentencing duties and membership of probation boards.

In dealing with over 95 per cent of criminal cases in England and Wales, magistrates have a key role to play in the criminal justice system, and have had for centuries. Magistrates are ordinary people, drawn from the local community, giving up their time and deemed to have the key qualities necessary to deal with offenders 'without fear, favour, affection or ill-will'.

The bench, as they are collectively known, will comprise equal numbers of men and women aged between 18 and 70, representatives of black and minority ethnic communities, employed or self-employed people from a wide variety of businesses and organizations, the retired and unemployed, etc. Diverse as every bench should be, when they come together to sit in court as tribunals of three people, they have a consistent structure to follow and sentencing guidelines to enable them to act as consistently as possible.

Some of the magistrates' courts are presided over by district judges. Formerly known as stipendiary magistrates, they sit alone in court and have backgrounds as professional lawyers. They often preside over the courts with a very heavy workload, or over legally complex trials. In busy urban areas, district judges become well known to the probation staff who work in court because they handle a large proportion of the cases where pre-sentence reports are requested.

The media are quick to criticize, but magistrates always work within the law, giving reasons for their decisions. Outcomes may not please everyone, but the appeal rate against magistrates' decisions is very low (less than 3 per cent), with less than 40 per cent of their decisions changed by the appeal court.

As a team of three, magistrates work together to reach what they believe is the most appropriate way of dealing with the defendant(s) in the case. For the more serious cases, magistrates rely on probation staff to find out more information on offenders and to recommend programmes they believe would benefit the offender in stopping a pattern of reoffending. For the persistent offender, for whom almost everything has been tried, custody may be the only option. To deprive someone of his or her liberty, and sometimes his or her family and employment, is not the easy task some may think it is. All magistrates have visited at least one prison, and the constant sound of jingling keys and the relief on coming back into the outside world are memorable experiences for most.

With three or four years' experience on the bench, there are 'career options' for magistrates – they can go on to do specialist work, such as that of becoming a member of the local probation board. Magistrates are motivated by a genuine wish to contribute to their local communities and to help to make them safer and better places to live.

Ann Flintham

Related entries

Court work; Criminal justice system; Probation boards.

Key texts and sources

The Magistrates' Association website (**www.magistrates-association.org.uk**) provides a wide range of information about the work of magistrates.

MANAGERIALISM

> Managerialism refers to the ascendancy of business management values and priorities within the public sector, and the corresponding decline in the influence and value base of the professions.

The term 'managerialism' is closely associated with new public management (NPM), which has generally been described as representing a paradigm shift in the values and priorities in public sector organizations: from an essentially needs-driven approach to public policy and provision to one that is largely resource driven.

The roots of public sector managerialism lay in 'new right' politics, coming to prominence in the mid-1970s, which advocated business thinking and entrepreneurialism within government and public services to drive out waste and increase efficiency. Managerialism has passed its 'high point', but a strong legacy remains and, in some quarters, including probation, it is really only now that the full impacts of the associated value shift are beginning to be felt.

NPM is characterized by seven doctrines (Hood 1991):

1. *Hands-on professional management in the public sector*: sharper accountability through more 'active, visible control of organizations from named persons at the top' (Hood 1991: 4).
2. *Explicit standards and measures of performance*: the setting of clear goals and performance targets and more thorough monitoring of achievements.
3. *Greater emphasis on output controls*: more orientation to results and correspondingly less preoccupation with procedures and inputs.
4. *Shift to disaggregation of units*: breaking up monolithic bureaucracies into manageably sized units, each operating as distinct budget/cost centres.
5. *Shift to greater competition in the public sector*: more contracting and public tendering processes to use rivalry as a key to better standards and lower costs.
6. *Stress on private sector styles of management practice*: a shift from the traditional public service ethos, adoption of more flexibility in hiring and rewarding personnel, and adoption of other private sector methods to incentivize efficiency and effectiveness.
7. *Stress on greater discipline and parsimony in resource use*: strong emphasis on cost-cutting, stronger resistance to union demands, limitations on compliance costs and commitment to the ethic of value for money and 'doing more for less'.

The legacy of all seven trends is apparent in the developing Probation Service, particularly in the period since the creation of the National Probation Service. Under this new structure, the work of the Probation Service has become more standardized and more centrally driven by corporate management priorities – for example, through a common framework for performance management. One obvious example of the stress on private sector styles was the adoption by the National Directorate of a quality management model – the European Foundation for Quality Management (EFQM), derived from the widely applied 'business excellence model' in the commercial sector.

Increasingly, the senior echelons of the national service have changed from dominance by a professionally qualified cadre of career practitioners to encompass a diverse range of corporate resource management specialisms (e.g. in finance, human resources and IT). Performance management, together with the associated regimes of performance indicators, target-setting, monitoring and reporting, became the new 'drivers', and the local areas came under unprecedented pressure to 'deliver' on centrally determined priorities and business plans.

Managerialist values – particularly a concern for 'parsimony in resource use' – were also clearly reflected in the move to develop standardized methods for the risk assessment of offenders, and in the refocusing of practice to more serious offenders with an associated withdrawal of initiatives for less serious and first-time offenders. The proposal to amalgamate probation with the Prison Service to form a single 'correctional services' agency was managerially inspired, as were proposals to introduce 'contestability' into probation provision and to encourage the creation of a market for voluntary and independent providers to compete with the existing public sector. Lord Patrick Carter was appointed from the world of business (rather than criminal justice) to advise the government on how to reduce reoffending. The Carter Report in 2003 led directly to the decision to establish a new National Offender Management Service (NOMS), linking probation and prisons into a single organizational framework and introducing 'contestability' (Hood's 'market competition') to raise standards and lower costs.

The suitability of managerialism in probation and criminal justice remains contentious – not least because of ideological differences – while its impact, with so many other contemporary changes in criminal justice, is hard to evaluate. Much of the potentially positive impacts of New Labour's increased investment in probation were blunted by plummeting morale and the loss of the service's capacity to achieve everything expected of it; by the distraction and protracted uncertainty about organizational restructuring under the NOMS proposals; by the enforced shift in the culture and ethos of the service (with which most longer-serving practitioners profoundly disagreed); by the relentless public pillorying of the service by the more punitive-minded populist press; and by the uncompromising stance adopted by ministers in relation to their managerial reform proposals.

Hughes (2003) sees managerialism as an understandable reaction to a growing recognition of the shortcomings of traditional public bureaucratic-driven approaches to public provision. Arguing that governments and taxpayers would always want to be satisfied 'that public ends are being served in an efficient and effective manner', he has suggested that new managerialist values within the public sector have been valuable, not least in raising important questions about public service provision and the role of government:

Managerialism does not mean usurpation of government by technocrats, a reduction in accountability or a diminution of democracy. All the managerial changes do is allow for public purposes to be carried out in a more efficient, cost-effective way, by providing more and better information to those making decisions

(Hughes 2003: 79).

Perhaps so in general terms. But within the more specific context of criminal justice and probation, the legacy of managerialism so far seems altogether less positive. As the incoming Home Secretary, Dr John Reid MP, chose to describe his new department as 'not fit for purpose' and his Probation Service as 'not up to the job', the legacy of a decade and more of managerialist values and initiatives seemed to many observers anything but rosy.

John W Raine

Related entries

Contestability; Discretion; National Offender Management Service (NOMS); National Standards; Performance management.

Key texts and sources

Faulkner, D. (2006) *Crime, State and Citizen: A Field Full of Folk* (2nd edn). Chichester: Waterside Press.

Hood, C. (1991) 'A public management for all seasons', *Public Administration*, 69: 3–19.

Hughes, O. (2003) *Public Management and Administration* (3rd edn). Basingstoke: Macmillan.

McLaughlin, K., Osborne, S. and Ferlie, E. (eds) (2002) *New Public Management: Current Trends and Future Prospects*. London: Routledge.

Nellis, M. (2002) 'Community justice, time and the new National Probation Service', *Howard Journal of Criminal Justice*, 41: 59–86.

MASCULINITY AND OFFENDING

'Masculinity' can be understood simply as biological fact, but it is more helpful to think sociologically of masculinities conceived of as intersecting sets of ideas and/or practices which constitute the actor as masculine through the act, the 'doing', of one or more masculinities.

Offending is sometimes nothing more or less than the interactions between competing masculinities. Differences can be nuanced, such as those between rival gangs in 'drug wars'; others can be more fundamental. For example, in May

2006, two men were convicted of the 'homophobic' murder of a third man. These assailants were 'doing' their masculinity in attacking their victim for 'doing' his own (and it is not so long since the masculinity of the victim, a gay man, was officially constructed as criminogenic).

The dynamics underpinning such an attack seem to draw on not only the significance of the victim's commonality with his attackers – he is a man, just as they are – but also his difference from them, which, apparently, in some way pollutes their masculinity as much as his. Perhaps the assailants were simply affronted by the presence of a gay man but, for some, the masculine turn to violence (1) implies the fragility of the masculine power that is thereby put into play and (2) sees the threat as the contamination of masculinity by effeminacy, or the feminine. Since most men are mostly raised by women, femininity, as a set of caring practices, is the essential precondition for the existence of masculinity. But in a male-dominated culture this is unpalatable since it draws attention to the relations of dependency in which masculinities are implicated. The violent suppression of this perceived threat to the autonomy and superiority of the masculine is one consequence. This is why the focus should be on issues around masculinity and attitudes towards femininity, rather than on offending as such when dealing, for example, with perpetrators of domestic violence. But the point – that the relations between masculinity and offending are many, complex and problematic – is of more general application.

Most violent street crime is committed by young males for whom displays of aggression, daring or rebelliousness articulate, paradoxically, both individuality and commonality (i.e. masculinity). By the same token, the commission of 'white collar' crime is also associated with a different, superficially more 'respectable' sort of masculinity.

There is a sense in which the criminal law and criminal justice system are designed to calibrate and modify examples of masculinities. Some are outlawed altogether, others are subject to prescribed limits or contexts, and some, acting within the set limits, are valorized or exemplified. In any case, it is impossible to separate the study of offending from the study of masculinities, even if the question 'why not all men?' cannot be answered satisfactorily.

Ralph Sandland

Related entries

Domestic violence; Gender.

Key texts and sources

Hood-Williams, J. (2001) 'Gender, masculinities and crime: from structures to psyches', *Theoretical Criminology*, 5: 37–60.
Messerschmidt, J. (1993) *Masculinities and Crime: Critique and Reconceptualization of Theory.* Lanham, MD: Rowman & Littlefield.
Messerschmidt, J. (2006) 'Masculinities and crime: beyond a dualist criminology', in C.M. Renzetti *et al.* (eds) *Rethinking Gender, Crime and Justice: Feminist Readings.* Los Angeles, CA: Roxbury.

MEDIATION

Helping people in dispute move towards an agreement, the terms of which are defined by the disputants themselves rather than by the mediator.

Mediation, often referred to as 'alternative dispute resolution' (ADR), is a way of resolving disputes, conflicts or differences of interest. Usually, a mediator helps the parties settle their differences, encouraging them to set the terms of their settlement themselves – which readily distinguishes mediation from *arbitration*. Mediation has become popular – for example, bringing victims and offenders together; using peers to address bullying in schools; resolving disputes between neighbours or in the workplace. Often presented as a 'new' alternative, a less formal way of settling differences than by 'traditional' legalistic routes, mediation itself has a very long history. Criminal justice practitioners need to be familiar with the different contexts where mediation operates and may want to include mediation within their own portfolio of skills. They also need to recognize that equality of power between two parties cannot be assumed, so that mediators must ensure that no participant is oppressed or disadvantaged.

Mediation has received a strong boost from the gathering global interest in restorative justice (RJ) and conciliation. In some countries, such as New Zealand, Canada and Australia, RJ and mediation play a much more important part in responding to crime than in the UK, where the emphasis is on punishing or treating the offender. The main purpose of mediation here is to bring the offender, victim and community together to repair the harm caused and to encourage discussion and negotiation between all the parties concerned. Although a penalty may then be set, it tends to have a much more specific pertinence to the offender and victim. In contrast to traditional court procedure, the approach is non-adversarial and usually results in a sense of having been involved in something meaningful. Because the aim of mediation in the criminal justice context is to restore relationships fractured by crime, there is a ready affinity with social reaction or labelling theory – the idea that 'deviants' can be made worse by the way other people react to them. By concentrating on repairing relationships, mediation can contribute to cooling things down, thereby lessening the risk of further offending.

In the UK, mediation is perhaps most often associated with divorce and separation. This is *family mediation* and can be concerned with issues related to the children and/or property and financial matters. Helping parents settle their disputes about where their children will live and how contact with the non-resident parent should be managed is what most people understand by family mediation. However, professional mediators, who practise their craft in the community, free from the auspices of the court, reserve the term *mediation* for what they do. They prefer to describe the work undertaken by Children and Family Court Advisory and Support Service (CAFCASS) officers, which is court directed, as *dispute resolution*.

Greg Mantle

Related entries

Conciliation; Restorative justice.

Key texts and sources

Liebmann, M. (ed.) (2000) *Mediation in Context.* London: Jessica Kingsley.

Mantle, G. (2004) 'Social work and child-centred family court mediation', *British Journal of Social Work*, 34: 1161–72.

Mantle, G., Fox, D. and Dhami, M. (2005) 'Restorative justice and three individual theories of crime', *Internet Journal of Criminology* (available online at **www.internetjournalofcriminology.com**).

MENTALLY DISORDERED OFFENDERS

Offenders and defendants who are or may be mentally disordered or who might benefit from referral to psychiatric services.

The relationship between mental disorder and crime is equivocal; the reasons are not hard to find. First, there is no single definition of 'mental disorder'. In England and Wales the term is currently used in legislation (Mental Health Act 1983) to cover mental illness, mental impairment, severe mental impairment and psychopathic disorder. Mental illness is not further defined in the Act, but is usually taken to include the more severe illnesses, such as the various presentations of schizophrenia and the affective disorders (depression and manic disorders). Some forms of neurotic illness may bring individuals within the Act's provisions. Under current legislation (although this *may* be changed), certain forms of sexual deviancy and addictive behaviours do not constitute disorder justifying compulsory admission to hospital unless associated with serious anti-social conduct. Secondly, some forms of mentally disturbed conduct fall outside the definition because they may not fulfil the criteria for compulsory admission. The term mental *disturbance* is therefore preferable.

Our understanding of these conditions is not helped by surrounding myths; such myths are unfortunately propagated by the media, leading to what Cohen helpfully described as 'moral panic'. One such myth concerns uncertainties about causation – described graphically by Othello: 'It is the very error of the moon; she comes too near the earth and makes men mad' (Act V, Sc. ii). A second, our fears of madness, is expressed by King Lear: 'O, let me not be mad, not that sweet heaven; keep me in temper; I would not be mad'. (Act I, Sc. v). A third is the intractable nature of some mental disturbances, as when Macbeth catechizes his wife's physician, demanding: 'Canst thou not minister to a mind diseas'd?' (Act V, Sc. iii). Such myths influence our understanding of the disturbing combination of 'madness' and 'badness'.

These irrational, if partly understandable, fears are powerfully evidenced in the media's response to the rare instances of homicides committed by those suffering from serious mental disturbances. A common misunderstanding is that the number of homicides committed by the mentally disturbed has markedly increased. In the UK, Taylor and Gunn (1999) have provided good evidence to refute such claims, and recent studies in New Zealand and Denmark have produced similar findings. The frequent assertion by mental health campaigners and politicians that deinstitutionalization has led to increased (notably violent) activity by the mentally disturbed oversimplifies a complex problem. Such assertions have no doubt fuelled concerns about so-called 'dangerous severe personality disorder'.

It can be seen, then, that the understanding and management of the various forms of mental disorder (disturbance) involve complex issues. This complexity is heightened when we endeavour to make connections between such disturbance and crime – two phenomena that are not directly comparable. Behaviours described as criminal vary over time. For example, adult (now defined as the age of 16) consenting male homosexual acts in private are no longer deemed to be crimes; attempted suicide ceased to be an offence in the 1960s. However, there are also certain trends in the opposite direction. For example, consider the wide-ranging legislation concerning the ingestion, possession and distribution of certain drugs, the proliferation of penalties for road traffic violations and the increase in powers to legislate against terrorism. Such developments can be likened to a 'see-saw', moving up and down as society's views change.

Differences of opinion about the causes of forms of mental disorder, particularly those

thought to have an association with crime, bring further complications. Szasz suggested that we all too frequently diagnose and treat as 'illness' certain behaviours that merely affront society. Others assert that mental illness has its foundations in social and familial pressures. At the other end of the spectrum are those who espouse a 'biological' causation. Some disorders – for example, some of the disorders of older age (such as the various forms of dementia) and disorders produced by infections, injury or hormonal imbalance – have a biological basis. Some forms of affective disorder (notably severe depression and manic states) and certain presentations of schizophrenic illness might be included in this categorization. 'Biology' and 'environment' are doubtless both influential.

Mental disorder may constitute complete or partial defences to criminal responsibility:

1. *A plea of insanity* (not guilty by reason of insanity): this fairly rarely used defence, if successful, will lead to total exculpation of criminal responsibility.
2. *Being under disability in relation to the trial* (formerly known as *unfitness to plead*): if the court accepts that the accused is too mentally disordered to be tried, a mental health disposal will result.
3. *A plea of diminished responsibility* to a charge of murder, on the grounds of an abnormality of mind (as defined in the Homicide Act 1957), where accepted, will lead to total judicial discretion in sentencing for manslaughter instead of murder. The diminished responsibility defence is controversial and could be modified if the Law Commission's proposals are accepted by the government. Abolition of the mandatory life sentence for murder, which finds favour with almost all involved in criminal justice and mental health, would resolve some of these controversies, but successive Home Secretaries have remained intransigent (see Blom-Cooper and Morris 2004).
4. *Pleas of mitigation of penalty* may be made in other cases, enabling courts to take into account an accused's mental state at the time of, or subsequent to, the offence.
5. *Diversion from the criminal justice system.* For some years the Home Office has encouraged the use of appropriate diversion from prosecu-

tion (usually to a mental health resource), which may take place prior to, during or immediately following court appearance or subsequent to sentence (for example, by transfer from prison to a secure hospital facility).

Probation staff will often find themselves involved in the latter two sets of circumstances, as well as in subsequent challenges of working with people who are or may be mentally disturbed, commonly in liaison with other psychological or psychiatric services.

Herschel Prins

Related entries

Dual diagnosis; Personality disorder; Psychopathy/psychopathic disorder.

Key texts and sources

Blom-Cooper, Sir L. and Morris, T. (2004) *With Malice Aforethought: A Study of the Crime and Punishment for Homicide*. Oxford: Hart Publishing.
Prins, H. (2005) 'Mental disorder and violent crime: a problematic relationship', *Probation Journal*, 52: 333–57.
Prins, H. (2005) *Offenders, Deviants or Patients?* (3rd edn). London: Routledge.
Prins, H. (2006) 'The law and mental disorder: an uneasy relationship', in K. Moss and M. Stephens (eds) *Crime Reduction and the Law*. London: Routledge.
Szasz, T. (1984) *Myth of Mental Illness*, New York: Harper Colophon.
Taylor, P. and Gunn, J. (1999) 'Homicides by people with mental illness', *British Journal of Psychiatry*, Jan 174: 564–5.
The diagnostic criteria for many mental disorders may be found at http://www.mentalhealth.com/.

MINISTRY OF JUSTICE

A new ministry, bringing together the functions of the Department for Constitutional Affairs with responsibilities hitherto held by the Home Office, including the National Offender Management Service (NOMS) and youth justice. The ministry is to have lead responsibility for criminal law and sentencing.

In March 2007, the Prime Minister announced that, from May 2007, a new Ministry of Justice was to take over the staff and responsibilities of the Department for Constitutional Affairs (formerly the Lord Chancellor's Department) and many of the functions hitherto managed by the Home Office – NOMS (including the Prison and Probation Services), youth justice and the Office of Criminal Justice Reform. The ministry will have lead responsibility for criminal law and sentencing. The Home Office retains responsibility for security, as well as for the police, crime reduction, drugs, immigration and asylum, identity and passports.

Hitherto, the government department with responsibility for probation had always been the Home Office. When John Reid became Home Secretary in May 2006, he described his department as 'not fit for purpose'. The proposed remedy was to separate the functions of security and policing, which remain with the Home Office, from the responsibilities for courts, criminal justice and the implementation of sentencing.

The distinguished former Lord Chief Justice Woolf expressed misgivings about the pace of the reform, saying that any rearrangement of the 'checks and balances' of the constitution should be considered very carefully and not rushed through. In particular, he reflected that the Lord Chancellor has traditionally enjoyed a close relationship with the judiciary and was anxious that this might be jeopardized when the new minister's portfolio was extended.

While the changes seem precipitate to some, the idea of a Ministry of Justice is scarcely new. The Liberal Democratic Party *Election Manifesto* of 1992, for example, included the idea. A number of reform groups have campaigned for this too, with the Legal Action Group insisting that it would improve the transparency and independence of appointments to the judiciary.

It is also to be noted that all European jurisdictions (except Spain) have a Ministry of Justice and, as a matter of constitutional principle, this is distinct from the Ministry of Internal Affairs/Interior. In France, the Ministère de l'Intérieur et de l'Aménagement du territoire is responsible for policing, while the Ministère de la Justice is in charge of judicial administration and the implementation of punishment. Similarly, in the German Federal government, the Bundesministerium des Innern is quite distinct from the Bundesministerium der Justiz.

When new member states join the Council of Europe, this separation is among the first principles on which the council insists; a formal separation of powers between the agencies of security and justice, including the implementation of punishment, is held to be an important human rights safeguard. It was more than a little ironic that the UK, one of the council's founder members, had almost alone retained a Home Office that held responsibility for penal affairs.

Probation has a key role in promoting public safety and crime reduction, and it remains to be seen how this will be affected by its formal separation from the government department charged with lead responsibility for these matters. Local collaboration between police and probation, for example, may be affected now that these agencies are to have quite distinct lines of accountability to central government. There are also some issues of constitutional principle that may be exposed and put to test under the new arrangements. For example, while some hold that judges should take account of pressures on the prison population, others have argued that 'judicial independence' requires that the judiciary retains the power to sentence as they think right, while the government should provide the required resources. These arguments will take on a new character when the same minister is responsible both for sentencing policy and for prisons. Whether this will be a good thing is a matter for debate. It is much too early to appraise the significance of the change; how the arrangements will develop over time is, at this point, a matter for speculation.

Rob Canton

Related entries

Criminal justice system; Judges; Probation in Europe.

Key texts and sources

Faulkner, D. (2006) *Crime, State and Citizen: A Field Full of Folk* (2nd edn). Winchester: Waterside Press (a wise consideration of the constitutional relationships).

The Ministry of Justice website is at **http://www. justice.gov.uk/index.htm**. The Prime Minister's announcement is at **http://www.homeoffice.gov.uk/ about-us/news/announce-future-home-office**. An

interview in which Lord Woolf expressed his concerns may be found at **http://news.bbc.co.uk/1/hi/ uk_politics/6586437.stm**. An instructive paper ('Prisons and the Ministry of Justice'), by Andrew Coyle, may be downloaded from **http://www.kcl. ac.uk/depsta/rel/icps/new.html**.

MOTIVATION

'Motivation is a *state* of readiness or eagerness to change, which may fluctuate from one time or situation to another. This state is one that can be influenced' (Miller and Rollnick 1991: 14).

Work with offenders is concerned with enhancing their motivation to change their offending behaviour, which is based on addressing criminogenic needs (risk factors that, if reduced, help to prevent offending). The offender manager/supervisor's role is to assess the offender's motivation at the assessment stage and enhance it throughout the order. Using the cycle of change, which sees change as a process, the supervisor can establish where on the cycle of change the offender is. He or she can then utilize skills in motivational interviewing to work with the offender on the actions to be taken towards change.

Motivation of the offender depends on several factors and the way in which the offender is experiencing life at any one time. Offenders' basic needs should be addressed first in order to engage them in offence-focused work. If someone has no food or accommodation then his or her motivation to cease offending will not be very high. At an emotional level, the need for instant gratification will be greater than the rational decision at a cognitive level to stop offending. Maslow's hierarchy of needs (1954) explores this concept in more depth. Prior to an offender beginning work on an accredited programme, the supervisor, as part of the pre-programme work, is asked to ensure that any obstacles to attendance on the programme or barriers to change are addressed. These could relate to literacy, drug or alcohol problems as well as logistical considerations, such as transport arrangements, work patterns and dependent care commitments.

Research into models of case management highlights the importance of the offender/supervisor relationship in enhancing the motivation of the offender to reduce his or her offending. Consistency, continuity, consolidation and commitment of the offender manager are important in delivering effective practice. Building up trust and respect, the worker's style and the quality of the relationship are highlighted as important factors. Many offenders view life as a series of unconnected events where they find it difficult to link consequences with behaviour. If a series of different people deliver separate components of the supervision plan, then this may collude with this view and provide little stability for the offender. Prosocial modelling by the supervisor – in terms of demonstrating empathy, clear values in relation to the harm caused by crime and the belief in the capacity of offenders to change – as well as empowering the offender to take control of his or her life and make decisions, plays an important role in increasing the likelihood of someone ceasing offending. Praise, reward, reinforcement of learning and being clear with the offender what the role of the offender manager is can be very helpful. The offender's motivation and loyalty may be enhanced by the supervisor's legitimate moral authority (legitimacy), reasonableness, fairness and encouragement: '[Reinforcing motivation requires the case manager] to provide a safe, consistent, reliable and firm working relationship' (Chapman and Hough 1998: 44).

Behavioural theories primarily focus on extrinsic motivation (rewards), while cognitive theories centre on intrinsic motivation (goals). The supervisor needs to elicit the decision to change from the offender since change cannot be forced: it depends on how much the offender wants to change, and the desire for change often relates to the discrepancy between what is happening and what one wants to happen. As this discrepancy increases, the willingness to change increases. It also needs to be the right time for change. By increasing the client's *self-efficacy* – the belief that he or she has the ability to carry out or succeed in a specific task – progress can be made. This also fits in with the importance of the offender manager's belief that offenders can change their behaviour: 'The task of the practitioner is to provide a safe empowering environment where the client can explore the conflicting factors in order to work out what truly matters' (Cherry 2005: 78).

The offender's diversity is very important in thinking about motivation. People have different life experiences and learning styles. It is said that offenders learn best through active, participatory styles of learning. Experiential learning is important in supervision programmes as offenders learn best through testing out theory and principles in the real world. This is why it can be argued that cognitive-behavioural programmes are better utilized in the community than in prison. Reinforcement of the work on accredited programmes by the case manager is also seen to enhance motivation. As learning styles can differ from person to person, it is important to assess this at the start of supervision so that work with the offender can be tailored accordingly (responsivity). Materials on accredited programmes also need to be appropriate to the gender, age and culture of the participants.

Research into desistance factors highlights the fact that many offenders are more likely to cease offending due to age, maturity, quality of their relationships, employment and training. Qualitative research has shown that changes in a person's sense of him or herself and an increasing concern for others and the future are also indicators of the likelihood of desistance. However, attitudes and motivation are also key factors, and an offender manager can increase the likelihood of an offender reaching this stage of transition by encouraging him or her to see the positives in his or her life as well as the factors that increase the risk of reoffending and harm to the public. Focusing on times when offenders have solved problems without resorting to crime by using techniques such as solution-focused interventions can increase the protective factors (such as health, employment, qualifications, partners and family ties).

'Community reintegration is the most critical process for achieving long-term change. It should be an essential element of a supervision plan' (Chapman and Hough 1998: 64). The environmental causes of crime – that is, 'social capital' and 'human capital' – are equally important. Relapse prevention work can help to increase the offender's own monitoring skills to reduce the opportunities for offending. The Probation Studies Unit's evaluation of the Think First Programme, 2000–02, distinguishes three distinctive aspects of motivation: attitudes to offending, non-compliance and the wish to change (Roberts 2004). These are influenced by positive factors as noted earlier, as well as prior criminal history. The most motivated had a mean age of 30, had less entrenched criminal careers and less strong criminal associations. Those offenders with better reasoning and thinking skills, learning abilities, communication and basic skills benefited most from the programme. Protective factors such as these and the ones noted earlier are also factors affecting compliance. Without attendance on the order, offending behaviour or motivation cannot be addressed.

Judy Hudson

Related entries

Compliance; Cycle of change; Diversity; Legitimacy; Motivational interviewing; Prosocial modelling; Responsivity.

Key texts and sources

Chapman, T. and Hough, M. (1998) *Evidence Based Practice.* London: Home Office.

Cherry, S. (2005) *Transforming Behaviour: Pro-social Modelling in Practice.* Cullompton: Willan Publishing.

Hopkinson, J. and Rex, S. (2003) 'Essential skills in working with offenders', in W.H. Chui and M. Nellis (eds) *Moving Probation Forward.* Harlow: Pearson Education.

Maslow, A.H. (1954) *Motivation and Personality.* New York, NY: Harper & Bros (available online in Davidmann, M. 'Motivation: summary' at http://www.solbaram.org/articles/motvtnsu.html).

Miller, W.R. and Rollnick, R. (1991) *Motivational Interviewing.* New York, NY: Guilford Press.

Roberts, C. (2004) 'Offending behaviour programmes: emerging evidence and implications for practice', in R. Burnett and C. Roberts (eds) *What Works in Probation and Youth Justice.* Cullompton: Willan Publishing.

Trotter, C. (1999) *Working with Involuntary Clients.* London: Sage.

MOTIVATIONAL INTERVIEWING

'Motivational interviewing is a directive, client-centered counseling style for eliciting behavior change by helping clients to explore and resolve ambivalence. Compared with nondirective counseling, it is more focused and goal-directed. The examination and resolution of ambivalence is its central purpose, and the counselor is intentionally directive in pursuing this goal' (Miller and Rollnick 2002: 6).

Motivational interviewing (MI) is a counselling approach, outlined by clinical psychologist William R. Miller in 1983, and developed in collaboration with Stephen Rollnick in the early 1990s. Initially used in the fields of alcohol and substance misuse, it rapidly came to be seen as an effective approach to the management and treatment of a range of compulsive/addictive behaviours, such as gambling, sex offending and eating disorders. By the beginning of the new century, randomized controlled trials were demonstrating its usefulness as part of compliance therapy in mental health and in the management of disease by general practitioners. It had also come to be advocated as 'the language of change' in offender management on both sides of the Atlantic, and as a way to avoid the false dichotomy of a 'care or control' approach in probation.

In their more recent work, Miller and Rollnick have stressed that the counselling style or philosophy – a therapeutic partnership or alliance – is more salient than the individual techniques that are used, emphasizing that confrontation of certain behaviours is an essential goal, but an ineffective interpersonal style. Applying this 'style' to addressing offending behaviour, David Hawkins (2002) has added that success in facilitating change 'occurs not by attacking the negative, but by fostering the positive'.

Rollnick and Miller have suggested that the MI philosophy should inform a number of worker skills or techniques. These are the target behaviours in MI training programmes:

- Seeking to understand the person's frame of reference, particularly via reflective listening.

- Expressing acceptance and affirmation.
- Eliciting and selectively reinforcing the client's own self-motivational statements, expressions of problem recognition, concern, desire and intention to change, and ability to change.
- Monitoring the client's degree of readiness to change, and ensuring that resistance is not generated by jumping ahead of the client.
- Affirming the client's freedom of choice and self-direction.

MI has been successfully adopted in a wide range of settings and cultures. Initial worker training is usually through in-service courses of between two and four days where emphasis is placed on the application of MI philosophy to practice skills and settings.

James Sandham and Mike Octigan

Related entries

Motivation; Prosocial modelling.

Key texts and sources

Clark, M.D. (2005) 'Motivational interviewing for probation staff: increasing the readiness to change', *Federal Probation*, 69: 22–8.

Fuller, C. and Taylor, P. (2003) *Toolkit of Motivational Skills*. London: National Probation Directorate.

Hawkins, D.R. (2002) *Power vs. Force: The Hidden Determinants of Human Behavior*. Sedona, AZ: Veritas Publishing.

Miller, W.R. and Rollnick, S. (2002) *Motivational Interviewing*. New York, NY: Guilford Press.

The 'official' MI website (**http://motivationalinterview. org/**) is a resource for training materials and for access to recent research findings.

MUBAREK INQUIRY

A public inquiry, set up in 2004, into the death of Asian teenager, Zahid Mubarek, attacked and killed by his cellmate in Feltham Young Offender Institution in 2000.

In the early hours of 21 March 2000, Zahid Mubarek was brutally attacked by his cellmate, Robert Stewart. He was clubbed about the head with a wooden table leg and died of his injuries.

It was soon discovered that Stewart had strong racist views and that he had bragged beforehand about committing a murder. He was subsequently convicted of Zahid's murder and sentenced to life imprisonment.

Stewart had a violent history, and his mental health had been questioned. The prison officers in Feltham had known of this background at the time. Questions immediately arose about how Zahid had been required to share a cell with a violent and racist offender with a disturbed background and a long criminal career.

The Prison Service recognized that it had failed, and both the Prison Service and the Commission for Racial Equality undertook investigations. In April 2004, following protracted legal proceedings, the Honourable Mr Justice Keith was appointed by the Home Secretary to carry out a non-statutory public inquiry.

The 692-page report of the inquiry was published in June 2006. It highlighted the deplorable conditions in Feltham. There had been a failure to implement the inspectors' recommendations and, following a visit in December 1998, the Chief Inspector of Prisons had said:

> This report … is, without doubt, the most disturbing that I have had to make during my three years as HM Chief Inspector of Prisons … the conditions and treatment, of the 922 children and young prisoners confined at Feltham are in many instances totally unacceptable. They are, in many instances, worse than when I reported on them two years ago and reveal a history of neglect of those committed to their charge.

The inquiry report paints a dismal picture of an institution degenerating into crisis, and highlights the core problems as staff shortages, overcrowding, poor industrial relations and racism. Explicit racism on the part of staff was prevalent at Feltham. The race relations management team were ineffective and had little appreciation of how bad race relations were.

The inquiry found that, in the six years that had elapsed since Zahid's murder, several of the systems and procedures that would have been recommended had been put in place. Examples were computerized information flow, new cell-sharing protocols and risk assessment tools.

However, the inquiry found a disconnection between aspiration and reality because of poor implementation.

The report made 88 recommendations for reducing the risks of violence in cells. They cover, among other subjects, cell-sharing practice, the flow of information, mentally disturbed prisoners, racism and religious intolerance. The report recommends extending the Stephen Lawrence Inquiry's definition of institutional racism to incorporate the concept of institutional religious intolerance.

The report concludes by emphasizing the increased risks when population pressure and understaffing combine to undermine decency.

David Hancock

Related entries

Macpherson Report; Personality disorder; Race and racism; Racially motivated offenders.

Key texts and sources

The full text of the Zahid Mubarek Inquiry report can be accessed at **www.zahidmubarekinquiry. org.uk.**

MULTI-AGENCY PUBLIC PROTECTION ARRANGEMENTS (MAPPAs)

> The framework under which agencies work together to reduce the risk of the serious reoffending behaviour of violent and sexual offenders.

The multi-agency public protection arrangements (MAPPAs) came into being in 2000 when the Criminal Justice and Court Services Act placed a statutory obligation on the Probation and Police Services in each area to establish arrangements for the purpose of assessing and managing the risks posed by certain offenders.

The Criminal Justice Act 2003 extended that obligation to include the Prison Service. The three criminal justice agencies are known as the 'responsible authority'. At the same time, other agencies were formally brought into the arrangements under a duty to co-operate measure. These are social services, youth offending teams, Jobcentre Plus, local education authorities, local housing authorities, registered social landlords, strategic health authorities, primary care trusts, NHS trusts and electronic monitoring providers.

There are four overlapping stages to a MAPPA:

1. The identification of MAPPA offenders.
2. The sharing of relevant information between agencies.
3. The assessment of the risk of serious harm.
4. The management of that risk.

The offenders who fall under a MAPPA are identified by three categories:

- *Category 1*: registered sex offenders for the period of their registration.
- *Category 2*: other sex offenders and violent offenders (sentenced to 12 months' imprisonment or more), usually for the period they are being supervised by probation.
- *Category 3*: other offenders who have been convicted of an offence which indicates that they are capable of causing serious harm to the public, and the responsible authority reasonably considers that the offenders may cause serious harm to the public (see the Criminal Justice Act 2003, s. 327 for a broader definition).

The MAPPA identifies three levels of risk management:

- *Level 1: ordinary risk management (MAPPA 1)* – used in cases where the risk posed by the offender can be managed by one agency without actively or significantly involving other agencies.
- *Level 2: local inter-agency risk management (MAPPA 2)* – used where the active involvement of more than one agency is required but where either the level of risk or the complexity of managing the risk is not so great as to require referral to Level 3. The meeting should be called when it is felt that risk of harm requiring multi-agency intervention is needed. Key triggers would include an escalation of identified risk or pre-release preparation. All relevant agencies who have a part to play in this should be invited, and a senior member of

staff from the most appropriate agency will convene this meeting. A core membership is recommended by the Home Office.

- *Level 3: MAPPP – multi-agency public protection panel (MAPPA 3)* – used for the management of the 'critical few'. This is defined as when the offender is assessed under OASys as being a high or very high risk of causing serious harm and presents risks that can only be managed by a plan that requires close co-operation at a senior level due to the complexity of the case and/or because of the unusual resource commitments it requires; *or*, although not assessed as a high or very high risk, the case is exceptional because the likelihood of media scrutiny and/or public interest in the management of the case is very high. These meetings usually take place on a monthly basis, with core membership at senior management level representing the responsible authority and duty to co-operate bodies. Normally the offender will have escalated from management at MAPPA 2 level. Arrangements for chairing these panels vary from area to area. Core panel members should receive full information in advance of the panel.

In deciding what level of risk management should be used to manage the risk posed by a MAPPA offender, consideration should be given to the nature of the risk and how it can be managed. The levels of risk management do not necessarily equate directly to levels of risk but, generally, the higher the assessed level of risk, the higher the level of management required.

Throughout the MAPPA process risks will be identified, approved assessment instruments used, victim issues considered and a risk management plan and/or licence requirements agreed. Regular reviews should take place when required. Information sharing must have lawful authority, be necessary, proportionate and ensure the safety and security of the information shared.

Risks cannot be entirely eliminated, but the principles of defensible decision-making must be applied. That means that all reasonable steps have been taken, reliable assessment methods have been used, further information collected and thoroughly evaluated, and decisions recorded and implemented. Finally, it must be demonstrated that policies and procedures have been followed using an investigative and proactive approach.

The MAPPA is reviewed and monitored by a strategic management board (SMB) in each area. Their principal activities are to monitor and evaluate the MAPPA; connect with safeguarding children boards and Crime and Disorder Reduction Partnerships; report, promote and develop the work of the MAPPA; review the arrangements; prepare a business plan; and identify the training and development needs of those working within the MAPPA.

The Secretary of State has appointed two lay advisers to each area (Criminal Justice Act 2003, s. 326(3)) to assist the MAPPA as full members of each SMB in the role of 'informed observers'. The SMB should usually meet not less than quarterly and is chaired by a senior manager (with strategic responsibilities) from one of the responsible authorities. It is recommended that duty to co-operate bodies be similarly represented on the SMB.

Risk management will never be a precise science. However, what the MAPPA process has achieved over the first five years of its existence is to provide a robust structure that incorporates the involvement of a wide range of agencies working collaboratively within each community to address dangerousness and increase public protection. It continues to evolve and is seen as a world leader in criminal justice.

Victoria Hodgett

Related entries

Assessment; Assessment instruments and systems; Dangerousness; Inter-agency work; Public protection; Risk assessment and risk management; Risk of harm; Sex offenders; Violent offenders.

Key texts and sources

Home Office (2003) *MAPPA Guidance* (NPD/057/2003). London: Home Office.

Home Office (2005) *Public Protection Framework, Risk of Harm and MAPPA Thresholds* (PC/10/2005). London: Home Office.

Kemshall, H., Mackenzie, G., Wood, J., Bailey, R. and Yates, J. (2005) *Strengthening Multi-agency Public Protection Arrangements (MAPPAs)*. Report 45. London: Home Office Research, Development and Statistics Directorate (available online at http://www.homeoffice.gov.uk/rds/pdfs05/dpr45.pdf).

N

NAPO

The trade union and professional association for family court and probation staff.

Napo, which acts as a trade union and a professional association, represents over 9,000 members in the Probation Service and Children and Family Court Advisory and Support Service (CAFCASS).

Napo, which was originally founded in 1912 as the National Association of Probation Officers, changed its name in 2001 to Napo – the Trade Union and Professional Association for Family Court and Probation Staff. The name change reflected the changes to the nature of Napo's membership and to the restructuring of the Probation Service in 2001, the same year that saw the establishment of CAFCASS as a separate organization.

Napo has always existed to represent the professional interests of its members, as well as to protect and promote the best interests of its members as employees. The trade union and professional association aspects of its work have been entwined from the outset. Napo may not have considered itself as a trade union in its early days. Its first strike was over probation trainee salaries in 1983, and it joined the Trade Union Congress (TUC) in 1984, but it was producing reports on pay and campaigning on pensions back in the 1920s.

As a trade union, Napo negotiates pay and conditions of service; provides advice and representation; provides education and training; promotes health and safety at work; and promotes equality at work.

As a professional association, Napo seeks to influence policies and practice in the criminal justice and family court systems and helps shape and develop training policies. It also promotes anti-racist and anti-discriminatory practice and policy.

As a campaigning group, Napo seeks to promote positive change in the criminal and family court systems through parliamentary lobbying and briefing, and the active use of the press and the media.

Examples of major actions in the past decade, many of which combine trade union and professional issues, include the following:

- The mid-1990s' campaign to restore a higher education-based probation officer qualification after its abolition by Michael Howard in 1995. This probation training campaign was run with the support of the probation employers, and included the organization of two lobbies of Parliament. The outcome was eventually successful, following the election of the Labour government in 1997 and the introduction, in 1998, of the Diploma in Probation Studies.
- The negotiations in the run-up to, and subsequent to, the introduction of CAFCASS and the restructuring of the Probation Service, with effect from 2001. This ensured that members' jobs and terms and conditions, and health and safety, were protected and promoted.
- The negotiations and campaign for probation staff to have manageable workloads. This led to strike action in a number of probation areas in 2003, and subsequent agreement to workload prioritization agreements and a national Workload Management Tool.
- The negotiations to harmonize terms and conditions of probation staff and to introduce a new pay structure based on job evaluation with effect from April 2006.
- The production of advice, guidance and training for members on a range of diversity and equal rights issues.

- The campaign, since the introduction of the Case Recording and Management System in 1996, for efficient information technology systems which are accessible to all.
- The campaign, and the production of advice for members, on changes to practice in the light of changing criminal justice legislation, policies and National Standards. This includes seeking to influence the development of professional tools, such as the OASys.
- The development and production of a practice guide on probation values.
- The negotiations with the National Probation Directorate, and the development of guidance for branches and members, on role boundaries and on the work appropriate to different grades in the service.

Following David Blunkett's announcement in January 2004 that the National Offender Management Service (NOMS) was to be created without any consultation following the Carter Report, Napo has been actively engaged in responding to developments and campaigning to save the Probation Service as a public service.

Napo does not oppose the concept of end-to-end case management between the probation and Prison Services, a concept based on long-established good probation practice, but has actively opposed the various structural models put forward for NOMS. Napo has campaigned against the model of contestability and competition that threatens to dismantle the whole Probation Service in order to allow the private and voluntary sectors to compete for probation work. Napo submitted an alternative structural model for NOMS based on the principle of partnership working.

Napo was actively involved in parliamentary briefings on NOMS; organized a lobby of Parliament and an early-day motion in support of the Probation Service; met regularly with Home Office and NOMS officials and ministers; and submitted responses to the various consultation exercises on NOMS. Napo policy is determined at its annual general meeting, which is held every October and is open to all members. Napo's National Executive meets six times

a year and is made up of representatives from each of its 37 branches. Napo also has a range of committees which pursue work on policies throughout the year, and a team of elected officers who act between meetings of the National Executives. There is a regular programme of conferences, seminars and training events on specific subjects for members. Napo has a small team of full-time staff that includes a general secretary, three assistant general secretaries, a research and information officer, a human resource manager and 12 administrators.

Judy McKnight

Related entries

Anti-discriminatory practice; National Offender Management Service (NOMS); Probation training; Probation values.

Key texts and sources

Publications include *Napo News*, a trade union magazine that is published monthly, and the *Probation Journal*, published four times a year by Sage Publications. This has established an acclaimed reputation, nationally and internationally, on the dissemination of good probation practice. Napo also has a website (**www.napo.org.uk**) on which details of publications can be found.

NATIONAL ASSOCIATION OF ASIAN PROBATION STAFF (NAAPS)

Naaps is the association for Asian staff in the National Probation Service. It embodies the needs and aspirations of Asian staff working at all levels and grades within the National Offender Management Service.

Naaps has grown and developed over the last 20 years. It adopted its current constitution in 2004, and this sets out the aims and powers of the association. Naaps is a professional association that exists to:

- promote an Asian perspective at all levels in the work of the National Offender Management Service (NOMS); and
- provide a support network for Asian staff in NOMS.

For the association to ensure the appropriate delivery of service in accordance with its prime objectives, the following powers have been agreed and are stated in the Naaps' constitution:

- Assisting the work of NOMS in developing national strategies and policies on all areas of diversity.
- Providing NOMS and its regions advice, guidance and information on diversity issues.
- Improving links with the Asian communities, and working in partnership with other associations in the criminal justice system in order to promote, lead and influence the race agenda.
- Ensuring that the religious and cultural needs of Asian staff are met.
- Working with the service to eliminate incidents of discrimination.
- Promoting the monitoring of service to all Asian service users, both offenders and employees.
- Ensuring the inclusion of Asian perspectives in all aspects of training and other business activities.
- Liaising with other agencies to ensure the meeting of targets and the completion of the objectives of the association.

Membership of Naaps is open to all staff who identify themselves as Asian and who are able to support the values and aspirations of the association. Associate membership is open to people employed in NOMS or related agencies who declare a wish to pursue the aims and objectives of Naaps and who are not eligible for full membership.

The day-to-day work of Naaps is conducted through a series of regional groups that meet regularly to discuss professional issues. There are national officers and a national executive committee that comprises the national officers and representatives from the regions. The main roles of the national officers are to ensure the proper running of the association and to represent the views of Naaps' members to government and other bodies. Naaps' representatives sit on a wide range of policy and consultative groups, and they enjoy the support of the employers' association. They have many opportunities to represent Asian perspectives in the formulation of policy and procedures.

The main event of the Naaps' year is the annual conference. The first of these was held in Birmingham in 2001 and, since that time, a succession of well attended conferences has been held. The annual conference is held in March and comprises professional discussion and debate as well as the annual general meeting (AGM) of the association. National officers are elected annually at the AGM.

Naaps believes that Asian staff suffer a different kind of discrimination: they are not only discriminated against for their skin colour but also their language, culture, dress and religion. In order to explore this further, Naaps sponsored a significant research initiative that reported in 2004. This was the first ever study of the views of Asian employees in the National Probation Service on issues of recruitment, retention and progression. The study was based on the analysis of 140 self-completed questionnaires and 38 individual interviews. The key findings were as follows:

- Respondents disapproved overwhelmingly of the description 'black'. Staff felt that this term had marginalized Asian staff and their perspectives. There was a call for informed and accurate terminology to reflect Asian staff identities.
- Asian staff reported a rift in their relationships with colleagues following recent terrorist attacks. Muslim respondents, in particular, had experienced Islamaphobia from colleagues and offenders. Staff wanted to assert that, despite the war on terror, they are not the enemy.
- More should be done to attract Asian staff. Although the respondents generally expressed an attraction to the interesting and challenging nature of probation work, many felt that the service is not as well known or understood in Asian communities as it should be. There is a need to reverse the limited community engagement by the service.

- Asian staff did not feel properly appreciated for the 'added value' they bring to the work of the service.
- Staff racism is still an issue. Staff reported discrimination from both colleagues and offenders, and it was of particular concern that this was reported to be greater from colleagues than from offenders.
- More management action is needed to achieve a consistent level of support across England and Wales. Respondents indicated that some limited support on issues of race, religion and culture had been offered to staff in keeping with local organizational policy. However, concern was expressed that some colleagues and managers were still not honouring local agreements about cover to attend support and professional meetings.
- Promotion and advancement should be based on merit, skill and competency. Some respondents had concerns about promotional opportunities and linked this to the way in which their religion and culture were perceived.

The issues raised in these key findings will probably be easily recognized by the majority of Asian staff working in probation, and it is the task of Naaps to continue to highlight these deficits and to suggest ways that these problems can be overcome.

Gurdev Singh

Related entries

Diversity.

Key texts and sources

Singh, G. and Heer, G. (2004) *Recruitment, Retention and Progression: The Asian Experience within the National Probation Service* (available on request from **gurdev.singh@nottinghamshire.probation. gsi.gov.uk**).

NATIONAL OFFENDER MANAGEMENT SERVICE (NOMS)

NOMS was established in 2004 following a major independent review of correctional services in England and Wales. The government's response, *Reducing Crime: Changing Lives*, was published soon after, resulting in the creation of NOMS. NOMS' purpose is to ensure a reduction in reoffending and improved public protection by ensuring a greater coherence in the way prisons and probation work together.

NOMS was created following the comprehensive correctional services review conducted by Patrick Carter in 2003 (the Carter Report). The review's focus was to recommend more effective ways of using scarce resources. He recognized an urgent need for the key correctional services to work more closely together and to deliver a service fit for purpose. NOMS was set up in 2004 to meet the paramount objective of public protection and reducing reoffending.

Instead of relying solely on line management, NOMS' aim is to establish a clear distinction between the purchaser of services and the providers. At its heart is the development of national and regional commissioning. The bulk of services will be commissioned at regional level, with the most resources and interventions concentrated on those offenders who present the greatest risk of harm and the greatest risk of reoffending.

In his review, Patrick Carter recognized that correctional services needed to be aligned towards tackling the reasons why people offend, with offender management being the mechanism for ensuring proper assessment and arranging interventions to meet need. The offender manager is to act as the 'glue' holding the sentence together. This will maximize the potential for protecting the public and reducing reoffending.

The Offender Management Model was tested through a pathfinder in the north-west of England and is the subject of three stages of evaluation, with the final evaluation to assess the impact on reducing reoffending. The early action research identified very positive feedback from prison and probation staff. Offenders valued being involved in their sentence plan, could see the purpose of it and welcomed the continuity of involvement with the offender manager and the supervisor. These are the key components of the model, so it was reassuring that the action research recognized this.

The Offender Management Model is supported by the two IT systems, OASys and C-NOMIS. OASys is the national assessment tool used by prisons and probation. The national database now holds over one million assessments and is proving invaluable in helping commissioners and providers identify what interventions are needed and for whom (see O-DEAT). The data will inform the regional and national reducing re-offending action plans, assisting other government departments such as health, education and employment to identify and meet the social exclusion needs of offenders. This needs to be an integral part of any strategy to reduce reoffending.

The second IT system is C-NOMIS. This consists of a single case record for every offender, shared by prisons and probation and enabling the offender manager and the offender supervisor to have instant access to information about offenders. This is critical to ensuring prisoners are held in a safe and decent manner, and are supervised properly and appropriately by the Probation Service while in the community. It is expected that the C-NOMIS roll-out will be completed in 2008, with the Offender Management Model being rolled out in prisons over a three-year period from 2006.

The government's paper *Reducing Crime: Changing Lives*, and the five-year strategy recognized that nobody should have the monopoly on providing services for offenders. If the system is to work both effectively and efficiently, a range of providers is needed, playing to their strengths, and who demonstrate their ability to deliver effec-

tively through a process of performance tests and competition. The recently published *Public Value Partnerships* sets out the vision and the practicalities as to how this might occur. Patrick Carter envisaged competition as providing the creative tension in the system, driving up quality and innovation, and driving out complacency. There are already a number of private prisons, and many recognize the role they have played in challenging performance. Probation, on the other hand, has experienced very little in the way of competition and, although many in probation are concerned with the impact this might have, the government recognizes the role that the private, and particularly the voluntary, sector can play. Some £4 billion is spent annually on prisons and probation in England and Wales, and it is essential there is confidence that every penny is well spent.

At the same time as introducing offender management and commissioning and contestability, NOMS has been introducing the National and Regional Reducing Re-offending Action Plans with their seven pathways. Each covers one of the main reasons that contribute to offending. The regional offender managers have been charged with turning these action plans into reality, working very closely with the government offices in the regions. Crime and Disorder Reduction Partnerships, local area agreements and local criminal justice boards are all critical to ensuring that all agencies recognize and play their part in public protection and reducing reoffending. NOMS, prisons and probation have all recognized that, whatever our best efforts, successful public protection and reduced reoffending are also dependent on working effectively in partnership with other agencies, both inside and outside the criminal justice system.

There is much to be achieved in NOMS. Prisons and probation have proud traditions going back over 100 years. To work together effectively needs not only good structures, performance and well directed resources, but it is also dependent on the determination and commitment of the staff who provide services to offenders, whether employed by the public, private or voluntary sectors. If they are empowered to do their jobs effectively and with innovation, the public will be better protected; fewer offenders will reoffend; and victims will recognize the impact on their safety, will have confidence in the system, and will acknowledge the success of prisons and probation.

Christine Knott

Related entries

Carter Report; C-NOMIS; Contestability; Interventions; Offender management; Probation trusts; Regional offender managers (ROMs).

Key texts and sources

Criminal Justice and Court Services Act 2000.
Bailey, R., Knight, C. and Williams, B. (2007) 'The Probation Service as part of NOMS in England and Wales: fit for purpose?', in L. Gelsthorpe and R. Morgan (eds) *Handbook of Probation.* Cullompton: Willan Publishing.
Morgan, R. (2007) 'Probation, governance and accountability', in L. Gelsthorpe and R. Morgan (eds) *Handbook of Probation.* Cullompton: Willan Publishing.
The following documents can be found on the NOMS website (**www.noms.homeoffice.gov.uk**):
Managing Offenders, Reducing Crime (December 2003).
Reducing Crime: Changing Lives (January 2004).
Offender Management Action Research (2005).
A Five Year Strategy for Protecting the Public and Reducing Re-offending (February 2006).
Offender Management Model (May 2006).
Public Value Partnerships (August 2006).

NATIONAL PROBATION RESEARCH AND INFORMATION EXCHANGE (NPRIE)

NPRIE is a non-accredited body that provides a forum for exchanging information, for discussing issues relating to research and information in the National Probation Service, and for encouraging co-operation, co-ordination and professional development among individual research and information units.

NPRIE's core role is to improve the quality of research and information management services in the National Probation Service (NPS). It endeavours to achieve this through a number of different approaches:

- Representation on national bodies and working groups.
- The co-ordination of responses from the NPRIE community to national consultations and other requests from national and regional bodies for advice and opinion.
- The provision of opportunities for research and information staff to have dialogue through a mixture of organized conferences, specialist interest groups and website developments.

Recent specific involvements have included the following:

- *C-NOMIS User Group:* assisting with specifying reporting requirements for the National Offender Management Service database.
- *eOASys User Group*: advice and comment on, among other things, connectivity, business processes and quality assurance.
- *NPS Research Advisory Group*: the introduction of the Project Quality Assurance Board, dissemination of the Home Office Research, Development and Statistics Directorate (RDS) competence-based training framework and training opportunities.
- *Data Standards and Reporting Group:* contributing to the definition of performance measures.
- Response to *consultation on the restructuring of probation.*
- Setting up a *special interest group for communications/PR officers.*
- Organizing the *NPRIE conference.*

NPRIE has a number of special interest groups dealing with research, information and communications.

Information and Library Management Group

This group is concerned with the management of information, knowledge and library services. The group advises on such issues as intellectual property rights, freedom of information and data protection.

Research Officer Group (ROG)

The group is open to anyone working in or with the NPS on the following subject areas: research, monitoring and evaluation, performance measurement and management.

Research – as distinct from information provision and management – in the NPS has revolved around the quest to find 'what works' (effective practice). A full description of how NPRIE research officers engage in evaluation also appears separately.

Research at the area level is often patchy, and the RDS is seeking to raise consistency and quality through its 'research standards', which advocate studies based upon randomized control trials. The ROG is working with the RDS to promote these standards among area research workers.

Communication Officers Group

A newly formed group to help communication professionals to share best practice, problems and issues in a flexible and fluid way. Being part of NPRIE is designed not only to help communication officers with their own interactions but also to improve the way research and information can be disseminated and understood.

Membership has expanded over the years to include representatives of probation area information managers and other key stakeholders in probation management information: the RDS Statistics Unit, Criminal Justice Information Technology, the National Probation Directorate (NPD) Performance and Planning Unit, the NPD Data Standards Unit, HMIP and, by correspondence, the NPD OASys (O-DEAT) and the RDS Programme Director. The group's brief was to advise the NPS and other related agencies on data gathering and reporting, and to support the production of a range of monitoring, evaluation and workload management information requirements.

In 2005 the group came within the remit of the NPD Regions and Performance Unit, and membership was widened further to include various policy leads.

NPRIE members seek to ensure that the Data Standards and Reporting Group influences decision-makers at the centre to apply the following principles in setting, defining and measuring information requirements:

- A focus on delivery of products/services.
- Fitness for business purpose, delivered at the required time.
- Iterative development and recognition of the need for partial solutions.
- A collaborative approach among all those involved in determining, implementing, supporting, monitoring and reviewing policy.
- Attention to the costs and benefits of meeting information requirements.
- Recognition of the importance of common data standards and definitions to enable comparability of information, both across probation areas and among criminal justice agencies.
- Attention to all aspects of the information systems required to support policy implementation, monitoring, review and evaluation, including attention to data and to reporting training and quality assurance.

In the beginning ...

NPRIE was founded nearly 30 years ago by the inspiration of Bill McWilliams (then Research Officer with South Yorkshire Probation Service). A committee was established that developed a way of working based around general meetings and the building up of relationships with the Home Office and the Association of Chief Officers of Probation (ACOP). An early contribution was to edit and publish through the Home Office a *National Directory of Projects*. Another consequence of this joint working included the introduction of form 20 for the recording and collection of case information.

In the early 1980s, NPRIE branched out and set up, with support from ACOP and the then Regional Staff Development Structure, the National Probation Research and Information Conference. Then NPRIE began running an 'information exchange' at ACOP national conferences.

NPRIE's relationship with ACOP developed as probation managers became more aware of the contribution that information can make to the functions of the service. The year 1996 saw the first of the one-day conferences. This was on the topic of assessment tools, and it drew an audience at least double the size that had been expected and helped managers, practitioners and civil servants explore the relative merits of different approaches.

NPRIE, as can be seen see from above, became more involved in many areas of service development, but it remains loyal to its core aims of sharing the dissemination of information, knowledge and good practice.

Finally, it should be noted that NPRIE functions on the voluntary contributions of its members (who have given their time) and on the contributions of the chiefs who have allowed and supported it.

Michael Slade

Related entries

Effective practice; Evaluation; Information strategy; National Probation Service for England and Wales; Research.

Key texts and sources

NPRIE's website (**www.nprie.info**) includes much more information about the organization, as well as annual reports, responses to consultation documents, the Glossary of Acronyms and Abbreviations (see Appendix I), the Probation Thesaurus, the Probation Gateway of Internet Resources and the National Research Collection (including area-level research).

NATIONAL PROBATION SERVICE FOR ENGLAND AND WALES

Created in 2001, the National Probation Service brought together 54 independent local probation services, reduced them to 42 coterminous with the police and gave them a national identity.

The Criminal Justice and Court Services Act 2000 created a unified National Probation Service (NPS) coterminous with the 42 police areas across England and Wales. The new NPS,

comprising 42 local probation boards that employed all the staff except the chief, led by a National Probation Directorate (NPD) within the Home Office, came into being on 1 April 2001. This largely devolved structure drove significant gains in performance against targets between 2001 and 2006 and can be seen as one of the successes of government during that time. By the end of the performance year 2005–6, seven of eleven service delivery targets set by ministers were achieved or exceeded, and the remaining four were within 10 per cent of the target.

A new post of Director of Probation was appointed for the first time in 2001. The director line managed all chief officers and, through this arrangement, the national service began to create a consistency not seen previously. The NPD, a new department of the Home Office, grew quickly alongside the NPS and provided an interface with ministers, set policy, provided leadership and determined priorities. In addition, a light-touch regional structure was created, and ten regional managers were appointed, one for each of the English regions and one for Wales. These posts had a co-ordinating function to ensure that regions added value and built an identity. The best examples of regional work involved collaboration to share resources and deliver some joint projects.

Chief officers were recruited centrally, as statutory office holders and members of the local board in the area to which they were appointed. They were accountable to the Director of Probation who was a civil servant. As accountable officers, chiefs were directly responsible for 'spending within the vote' (delivering the priorities of government) and financial probity. The potential tension between these responsibilities and being members of local boards was resolved by making it clear that a board could not require a chief to take action that would place the chief in conflict with the director.

The new national service used a formula to distribute resources alongside a parallel business planning cycle based on the financial year. In the early years, national targets were agreed with ministers and divided pro rata according to resources.

Delivery against targets was encouraged through a 'cash linking' process whereby failure to achieve targets had a negative impact on the area budget for the following year. This 'penalty'-based approach was later rebranded a 'performance bonus scheme', though it continued to work in much the same way. Once the scheme was established, which took about three years, approximately £30 million of the national budget (at that stage about 4 per cent) was distributed or withheld through this approach. It is a mark of the effectiveness of the scheme that, in 2005, 39 of the 42 areas received a performance bonus, in marked contrast to the first year of operation when only one area received it.

The NPD has had extensive dialogue with ministers about what were the key priorities and what was achievable. Usually this approach has brought with it negotiated manageable targets, though sometimes ministers have exercised their prerogative to establish 'stretch' around specific priorities and have set a higher level of achievement. This was particularly evident in the setting of basic skills targets where a step change in delivery was wanted. Between 2003 and 2006 the target for offenders achieving basic skills awards increased ten fold from 1,000 to 10,000; across the same period, the end-of-year performance increased from 848 to 14,930.

Policy changes have been significant over the same period, and the NPS played a key role in influencing and contributing to policy.

The profile of drug related crime has continued to rise in recent years, and the concept of mandated treatment has emerged strongly, representing a policy shift from drug-using offenders having to 'want to change' in order to be seen as treatable to the compulsory treatment that came through drug treatment and testing orders (DTTOs) once offenders consented in court. Completion rates for DTTOs and more recently drug rehabilitation requirements have continued to rise, and research has shown that mandated treatment is no less effective than voluntary treatment. Hepburn (2005) reviewed the research literature and concluded that exposure to drug treatment significantly reduces drug use and criminal behaviour and that there was no difference in the effectiveness of mandated treatment and treatment attended voluntarily in reducing recidivism. The review cites a number of studies that demonstrate that those mandated to treatment began treatment sooner and stayed in treatment longer – two factors generally associated with a positive outcome.

Drug testing has been expanded and is now used in a targeted way in the management of offenders, particularly in key groups (for example, approved premises residents and prolific offenders). Probation has worked extensively with the National Treatment Agency (NTA) to make treatment more widely available and, through the NTA and the Drug Intervention Programme, access has increased significantly. Probation chiefs have been members or sometimes chairs of drug action teams (DATs) and have used this position to ensure access to treatment for drug-using offenders. Again this has seen a policy shift where treatment is aligned with reducing crime, rather than being seen as driven by the health of the individual. In the best examples, DATs have been able to co-ordinate activity across agencies, so where, for example, there is police action to stem supply, there is a consequent increase in treatment capacity. The focus on drugs has led to a lack of access to services for alcohol treatment. Lacking the same concerted drive for alcohol to be seen as a priority, treatment services remain inadequate.

There have also been several initiatives where probation has been a key player in developing work with offenders within communities. The Prolific and other Priority Offender (PPO) initiative allowed communities, represented by Crime and Disorder Reduction Partnerships in England and Community Safety Partnerships in Wales, to identify the group of offenders who committed the greatest volume of crime and caused the greatest difficulty for people locally and to focus on them intensively. This was a key shift from previous national attempts to define a prolific offender category, none of which had had overall national relevance. Probation staff have been the 'offender managers' of this group and have fostered the close inter-agency working that characterizes this scheme. Home Office research suggests some promising early results, including a 10 per cent reduction in recorded convictions for the first PPO cohort compared with the six months prior to the start of the scheme.

During 2005, the Community Payback initiative was launched that created a policy shift in the management of unpaid work. The new components of Community Payback included establishing a consultative process to allow the community a say in how offenders should pay back, and it began the process of making the work and the projects much more visible. A year on, the best payback projects tend to be those that are undertaken with other partners in communities that have an effective consultative process. Community Payback was rolled out across England and Wales with considerable positive local publicity during the period May–November 2005.

Perhaps the greatest policy shift in recent times has been the extent of collaboration between probation and police. Since the late 1990s and through the author's own experience as a chief, this is a relationship that has grown in strength enormously, significantly assisted by the requirement that probation areas shared police force boundaries from 2001. The author firmly believes that probation areas would describe the police as their most significant partner in the community-based management of offenders. This close working relationship involves information sharing and direct working together with key offender groups, most notably PPOs and public protection cases. Police and probation staff work alongside one another, sometimes in the police station, sometimes in the probation office. Discussion about those offenders who cause significant harm to others regularly takes place in all 42 police/probation areas through the multi-agency public protection arrangements, always with both agencies present.

The Probation Service in England and Wales is currently undergoing more change that builds on the success of the last five years and moves forward into different structures that will be based on greater partnerships and new commissioning arrangements. Public protection stemming from the close work with the police will be at the heart of this change, and there will be a very significant demand for continued performance improvements.

Roger Hill

Related entries

Chief officers; Crime and Disorder Reduction Partnerships; National Offender Management Service (NOMS); Performance management; Probation boards.

Key texts and sources

Criminal Justice and Court Services Act 2000.
Bailey, R., Knight, C. and Williams, B. (2007) 'The Probation Service as part of NOMS in England and Wales: fit for purpose?', in L. Gelsthorpe and R. Morgan (eds) *Handbook of Probation*. Cullompton: Willan Publishing.
Hepburn, J.R. (2005) 'Recidivism among drug offenders following exposure to treatment', *Criminal Justice Policy Review*, 16: 237–59.
Morgan, R. (2007) 'Probation, governance and accountability', in L. Gelsthorpe and R. Morgan (eds) *Handbook of Probation*. Cullompton: Willan Publishing.
The National Probation Service Performance Reports 8 and 20 are available online at **www.probation. homeoffice.gov.uk/output/page34.asp**.

NATIONAL STANDARDS

National Standards specify core probation tasks and when they must be carried out. The latest (2005) edition is based on the principles of offender management and the requirements of the Criminal Justice Act 2003.

National Standards prescribe how offenders are to be supervised and managed. They stipulate the process and timeliness of the allocation of new cases, first appointment, assessment, frequency of contact, sentence planning and review. They also cover the standard of reports, including pre-sentence reports. More recent editions specify standards for offenders' behaviour.

National Standards were first issued in 1989 in relation to community service (unpaid work). This represented a development in the Home Office's guidance to Probation Service. As independent bodies corporate, probation committees had been largely responsible for their own policy and practice. The *Statement of National*

Objectives and Priorities (1984), which required services to respond with their own local statements, was an early sign that the Home Office was becoming more assertive in its management of probation, changing the balance between the national and the local. The promulgation of a full set of standards in 1992, to support the implementation of the Criminal Justice Act 1991, represented a further significant step towards the national regulation of practice.

National Standards were intended to enhance quality, constituting an essential assurance to courts about how orders would be implemented and what they might expect from the Probation Service; they increased consistency, so that the character and frequency of dealings with the service no longer depended on the judgement (and perhaps idiosyncrasies) of the supervising officer; and they also made it very clear to offenders what was expected and what would follow in the event of non-compliance.

Critics object that, by prescribing a 'standard' experience without regard to the many ways in which offenders are differently situated – for instance, the different demands that community supervision make upon them – the standards overlook the diversity of offenders, mistaking sameness for consistency and fairness. Diversity calls for practitioner discretion, within a framework of accountability, but, while professional discretion certainly remains, it has been progressively circumscribed in successive editions of the standards. Arguably, too, National Standards denied a busy service the opportunity of managing an overwhelming caseload: instead of being able to target its resources on the basis of the risk principle and criminogenic need, the standards took away this latitude in favour of a standard experience for all.

National Standards have never been evidence-based, and conformity with these standards, while plausibly a measure of efficiency, must not be taken to be a measure of effectiveness. Reports and inquiries have sometimes mistaken conformity with standards as an indication of high-quality practice. As the basis on which staff would be held to account for their practice, standards had considerable potential, but their decisive importance as targets in performance management, inspection and inquiries has led to a mechanistic and often defensive implementation.

Rob Canton and Tina Eadie

Related entries

Accountability; Criminal Justice Act 1991; Discretion; Diversity; Performance management.

Key texts and sources

Canton, R. and Eadie, T. (2005) 'From enforcement to compliance: implications for supervising officers', *Vista*, 9: 152–8.

Hopley, K. (2002) 'National Standards: defining the service', in D. Ward *et al.* (eds) *Probation: Working for Justice* (2nd edn). Oxford: Oxford University Press.

The National Standards are available online at **http://www.probation.homeoffice.gov.uk/files/pdf /NPS%20National%20Standard%202005.pdf.**

O

OASYS DATA EVALUATION AND ANALYSIS TEAM (O-DEAT)

A team of analysts and social researchers within the OASys team who examine the quality of completed OASys assessments and test the reliability, validity and predictive ability of OASys as a risk–needs assessment tool. O-DEAT also produces information for operational use and policy development within the National Offender Management Service (NOMS) and contributes to research on offenders undertaken within the Home Office and within the wider research community.

OASys is an effective tool for use in the assessment and management of offenders to the extent that it is both a reliable and valid measure – that is, it consistently measures what it is designed to measure in a verifiably robust way. There were three pilot studies of OASys in the Prison Service and National Probation Service, beginning in 1999, during which data were collected and analysed to inform further development. The research focused on testing and improving different types of reliability and validity of OASys at each stage of the pilot. O-DEAT continues research to evaluate and improve OASys, with projects, for example, looking at the extent to which OASys is used consistently by different assessors (inter-rater reliability) and how successfully it predicts the likelihood of violent and non-violent reoffending (predictive validity). O-DEAT's findings are used to improve guidance to assessors and managers and sometimes to amend the content of OASys.

The quality of data in OASys assessments is of the utmost importance as data affect the value of using assessments in both making defensible decisions in managing offenders' risks and needs, and in research. O-DEAT reports on the extent of missing information in completed OASys assessments to aid OASys managers in improving the quality of assessments.

Having established the quality, reliability and validity of OASys in assessing offenders, O-DEAT produces reports in the form of profiles, summarizing offenders' likelihood of reoffending, risk of harm (to self and others) and level of criminogenic needs. O-DEAT can further divide the data into subgroups summarizing risks and needs by offence type, gender, ethnicity, region, area, establishment, etc. The summary findings apply only to offenders with completed OASys assessments, although O-DEAT is exploring the extent to which OASys data are representative of the population of offenders in NOMS. Some of O-DEAT's production of offender profiles is being superseded by the OASys National Reporting System, which allows standard reports to be generated at regional and local levels. O-DEAT continues to meet requests for the tailored analysis of data for use in management information, commissioning, performance measurement and research.

Mia Debidin

Related entries

Criminogenic needs; Offender Assessment System (OASys); Research.

Key texts and sources

Published findings of the OASys evaluation include the following:
Howard, P. (2006) *The Offender Assessment System: An Evaluation of the Second Pilot. Home Office Research Findings* 278. London: Home Office.

Howard, P., Clark, D. and Garnham, N. (2006) *An evaluation of the Offender Assessment System (OASys) in Three Pilots, 1999–2001*. London: Home Office (available online at http://www.noms.homeoffice.gov.uk/downloads/oasys-210606.pdf).
Publication of the findings from O-DEAT research on the inter-rater reliability of OASys and on the prediction of reoffending from OASys scores is expected in 2007.

OFFENDER ASSESSMENT SYSTEM (OASYS)

OASys is a national system for assessing the risks and needs of an offender. It is designed to:

- assess how likely it is for an offender to be reconvicted;
- identify and classify offending-related needs;
- assess risk of harm to others and to self;
- assist with the management of risk of harm;
- link the assessment to the sentence plan;
- indicate the need for further specialist assessments; and
- measure change during the period of supervision/sentence.

The electronic version of OASys, known in probation as eOASys, allows for assessments to be passed between probation areas and between probation offices and prison establishments.

Background

OASys – short for the Offender Assessment System – was developed as an assessment instrument jointly by the National Probation Service (NPS) and the Prison Service with the intention that it should be used in both services.

The development of OASys began in 1999 after an analysis of existing assessment systems demonstrated that none fully met the needs of the Prison Service and NPS. OASys was initially rolled out in the NPS as a paper-based system, but the intention was always that an electronic version would be developed that allowed assessments to be exchanged between both services. Because of their different IT infrastructures, the Prison Service and NPS separately developed their own OASys IT systems. The two systems began to be rolled out from 2003 and were connected to one another in stages between 2004 and 2006. All the NPS areas and the publicly owned prisons were connected by April 2006. Work to connect the contracted-out prisons is ongoing.

What is OASys?

Using evidence-based research, OASys assesses the likelihood of reconviction, risk of harm and offending-related factors (or 'criminogenic needs'), such as poor educational and employment skills, substance misuse, relationship problems and problems with thinking and attitude. The OASys assessment enables a sentence plan to be prepared. Completed at pre-sentence report (PSR) stage in many cases, OASys informs probation's sentencing advice to the courts. Used in the ongoing offender management of sentenced offenders, both in custody and in the community, it helps practitioners make sound and defensible decisions about managing risk and tackling need. OASys enables better targeting to accredited programmes and other interventions than was hitherto possible, increasing the chances of those interventions having a beneficial impact.

OASys also provides, on an ongoing basis, a wealth of information that can inform national and local research into, for example, criminogenic profiles in particular areas and the impact of specific interventions on reconviction rates (see O-DEAT). It thus assists both probation areas and prison establishments in managing their offender populations to enable them to match resources with identified need to the maximum effect.

Which offenders are assessed using OASys?

The following are assessed:

- Offenders subject to court-ordered standard delivery PSRs.
- Offenders on community orders (see Supervision of offenders).

- Offenders on licence from prison.
- Hostel residents (in approved premises) who are subject to an order, licence or on bail.
- Young offenders serving one month or more in custody and adults serving one year or more in custody.

The five main components of OASys

The five main components of OASys are as follows:

1. Risk of reconviction and offending-related factors – including offending information both past and current, social and economic factors and personal factors. All these sections are scored. The higher the score, the more likely the factor is related to offending. There is also a section on health in this component but this section is not scored.
2. Risk of serious harm to others, risks to the individual and other risks.
3. The OASys summary sheet.
4. The Sentence plan.
5. Self-assessment.

1. Offending information

This component examines current and previous offences. Research clearly indicates that criminal history is the best predictor of future conviction.

Social and economic factors

The *accommodation* section looks at whether accommodation is available, the quality of that accommodation and whether its location is a problem.

Offenders are generally less well educated and trained than other groups in society. They are more likely to be unemployed, have a poor history of employment and express a dislike of the work ethic. The *education, training and employability* section explores this area. The *financial management and income* section deals with income and how it is managed. This is an indicator of general ability to cope and relates, in turn, to reoffending.

The *relationships* section assesses whether the offender's satisfaction with his or her relationships, and the stability of those relationships, relates to his or her offending behaviour. The *lifestyle and associates* section examines aspects of the offender's current lifestyle. A clear link exists between how offenders spend their time, the people they mix with and the likelihood of reconviction.

The *drug misuse* section identifies the extent and type of any drug misuse and its effects on an offender's life. Research consistently links misuse of drugs with reoffending. The next section considers whether *alcohol misuse* is a significant factor in previous or current offending. Alcohol is often linked with risk of harm and is a factor in much violent crime.

Personal factors

The *emotional wellbeing* section examines the extent to which emotional problems interfere with the offender's life and whether this is associated with risk of harm to him or herself or others. Mental health problems (such as anxiety and depression) relate to offending for certain groups.

The *thinking and behaviour* section assesses the offender's application of reasoning, especially to social problems. Research indicates that offenders tend not to think things through, plan or consider the consequences of their behaviour and do not see things from other people's perspectives. Those with a number of such 'cognitive deficits' will be more likely to reoffend and benefit from cognitive-behavioural methods.

The *attitudes* section considers the offender's attitude towards his or her offending and towards supervision. A growing body of research demonstrates that pro-criminal attitudes are predictive of reconviction. Tackling attitudes can reduce the likelihood of reconviction.

The *health and other considerations* sections does not contribute to assessing the likelihood of reconviction or risk of harm. Assessors use this section when considering suitability for a community sentence (which may involve physical work), electronic monitoring and programmes. This information will mainly be used by the NPS but it also assists the Prison Service in sentence planning and in determining suitable allocations to work.

2. Risk of serious harm, risks to the individual and other risks

This part of OASys includes the following:

- A screening section (designed to indicate whether a full risk analysis should be completed).
- A full analysis section, including a risk management plan (see Risk assessment and risk management).
- A harm summary section.

It addresses risk of harm to:

- the public (public protection);
- adults known to the offender;
- staff;
- prisoners;
- children;
- the offender him or herself (including self-harm and suicide; coping in a custodial or hostel setting; vulnerability).

It also addresses other risks, such as escape/abscond from custody, control issues and breach of trust.

OASys uses four levels of risk of serious harm:

1. *Low*: current evidence does not indicate the likelihood of causing serious harm.
2. *Medium*: there are identifiable indicators of risk of serious harm. The offender has the potential to cause serious harm but is unlikely to do so unless there is a change in circumstances (for example, failure to take medication, loss of accommodation, relationship breakdown and drug or alcohol misuse).
3. *High*: there are identifiable indicators of risk of serious harm. A potential event could happen at any time and the impact would be serious.
4. *Very high*: there is imminent risk of serious harm. A potential event is more likely than not to happen imminently. The impact would be serious.

The risks to self include self-harm and suicide, and other risks, such as the risk of absconding,

are not graded but are highlighted as needing to be considered.

3. OASys summary sheet

This component shows 'at a glance' what risks and needs relating to the offender have been identified. It shows the main areas of work that need to be included in the sentence plan and risk management plan.

4. Sentence planning

The various elements of OASys are drawn together in a component that looks ahead to the management of the offender throughout his or her sentence and leads to the preparation of a sentence plan. This plan is reviewed at regular intervals depending on the type of order/sentence the offender is subject to and the risks he or she is deemed to pose.

5. Self-assessment

OASys contains a self-assessment questionnaire which gives the offender an opportunity to record his or her views. It provides the offender manager with a useful insight into how offenders see their lives and their offending behaviour. Research suggests that offenders tend to recognize their problems, and there is an evidential link between reconviction and the degree of difficulty they report. The self-assessment questionnaire contributes to the sentence plan prepared by probation or prison staff.

Triggers for further assessments

OASys is an excellent assessment system but it does not provide the level of detail needed in every case. OASys prompts the assessor to recognize where a more detailed – specialist – assessment is necessary. Specialist assessments include:

- sex offender;
- violent offender;
- basic skills (Education, Skills for Life);
- drugs;
- alcohol;
- mental health (mentally disordered offenders);

- dangerous and severe personality disorder; and
- domestic violence.

Confidentiality

The OASys assessment will normally be shared with the offender. However, any information that ought not to be seen by the offender – victim details, for example – would be recorded in the *confidential* section of OASys (see Case records; Data Protection Act 1998).

OASys IT

The NPS and Prison Service OASys IT systems allow assessments to be passed from probation area to probation area and between the NPS and the Prison Service.

Once an assessment is completed, the electronic system allows for reviews to be done by 'cloning' information from the previous assessment into the current one and allows the assessor to change only what needs changing. The system is designed in such a way that countersignatures are required for certain assessments (such as those for offenders deemed to pose a high risk of serious harm) before an assessment is deemed to be complete.

Court report template

In 2005 the National Probation Directorate in the Home Office promulgated a new court report framework for the NPS (PC 18/05) which introduced greater standardization in the provision of PSRs across England and Wales. Within eOASys it is now possible to produce a standard delivery report from an OASys assessment. This has helped in raising the standard of both assessments and court reports and has an important role to play in underpinning the new framework and in supporting the successful implementation

of the Criminal Justice Act 2003. A single revised version of the PSR template in OASys, replacing the two versions originally deployed, was introduced in August 2006.

Liz Holden

Related entries

Assessment; Assessment instruments and systems; Criminogenic needs; Interventions; OASys Data Evaluation and Analysis Team (O-DEAT); Offender management; Pre-sentence report (PSR); Risk assessment and risk management; Risk of harm.

Key texts and sources

Aubrey, R. and Hough, M. (1997) *Assessing Offenders' Needs: Assessment Scales for the Probation Service.* Home Office Research Study 166. London: Home Office.

Aye Maung, N. and Hammond, N. (2000) *Risk of Reoffending and Needs Assessment: The User's Perspective.* Home Office Research Study 211. London: Home Office.

Burnett, R., Baker, K. and Roberts, C. (2007) 'Assessment, supervision and intervention: fundamental practice in probation', in L. Gelsthorpe and R. Morgan (eds) *Handbook of Probation.* Cullompton: Willan Publishing.

Howard, P., Clark, D.A. and Garnham, N. (2006) *The Offender Assessment System: An Evaluation of the Second Pilot.* RDS Findings 278. London: Home Office.

Kemshall, H. (2003) *Understanding Risk in Criminal Justice.* Buckingham: Open University Press.

Raynor, P., Kynch, J., Roberts, R. and Merrington, M. (2000) *Risk and Need Assessment in Probation Services: An Evaluation. Home Office Research Study* 211. London: Home Office.

Zamble, E. and Quinsey, V.L. (1999) *The Criminal Recidivism Process.* Cambridge: Cambridge University Press.

OFFENDER MANAGEMENT

1. At a macro and general level, the processes and arrangements for handling offenders from arrest through to the completion of sentences.
2. The particular strategy and arrangements for the above proposed by the Correctional Services Review of 2003, and adopted by the government in 2004.
3. At a micro level, handling individual offenders in accordance with the Offender Management Model.

Origins

The Carter Report introduced the term 'offender management'. It is not a term that can be found in common usage prior to this. It can also be a confusing term, sometimes referring to the entire national framework for handling offenders, at other times referring to the contribution of the correctional services and at yet others to processes for handling individual offenders.

General use of the term

At its most general, the term is used to refer simply to the entire network of roles, processes and structures for managing offenders in any jurisdiction. More narrowly, it refers to the specific contribution of the correctional services to this network. In either usage, the term does not imply any particular methodology or approach.

Specific meaning at a macro level

In the Carter Report the 'new approach to offender management' had three integrated and interdependent strands:

1. The Rebalancing Sentencing initiative was to secure a shift in sentencing away from short periods of custody into community sentences, and from community sentences to fines. The establishment of the Sentencing Guidelines Council and a programme of routinely providing sentencers with cost and effectiveness information were intended to achieve this.

2. The second strand was to implement an 'end-to-end' approach to managing individual offenders. There would be a single organization – NOMS. Offender managers would manage individual offenders and be accountable through regional offender managers to a National Offender Manager.

3. The third strand – contestability – was to introduce a regional commissioning framework through which, over time, the voluntary and community sector, and the private sector, would compete for correctional work.

The Offender Management Model

It was the NOMS Offender Management Model (in 2005) which added the next level of detail. This is a much more specific use of the term. Offender management is the name given to the case management model designed to meet the needs of the correctional system in England and Wales. In the process of implementing the model, the awful verb 'to offender manage' evolved, meaning 'to deal with an offender in accordance with the Offender Management Model'.

The Offender Management Model (see Figure 5) is just that – a model. It builds from an 'offender journey' through the correctional system. It is couched in new, agency-neutral language and terminology. The 'journey' is community based and made up of an individualized combination of length, punitive, rehabilitative and restrictive elements, to which the various different providers make their own unique contribution. The punitive element may range from keeping supervision appointments to long-term custody. The approach is person centred, rather than task or environment focused.

The ASPIRE acronym is used to refer to the backbone of the process, and simultaneously defines the role of the offender manager within it:

Assess Sentence Plan Implement Review Evaluate

A universal national assessment instrument (OASys) already existed to codify the A, SP, R and E of ASPIRE. Integrating OASys into the formally approved case management process countered the risk of assessment being seen, and managed, as an isolated task.

Figure 5 The Offender Management Model

The implementation element in ASPIRE stresses a teamwork approach to individuals (as opposed to caseloads) and the establishment of improved communication systems to support that teamwork:

- A delivery team (the Offender Management Team) is composed of an offender manager, offender supervisor, key workers and a case administrator. This is an inclusive concept. For example, it recognizes the valuable role played by administrative staff, previously almost invisible in the external profile of the correctional services (see Figure 6).

- It validates the appointment of Probation Service officer-grade offender managers. The providers of interventions (key workers) are team members and partners, not 'contractors'. Offender supervisors are particularly important during custodial periods, delivering the day-to-day contact which cannot be delivered by a community-based offender manager. Throughout 2005–6, prisons and probation areas reconfigured their working arrangements to support the Offender Management Team concept by locating staff in small, cross-grade units, with various titles like 'triads', 'clusters' or 'offender management units'.

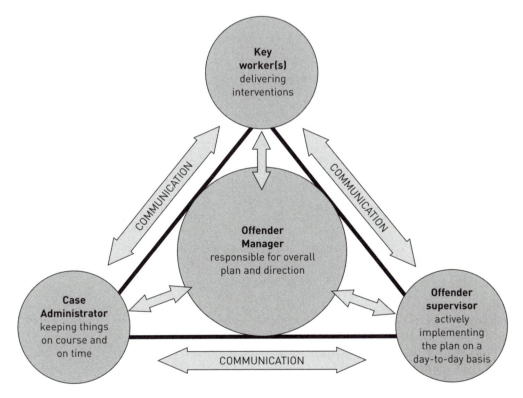

Figure 6 The Offender Management Team

- A new communication system and case record – called C-NOMIS – was developed based upon the Offender Management Model. Implementation commenced in December 2006. C-NOMIS contains a single record for each offender in the NOMS 'family' of services and enables designated members of each offender's Offender Management Team to communicate in real time across the boundaries of agency and geography.
- The lessons from effective project management are applied to the work of the Offender Management Team under the subtitle of 'Every case is a project'.

Tiering

Tiering is a 'model within a model'. It introduces a single framework for turning the two principles – 'resources follow risk' and 'least necessary' – into an operational construct for resourcing the case management (as opposed to the interventions) function of individual cases. Arguably its catchy 'PUNISH, HELP, CHANGE and CONTROL' language provides a contemporary NOMS 'strapline' replacing probation's 'ADVISE, ASSIST

and BEFRIEND'. A set of national rules breaks down the offender population into four tiers, each attracting a different case management approach (called 'PUNISH, HELP, CHANGE or CONTROL') requiring different time allocations and different offender manager competences and accountability (see Figure 7).

Finally, the model uses 'the 4 Cs' to define how the correctional process needs to be experienced by offenders for maximum impact. The 4 Cs are:

Continuity Consistency Commitment Consolidation

The importance of these features emerges consistently from effective practice and desistance research. Continuity has two dimensions – continuity of treatment (sometimes called integrity) and continuity of relationship. It is a desirable precondition (though not a guarantee) for consistency, commitment and consolidation, and is particularly important at the transition from custody back into the community. Work is underway to find ways of measuring whether offenders experience the 4 Cs as a proxy for reduced reoffending and public protection.

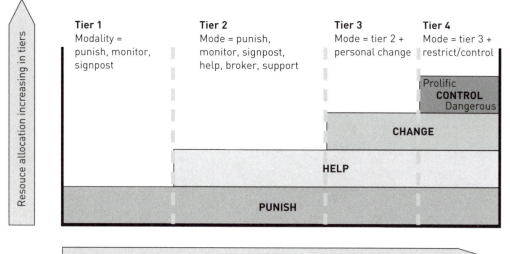

Figure 7 The four tiers of the offender population

Implementation

Agreeing a single, agency-neutral case management model was no mean feat. The term alone was laden with controversy. For some, the word 'offender' excessively labelled those with whom NOMS works; for others, 'management' implied a depersonalization or objectification of those people. The use of the term 'management' in relation to the roles of front-line practitioners was always liable to bring with it industrial relations complications.

Beyond the adoption of the model as policy, its implementation would always be a sterner test. The implementation plan was broken into phases from April 2005 to December 2008, though dates were not set for the inclusion of short-sentence and remand prisoners in the programme.

Carter's vision was that a more effective model of offender management would be funded by reducing the demand for prison places and community sentences. This was to be accompanied by a better balance between the regional demand for, and supply of, prison places. Supported by C-NOMIS and a national network of video communication technology, this would make the offender management of serving prisoners by community-based offender managers more feasible.

By the beginning of the implementation of phase II of offender management (the first tranche of the prison population), none of these preconditions had been satisfactorily met. Additionally, one of the other Carter strands – the introduction of contestability – had proved to be a hugely preoccupying issue for the National Probation Service.

Impact of the Offender Management Model

Little can be said in the early stages about the impact of offender management in terms of its outcomes with offenders. Any impact on re-offending rates will take several years to identify.

What was clear from the early months of implementation was that the Offender Management Model carried substantial support among staff and offenders. The PATHFINDER (November 2005–March 2007) project established that practitioners, partners and offenders at all levels and in all agencies viewed it as 'the right way to do things'. Implementation was driven by a network of multi-agency regional implementation groups. These were characterized by high levels of energy and commitment, and a positive, problem-solving approach. Such determined collaboration on a single, universal change initiative was unprecedented.

When, on 6 November 2006, phase II of the implementation of offender management began, an Offender Management Unit came into being in every prison in the country, populated by offender supervisors. The ASPIRE responsibility began to be allocated to community-based offender managers who set about establishing and reviewing sentence plans in custody.

One of the objectives of the introduction of NOMS was to 'break down the silos of prison and probation'. The Offender Management Model had already made a substantial contribution to the achievement of that objective.

Tony Grapes

Related entries

ASPIRE; Carter Report; Case management; C-NOMIS; Desistance; Effective practice; Interventions; National Offender Management Service (NOMS); Offender management as seen by other agencies.

Key texts and sources

Bailey, R., Knight, C. and Williams, B. (2007) 'The Probation Service as part of NOMS in England and Wales: fit for purpose?', in L. Gelsthorpe and R. Morgan (eds) *Handbook of Probation.* Cullompton: Willan Publishing.

Burnett, R., Baker, K. and Roberts, C. (2007) 'Assessment, supervision and intervention: fundamental practice in probation', in L. Gelsthorpe and R. Morgan (eds) *Handbook of Probation.* Cullompton: Willan Publishing.

Holt, P. (2000) *Case Management: Context for Supervision.* Leicester: De Montfort University (for origins of the 4 Cs) (available online at **http://www.dmu.ac.uk/Images/Monograph%202_tcm2-35042.pdf**).

The NOMS Offender Management Model (Version 1.1) and the *Action Research Report* on the PATHFINDER can be found on the NOMS website (**www.noms.homeoffice.gov.uk**).

OFFENDER MANAGEMENT AS SEEN BY OTHER AGENCIES

Inter-agency perspectives on offender management.

As the National Offender Management Service (NOMS) implements the Offender Management Model, it is essential to consider whether that approach is consistent with case management in other related sectors, notably child protection, mental health and drug treatment. How can the Offender Management Model and the case management/care co-ordination arrangements in related sectors work together to avoid confusion and add value to each other?

Terminology

NOMS and the Probation Service use the term 'offender manager' for the role of 'case manager' or 'care co-ordinator'; 'offender management' for 'case management' or 'care co-ordination'; and 'sentence plan' or 'supervision plan' for the 'case' or 'care plan'. In this entry, the terms 'case plan' and 'case management' will be used throughout but should be interpreted to cover the equivalent roles and systems operating in criminal justice and treatment services.

Core elements of offender management

The Offender Management Model espoused by NOMS has at its core the following elements:

- A separation of 'case management' functions from 'interventions'.
- 'Case management' includes proper assessment and case planning, as well as oversight of the delivery of the case plan and action where the plan may break down.
- 'End to end' case management with a single 'case manager' to ensure continuity of interventions.
- Assessment is holistic and evidence based, through the OASys tool.
- 'Case management' regards motivational inputs as an essential feature of the role (see Motivation) and values-planned programme completion as a key outcome.

- Enhanced arrangements for case planning and plan delivery exist in priority cases, such as high-risk multi-agency public protection arrangement (MAPPA) cases. These arrangements are designed to ensure co-ordinated inter-agency action to support effective case management and interventions.
- Interventions are developed in line with the evidence base and include cognitive-behavioural programmes and interventions through 'wrap around' services (for example, around accommodation and employability needs).
- Interventions are concerned not simply with the delivery of a specified programme but with a process of behavioural and attitudinal change in which key criminogenic needs are tackled.
- The case management process is subject to quality assurance mechanisms through the Probation and Prison Services and through inspection and audit processes.
- User involvement is reflected in the case management process, specifically by recorded involvement in case planning.
- Case management is responsive to diversity issues and needs.

Other case management approaches

Other approaches use a different language but the core elements above apply:

- Drug treatment interventions are subject to clinical governance arrangements and increasingly formal case management frameworks.
- While drug treatment would focus on behavioural factors other than (but where appropriate inclusive of) criminogenic ones, behavioural and attitude change are at the heart of effective drug treatment.
- Drug treatment is being built on an evidence base that recognizes motivational inputs, programme interventions, user involvement and effective community integration as core components. Retention in, and planned completion of, treatment are key indicators for effectiveness.
- Child protection work operates under the national 'framework for assessment' rather than OASys.

- The case management function is held by the 'key worker' in child protection interventions.
- Mental health treatment operates under the Care Programme Approach (CPA). This approach embodies the same elements as set out above but, of course, focused on mental health improvements.
- Assessment, Care in Custody and Teamwork (ACCT) plans operate in prisons where there are suicide risks and involve identified case managers and case plans naming those responsible for specific actions.

Hierarchy of models

In order to prevent confusion and duplication of activity, it is important that all agencies recognize the following hierarchy according to which the models must operate. The hierarchy does not imply that agencies can dispense with the structures they operate as individual agencies. It does, however, provide an opportunity to reduce duplication and confusions about case management, and the potential to use case planning and review meetings to meet the demands of more than one case management structure:

1. Child protection is the paramount responsibility of all agencies. Where children are at risk, the child protection system must take priority.
2. Public protection takes priority when dealing with cases that meet the criteria for a MAPPA. A MAPPA case management system should take priority.
3. Within prisons, ACCT plans need to be prioritized when there are suicide risks.
4. Other priority cases identified because of the damage being caused to society are supervised within Prolific and Priority Offender (PPO) arrangements. Where the above three categories do not apply, PPO premium service case management systems take priority.
5. Where cases are subject to statutory supervision under a court order or licence, the offender management model should take priority and the case management role would be held by a probation officer/offender manager.
6. Where cases are in receipt of treatment for mental illness, a judgement will need to be made in each case as to which case management system structure can most effectively meet the needs of the patient and protect the community, and should therefore be the lead system. Drug users suffering from severe and enduring mental illness would be subject to CPA case management.
7. Other cases subject to drug treatment would fall within case management arrangements through treatment providers and criminal justice intervention teams (CJITs). These work within the Drugs Intervention Programme (DIP), which seeks to engage and retain problematic drug-using offenders in treatment.

Partnerships and inter-agency work add value, but the complexities must be understood and addressed. This hierarchy of priorities that emerges from a consideration of the priorities in different agencies presents both opportunities and challenges for those involved in offender management. The opportunities rely on offender managers being sensitive to the ways in which other public services will see the needs of specific offenders who may access other services that will be useful in reducing criminogenic propensity. The challenges lie in recognizing the priorities of others and in establishing common understandings about responsibilities, sharing and liaison in different professional settings.

David Skidmore

Related entries

Child protection; Inter-agency work; Multi-agency public protection arrangements (MAPPAs); National Offender Management Service (NOMS); Offender management; Partnerships; Public protection.

> ### Key texts and sources
>
> See the sources in the related entries.

OFFENDER PERCEPTIONS

How offenders perceive probation officers and the Probation Service.

If you want to know something about the ways in which offenders interact with their probation supervisors, what motivates them and how they perceive their own experience, then the best way is to ask them and to talk with them and with those most closely concerned. Yet the rigorous investigation and analysis of offenders' perceptions of and opinions about probation, or about criminal justice generally, received virtually no attention before 1980, either in academic research or in administrative processes. Indeed, the notion still appears to be alien to ministerial thought, even though the research has proved instructive and its findings are consistent.

Offender perception studies usually adopt a qualitative rather than a quantitative approach, with the objective of disclosing and examining key topics and themes embedded in offenders' experience. While this method of research has its limitations, the richness of the material provides considerable insight into the factors leading towards the successful completion of a probation programme – or its early failure – and so potentially helping to enhance the quality of intervention.

Studies have adopted a number of different approaches, but findings have been remarkably consistent. While the sanctions inherent in probation supervision can assist in establishing and maintaining the relationship between an offender and the supervisor, it is the *quality* of that relationship that has been found to determine – for good or for ill – the dynamics and interaction.

While none of the studies suggested that the quality of the relationship of itself *determines* a successful outcome, all of them indicated that where offenders experienced a supervisor's sustained practical interest and concern and were treated as persons deserving respect, alongside a rigorous challenge to their offending behaviour, there was at least the *basis* for a successful outcome in terms of completion and reduced reoffending. Certainly, humiliation, whether deliberate or unintentional, was a negative force driving persistent serious offenders deeper into anti-social behaviour, and was usually associated with an unsuccessful outcome.

Several studies show that offenders value:

- sustained interest from a practitioner;
- being treated as a person and with respect (including respect for the several dimensions of diversity and responsivity);
- rigorous challenge to offending behaviour; and
- trust, integrity, honesty, listening, being held to account and a non-judgemental approach.

Rex (1999) found that the following played a significant part in the supervisory relationship and in subsequent desistance from offending:

- Negotiated engagement and partnership in problem-solving.
- Support and encouragement.
- Efforts to improve reasoning and decision-making.
- Personal and professional commitment of workers to the change process and to the recommended programme.
- Attention to the personal and social problems of offenders.
- Feelings of loyalty, commitment and accountability to the probation officer.
- Reinforcement of prosocial behaviour (see Prosocial modelling).
- All staff displaying a genuine interest in offenders' well-being.

Conversely, if the supervisor was seen as overbearing, co-operation would be withdrawn and, even if they still attended appointments, offenders might withhold information or even try to mislead the probation officer.

These research findings have important implications for compliance and for all aspects of probation practice.

Roy Bailey

Related entries

Compliance; Diversity; Effective practice; Legitimacy; Motivation; Public attitudes to probation; Research.

Key texts and sources

Beaumont, B. and Mistry, T. (1996) 'Doing a good job under duress', *Probation Journal*, 43: 200–4.

Chigwada-Bailey, R. (1997) *Black Women's Experiences of Criminal Justice*. Winchester: Waterside Press.

Kemshall, H., Dominey, J., Knight, V. with Bailey, R. and Price, A. (2004) *Offender Perception Data Project*. Leicester: De Montfort University.

Rex, S. (1999) 'Desistance from offending: experiences of probation', *Howard Journal of Criminal Justice*, 38: 366–83.

OLDER OFFENDERS

The terms 'elderly', 'elder', 'older' or 'in later life' are used in the literature to describe prisoners who are 50 and above. (Using 50 means that women will not be excluded from policy consideration – there are very few women aged 60 or older in prisons or subject to community penalties.)

Ageing, in penal policy, is not seen to be an issue which, in itself, reflects how the age and crime relationship has been constructed within the criminal justice system. The most common offences for the older female age group are violence against the person and drug offences. In comparison, the most common offences for men in this group are sexual offences, violence against the person and drug offences. The numbers of older offenders in prison are increasing as more and more people are receiving longer mandatory sentences, while changes in arrest and prosecution practices and revised sentencing policies have also led to an increase in the older prison population. The general rise in the number of men who have been convicted in later life for sex-related offences, including those charged with 'historical offences' (committed two or three decades ago), contributes to this trend.

Since older prisoners are relatively few in number (approximately 6,500 over 55 years of age in a prison population of around 80,000), the majority of prisons in England and Wales have not been designed with the older prisoner in mind. The absence of basic facilities (such as hav-ing a 24-hour medical centre on site, ground-floor rooms, adequate resettlement programmes, activities for daily living, etc.), results in a situation where women and men in later life are left without any form of purposeful activity. Purposeful activity, including employment or work-based training, is limited because there is no statutory requirement for those over 60 to work, and activities outside the cell are often not available to the less mobile and certainly the infirm. Prisoners over the age of 60 who do not work will receive the minimum weekly wage entitlement (not enough to buy a pouch of tobacco).

Prior to discharge, arrangements for a single multidisciplinary assessment should be made to identify needs and develop inter-agency co-operation with primary care trusts, probation and social services. This fits in with the offender management approach adopted by National Offender Management Service. Older prisoners experience social exclusion and can be very anxious and apprehensive over their supervision or licence details. They often get confused over what is expected of them and how they are going to meet these expectations. It is important to ensure that information is effectively communicated and that it is understood. Many older prisoners have no family or community links, making resettlement harder, and are more likely to become institutionalized. They often have a multiplicity of healthcare issues, have not benefited from prison programmes (which are not geared to the needs of older prisoners – especially offending behaviour, education and employment programmes) and may have limited funds during sentence, as retirement pension is suspended.

Azrini Wahidin, Sally Wentworth-James and Stuart Ware

Related entries

Diversity; Offender management; Prison; Resettlement; Social exclusion.

Key texts and sources

Wahidin, A. and Cain, M. (eds) (2006) *Ageing, Crime and Society*. Cullompton: Willan Publishing.

P

PAROLE BOARD

The Parole Board is the independent body that protects the public by making risk assessments about prisoners to decide who may safely be released into the community and who must remain in or be returned to custody.

Legal framework

The Parole Board was established under the provisions of the Criminal Justice Act 1967 to advise the Home Secretary on the early release of prisoners. The Criminal Justice and Public Order Act 1994 established the Parole Board as an executive non-departmental public body.

Under the terms of the Criminal Justice Act 1991 and the Parole Board (Transfer of Functions) Order 1998, the Parole Board has delegated authority to decide applications for parole for those sentenced on or after 1 October 1992 to a determinate sentence of from 4 to less than 15 years. The 1991 Act, as amended by the Crime (Sentences) Act 1997 and the Criminal Justice Act 2003, also gives authority to the board to direct the release of life-sentence prisoners (lifers) and those serving sentences for public protection (see Dangerousness). For other classes of prisoner, the board makes recommendations to the Secretary of State.

The board is guided in its work by directions issued to the board by the Home Secretary in regard to life-sentence prisoners and determinate-sentence prisoners. Procedures for the release of life-sentence prisoners and those serving sentences for public protection are governed by the Crime (Sentences) Act 1997, as amended by the Criminal Justice Act 2003 and the Parole Board Rules 2004.

Types of cases

The Parole Board currently has responsibility for considering the following types of case:

- *Life-sentence prisoners*: most cases are considered at an oral hearing by a three-member panel composed of a judge, a psychologist or psychiatrist and an independent, probation or criminologist member.
- *Determinate-sentence prisoners serving sentences of between 4 and 15 years sentenced before 4 April 2005*: considered by paper panels that can direct release.
- *Determinate-sentence prisoners with sentences of 15 years and over sentenced before 4 April 2005*: considered by paper panels that make recommendations to the Secretary of State on release.
- *Life-sentence recalls*: considered either on paper as a recommendation to the Secretary of State or subsequently at oral hearings to consider representations against recall.
- *Determinate-sentence recalls*: cases are initially decided on the papers although, following the case of Smith and West, the prisoner has the right to opt for an oral hearing to make representations against recall.
- *Extended-sentence representations against recall*: considered at an oral hearing and, should the representations be rejected, subsequent annual reviews.
- *Indeterminate sentences for public protection (IPP) for prisoners sentenced after 1 April 2005*: considered in the same way as life-sentence prisoners with three-member oral hearings.
- *Extended sentences for public protection (EPP) for prisoners sentenced after 1 April 2005*: considered in the same way as determinate-sentence cases by paper panels.

Members of the board

In 2006–7 there were 176 members of the board composed of the following categories:

- Chairman and salaried members (3).
- Judges (47).
- Psychiatrists (20).
- Psychologists (18).
- Probation Officers (11).
- Criminologists (6).
- Independents (71).

Workload

The board considered a total of 19,402 cases during 2005–6. This compared with 18,583 in 2004–5, up by 4.4 per cent. This modest increase in overall cases masks the massive 41 per cent increase in resource-intensive oral hearings, which follows a 31 per cent increase the previous year. Case law and legislative changes are turning the board into an increasingly tribunal-based organization with responsibility for dealing with the most serious and dangerous offenders.

A total of 1,900 oral hearings took place in 2005–6. This compared with 1,341 in 2004–5, up by 42 per cent, and follows on from the House of Lords decision in the Smith and West case to allow prisoners an oral hearing to make representations against recall. The year 2006–7 will see a continued increase in the number of oral hearings as the new indeterminate sentences for public protection, brought in by the Criminal Justice Act 2003, start to filter through.

The board received a total of 7,528 parole applications during 2005–6. This compared with 7,297 in 2004–5, up by 3.2 per cent. The number of discretionary conditional release (DCR) cases is expected to begin to fall from 2006–7 as these sentences start to be phased out under the Criminal Justice Act 2003, being largely replaced by automatic parole at the halfway point for determinate-sentence cases.

A total of 9,296 recall cases were considered during 2005–6. This compared with 9,320 in 2004–5, down by 0.3 per cent. This number is expected to rise as the percentage of prisoners recalled to prison increases, often for reasons other than further offences.

The use of indeterminate and extended public protection sentences by the courts, under the provisions of the Criminal Justice Act 2003, has been even greater than expected, and over 1,000 had already been imposed by March 2006.

Tim Morris

Related entries

Criminal Justice Act 2003; Extended sentencing; Licence; Lifers; Public protection; Resettlement; Risk assessment and risk management.

Key texts and sources

Arnott, H. and Creighton, S. (2006) *Parole Board Hearings – Law and Practice.* London: Legal Action Group.
Padfield, N. (ed.) (2007) *Whom to Release? Parole, Fairness and Criminal Justice.* Cullompton: Willan Publishing.
See also the Parole Board's website (**www.paroleboard.gov.uk**).

PARTNERSHIPS

Arrangements made by an offender manager or probation board to work together with others in order to protect the public or reduce reoffending.

Partnerships to meet the needs of individual offenders

When an offender manager prepares a supervision plan for a new offender, it usually becomes clear that the offender manager can carry out certain tasks personally during the course of supervision. However, it is frequently the case that additional tasks are identified to protect the public or to reduce the risk of reoffending which need to be done by others. These tasks may be specialist interventions, such as an accredited programme, or they may be initiatives to tackle the criminogenic environment in which the offender lives. Such work may focus on employment, housing or leisure activities (see Criminogenic needs).

In cases like these, the supervising officer will build into the supervision plan elements that can only be provided by other people. Other examples might involve residence in approved premises or counselling and testing by an independent drugs agency. As the Probation Service moves towards the structural separation of offender managers and those providing interventions, it is increasingly likely that elements of supervision plans will be carried out by staff in other, partner, organizations.

Offender managers have always looked beyond the staff of their own service to provide what is needed to prevent reoffending and protect the public. Accommodation providers in both the public and private sectors have been long-term partners. Employers, trainers and educationalists similarly have always contributed effectively to supervising offenders. Health professionals in mental health and in substance misuse teams often have a part to play. The list of those who can contribute to an offender's supervision plan would be extensive, and the examples quoted here are not an exhaustive list. Offender managers are now guided by the OASys assessment structure, which identifies all those areas where intervention is indicated for the supervision plan.

A typical supervision plan is likely to comprise services provided personally by the offender manager, services provided by other probation colleagues and services provided by other public and private sector staff. Until now a co-operative culture of partnership and sharing has existed between the range of public and voluntary sector staff working with offenders. New commissioning arrangements will introduce a commercial market-oriented culture (see Contestability). The effects of this are at present unknown and will need to be monitored. There may be some confusion as previous 'partners' come to see each other as 'competitors'. The most important criterion in evaluating the effectiveness of the changes will be the overall effect on offender behaviour as measured by risk to the public and by reoffending rates.

Formal multilateral partnerships at agency level

Because of the close relationship between probation and the public services addressing the causes of crime, it is not surprising that, over the years, a number of statutory requirements and other formal arrangements have been placed on probation boards by the government.

One of the most long-standing statutory requirements is for probation areas to contribute to child protection. At the local safeguarding children boards (LSCBs) in each county or unitary authority area, police, local authority (social services and education), health, voluntary sector and probation managers work together to define required practice and protocols for all relevant agencies to promote the welfare and safety of children. Each LSCB has its own protocols and procedures, based on national models, about how to assess and respond to children at risk.

Probation staff are required to undertake training in the LSCB procedures, and to follow the protocols and procedures of the LSCB in all their work with offenders. Probation managers contribute to the arrangements through their work at LSCB meetings and review panels.

The statutory requirements of the multi-agency public protection arrangements (MAPPAs) ensure that the relevant agencies work together to minimize the risk posed to the public by dangerous offenders. The responsible bodies are the police and the Probation and Prison Services, and the participating authorities, with a duty to co-operate, include local authorities (housing and social services), health (including forensic services) and youth offending teams. These arrangements are designed to ensure that, as far as possible, each public sector worker who comes into contact with someone who is a serious risk to the public knows what to do to minimize the risk. For the highest-risk offenders, senior managers of the agencies will be co-operating to agree a plan and review its implementation at regular intervals.

Youth offending teams (YOTs) comprise staff from social services, police, education, probation and health, seconded to a specialist team concentrating on the supervision of young people. The seconded staff develop a real specialist skill in working with young people under the age of 18 years, and they also draw on the knowledge and expertise that rest in their seconding organization. This makes for a very resourceful team approach.

The Crime and Disorder Reduction Partnerships (CDRPs) are a further statutory partnership. They pool the data from police, local authorities and probation in order to analyse crime patterns and identify strategies which inform police priorities and local authority initiatives. The list of partners includes the health service in every area and, in some areas, a wider range of partners is drawn in, including the courts, the services to victims, the fire service and the Crown Prosecution Service. Crime-mapping exercises usually show that the greatest concerns are concentrated in small parts of a local authority area. These neighbourhoods will probably be receiving special initiatives from several parts of the public service (for example, regeneration, health and education). The CDRP will seek to ensure that these initiatives are co-ordinated and that gaps in provision can be filled. The partnership will also try to maximize the crime prevention potential of these initiatives.

CDRPs are also responsible for the delivery of the Prolific and other Priority Offender schemes. These include arrangements to target the most damaging offenders within communities and to ensure rigorous enforcement of supervision arrangements jointly between police and probation, with proactive prevention strategies among the key partners.

Several significant partnerships arise from government initiatives where there is no supporting legislation. The criminal justice boards and the drug action teams are the principal examples in this category. Both are very significant drivers of priorities and probation practice. Probation boards are also involved in multi-agency partnerships regarding accommodation (Supporting People), employment, training and education, and various aspects of the health services. Finally, with the establishment of regional offender managers, regional reducing reoffending action plans have been developed

and are overseen by partnership boards in which probation has a significant role.

It has been said that there is a plethora of overlapping partnerships. Each requires the identification of priorities, the implementation of an action plan, the monitoring of performance and inter-agency work. In each case the agendas and the framework used are desirable, but partnerships have become so numerous and so complex that sometimes it has become impossible to maintain coherence and focus. This observation applies particularly to a small organization such as probation.

Partnership requirements are the natural consequence of recognizing the connection between different aspects of social policy. 'Joined-up government' is an appropriate response to seeking to reduce 'the causes of crime'. However, the difficulty of implementing cohesive social investment should not be underestimated. Developing partnerships can so easily be undermined by a new 'initiative' focused on one problem or agency, especially when it is called for in the absence of an understanding of how current systems of provision are operating.

Bilateral partnerships

Probation committees had, for many years, allocated a part of their budget for the purchase of services from other organizations. Accommodation providers and voluntary organizations were given grants to meet the needs of the offenders being supervised in the area. Often it was a condition of receiving the grant that a probation staff member joined the management committee of the voluntary body. In this way many positive partnerships between the voluntary sector and the Probation Service developed over the years.

In the 1980s, the government began to specify a proportion of the budget that had to be allocated to this purpose. The proportion increased in the early 1990s. For many committees the financial restrictions of the period necessitated a curtailment of spending on in-house services and an expansion of partnership spending in order to meet the required quota. For this reason the partnership budget was seen by some as probation's version of 'privatization'.

With the arrival of the National Probation Service in 2001, the boards were required to have a partnership plan and to set aside funding for it. However, the quota was dropped and boards had more freedom to decide for themselves. Typically a partnership plan will cover some specialist accommodation providers outside the 'Supporting People' arrangements, employment, training and education initiatives, services for drug and alcohol counselling, and services to meet the diversity needs of offenders. A partnership quota of 10 per cent of the area budget is now being restored for the year 2007–8, as the government moves to develop a plurality of providers.

David Hancock

Related entries

Contestability; Crime and Disorder Reduction Partnerships; Criminal justice boards; Criminogenic needs; Inter-agency work; Interventions; Local authorities; Multi-agency public protection arrangements (MAPPAs); National Offender Management Service (NOMS); Offender management; Youth offending teams.

Key texts and sources

Rumgay, J. (2007) 'Partnerships in probation', in L. Gelsthorpe and R. Morgan (eds) *Handbook of Probation*. Cullompton: Willan Publishing.
Partnership expenditure is clearly shown in each probation board's annual report, and this can often be accessed via the probation area website. The statutory and non-statutory partnerships often publish annual reports that can usually be accessed on the web.

PENAL POLICY

The strategies adopted by national governments in response to offending behaviour, particularly those that involve the use of formal sanctions directed against individual lawbreakers as opposed to more broadly based preventive measures.

The direction and content of penal policy are not automatically 'determined' in response to external factors such as rising or falling crime rates, but are always a matter of conscious political choice. How that choice is exercised – the policy-making process – may be influenced by various constituencies including professionally trained penal experts, elected politicians, pressure groups, the media, the general public (for example, in plebiscites or referenda) and a variety of policy entrepreneurs. The latter may include lobbyists representing commercial interests or those of voluntary or non-statutory organizations. The influence of these different constituencies is likely to vary from one country to another, and also over time within a given country.

A variety of broad penal policy approaches can be identified, the relative influence of which again varies with regard to both time and place. The first is the 'welfare model', which stresses the importance of taking action that is intended to benefit offenders and the wider community by contributing to their reform or resocialization. The second is the 'justice model', which places a high value on procedural safeguards for defendants and favours the consistent and proportionate application of punishment according to the offender's 'just deserts'. A third approach is the 'minimum intervention' model, which favours the avoidance, where possible, of formal interventions including not only the use of custody but also prosecution and even compulsory welfare measures. A fourth approach, the 'restorative justice' model, seeks to ensure that offenders undertake appropriate acts of reparation for the benefit of victims or the community, encourages dialogue between offenders and their victims, and promotes measures that will help to reintegrate offenders into the community. A fifth and final approach, the 'neo-correctionalist' model, favours an uncompromisingly harsh and punitive response with regard to convicted offenders augmented by tough restrictions placed on those who are perceived to be at risk of offending.

An international comparative study of 12 different countries by Cavadino and Dignan (2006) found that important differences in the type of political economy were reflected in both the policy-making process and the content of penal policy. Very briefly, penal policymaking in countries with neoliberal political economies is more susceptible to populist pressures and tends to favour neo-correctionalist approaches. Countries with more corporatist political economies are more likely to leave penal policymaking in the hands of elite professional experts, tending to favour approaches associated with welfare, justice or minimum intervention models.

James Dignan

Related entries

Criminal justice system; Probation in Africa; Probation in Europe; Probation in the USA and Canada.

Key texts and sources

Cavadino, M. and Dignan, J. (2006) *Penal Systems: A Comparative Approach.* London: Sage.
Jones, T. and Newburn, T. (2005) 'Comparative criminal justice policy-making in the United Kingdom and the United States: the case of private prisons', *British Journal of Criminology*, 25: 58–80.
Tonry, M. (2001) 'Symbol, substance and severity in western penal policies', *Punishment and Society*, 3: 517–36.

PERFORMANCE MANAGEMENT

Management activity that focuses the work of an organization on the achievement of a limited number of numerical targets. This can be a great asset in achieving desired results. For organizations that work in a complex environment, performance management can produce perverse outcomes, especially if the targets focus on process rather than outcome.

The role and workload of the Probation Service grew to such an extent in the twentieth century that, by 2000, approximately 250,000 court reports were written each year and over 200,000 offenders were being supervised. The Probation Service had become a complex professional organization working predominantly with adult offenders, many of whom had committed serious crimes.

In the years leading up to the formation of the National Probation Service (NPS) in 2001, there were increasing calls for the service to demonstrate that it was performing well. The arrival of National Standards had, for the first time, provided an undisputed benchmark for the service to use in measuring whether or not it had delivered consistent services to the recognized standard. During the 1990s, HM Inspectorate of Probation conducted a series of area inspections focusing on performance. These examined levels of compliance with National Standards, the quality of work with offenders and success against national targets. In another initiative the Association of Chief Officers of Probation led several audits of the enforcement of community orders and licences.

In 2000 the Criminal Justice and Court Services Act established the NPS as a unified service for England and Wales. The chief officers were employed by the Home Office and directly accountable to a new Director of Probation. This meant that there was a clearer focus to the work of the service, and accountability to ministers for performance became more apparent.

Performance targets were set for each area depending on its size and, at first, these concentrated on the ever-significant issue of enforcement and on establishing the new accredited programmes. Implementing the new drug treatment and testing order (DTTO) in a consistent pattern across England and Wales also featured in the selection of targets, as did indicators of competence in relation to diversity issues. The targets went hand in hand with the establishment of new monthly data-collecting routines in all areas. The performance of each area was fed back promptly via the national 'performance reports' published on a quarterly basis. This transparency concentrated the minds of managers and probation boards, especially as the most telling data were often presented in the form of national 'league tables'. The organizational culture of the NPS soon adjusted to the imperative of performing well in relation to the targets. The desire to be perceived as performing well was reinforced by a system of financial penalties for performing badly. This system was soon amended to one of providing cash incentives for doing well, but the effect was the same. Areas simply had to meet targets in order to maintain the budget and pay staff.

It became vital for areas to hit performance targets if they were to maintain their funding. The targets are now spread over a wide range of work. In the year ending March 2007, the performance bonus scheme was triggered by good performance on the following variables:

- Some 90 per cent of OASys sentence plans, risk of harm assessments and risk management plans completed in five days for high risk of harm offenders and prolific and other priority offenders.
- Some 90 per cent court reports on time.
- Enforcement action taken.
- Appointments attended.
- Compliance.
- Unpaid work completions.
- DTTO/drug rehabilitation requirements completed.
- Accredited programme completions, including specified numbers of sex offenders and domestic violence offenders.
- Level of staff sickness absence.
- Basic skills starts.
- Offenders placed in employment.
- Employment sustained for four weeks.
- Race and ethnic monitoring data, accurate and on time.

For a medium-sized area, performance on these criteria leads to the awarding or withholding of a performance bonus of about half a million pounds. This places about 25 jobs at risk in the event of poor results. This is equivalent to about 5 per cent of the total staffing of an area. Loss of confidence and reputation is also associated with a poor performance. The spotlight shines on the weaknesses of a 'poorly performing' area at the expense of its strengths, and this can lead to a spiral of decline, rather than improvement.

This management methodology is now common throughout the public sector and has led to improved overall performance. However, the practice of removing resources from an area means that the local community might ultimately receive an even poorer service from an organization that is intrinsically weak. In the early years of the NPS, poorly performing areas received some help in the shape of additional 'performance improvement teams'. These added both impetus and resource, and were seen to be quite effective. However, their availability tended to undermine the true culture of performance incentives, and their use was discontinued after a few years.

Within the NPS there is frequent criticism of some of the targets, and there is always a danger that some of them create perverse incentives. The National Probation Directorate (NPD) played a major role in advising ministers on the targets, and it attempted to align them to the principles of effective practice that were the cornerstone of its strategy. Thus key targets were set around the completion of accredited programmes. The focus on social exclusion, reflected in a series of government reports, led to the National Reducing Re-offending Action Plan. This resulted in targets relating to basic skills, accommodation and training. The concerns of ministers were evident in the priority given to improving the enforcement of community orders and licences.

The NPS has made remarkable progress and has consistently achieved the targets set by focusing on the business processes and by promoting a culture in the service that recognizes the importance of targets. In 2005, a new set of targets for improving public protection was introduced following a number of high-profile cases that had damaged public confidence.

The prominence of a target-based performance management culture could not have been sustained without significant advances in the collection of data. All areas collect data in a consistent way. This enables the NPD to publish national data broken down into regional and area figures. A weighted scorecard makes comparisons of area performance against the key targets. Although this inevitably creates relatively 'poor performers' and generates concern among staff who do not like such rigorous central direction, it does allow areas to benchmark themselves. It can also promote the spread of good practice. By 2006 the NPS's performance against the targets set by ministers had reached record levels with virtually all the targets being achieved.

However, the limitations of this approach to performance management became evident when the Home Secretary strongly criticized the NPS in November 2006. He said the performance of the Probation Service was 'poor or mediocre' in too many areas. He was concerned over a number of high-profile cases where offenders under supervision had committed serious further offences. He was also concerned about the number of offenders who reoffended while under supervision. While the NPS and its leadership found these criticisms unsettling, it was undeniable that they reflected wider concern in the media and the public.

In 2007–8 the weighted scorecard, which is based on an aggregation of the 13 principal performance targets on which the performance bonus is calculated, is to be replaced by a new, more comprehensive index, comprising up to 30 variables. This will compute a wide range of data and is described as a 'holistic framework for assessing quality'. This performance portfolio comprises measures of public protection work, of offender management and of various measures of efficiency and effectiveness. In addition to these the index will incorporate about ten separate measures of quality in relation to interventions. On completion of the detailed calculations to reach a score in this system, areas will then be placed in one of four bands, from excellent to poor. This comprehensive system still begs the question of whether meeting targets guarantees quality in probation work. Can quality be determined entirely through measurable variables?

As to the future, the government has introduced legislation to reform the NPS as part of the Management of Offenders Bill 2007. Probation areas will become independent probation trusts if they met minimum requirements set by the National Offender Management Service (NOMS). Commissioning and the use of contracts that specify outputs/outcomes will become the basis of managing performance through the network of regional offender managers (ROMs). The use of targets will remain, and they will be written into the contracts between the ROM and the areas/trusts. This approach can also align targets more closely to local need as identified by the ROM. It is clear that performance in relation to public protection and reduction in the levels of reoffending will be the crucial measures of reputation and success in the forthcoming commissioning environment.

Roger McGarva

Related entries

Accountability; Chief officers; Contestability; External audit; Internal audit; Managerialism; National Probation Service for England and Wales; Probation boards; Probation trusts; Regional offender managers (ROMs).

Key texts and sources

Bailey, R., Knight, C. and Williams, B. (2007) 'The Probation Service as part of NOMS in England and Wales: fit for purpose?', in L. Gelsthorpe and R. Morgan (eds) *Handbook of Probation*. Cullompton: Willan Publishing.

Performance management data are published quarterly in the NPS performance reports, which can be found on the website **www.probation.homeoffice. gov.uk.**

PERSISTENT AND SERIOUS OFFENDERS

> A subgroup of offenders, identified through the persistence and/or seriousness of their offending.

The long-standing political interest in identifying and tackling persistent offenders appears to have gathered impetus in recent times. For example, the 2004 Home Office strategic plan stated that, 'In any one year, approximately 100,000 people commit half of all crimes and just 5,000 people commit about 9 per cent of all crimes – around one million crimes in total'. Consequently, there have been a number of attempts at identifying persistent offenders. For example, in the early 1990s, Ann Hagell and Tim Newburn studied a sample of over 500 young people who had been arrested at least three times in the last year. Within this sample, they found that no two definitions led to the identification of the same individuals. They thus concluded that any definition of persistence would tend to be arbitrary, and that sentencing on the basis of a definition of persistence would potentially involve a degree of inequity.

Further consideration was given to persistent offenders in the Carter Report, using research conducted for the Home Office White Paper, *Criminal Justice – the Way Ahead* (2001). The research defined persistent offenders as those who had accumulated at least three convictions during their criminal careers. These offenders, it was calculated, formed about 10 per cent of the active offender population at any one time, and over their careers accumulated at least 50 per cent of all serious offences. However, it was recognized that the persistent group was not stable, with 40 per cent of persistent offenders desisting from offending without official intervention and many being replaced each year by new persistent offenders.

It is perhaps not surprising, therefore, that there is no commonly accepted definition of 'persistence' and that differing demarcations have been employed. These include the following:

- Three or more offences in the past 12 months.
- Four or more offending episodes in the past 12 months.
- Three or more previous sentencing offences, with a subsequent arrest within three years of the last sentencing occasion.

Even more recently, the national implementation guide for the Criminal Justice Act 2003 states very simply that persistent offenders are 'those who continue to offend over a period of time'. Interestingly, these offenders are distinguished from 'prolific' offenders, defined as 'those who offend with a high frequency, possibly committing a range of different offences, and rapidly building up a substantial history of convictions'. In September 2004, the Home Office launched a national Prolific and other Priority Offender (PPO) strategy, requiring a PPO scheme to be established in every Crime and Disorder Reduction Partnership in England and Wales. In general, PPO schemes identify potential offenders and then apply a scoring matrix to prioritize cases. However, the criteria used in the matrices have varied considerably between schemes, usually according to local priorities and crime reduction targets.

Persistent offenders are often grouped together, with those committing serious offences assigned to one high-risk group. However, the assumption that persistent offenders are those committing the most serious offences would appear to be often mistaken, with research studies indicating that persistent offenders are not disproportionately engaged in serious offending. Importantly, the generic risk/needs assessment instruments for both young and adult offenders (ASSET and OASys, respectively) have separate components for identifying those offenders who have a high likelihood of reconviction and those who present a high or very high risk of serious harm.

Whether emphasis should be placed upon identifying persistent or serious offenders is debatable. The increasing focus on persistence rather than seriousness can be seen as representing a shifting from acts to people, and has been criticized as potentially violating the principle of proportionality in sentencing. It can therefore be argued that notions of persistence and seriousness should be combined to ensure that persistent offenders have been convicted of sufficiently serious offences to warrant higher levels of intervention.

The focus on persistent offenders is thus questionable on a number of grounds: (1) the arbitrary definitions of persistence; (2) the transitory nature of persistence; (3) the reliance on official statistics; and (4) the disregarding of seriousness. It should not be assumed, however, that defining 'seriousness' and identifying a homogeneous group of serious offenders are without complication. More specifically, identifying the relative seriousness of different offences is difficult. While there is a standard list of violent and sexual offences and some offence types seem more serious than others by virtue of their description, for many offences relative seriousness is likely to vary according to what actually took place. In the 2003 Crime and Justice Survey, serious offenders were defined as those who had committed any of the following specified offences in the last 12 months: theft of a vehicle, burglary, robbery, theft from the person, assault resulting in injury and selling Class A drugs.

There is also a close relationship between identifying persistent and/or serious offenders and identifying high-risk offenders. The interest in measuring risk has recently gathered pace, particularly following the decline of the rehabilitative model in the late 1970s and the consequent emergence of an actuarial model of risk management which classifies groups according to levels of dangerousness (see Actuarialism). But this strategy is open to criticism, notably because of the difficulties in predicting further offending and identifying high-risk offenders. Such problems exist even with persistent offenders, and the difficulties become more pronounced the more specific the type of risk or offence being assessed. Whether those offenders who commit the more serious offences should necessarily be deemed high risk is particularly controversial. There are further concerns that the attempted targeting of persistent and/or high-risk offenders is resulting in the detrimental labelling of a subgroup of offenders as 'innately criminal'. The most immediate danger of labelling is one of stigmatization, encouraging offenders to develop a tough 'macho' criminal self-image and consequently living up to the labels attached to them.

Robin Moore

Related entries

Assessment instruments and systems; Carter Report; Crime and Disorder Reduction Partnerships; Police; Prolific and other priority offenders; Public protection; Reconviction.

Key texts and sources

Farrall, S., Mawby, R.C. and Worrall, A. (2007) 'Prolific/persistent offenders and desistance', in L. Gelsthorpe and R. Morgan (eds) *Handbook of Probation*. Cullompton: Willan Publishing.
Hagell, A. and Newburn, T. (1994) *Persistent Young Offenders*. London: Policy Studies Institute.
HM Chief Inspector of Constabulary, HM Chief Inspector of Probation, HM Chief Inspector the Crown Prosecution Service, HM Chief Inspector of the Magistrate's Courts Service and HM Chief Inspector of Prisons, Audit Commission (2004) *Joint Inspection Report into Persistent and Prolific Offenders*. London: Home Office Communications Directorate.
Moore, R., Gray, E., Roberts, C., Taylor, E. and Merrington, S. (2006) *Managing Persistent and Serious Offenders in the Community: Community Programmes in Theory and Practice*. Cullompton: Willan Publishing.

PERSONALITY DISORDER

Personality disorder is a common form of mental disorder with a high prevalence in offender management settings, requiring an understanding of its relationship to other mental disorder, risk and the use of multi-agency working.

Most probation officers will be familiar with the term 'personality disorder' (PD), although few, despite a long-standing expertise in managing high-risk offenders, will feel confident in understanding the concept in context with other forms of mental disorder or how it influences supervision and risk. PD can be defined in several ways but, essentially, represents enduring patterns of thinking, feeling, interpersonal style and impulse control which deviate markedly from cultural norms, leading to considerable personal distress and disruption in most aspects of the individual's life and/or of those around him or her. It usually manifests in adolescence, and the aetiology probably includes biological (such as genetic), social (such as socio-economic disadvantage) and psychological (such as trauma/abuse or abnormal attachments) factors. As individuals with PD can sometimes, but not always, pose a risk to others (as well as themselves), they can become known to probation services through offence-related behaviour.

PD is relatively common. Between 5 and 10 per cent of people in the community would meet the clinical ('diagnostic') criteria using recognized classification systems, and most would not be offenders. There are several sub-types with their own characteristics, such as borderline or paranoid PD, but the most commonly known to criminal justice agencies is anti-social PD. Between 50 and 78 per cent of adult prisoners meet the criteria for at least one PD and similar proportions are found in secure psychiatric settings. Despite this, until recently there has been no concerted or systematic response to treatment or service delivery.

Along with mental illness (see Mentally disordered offenders) and learning disability, PD ought to sit squarely in the domain of mental health services. Historically, however, most health agencies have, perhaps understandably due to the acute risks and often clearer treatment needs, prioritized mental illness over PD. Coupled with an inadequate evidence base regarding effective treatments or outcome and with restrictions by psychiatrists in the use of the Mental Health Act (1983) for individuals with PD (who have to be deemed 'treatable' to be detained under the Mental Health Act, not always a clear issue), most offenders with PD will probably have more contact with probation than mental health services.

Depending on the type of disorder, individuals with PD can exhibit a range of abnormal behaviour which can relate to offending. Probation practitioners may recognize impulsiveness or risk-taking, emotional dysregulation (volatility), abnormal core beliefs (such as paranoid hyper-sensitivity) or characteristics similar to psychopathy, where behavioural irresponsibility and instability are allied with low empathy and callous unconcern. Other pathways to mental health services (and sometimes probation settings) for individuals with PD occur through associated maladaptive coping strategies, such as substance misuse. PD also increases the likelihood of developing other mental disorder, including mental illness, sometimes leading to difficulty in diagnosis and referral for appropriate treatment. Hence, it is possible to see how a probation officer, whether working in a prison, with drug treatment and testing orders, through multi-agency public protection arrangements (MAPPAs) or in generic community settings could be unwittingly managing individuals with PD.

Until recently, the pockets of expertise in managing PD were based in secure psychiatric services, with some notable exceptions, such as prison-based 'therapeutic community' approaches (such as at Grendon Underwood or Dovegate Prisons) or community-based services (such as at Henderson Hospital, now a prototype for several similar services). Since 2003, following the publication of *Personality Disorder: No Longer a Diagnosis of Exclusion*, all mental health trusts are required to develop services for individuals with PD, some of which have working relationships with criminal justice agencies, although provision remains patchy.

Around the same time, a government initiative involving NHS and Home Office services was developed for so-called dangerous and severe personality disordered (DSPD) individuals, a small group of mainly men who, despite their high-risk and PD, were often excluded from mental health services over concerns about treatability. Although the initial phase has involved the opening of specialist units in high-secure hospitals (Rampton and Broadmoor) and prisons (Whitemoor and Frankland), it is likely that, in time, DSPD individuals will be referred 'downstream' to the community, requiring supervision from mental health and probation services.

Although many probation staff may feel underprepared to help in the supervision of offenders with PD, it may be reassuring to consider how traditional probation supervision approaches overlap with the broad initiatives for managing PD. There is a consensus that psychological approaches are probably beneficial, with similarities between the 'what works' (predominantly cognitive-behavioural/social learning) approaches for offender management and applied interventions for PD. Similarly, supervision adopting a longer-term, relatively intensive, structured (including psychologically boundaried) and multi-agency approach is likely to be feasible and familiar for most probation practitioners. At the same time the interpersonal problems associated with PD can be major impediments in supervision, often providing a clue to an unrecognized personality problem.

What might be less comfortable for many probation practitioners is the recognition of symptoms and risk-related behaviour (e.g. mood changes leading to self-harm). Here, rather than an expectation that a probation practitioner should be solely responsible for assessment and treatment, a basic knowledge of PD issues would be appropriate. Probation staff should also know how and when to seek help – to be a 'safe pair of hands' – referring to specialist services such as a community forensic mental health team. Such joint working should become increasingly common at the outset of supervision.

In summary, PD is common among offenders and will therefore be part of everyday probation practice. With improved assessment procedures, including risk assessment such as OASys, recognition of the problem will undoubtedly increase. Although specialist services are available, not all cases will require specialist supervision, so that all probation practitioners need to have a working knowledge of the core features of PD and an overview of useful interventions available.

John Milton

Related entries

Cognitive-behavioural; Dual diagnosis; Mentally disordered offenders; Psychopathy/psychopathic disorder; Risk assessment and risk management; Therapeutic community.

Key texts and sources

Personality Disorder: No Longer a Diagnosis of Exclusion is available online at **http://www.dh.gov.uk/assetRoot/04/05/42/30/04054230.pdf**. A good introductory text is available online: *Understanding Personality Disorder: A Report by the British Psychological Society* (**http://www.bps.org.uk**). For the DSPD Programme, see **http://www.dspdprogramme.gov.uk/home**.

POLICE

A public body responsible for building safer and more secure communities. It is the agency for the maintenance of order, the detection of crime and the arrest of alleged offenders. It is organized into 43 areas in England and Wales, which are virtually coterminous with probation areas.

The level of contact and partnership between police and probation staff has increased significantly in recent years. The traditional myth that the police are against the offender and probation are for the offender may linger in public consciousness, but in reality this was always a gross oversimplification, and new shared practice and values have been developing rapidly.

The Crime and Disorder Act 1998 was a crucial milestone for strengthening inter-agency working. This provided key 'responsible authorities', such as police and probation, with an unambiguous right to exchange information about individuals in the interests of community safety and crime reduction, on a basis proportionate to data protection and human rights safeguards.

During the 1990s various probation and police services developed 'prolific offender' projects. The key hallmarks of these schemes are the careful screening and scrutiny of individuals who are known, or suspected, to be engaged in frequent crime, particularly theft, burglary and robbery.

This was largely based on the innovatory Dutch 'Dordrecht' police and probation partnership scheme. Typically, the courts or the releasing prison require the individual to understand that he or she will be subject to surveillance and frequent supervisory contacts, normally four per week. The supervisory team normally consists of a probation officer, a police officer and a community drugs nurse. They constitute a formidable trio. These schemes are now generalized as Prolific and other Priority Offenders schemes.

Legislation in 2001 consolidated partnership arrangements between police and probation (and subsequently prisons) for the purpose of the assessment, supervision and surveillance of high-risk offenders in the 42 criminal justice areas – the multi-agency public protection arrangements (MAPPAs).

Good liaison between police and probation is necessary to ensure offenders are arrested promptly once a decision has been made to revoke a parole licence or to arrest someone who is living in approved premises and is in breach of bail conditions. If the person is assessed as dangerous to individuals or to the public, the need for careful joint work is essential.

Police and probation work together in the 42 criminal justice boards of England and Wales. Here the focus on timeliness and on 'narrowing the justice gap' means that both agencies have to collaborate to reach the standards required. There are shared agendas in the youth offending teams, in victim contact work and in child protection work.

These partnerships depend on trust and confidence developing at local and agency level. Possible future developments (such as a breakdown in the current agency coterminosity or the submission of probation services to 'contestability') could damage the types of joined-up agency activity described above.

David Walton

Related entries

Community safety; Criminal justice boards; Multi-agency public protection arrangements (MAPPAs); Prolific and other priority offenders.

Key texts and sources

This entry is based on the author's paper on this subject in *Criminal Justice Matters*, (2006), Vol. 63. 20–1.

Hope, T. and Sparks, R. (eds) (2000) *Crime, Risk and Insecurity: Law and Order in Everyday Life and Political Discourse.* London: Routledge.

Newburn, T. (ed.) (2003) *Handbook of Policing.* Cullompton: Willan Publishing.

See also the Home Office's and area police forces' websites.

POPULIST PUNITIVENESS

A term originally coined 'to convey the notion of politicians tapping into, and using for their own purposes, what they believe to be the public's generally punitive stance' (Bottoms 1995: 40).

The term 'populist punitiveness' was first used in a 1995 essay by Anthony Bottoms and has subsequently become widely adopted. Some commentators have used the phrase to refer in a general way to punitive public attitudes to sentencing and the penal system; however, in the original source, the author specifically differentiated the concepts of 'public opinion' and 'populist punitiveness'.

Bottoms's essay was concerned principally 'to sketch the main movements of thought that seemed to underpin much of modern sentencing change in different countries [and] to try to understand why these movements of thought have been occurring' (1995: 18). He located populist punitiveness within the general social changes occurring in the development of 'late modern societies', a theme that was subsequently more fully developed in David Garland's classic work, *The Culture of Control* (2001).

A dictionary definition of 'a populist' is 'a member of a political party claiming to represent the common people' (*Longman's Dictionary*).

Accordingly, one feature of populist punitiveness is that a politician using this approach frequently 'denigrates expert and professional elites and claims the authority of "the people", of common sense, of "getting back to basics"'(Garland 2001: 13). Another feature is that those adopting a populist punitive approach tend to represent the general public's attitude to crime as straightforwardly punitive. In fact, however, empirical research on public attitudes to the punishment of offenders reveals quite a complex picture. To generalize, when survey questions are short, general and unspecific, considerable public support for punitive policies is usually evident. However, when survey instruments provide more details of the circumstances of the offence and the offender, or ask victims about appropriate sentences for offences committed against them, more nuanced views are frequently expressed, and the suggested sentence is normally much closer to the actual practice of the courts (Roberts and Hough 2005). Politicians attracted to populist punitiveness tend to ignore these complexities and to focus on the simple picture derivable from general and 'headline' surveys.

Why is populist punitiveness an attractive strategy for politicians? In contemporary democracies, all political parties regularly commission private opinion polls and focus groups. Responding to the public's views, as expressed in such exercises, can be seen as likely to improve electoral prospects and as providing enhanced legitimacy for the politicians in question, both among the public and in the estimation of politicians themselves (on which see Barker 2001). For these reasons, populist punitive strategies can be attractive to some politicians irrespective of the utilitarian value of such strategies in reducing crime. Hence, such strategies can sometimes be deployed cynically. Nevertheless, there is no doubt that some populist punitive politicians do sincerely believe that more punitive penal policies will reduce crime, principally through the assumed incapacitative and general deterrent effects of the greater use of imprisonment. (For a summary of empirical evidence relating to such claims, see Bottoms 2004.)

As noted in the entry on penal policy, there is evidence that 'policy-making in countries with

neoliberal political economies is more susceptible to populist pressures'. As Philip Bobbitt (2002: ch. 10) has suggested, in a world of globalized capitalism, the governments of neoliberal nations tend to see the role of the state as limited and its function as being that of the 'market state', which promises to maximize choice for its citizens in relation to public services (such as health and education) and public policies, in a manner analogous to that of 'consumer choice' in private markets. Politicians in such states are therefore perhaps more likely to adopt populist punitiveness approaches. By contrast, countries with a stronger 'state tradition' may see less need to pay special attention to the specific ('consumerist') views of the general public, and to place more weight on the views of judges, academic experts and so on.

An obvious potential problem for politicians in adopting a populist punitive stance is that such an approach might encourage an almost infinite progression (i.e. perceived public punitiveness → more punitive policies → perceived further public punitiveness, etc.). Such progressions will eventually come into potential conflict with resource constraints (e.g. the fiscal costs of a much expanded prison population), with possibly complex political consequences. One way of attempting to retain the advantages of populist punitiveness, while mitigating the resource problems, is to adopt a policy of bifurcation.

Anthony Bottoms

Related entries

Bifurcation; Penal policy; Public attitudes to probation.

Key texts and sources

Barker, R. (2001) *Legitimating Identities: The Self-presentation of Rulers and Subjects.* Cambridge: Cambridge University Press.
Bobbitt, P. (2002) *The Shield of Achilles.* London: Penguin Books.
Bottoms, A.E. (1995) 'The philosophy and politics of punishment and sentencing', in C.M.V. Clarkson and R. Morgan (eds) *The Politics of Sentencing Reform.* Oxford: Clarendon Press.

Bottoms, A.E. (2004) 'Empirical research relevant to sentencing frameworks', in A.E. Bottoms *et al.* (eds) *Alternatives to Prison.* Cullompton: Willan Publishing.

Garland, D. (2001) *The Culture of Control.* Oxford: Oxford University Press

Roberts, J.V. and Hough, M. (2005) *Understanding Public Attitudes to Criminal Justice.* Maidenhead: Open University Press.

POVERTY

Poverty is a politically contentious topic, currently regarded as a relative condition and defined as living on less than 60 per cent of average household incomes. Traditionally viewed in criminal justice policy as a key contextual factor in explaining offending, this focus has recently altered and diminished radically.

Poverty, one of the most enduring characteristics of the population with whom the Probation Service has its dealings, has become one of those topics that is almost never mentioned in polite probation circles. This disappearance is all the more striking because, less than 20 years ago and in some ways less propitious circumstances, poverty received consistent attention in both policy and practice arenas. Very little hard, current information therefore exists about the extent and nature of poverty among Probation Service users, but some estimates can be made from previous research applied to what is known more generally about contemporary conditions.

Direct interest in the impact of poverty on probationers and the services provided to them peaked during the Thatcher era when mass unemployment and cuts in benefit entitlement combined to exacerbate and concentrate poverty among already-disadvantaged communities. Research at Lancaster University, commissioned by the Association of Chief Officers of Probation, suggested many probationers experienced deep and enduring poverty, worsened by changes in social security provision (such as the introduction of the Social Fund). Such findings were launched into a hostile governmental climate. Ministers during the 1980s had concluded that poverty no longer existed in the UK, dismissing the concerns of what they pejoratively called the 'poverty lobby' as mere inequality. Nor was inequality a bad thing; rather, it provided the engine for economic progress. Entrepreneurial, risk-taking, wealth-creating individuals were to be rewarded by tax cuts and other advantages, while the low-skilled and unemployed were reaping the consequences of their own lack of motivation and deficient energies, and were in need of remotivation by a lean regime of state assistance, meanly administered. The term 'poverty' literally disappeared from official government publications at a time when, uniquely in the post-1945 period, the living standards of the poorest tenth of the population – where Probation Service users were concentrated – were in absolute decline. Local probation services responded with anti-poverty strategies concentrating upon income maximization and employment finding.

Meanwhile, the impact of growing poverty was felt very directly in the courts. The use of fines, long the staple disposal of courts in England and Wales, fell from 39 per cent of all offenders sentenced in 1988 to 28 per cent in 1999, as magistrates applied the commonsense understanding that the impact of financial penalties was felt disproportionately among those who had the least, combined with the pragmatic belief that there was little hope of extracting payment from those already unable to meet the most modest everyday obligations.

Ironically, the election of a New Labour government in May 1997 rehabilitated the notion of poverty in general, while eliminating it as a focus for probation activity. The Treasury insisted that work was the best form of welfare, devising a series of 'supply side' measures designed to improve skill levels and assist individuals back into employment. This policy could be criticized on a variety of grounds, both internal (in terms of its effectiveness) and external (in terms of the coercive edge applied to its persuasive strategies) and, more generally, as a disguised means of subsidizing the lowest paying of employers. Nevertheless, in its own terms, the policy has been remarkably successful. Less than 20 years after mass unemployment had been explained by government as the necessary price for competing in the global economy, unemployment had fallen to levels not seen since the mid-1970s, while employment, in terms of new jobs created, had grown even faster. Underpinning the welfare-to-work strategy was a belief that work had to be made to pay. The minimum wage, and wage subsidies in the form of tax credits, were meant to ensure that the 'hard-working families' of New Labour mythology were always recognizably better off in work than out of it.

For particular groups within the population – pensioners and families with children most especially – poverty has accordingly fallen substantially since 1997. Standards of living have improved fastest among the least well off, and the accelerating inequality of the last quarter of the twentieth century has been halted and, in a very preliminary way, reversed.

Yet underpinning the New Labour approach has been a new willingness to distinguish between those who, in Prime Minister Blair's words, 'play the game by the rules' and those who do not. For the former, state services, including income maintenance services, have become more generous. For the latter, the opposite approach has been deployed. 'Toughness' on those who offend has, therefore, not been confined to the courtroom. It extends into a wider range of public services, where a 'less eligibility' principle sits easily with the new 'responsibilization' of contemporary probation practice. Poverty, alongside other structural factors such as poor housing and health inequality, has been relegated to the status of a never-to-be-condoned 'excuse', and a condition to be overcome by individual endeavour rather than collective action. Where it does emerge in contemporary research it is almost always as a background factor, in relation, for example, to drug abuse or domestic violence, rather than as a topic in its own right.

Probation practice, then, finds itself concentrated among those who have done least well out of the generally improving New Labour picture. Single men, and those at the very sharpest end of disadvantage, have benefited the least from anti-poverty measures and are treated, in social policy terms, as the least deserving. Rather than speaking up for users in these circumstances, contemporary Probation Service approaches fall in with, and reinforce, the general picture. Poverty has become a taken-for-granted condition and one for which individuals themselves are largely to blame. It is, at once, both one of the most striking changes of the past 20 years and one of the most dismal.

Mark Drakeford

Related entries

Criminogenic needs; Social capital; Social exclusion.

Key texts and sources

Smith, D. and Stewart, J. (1997) 'Probation and social exclusion', *Social Policy and Administration*, 31: 96–115.

See the Howard League's website (http://www.howardleague.org.uk/).

PRACTICE DEVELOPMENT ASSESSORS

Practice development assessors (PDAs) are professionally qualified and occupationally competent probation officers who teach, guide and assess trainee probation officers for the Diploma in Probation Studies qualification (DipPS).

All those appointed as PDAs are required to have a minimum two years' experience working as a probation officer. In addition, they must undertake additional assessor qualifications (A1) in order to assess the National Vocation Qualification (NVQ) Level 4 in Community and Criminal Justice, as required by specified awarding bodies such as City and Guilds, to ensure objectivity, rigour and fairness in assessment. PDAs work with the NVQ Assessment Centre to assess and evaluate trainees' competence in line with the requirements of the NVQ assessment procedures and regulations relating to the DipPS.

Many PDAs are involved in the quality assurance of the NVQ process, holding the qualification (V1) required to undertake internal verification and to monitor and quality assure NVQ processes and procedure in their local area on the Assessment Centre's behalf.

The role of PDAs varies across regional training consortia. However, all PDAs are required to allocate, support and assess the practice-based work of trainees. PDAs work with areas to provide trainees with a variety of learning opportunities, allocating work appropriate to their progress in the programme and to their learning needs. They hold a pivotal role in liaising with key stakeholders in the programme, university tutors, area staff and the regional consortium. PDAs play a central role in monitoring the progress of trainees throughout the two-year programme and, where necessary, working with local performance management procedures when trainees are underperforming.

PDAs work in collaboration with the university provider, the regional consortium and areas to integrate the academic and practice-based aspects of the programme, providing learning opportunities for trainees to link theory to probation practice. The role of the PDA is to assist trainees to apply theoretical knowledge and methods in their practice and to encourage them to develop a critical and reflective approach to their work. Therefore it is important that PDAs keep up to date with current practice, legislation and national and local policies.

To enhance the integration of the programme, PDAs meet with the tutor regularly to confirm progress and, where necessary, are involved in action plans to address any difficulties. In some regions, they may support the student in his or her learning and may mark any portfolios of practice evidence jointly with the tutor. The work of PDAs ensures that an effective, inclusive and imaginative approach to working with diversity and anti-discriminatory practice is embedded into the DipPS.

PDAs contribute to the development and evaluation of the trainee programme. Attendance at consortium and university meetings and work groups allows PDAs to raise local issues and share ideas, as well as ensuring consistency of practices, in line with programme guidelines. In many areas PDAs' assessment skills are also put

to use in the recruitment and selection process for trainees.

Michelle Walters

Related entries

Probation training; Regional training consortia.

Key texts and sources

Whitehead, P. and Thompson, J. (2004) *Knowledge and the Probation Service: Raising Standards for Trainees, Assessors and Practitioners.* Chichester: Wiley.

PRE-SENTENCE REPORT (PSR)

A report requested by the court from the Probation Service or youth offending team prior to sentencing. The report provides an analysis of the offence(s), relevant information pertaining to the offender and an assessment of the offender's risk of harm and reoffending. It concludes with a clear and realistic proposal for sentence.

The preparation of PSRs is a key task of the Probation Service and probation officers. Each year the service will assist magistrates and judges in their sentencing decisions through the preparation of about 246,000 PSRs in England and Wales. The provision of reports has been a central part of the Probation Service's work since its very earliest days, a key function being to assist in the sentencing process. Such reports were first enshrined in legislation in the Powers of Criminal Courts Act (PCCA) 1973. The purpose of a 'social inquiry report' (SIR) was to 'enquire … into the circumstances or home surroundings of any person with a view to assisting the court in determining the most suitable method of dealing with the case' (PCCA 1973, Sch. 3, para 8(1)). However, there was no prescriptive guidance on their structure or content. SIRs consequently varied considerably across the country and tended to concentrate on the offender's circumstances and history, paying less attention to the offence(s) and future risk.

The Criminal Justice Act (CJA) 1991 brought about a major change, with PSRs replacing SIRs. A PSR was to be prepared with 'a view to assisting the court in determining the most suitable method of dealing with the offender' (CJA 1991, s.3(5)). This was not just a change in name, however, but represented a major departure in terms of the terminology, style, content and format of court reports. PSRs were to be more offence focused, were only to contain information on the offender which was demonstrably 'relevant' to the offence(s), were to make explicit assessments about the risk posed and were to put forward a 'proposal' for sentence (rather than the term 'recommendation' previously used in SIRs). Subsequent National Standards laid down the specific section headings to be contained in all PSRs, and what each section should cover.

While there have since been legislative amendments to the relevant sections of the PCCA 1973 and national policy developments with regard to PSRs, the format remains largely as outlined in the CJA 1991 and related National Standards (see below). The standard adjournment time for the preparation of the full written report remains 15 working days in most cases. However, the pressure on courts to reduce overall adjournment times and the political need for 'swift' justice have led to some local agreements reducing the adjournment times in certain cases. It also became national policy in 2006 to allow only 10 working-day adjournments for defendants remanded in custody. This, together with the increasing complexity in preparing PSRs, the need to complete the OASys assessment before preparing the final document and the increase in numbers of reports requested, has put considerable workload pressures on the writers of PSRs.

Other, shorter-format reports providing information on offenders and proposals to courts have been developed in response to increasing demand. These initially ranged from verbal reports following short interviews done on court premises and presented on the day by court-based probation staff, to short, often 'tick-box'-style reports produced for the court either

on the same or following day. Practice in this area developed differentially across England and Wales. In 1999 the specific sentence report (SSR) was introduced. However, in practice, courts requested SSRs in some cases which had not previously attracted a request for a report, while continuing to require similar numbers of PSRs, hence increasing report demand overall.

The Criminal Justice Act (CJA) 2003 brought in many significant changes when its provisions were implemented in April 2005. Its definition of a PSR appears similar to previous Acts. Section 158 states:

> *(1)* In this Part 'pre-sentence report' means a report which –
>
> > *(a)* with a view to assisting the court in determining the most suitable method of dealing with an offender, is made or submitted by an appropriate officer, and
> >
> > *(b)* contains information as to such matters, presented in such a manner, as may be prescribed by rules made by the Secretary of State.

However, most significantly it removed the requirement for PSRs to be *written*. This change, together with the 'prescribed … rules' was contained in PC 18/2005 *Criminal Justice Act 2003 – New Sentences and the New Report Framework*. This outlined three 'versions' of a PSR, which would all fulfil the statutory requirement:

1. *Oral report*: provided to a court in very limited and specific circumstances where a written report is not deemed necessary.
2. *Fast delivery report (FDR)*: this replaced the SSR. Normally it is to be completed on the day, but may be completed in up to five days. PC 18/2005 contained an FDR template which is to be used for all FDRs. It is largely 'tick-box' in format, with spaces for small sections of text, finishing with a larger text section containing the proposal. There is very clear guidance that FDRs should only be used in specific types of cases and offender circumstances: with a low risk of harm and reoffending; when only a lesser complex sentence is being proposed; and when a full-length PSR would previously have been requested.

3. *Standard delivery report (SDR)*: this largely replicates the format and content of the traditional PSR.

The following sections largely relate to the preparation of SDRs, although the practice issues for writers of FDRs are similar. The headings for both FDRs and SDRs remained those which date back to the inception of PSRs.

Sources of information

In the vast majority of cases, the report writer will conduct a face-to-face interview with the offender, usually on probation premises or at a local prison if remanded in custody. While this remains the key part of the information-gathering and assessment process, the report writer will wish to use a wide range of information sources, including information on the offence(s) details and previous convictions provided by the Crown Prosecution Service and police; probation and other agency records; contact with any other agencies whether already involved or who might contribute to future interventions; contact with other family members or significant others; and verified information concerning the offender's circumstances. All information sources must be detailed in this section of the PSR.

Offence analysis

The court is already aware of the details of the offence(s). It is therefore important for the PSR author to avoid a narrative in this section. In essence, the court wants to know why *this* offender committed *this* offence (*these* offences) at *this* time. This will include comments on the circumstances surrounding the offence(s), on the level of culpability, on the offender's attitude and victim awareness, and on an assessment of the key factors underpinning the offending behaviour.

Offender assessment

This section looks at previous patterns of offending, responses to previous sentences and relevant issues relating to the offender's history and current circumstances. It will explore such issues as accommodation, basic skills needs, employment, mental/physical health, substance misuse, community ties, etc.

Assessment of risk of harm to the public and likelihood of reoffending

This is a key section that relates information in the previous two sections to an assessment of the risk of reoffending and risk of harm to others and self. This is a vital section which contains assessments with significant implications for sentencing and the future management of the offender, particularly if a public protection sentence is a possibility within the provisions of the CJA 2003. This section must therefore be clearly constructed and well evidenced.

Conclusion

This should follow on logically from the substance of the report. The proposal needs to reflect the seriousness of the offence(s), the risk posed and the intended purpose(s) of sentencing outlined by the adjourning court. The sentencing provisions of the CJA 2003 make this an increasingly complex section to compose.

While the skill of the officer in writing reports is key to the quality of the final document, his or her skills in interviewing, information gathering, assessment and planning are equally crucial. The preparation of a PSR, then, from initial allocation through to submission of the completed document, represents the author's use of most of the key skills employed by probation officers in all their work. The development of those skills is central to current probation officer qualifying training. It is therefore a matter of significant importance to the majority of those within and associated with the Probation Service that the preparation of the PSR, particularly the standard delivery pre-sentence report, remains the task of probation staff who hold the relevant qualification.

Bob Bearne

Related entries

Court work; Criminal Justice Act 1991; Criminal Justice Act 2003; Crown Prosecution Service; Judges; Magistrates; Offender Assessment System (OASys); Victim awareness.

Key texts and sources

Powers of the Criminal Courts Act 1973.

Criminal Justice Act 1991.

Criminal Justice Act 2003.

Haines, K. and Morgan, R. (2007) 'Services before trial and sentence: achievement, decline and potential', in L. Gelsthorpe and R. Morgan (eds) *Handbook of Probation.* Cullompton: Willan Publishing.

Home Office (2005) *National Standards 2005* (Probation Circular 15/2005). London: Home Office.

Home Office (2005) *Criminal Justice Act 2003 – New Sentences and the New Report Framework* (Probation Circular 18/2005). London: Home Office.

PRISON

> Imprisonment is the most extreme punishment available to sentencers. The prison population has risen steeply in recent decades. One of the main aims of the National Offender Management Service (NOMS) is to ensure that the time someone spends in prison is part of an integrated overall approach to the reintegration and rehabilitation of offenders.

In October 2006, the prison population in England and Wales stood at an all-time high of around 80,000 offenders, held in over 140 prisons. This compares with less than 46,000 in 1992. The number of prisoners has increased particularly rapidly in recent years, rising by 15,000 in the last five or so years alone, leading to chronic overcrowding. Many cells designed for one person have been fitted with bunk beds, and less staff time for each prisoner means that access to basic needs (such as showers and phone calls) is more limited. Prisoners are often moved around the prison estate to make room in the most pressurized prisons and areas, making visits and the completion of offending behaviour programmes and educational courses difficult. Prisoners may also be held in the wrong type of prison for their security classification.

All this has had a negative impact on the ability of prison staff to provide safe and decent conditions and to provide purposeful regimes (see HM Inspectorate of Prisons 2005, 2006). These difficulties are reflected in the reconviction rates, with some two thirds of prisoners being reconvicted within two years of release (Prison Reform Trust 2006). The financial costs of imprisonment are considerable, but there are also very real social costs for prisoners and their children and families. Imprisonment often undermines factors related to desistance, and ex-prisoners are very much more likely than average to experience difficulties related to social exclusion.

The problem of rising prison numbers was one of the main drivers behind the creation of NOMS, an explicit aim of which was to stabilize the prison population and increase the use of community penalties. NOMS exemplified the move away from what became known as the 'prison works' approach, propagated by Michael Howard, Home Secretary between 1993 and 1997. However, the aim of achieving a levelling off of prison numbers has proven hard to achieve. The government has announced its intention to provide 8,000 more prison places; meanwhile, when the prison estate reaches capacity, emergency measures (often detention in police cells) have to be introduced.

The apparent preference of sentencers for custodial rather than community sentences has led to the political demand for 'tougher' community sentences. One aspect of this is more stringent enforcement practice, which has in itself led to greatly increased rates of recall to custody. Rising prison numbers are also explained by increasing punitiveness and by developments such as mandatory sentences and indeterminate sentences of imprisonment for public protection (Criminal Justice Act 2003, s. 225), both of which have boosted the numbers of long-term prisoners.

Although they had usually carried out some degree of risk assessment and management work, until relatively recently prison probation teams were generally viewed as providing a 'welfare' service. For example, they gave prisoners practical assistance with housing and employment, and offered support and counselling. As in the community, these functions are now usually carried out by specialist agencies, and the seconded probation officer's role has become more focused on statutory work (such as writing parole assessment reports) and contributing to the running of accredited programmes. Within the Probation Service, the work of seconded probation staff has been a relatively minor specialism, and is arguably still little understood by community probation staff.

This kind of separation is being challenged by NOMS, and offender management is seen as a means of linking together the Prison and Probation Services to provide a coherent overall approach to work with offenders. A new information management database, C-NOMIS, is being introduced to improve communication across services, and prisons are in the process of developing offender management units, containing both prison and seconded probation staff. Probation offender managers in the community responsible for overseeing and co-ordinating the entirety of offenders' sentence plans will also need to become more familiar with the workings of prisons and with the impact of the prison environment on the aims of rehabilitation and reintegration.

There are major challenges here, not only in practical terms but also in changing the mindset of probation and prison staff who may have misunderstandings, prejudices and genuine concerns about each other's roles and historical functions. Although the stated purpose of prison has varied, its most easily understood goal has been the incapacitation of offenders (others include deterrence, retribution and rehabilitation – see Punishment (aims and justifications)). This basic function has strong public and political legitimacy and, as long as it is carried out, offender management could in theory have a minimal impact on the day-to-day working lives of most prison staff. However, the management and delivery of probation services are being restructured on a far more fundamental level. The ethos of the Probation Service has traditionally been based on the notions of redemption and rehabilitation, and the service has been sceptical of and at times actively hostile towards the validity of prison as a rehabilitative experience. This perspective is not only based on prejudice but also on some genuine limitations of the prison environment.

Carlen (2002) describes a process of 'carceral clawback', whereby the nature of the prison system confounds rehabilitative work by reverting back to the most basic purpose of containment and the perceived requirements of control and security. She argues that the fundamental nature of prison should not be obscured by talk of rehabilitation or self-improvement, which encourages sentencers to think that prison is a positive option for reducing reoffending. Rather, she argues, prisons should be seen starkly as places designed to confine, where any other constructive impact is minimal.

The current crisis situation in prisons may provide some support for this view, as overcrowding inhibits efforts to focus on end-to-end offender management because prison managers are concentrating on providing regimes of basic decency. In any event, if the NOMS project is to work to any degree, it is indisputable that probation staff will have to be far more aware of the world of prisons.

Hindpal Singh Bhui

Related entries

National Offender Management Service (NOMS); Offender Assessment System (OASys); Offender management; Prison probation teams; Rehabilitation; Reintegration; Resettlement.

Key texts and sources

Carlen, P. (2002) 'Women's imprisonment: models of reform and change', *Probation Journal*, 49: 76–87.

Coyle, A. (2005) *Understanding Prisons*. Maidenhead: Open University Press.

HM Inspectorate of Prisons (2005) *Annual Report, 2003–4*. London: Home Office.

HM Inspectorate of Prisons (2006) *Annual Report, 2004–5*. London: Home Office.

Matthews, R. (ed.) (1999) *Imprisonment*. Dartmouth: Ashgate.

Prison Reform Trust (2006) *Bromley Briefings: Prison Fact File* (available online at **http://www.ws3. prisonreform.web.baigent.net/uploads/documents/ factfile1807lo.pdf**).

The Prison Service website (**http://www. hmprisonservice.gov.uk/**) contains much valuable information, as does HM Inspectorate of Prisons' website (**http://inspectorates.homeoffice.gov.uk/ hmiprisons/**).

PRISON PROBATION TEAMS

Groups of probation staff, employed by the local area probation board, seconded to work in prison establishments in accordance with an annual contract agreed between the governor and the local chief officer of probation.

Probation staff have worked in prisons since the mid-1960s when the former 'welfare officers' were assimilated into the Probation Service. The welfare officers had assisted prisoners with welfare and resettlement issues. As probation officers took over this role, their focus was directed more to casework and assessment, although the term 'welfare' lingered for many years in some prisons. The main duties became ones of counselling prisoners in relation to their future behaviour and compiling assessment reports, especially for the parole system which developed significantly during the 1970s (see Parole Board). Prison probation officers also ensured that prisoners were linked to community-based probation officers before release, especially if the prisoner was to be released on licence.

The strictly 'welfare' functions were transferred to prison staff who developed 'personal officer' schemes through which designated prison officers took an increasing interest in the personal affairs of a group of prisoners.

In the mid-1990s a new system was introduced to agree the role and size of the prison probation team through an annual contract between the governor and the local chief probation officer. Previously a national formula had allocated a number of probation officers to each establishment on the basis of its size. The devolved contract system ensured that there was more focus on the tasks and output of probation staff than had been the case previously. There also developed a stronger sense of joint ownership. Differential developments took place that reflected the varying needs of different prisons and the preferences of individual governors, who had to pay for the service from their devolved prison budget. Before then the cost of probation in prison was met by a central payment from the Home Office to probation areas. Nevertheless, the net effect was a growth in the contribution of probation staff to prisons and a considerable extension of the roles and tasks in which they were involved.

In many prisons today probation staff fulfil key assessment and offender management duties, contributing to decisions regarding parole, release on home detention curfew, release on temporary licence, home leave, etc. In many local prisons they act as the link with outside resources that contribute to the resettlement and rehabilitation of short-term prisoners. Some prison probation teams have forged good links with the benefits system, accommodation and employment providers, etc., to the extent that these agencies come into the prison and provide surgeries for those about to be released.

Prison probation teams also work closely with health providers, especially in the areas of mental health and substance misuse. Many prisons have Counselling, Assessment, Referral, Advice and Through-care (CARATs) workers who work with drug-misusing prisoners.

In prisons holding more long-term prisoners, probation staff are acting as tutors and treatment managers for the accredited programmes run in the prison. In many prisons the programme-delivering team comprises individuals drawn from the prison staff, the psychology department and the probation department. Prisons are set challenging targets for the completion of offending behaviour and sex offender treatment programmes, and many probation staff have been recruited to prisons to deliver these.

The introduction of offender management into prisons is changing the shape of prison probation teams. While for most prisoners their offender manager will be a community-based probation officer, the prison will provide an offender supervisor for the part of the sentence served in custody. Prisons have been establishing 'offender management units' and, in many prisons, the prison-based probation staff have been filling roles in offender management. These changes are increasing the proportion of Probation Service officers who are working in prison probation teams as offender supervisors.

Another notable development in the last decade is the extent to which senior probation officers, responsible for the prison probation team, are moving into senior management positions in the prison as part of the governor's management team. Posts such as 'head of resettlement' are now frequently held by probation staff, seconded by the local probation board, usually for a time-limited period of about four years.

David Hancock

Related entries

Licence; Mubarek Inquiry; National Offender Management Service (NOMS); Offender management; Parole Board; Prison; Rehabilitation.

Key texts and sources

Home Office (2006) *Offender Management for Custodial Sentences* (Probation Circular 09/2006). London: Home Office.
Home Office/NOMS (2006) *Offender Management Model.* London: Home Office.

PRISONS AND PROBATION OMBUDSMAN

The Prisons and Probation Ombudsman investigates complaints from those whose grievances have not been resolved through the internal Probation Service complaints process. He also investigates the deaths of residents of approved premises.

Until 2001, offenders under supervision had no access to an independent complaints investigator if they had a grievance against the Probation Service. However, in April that year, the remit of the (then) Prisons Ombudsman was extended, and his office was rebadged to include probation. In April 2004, his terms of reference were further increased to take in the investigation of the deaths of those resident in approved premises.

The ombudsman has reported that those most likely to complain about probation are people currently in prison, rather than those currently on licence or serving a punishment in the community. In common with other ombudsman systems, complainants must first have exhausted the internal remedies. However, most potential complainants have in fact not completed the internal system and are referred back before the ombudsman can intervene. In successive annual reports, the ombudsman has criticized the Probation Service because those on supervision seem not to know how to pursue a complaint or are fearful of the repercussions.

The total number of complaints the ombudsman receives about probation remains small compared with his prison caseload. However, while the numbers are not great (in 2005–6, just 307 probation complaints were received compared with over 4,000 for prisons), the issues they raise are important. A significant proportion concern the content of pre-sentence reports and reports for the Parole Board. The ombudsman has said that his probation complaints often have a more personal character than those about prisons. Complainants tend to criticize the specific actions of a named probation officer rather than being directed at systematic failures, as is the case with prison complaints.

The ombudsman's fatal incidents remit encompasses all deaths of approved premises residents – whether self-inflicted, accidental, from natural causes or homicides. During 2005–6, there were 17 such deaths. Three were from natural causes, six were apparently self-inflicted (see Self-harm; Suicide) and seven were a result of substance misuse. One death had not been classified. Many of those leaving prison are at special risk of overdose if returning to intravenous drug abuse.

The investigation reports are published, in anonymized form, post-inquest. Many can already be found on the ombudsman's website which will, in time, build to form a unique archive. Several reports have drawn attention to a failure to transfer information about risk following an offender's release from custody. Although generally impressed by the level of support given by hostel staff to high-risk and vulnerable residents, the ombudsman has also found hostels where staff were unclear about procedures and ill-equipped to deal with emergencies.

Stephen Shaw

Related entries

Approved premises; Complaints; Parole Board; Pre-sentence report (PSR); Self-harm; Suicide.

Key texts and sources

The Ombudsman's own annual reports are the best source of information. He also publishes a quarterly digest of cases: *On the Case*. These documents, plus the anonymized fatal incident investigation reports, are available online at http://www.ppo.gov.uk.

PRIVATIZATION

A process whereby the government transfers responsibility for the provision of a public service from public sector staff groups to private companies.

Although the Home Office is actively pursuing an agenda of introducing privatization and competition into the Probation Service, no business case has been produced to justify the strategy. Nor has evidence been put forward to suggest it would reduce reoffending or enhance public protection. Were the Home Office to examine the existing record of private sector involvement in the provision of either prisons or probation work, then perhaps it would review its thinking.

The government has made much in the recent past of the success of privatization in the prison system. It has claimed that the project has driven up standards and improved the dignity agenda. However, there is no evidence for this, and the National Audit Office report in 2005 was inconclusive. The private sector has only been involved in new prisons and has not faced the disadvantage of chronic overcrowding in Victorian buildings. It has benefited from new technology and modern design.

The private sector has driven down costs. The think-tank 'Catalyst' produced a report in the summer of 2004 which found that public sector prison officers' pay was on average, 51 per cent greater than their private sector counterparts. When the value of pensions and holiday benefits were added, the difference rose to 70 per cent. Staff turnover rates are ten times greater in the private sector.

Private sector involvement in the Probation Service has been fairly disastrous. In 2002, the Home Office privatized hostel (approved premises) facilities, including cooks, cleaners and maintenance staff. Costs rose by 62 per cent.

The decision was also taken to privatize the management and maintenance of all probation premises. This led to an immediate increase in cost of 35 per cent.

Both privatized projects were then characterized by a fall in service standards. Staff have recorded a catalogue of problems, which have included numerous complaints about standards of hygiene in kitchens. A Brighton hostel was forced to call in environmental health officers because of the state of the kitchen. There had been no cook for a lengthy period and, when a cook eventually came, there was no food. Food was eventually purchased at a supermarket at Peterborough and delivered to the hostel. Another hostel in London needed its boiler switching on: the company sent a carpenter from Portsmouth. In contrast, one of the Sheffield hostels needed roof repairs and a boilerman was sent. A call-out from a hostel in Newcastle resulted in a contractor travelling from Chester to mend a broken toilet.

It is some satisfaction and relief to note that the catering contract will, from 2007, almost certainly be brought back in-house.

In conclusion, there is absolutely no evidence that the private sector is likely to run the probation services more efficiently. What the evidence does suggest, however, is that privatization may be successful in driving down the terms and conditions of staff and depressing service delivery standards.

Harry Fletcher

Related entries

Carter Report; Contestability; National Offender Management Service (NOMS); Probation trusts.

Key texts and sources

The National Audit Office report can be found at www.nao.org.uk/publications/naoreports/ 02-03/0203700.pdf
A summary of the Catalyst Report can be found at www.labournet.net/other/ 0406/catalyst.html.

PROBATION

The term 'probation' – derived from the Latin noun *probatio*, meaning a period of proving or testing – is both the name of a court disposal (now renamed in England and Wales) and of services which administer such orders. Offenders who are placed on probation are given an alternative to harsher sentences, allowing them to remain in the community under supervision, subject to specified conditions. The concept has symbolic significance because of its association with certain principles and values.

It is a tribute to the resilience of traditional probation values that the National Probation Service of England and Wales in the first decade of the twenty-first century retains the concept of 'probation' within its title, even though probation orders no longer exist as such, and despite the efforts of successive governments to change the name. Although the policies and objectives of the service have undergone much revision, the name carries strong symbolic value and, therefore, at a time of immense change, provides some continuity with the purposes and principles of the service in the past. Depending on perspective, it is a rubric that may be regarded as either sacrosanct or anachronistic.

The nature of probation as a court disposal is variable across time and country, but the following definition captures common characteristics:

> *probation is a system of dealing ... with ... persons found guilty of crimes of lesser gravity ... wherein these, instead of being sent to prison or otherwise punished, are released on suspended sentence during good behaviour, and placed under the supervision of a probation officer, who acts as a friend and adviser, but who, in case of the failure of the probationer to fulfil the terms of his probation, can report him back to the court*
>
> (*Oxford English Dictionary*).

This court order has long been associated with alternatives to harsher sentences. Being a substitute for prison is part of probation's long-term identity:

> without the prison, it would have been difficult for probation to assume an identity as a penal provision because prison was the main form of punishment and probation was instead of punishment. It was in this sense therefore that it was always an alternative to imprisonment, and the theory and practice of probation cannot be fully articulated outside that function'
>
> (Vanstone 2004: 21–2).

More broadly, probation has been imposed instead of punishment; in England and Wales, it was not until the Criminal Justice Act 1991 that probation became a penalty in its own right, changing the ethos of a probation order to punishment in the community. Probation orders were renamed community rehabilitation orders in 2000 and further changes were introduced by the Criminal Justice Act 2003. For offences committed since April 2005, the nearest equivalent to the old probation order is a community order with the requirement of 'supervision'.

Precursors of probation as a practice can be traced to English criminal law of the Middle Ages when courts first made use of 'binding over' and 'recognizance' – payment of a fee as a collateral for a period of release during which the accused could take measures to secure pardons or lesser sentences. The word 'probation' became embedded in penal terminology during the nineteenth century – in the USA with the Massachusetts Act 1878, and in the UK with the Probation of First Offenders Act 1887. The duty of probation officers to 'advise, assist and befriend', specified in the Probation of Offenders Act 1907, served, in effect, as a mission statement for probation work over the next eight decades.

The concept of probation is applied internationally to identify comparable services and community sanctions, although the formal characteristics vary. The UK system has served as a world leader. It is fair to argue that 'The Probation Service, as a title, embodies the values of a service and a profession that is internationally recognised and respected' (McKnight 2005: 4). Moves to relabel the service as the Community Rehabilitation and Punishment Service, and to 'expunge' the concept of probation, met with entrenched resistance (Nellis 2004). Similarly, following the creation of the National Offender Management Service, practitioner representatives have asserted that the concepts of 'offender management' and 'probation' are not interchangeable (McKnight 2005).

What's in a name? 'Probation' is symbolically loaded. It is a brand name that has international recognition and that is a 'potent symbol of the organisation's social work heritage and aspirations' (Nellis 2004: 120). It serves as a bridge linking the modernized service with what it has stood for over the decades: humanitarian ethics, the rehabilitative ideal and social work values. In its early years, the Probation Service epitomized progressive penal practices and it developed as 'the exemplar, the paradigm, of the welfarist approach to dealing with crime and offenders' (Garland 1997: 2). Its method and focus have been a personalized approach addressing the psychosocial problems underlying offending, and orientated towards bringing out the good in people and promoting self-control but, until recently, orientated away from punishment and imposed surveillance. While other labels might be helpfully adopted, such as 'community justice', the name 'probation' is like a talisman to defend against being more fully implicated in the worst excesses of the culture of control, and marking the limits to which the service is prepared to go in adapting to the government's programme of modernization.

Ros Burnett

Related entries

Community justice; Criminal Justice Act 1991; National Probation Service for England and Wales; Offender management; Probation values; Punishment in the community; Rehabilitation; Supervision of offenders.

Key texts and sources

Garland, D. (1997) 'Probation and the reconfiguration of crime control', in R. Burnett (ed.) *The Probation Service: Responding to Change. Proceedings of the Probation Studies Unit First Colloquium.* Oxford: University of Oxford Centre for Criminological Research.

McKnight, J. (2005) *NOMS – the Vision, the Blueprint and an Alternative: Napo's Response.* London: Napo (available online at **www.napo2.org.uk**).

Nellis, M. (2004) '"Into the field of corrections": the end of English probation in the early 21st century', *Cambrian Law Review*, 35: 115–33 (available online at **http://www.aber.ac.uk/clr/**).

Vanstone, M. (2004) *Supervising Offenders in the Community: A History of Probation Theory and Practice.* Aldershot: Ashgate.

PROBATION BOARD FOR NORTHERN IRELAND

The key mandatory functions of the Probation Board for Northern Ireland (PBNI) are to provide an effective and efficient probation service, to make arrangements for offenders to perform work under community service orders and to undertake social welfare duties in prison. In 2007 the Committee on the Programme for Government agreed that probation matters in Northern Ireland would be the responsibility of the devolved Assembly, so it is likely that Northern Irish probation will continue even further to take on its own distinct character.

For many years probation practice in Northern Ireland was closely related to that in England and Wales, with similar training and legislation. However, the combination of the rapid changes to probation practice in England and Wales and the advent of devolution in Northern Ireland has led to a greater separation and difference between the two jurisdictions.

Although its history cannot be traced to as early a date, the nature of the origins of probation in Northern Ireland is similar to that of probation in England and Wales. In the post-war period altruistic volunteers were tasked by the courts to help young people to stay out of trouble. This work was given a more formal remit by the appointment of the first probation officer in the mid-1950s. The service developed over the next 15 years with an increase in the number of officers appointed and an eventual requirement that those appointed should undertake social work training. Having originally been part of the Ministry of Home Affairs and then the Northern Ireland Office, the PBNI was created by the Probation Board (Northern Ireland) Order 1982.

The PBNI is a community-based board with the status of a non-departmental public body. It has a number of functions laid down in the legislation. To:

- carry out assessments and provide court reports;
- supervise offenders in the community; and
- work in prisons providing a range of services.

The PBNI also funds organizations that provide hostels for offenders and runs various community projects, addressing the offending behaviour of those under PBNI supervision. The organization's stated purpose is to protect the public by working with courts, other agencies and partners to reduce reoffending and integrate offenders successfully back into the community. Its aim is to help reduce crime and the harm it does, and its vision is to achieve excellence in the assessment and management of offenders.

Along with all other aspects of the criminal justice system, the PBNI was considered by the Criminal Justice Review Group in 2000, following the Good Friday Agreement. The review recommended that the Probation Service be reconstituted as a Next Steps agency, with the responsible minister supported by an advisory board. While recommending much closer links between prisons and probation, it rejected the suggestion of merger. These suggestions will be considered by the Northern Ireland Executive after the devolution of criminal justice matters.

The Northern Ireland Office commissioned a strategic review of the PBNI in 2004, and the recommendations of this review influenced subsequent corporate planning.

The main differences between the PBNI and probation areas in England and Wales relate to training and community development. Probation officers in Northern Ireland are still required to hold a social work qualification, and there do not appear to be any immediate plans to change this. Some 20 per cent of the PBNI's annual budget (up to £2 million) is allocated towards community development. The board seeks to work closely with statutory, community and voluntary organizations in order to achieve its purpose. Examples of partnership projects include IMPACT (Inclusive Model of Partnership Against Car Crime), the Course for Drink Drive Offenders (CDDO) and Men Overcoming Domestic Violence (MODV).

Brian Stout

Key texts and sources

Criminal Justice Review Group (2000) *Review of the Criminal Justice System in Northern Ireland* (available online at **http://www.nio.gov.uk/criminal-justice**).

Gadd, B. (1996) 'Probation in Northern Ireland', in G. McIvor (ed.) *Working with Offenders*. London: Jessica Kingsley.

O'Mahony, D. and Chapman, T. (2007) 'Probation, the state and community – delivering probation services in Northern Ireland', in L. Gelsthorpe and R. Morgan (eds) *Handbook of Probation*. Cullompton: Willan Publishing.

See also the PBNI website (**http://www.pbni.org.uk/index.htm**).

PROBATION BOARD SECRETARIES

Office holders appointed by probation boards to advise on legal, governance and policy issues. They must have independent direct access to the board and always be in a position to be able to render advice as an independent officer.

The Home Office has advised probation boards that they must have all reasonable and relevant information available to them in order to reach lawful decisions. Prior to 2001, chief probation officers were responsible for the day-to-day management of probation services, with the committees exercising oversight functions. However, the creation of probation boards in 2001 resulted in all probation functions being exercised in the name of the board. The requirements for probation officers to perform certain functions was replaced by a provision that enabled boards to authorize any of their officers or, alternatively, persons belonging to other organizations, to carry out the duties of officers of boards. This led to some changes in the relationships, with the secretary becoming the board's (including the chief officer's) primary representative, and its 'eyes and ears'.

A prime role of the secretary is protecting the board from legal challenge and ensuring that contractual procedures and terms entered into on behalf of the board are appropriate in terms of contractual probity and liability. Additionally there is the monitoring officer role in relation to the board's own procedures, and the various duties prescribed in standing orders and codes of conduct.

The crucial competency is an ability to identify a broad range of legal problems and to be able to judge whether it is in the best interests of the board whether these should be dealt with directly or procured outside (e.g. counsel). Boards are directly responsible for substantial staffing complements and, in the modern world, this leads not only to reputational risks around employment law but can also result in almost unlimited financial exposure. Secretaries perform a critical role in advising boards at appeal level in disciplinary and grievance issues, and those who are also legal advisers undertake the legal work arising from employment tribunals.

The job of secretary can be an isolated and exposed role, and he or she may have to make judgements which can be extremely unpopular, so the secretary requires a constitution that is able to withstand quite insidious pressures on occasion. Manoeuvring through such currents requires a degree of diplomacy and steadfastness without appearing partisan.

It is, perhaps, unfortunate that the present regime within the National Offender Management Service/National Probation Directorate makes no effort to use the Secretaries

Group as an early-warning system for concerns. This would be of benefit to all, as experienced secretaries are skilled at conflict prevention, enjoying, as they do, a degree of detachment from operational management.

Richard Steer

Related entries

Probation boards; Probation board treasurers.

Key texts and sources

The provision for secretaries is contained in Schedule 1, para. 7 of the Criminal Justice and Court Services Act 2000. The regulations made under para. 7 are in SI 786 2001 (*The Local Probation Boards (Miscellaneous Provisions) Regulations 2001*).

PROBATION BOARD TREASURERS

Each probation board must appoint a treasurer. It is the treasurer's duty, as the source of independent expert advice on financial matters, to support and advise the chief officer in the role as accountable officer for the board.

The post and role of treasurer are important in the management and accountability of both the local probation board and the local service. The Criminal Justice and Court Services Act 2000 (Schedule 1) provides for regulations to be made for the appointment of a treasurer by each probation board and for the specification of any conditions to be fulfilled for such an appointment, including the tenure of office. A treasurer must be a member of an approved accountancy body (as defined within the Local Government Act 1988). This means that individuals will have an obligation to keep up to date with professional practice and will also be bound by codes of ethics and practice set by the relevant accountancy body.

The specification of requirements and responsibilities for board treasurers marked a significant departure from previous arrangements where committees generally operated within a local authority accounting framework. This changed to a central government one in 2001 with the creation of the National Probation Service and the ending of financial support by local authorities. Many more services now have their own directly employed treasurers.

The treasurer is directly accountable to the chief officer. It is the chief officer who is the local board's accountable officer and is therefore personally responsible for propriety and regularity in the management of the public funds and assets delegated to him or her. The treasurer, as an independent and experienced professional, provides support and advice to the chief officer in this role.

The treasurer has the right of independent access to the chair and to the board (and, indeed, to the National Director in extreme cases). The treasurer has the right to attend board meetings and the meetings of any committee or group established by the board that has devolved authority for decisions on financial matters. The treasurer must attend the audit committee that all boards are required to establish.

The specific responsibilities attaching to the role of treasurer are identified in the National Probation Directorate's *Management Statement and Financial Memorandum*. In day-to-day terms, effective discharge of these responsibilities means working with senior management and other officers across the service and with a range of external partners. This direct management role is now commonly reflected in the operational designation of treasurers as 'directors of finance'.

Brian Kerslake

Related entries

Probation boards; Probation board secretaries.

Key texts and sources

Home Office (2001) *National Probation Service Management Statement and Financial Memorandum*. London: Home Office.
Various publications by the Probation Boards' Association provide information about the general financial context (see their website: **www.probationboards.co.uk/**).

The Chartered Institute of Public Finance and Accountancy (CIPFA) (**www.cipfa.org.uk**) has produced guides to the role of the chief finance officer, in both local government and health.

PROBATION BOARDS

Bodies corporate responsible for the delivery of probation services and the employment of probation staff in an area.

Probation boards were created, as part of the National Probation Service on 1 April 2001, by the Criminal Justice and Courts Act 2000, and the Home Secretary became responsible for the funding and performance of the service. The aim of the government at this time was to make criminal justice agencies coterminous in 42 areas. Hence the Crown Prosecution Service, the Police Service, the Courts Service and Probation all had matching geographic areas, and local criminal justice boards were later formed to help promote closer working relationships between the agencies.

Each board must operate within the provisions of the Act and relevant subordinate legislation, and must comply with any directions given by the Secretary of State. Probation boards are corporate bodies, enjoying their own 'legal personality' but also being subject to numerous restrictions, particularly those contained in Schedule 1 of the Act and in the management statement/financial memorandum which was issued by the Secretary of State in May 2001.

Paragraph 2 of Schedule 1 to the Act provides that each board is to consist of a chairman, a chief officer and not fewer than five other members. Each of the new boards were, in fact, established with 15 members, regardless of the area or the budget. Each new board was encouraged to have four continuing members from the former committees, four magistrates, one judge (appointed by the Lord Chancellor), two local authority members, and the remaining positions filled by members of the local community. Appointments were made against a published schedule of competencies. The process was monitored by the Office of the Commissioner of Public Appointments.

West Mercia Area was an amalgamation of two services (Shropshire, together with Herefordshire and Worcestershire), making a service covering two county councils and two unitary authority areas. The competition for places on the board was stiff. The author was notified of her appointment in November 2000 and was then involved in the appointment process for board members, including the chief officer.

During the transition period from committees to boards, transitional management steering groups were formed to put business plans in place for the new service, to set budgets and to look at ways of minimizing the disruption that creating a new service would necessarily cause. In the case of West Mercia, the change necessitated the building of a new head office in the middle of the new area at Kidderminster.

The probation board is the employing body of all staff in its area. Community members of the board are paid an hourly rate for board duties, currently standing at £15 an hour, plus travelling expenses and preparation time. The chair and the chief officer who, like the other board members, are appointed by the Home Secretary, are paid a salary by the Home Office, and are statutory office holders rather than employees. The judge is appointed by the Lord Chancellor and does not draw a payment for his work on the board. The board currently has five women and nine men from diverse backgrounds.

Boards were created to set the strategic direction of the service locally and to hold the chief officer to account for service delivery in the area. Regular board meetings are held and are open to members of the public. The financial memorandum was issued at the outset, and boards were directed to adopt this document on 1 May 2001. All boards are required to have an audit committee.

The West Mercia Board also has a Human Resources Committee and a Joint Negotiating Consultative Committee that meets with the unions, together with a Performance Committee that specifically monitors the service's performance in relation to targets set by the government. The West Mercia Board has a 'Risk register' where matters of concern to the board, whether financial, reputational or business risks, are recorded. This register is reviewed at every board meeting and changes in the items listed are noted.

Various board members have lead responsibility for different areas of work (e.g. a lead member for training, governance, health and safety, and property strategy). These members will attend various meetings and report back at board meetings. Board members also contribute significantly to maintaining links with the community by sitting on Supporting People boards and strategic partnership boards in the area, and by keeping an interest in a designated area within West Mercia.

From the outset the board has recognized that good liaison with sentencers was crucial. Local probation forums were formed at each local court centre comprising local magistrates and local probation staff. The board then established a structure to co-ordinate the local forums.

With the arrival of the National Offender Management Service (NOMS), the West Mercia Board is now considering setting up a further subcommittee to review the commissioning, monitoring and performance of contracts with partner agencies. The new role of regional offender manager (ROM) has also profoundly changed the strategic focus of the board. Two service-level agreements were signed by the board chair, on behalf of the board, on 29 March 2006 with the ROM: one for offender management and the other for interventions in West Mercia. However, at this time performance and targets are still governed by the National Probation Directorate (NPD). This tripartite relationship can mean tensions that are not easy for the board to resolve.

The majority of the West Mercia Board members were appointed on 1 April 2001 and subsequently were reappointed in April 2004. On 1 April 2007, all these members and the board chair came to the end of a six-year contract, the maximum allowed in the legislation.

The government has now recruited new board members who took over from 1 April 2007 and has announced that it will introduce legislation to transform the boards into probation trusts, reflecting a move from a predominantly employing role to a commissioning one.

Patricia Bradbury

Related entries

Chief officers; National Offender Management Service (NOMS); National Probation Service for England and Wales; Probation Boards' Association (PBA); Probation board secretaries; Probation board treasurers; Probation trusts; Regional offender managers (ROMs).

Key texts and sources

The 'Local probation boards standing orders' issued by the Secretary of State as a direction for implementation from 1 April 2003.

Morgan, R. (2007) 'Probation, governance and accountability', in L. Gelsthorpe and R. Morgan (eds) *Handbook of Probation*. Cullompton: Willan Publishing.

PROBATION BOARDS' ASSOCIATION (PBA)

The Probation Boards' Association is the national employers' organization for probation in England and Wales. It represents the interests of the 42 local boards that employ the staff and that are charged under statute with providing probation services.

The PBA was formed in April 2001 to coincide with the changes brought about by the Criminal Justice and Courts Services Act 2000. The Act replaced probation committees by smaller boards of up to 15 people, including a chair, the chief officer and a judge. The Act also referred to a National Probation Service and changed the status of chief probation officers from locally employed staff to statutory office holders, appointed by the Home Secretary. In effect they became civil servants, accountable to the Secretary of State, but also members of the local probation board, responsible for the work of the service in its geographical area.

The probation committees consisted mainly of magistrates, ensuring that the service kept a close relationship with a true customer for its services, and thus a consistently high user-approval response was achieved. One of the unforeseen consequences of the Act was to divert attention away from this vital relationship and to focus the service on civil-service-set targets. However, the well considered competencies set for the new appointments to boards ensured a good mix of skills, while retaining a few sentencers within the membership. As such the new boards could claim to be more representative of the communities they serve.

The PBA is a private company limited by guarantee, and each local board is entitled to membership. From the start, the association strove to involve as many individual board members as possible, utilizing their skills at a national level. The three areas on which the PBA has concentrated have been local governance, employment issues and the promotion of the service. The PBA has also sought to develop partnerships with other appropriate organizations.

As the national employers' body, the negotiation of pay and conditions and related matters has remained the core of the association's work. For example, far-reaching changes of the national pay and reward review were introduced in 2006 after lengthy and productive negotiations with the unions and the Home Office.

In other areas of national work, the PBA has produced a range of events, conferences, workshops and publications. It has formed alliances with other organizations in the criminal justice system and with those providing support for it or commentary on it. Local board members contributing their time and skills to three working groups has enhanced the work of the PBA. More recently, the association has been active in various aspects of the news media, promoting the work of the service, defending it from less well informed criticism and explaining its purposes. This has been especially necessary in the wake of high-profile media storms concerning serious further offences committed by offenders under the supervision of probation staff.

The PBA combines the work of the former Central Council of Probation Committees with some aspects of the disbanded Association of Chief Officers of Probation. It was established at the same moment that a National Probation Directorate (NPD) was formed within the Home Office, replacing the small unit that had overseen policy and strategy. The NPD grew rapidly and developed into a headquarters for a national service, albeit one comprising 42 independent bodies corporate. This position led, unsurprisingly, to areas of uncertainty and tension. The emergence of top-down management control by the NPD raised questions about the practicalities of truly local governance. This has yet to be resolved and has been compounded as another layer of Home Office oversight, the National Offender Management Service (NOMS), came into being in 2004.

Following the Carter Report in 2004, the Home Office announced that the Probation Service would, in effect, merge with the Prison Service and both would be subject to 'contestability', a government term for the introduction of private companies into public sector operations. After two and a half years no merger has taken place, but NOMS has grown considerably in size with a major headquarters (in addition to the headquarters of the Prison Service, which has agency status) and ten regional offender managers, whose job it might be to oversee the contestability regime. There has been delay and confusion surrounding the rationale and future of NOMS, and no legislation to achieve its purposes was brought to Parliament before 2007. Opposition to the structures and possible methods of NOMS has been widespread.

The PBA inevitably regarded the advent of NOMS as the most important issue for the service at its centenary in 2007. It has argued that a 'mixed economy' of public, private and voluntary sector involvement could only be to the advantage of probation and the criminal justice system as a whole. However, it has stressed that commissioning for most operational matters should remain 'close to the business' and not at a regional or national level. Indeed, the concept of localism, well regarded in government policy generally, remains at the heart of the vision that the PBA holds for the future of the service. At the time of writing the current Home Secretary has insisted that some form of contestability will go ahead, but that NOMS will halve in size. The future of the NPD remains uncertain.

Inherent in the plans for NOMS is a move from local boards to trusts. Little seems to be known of what might be entailed in the change, the only comments having concentrated on describing them as 'more like businesses' and implying that representation of local interest would be of little importance and a handicap to competitiveness. More seriously for the PBA and the concept of local people's increased involvement in the work of probation has been the view from NOMS that parts of the service might not remain in public control but move to the commercial sector.

Martin Wargent

Related entries

Association of Chief Officers of Probation (ACOP); Central Council of Probation Committees (CCPC); Chief officers; National Offender Management Service (NOMS); National Probation Service for England and Wales; Probation boards; Probation board secretaries; Probation board treasurers; Probation trusts.

Key texts and sources

Changes in probation work since 2001 have been the subject of a wide variety of books and articles. Much of the material most relevant to the Probation Boards' Association can be found on its comprehensive website (**www.probationboards.co.uk**).

PROBATION IN AFRICA

Africa is a vast continent with many different legal systems. The administration of justice and punishment in northern countries is quite different from practices in the south, often reflecting diverse colonial and cultural legacies. This entry considers aspects of probation practice in the countries of the South African Development Community (SADC), particularly the Republic of South Africa.

In South Africa and, indeed, in the region, there are two very different streams of thought with regard to probation. Correctional services view probation from a penal perspective (i.e. the supervision of an offender or accused outside a prison setting, either during the pre-trial phase or as a sentence or part of a sentence). The Correctional Services Act (1998) in South Africa thus makes reference to 'being on probation' and to 'probationers', though not to 'probation officers'.

Social development practitioners, on the other hand, see a much broader role for probation. In South Africa a 'probation officer' is a qualified social worker employed by the state. Probation services focus on a continuum of social services and support to people (and particularly youth) in the criminal justice system – from assessment at the time of arrest, to diversion services, pre-sentence work, after-care and monitoring. Probation officers, then, are social workers, appointed by the Minister of Social Development, and officers of every magistrates' court.

The main components of probation officers' work include the following:

- The prevention of crime, focused on the family, school and broader community.
- Pre-trial intervention, including offender–victim mediation programmes, diversion programmes and services to offenders' families.
- Awaiting trial interventions, including services to children awaiting trial in custody, support of parents/guardians and residential care.
- The trial and sentencing phase, comprising conducting pre-trial and pre-sentence investigations and supplying information to courts. (This forms the bulk of the work of state-appointed probation officers.)
- After-care and supervision, focusing on the supervision of offenders in a variety of programmes under a probation order, such as community service, skills training and family reconstruction and, occasionally, supervising probationers.

Some of these tasks are undertaken by assistants. Probation officers could, in addition, undertake tasks related to the care and supervision of children who have been sentenced to community-based sanctions, but this does not form the bulk of their work. They also have no involvement with convicted persons serving sentences of correctional supervision under the Correctional Service Act who would be monitored by 'correctional officers' employed by the Department of Correctional Services. Correctional officers are not required to have a social work qualification. While they may make recommendations about the suitability of persons for community corrections, they are not permitted to draft formal pre-sentence reports for the court.

South Africa arguably has one of the most established probation services in sub-Saharan Africa. Probation is governed by the Probation Services Act (116 of 1991). An amendment to the Act (2002) introduced concepts such as 'diversion' and 'restorative justice' and provided for assistant probation officers. It also established home-based supervision as an alternative to pre-trial detention and provided legal recognition for reception, assessment and referral centres.

Ten years ago there were no probation officers in South Africa. There are now 600. South Africa has thus made considerable progress towards creating a dedicated probation service through such initiatives as specific probation training, at both undergraduate and tertiary levels.

The majority of African countries are signatories to both the Kampala and Kadoma declarations, which introduce the notion of community service and the promotion of alternatives to incarceration in direct response to prison overcrowding. The focus of much community-based sentencing in Africa is on community service orders. It has been said that community service, with its emphasis on reparation, fits well with cultural traditions of making amends as a response to wrongdoing. Becoming a signatory to these conventions could be seen as implicit recognition of the need for the appointment of persons to oversee this process – whether or not such staff are to be known as 'probation officers'. Arguably, the signature and ratification of these declarations place an obligation on states to adopt these provisions.

Similarly, all African countries except Somalia are signatories to the United Nations Convention on the Rights of the Child (CRC) and, therefore, in theory at least, use prison as a measure of last resort. Countries such as South Africa,

Mozambique, Namibia, Ghana, Uganda, Lesotho, Kenya and Swaziland are accordingly all developing new systems for the management of children in the welfare and criminal justice systems. There is often statutory provision for the appointment of social workers, although no explicit reference to probation. For the most part, probation is seen as an extension of generic social work rather than a dedicated profession.

While there has been progress in legal reform, there are severe resource constraints and a dire shortage of social workers in almost every African country. Of the 40 heavily indebted poor countries (HIPCs), the vast majority are in Africa. Many countries are grappling with basic issues, such as the establishment of a birth registration system and access for children to basic nutrition, health and education. There are very few institutional facilities or alternatives to prison for children. The development of probation would be one of many priorities in countries such as this. They would probably lack the capacity to assign staff to this function and, indeed, there might be little point in introducing a fully fledged probation service into a system that lacks the infrastructure and resources to implement, monitor and oversee it.

Through the influence of organizations such as UNICEF, many African countries are now starting to recognize the role that social workers need to play in the criminal justice system. The challenge lies in how alternatives to incarceration, for both adults and children and the associated tasks of assessment, supervision and monitoring, are to be promoted in such a context.

Louise Ehlers

Related entries

Probation training; United Nations.

Key texts and sources

The Kampala Declaration on Prison Conditions in Africa (1996) is available online at **www.chr.up.ac.za/hr_docs/african/docs/other/other15.doc**.

Kadoma Declaration on Community Service Orders in Africa (1997) is available online at **www.chr.up.ac.za/law_of_africa.html**.

http://www.capegateway.gov.za/eng/pubs/public_info/W/47585.

PROBATION IN EUROPE

The essence of probation seems to be the combination of a conditional suspension of punishment and the supervision of offenders in the community. European probation systems vary in the emphasis they give to these ideas. In the Anglo-American tradition, rehabilitation through supervision has tended to be the more emphasized; in the civil law codes of continental Europe, suspension – deterrence through the prospect of future punishment – is quite as fundamental as any rehabilitative aspiration.

Current practice and themes

A long tradition of sharing ideas about probation practice in Europe (notably in recent years through the CEP (Conférence permanente européenne de la Probation), the Council of Europe and many other networks), as well as marked political, social and cultural affinities in different regions, has led to a number of similarities in probation principles, methods and organizations across Europe. At the same time, since penal policy is the upshot of a complex of political, economic, social and cultural factors, interacting in unpredictable ways, there are tendencies towards difference as well.

Walters (2003) usefully identifies a number of themes in contemporary European probation. Among these is a move 'from welfare to corrections'. A definitive survey of European probation practice (van Kalmthout and Derks 2000) found a tendency in 'almost all countries' away from social work concepts and values and towards an alignment with the goals of other criminal justice agencies – notably, risk management, public protection and punishment. At the same time, however, 'it is clear that the job of providing guidance, care and assistance is still the most important one of probation services' (2000: 17), and many services continue to characterize their work as a type of social work (see Scotland: criminal justice social work) and provide social work training for staff (see, for example, Probation Board for Northern Ireland).

A second theme is a 'more scientific' approach to practice. Effective practice research, cognitive-behavioural approaches and the use of accredited programmes are being taken up in most European jurisdictions. Many of these initiatives originated in Canada and have come to Europe, often via England. OASys and other systematic assessment instruments of English provenance have been exported and widely taken up elsewhere. Walters (2003) notes that Scandinavian countries, Switzerland and other jurisdictions have also been influential 'exporters' in furthering this development.

In almost all the probation systems of western Europe, practice has historically centred on the offender. Over time, it has become essential, ethically and politically, to respond to victims. Austria, Belgium, Norway and parts of Germany have made considerable progress in developing victim–offender mediation and other restorative approaches, but many jurisdictions have struggled to accommodate victim-centred work in an essentially offender-centred organization. The newer services – for example, in the Czech Republic, Latvia and Turkey – have established principles of reparation and mediation in the foundations of their organization. In addition to many other advantages, this recognition of the rights of victims gives services greater credibility and commands the trust of the public.

Voluntary organizations have often been the ancestors of state probation provision and remain extensively involved in many jurisdictions. The Salvation Army, for example, is of central importance to probation work in the Netherlands. Services also use volunteers in different ways. In many southern European countries, for example, there is extensive participation of volunteers – with their connections to community organizations, formal and informal – in supervising offenders. At best, such practices represent the critical involvement of the community in working with offenders and promote social inclusion.

Walters (2003) convincingly describes community service as 'the most successful innovation of the last quarter of the twentieth century in the field of criminal sanctions'. Practice is similar in most jurisdictions, trying to maintain a balance between rehabilitation, punishment and reparation. The measure is used imaginatively to avoid custodial sentences: it is quite widely used, for example, in Germany as a penalty for non-payment of fines.

In eastern Europe, many countries have looked to find ways of managing very severe prison overcrowding and are trying to develop probation systems in response – despite the very meagre evidence that the provision of 'alternatives' is effective in reducing the prison population.

Challenges and changes

Many countries face a problem of legitimacy in relation to public attitudes to probation. Almost all northern and western European jurisdictions are experiencing increases in their prison populations. The (punitive) credibility of community sanctions and measures is a challenge everywhere and, without such credibility, the public may lack confidence in non-custodial measures and the courts may be reluctant to use community sanctions to their fullest potential. Credibility is important, but is more likely to be achieved by a clear statement of the objectives of probation practice and through the services' openness and integrity than by any (doomed) attempt to make probation as prison-like or punitive as possible.

All services are trying to respond to the challenges of diversity: service that is appropriate and relevant for women offenders may not be assumed to be the same as for men, for example, and the distinctive needs of different cultural and ethnic groups call for principled changes in practice. There has been a great deal of movement and migration in the continent in recent years and there is an increasing awareness of the particular circumstances of non-nationals in the criminal justice system. Terms like 'community' and 'reintegration' have a quite different significance for non-nationals, and this has important implications for probation practice.

Most services have experienced extensive change in recent years, and there is no prospect of the pace of change slowing down. Criminal justice policy will always have to react to changes in political, economic and social context, and these influences are themselves changing rapidly. The effect of this on probation practice is often unhelpful – changes need to be made before practices have become properly established or had an opportunity to be evaluated – and such volatility can be destabilizing. European services will have to be clear and resolute in their purpose and at the same time sufficiently flexible to respond to change.

Rob Canton

Related entries

Community; Conférence permanente européenne de la Probation (CEP); Council of Europe; Diversity; Effective practice; Legitimacy; Offender Assessment System (OASys); Probation Board for Northern Ireland; Public attitudes to probation; Scotland: criminal justice social work; Social exclusion; Social work; Victims; Volunteers; United Nations.

Key texts and sources

Cavadino, M. and Dignan, J. (2006) *Penal Systems: A Comparative Approach.* London: Sage.

Hamai, K., Villé, R., Harris, R., Hough, M. and Zvekic, U. (1995) *Probation Round the World: A Comparative Study.* London: Routledge.

van Kalmthout, A. and Derks, J. (eds) (2000) *Probation and Probation Services – a European Perspective.* Nijmegen: Wolf Legal Publishers.

van Kalmthout, A., Roberts, J. and Vinding, S. (eds) (2003) *Probation and Probation Services in the EU Accession Countries.* Nijmegen: Wolf Legal Publishers.

Walters, J. (2003) 'Trends and issues in probation in Europe.' Paper delivered to the PACCOA conference, Hobart, Tasmania, 1 September (available online at http://www.paccoa.com.au/).

PROBATION IN THE USA AND CANADA

Probation is an integral part of community corrections in both Canada and the USA. How probation is delivered, however, varies considerably in the different jurisdictions in each country.

A complete study of probation in North America would require knowledge of how probation is delivered, within what criminal justice framework and guided by what kind of approach to offender management – all of which is highly dependent on a range of local, regional and national characteristics. Such characteristics might include demography (e.g. rural vs. urban populations), geography (e.g. remote vs. accessible) and history (especially a history of immigration, including internal migration). There are, of course, some distinct differences between the USA and Canada, and combining the two countries in this short piece is not intended to minimize or overlook those differences.

History

Probation in North America is generally recognized as having begun, at least in some formal sense, with John Augustus, the nineteenth-century Boston shoemaker who began the process of convincing judges to suspend sentence on convicted offenders in return for a promise of good behaviour. The expansion of probation as a sanction available to the courts began in the final years of the nineteenth century as both Canada and the USA made provision for young persons to be tried in courts separate from adults, and to be subject to sanctions, especially community-based ones, that provided a greater focus on the 'welfare' of the young person. Thus the growth of the juvenile court, more or less simultaneously from Chicago and Toronto outwards across both countries, spurred the idea of probation officers being attached to juvenile courts. Although some places (for example, Massachusetts) had probation officers in adult courts earlier, the development of adult probation services was encouraged by the expansion of probation at the juvenile level.

Fragmentation of delivery

A major aspect of probation in the USA is the multitude of levels of government (and, indeed, parts of government) that might provide probation services. Municipalities, counties, states and the American federal government all provide probation services. In some cases, they are attached to the court system (the US federal probation system is a case in point), whereas in other jurisdictions they are part of government at the various levels indicated above. Legislative foundations for probation are usually based in state or federal law. In Canada, each of the ten provinces and three territories is responsible for the delivery of probation services, but not the Canadian federal government. However, Canadian federal legislation provides the legislative foundation for probation across the country. Thus in both countries service delivery is not subject to national direction and much more under the control of some local or regional jurisdiction.

Youth and adult probation

Both the USA and Canada continue to have strong juvenile probation systems. In some jurisdictions probation officers could have mixed youth and adult caseloads, while in other places there may be quite separate services providing probation supervision to adults and youths.

No one discipline ever had the monopoly on probation training that social work had in England and Wales (and continues to have in Scotland), but social work was an important discipline in probation work in both countries, particularly in the period immediately after the Second World War. But the de-emphasis of psychotherapeutic approaches to offender management in the 1970s meant that what social work was (mistakenly) thought to offer was perhaps of less importance than the perceived need for a broad-based foundation in social sciences. Whether or not that is currently a part of a university-based degree programme (as is the case in most parts of Canada) or some other post-secondary qualification (more prevalent in the USA) depends on the jurisdiction.

Lastly, there has emerged, especially in the USA, an emphasis on probation work as being part of a criminal justice system-wide focus on offender compliance. Electronic monitoring and drug testing are seen in some parts of North America as very much the norm in contemporary probation practice. This has also led to the practice in many jurisdictions in the USA of probation officers (or specialized units within probation services) trained in firearms use. In some American states, probation officers are armed as a matter of course. Most probation officers in both countries are designated as 'peace officers' and, as such, have powers of arrest beyond those of the ordinary citizen.

Denis Bracken

Related entries

Compliance; Electronic monitoring; Probation training.

Key texts and sources

Bracken, D. (2005) 'Developments and trends in Canadian probation', *Vista*, 10: 99–108 (a contemporary review, partly based on a survey of the directors of probation in nine Canadian provinces and two territories).

Clear, T. and Rumgay, J. (1992) 'Divided by a common language: British and American probation cultures', *Federal Probation*, 56: 3–11 (somewhat superseded by recent developments, but still a good discussion of the differences between the two countries).

The journal, *Federal Probation*, covers both American and international issues. See also the websites of the American Probation and Parole Association (**http://www.appa-net.org**) (mostly American but some Canadian information), the Probation Officers Association of Ontario (**http://www.poao.org/**) and the British Columbia Probation Officers Association (**http://www.vcn.bc.ca/bcpoa/BCPO2003.htm**).

PROBATION OFFICERS

An offender manager with a qualification in Probation Studies (or the equivalent) employed by a probation board to undertake a range of statutory duties related to the assessment and supervision of offenders.

'Main grade' probation officers work directly with offenders subject to community penalties (including supervision, unpaid work, and drug and alcohol treatment) and also with those sentenced to custody, both during and after their release. The aim is to reduce the likelihood of further offending, to reduce risk of harm to the public and to promote rehabilitation.

What a probation officer does can be divided into two broad categories: first, the preparation of reports on offenders (to assist courts with sentencing and to contribute to decisions on early release from custody); and, secondly, the management, supervision and enforcement of community orders and prison licences. *How* this is done is by carrying out a detailed assessment of the causes of the offending and, in discussion with the offender, devising and implementing supervision plans aimed at removing those causes. Assessments and plans are regularly reviewed and adjusted according to the offender's progress.

Probation officers are assisted in their assessments by assessment instruments but, to make proper use of these tools, they need to have good interviewing skills and a thorough understanding of human behaviour. Expertise in assessment – more specifically an assessment of the risk of harm and of reoffending – is the distinctive strength of the Probation Service, and it is this skill and responsibility which primarily distinguish the probation officer from the probation service officer.

Throughout the service's history there have been debates about the perceived conflict between the duty to control offenders under supervision and the duty to care for them. Probation officers need knowledge of methods and techniques, often drawn from psychology, to motivate and sustain offenders in changing their behaviour. Crucial to the success of all probation methods is establishing an empathetic relationship in which the offender feels valued and listened to. The first probation officers were charged to 'advise, assist and befriend', and it was not until 2000 that this duty was formally removed. Even though it has been replaced by the language of punishment and correction, the importance of the officer/offender relationship is stressed in the case management approach described in the National Offender Management Service (NOMS) Offender Management Model.

Historically, probation officers worked mostly alone and with a considerable degree of autonomy. While this enabled the development of some imaginative practice, it also led to much inconsistency. Probation officers now work mostly in teams, managed by a senior probation officer. National Standards and regular monitoring and inspection by line managers and Her Majesty's Inspectorate have aimed to counteract poor practice and to hold probation officers accountable for their work. The supervision of individual offenders is often shared with probation service officers and carried out in partnership with a range of other agencies. Role relationships are evolving as NOMS develops, and it remains to be seen how radically the new tasks of offender management alter the probation officer's role.

Kathy Ferguson

Related entries

Interventions; Offender management; Probation service officers; Senior probation officers.

Key texts and sources

Bailey, R., Knight, C. and Williams, B. (2007) 'The Probation Service as part of NOMS in England and Wales: fit for purpose?', in L. Gelsthorpe and R. Morgan (eds) *Handbook of Probation*. Cullompton: Willan Publishing.

Whitehead, P. and Statham, R. (2006) *The History of Probation: Politics, Power and Cultural Change, 1876–2005*. Crayford: Shaw & Sons.

PROBATION SERVICE OFFICERS

An employee of a probation board who is not a qualified probation officer but who is appointed to undertake a range of duties related to the management and supervision of offenders.

Though not qualified as probation officers, probation service officers (PSOs) undertake the direct supervision of a wide range of offenders. They are given training in assessment and some methods of working with offenders. Those placed in offender management teams have their own caseload and work with offenders in much the same way as their qualified colleagues. The practical distinction between PSOs and probation officers is primarily that of expertise in (and responsibility for) risk assessment: unqualified officers should not supervise offenders assessed as posing a high risk of harm nor those requiring a high level of intervention to reduce these risks. However, as risk is not static nor risk assessment an exact science, this distinction is sometimes blurred. PSOs do not currently write full pre-sentence reports or parole reports, though they do make assessments for the release of prisoners on home leave or home detention curfew and, in some areas, provide oral or fast-delivery reports to courts on low-risk offenders.

From the 1960s, as the work of the service expanded, unqualified staff were employed as 'ancillaries' to assist with the practical needs of offenders, such as housing or benefits claims. Probation officers were anxious about the work of PSOs compromising their professional status or undermining their casework relationships, so tasks given to ancillaries (later renamed probation service assistants) were quite limited. Nevertheless, assistants soon became integrated into teams and established as court duty officers and community service officers.

The most significant event in the development of the modern role occurred in 1998. The Home Office decision in 1995 to change probation training led to four years in which there were markedly reduced numbers of newly qualified officers. To deal with the resulting severe staffing shortages, the Teesside Probation Committee sought to establish a new grade of staff to supervise lower-risk offenders, whose principal need was support. This would free qualified probation officers to concentrate on higher-risk offenders needing skilled intervention. The National Association of Probation Officers (see Napo) initiated a High Court action claiming the new grade would be doing work which must, in law, be reserved to probation officers. The association lost the action and the new grade was established.

PSO is not a trainee grade, though PSOs can undertake a National Vocational Qualification (NVQ) in criminal justice. As well as working in offender manager teams, PSOs can move into specialist roles, such as accredited programme tutors, unpaid work officers, approved premises workers and breach officers. PSOs are supervised by and accountable to a senior probation officer. Under the National Offender Management Service (NOMS) Offender Management Model, the distinction between probation officers and PSOs is further blurred as either can be designated an offender manager.

Kathy Ferguson

Related entries

Napo; Probation officers; Probation training; Senior probation officers.

Key texts and sources

Bailey, R., Knight, C. and Williams, B. (2007) 'The Probation Service as part of NOMS in England and Wales: fit for purpose?', in L. Gelsthorpe and R. Morgan (eds) *Handbook of Probation.* Cullompton: Willan Publishing.
The Teesside judgment is described in Whitehead, P. and Statham, R. (2006) *The History of Probation: Politics, Power and Cultural Change, 1876–2005.* Crayford: Shaw & Sons, pp. 194–6.

PROBATION TRAINING

'Probation training' has, historically, been taken to refer to qualifying training to become a probation officer. The term should refer more broadly to training for all staff in the service.

As early as 1922 it was agreed that the probation officer qualification should be located within a social science framework in higher education (HE). In 1930 the Home Office introduced the first probation officer training course and, in 1946, a training centre was established at Rainer House. Subsequently, probation training became located within social work education via the Certificate of Qualification in Social Work (CQSW) and then the Diploma in Social Work (DipSW). Following much controversy and a two-year gap in provision, a new employment-based qualification was established in 1998: a Diploma in Probation Studies (DipPS), combining a National Vocational Qualification (NVQ) Level 4 with an honours degree.

Criticism of the former training focused on the perceived lack of criminological input, an overemphasis on issues related to anti-racism and diversity, and an implicit link between this and the failure to recruit a more experienced and 'male' workforce (Knight 2002). (Ironically, recent inquiries and thematic inspections have criticized criminal justice agencies for their lack of attention to diversity issues.) The probation officer qualification has continued to dominate most of the debates although, in recent years, the absence of training for the growing group of staff employed as probation service officers (PSOs) has become a focus of concern, as the traditional role boundaries between such staff and probation officers begin to blur. A continuing unanswered question in the evolving framework of the National Offender Management Service (NOMS) is what the expectations of probation officers are at the point of qualification and, leading on from this, what is realistic to expect of staff who lack relevant role-specific qualifications (Knight 2002).

The DipPS programme is delivered via contractual arrangements between the National Probation Service (NPS), managed by regional training consortia, and five universities. It is delivered in a 24-month period by a mixture of taught, distance and e-enabled learning. The purchaser/provider split of these arrangements has caused some tensions, although most have evolved into 'partnerships' in order to manage curriculum development, to reflect changes in policy and to manage performance where trainees are struggling to complete the programme.

The strengths of an employment-based model of learning and development include the potential for a robust interrogation between theory and practice, an opportunity to apply and critique current research on effective practice and a close correlation between learning and improved competence. Employers are directly involved in recruitment and selection, in supporting their staff to be learners and in assessment and quality assurance of some of this learning. Distance learning offers flexibility to meet a range of learning needs and openness in terms of curriculum design and delivery. The increasing use of information and communication technology (ICT) is a powerful tool for learning as long as care is taken with students with particular learning needs (for example, dyslexia), but its development has been somewhat inhibited by the limitations of the Probation Service's implementation of ICT and web-based access.

Concerns about a work-based model of learning include the risk that learning becomes 'training' rather than education in its true sense and that, as employees, trainee probation officers (TPOs) are required to demonstrate 'competence' (via the NVQ model) rather more than critical analysis and reflection on their practice. This risks a focus on 'underpinning knowledge' for instrumental purposes as opposed to the more 'overarching' knowledge described by Nellis as placing tasks 'within a breadth and depth of thought about the ever changing contours of criminal justice policy' (2001: 423). The priorities of managerialism, reflecting the governmental drive for competence-based education, risk producing staff who are technically competent but lack the values and vision to continue to develop and evolve 'evidence-based' practice in work with offenders.

The development of NOMS has led to continuing uncertainty about the future of probation training and, while the current DipPS looks set to continue until 2009, the expectation, outlined by the Chief Executive of NOMS, is that an alternative offender management qualification will be in place by 2008, and that this will be a 'flexible qualification pathway that is linked to the tiered model of offender management'. Universities have been campaigning for such a route that would build on the National Qualification Framework and identify a continuum of programmes: a certificate programme (level one of a degree) to meet the learning and development needs of PSOs working up to tier 3 of the new risk framework; a progression route on to a degree programme similar to the current DipPS for staff working at risk tier 4; and a post-graduate, post-qualifying route for staff working with the most complex and challenging people (e.g. sex offenders) and as managers.

The current lack of continuing professional development opportunities for experienced staff is perhaps as serious as the lack of externally validated qualifications for the increasing numbers of PSO staff. Such a model, delivered by a combination of in-house workshops and university-led distance/e-enabled academic modules, would enable staff to have clear progression routes and to step in and out of training without taking cuts in pay or periods out of employment in order to qualify. It would match roles to qualifications and identify the specific knowledge and skills required to work with different categories of risk and need. The fear that a competence model of learning would limit the ability of staff to instrumental competence rather than critical reflection could be countered by a robust HE sector's continuing involvement in delivery and the constant updating of learning packages with current research evidence on effectiveness. This links to complex and far-reaching debates about the role and purpose of vocational training in HE and requires ongoing vigilance, campaigning and collaboration in HE, and a proper evaluation of what is required of training and of its outcomes for different grades and roles.

Charlotte Knight

Related entries

Diversity; Practice development assessors; Probation officers; Regional training consortia.

Key texts and sources

Bailey, R., Knight, C. and Williams, B. (2007) 'The Probation Service as part of NOMS in England and Wales: fit for purpose?', in L. Gelsthorpe and R. Morgan (eds) *Handbook of Probation*. Cullompton: Willan Publishing.

Knight, C. (2002) 'Training for a modern service', in D. Ward *et al.* (eds) *Probation: Working for Justice*. Oxford: Oxford University Press.

Nellis, M. (2001) 'The new probation training in England and Wales: realising the potential'. *Social Work Education*, 20(4): 415–32.

Nellis, M. (2003) 'Probation training and the community justice curriculum', *British Journal of Social Work*, 33: 943–59.

PROBATION TRUSTS

Probation trusts are proposed as replacements for probation boards.

This new type of probation body was first identified in the Home Office consultation paper, *Restructuring Probation to Reduce Re-offending*, which set out how the government intended to introduce commissioning and contestability into the provision of probation services and the organizational changes that would be required. It was published in October 2005. The paper supplied some of the missing detail about how the National Offender Management Service (NOMS), formed following the Carter Report, will operate.

Trusts, said the paper, would replace probation boards and operate with greater independence from the centre. Unlike probation boards, trusts would not have a statutory duty to provide probation services but would become one of a number of possible providers of probation services under contract to the Secretary of State. It was made clear that their continued existence would depend on their ability to contribute to the reduction of reoffending and thereby to win business from the commissioners – the regional offender managers to whom trusts would be accountable for performance against contract.

Although boards and trusts might look superficially similar at the outset, the new probation bodies would be very different entities from the existing ones and, therefore, to avoid confusion, the new terminology, according to the paper, was intended to reflect this change.

Reaction to the consultation paper was universally hostile and much of the criticism centred on the proposal for trusts as provider-only bodies. The Probation Boards' Association (PBA) provided a focus for these concerns, believing that the transfer of statutory duties away from local probation bodies to the Secretary of State represented a centralization of powers to the detriment of local accountability. By removing the commissioning of services from the locality to the much more remote level of the region would, argued the PBA, make it difficult for probation services to be responsive to community needs and to work effectively in local partnerships. The PBA also drew attention to the contradiction presented by changes to other public services, notably in health services where the design and commissioning of service are increasingly moving from primary care trusts, already area-based, down to general practice, and in local government which has been promised greater devolved powers.

Partnership working across public, private and voluntary sectors, stimulated and managed by probation boards, was the preferred way forward, according to the PBA and its members, and not contests arranged by regional managers in which the public sector trusts would be but one contender.

However, the government was not for turning, and the Offender Management Bill, which had its second reading in December 2006, provides for trusts to be set up to enter into contracts with the Secretary of State. Local probation boards constituted under the Criminal Justice and Court Services Act 2000 would be abolished.

Defining a probation trust as 'a body corporate', the bill says it is not to be regarded as the servant or agent of the Crown or as enjoying any status, privilege or immunity of the Crown. A trust shall consist of 'a chairman and not less than four other members appointed by the Secretary of State' and a chief executive.

The Secretary of State would determine the remuneration to be paid to appointed members, and a trust would have a chief executive appointed by the members on terms determined by them. But this would not apply to the appointment of the first chief executive or the determination of terms, if the Secretary of State chose to decide these. While staff employment terms were for the trusts to decide, pay and expenses and pensions required Secretary of State approval.

The bill envisages trusts having powers to do anything, including acquiring and disposing of property, which facilitates or is conducive to the achievement of its purposes. But a trust would not be able to hold land or borrow money or invest money without Secretary of State approval and would have a duty to comply with any directions given by the Secretary of State.

There is a clear intention that trusts should be business focused with members having commercial and business experience. As such they would be markedly different from the boards that, it is intended, should be replaced. The membership of the current probation boards is intended to ensure that a range of skills can be brought to the governance arena and also that the geography and diversity of the community served are broadly represented. Where practicable, probation board membership should have four magistrates and two local authority councillors as well as a judge, and boards can have up to 15 members.

As a preparatory move for the new world of trusts, the composition of boards was amended by statutory instrument change in December 2006. The change removed the 'as of right' places for magistrates and councillors and reduced the quorum for boards.

Many have seen this as a retrograde and premature step paving the way for trusts in advance of legislation being put in place, and the move was not without its opponents, including in the House of Lords.

The government has said it envisages the public sector Probation Service continuing to play a central role, particularly in relation to offender management. But other providers from other sectors should have the opportunity to show what they can do, especially with regard to interventions work. Contracts would be awarded on the basis of performance, and providers who demonstrate effectiveness and value for money can expect multi-year contracts.

Should the legislation be passed it is not intended that all boards will move straightaway to trust status. Trusts would be phased in. The autonomy that trust status is said to confer is one that would first have to be earned by strong performance.

John Raine

Related entries

Carter Report; Contestability; Interventions; National Offender Management Service (NOMS); Offender management; Probation boards.

Key texts and sources

See the sources mentioned under Probation boards; Probation Boards' Association (PBA).

PROBATION VALUES

The moral principles and penal ideals that inform the strategies and practices of the Probation Service.

The phrase 'probation values' is of relatively recent coinage, although discursively it presumes the existence of an enduring probation tradition. It developed in the context of late twentieth-century crises about the purpose and function of probation in England and Wales, and was intended to bestow a distinct moral identity on the service when its tradition was under serious attack. Historically, because the service had always been a relatively small organization and only ever approximated to an independent profession, it had traditionally characterized itself as an active practical expression of principles embedded in other institutional domains (first the Christian Church, later social work and penal reform, and the welfare state more generally) rather than claiming to possess a distinctive ethical standpoint of its own. From the moral penumbra of these larger bodies, probation drew legitimacy and prestige. Over the years, written descriptions of values have been legion, but 'probation values' as such were never formally codified into a credo to which all staff were required to subscribe, and it is difficult to know with accuracy what 'habits of the heart' prevailed among individual officers. The service, however, never effectively projected a compelling and persuasive image of what it stood for into the public domain, too easily allowing itself to be caricatured as 'a *mere* welfare service for offenders'. The 'probation values' debate of recent years has tried, often desperately, to improve on this but, as the term 'probation' increasingly loses favour in England and Wales, if not necessarily elsewhere in the world, it seems likely that future debates will focus on the kinds of moral values that might conceivably be infused into the concept of 'offender management'.

Values (in this context) are normative statements that can and should be embodied in both the aims and methods of an organization or profession. They ostensibly signal the moral nature of their aspirations, goals, objectives and practices. Arguably, however, before any values can be embodied in such entities, they have to be understood and upheld by their individual members. At root, values are personal moral commitments (like a passion for justice) – beliefs about what it is right to do and good to be. They are expressions of character and conscience, manifestations of what a person stands for or stands against. Traditionally, the Probation Service recruited 'mature' people precisely because of the values they already possessed, rather than an organization which sought to impose a ready-made moral code on them. Probation professionalism has largely consisted of honing and directing those personal moral principles, matching them to liberal penal ideals which were themselves shaped by a desire to resist unnecessary punitiveness – particularly reducing the use of imprisonment – or to avoid it altogether. Historically, the precise moral contours of the Probation Service's public commitments have been affected by broader debate among its professional associations, the universities associated with staff training, academic criminologists, government agencies, legislators and national and international penal reform bodies. Different voices have been dominant at different times.

Proto-probation values were framed in terms of Christian theology. The nineteenth-century police court missionaries believed that, by saving souls, denouncing sin and promoting temperance (with a little practical help), they would reduce both crime and the use of imprisonment. Theirs was a stern compassion, an attitude of hating the sin but loving the sinner. In somewhat attenuated form this outlook was incorporated into the Probation of Offenders Act 1907, which conceived of a probation order as an alternative to punishment and defined its aim as 'advise, assist and befriend'. From the 1930s onwards, in order to gain credibility in a more secular society, the Probation Service formally distanced itself from evangelical language and sentiments, although key speakers at its half-centenary in 1957 still celebrated and commended it as a profound and worthwhile expression of Christian social ideals. Even today, some people's motivation for joining the service remains faith based, although not necessarily Christian, because elements of all the world's major faith traditions emphasize compassion for the poor and the redeemability of most lawbreakers.

The post-World War Two Probation Service derived its penal ideals from liberal humanism – the belief that, through education and/or treatment and therapy, and the incremental achievement of social justice, the character and behaviour of most individual offenders could be improved. Specifically, it defined itself as social work, adopting the same generic values as agencies which worked with problem families, the mentally ill, the disabled and the old – namely, respect for persons, client self-determination and non-judgemental attitudes. These required the forging of a relationship between the worker and the 'client', whose assumed latent desire to cease offending would be kindled by the ministrations of a skilled helper. To the ethical ingredients of an effective relationship – genuineness, warmth and empathy – common to all social work occupations, the Probation Service added the need to balance 'care and control'. Liberal social work values, however, have always privileged the welfare of offenders and, while this aligned the service with philosophers who saw rehabilitation as a penal principle above all others, it did so, eventually, at the price of isolating probation from broader – and often normatively sophisticated – debates on crime control, especially those which emphasized the needs, rights and interests of victims.

In the 1980s, liberal social work values were somewhat dramatically reconfigured into anti-discriminatory and anti-oppressive values, in order to challenge the structural injustice and institutionalized discrimination faced by social work clients. Napo was to the fore of a movement that sought to address racism and sexism in criminal justice, which had the indirect effect of restoring concern for (some) crime victims to the probation agenda. Initially, the focus was on abused women and rape victims; later on the victims of 'hate crime' more generally. Such crimes exposed the moral limitations of a (liberal) non-judgemental stance and made censure, if not punishment, into an ethically acceptable aspect of probation practice. In general, however, the anti-discriminatory turn in probation values was no more able to engage constructively with emerging developments in crime policy – the 'punishment in the community' initiative – than liberal humanist values had been. Neither set of values sounded morally engaged with crime as a social problem, or as people experienced it in high-crime areas. New moral ideals – 'community safety' and 'public protection' – emerged in political and academic debate, with which the Probation Service was rather slow to come to terms.

Managerialism in the Probation Service introduced a shift from *character-driven values* to *system-driven values*, which are, in fact, of a different – lesser – order. Managerialism aims at the meticulous regulation of all organizational procedures and staff behaviour, ostensibly in the service of a larger goal or target. It erodes the idea of autonomous, ethical professionalism. Normative commitments to efficiency (the simplification and acceleration of procedures), economy (value for money) and effectiveness (the achievement of pre-specified outcomes) subordinate traditional moral values, reducing them to matters of merely private concern among staff. Character-driven values cannot thrive in a managerialized environment and are supplanted by normative claims about consumer orientation,

customer satisfaction and a quality service. These, however, are *impersonal and transactional*, rather than *personal and relational* – they neither achieve nor intend genuine moral engagement with the person being dealt with. Probation employees are expected to do little more than articulate organizational credos in their work, regardless of whether their heart is in them.

It is in the context of both the moral vacuum created by managerialism and the insistent demands of state-orchestrated 'populist punitiveness' that discourse on 'probation values' has latterly come to the fore. While there is an undoubted need to identify and affirm genuine moral values which should inform the supervision of offenders, whether instead of, or after, a period of imprisonment, it may soon be anachronistic to call them 'probation values' simply because the Probation Service itself may cease to exist. In Scotland, a probation order survives, but there has been no Probation Service there since 1970, and ethical debate is still conducted in terms of '(criminal justice) social work' values. 'Offender management', an ascendant term in both countries, may be difficult to infuse with moral values because the inherent elasticity of the term 'management' permits almost any practice. Some commentators have argued that human rights might curtail any excesses to which offender management may be prone, but human rights are rights of last resort, rights which individuals have when all else fails, and probation was surely there to ensure that, in the case of offenders, 'all else' does not fail. Discourses around community justice, restorative justice, desistance and rights-based rehabilitation all offer intellectually promising ways of revitalizing what were once called 'probation values', but only if they are presented to the wider world as serious ways of engaging with crime in all its harmful manifestations will they have a chance of withstanding the punitive turn in contemporary penal policy.

Mike Nellis

Related entries

Community justice; Human rights; Managerialism; Social work.

Key texts and sources

Bailey, R., Knight, C. and Williams, B. (2007) 'The Probation Service as part of NOMS in England and Wales: fit for purpose?', in L. Gelsthorpe and R. Morgan (eds) *Handbook of Probation*. Cullompton: Willan Publishing.

Canton, R. (2007) 'Probation and the tragedy of punishment', *Howard Journal* (forthcoming).

Chui, E. and Nellis, M. (2004) *Moving Probation Forward: Theory, Policy and Practice*. London: Pearson Longman.

Gelsthorpe, L. (2007) 'Probation values and human rights', in L. Gelsthorpe and R. Morgan (eds) *Handbook of Probation*. Cullompton: Willan Publishing.

McNeill, F. (2006) 'A desistance paradigm for offender management', *Criminology and Criminal Justice*, 6: 32–64.

Rex, S. (2005) *Reforming Community Penalties*. Cullompton: Willan Publishing.

PROLIFIC AND OTHER PRIORITY OFFENDERS

The Prolific and other Priority Offender (PPO) Strategy is a single, coherent initiative in three complementary strands to reduce crime by targeting those who offend most. The three strands are called 'prevent and deter', 'catch and convict', and 'rehabilitate and resettle'.

This initiative developed from pioneering police/probation partnerships that had been established in the mid-1990s. Based on Dutch experience, joint teams of police and probation staff set out to identify prolific offenders who were responsible for volume crime in specific neighbourhoods. Burglars and car thieves were usually the focus of this targeting. Those offenders who were placed on the scheme were offered very intensive supervision by the probation staff. Four or more contacts per week were generally required. The supervision was especially focused on providing routes out of crime, often in conjunction with other specialists, such as drug treatment workers. It was made clear to

these offenders that, in addition to the intensive supervision and support, they would be kept under surveillance by the police so that if they did reoffend, there would be a very high chance of detection and reconviction. A high level of resourcing was applied to the work, and the approach was summarized in the phrase 'go straight or get nicked'.

As this type of work developed there were variations in the formula used to identify offenders to be placed on the scheme. In some cases fixed criteria of so many convictions over a stated period of time were used; in other cases more flexibility was employed, based on police intelligence and probation assessment. Many prolific offenders were identified while they were serving prison sentences, and intensive pre-release work took place to plan the resettlement strategy and to ensure that these offenders were clear that they would be subject to both intensive supervision and surveillance on release. Licence conditions were imposed in accordance with the intensive reporting regime of the scheme, often including electronic monitoring and drug testing. Enforcement action was taken where there was a lack of co-operation.

This led to a very high rate of recall to prison for breach of licence. It was frequently the case that a very large proportion of the offenders on the prolific offenders schemes were in prison, either freshly sentenced for new offences or recalled to prison for breach of licence. Thus the outcomes of the scheme might have been better in terms of community safety and keeping high-volume offenders off the streets, rather than in terms of resettlement and rehabilitation. While it was not widely stated at the time, the effect of the schemes may have been similar to the use of the 'preventive detention' sentences used in the 1950s (see Extended sentencing).

These schemes were designed to do everything possible to increase the likelihood that reoffending would be detected and converted into reconviction. This was very much in line with 'narrowing the justice gap', the top government priority for the inter-agency work led by the criminal justice boards in the initial years of this century. All agencies recognized the merit of this and committed to doing everything possible to ensure that crime was detected and processed through the criminal justice system as effectively and speedily as possible, thereby seeking to reduce the size and burden of undetected crime. However, it was also noted that this objective was not fully consistent with the aim of reducing reconviction rates, and this anomaly highlighted that government targets can work against each other.

This was the context in which the current initiative for PPOs was formed and implemented throughout England and Wales. The 'prevent and deter' strand of the strategy aims to prevent high-risk young offenders from becoming increasingly involved in criminal activity. The strand is delivered by the youth offending teams through a series of interventions and partnerships with community-based initiatives that address the reasons that underlie the offending. It seeks to engage them in positive activity and to steer them away from crime.

The 'catch and convict' part of the scheme is designed to ensure that all the relevant criminal justice agencies prioritize PPOs in their work. The offenders included in the scheme will have been selected using inter-agency intelligence as the ones causing most harm to the community. 'Catch and convict' ensures that the most thorough and timely practice is deployed to ensure effective investigation, charging and prosecution of PPOs. All areas adopt a Criminal Justice System Premium Service, which ensures that these offenders are consistently prioritized throughout the criminal justice system.

The 'rehabilitate and resettle' part of the overall scheme aims to provide the offenders on the scheme with the very best chance of changing their behaviour and becoming rehabilitated. It is based on a multi-agency team offering attractive services to motivate and provide realistic routes out of crime. Police, probation and drugs agencies form the core of most teams, and the offender manager has the job of devising a sentence plan on the basis of OASys that provides enough opportunities to change those offenders who are most at risk of reoffending. In offender management terms, these offenders are managed at tier 4, the most intensive level. A typical programme for an individual offender might contain components of electronic monitoring,

drug treatment and testing, an accredited programme, work on employment, training and education, and a volunteer mentor to support with budgeting and leisure-time activities.

There is one designated PPO in each Crime and Disorder Reduction Partnership (CDRP) area. This gives all the partners in the CDRP an influence and a stake in the scheme. This can be very useful in maintaining local authority political support and in accessing certain public services, such as health and housing. On average, 15 or 20 offenders are included in each PPO scheme, although in large CDRP areas (i.e. the big cities) the numbers are substantially higher.

David Hancock

Related entries

Assessment; Crime and Disorder Reduction Partnerships; Inter-agency work; Interventions; Offender management; Partnerships; Persistent and serious offenders; Police; Reconviction.

Key texts and sources

Farrall, S., Mawby, R.C. and Worrall, A. (2007) 'Prolific/persistent offenders and desistance', in L. Gelsthorpe and R. Morgan (eds) *Handbook of Probation*. Cullompton: Willan Publishing.

Home Office (2006) *Further Guidance on Prolific and Priority Offenders (PPOs)* (Probation Circular 30/2006) (available online at **www.homeoffice. gov.uk/output/page31.asp**).

PROSOCIAL MODELLING

The process by which the practitioner engages the offender in an empathetic relationship within which he or she actively reinforces prosocial behaviour and discourages antisocial behaviour and attitudes, particularly by acting as a good, motivating role model.

Prosocial modelling has become a core element of work with offenders, having been shown to be effective in helping to reduce offending. In a study in Australia, Trotter (1999) demonstrated that, after a consistent application of prosocial modelling, probation officers were half as likely to have offenders who went to prison for breaching their orders. He has also demonstrated that the approach works with others, including high-risk offenders and drug users. Prosocial modelling was a key element in the introduction of enhanced community punishment in 2003–4, when a significant training programme for all community service staff was implemented (see Unpaid work).

Prosocial behaviour is not just the opposite of anti-social behaviour but includes many of the other behaviours that make it possible for us to live together in society, like being polite, respectful, punctual, apologizing for mistakes and so on.

Working prosocially is ethical and respectful, valuing offenders as individuals. It is optimistic about the possibility of change and seeks to engage them as a partner in the change process. It is a strengths-focused model, looking to reinforce what is right (often by using affirmations and rewards) before looking to sanction what is wrong. However, it is underpinned by values often demonstrated as rules which are made transparent to the offender and reinforced consistently by the practitioner.

Prosocial modelling is popular with practitioners because it makes sense – it feels like the right way to behave – but it also gives them strategies to behave in this 'right way' both individually and as teams in their work with clients and each other. It is sometimes criticized as 'only common sense', but this expression is usually used to describe something done in a subconscious or taken-for-granted way, while the consistent, sustained prosocial modelling required to be truly influential is hard work and requires conscious re-examination and reinforcement from all members of a team.

One of the principal ways in which we learn new behaviours is by observing other people (see also Cognitive-behavioural). In every interaction with offenders, practitioners have the opportunity to act as positive role models and to demonstrate the behaviours and attitudes that they are encouraging in those offenders. Learning is more likely to take place if the activity being modelled is one that the learner thinks is important and the person doing the modelling has the observer's respect. To be a good role model the practitioner needs to be clear about underlying values and clear with the offender about expectations of values and behaviour.

Among the behaviours and attitudes to model and impart are the following:

- *Respect for the individual*: I am genuinely interested in you and I want to try to understand your point of view.
- *Respect for the law and for rules*: one of the most important concepts in prosocial modelling is the legitimate use of authority. This means being transparent about what the rules are and applying them consistently and fairly. In order to do this, practitioners need to be open and transparent with themselves and offenders about the values underpinning their work and how these manifest themselves in their practice.
- *Punctuality*: Trotter demonstrated that practitioner punctuality has a huge impact on client outcomes.
- *Reliability*: I will do what I said I would do unless there is a very good reason and, if this is the case, I will explain why I have not done it.
- *Consistency*: I will try to treat you the same over time and also treat others the same from one to another as far as I can, bearing in mind their individual needs.
- *Fairness*: I will try to treat you according to your needs and not make unreasonable demands.
- *Putting things right*: if I make a mistake I will say so, put it right and apologize. (A very useful piece of learning for offenders whose offences often result from the escalating consequences of one mistake.)
- *Assertiveness*: in my interactions with others I will aim for a win–win. I will be clear about what I am thinking and feeling and want to happen, but I will also try to understand what you are thinking and feeling and what you want to happen.

The term 'prosocial modelling' has come to describe something broader than just acting as a positive role model and is perhaps described more accurately as 'prosocial practice'.

In order to engage with offenders, staff need to develop honest and empathetic relationships with them, demonstrating a genuine concern for the person, persistence and optimism about his or her capacity to change. They need to be clear and open about their roles and the purpose and expectations of any interventions. Staff need to work actively in partnership with offenders to help them to change by increasing their motivation, coaching them in new skills, clear objective setting, planned and negotiated problem-solving, and the monitoring of progress.

Prosocial practice treats the offender as an individual and values his or her differences and similarities to others. This includes avoiding stereotyping and valuing diversity of ethnicity, cultural experience, gender, sexuality, differing abilities, etc., as well as working at an appropriate level for the offender's speaking and listening abilities (see Responsivity), and working with different thinking and learning styles.

Prosocial modelling is both a way of thinking and behaving and a series of strategies; it helps practitioners to do this consistently and actively and thus fundamentally underpins engagement with offenders. These same principles can be applied to the behaviour of managers and to organizations (described as organizational modelling) and, when it is in place throughout the organization, it is a powerful force to ensure consistent good practice and effective teamwork.

Sally Cherry

Related entries

Cognitive-behavioural; Diversity; Learning styles; Motivation; Responsivity.

Key texts and sources

Cherry, S. (2005) *Transforming Behaviour: Pro-social Modelling in Action.* Cullompton: Willan Publishing.
Rex, S. and Matravers, A. (eds) (1998) *Pro-social Modelling and Legitimacy.* Cambridge: Institute of Criminology, University of Cambridge.
Trotter, C. (1999) *Working with Involuntary Clients.* London: Sage.

PSYCHOPATHY/PSYCHOPATHIC DISORDER

> Attempts to define psychopathy and its terminology have gone through a number of changes. This entry is concerned with *criminal psychopathy*: there are those who demonstrate this disorder who do not necessarily come to the attention of the criminal justice and forensic mental health systems.

The problem involved in trying to describe the psychopath adequately was once stated in the expression 'I can't define an elephant, but I know one when I see one'. The term (see Figure 8 for developments in terminology) emerged in the nineteenth century (when it did not carry the pejorative overtones and undertones acquired later) to describe the 'hard to like', 'the unloved, the unlovable and the unlovely'. Such descriptions attest to the need for workers to confront their own 'demons' when dealing with those labelled 'psychopath'. It is very important to note that the legal category 'psychopathic disorder' (introduced by Mental Health Act 1959 and restated in the 1983 Act) does not equate necessarily with clinical diagnostic criteria.

Manie sans delire (madness without delirium or delusion) → Moral insanity → Moral imbecility (defectiveness) → Constitutional psychopathic inferiority → Neurotic character → Psychopathy → Sociopathy (USA) → Anti-social personality disorder → Dissocial personality disorder → Dangerous severe personality disorder

Figure 8 Psychopathy: developments in terminology

The most important characteristics and behaviour of those adjudged to be psychopathic may be summarized as follows. Psychopaths lack affective and effective bonding attachments; their offending starts early (often as childhood behaviour disorder) and is rapidly continuous and frequently includes violence;

they employ tactics of lying and evasion, and are highly manipulative; they create chaos not only for themselves but, more importantly, also for all around them; they need frequent 'highs' to negate the loneliness and emptiness of their lives; and they defy our best 'treatment' efforts.

Much attention has been paid to causal factors and classifications. Some have regarded the condition as a true illness. Others have described it as 'elusive' (Lewis) and 'fuzzy at the edges and in need of refinement' (Roth), or even as a term of dislike masquerading as a diagnosis. Coid suggests that it is best to describe psychopathic disorder in the plural rather than as a single and discrete entity.

Are psychopaths born or made? Environmental pressures are important but do not entirely explain why, for example, one sibling in an entirely normal and law-abiding family develops psychopathic characteristics. Neurobiological and neuro-chemical factors have been adduced recently to explain an inability (starting in infancy) to develop emotional attachment and responsiveness (Blair 2003). (In her novel, *We Need to Talk about Kevin* (2003), Shriver provides a remarkable insight into this early failure in emotional bonding.) It can be conjectured that failure in bonding may be less a parental failure than a primary neurological 'fault' in the infant which makes for a 'failure to bond' child.

What can workers achieve with psychopathic offenders? There are three key interventive activities. First, *consistence* – the worker's capacity to foster a relationship despite the psychopath's attempts at rejection, evasion, hostility and manipulation. Secondly, *insistence* – insisting that reasonable demands for change are met despite the offender's excuses and prevarication. The third is *persistence* – the capacity to 'hang in there' despite the offender's evasive tactics, which will *sometimes* bring rewards if pursued over long periods of time.

Herschel Prins

Related entries

Mentally disordered offenders; Personality disorder.

Key texts and sources

Detailed references to the texts cited may be found in the following:

Blair, R.J.R. (2003) 'Neurobiological basis of psychopathy', *British Journal of Psychiatry*, 182, 5–7.

Moss, K. and Prins, H. (2006) 'Severe personality (psychopathic) disorder: a review', *Medicine, Science and the Law*, 46: 190–207.

Prins, H. (2005) *Offenders, Deviants or Patients?* (3rd edn). London: Routledge.

PUBLIC ATTITUDES TO PROBATION

The public's views about the Probation Service as an institution and about the effectiveness and fairness of its work. Public attitudes about probation work can affect the extent to which sentencers use community penalties and political decisions about funding.

People are generally poorly informed about probation work, as they will admit in surveys. Almost four out of five people say they know little or nothing about probation. Despite this, many people have strong views about the punishment of offenders and the use of community penalties.

According to the British Crime Survey (BCS), only a quarter of people think that the Probation Service does a good job. The police are rated higher and the youth courts lower. The BCS has consistently shown that people tend to associate community sentences with lenient sentencing. At one level, the public think that the courts are too soft on crime and that sentencers are out of touch with what ordinary people think. The International Criminal Victimization Survey suggests that Britain is more tough-minded than many other countries.

However, these 'top of the head' views reflect the fact that people consistently underestimate the extent to which the courts actually send people to prison. Media reporting of crime and punishment is thought to be one of the main reasons why people think that sentencing is too soft. If people are given more time to consider specific cases, a different picture emerges, however.

When asked to 'sentence' offenders themselves, people's responses are much more in line with sentencing practice. Public attitudes emerge as more nuanced and less in favour of imprisonment. For example, the BCS has found that large minorities of the public favour non-custodial penalties for an adult burglar with previous burglary convictions – the sort of offender who now falls within the scope of a mandatory three-year prison sentence for burglary.

The most popular community sentences are those that require the offender to pay compensation to the victim or perform work for the community. The work of the Probation Service towards rehabilitation is probably least well understood, although drug treatment for addicted offenders secures widespread support.

Making the conditions of a community sentence salient to the public promotes acceptance of these sanctions, and increasing public awareness of alternative sanctions also promotes public support for these dispositions. Not surprisingly, support for the use of community-based sanctions declines as the seriousness of the offence or the number of the offender's previous convictions increases.

The dilemma facing politicians is this: however ill-informed voters may be about crime and punishment, it is these poorly informed attitudes that they take with them to the ballot box. In an increasingly populist climate of debate about law and order, too few politicians are prepared to fight the corner of the Probation Service.

Mike Hough

Related entries

Community penalties; Legitimacy; Punishment (aims and justifications).

Key texts and sources

Allen, R. and Hough, M. (2007) 'Community penalties, sentencers, the media and public opinion', in L. Gelsthorpe and R. Morgan (eds) *Handbook of Probation*. Cullompton: Willan Publishing.

Roberts, J. and Hough, M. (eds) (2002) *Changing Attitudes to Punishment: Public Opinion, Crime and Justice*. Cullompton: Willan Publishing.

Roberts, J. and Hough, M. (2005) *Understanding Public Attitudes to Criminal Justice*. Maidenhead: Open University Press.

An interesting attempt to promote probation may be found at **http://www.brightplace.org.uk/pdfs/mie.pdf**.

PUBLIC PROTECTION

Actions taken by offender managers and others to protect the public from the risk of serious harm posed by some offenders.

Public protection work is the top priority of offender managers and the work of the National Probation Service. The arrival of new tools is providing greater consistency between practitioners, as is the formalization of inter-agency arrangements. Failures to implement best practice have led to a number of recent high-profile criticisms. This has galvanized work to improve practice, monitoring and training in this critically significant area of work.

Responsibility for public protection work within the National Offender Management Service (NOMS) headquarters lies with the Public Protection Unit. This unit develops strategy, identifies targets and priorities, and supports practice in the field. It has separate teams dealing with:

- multi-agency public protection arrangements (MAPPAs) and mental health;
- critical public protection casework;

- serious further offences;
- sex offenders strategy;
- domestic abuse (domestic violence);
- child protection;
- victims;
- pre- and post-release operational policy and practice; and
- approved premises.

In practice, good public protection depends on practitioners and managers implementing best practice in every case. Every offender coming under the supervision of the National Probation Service must be subject to an OASys assessment. There is an initial screening section, which will indicate whether a full analysis is needed; if so, it must be completed. The full 'Risk of serious harm' analysis enables the practitioner to assess the risk in relation to the public, adults known to the offender, staff, prisoners, children and self. It will place the offender in one of four categories: low risk, medium risk, high risk or very high risk. Medium risk indicates that there are significant risk factors that are held in check by the offender's current circumstances. If there is a change in those circumstances (e.g. employment, place of residence, abstinence from drugs or alcohol, medication used), a change in designation to high risk or very high risk might be indicated. High risk means that there are identifiable indicators of serious harm, and that a potential event could happen at any time and that the impact would be serious. The very-high-risk category indicates that there is imminent risk of serious harm. A potential event is more likely than not to happen imminently and the impact would be serious.

Serious is defined in OASys as 'a risk which is life threatening and or traumatic, and from which recovery, whether physical or psychological can be expected to be difficult or impossible'.

Not only does the OASys assessment lead to a decision on the level of risk of serious harm but it also leads the practitioner to generate a 'risk management plan' which will state what needs to be done to reduce and control the risks that have been identified. Frequently the skills and resources of other agencies will need to be harnessed in order to protect the public. This might mean medical treatment, or police surveillance or co-operative monitoring by a family member. The MAPPAs provide the statutory basis for the operation of these partnerships.

In summary, then, good practice means that practitioners have assessed risk of harm using OASys and other specialist assessment tools, written a risk management plan, implemented the plan, and reviewed the circumstances of the offender and the implementation of the plan on a regular basis throughout the period of supervision.

The National Probation Service Business Plan for 2005–6 included protecting the public from harm as a priority. To support this a performance target (PT1) was introduced to the weighted scorecard. The target was that 90 per cent of risk of serious harm assessments, risk management plans and OASys sentence plans on high-risk offenders are completed within five days of the commencement of the order or release into the community. The performance of each area in relation to these criteria began to become more transparent, and areas lost income if they were deficient.

In early 2005, concern arose that too many cases were being referred to the local MAPPA for management at level 3 (i.e. by the MAPP panels). While OASys assessments were accurately defining risk in an increasing number of cases as 'high' or 'very high', it had to be recognized that many of these cases did not constitute the 'critical few'. Level 3 is reserved for those few cases which require an inter-agency risk management plan agreed by the senior managers of the participating agencies. Cases needing this procedure are defined as those of great complexity or those requiring the commitment of resources which is beyond the remit of middle managers. Further guidance was issued in PC 10/2005.

This circular also introduced a set of headings to be used in drawing up risk management plans:

1. *Other agencies involved*: a brief outline of the activity of each agency that can be shared with the offender.
2. *Existing support/controls*: in place or can be activated if the offender is being released into the community.
3. *Added measures for specific risks*: for example, reference to work with the Victim Contact Unit where appropriate.
4. *Who will undertake the actions and by when*: cross-reference to any recent or planned MAPPA meeting.
5. *Additional considerations/requirements to manage the specific risks.*
6. *Level of contact* (including frequency of home visits).

These headings have been incorporated into the 'Risk management plan' section of OASys, and guidance on their use is contained in the revised Chapter 8 of the OASys manual, issued under PC 36/2006.

In June 2005 guidance was issued regarding the new sentencing provisions of the Criminal Justice Act 2003 for offenders considered to represent a continuing 'significant' risk of serious harm to the public. The provisions apply to 'specified' offences of sex and violence listed in Schedule 15 of the Act. This includes every indictable-only and either-way offence of sex and violence. Serious offences, for the purposes of these provisions, are 'specified' ones that are punishable with either life imprisonment or with a sentence of ten years or more. In deciding whether one of the new sentences is appropriate in these cases, the court has to decide whether there is a 'significant risk to members of the public of serious harm occasioned by the commission by him of further such offences'. Serious harm is defined here as 'death or serious personal injury whether that is physical or psychological'. This definition differs a little from the OASys definition quoted above, but the two definitions are seen as comparable. (More about these public protection sentences can be found under Dangerousness; Extended sentencing.)

In the light of growing concern about failures in public protection practice, two initiatives were established in June 2005. PC 48/2005 published an OASys quality management plan and required areas to draw up improvement plans accordingly. PC 49/2005 published a national action plan for the assessment and management of risk of harm. This called for action at regional and area level to achieve sustained improvement in the consistency, timeliness and quality of the assessment and management of risk of harm.

Damien Hanson and Elliot White were convicted of the murder of John Monckton and the attempted murder of his wife, Homeyra Monckton, in December 2005. Following an investigation of poor practice, five key recommendations were made by Her Majesty's Chief Inspector of Probation:

1. *Doing the job properly*: NOMS must demonstrate that practice and procedures are followed in every case.
2. *Lead responsibility in managing cases*: there must be continuity and clarity of lead responsibility, particularly for high risk of harm offenders.
3. *Updating Parole Board decisions*: the Parole Board should specify what should happen in situations where release is dependent on a requirement which in practice cannot be met.
4. *Improving risk of harm work nationally*: areas must ensure that structures support risk of harm work.
5. *Future independent reviews*: in exceptional cases of serious further offending, HM Inspectorate of Probation should undertake and publish a formal review.

Areas were required to implement action plans designed to cover the above points. Later in 2006, a revised and comprehensive 'risk of harm guidance and training resource pack' became available, and steps were taken to ensure that all staff with relevant responsibilities undertook training based on this material.

David Hancock

Related entries

Dangerousness; Extended sentencing; HM Inspectorate of Probation; Multi-agency public protection arrangements (MAPPAs); Offender Assessment System (OASys); Risk assessment and risk management; Risk of harm; Serious further offences; Supervision of offenders.

Key texts and sources

The following NPD circulars are available online at **www.probation.homeoffice.gov.uk/output/page31.asp:**

10/2005 *(Public Protection Framework, Risk of Harm and MAPPA Thresholds).*

48/2005 *(Offender Assessment System Quality Management Plan).*

49/2005 *(Assessment and Management of Risk of Harm Plan).*

15/2006 *(Guidance on the Implementation of Practice Recommendations Arising from an HMIP Independent Review of a Serious Offence Case).*

22/2006 *(Implementation of the Risk of Harm Guidance and Training Resource Pack).*

36/2006 *(OASys Manual* – revised chapter on risk of serious harm (ch. 8)).

Home Office (2005) *National Guide for the New CJA Sentences for Public Protection.* London: Home Office.

Kemshall, H. and Wood, J. (2007) 'High-risk offenders and public protection', in L. Gelsthorpe and R. Morgan (eds) *Handbook of Probation.* Cullompton: Willan Publishing.

PUNISHMENT (AIMS AND JUSTIFICATIONS)

Punishment involves a deliberate infliction of hardship or an imposition (a loss of liberty or rights) on wrongdoers, by a recognized authority, as a censure for the wrong done. This calls for an account of its purposes and justifications.

Since it is the duty of the state to protect its citizens and safeguard their rights, the imposition of punishment for crimes raises questions about the circumstances when and the extent to which punishment may be justified, as well as about its purposes.

The conventional initial distinction is between retributive and reductive accounts. *Retributivism* (sometimes called the *justice model*) holds that punishment is an intrinsically appropriate response to wrongdoing, that offenders should be dealt with as they deserve: the proper punishment is that which matches the offence. *Reductivism* sets for punishment the objective of contributing to a reduction in future offending.

Retributivism characteristically determines the due amount of punishment by reference to the seriousness of the offence as a function of harm done and the offender's responsibility. Since crimes and punishments are incommensurate – there is no common metric by which to calibrate offence seriousness and weight of punishment – it seems difficult to ensure that punishment is fittingly matched to crime. It may, however, be possible to rank crimes in order of seriousness, to rank punishments (perhaps according to the weight of imposition or loss of liberty) and to read across from one scale to the other. The penal tariff thus constructed is a device to ensure ordinal proportionality – that like crimes are punished alike and that the more serious crimes are awarded the heavier penalties.

Yet offences, depending on variables of responsibility and harm done, may differ in an indefinite number of ways, complicating the idea of 'like offences', while considerations can be advanced to show that an offence is a less or more serious instance of its kind. These mitigating or aggravating factors typically relate to harm (the damage done was not so bad, the effect on the victim was particularly serious) and responsibility (the offender was provoked, the offence was carefully planned). A further consideration (although relatively neglected in the literature) is the impact of the offence: if punishment is to be in proportion to the wrong done, then the real impact of the penalty, different upon different people, cannot justly be ignored. Considerations of this kind are also often advanced in mitigation (for example, imprisonment of this defendant will result in unemployment or homelessness).

Even those who seek another justification for punishment recognize that it must always be relevant, even if not necessarily decisive, to protest that a punishment is excessive (or too lenient). *Limiting retributivism* refers to the principle that, even where other aims are pursued, desert sets upper and lower limits on the penalty.

Reductivism is an inelegant word for a variety of accounts that share the idea that punishment should try to reduce the incidence of crime. Reductive accounts often have their origin in the view that the hardship of punishment can only be justified to the extent that, by reducing offending, there is a net reduction in harm overall. In some accounts, punishment that goes beyond that required to reduce offending is by definition gratuitous and unjustified. The most persuasive reductive versions thus incorporate a *principle of parsimony*: to impose as light a punishment as is consistent with achieving reductive objectives.

The main mechanisms by which such reduction might be achieved are as follows:

- *Individual deterrence*: the idea that a punitive experience (like a short, sharp shock) or a vivid prospect of punishment (perhaps a suspended sentence) might dissuade someone from further offending by frightening him or her off (the root meaning of 'deterrence').
- *General deterrence*: that others contemplating a crime, but knowing of the punishment that awaits offenders, should refrain through fear of this penalty.
- *Rehabilitation*: this refers to a range of interventions which try to reduce reoffending by influencing the offender's motivation or inhibitions or attitudes or abilities; less ambitious than deterrence, since it aspires to influence only the individual offender, it is also more ambitious in that it tries to influence the offender's own propensities and does not rely principally on fear of penalty (which, after all, gives a reason not to be caught rather than a reason to refrain).
- *Incapacitation*: this relies not on the offender's psychology but imposes constraints to prevent offending. While electronic monitoring and even driving disqualification can be considered as to some degree incapacitative,

prison is the plainest example. Some argue that it is possible and defensible to identify and incapacitate (imprison) those most likely to offend prolifically. Others claim that our capacity to make such assessments is less reliable than is sometimes thought; that criminal careers are often shorter than appreciated by proponents of incapacitation; that high levels of incarceration would be needed to achieve quite modest reductive gains; and that incapacitation is rarely ethically justifiable.

Since these approaches set out to achieve a reduction, they are – at least in principle – amenable to empirical inquiry about their effectiveness, although the methodological difficulties are formidable. (Retributive punishment may not be investigated in this way since there is nothing it sets out to achieve beyond a fitting match between crime and punishment.) Deterrence makes assumptions about how people reason, but do people reason in this way? Is fear of a relatively remote punishment enough to deter – especially if the prospect of apprehension seems unlikely? Might anger, distress or intoxication distort rational calculation? It is hard to find evidence to show that increases in the amount of punishment achieve deterrent gains.

There are also intractable debates of ethical principle between retributivists and reductivists. Reductivists say that retributive punishment is pointless and gratuitous. Retributivists counter that, to punish someone beyond desert to influence others, looks like using someone as a means rather than an end in itself; that to detain someone for a period longer than deserved by his or her offence to incapacitate him or her amounts to punishing that person for something he or she has not (yet or ever will have) done; and that rehabilitation undermines notions of responsibility by assuming that wrongdoing arises from personal shortcomings rather than culpable choice.

Retributivism respects our strong moral intuitions that it is repugnant to punish innocent people; that punishment should be in proportion to desert; that more serious crimes should receive weightier punishments; and that like cases should be treated alike. Reductivism recognizes that, presumably, the whole point of a criminal justice system is to reduce the incidence of offending, and its punishing practices should contribute to this. Retributivism typically invokes justice; reductivism appeals to a social utility, like public protection. Each captures something important about punishment that seems to elude the other. Attempts have therefore been made to reconcile them. For example, perhaps the justification for the *institution* of punishment is essentially reductive, but the sole and sufficient justification for the *distribution* of punishment in particular cases (whom and how much) must be retributive.

It is certainly true that neither broad approach can give much guidance about *amounts* of punishment: a conception of a retributively apt punishment differs across different societies and changes over time so that it is largely a matter of convention or habit; while if (for example) there is an amount of punishment that deters, with respect to the principle of parsimony, no one knows what it is.

Restorative justice tries to transcend these debates by urging that responses to crime should respect the interests of victim, perpetrator and community. The Criminal Justice Act 2003 (s. 142) includes reparation – righting the wrong by making amends – together with punishment and reductive considerations among the statutory purposes of sentencing, while not saying which should prevail when these several purposes indicate different sentences.

Punishment is irreducibly an institution of *censure*. In attributing blame there are accordingly things that punishment *says* as well as what it does, and there has been recent interest in punishment as communication – what punishment tries to communicate, to whom, how this is accomplished and whether these communications are 'heard'.

David Garland has influentially suggested that philosophers tend to bring to these debates an insufficient appreciation of the character and significance of punishment practices:

> Punishment is, on the face of things, an apparatus for dealing with criminals ... But it is also ... an expression of state power, a statement of collective morality, a vehicle for emotional

expression, an economically conditioned social policy, an embodiment of current sensibilities, and a set of symbols which display a cultural ethos and help create a social identity

(1990: 287).

Since punishment aims for so much – and sets for itself objectives that are mostly beyond it – the practices of punishment typically occasion dispute, frustration and disappointment.

Rob Canton

Related entries

Criminal Justice Act 1991; Desistance; Halliday Report; Punishment as communication; Rehabilitation; Reparation; Sentencing Guidelines Council.

Key texts and sources

Cavadino, M. and Dignan, J. (2002) *The Penal System: An Introduction* (3rd edn). London: Sage (chs 2 and 3).

Duff, A. and Garland, D. (eds) (1994) *A Reader on Punishment.* Oxford: Oxford University Press.

Garland, D. (1990) *Punishment and Modern Society.* Oxford: Oxford University Press.

PUNISHMENT AS COMMUNICATION

The idea that the proper purpose of punishment is to communicate, to the offender and others, the condemnation that crime deserves.

It has often been noted that punishment has a communicative aspect: a fine is not intended to be understood simply as a tax or charge on criminal conduct – it condemns that conduct as wrongful. Some theorists make such communication crucial to the justification of criminal punishment: the purpose of punishment is to communicate the censure that crime deserves. This explains the retributivist slogan that the guilty deserve to suffer, and that the point of punishment is to impose that deserved suffering. What the law defines as crimes are wrongs which concern the whole community. Those who commit such wrongs deserve to suffer censure from their fellow citizens, whose values they have flouted and whose interests they have threatened; conviction and punishment impose that suffering on them. Punishment as communication also has a forward-looking, preventive aim: if offenders come to understand and accept the censure, they will recognize that they should refrain from crime in future; the effective censure of past wrongdoing dissuades people from future wrongdoing.

The central challenge for communicative theorists is to explain why the communication of deserved censure should take the material form of burdensome punishment. Censure could be communicated by a suitably serious form of words (in a speech from the judge, for instance) or by purely symbolic punishments which are burdensome only because of what they mean (a thief could be required to have a notice condemning his crime fixed to his bathroom mirror for a certain period). So why should we communicate it through the imposition of material punishments – deprivations of liberty, money or time – which are burdensome independently of their meaning? Must we say (as some theorists argue) that, while a central aim of criminal punishment is to communicate deserved censure, the rationale for choosing these modes of communication lies in deterrence rather than moral persuasion – that we choose these burdensome modes of communication because the prospect of such burdens might deter those whom mere censure would not persuade to desist from crime?

Perhaps not: by considering probation (understood as punishment) and other non-custodial punishments such as unpaid work, we can see how to explain some kinds of punishment in more thoroughly communicative terms. By requiring offenders to undertake community service, we try to make clear to them why their fellow citizens regard what they did as wrong. The time they must spend undertaking the order (and perhaps the work that they must do, as when those guilty of vandalism must clean up the effects of vandalism) is intended to focus their attention on their offence and its implications, in a way that merely verbal admonitions or purely symbolic punishments might fail to do. By undertaking

such work, offenders can also make symbolic, apologetic reparation to the community whose values they flouted.

The Probation Service is central to punishment on this view. Probation officers' responsibility is to persuade offenders to face up to the implications of their offending – to try to ensure that the right messages are communicated and understood. That responsibility also includes trying to help the offender avoid crime in future, and offering help with whatever problems were related to the past offending. Part of the message of punishment is 'You must avoid such wrongdoing in future' but, if we are to communicate that message to offenders in this way, we must also offer them help in responding appropriately to it. In a reformed penal system, probation officers could also be involved in sentencing negotiation – in working out with the offender, and other affected parties including the victim, an appropriate sentence to mark the community's condemnation of the crime and to make moral reparation. A probation order tells offenders that their crimes put into question their commitment to the community's values and requires them to undertake this burdensome punishment as a way of coming to terms properly with their crimes and finding how to avoid their repetition.

Two further points about punishment as communication are important. First, it requires us to attend carefully to the meanings of different modes of punishment, and thus gives us further reason to limit our use of imprisonment. The message of imprisonment is exclusion – that the offender has by his or her offence excluded him or herself from community with his or her fellow citizens, but that is a message we should be very slow to communicate.

Secondly, communicative punishment presupposes that the offender is a member of a political community, whose values he or she has flouted, by whom he or she is now censured and with whom he or she is to be reconciled by undergoing punishment. If we are to claim the right to condemn the offender for his or her crime, we must claim that the offender, is a fellow citizen who is answerable to us for his or her violations of the values that define our political community, and that we have collectively treated him or her as a fellow citizen. If this is not true (and it is arguably not true of many who appear in our courts) – if the offender has been excluded from various rights and benefits of citizenship and has not been treated by the state or his or her fellow citizens with the concern and respect that we owe each other – our collective right to punish him or her is undermined. A communicative account of punishment illuminates a serious problem about the legitimacy of punishment in societies characterized by social injustice and exclusion – a problem that makes the probation officer's task even more demanding since it now includes a responsibility to help offenders to speak to the wider society about the injustices they have suffered, and to begin to work through the implications of those injustices.

Anthony Duff

Related entries

Citizenship; Community; Punishment (aims and justifications).

Key texts and sources

Duff, R.A. (2003) 'Probation, punishment and restorative justice', *Howard Journal of Criminal Justice*, 42: 180–97.
Feinberg, J. (1970) 'The expressive function of punishment', in his *Doing and Deserving*. Princeton, NJ: Princeton University Press.
von Hirsch, A. (1993) *Censure and Sanctions*. Oxford: Oxford University Press.

PUNISHMENT IN THE COMMUNITY

A challenge to the assumption that only prison constitutes proper punishment, punishment in the community expresses the idea that demanding and credible punishment can take place in the community, where a deserved penalty can be given effect while some of the damaging consequences of imprisonment are avoided.

The size of the prison population of England and Wales has been recognized as a problem since at least the 1960s. More recently, the increasing politicization of crime and punishment has made politicians anxious to avoid any imputation that they are 'soft on crime'. The idea of punishment in the community first came to prominence in the late 1980s when the Conservative administration struggled to square this circle by asserting the importance of punishment, while at the same time insisting that it need not take place in prison.

A probation order, historically, was legally not a sentence, but *instead of* a sentence and so not a punishment but *instead of* punishment. It always made demands upon the probationer, and failure to comply might lead to enforcement and eventually a return to court and a liability to be sentenced. Nevertheless, the probation order enjoined probation officers to 'advise, assist and befriend' those under their supervision. Conceived as a moral mission or a therapeutic intervention (or even simply as help), this remit seemed very different from punishment. Probation officers, then, have often been discomfited by political attempts to characterize their work as punishment. Some new responsibilities – for example, parole supervision or community service – were therefore viewed suspiciously by probation officers at introduction and this was aggravated because it was expedient for legislators and policymakers to emphasize precisely their punitive and controlling character in an attempt to promote the credibility of the new measure.

At the same time, the public, accustomed to thinking of punishment as involving imprisonment, are supposedly sceptical about whether punishment in the community could – perhaps even in principle – afford the same punitive weight or public protection as prison. Attempts to address this scepticism have emphasized the punitive character of punishment in the community – its demanding content and rigorous enforcement – and the possibility of ensuring public protection in a community setting.

The logic of the Criminal Justice Act 1991 was that all penalties, including those in the community, could in some sense be conceptualized as involving a loss of liberty, and that this should (usually) be in proportion to the seriousness of the offence – a principle of retributive punishment. Probation has been variably successful in making the case in this way, sometimes emphasizing instead that community sentences make claims on an offender's sense of responsibility and entail the discomfort of demands for personal change. In that respect, the argument runs, prison is less of a punishment since it allows people to evade their responsibilities – for managing their own circumstances and meeting obligations of social participation in relation to family, accommodation and employment. Again, a case for punishment in the community can be made on the basis that it is in the community that offenders normally reside and it is here that they must develop a law-abiding lifestyle. Prison, by contrast, can delay processes of maturing and create problems of its own that militate against successful resettlement. Many factors thought to be related to desistance are undermined by the experience of incarceration.

The concept of punishment in the community occupies a hazardous political place. It is vulnerable to attack from those who support higher levels of incarceration. More surprisingly, it is sometimes viewed with suspicion by liberals who see punishment *in* the community as an extension of projects of 'discipline' and surveillance into the community – or even, when these disciplinary devices are more widely extended, punishment *of* the community.

If the expression raises interesting questions about the character and philosophy of punishment, the meaning of community is no less significant. The term 'community' is used somewhat promiscuously in penal policy and, while one might expect there to be some conceptual connection between (say) punishment in the community and community crime prevention, the links are not obvious. Community here means, at the least, not in prison, but some urge the value of broadening its connotations, suggesting that the community is not just the venue for punishment but could and should be actively involved in the response to crime (community justice).

The specific penalty in which this idea is most richly expressed is community service (unpaid work). Probation supervision is private and invisible; community service is striving to make itself more visible and to show that the community is not only the place where the punishment is carried out but is also a beneficiary of the process. Part of the rationale is that the community can see – in the way that offenders make tangible amends for the wrongs they have done – that these are people who have a contribution to make and have earned their requalification as respected members of the community.

On the other hand, while these ideas seem progressive, traditional and contemporary community responses to crime should not be assumed to be liberal or inclusive; spontaneous expressions by (some members) of the community towards (some of) the offenders in its midst can take a hostile and aggressive form. Whenever the idea of community is invoked in these debates, a large question is whether offenders are to be considered as members of the community or whether the community closes ranks to exclude them.

Finally, while community sentences are widely used in England and Wales, their relationship with the size of the prison population is uncertain. It is not easy to show that a reliance on extending the use of community punishment is a plausible strategy for reducing the number of people in prison.

Rob Canton

Related entries

Community justice; Criminal Justice Act 1991; Punishment (aims and justifications).

Key texts and sources

Bottoms, A., Gelsthorpe, L. and Rex, S. (eds) (2001) *Community Penalties: Changes and Challenges.* Cullompton: Willan Publishing.

Mair, G. and Canton, R. (2007) 'Sentencing, community penalties and the role of the Probation Service', in L. Gelsthorpe and R. Morgan (eds) *Handbook of Probation.* Cullompton: Willan Publishing.

Worrall, A. and Hoy, C. (2005) *Punishment in the Community: Managing Offenders, Making Choices* (2nd edn). Cullompton: Willan Publishing

R

RACE AND RACISM

A race is a group of people believed to have biological characteristics in common that differentiate them from other races. Critics of this idea hold race to be a social construct rather than a scientific classification. Whether or not there are any rational grounds for such classifications, the belief in race is a precondition of racism – the prejudicial treatment of individuals or groups on the basis of their 'race'.

The classification of human beings into 'races' seems to have no genetic or biological basis. Racial categories seem based on arbitrary differentiations, typically skin colour or other aspects of appearance. Historically, the project of racial classification has nearly always been undertaken in an attempt to demonstrate the superiority of some races over others, with white/European/Caucasian peoples set at the top of an imagined hierarchy. This ranking becomes a justification for imperialism, colonization, slavery and other modes of oppression and exploitation. Assigning people to racial or ethnic categories, based on supposed cultural or national similarities, invariably entails overgeneralizing, the use of stereotypes and the making of assumptions.

Whatever the realities of race, the existence of racism is incontrovertible. Racism, which depends on a belief in the possibility of racial differentiation, involves a combination of prejudice and power. Racism can take a number of forms and operates with different sets of stereotypes and assumptions that manifest themselves in different ways. Discussions of black and minority ethnic offenders should always bear in mind the ethnic and cultural diversity of this

'group'. Indeed, the complexities of racism go beyond oppressive behaviour by white towards black people. Localities, demographics and economic, cultural and political factors all have an impact upon the manifestations of racist behaviour. Accordingly, anti-discriminatory practice must engage with these complexities, as well as recognize that racism is often compounded by sexism and other forms of discrimination.

The experience of racism is likely to have been encountered by most black and Asian people, ranging from condescension, exclusion and blocked opportunities to racial harassment and hate crime perpetrated by racially motivated offenders. All criminal justice agencies and the system in general are said to have racist aspects: black people have reported being over-policed as (supposed) offenders and under-protected as victims, while many defendants and offenders describe unfair treatment on racial grounds. These experiences must be taken seriously in all work with black and minority ethnic offenders. Members of staff, too, report experiences of racism within their own organizations.

Sometimes racism is a deliberate and, indeed, flagrant act or attitude of prejudiced individuals. Other forms of racism are more subtle. The concept of 'institutional racism' was given authoritative definition in the Macpherson Report, which recognizes an organization's collective failure that 'can be seen or detected in the processes, attitudes and behaviour which amount to discrimination through unwitting prejudice, ignorance, thoughtlessness and racist stereotyping which disadvantage minority ethnic people'. Yet the essence of institutional racism is not so much that it is unwitting – how often can organizations plead that discriminatory practice is unwitting when, in some cases, this has been repeatedly drawn to their attention? – but that it is somehow embedded in the practices of the organization, enduring through changes of personnel.

Anti-racist practice, like all sound anti-discriminatory practice, must originate in the willingness of white people to examine their own behaviour and attitudes, an ethical commitment to change and a reflective understanding of the systems and processes to implement change where necessary.

Rob Canton

RELATED ENTRIES

Anti-discriminatory practice; Black and minority ethnic (BME) offenders; Diversity; Hate crime; Macpherson Report; Mubarek Inquiry; Racially motivated offenders.

Key texts and sources

Calverley, A., Cole, B., Kaur, G., Lewis, S., Raynor, P., Sadeghi, S., Smith, D., Vanstone, M. and Wardak, A. (2004) *Black and Asian Offenders on Probation.* Home Office Research Study 277 (available online at **http://www.homeoffice.gov.uk/rds/pdfs04/hors277.pdf**).

Gelsthorpe, L. and McIvor, G. (2007) 'Difference and diversity in probation', in L. Gelsthorpe and R. Morgan (eds) *Handbook of Probation.* Cullompton: Willan Publishing.

HMIP (2004) *Towards Race Equality: Follow up Inspection Report.* London: Home Office.

Lewis, S., Raynor, P., Smith, D. and Wardak, A. (eds) (2006) *Race and Probation.* Cullompton: Willan Publishing.

Macpherson, Sir W. (1999) *The Stephen Lawrence Inquiry* (available online at **http://www.archive.official-documents.co.uk/document/cm42/4262/4262.htm**), especially ch. 6.

For reports under the Criminal Justice Act 1991 (s. 95), see **http://www.homeoffice.gov.uk/rds/pubsstatistical.html**.

RACIALLY MOTIVATED OFFENDERS

Those offending on account of their hatred of people whose racial background is different from their own.

The issue of racially motivated offending has become one of serious public concern in the past 20 years. Increased reporting by victims and perhaps increased incidence were propelled into the forefront of political debate by the murder of Stephen Lawrence in 1993 and the subsequent campaign of his parents. Governments have been quick to condemn and prohibit, but less energetic in developing strategies to deal with the offenders. The Probation Service has had to face the problems of dealing with some of the perpetrators and victims. Many areas, therefore, developed specific policies and practices, often in collaboration with other local organizations.

These policies recognized a number of key characteristics of racially motivated offending. It is targeted in many cases. It is generally physical, verbal or property violence, often committed by groups of perpetrators. Its victims often suffer repeated instances in short periods of time, frequently in or close to their home. It manifests in a continuum from verbal abuse to murder. As a result, the lives of its victims can be dramatically blighted. Its perpetrators often claim a quasi-rational justification for their actions. This is sometimes directly supported by extreme political groups and, more often, implicitly by some mainstream media and politicians.

Probation areas were faced with adjusting their assessment and intervention activities to deal with the offenders, recognizing one familiar offender characteristic: the need to exercise power over his or her victim. Most probation areas have taken the view that, when racist attitudes have played a significant part in the offending behaviour of an individual, the risks of harm and reoffending posed by that offender are increased. The consequence of this has been a recognition that the underpinning attitudes and beliefs have to be tackled and changed. Until 1998 this strategy had no basis in legislation or regulation. Challenges to offenders almost always brought denials of racist attitudes, generally supported in courts by their advocates and sometimes, therefore, eliciting criticism from sentencers.

Following the publication of the Macpherson Report there were significant annual increases in the level of reporting of racially motivated offending to the police. The introduction of racially aggravated offences brought the issue of the offender's motivation into the legitimate purview of criminal justice agencies, but failed to capture the real extent of the issue and its incidence. There remained a vacuum in relation to the expectations on probation staff dealing with the perpetrators. The Association of Chief Officers of Probation (ACOP) in the Midlands produced a manual in 1998 called *From Murmur to Murder*. This has been widely used by probation areas since, but has never been formally adopted centrally.

Meanwhile the context has moved on rapidly. Other groups are victimized in similar ways, notably some religious groups and homosexual people. The international context has clearly demonstrated that the notion of racially motivated offending as a post-colonial manifestation of white supremacy is insufficient. The terminology of hate crime is now increasingly used, building on the understanding drawn from work with racially motivated offenders and applied to behaviours that have similar characteristics.

John Kay

RELATED ENTRIES

Hate crime; Macpherson Report; Race and racism.

Key texts and sources

HM Inspectorate of Probation (2005) *An Effective Supervision Inspection Programme Thematic Report: 'I'm not a Racist but...'* London: Home Office (available online at **http://www.ncblo.co.uk/ documents_download/HMIP%20I'm%20not%20 really%20a%20racist%20but%20RMOs.pdf**).

Kay, J. and Gast, L. (1998) *From Murmur to Murder*. Birmingham: Midlands Probation Training Consortium (a resource pack for probation staff, including a substantial bibliography).

RECONVICTION

Further findings of guilt recorded against offenders after an earlier conviction and sentence and, in this context, especially during or after a period of supervision or imprisonment. Reconviction is a proxy measure for reoffending.

The whole idea of 'effective practice', the idea of sentences 'working' or not, depends on some specification of (or assumption about) their intended effect. Among the principal aims of probation (and other penal interventions) is a reduction in the reoffending of those under supervision, and this is conventionally measured by monitoring reconviction.

The first difficulty is that reoffending is not the same as reconviction. Many offences do not lead to conviction (see Attrition), as we know through victim surveys and self-reports (accounts by offenders of their own behaviour). This is more true of some types of offence and offender than others – for example, there is reason to think that some sex offenders commit many more offences than come to the attention of the police or lead to conviction. The same is true of domestic violence. It seems almost certainly to be true of many kinds of white-collar crime and crimes of the powerful.

Since so much offending does not lead to conviction, if a group is subject to particular scrutiny or surveillance, more detection and conviction are likely to result – a rise in convictions which may not necessarily correspond to an increase in the incidence of their offending. For example, offenders in projects for prolific and other priority offenders may be more likely to be detected in their offending, leading to a higher rate of reconviction, which may mislead about the true impact of the project.

A further shortcoming in using simple reconviction (conventionally recorded within a two-year follow-up period) as 'the' measure of effectiveness is that it cannot capture important changes in *frequency* or offence *seriousness*. A reconviction within two years may be regarded as a 'failure' but, if there has been an increase in the interval between offences or if offences are less serious, then this is plainly at least some kind of success. For that matter, there may be other changes, of which reconviction is an uncertain indicator, that are also legitimate objectives in the supervision of offenders – for instance, change of attitude, reduction in criminogenic needs or improvement in employment prospects.

The effect of an intervention is typically assessed by comparing actual with predicted reconviction. The Offender Group Reconviction Score (OGRS) is used to predict reoffending. An input of a specified number of variables generates a 'score' – a percentage probability of reconviction. While this is reliable for groups in the aggregate, it is of limited use in the individual case. Suppose, for example, OGRS yields a score of 70 per cent for a particular offender. What this means is that, of 100 people relevantly matched – mostly on criminal history variables – 70 will be reconvicted within two years and 30 will not. OGRS does not say whether this person is one of the 70 or one of the 30, how soon or how seriously he or she may reoffend or, crucially, what might be done to make a difference. The assessment is 'accurate' but disconnects risk assessment from its management (see also Actuarialism; Risk assessment and risk management).

It is tempting to use reconviction rates to decide which forms of intervention are more effective (prison compared with community supervision, say, or supervision with or without an accredited programme). One difficulty here is that it is rarely possible to be confident that like is being compared with like. Courts must dispense justice, so assigning offenders randomly to different interventions – sometimes considered a 'gold standard' of research into effects – will be unacceptable in practice. There are likely to be many differences in the characteristics of those sent to prison and those made subject to community penalties.

Causal connections are also extremely difficult to disentangle. For example, if a programme appears to lead to a reduction in reconviction, can this be said to be a consequence of the programme? Or might it be that a sustained resolve to stop offending is responsible for the individual's completing of the programme? It is certainly possible to exaggerate the impact of any intervention on reconviction. As McNeill and Whyte put it: 'Reconviction is strongly associated with the chronic and serious problems of disadvantage, marginalisation and exclusion that commonly characterise the lives of both prisoners and those subject to community penalties' (2007: 43), and these factors may well be more influential than the impact of interventions. There are also well established factors associated with reconviction that are not amenable to the influence of intervention – men, for example, are more likely to be reconvicted than women, younger people than older people.

The reliability of reconviction data cannot be assumed. The relevant databases are no more infallible than any other such artefact. Notoriously, too, there is the problem of 'pseudo-reconvictions' – offences which only come to court after the sentence, but were in fact committed before the intervention and which, accordingly, the intervention can in no way affect. Unless carefully identified, these can distort an understanding of an intervention's effects.

For all the contingencies and doubts, reconviction remains as good a proxy measure as there is to gauge reoffending, and reoffending must be a matter of great significance to people who need to evaluate the effects of their practice. Reconviction, however, is a 'headline' figure – like clear-up rates for the police – and, like all such figures, often does not get the careful interpretation it requires.

Rob Canton

RELATED ENTRIES

Actuarialism; Assessment instruments and systems; Attrition; Desistance; Desistance studies vs. cognitive-behavioural therapies: which offers most hope for the long term?; Effective practice; Evaluation; Research; Risk assessment and risk management.

Key texts and sources

Cuppleditch, L. and Evans, W. (2005) *Re-offending of Adults: Results from the 2002 Cohort. Home Office Statistical Bulletin* 2505 (available online at **http://www.homeoffice.gov.uk/rds/pdfs05/hosb2505.pdf**).

Hedderman, C. (2007) 'Past, present and future sentences: what do we know about their effectiveness?', in L. Gelsthorpe and R. Morgan (eds) *Handbook of Probation.* Cullompton: Willan Publishing.

Hine, J. and Celnick, A. (2001) *A One Year Reconviction Study of Final Warnings.* London: Home Office (available online at **http://www.homeoffice.gov.uk/rds/pdfs/reconvictstudywarn.pdf**).

Mair, G., Lloyd, C. and Hough, M. (1997) 'The limitations of reconviction rates', in G. Mair (ed.) *Evaluating the Effectiveness of Community Penalties.* Aldershot: Avebury.

McNeill, F. and Whyte, B. (2007) *Reducing Reoffending: Social Work and Community Justice in Scotland.* Cullompton: Willan Publishing.

Merrington, S. and Stanley, S. (2007) 'Effectiveness: who counts what?', in L. Gelsthorpe and R. Morgan (eds) *Handbook of Probation.* Cullompton: Willan Publishing.

REGIONAL OFFENDER MANAGERS (ROMS)

Appointees charged with the responsibility for the provision of correctional services in the nine regions of England and in Wales.

The National Offender Management Service (NOMS) exists to reduce reoffending and to increase the protection of the public, particularly from those who have committed sexual or violent offences. Its origins lie in Patrick Carter's analysis (the Carter Report) that end-to-end offender management, better commissioned service delivery, the rebalancing of sentencing and more competition in the provision of correctional services would serve to meet that aim.

The nine regional offender managers (ROMs) and the Director of Offender Management for Wales have a key role in all these functions. They provide an opportunity to ensure that effective services in prisons and community sentences are properly planned and delivered to offenders in line with the sentencing patterns of the courts. Only by delivering to high standards those interventions that are known to have the best chance of turning offenders away from crime will sentencer and public confidence in the correctional process be established, and help achieve NOMS' overall aim.

However, sentences – whether custodial or community based – will not usually, of themselves, deflect offenders from crime. Many offenders require integrated, accessible supporting services which address the factors underpinning an offending lifestyle. Consequently, the ROM is also responsible for reducing reoffending strategies and delivery plans at regional level. These seek to gain buy-in to the reducing reoffending and public protection agendas from the plethora of regional and local agencies – concerned with drugs, housing, education, training and employment, children and families, health, etc. – that deliver or commission those services. The ROM is not precious about who actually delivers community or prison sentences as long as they satisfy the requirements of the courts and meet the necessary standards of security, safety, decency and respect.

NOMS is keen to develop a culture of creativity in correctional services which sees new providers and new combinations of existing and new providers offering ways of delivering sentences more effectively and with sensitivity to the diverse characteristics of the offenders with whom they work on the community's behalf. Clearly, the principal providers in the first years of NOMS will be the National Probation Service and HM Prison Service, but there are plans to extend that provider base to more private and voluntary and community sector agencies (see Contestability).

The ROM's essential commissioning role is to assess demand for provision (from sentencing decisions), the aggregated needs of offenders (from OASys) and the capacity of providers, and then to produce challenging targets for those providers to achieve in the delivery of services. Additionally, the ROM will have an increasing role in the joint commissioning of allied services – education, training and employment, offender healthcare and drug treatment provision, for example. This recognizes that it is those services that can have a major positive impact on the likelihood of offenders sustaining crime-free lives in the future.

Steve Murphy

RELATED ENTRIES

Carter Report; Contestability; Interventions; National Offender Management Service (NOMS); Offender management; Privatization.

Key texts and sources

See key texts and sources at related entries.

REGIONAL TRAINING CONSORTIA

Consortia of probation boards through which key training and development activities are managed and delivered, especially the recruitment and qualifying training of probation officers, assessment and accreditation of probation staff for vocational awards and the training of accredited programmes tutors.

Regional training consortia are consortia of area probation boards. Established and approved by the Home Office in 1998, their original role was to:

- assist in the selection of staff;
- manage collaborative staff training and development; and
- manage the assessment and accreditation of staff.

Although it was anticipated that the consortia would, in the longer term, come to have a role in developing and delivering training for a wide range of probation staff, their first task was to implement the new qualifying probation training arrangements. The first cohort of 250 trainee probation officers duly commenced the two-year Diploma in Probation Studies programme, managed by consortia in collaboration with a contracted university provider.

The functions of consortia were further amplified in subsequent probation circulars, notably PC 32/2000 on accredited programmes and PC 41/2005 on probation service officers. Until 2001, the Home Office Probation Unit (and subsequently the National Probation Directorate) provided the core funding for consortia and set a central strategic direction. Regionally, however, it was evident that some areas, and thus regions, gave different priority to regional collaboration on training and development. While development has been broadly consistent, there has accordingly been some variation.

The consortia carried on the tradition of the former regional staff development units (RSDUs). Those units had managed and delivered extensive training and development programmes for staff, notably for newly qualified probation officers, and induction and development training for all new managers. When the RSDUs ceased to exist, their role of providing a regional lead on training and development was eventually taken on by ten regional human resource management advisers, working to the Home Office Probation Unit. By the time the National Probation Directorate (NPD) was established in 2001, only one of those posts remained. As central capacity declined, the regional training consortia progressively took on key lead roles in important areas of human resource development.

A National Consortia Directors' Forum was established and this has contributed to national policy, providing consistent management of national processes, and liaising with NPD, National Offender Management Service (NOMS) and Prison Service colleagues at a senior level. The directors arrange an annual national conference for regional training consortia staff.

A rigorous review of regional training consortia in 2001 spoke highly of their achievements and of their potential. By 2005, regional training consortia had trained over half the current probation officer workforce, were processing in excess of 8,000 applications to be a trainee probation officer each year, had achieved fully compliant status as National Vocational Qualification (NVQ) assessment centres, were progressing over 800 probation service officers per year through a core training programme, and had managed and delivered accredited programme training for all tutors running programmes.

Ian Macnair

RELATED ENTRIES

Accredited programmes; Practice development assessors; Probation boards; Probation service officers; Probation training.

Key texts and sources

Home Office (1999) *Diploma in Probation Studies.* London: Home Office (contains all the relevant PCs).
Home Office (2002) *Better Quality Services Review.* London: Home Office/National Probation Service Training Consortia.

REHABILITATION

A broad concept that denotes a wide variety of interventions aimed at promoting desistance and/or the symbolic restoration of a former offender to the status of a law-abiding citizen.

The rehabilitation of offenders has been at the heart of the Probation Service's mission since its inception. However, as a concept, rehabilitation is surprisingly difficult to pin down, such that, when different writers, theorists or practitioners refer to it, there is quite a good chance that they are not talking about the same thing. This is at least in part because it can be understood both as a general objective or goal and as a process or set of practices.

According to a dictionary definition, rehabilitation is closely associated with the notion of 'restoration': that is, a return to a former (desirable) state or status. This is arguably a useful starting point for thinking about the rehabilitation of offenders. In this context, rehabilitation can have both behavioural and symbolic dimensions. In behavioural terms, rehabilitation implies desistance from offending. In other words, a 'rehabilitated offender' is usually understood to be a person who has a history of offending but has now put his or her offending behind him or her, and 'rehabilitative' interventions similarly imply a goal of reducing reoffending or promoting desistance. But the notion of rehabilitation also has a symbolic dimension, such that the cessation of offending implies a return to a former status: that of a law-abiding citizen who is accepted by and enjoys the same rights as other members of the community. In other words, rehabilitation can imply not just behavioural change but also a symbolic process whereby an individual is permitted to shed the negative label of 'offender' (see Reintegration).

At the heart of rehabilitation is the notion of *corrigibility*: that is, a belief in the propensity of (at least some) offenders to change 'for the better'. However, that belief has manifested itself in a wide variety of practices which have claimed 'rehabilitative' effects. Ideas associated with the rehabilitation of offenders have a long history and date back at least to the late eighteenth century, when the penal reformer, John Howard, put forward plans for a national system of penitentiaries designed to bring about the moral and spiritual improvement of prisoners. Subsequently, the development of probation reflected a growing commitment on the part of the state to rehabilitation as an alternative to punishment for 'suitable' (usually young or unpractised) offenders. Under the influence of the developing science of psychology, rehabilitation in the post-war period became a more secular enterprise, and both rehabilitation and probation came to be synonymous with 'treatment'.

During the 1960s and 1970s, however, the 'treatment model' was discredited, and faith in the possibility of achieving the rehabilitation of offenders declined. This was largely because, by this time, there was an accumulation of evidence that probation, among other sanctions, was not producing the reductions in reoffending rates which had been taken for granted. The treatment model was also criticized for its portrayal of the offender as a passive recipient of 'help' rather than an active participant in the process of rehabilitation. The Probation Service did not, however, turn its back on the quest for rehabilitation: it simply looked to other approaches to help its clients desist from crime. Rehabilitative practice became much more eclectic, as probation staff experimented both with new psychologically inspired approaches (such as behavioural and cognitive-behavioural interventions) and other, more practical approaches which paid more attention to the social and economic barriers to desistance, such as unemployment, debt, accommodation and other such issues. In this period the service also took responsibility for the new community service order (now unpaid work), which was thought to have rehabilitative potential.

In theoretical terms, the downfall of the treatment model produced a number of attempts to recast rehabilitation not as a therapeutic process of punishment but, rather, as an *antidote to* punishment. So-called 'rights-based' rehabilitation is based on the notion that, just as the state has a right to punish wrongdoing, so the offender has a corresponding right not to be unduly disadvantaged by the experience of punishment (imprisonment in particular). It is argued that any handicaps or damage created by punishment ought therefore to be offset by 'rehabilitative' measures.

The 1990s, however, witnessed a revival of the notion of *rehabilitative punishment* in the context of an international 'what works?' movement which has reasserted the effectiveness of a new breed of – mainly cognitive-behavioural – treatment programmes in reducing reoffending. In some of the literature this has been referred to as 'new rehabilitationism'. But this new, treatment-centred version of rehabilitation has not been without critics. For example, it has been criticized for focusing too heavily on endogenous factors in crime causation, while potentially ignoring some of the wider social and practical

problems offenders face that inhibit desistance. This reminds us that there is more to rehabilitation than the administration of 'treatment'. It has also been criticized for presenting a rather negative image of offenders as sources of risks, needs and problems which must be tackled or addressed. An alternative contemporary model of rehabilitation is the so-called 'strengths-based' approach, which views the offender as an active participant in the process of rehabilitation and asks what positive contribution he or she can make to the community.

In the context of the Probation Service's official purposes, rehabilitation has never disappeared but, since the 1970s, its importance has diminished. Where rehabilitation was once the central *raison d'être* of the service's work, it is now just one objective alongside others, and is arguably subordinate to those of public protection, risk management and enforcement.

Gwen Robinson

RELATED ENTRIES

Desistance; Reintegration; Supervision of offenders.

Key texts and sources

Crow, I. (2001) *The Treatment and Rehabilitation of Offenders.* London: Sage.

Lewis, S. (2005) 'Rehabilitation: headline or footnote in the new penal policy?', *Probation Journal*, 52: 119–35.

Maruna, S. and Ward, T. (2006) *Rehabilitation. Key Ideas in Criminology Series.* London: Routledge.

Raynor, P. and Robinson, G. (2005) *Rehabilitation, Crime and Justice.* Basingstoke: Palgrave Macmillan.

REINTEGRATION

A process that follows a period of formal punishment (usually imprisonment) whereby the ex-offender resumes life as a member of the community.

Reintegration is a rather general term that has close links with the concept of rehabilitation. In the criminal justice context, reintegration is most commonly applied to prisoners on release from custody, and is generally understood as a process that seeks to aid the transition to life in the community, while also minimizing the likelihood of reoffending. In the USA the preferred term is 're-entry'. Attempts to facilitate the reintegration of ex-prisoners have been a part of the work of the Probation Service throughout its history and, in the context of a transition to the National Offender Management Service (NOMS) and an increasing emphasis on 'joined-up' working between prisons and probation, it is an area of work which is set to expand (see also Resettlement).

Reintegration has both symbolic and practical dimensions. Symbolically, reintegration can denote the acceptance of the offender as a law-abiding member of the community: that is, his or her 'requalification' as a citizen. This is central to the spirit of the Rehabilitation of Offenders Act 1974, which specifies (according to sentence type/length) 'rehabilitation periods' after which most ex-offenders are not required to disclose their convictions when applying for employment, insurance and the like. This process of symbolic reintegration is also central to some versions of restorative justice, which see offender reintegration as part of a reciprocal process which follows censure (shaming) and the expression of remorse on the part of the offender (Braithwaite 1989). However, reintegration is a term that also has more *practical* connotations, denoting not only attempts to help offenders access practical services relating to employment, education, accommodation, etc., but also efforts to (re-)involve former offenders in networks of prosocial opportunities and relationships in the community with the aim of helping them achieve and/or maintain a non-offending lifestyle. Work of this type is sometimes referred to as the building of 'social capital' or the promotion of 'social inclusion', and this, too, has a long history in probation practice.

Reintegration is a slightly problematic term when applied to ex-offenders in that it assumes that individuals were suitably 'integrated' prior to a period of punishment. Yet prisoners are a socially excluded group who typically have a history of multiple social and economic disadvantages and do not necessarily enjoy strong, supportive personal and social relationships. It also assumes that the communities to which offenders return have the resources and the will to assist with the reintegration process. Reintegration is also particularly problematic in respect of those offenders – most notably those convicted of serious sexual and violent offences – who pose an ongoing risk to the community. Multi-agency public protection arrangements (MAPPAs), for example, subject some high-risk offenders to intensive monitoring and surveillance precisely because their 'integration' into the community is deemed problematic.

Gwen Robinson

RELATED ENTRIES

Citizenship; Rehabilitation; Resettlement; Restorative justice; Social exclusion.

Key texts and sources

Braithwaite, J. (1989) *Crime, Shame and Reintegration.* Cambridge: Cambridge University Press.

Maguire, M. (2007) 'The resettlement of ex-prisoners', in L. Gelsthorpe and R. Morgan (eds) *Handbook of Probation.* Cullompton: Willan Publishing.

Maruna, S. and Immarigeon, R. (eds) (2004) *After Crime and Punishment: Pathways to Offender Reintegration.* Cullompton: Willan Publishing.

Social Exclusion Unit (2002) *Reducing Re-offending by Ex-prisoners.* London: Office of the Deputy Prime Minister (available online at **http://www. socialexclusionunit.gov.uk/downloaddoc. asp?id=64**).

REMAND SERVICES

Remand or pre-trial services that exist to divert offenders from an unnecessary custodial remand.

The Probation Service has a significant contribution to make in the area of remand services. Sometimes the objective of avoiding unnecessary custodial remand is achieved by assisting the courts (judges and magistrates, as well as other court personnel) to make better and more effective decisions; sometimes it is achieved through the direct provision of services (bail support or supported bail accommodation) and the promotion of these in the courts; and sometimes it is achieved through professional conflict, as one agency seeks to achieve change in the decisions made by others. Remand services are clearly identified as a central activity of probation services throughout Europe and beyond. The main services designed to divert defendants from custodial remand are as follows.

Bail information

This involves the provision of information to the court or the Crown Prosecution Service (CPS) concerning a defendant's social and material circumstances, including risk of harm to the public, to enable more informed decisions about bail to be made. Independent, verified information which attends to the CPS's misgivings about bail may influence their application to the court and perhaps lead them to withdraw objections to bail. Arguably, the original priority of avoiding custodial remand for vulnerable groups (for example, mentally disordered offenders) and/or those disproportionately represented in the prison system (including black and minority ethnic offenders) has been superseded by a preoccupation with public protection.

Bail support

This had its origins in work with younger offenders, but later extended to adult defendants. It involves providing services, sometimes including accommodation provision and, in appropriate cases, initiating contact with drug services through arrest referral schemes. Most commonly it comprises assistance and stabilizing support which address objections to bail and provide support to a defendant on bail. Bail support goes beyond bail information in seeking to address the two major reasons for objecting to bail: the seriousness of the offence and the likelihood that the defendant will commit further offences while on bail. This is designed to give magistrates and judges greater confidence in a non-custodial remand.

Bail hostels

These provide structured living accommodation in a supportive regime that places firm boundaries around a defendant's behaviour, often involving a curfew and a no-drink or drugs policy (see also Approved premises). Bail hostels, therefore, are to be used as an alternative to custody. They can keep people in employment; maintain links between defendants and their families; confront offending behaviour; repair damaged relationships; and prepare defendants for independent living in the community. They are a halfway house between bail in the community and a remand in custody.

Although remand services are variably deployed across the country, their potential is considerable and so far insufficiently realized: 'A vision for the future of the Probation Service is one in which a fully articulated set of court focused remand services, firmly located within the public protection and effectiveness agendas, can be mobilised to reduce, wherever possible, unnecessary and inappropriate remands in custody' (Haines and Octigan 1998). Notwithstanding this, remand services continue to be vulnerable to changes in policy, and other priorities have sometimes deflected attention away from their development.

Mike Octigan

RELATED ENTRIES

Approved premises; Court work; Crown Prosecution Service (CPS).

Key texts and sources

Drakeford, M., Haines, K., Cotton, B. and Octigan, M. (2001) *Pre-trial Services and the Future of Probation.* Cardiff: University of Wales Press.
Haines, K. and Morgan, R. (2007) 'Services before trial and sentence: achievement, decline and potential', in L. Gelsthorpe and R. Morgan (eds) *Handbook of Probation.* Cullompton: Willan Publishing.
Haines, K. and Octigan, M. (1998) *Reducing Remands in Custody: The Probation Service and Remand Service.* London: ACOP.

REPARATION

The making of amends by an offender to a victim or his or her community in order to repair the harm caused by his or her offence. This might be by way of an apology, compensation or carrying out unpaid work. Reparation practice is most developed in relation to working with young offenders.

Reparation has become increasingly significant in the criminal justice system in recent years. The Criminal Justice Act 2003 instated reparation as one of the five purposes of sentencing. The Home Office regards community penalties as beneficial for lower-risk offenders, allowing for a combination of punishment with 'changing offenders' behaviour and making amends'. Repairing the harm caused by crime is therefore an important feature of sentencing.

The 2003 Act also introduced a number of requirements that can be selected to make up an offender's community sentence. Unpaid work is a key requirement to which offenders may be sentenced in order to allow them to make reparation to victims and the wider community.

The other principal measures of reparation are reparation orders and conditional cautions. Reparation orders are only available for young offenders and may involve learning about the impact of crime on victims, apologies to victims or carrying out unpaid work. The Together Academy website states that the aim of a reparation order is to ensure that 'young offenders understand the consequences of their offending and take responsibility for their behaviour'.

The conditional caution, only available for adults, allows offenders to avoid going through the criminal justice system. The difference between a traditional caution and a conditional caution is that the latter includes 'the imposition of specified conditions [which] will be an appropriate and effective means of addressing an offender's behaviour or making reparation for the effects of the offence on the victim or the community'. Conditions might include repairing the physical damage caused by his or her offence, making financial restitution or attempting to repair the harm caused to the victim by apologizing.

The 'message' of reparation is forward looking and readily understandable (see Punishment as communication). Among its benefits for communities is that it allows them to see offenders making amends. (There have been calls at various times for offenders carrying out unpaid work to be made more visible to the public through the use of identifying clothing, such as orange vests.) When reparation involves direct contact, victims have the chance to find out why the offender committed the offence, which can help reduce their fear of further victimization in the future. Offenders can discover the real impact their behaviour has had on others and given the opportunity to make amends.

Reparation can also be one element or aim among the many purposes of restorative justice.

Hannah Goodman

RELATED ENTRIES

Criminal Justice Act 2003; Punishment as communication; Restorative justice; Unpaid work.

Key texts and sources

Crown Prosecution Service *Conditional Cautioning* (available online at http://www.cps.gov.uk/publications/others/conditionalcautioning04.html).n.d.

Home Office *Justice and Prisons* (available online at http://www.homeoffice.gov.uk/justice/what-happens-at-court/sentencing/).n.d.

Home Office *Restorative Justice* (available online at http://www.homeoffice.gov.uk/crime-victims/victims/restorative-justice/).n.d.

Together Academy *Reparation Orders* (available online at http://www.together.gov.uk/article.asp?c=169&displayCat=no&aid=1250).n.d.

RESEARCH

Research means finding out, usually by referring to a range of sources. Academic research aims to produce knowledge and to test and develop theories and understanding in accordance with established reliable and valid principles and procedures. Social research addresses questions about the social world, bringing its own particular problems and potentials.

Research and probation

Research has played a key role in the recent history of the Probation Service, when findings have emerged in a particular political climate to be taken up by policymakers to influence practice. Though much criticized and subsequently recanted, Martinson's infamous 'nothing works' study (1974) reviewed over 200 rehabilitative programmes in America and concluded that they made little difference to subsequent reoffending. In England, Brody (1976) also found scant evidence of effectiveness.

This led to two important and related movements: first, a search for evidence that rehabilitation and probation *did* work; and, secondly, a call for more and better research that would provide the desired evidence of effectiveness. This became known as the 'what works' project and was taken up with gusto by HM Inspectorate of Probation in the mid-1990s with the commissioning of a review of effective practice (Underdown 1998), a guide to effective practice (Chapman and Hough 1998) and a guide to evaluation (Merrington and Hine 2001).

The concern for better evidence, combined with the increasing managerialism in the Probation Service, reinforced two major related developments. The first was the introduction of statistical and management information systems, which have become ever more detailed and sophisticated as technology has improved. The second was an increase in the amount and type of evaluation undertaken about the work of the service. At first this was piecemeal, under-taken at the behest of individual services, either by their own in-house researchers or by contracting external researchers. There was also an increase in the evaluation of probation practice commissioned and undertaken by the Home Office, culminating in the Pathfinder programme – part of the Home Office Crime Reduction Programme in 1998, piloting a range of initiatives to develop effective practice.

Some types of research

Evaluation

This is an everyday word with many meanings, all of which have some reference to an assessment of value or worth. In the 'what works' initiative, it is defined as 'finding out whether the programme is achieving its objectives' (Chapman and Hough 1998: 9). In many cases, however, evaluation focuses narrowly on the outcome of reducing offending, with all the difficulties this entails. Evaluation uses the same process and methods as those used in social research and, importantly, the same principles for data integrity apply. Social research methods provide a toolbox, each tool having its function and benefit and to be chosen to meet the purpose and needs of the particular evaluation most appropriately.

Applied research

This research is undertaken when the clear purpose is to inform policy and practice development and decision-making. Evaluation is a specific type of applied research, and good evaluation demands the rigorous application of research standards.

Practitioner research

This is undertaken by or in close collaboration with practitioners about their practice, addressing their own immediate concerns. While often small scale and innovative, such research should be guided by the same principles and standards as larger investigations. Such research is often iterative in informing and developing practice and, in such circumstances, is called action research.

Characteristics of good research

Research should be guided by the core principles of reliability, validity and generalizability:

- *Reliability* describes the extent to which a measure can be relied upon – its dependability. It is about consistency of instruments and methodology. There are established statistical means of measuring reliability in quantitative studies.
- *Validity* is the extent to which the research or instrument measures what it was designed to measure (e.g. does an intelligence test really measure intelligence or the ability to complete intelligence tests?). There is a substantial debate about the discriminatory nature of such instruments, which have frequently been developed using samples of white, middle-class male respondents. A good example of the question of validity particularly relevant for probation evaluations is the use of reconviction data as a proxy measure of reoffending.
- *Generalizability* is about the extent to which findings are applicable to other groups and settings. This often relates to the question of sampling and the choice of cases to include in the research, where the aim is that the cases should be as representative as possible of the wider group being sampled ('the population'). Relevant factors are the size of the sample and the means by which it is chosen. In programme evaluation this frequently comes down to the question: 'will similar results be obtained from future runs of this programme?' The answer is never straightforward. In realistic evaluation terms (Pawson and Tilley 1997), the process is about identifying what works for whom in what circumstances, and generating some explanation which can build and extend theoretical understandings in a way that is generalizable.

Current controversies

Quality of research

Some of the failures of research to provide appropriate evidence of 'what works' are being attributed to the quality of the research itself and a call for more rigour. The 'gold standard' – the use of random control trials – is often not attainable. The Home Office has issued its own standards (Home Office 2004) and a circular (PC 59/2005) requiring an audit of research activity and instructions related to the commissioning and undertaking of research locally.

The qualitative–quantitative question

A debate with a long history and sometimes called a 'paradigm war' is the question of whether qualitative or quantitative methodologies are most appropriate for addressing social research questions. This question links very strongly with what is viewed to be high-quality research. Some advocate experimental or quasi-experimental approaches with a focus on outcome. Others argue that it is of more value to understand the context and mechanisms whereby outcomes are achieved or not, thus generating transferable knowledge. This usually requires a more qualitative methodology. While most researchers now accept that both approaches can be valuable and use the more appropriate for the question being addressed, combining qualitative and quantitative in a mixed methods design, it is quantitative research that is most likely to have an impact on policymakers, with qualitative research often perceived as idiosyncratic or 'subjective'.

The limits of 'what works'

The results of the Pathfinder programmes are now emerging, but are inconclusive, calling the project into question. Some question the rigour of the methodology employed (Merrington and Stanley 2005), while others argue that the search for 'evidence-based practice' is theoretically flawed (McDonald and Gray 2006). All aspects of research rest on a series of assumptions and subjectivities which are more recognized by some research approaches than others. These assumptions relate to the questions that can and should be researched as well as the choice of methodologies employed to address them. The theoretical flaw alluded to is the belief that 'what works' can be identified through sufficient and suitably rigorous research (ideally random-controlled trials). Alternative approaches believe that the complexities of human behaviour mean that there is no simple answer to 'what works' and that understanding the cessation of offending requires a different approach, such as used in 'desistance' research. The 'what works' project has provided useful learning points, but has perhaps reached the limits of what it can reveal.

Jean Hine

RELATED ENTRIES

Effective practice; Evaluation; Reconviction.

Key texts and sources

Brody, S. (1976) *The Effectiveness of Sentencing. Home Office Research Study* 35. London: HMSO.

Chapman, T. and Hough, M. (1998) *Evidence Based Practice: A Guide to Effective Practice*. London: Home Office.

Home Office (2004) *Home Office RDS and YJB Standards for Impact Studies in Correctional Settings* (available online at **http://www.homeoffice.gov. uk/rds/pdfs04/rds_correctional_standards.pdf**).

Martinson, R. (1974) 'What works? Questions and answers about prison reform', *The Public Interest*, 35: 22–54.

McDonald, C. and Gray, M. (2006) 'Pursuing good practice? The limits of evidence based practice', *Journal of Social Work*, 6: 7–20.

Merrington, S. and Hine, J. (2001) *A Handbook for Evaluating Probation Work with Offenders*. London: Home Office (available online at **http:// inspectorates.homeoffice.gov.uk/hmiprobation/ docs/whole.pdf**).

Merrington, S. and Stanley, S. (2005) 'Some thoughts on recent research on pathfinder programmes in the Probation Service', *Probation Journal*, 52: 289–92.

Pawson, R. and Tilley, N. (1997) *Realistic Evaluation*. London: Sage.

Underdown, A. (1998) *Strategies for Effective Offender Supervision*. London: Home Office.

RESETTLEMENT

Beginning inside the prison – some would say even from the first day of sentence – 'resettlement' is the process of reintegration back into the community in a positive and managed way. It continues after release and is the core component of a period of supervision on licence, because it targets the criminogenic risks of an offender and aims to reduce them. Good resettlement should decrease the risk of reoffending and, in the case of dangerous offenders, limit the risks posed.

When an offender has served a custodial sentence and is coming up for release, plans will be made for his or her resettlement into the community. Accommodation and employment, reconnecting with family and friends, continuing work on offending-related behaviours and risks are all part of resettlement. Resettlement into the community is important because a prison sentence breaks linkages, which are essential for successful crime-free living in the wider world. The extent to which a person has had these prior to custody will vary, and it is the role of the offender manager or nominated individual to assess need and risk and create a plan with the offender for his or her release.

The basis of good resettlement is an individual assessment of risk and need – via OASys – together with an agreed plan of action with the offender him or herself, usually recorded in the form of a sentence plan. The resettlement arrangements will take account, first and foremost, of the risk of harm to the public. Risk assessment and the management of offenders subject to multi-agency public protection arrangements (MAPPAs) may lead, for example, to the offender being released subject to particular residence conditions on a licence. The MAPPA status of an offender is actioned by prisons six months prior to release, or at the first parole hearing, whichever is the sooner.

The professional responsible for resettlement of an offender will vary. Currently, prisoners over 21 years old and subject to less than 12 months' custody are released without statutory supervision in the community by the Probation Service. For this group, resettlement plans are made by the releasing prison establishment. Resettlement units in establishments such as Nottingham Prison (winners of a Butler Trust award in 2005) work with individual offenders to try to ensure accommodation and employment or training are secured.

For offenders under 21 years but over 18, and offenders who have served a sentence of over 12 months, Probation Service supervision while on licence is required. This enables resettlement work in prison to be followed up systematically by ongoing work by the Probation Service. The recognition of the importance of this 'through the gate' continuity to the success of resettlement is enshrined in the Custody Plus sentence created in the Criminal Justice Act 2003, although to date not implemented. This sentence will see the Probation Service supervising all post-sentence prisoners regardless of age or length of sentence.

As the Offender Management Model continues to be phased in, increasing numbers of prisoners will have a nominated offender manager (probation worker based in the community) who will be responsible for the end-to end management of the case. By January 2007 the model had been implemented so that high risk of harm cases and persistent and other priority offenders now have offender managers in the community. They are responsible for resettlement, via sentence planning and OASys-based risk assessment.

As outlined above, some offenders will be subject to a period of supervision following release from custody, and this will be under the terms of a licence. The licence should take into account the specific risks and needs in the case and, as part of preparation for release, consideration should be given to the conditions imposed

upon an individual through his or her licence. For example, the basic terms of the licence to 'live where reasonably approved' may be enhanced to state a specific address, such as approved premises. In many cases, the licence will be set by the governor of the releasing establishment, in conjunction with the Probation Service. In cases subject to parole, the setting of additional licence conditions is taken forward via the parole report process, and the conditions are likely to address public protection issues. For example, in appropriate cases an offender may be required to undertake a sex offender treatment programme.

During the late 1990s, the work of the social exclusion unit began to offer evidence to enhance what was already described in work such as Maslow's hierarchy of needs or the triangle of offender needs, and this research now forms the basis of regional reducing reoffending delivery plans (RRDPs). These plans have at least seven pathways: accommodation and support; education, training and employment; health; drugs; finance, benefit and debt; children and families; and attitudes, thinking and behaviour. Each has been shown to have an impact upon social exclusion and, in terms of reoffending, is likely to impact on reoffending if addressed.

RRDPs are lead by the regional offender manager (ROM) and are a means of joining together other government departments, private sector and third sector organizations to meet the needs of offenders better and thereby reduce reoffending. They encourage 'through the gate' delivery of services, because offenders often experience 'assessment fatigue' caused by multiple changes of providers of service, such as basic skills work.

Finally, a word on population management. At time of writing, the prison population is over 80,000. Prison places have been traditionally managed as part of a national estate, with a steady northward movement of prisoners from the south east and London, since those regions are unable to house all their own prisoners. This has implications for resettlement as offenders often spend their pre-release time many miles from home. This may mean limited or no visits from everyone, including their offender manager. Many third sector organizations, such as Lincolnshire Action Trust, which offers specialist services needed for successful resettlement, are geographically based. It can be hard for them to undertake pre-release visits to contribute to the release plan.

This issue of 'closeness to home' has been signalled as a desirable objective for many years. While the Prison Service recognizes the benefits that progress on this would mean for the resettlement agenda, overriding operational considerations, especially at times of prison overcrowding, mean that many prisoners complete their prison sentences in establishments very far from their home area. Little has been done to implement the ideal of 'community prisons' that has been promoted in the past.

With the development of the regional commissioning of services for offenders, the issue of population management in a region has come to the fore. It is not an easy problem to solve, although it is acknowledged that, without its resolution, the management of resettlement continues to be problematic.

Jo Mead

RELATED ENTRIES

Criminogenic needs; Interventions; Licence; Offender management; Parole Board; Public protection; Rehabilitation; Reintegration; Risk assessment and risk management; Social exclusion; Triangle of offender needs.

Key texts and sources

HM Inspectorate of Probation (2001) *Through the Prison Gate* (available online at **http://inspectorates. homeoffice.gov.uk/hmiprisons/thematic-reports1/ prison-gate**).

Maguire, M. (2007) 'The resettlement of ex-prisoners', in L. Gelsthorpe and R. Morgan (eds) *Handbook of Probation.* Cullompton: Willan Publishing.

RESPONSIVITY

Ensuring that all interventions, programmes and activities with offenders are run in a way that is engaging, encourages full participation and takes account of issues of identity and diversity.

The responsivity principle emerged from the research into effective practice for reducing recidivism undertaken in the 1980s and 1990s: the 'what works' research. Chapman and Hough (1998) state that 'Effectiveness research indicates that programmes which match staff and offenders' learning styles and engage the active participation of offenders are likely to be more effective'. In essence, responsivity is about ensuring that all work with offenders is undertaken in a way that enables offenders to be involved, to participate and to learn.

Other commentators make a distinction between general and specific responsivity. For example, Andrews (1995) describes general responsivity as the matching of the styles and strategies of interventions with the learning styles, motivation, aptitudes and ability of offenders. He identifies structured behavioural, social learning and cognitive-behavioural strategies as among the approaches most likely to be effective and highlights the importance of high-quality interpersonal relationships to the intervention process.

Specific responsivity focuses on factors particular to the individual (for example, race and ethnic origin, gender, language, culture and age). Ensuring that interventions and programmes are accessible to and appropriate for all offenders is a key component of anti-discriminatory practice and a consequence of following the responsivity principle. For example, programmes need to be run in ways that are suitable for those with childcare responsibilities, who are in employment, who are not able to read or write, whose first language is not English or who may fear isolation or discrimination in a group setting.

The concept of responsivity has not been as widely researched and theorized as some other aspects of the effective practice initiative. Chapman and Hough (1998) identify a number of factors likely to increase participation in programmes. These include the worker's style, legitimacy and prosocial modelling, recognizing change as a process, setting positive objectives, emphasizing the concrete and practical, and motivational interviewing. The responsivity principle makes it clear that those working with offenders should be able to build positive relationships that encourage motivation, reinforce prosocial attitudes and model anti-criminal approaches.

A link has been made between learning styles and responsivity asserting that the majority of offenders have an activist learning style. This has led to a favouring of interventions and programmes that are active and participatory rather than either formal and instructive or unstructured and reflective. Some commentators, however, question whether the evidence does support the use of learning styles in this way and express concern about the labelling of offenders as non-reflective activists.

A further challenge for practitioners is to combine the principle of responsivity with the demands of programme integrity and the need to ensure that interventions are delivered as intended by their creators. Ensuring that interventions take account of the motivation, aptitudes and abilities of offenders may require making changes to planned and structured sessions.

The responsivity principle also has implications for the training and deployment of staff. Good practice requires that staff have the skills needed to develop motivation and to enable offenders to commence and complete programmes and other interventions. Additionally, it is argued that understanding the skills, interests and styles of workers allows for the more effective matching of offenders with staff.

In conclusion, responsivity is a reminder that positive change and a reduction in reoffending are most likely if people are motivated and encouraged to participate in appropriate and relevant programmes. Such interventions and programmes require staff who are able to build constructive working relationships with offenders and who respond well to issues of discrimination and diversity.

Jane Dominey

RELATED ENTRIES

Cognitive-behavioural; Diversity; Effective practice; Learning styles; Legitimacy; Motivation.

Key texts and sources

Andrews, D. (1995) 'The psychology of criminal conduct and effective treatment', in J. McGuire (ed.) *What Works: Reducing Reoffending. Guidelines from Research and Practice.* Chichester: Wiley.

Annison, J. (2006) 'Style over substance: a review of the evidence base for the use of learning styles in probation', *Criminology and Criminal Justice*, 6: 239–57.

Chapman, T. and Hough, M. (1998) *Evidence Based Practice: A Guide to Effective Practice.* London: Home Office.

Cherry, S. (2005) *Transforming Behaviour: Pro-social Modelling in Practice.* Cullompton: Willan Publishing.

Kennedy, S. (2001) 'Treatment responsivity: reducing recidivism by enhancing treatment effectiveness', in L. Motiuk and R. Serin (eds) *Compendium 2000 on Effective Correctional Programming.* Ottawa: Correctional Services Canada (available online at http://www.csc-scc.gc.ca/text/rsrch/compendium/2000/chap_5_e.shtml).

RESTORATIVE JUSTICE

Approaches that aim to hold offenders accountable for their offences while seeking to repair the harm visited upon victims by the commission of the offence.

'Restorative justice' is seen by Marshall as 'centrally about *restoration*: restoration of the victim, restoration of the offender to a law-abiding life, restoration of the damage caused by crime to the community' (1999: 7), while Dignan (2002) proposes that its key attributes are the principle of 'inclusivity', the balancing of interests, non-coercive practice and a problem-solving orientation. Restorative justice differs from 'traditional' justice in so far as it is 'victim driven' or 'victim focused'.

Restorative justice approaches

A variety of practices and approaches can be described as 'restorative justice'. Each puts an emphasis on reparation or making amends, and outcomes (or agreements) include written or verbal apologies, financial restitution or unpaid work for the victim or the community. Approaches differ in the relative significance placed upon the victim, offender and 'community' in that process. They also differ in terms of their relationships to the formal criminal justice process, some having their basis in legislation while others – because they are predicated upon principles of voluntarism and non-coercion – operate more informally. The legislative context and location in the criminal justice system have a bearing on how restorative justice initiatives operate and on whom they are targeted. The extent to which they represent a 'mainstream' response to offending differs across jurisdictions, though they typically remain relatively marginalized in relation to traditional criminal justice processes.

Victim offender mediation and reparation, originating in US Mennonite communities, involves skilled mediators facilitating an exchange between victim and offender, aimed at providing an explanation for the offence, enabling the offender to appreciate the impact of the offence and reaching an agreement as to how the offender will repair the harm. It most typically operates semi-independently of criminal justice agencies, dealing with juvenile offenders and with relatively minor offences.

Family group conferences, which originated in New Zealand, seek to involve a wider constituency (including 'supporters' of both the victim and the offender) in discussion of the offence and decision-making about the actions to be undertaken by the offender to make amends. It is used in a number of countries, including Australia, where it was initially police led and based on 'reintegrative shaming'.

Similar in many respects to conferencing, circle sentencing was first developed in the Yukon, Canada, based on the traditional sanctioning and community healing processes of First Nation people in Canada and American Indians in the USA. The circle may include, in addition to the offender and victim, family and friends of both, criminal justice and social services personnel and interested members of the community. Speaking in turn through a symbolic 'talking piece', members of the circle seek to gain an understanding of the offence and to identify how the affected parties can be healed and further crimes prevented.

Finally, community panels of various types have been established in a number of jurisdictions. These typically involve trained members of the community deciding upon the course of action to be taken by the offender to make reparation for the offence.

Some restorative justice approaches – for example, police-led conferencing – have been criticized for their failure to take account of the economic, personal and social context in which the offending occurred. Concern has also been expressed that offenders may be stigmatized by participation in some types of restorative justice processes and that they may be susceptible to 'net-widening'. Moreover, the relevance of difference and diversity to restorative justice practices has largely been unexplored.

Restorative justice in the UK

In the UK there has been growing political interest in the potential of restorative justice, though provision is currently uneven and disparate. Reparation orders and youth panels were introduced for juvenile offenders in England and Wales by the Crime and Disorder Act 1998, while referral orders were brought in under the Youth Justice and Criminal Evidence Act 1999. The latter enable young people pleading guilt to a first conviction to be referred to a youth offending panel, who will agree a contract with the young person that is intended to include an element of reparation to the victim or to the wider community and that will be supervised by the youth offending team. However, the level of victim participation in these panels has been found to be low, and reparation in the context of both referral and reparation orders (the latter imposed by magistrates) more commonly takes the form of unpaid work for the community rather than direct reparation to the victim of the offence (Crawford and Newburn, 2002; Dignan 2002).

The introduction of family group conferencing in England and Wales has been *ad hoc*, non-statutory and primarily police driven. The first such scheme, based on the Australian model, was established by Thames Valley, where restorative cautioning was introduced as an alternative to the traditional cautioning system for juveniles who had committed minor offences. Most conferences were not attended by the victim and most agreed outcomes involved a written or oral apology, rather than financial restitution or unpaid work. The approach may have been susceptible to 'net-widening' since it represented a change to existing processes rather than an alternative to prosecution.

An evaluation of practice in England and Wales found a tendency to over-rely on community reparation and a low level of direct involvement of victims in meeting with their offenders (Wilcox and Hoyle 2004). However, in restorative justice initiatives established by the Home Office – often with more serious offences and with adults serving prison or community sentences – levels of victim participation were found to be high, especially in cases involving young offenders (Shapland *et al.* 2006).

In Scotland, restorative justice options have tended to be small in scale and located towards the lower end of the spectrum of offence and offender seriousness, though they are now being introduced more widely as part of the government's response to 'anti-social behaviour' and youth crime. In Northern Ireland, by contrast, restorative justice has been introduced on a legislated basis (via a newly established Youth Conference Service) as the primary method for dealing with young offenders.

Evidence of effectiveness

Proponents of restorative justice argue that it is inappropriate to restrict assessment of its effectiveness to measures of recidivism since it embraces broader aims. The evidence base for restorative justice is still rather rudimentary and, overall, the findings in relation to recidivism are inconclusive. However, such approaches have been shown to produce other benefits for offenders, victims and the community. For example, most cases involve an agreement for reparation being reached and most of these are subsequently fulfilled; levels of victim satisfaction are generally high; and most offenders are satisfied with how they have been dealt with, viewing both the process and outcomes as fair.

How offenders experience restorative justice approaches and how well they are able to promote their reintegration in the community may be related to their success in reducing recidivism, and initiatives that deal with more serious offences may be more effective in this respect. In the UK, public support for the use of restorative justice appears high, especially in relation to relatively minor offences and offenders. However, victims of more serious offences appear to benefit more from restorative justice processes, indicating an apparent tension between public tolerance and what victims may have to gain.

Gill McIvor

RELATED ENTRIES

Community justice; Diversity; Mediation; Punishment (aims and justifications); Punishment as communication; Reparation; Unpaid work; Victims.

Key texts and sources

Crawford, A. and Newburn, T. (2002) 'Recent developments in restorative justice for young people in England and Wales: community participation and representation', *British Journal of Criminology*, 42: 476–95.

Dignan, J. (2002) 'Reparation orders', in B. Williams (ed.) *Reparation and Victim-focused Social Work. Research Highlights in Social Work* 42. London: Jessica Kingsley.

Johnstone, G. (ed.) (2003) *A Restorative Justice Reader*. Cullompton: Willan Publishing.

Johnstone, G. and Van Ness, H. (eds) (2006) *Handbook of Restorative Justice*. Cullompton: Willan Publishing.

Marshall, T.F. (1999) *Restorative Justice: An Overview*. London: Home Office Research Development and Statistics Directorate (available online at http://www.homeoffice.gov.uk/rds/pdfs/occ-resjus.pdf).

Shapland, J., Atkinson, A., Atkinson, H., Chapman, B., Colledge, E., Dignan, J., Howes, M., Johnstone, J., Robinson, G. and Sorsby, A. (2006) *Restorative Justice in Practice – Findings from the Second Phase of the Evaluation of Three Schemes*. Findings 274. London: Home Office (available online at http://www.homeoffice.gov.uk/rds/pdfs06/r274.pdf).

Wilcox, A. and Hoyle, C. (2004) *The National Evaluation of the Youth Justice Board's Restorative Justice Projects*. London: Youth Justice Board (available online at http://www.yjb.gov.uk/Publications/).

RISK ASSESSMENT AND RISK MANAGEMENT

Risk assessment is the assessment of the likelihood and impact or harm of (re)offending; risk management is the reduction of the likelihood and/or impact of the risk of offending.

Risk assessment and risk management are now core tasks for the Probation Service and for the National Offender Management Service (NOMS). This includes various risks, but most importantly the risk of reoffending and the risk of harm an offender might cause. Throughout the 1990s, the Probation Service was tasked with assessing the likelihood of reoffending and targeting its interventions, programmes and resources at those most 'at risk' of offending. More recently this focus on the risk of reoffending has been subsumed under a broader requirement to deliver 'public protection' and to reduce risks to victims and the public through the supervision of offenders. Integral to this work is the accurate assessment and the effective management of risk.

Traditionally, there have been two approaches to risk assessment:

1. *Actuarial*: based on statistical techniques for assessing probability, where a probability 'score' (of reoffending or of the risk of harm) is usually produced. Actuarial techniques, using 'static' factors, are the most reliable, but are based on aggregates of the population and have limitations in predicting the riskiness of individuals.

2. *Clinical*: based on professional judgement and in-depth interviewing. This can be very helpful in refining the scores of actuarial tools in the light of additional knowledge and in planning interventions. Clinical techniques, using 'dynamic' factors, are generally less reliable, due mostly to the bias and error of the assessor.

Most recently, structured, holistic assessment instruments combining actuarial and clinical techniques have been developed (OASys, for example, combines the actuarial tool Offender Group Reconviction Score (OGRS) with structured interviewing and assessment techniques). However, the limitations of risk assessment and prediction are still much debated, and the difficulties in accurately predicting the risk of reoffending and serious harm can be acute. Two types of inaccuracy can result: false-positives and false-negatives.

False-positive assessments are those which predict that an offender will reoffend but the offender subsequently does not. This error can result in offenders being detained longer in prison than necessary or being subject to restrictive and intrusive supervision in the community.

False-negative assessments are those which predict that an offender will not reoffend but the offender subsequently does. This can result in offenders being paroled and then reoffending quickly and sometimes dangerously in the community, and offenders receiving less supervision and less intensive programmes than they should. As importantly, it can, in extreme cases, result in further victims, harm to the public and disrepute for practitioners and their agencies.

Risk assessment is not an accurate science. Most risk assessment tools have an average accuracy rate of 60–70 per cent. (A tool with 60 per cent accuracy for predicting reoffending when applied to a particular individual has a chance of being correct 6 times out of 10.) There are a number of other factors that affect the accuracy and reliability of risk assessment.

Risk assessors may be prone to error and bias in their judgements, by over-identifying with some risks and being more tolerant of others;

and tools may not be used with integrity over time. Short cuts in assessment can lead to error. In addition, the risky behaviours requiring assessment and prediction are often prone to low base rates – they occur relatively infrequently and are therefore difficult to predict statistically.

These difficulties with risk assessment and its accuracy have resulted in an intense ethical debate about its use in criminal justice. However, it is now firmly rooted in the work of NOMS, and much effort has been expended on pursuing more accurate risk assessment tools. The Risk Management Authority in Scotland has helpfully rated tools in terms of predictive accuracy and reliability. While risk assessment tools have formalized the process and increased accuracy, tools that produce scores may require some revision in the light of further information on offending behaviour, social context and victim-targeting available to the risk assessor.

Risk management cannot guarantee to prevent risk. It can only attempt to reduce the likelihood that risky behaviours (in this case offending) will occur, or reduce the impact of those behaviours if they take place (e.g. the level of harm caused by the offence). Harm reduction rather than elimination of risk is the key aim. While it is now generally accepted that victim rights and public protection will usually outweigh offender rights, risk management should be just, proportionate and fair. Risk management plans draw on a range of interventions, including accredited programmes which attempt to reduce reoffending. Such interventions concentrate on 'criminogenic needs' – risk factors that directly contribute to the offender's offending. Anti-social thinking patterns are also targeted, and offenders are encouraged to identify and change problematic behaviours.

Some risk management plans will also aim to reduce the opportunities to offend – for example, by using restrictive conditions that prevent an offender from approaching particular places, being out beyond curfew hours or from re-approaching known victims. For very serious offenders intensive risk management packages are delivered (see Multi-agency public protection arrangements (MAPPAs)). These are often delivered by agencies working together – for example, police and probation – and may comprise satellite tracking of offenders, supervised accommodation in a hostel, intensive treatment programmes and high levels of monitoring and reporting. Risk management plans should be well matched to the risk factors presented and delivered as intended. Risk assessment should be an ongoing process throughout the period of contact with the offender, and staff should respond to escalating risk and deteriorating behaviour quickly. Risk management plans that 'fail' can result in further offending. Where this results in death or injury, the case may be investigated through a serious further offence review.

Risk management plans that are well balanced between restrictive conditions, support to the offender and with a treatment component tend to work best. Where possible, good practice recommends that offenders are actively engaged in their risk management plan and should discuss it with their supervisor. However, in some instances this may not be possible because it will compromise the safety of others (potential victims) or undermine risk management by revealing surveillance or monitoring processes. Again, the delivery of risk management plans requires balance, integrity of delivery and responsiveness to changing circumstances.

Hazel Kemshall

RELATED ENTRIES

Actuarialism; Assessment instruments and systems; Dangerousness; Multi-agency public protection arrangements (MAPPAs); Public protection; Risk of harm; Risk society.

Key texts and sources

Kemshall, H. (2003) *Understanding Risk in Criminal Justice.* Buckingham: Open University Press.
Kemshall, H. and Wood, J. (2007) 'High-risk offenders and public protection', in L. Gelsthorpe and R. Morgan (eds) *Handbook of Probation.* Cullompton: Willan Publishing.
Risk Management Authority (2005) *Risk Assessment Tools Evaluation Directory (RATED)* (available online at www.RMAscotland.gov.uk).
The CD-ROM, *Risk of Harm Guidance and Training Resources* (commissioned from De Montfort University by NOMS), is available through prison/probation intranets.

RISK OF HARM

One of a number of key concepts central to issues of public protection, risk of harm refers to the likelihood that an offence causing physical or psychological harm may occur. It is often used interchangeably with 'risk of serious harm', although they should have different definitions, relating to the impact or degree of harm of the criminal behaviour.

The assessment of risk of harm has become a cornerstone of sentencing and public protection activity. 'Risk of harm' and 'risk of serious harm' are important entries in the increasingly large lexicon of risk (risk of self-harm, risk management planning, risk to children, etc.). Clarity of definition is essential and analysis must be specific (e.g. who is at risk, under what circumstances, what are the likely triggers and what the likely behaviour?). These are the prerequisites of risk management, planning and defensible public protection measures.

The use of the term in official reports, legislation and policy does not provide the necessary clarity. For example, in their serious further offence inquiry into the murder of John Monckton by Damien Hanson and Elliot White, who were under probation supervision, HM Probation Inspectorate defined risk of harm as the 'probability that [the offender] may behave in a manner that causes physical or psychological harm (or real fear of it) to others'. Yet OASys uses 'risk of harm' when the likelihood that a relevant offence will occur is assessed as low, and 'risk of serious harm' when this likelihood is medium to very high. This confuses the probability that an offence will occur with the potential impact or degree of harmfulness of the offence.

In the revised Chapter 8 of OASys (Home Office 2006), the references are all to serious harm, which is defined as 'an event which is life-threatening and/or traumatic, and from which recovery, whether physical or psychological, can be expected to be difficult or impossible'. This definition is appropriate to the public protection and victim protection duties of the probation, prison and police services.

The Criminal Justice Act 1991 (s. 1[2](b)) provided for a custodial sentence 'to protect the public from serious harm' where a violent or sexual offence had been committed, while s. 2[2](b) allowed the court to impose a longer than commensurate custodial sentence 'where necessary to protect the public'. This theme of public protection against serious harm is continued in the Criminal Justice and Court Services Act 2000 (s. 67) through the establishment of multi-agency public protection arrangements (MAPPAs). The Criminal Justice Act 2003 (s. 224) contains its own definition. Here '"serious harm" means death or serious personal injury, whether physical or psychological'. The indeterminate sentence of imprisonment for public protection, created by this Act, can only be imposed if the court 'is of the opinion that there is a significant risk to members of the public of serious harm occasioned by the commission by him of further specified offences' (and for which the offender cannot be sentenced to life imprisonment).

Gill Mackenzie

RELATED ENTRIES

Assessment; Criminal Justice Act 2003; Dangerousness; Extended sentencing; HM Inspectorate of Probation; Multi-agency public protection arrangements (MAPPAs); Offender Assessment System (OASys); Public protection; Risk assessment and risk management; Risk society; Serious further offences.

Key texts and sources

Home Office (2006) *OASys Manual* (PC 36/2006). London: Home Office.

Kemshall, H. (2003) *Understanding Risk in Criminal Justice.* Buckingham: Open University Press.

Kemshall, H. and Wood, J. (2007) 'High-risk offenders and public protection', in L. Gelsthorpe and R. Morgan (eds) *Handbook of Probation.* Cullompton: Willan Publishing.

Prins, H. (1999) *Will They Do it Again? Risk Assessment and Management in Criminal Justice and Psychiatry.* London: Routledge.

Scott, P. (1977) 'Assessing dangerousness in criminals', *British Journal of Psychiatry*, 131: 127–42.

HM Inspectorate of Probation independent reviews (including Damien Hanson and Elliot White, and Anthony Rice) are available online at **http://inspectorates.homeoffice.gov.uk/hmiprobation/inspect_reports/serious-further-offences/**. The CD-ROM, *Risk of Harm Guidance and Training Resources* (commissioned from De Montfort University by NOMS), is available through prison/probation intranets.

RISK PRINCIPLE

The risk principle states that offenders should be provided with supervision and treatment levels proportionate to the level of perceived risk and the likelihood of reoffending.

Together with the criminogenic need and responsivity principles, the risk principle is part of a core assessment model informing a range of interventions that were developed as part of the 'what works' (effective practice) initiative. The risk principle states that the higher the risk of reoffending, the more intensive and extended the supervision programme should be. The level of 'dosage' depends on the level of assessed risk. The need to quantify and assess the level of risk accurately prompted the introduction and development of assessment instruments. Risk was to be assessed both as the risk of reoffending and risk of harm to the public. Two main assessment tools emerged: the Offender Group Reconviction Score (OGRS), which depends on static factors, and the Offender Assessment System (OASys), which incorporates OGRS as well as assessing dynamic factors. The development and prominence of these tools were also driven by the increasing sophistication of information technology.

OGRS used quantitative analysis to compile statistical tables based on an 'analysis between prior history and subsequent rates of conviction in a large sample of offenders' (Bottoms *et al.* 2001: 7–8). The ACE assessment tool (and ASSET for young offenders) were precursors of OASys. These assessment tools converged with the government agenda, after 1997, of targeting scarce resources where they were deemed to be most effective, resulting in the slogan 'resources follow risk'. This was to be the principle of resource allocation in which offenders were categorized into a number of levels of risk, from high to low.

The Offender Management Model is similarly influenced by these principles. Once again developments in information technology (IT) strongly assisted in driving the agenda forward: C-NOMIS is an integrated IT system designed to ensure that information follows the offender throughout the 'seamless sentence'. The risk principle remains the axis around which resource allocation in the Probation Service revolves.

The prominence of the risk principle raises a number of ethical issues. It may subvert the sentencing principle of proportionality. Thus an offender may be sentenced, not in proportion to the seriousness of the offence, but in proportion to assessed risk (see Punishment (aims and justifications)). Risk is a socially constructed and subjective concept and assessment may also be influenced by a number of other factors. False-positives (those assessed as high risk who turn out to be 'safe') and negatives (those who commit serious offences having been assessed as lesser risk) may result from the incorrect input of data or the bias of the supervising officer, and this may result in differential sentencing and resource allocation. Such errors reflect the shortcomings of the assessment instruments, which cannot predict the behaviour of an individual; they assign the individual to a group with a determinate probability of reconviction, but any individual in that group may not conform with that group's characteristics in terms of future behaviour.

Discriminatory factors may also have an impact on the assessment of risk. Individuals diagnosed as suffering from mental illness may be subject to an incorrect assessment based on perceptions of dangerousness and risk. Gender may also be a factor. Women offenders who conform to a stereotype of passivity and contrition may be judged to deserve help; those who do not conform in this way may be viewed as deserving of punishment and to pose a greater risk. Race, religion and culture may also affect the construction of risk and result in incorrect assessments – particularly so given that the assessment tools are based on research that is based largely on white male offenders within the specific culture of North America.

The label 'high risk' in itself may be discriminatory and excluding. Sex offenders, for example, because of the nature of their offences, raise major questions about the balance between risk assessment and human rights. This is especially important at a time when public protection work by relevant agencies is better co-ordinated than it has ever been.

Working in a 'risk society' has placed increased responsibilities on the criminal justice system and widened its remit, putting pressure on practitioners. 'Scientific' tools cannot produce certainty. There is a danger that the focus on risk across the spectrum excludes or marginalizes other important concepts, such as proportionality in sentencing, desistance from offending, the rehabilitation and reintegration of offenders and issues around diversity. The voices of practitioners, victims and offenders may also be in danger of remaining unheard.

David Phillips

RELATED ENTRIES

Assessment; Assessment instruments and systems; Criminogenic needs; Diversity; Effective practice; Offender management; Responsivity; Risk assessment and risk management; Risk society.

Key texts and sources

Bottoms, A., Gelsthorpe, L. and Rex, S. (eds) (2001) *Community Penalties: Change and Challenges.* Cullompton: Willan Publishing.
Kemshall, H. (2003) *Understanding Risk in Criminal Justice.* Buckingham: Open University Press.
Robinson, G. (2003) 'Risk and risk assessment', in W.H. Chui and M. Nellis (eds) *Moving Probation Forward: Evidence, Arguments and Practice.* London: Pearson Longman.

RISK SOCIETY

Within the field of criminal justice, the 'risk society' is manifested as a series of intersecting and overlapping trends, tendencies and techniques, centred on the assessment and management of risk, which shape the practices of agencies and practitioners.

Beck (1992) introduced the concept of the 'risk society' in his depiction of late twentieth-century modernity as beset by the unforeseen and unanticipated impacts of technological advances and innovations (pollution, nuclear waste and the proliferation of weapons of mass destruction and so forth).

Discourses of risk can be seen as operating at *political, organizational* and *practical* levels. Some link the emergence of pervasive notions of risk with the rise of neoliberal politics. Politicians, increasingly risk averse and fearful of resultant media criticism, have introduced programmes of micro-management aimed in particular at various sites of risk. Such programmes are closely related to the dominance in neoliberal discourse of managerialism, with its core beliefs in centralization, bureaucratization and the replacement of discursive professional activities with non-narrative technical solutions.

The changes in probation have been profound, resulting in a hierarchical structure in which organizational success is identified as much in terms of procedural compliance as with its actual impact on offending. Practice has been reshaped, with assessment increasingly organized around risk assessment instruments. The heavy pressure on practitioners to complete this lengthy assessment tool creates a situation similar to the problem in aviation of increased technology in the cockpit, with staff spending too much time 'heads down' and too little time 'heads up' with their eyes on what is actually happening in the real world. Other manifestations of the risk society include increasing organizational defensiveness in anticipation of litigation – and financial penalty and/or compensation should the organization be found to have taken insufficient care to guard against error. There is an associated emphasis on citizens rights vis-à-vis formal organizations.

Within criminal justice, the notion of risk as a way of categorizing and discussing individuals can also lead to the treatment of risk categories as being real entities in themselves, rather than as technical shorthand for the wide variety of circumstances, problems and issues which are found in varying permutations and with varying degrees of complexity in the lives of those the Probation Service works with. It is disturbing to find descriptions in pre-sentence reports of offenders being, for example, of 'medium risk of reoffending with a low-medium risk of serious harm'. Using such categories to convey information to sentencers seems fraught with interpretive difficulties and also serves to decontextualize the messy reality of life into what, superficially, appear to be 'scientific' categories.

More generally, as Hudson (2003) argues, the salience of risk in criminal justice may adversely affect the likelihood and possibility of justice. Feely and Simon (1994) have also addressed the emergence of actuarialism. The reduction of offenders to such statistical ciphers seems to have contributed to the thinking underlying the redesignation of probation in terms of 'offender management' whereby issues of justice, social exclusion and rehabilitation give way to a technicized approach in which abstract terms provide the rationale for action.

Mark Oldfield

RELATED ENTRIES

Actuarialism; Assessment instruments and systems; Managerialism; Social exclusion.

Key texts and sources

Beck, U. (1992) *Risk Society: Towards a New Modernity.* London: Sage.
Feeley, M. and Simon, J. (1994) 'Actuarial justice: the emerging new criminal law', in D. Nelken (ed.) *The Futures of Criminology.* London: Sage.
Hudson, B. (2003) *Justice in the Risk Society.* London: Sage.
Oldfield, M. (2002) *From Welfare to Risk: Discourse, Power and Politics in the Probation Service. Issues in Crime and Community Justice Monograph* 1. London: Napo.
O'Malley, P. (1992) 'Risk, power and crime prevention', *Economy and Society*, 21: 252–75.

S

SCOTLAND: CRIMINAL JUSTICE SOCIAL WORK

Scotland has had its own distinctive criminal justice system since before the Act of Union in 1707. Since 1999, crime and justice legislation has been devolved to the Scottish Parliament. The Scottish Executive Justice Department plays the lead role. Crime and justice have moved centre-stage in Scottish political life, and a cascade of consultation papers, initiatives and bills has ensued, some of them heralding fundamental changes.

Historical context

Scottish arrangements for supervising offenders in the community have been distinctive since their beginning. Probation appears to have begun in Scotland in 1905 as a Glasgow-based pilot scheme inspired by earlier American initiatives. Rather than being located within charitable or religious organizations, the Glasgow scheme was police based, involving the appointment of plain-clothes officers to assist magistrates' sentencing deliberations and to supervise offenders in the community. Concern about high rates of imprisonment (particularly for fine default) in Glasgow and in Scotland was the stimulus for this innovation.

The Probation of Offenders (Scotland) Act 1931 signalled a shift towards the emerging notion of 'treatment' through social casework and prohibited the appointment of police officers as probation staff. The Act also established local probation committees and a Central Probation Council to advise the Secretary of State.

Despite some early successes and the extension of powers to use probation in 1949, the courts were reluctant to use probation for adults. Although the service expanded considerably in the 1960s and acquired new throughcare responsibilities, the Scottish probation services were disbanded following the Social Work (Scotland) Act 1968. This was partly because the low numbers of adults on probation meant that separate probation services would have been unsustainable in some areas (once juveniles became the responsibility of the new generic social work departments) and partly because probation officers were among the best trained social workers and, accordingly, were much needed in the new departments.

The 1970s and 1980s represented a period of comparative neglect for probation in Scotland. Although community service emerged as a credible disposal (after a successful pilot scheme), the numbers of probation orders declined and, much to the consternation of some sheriffs, criminal justice work became a low priority in many hard-pressed social work departments struggling to cope with ever-expanding childcare and protection work. To remedy this and to address a penal crisis resulting from prison overcrowding, the Scottish Office introduced 100 per cent central funding for most criminal justice social work services in 1991. The first National Objectives and Standards (NOSs) were issued at this time.

The focus of the initial NOSs was on reducing the unnecessary use of custody by promoting community disposals in general and direct alternatives to custody in particular. Restoring credibility was clearly linked to developing approaches to supervision that were effective in reducing reoffending. Indeed, a practice guidance supplement to the original NOSs succinctly outlined the evidence about 'what works?', signalling a shift towards a 'responsibility model' (Paterson and Tombs 1998) which recognized that offenders should be held accountable for their choices, albeit that these choices should be understood within their social context. In most local authorities, specialist teams and new management structures were created to drive forward the reforms and the (re-)development of practice. However, in Scotland, alongside this focus on effective practice to 'responsibilize' offenders and reduce reoffending, the welfare tradition proved durable and was progressively recast, in policy terms, in an ongoing concern to minimize the social exclusion of offenders.

By the late 1990s, research was beginning to suggest that, although the 100 per cent funding initiative had driven up standards and, with them, the use made of probation and community service, there had been no discernible impact on the rate of imprisonment. At the same time, earlier changes in release arrangements, alongside other social and political pressures, led to a shift in policy towards risk, public protection and reducing reoffending rather than reducing the use of imprisonment. The 1998 consultation paper – *The Tough Option* – declared that 'our paramount aim is public safety' . The consultation was, however, mainly concerned with the reorganization of services and led to the establishment of 11 'groupings' of local authorities in 2002.

Recent developments and future prospects

During the 1990s and especially since devolution, there have been many new initiatives, new policy statements and new pieces of legislation. Scotland has seen the introduction of supervised attendance orders (as an alternative to prison for fine defaulters and, in some cases, as an alternative to fines); the introduction of restriction of liberty orders (involving electronic monitoring); the piloting of drug treatment and testing orders and of specialist drugs courts; the piloting of a Domestic Abuse Court; the piloting of new youth courts for 15–18-year-olds involved in persistent offending; and the establishment of a Risk Management Authority (with a wide remit around policy advice, research, developing best practice, standard-setting, accreditation both of tools and of risk assessors, and approving specific risk management plans in serious cases). There

has also been much debate about the imprisonment of women, largely stimulated by a series of suicides in Scotland's only women's prison, Corton Vale. More recently, policy attention and debate have focused on the release arrangements for prisoners; the Scottish Executive has recently published proposals which would mean that anyone serving more than 14 days in custody will be subject to some form of post-release supervision.

Attempts to develop evidence-based practice have resulted in the introduction in 1993 of a Masters degree (an advanced social work professional qualification) in criminal justice social work, the establishment in 1999 of the Criminal Justice Social Work Development Centre for Scotland, the development from 1998 of the Getting Best Results Initiative (which brings together stakeholders to lead, direct and co-ordinate the development of practice) and, more recently, the establishment of an Effective Practice Unit in the Community Justice Division of the Justice Department. In 2006 the Scottish Accreditation Panel for Offender Programmes was also established, replacing earlier separate systems for prisons and social work. Many of these developments are broadly similar to those in England and Wales, although the Scottish approach, thus far, has been less centralized and prescriptive, relying on the co-operation of the local authorities and other stakeholders. Moreover, it has perhaps been more inclusive in its consideration of the evidence on which practice should be based. Thus, for example, while 'what works' studies have greatly informed developments, the emerging evidence about desistance and how best to support this process has also found a receptive audience.

The most significant changes for probation in Scotland since the 1968 Act are now being enacted. These changes were signalled in the 2003 parliamentary election when the Scottish Labour Party proposed to establish a single correctional agency combining prisons and criminal justice social work. In the Labour–Liberal Democrat coalition agreement which followed the election, this position was moderated and a consultation ensued. After a sometimes heated debate in which the Convention of Scottish Local Authorities argued that no case for change had been made while the First Minister insisted that 'the status quo [was] not an option', a compromise emerged, later enshrined in the Management of Offenders (Scotland) Act 2005. In line with the Act's provisions, eight Community Justice Authorities (CJAs) were established (with effect from April 2006) to facilitate strategic planning across areas and between partner agencies, with some agencies (including the local authorities, police, courts, prosecution, prisons, Victim Support Scotland, health boards and relevant voluntary agencies) having a statutory basis for their involvement in the partnership. In the first year their primary responsibility was to produce a strategic area plan in consultation with partner bodies. Thereafter their responsibilities will include the allocation of resources and the monitoring of criminal justice social work services.

The CJAs' local plans must be approved by a National Advisory Body on Offender Management, chaired by the Justice Minister, which was also established in March 2006 with a membership consisting of representatives from the Convention of Scottish Local Authorities, the Association of Directors of Social Work, the voluntary sector, Victim Support Scotland, Association of Chief Police Officers in Scotland (ACPOS), the Parole Board, the Risk Management Authority and a range of experts. Its role is to develop and review the national strategy for managing offenders, to provide advice to enhance offender management practice and to support the work of the new CJAs. The first National Strategy on Offender Management (Scottish Executive 2006) was published in May 2006. Apart from its predictable focus on end-to-end offender management, there is a strong and welcome reassertion of the social inclusion agenda but a worrying silence on reducing the use of custody.

Therefore, while recent policy developments signal a closer role for central government and other agencies in determining the strategic direction of offender management in Scotland, Scottish policy has, against strongly voiced opposition, stopped short of the organizational changes brought about through the creation of the National Offender Management Service in England and Wales. That said, while Scotland still retains aspects of its different probation and social work traditions, there is also evidence of significant policy transfer from south of the border. How this will play out within the new arrangements and after the 2007 Scottish parliamentary election remains to be seen.

Fergus McNeill and Gill McIvor

RELATED ENTRIES

Desistance; Effective practice; Scottish courts and sanctions; Social work.

Key texts and sources

McIvor, G. and McNeill, F. (2007) 'Probation in Scotland: past, present and future', in L. Gelsthorpe and R. Morgan (eds) *Handbook of Probation.* Cullompton: Willan Publishing.

McNeill, F. and Whyte, B. (2007) *Reducing Reoffending: Social Work and Community Justice in Scotland.* Cullompton: Willan Publishing.

Paterson, F. and Tombs, J. (1998) *Social Work and Criminal Justice. Volume 1. The Policy Context.* Edinburgh: HMSO.

Robinson, G. and McNeill, F. (2004) 'Purposes matter: the ends of probation', in G. Mair (ed.) *What Matters in Probation.* Cullompton: Willan Publishing.

Scottish Executive (2006) *Reducing Reoffending: National Strategy for the Management of Offenders.* Edinburgh: Scottish Executive.

CJScotland (**www.cjscotland.org.uk**) provides a wealth of information about current developments. The Criminal Justice Social Work Development Centre for Scotland's website (**www.cjsw.ac.uk**) contains a wide range of resources, including the National Standards.

SCOTLAND: YOUTH JUSTICE

The youth justice system in Scotland deals with young people, aged 8–18 years, involved in offending. Decision-making is undertaken by children's hearings and, to a lesser extent, by criminal courts.

The Children (Scotland) Act 1995 provides the current statutory framework for the system of youth justice in Scotland: young people subject to compulsory measures (supervision) because of offending are designated 'looked-after children' and 'children in need'.

The children's hearing system is based on the philosophy of justice advocated by the Kilbrandon Committee (1964) which recommended an extra-judicial system to replace juvenile courts. This is a unified system for dealing with young people above the age of criminal responsibility (8 years) alleged to have committed criminal offences, and for all children considered in need of care and protection.

The system separates the functions of adjudication and disposal. The criminal process has two fundamental functions: the adjudication of the legal facts – whether or not an offence has been established beyond reasonable doubt – and how best to deal with the young person once the facts have been established. The latter is the responsibility of a children's hearing. Consequently, a hearing has no power to determine questions of innocence or guilt. This remains the responsibility of the criminal court.

The Lord Advocate retains powers to prosecute all young people between 8 and 16 years in criminal courts under the Criminal Procedures (Scotland) Act 1995. No child under 13 can appear in court without the explicit direction of the Lord Advocate and no young person aged 13–16 can appear without the explicit direction of the procurator fiscal in consultation with the Children's Reporter. Categories of offences considered for prosecution relate to serious offences (cases of murder, rape and armed robbery), some offences under road traffic legislation for those over the age of 14, which can result in disqualification, and offences committed with an adult. Summary courts can refer young people under the age of 17 years 6 months back to a children's hearing for advice or disposal. Fewer than 100 children under 16 were prosecuted in Scottish courts in 2005.

In 2004 the Scottish government established a pilot youth court as part of the adult criminal court to deal with young people aged 16–17 (and 15 year olds in exceptional cases) following Council of Europe criticism that this age group was routinely dealt with by adult criminal courts.

A children's hearing is a tribunal consisting of three lay panel members (at least one man and one woman), one of whom acts as chairperson. Panel members are trained members of the community appointed by the First Minister initially for up to five years. Children's hearings are usually held close to the young person's home area with the intention that decisions are taken by members with personal knowledge of the child's community. The procedure (including decision-making) is conducted in front of all the participants, usually in a round-table discussion. A majority decision is sufficient, and the chairperson is required by law to share the substance and reasons for all decisions with the family directly and in writing.

The Children's Reporter is a key figure in dealing with youth crime. The reporter decides if there is a *prima facie* case and if the young person may be in need of 'compulsory measures' and thus referred to a hearing. The existence of an offence does not in itself indicate that a young person may be in need of 'compulsory measures', and the most common outcome of a referral to the reporter is 'no formal action'. The reporter may decide to refer the young person to the local authority for assistance on a 'voluntary agreement'. Anyone can make a referral to the reporter though, in practice, most referrals come from the police.

Normally, the young person must attend a hearing, and the attendance of parents is also compulsory. A local authority youth justice or childcare social worker will be present to provide a professional assessment, to advise the tribunal and to support the young person and his or her family. Others may attend with the permission of the chairperson and the agreement of the family (e.g. school teachers or residential social workers).

Representation for the child at a hearing is encouraged and need not be legal representation, since the role is non-adversarial and aimed at assisting the young person understand and participate in the process. Legal aid is available to young people and their parents to assist in preparation for a hearing but is available at the hearing itself only under special circumstances. Cases can go to the criminal court for 'proof' where the facts are disputed or the offence denied, where the child is unable to understand the evidence against him or her or for appeals against the outcome. Legal aid is available to all young people and parents for these appearances.

A hearing has no powers to imprison, fine, order compensation or impose a community sentence. However, the disposals that are available include powers of compulsory supervision (including a wide range of conditions, such as reparation and mediation) or attendance at offence-focused or educational programmes. Residential conditions can also be inserted and may include confinement in secure accommodation. The hearing must review all supervision requirements within a year or they automatically lapse.

The stated aim of the hearing remains that of involving parents in a non-coercive way in order to 'strengthen, support and supplement ... the natural beneficial influences of the home and family'. Local authorities have a corporate responsibility to provide services and each has a multidisciplinary strategic group responsible for planning services for young people who offend, within an integrated framework of children's services. A youth justice co-ordinator and specialist youth justice teams, generally located within 'children and family services' divisions, are responsible for day-to-day service provision.

Bill Whyte

RELATED ENTRIES

Scotland: criminal justice social work; Scottish courts and sanctions; Young offenders.

Key texts and sources

Lockyer, A. and Stone, F. (eds) (1998) *Juvenile Justice in Scotland: Twenty Five Years of the Welfare Approach.* Edinburgh: T. & T. Clark.

McGhee, J., Mellon, M. and Whyte, B. (eds) (2004) *Addressing Deeds: Working with Young People who Offend.* London: NCH.

Norrie, K. (2005) *Children's Hearings in Scotland.* Edinburgh: W. Green.

SED (1966) *Social Work in the Community.* Edinburgh: HMSO.

SCOTTISH COURTS AND SANCTIONS

There are three levels of criminal courts in Scotland – the High Court, the sheriff Courts and the district Courts – and two methods of prosecution – solemn and summary procedure – which determine the sentencing powers of the Scottish criminal courts. The High Court hears cases only on solemn procedure; the sheriff courts can hear cases using both methods; and the district Courts hear cases only on summary procedure.

Introduction

Criminal procedure is mainly regulated by the Criminal Procedure (Scotland) Act 1995 (CP(S)A) and is divided into solemn and summary procedures. Solemn procedure involves the most serious of criminal cases and may ultimately lead to a trial on indictment, either before a judge in the High Court or before a sheriff in one of the sheriff courts. Trials under solemn procedure are conducted with a jury. Summary procedure is used for less serious offences and may ultimately lead to a trial before a sheriff or, in district courts, before a bench of one or more lay justices of the peace. Trials under summary procedure are conducted without a jury. The procedure affects the sentences available to the court on conviction. The vast majority of cases in Scotland are dealt with under summary procedure.

Scottish courts

The High Court of Justiciary is the supreme court in Scotland and is a trial court for major crimes and an appeal court for all crime. It consists of the Lord Justice General, the Lord Justice Clerk and a number of lords commissioner of justiciary (judges). For trials, a High Court judge usually sits alone. In appeals, the High

Court usually sits with a bench of three judges, although a bench of five or more can be convened for certain review purposes. The High Court has exclusive jurisdiction in cases of murder, rape and treason, and most very serious offences will be tried there. It will also deal with those cases that have been remitted for disposal. The High Court has powers to pass acts of adjournal to regulate the workings of lower courts (e.g. the format of a probation order is specified by an act of adjournal) and, when considering appeals, can set sentencing guidelines. The High Court hears all criminal appeals – against conviction and against sentence. It also deals with bail appeals. There is no further appeal from the High Court.

Sheriff courts deal with the bulk of criminal matters in Scotland. Sheriffs are professional judges appointed by the Crown. When dealing with cases on solemn procedure, sentencing powers are restricted to a maximum custodial sentence of three years' imprisonment. However, cases can be remitted for disposal to the High Court. On summary procedure, sentencing powers are generally restricted to a maximum custodial sentence of six months, and to a 'level 5' fine.

District courts are local courts dealing with minor crime and offences. Judges in the district court, known as justices or magistrates, are trained lay appointees. The district court has a maximum power of 60 days' imprisonment, and fines not exceeding 'level 4'.

Administration

The Scottish Court Service, an executive agency of the Scottish Executive Justice Department, is responsible for the administration, organization and staffing of the criminal courts. District courts are the responsibility of individual local authorities, who appoint solicitors or advocates to act as clerks of each district court. The clerk of court acts as a legal adviser to the lay justices dealing with cases in the district courts – advising on matters of law, practice and procedure but taking no part in decisions on conviction and sentence.

Prosecution in the courts

The choice of whether to prosecute a case under solemn or summary procedure is made by the prosecution service, known as the Crown Office and Procurator Fiscal Service. The Lord Advocate is responsible for the service and is assisted by the Solicitor General and a number of law officers known collectively as Crown Counsel. The Lord Advocate and the Solicitor General are both political appointments and are members of the Scottish government. Local prosecutors are officers of the Lord Advocate and known as procurators fiscal (originally 'the fiscal' was an officer responsible for all monies and financial matters connected with the sheriff courts). The police report alleged crimes to the procurators fiscal, who decide whether or not to prosecute. Private prosecution is all but unknown, though it is technically possible in the High Court.

Disposals and sanctions

A wide range of disposals are available to the criminal court, many of which involve criminal justice social work supervision. The following is a brief summary of the main measures available to the courts:

- *Absolute discharge*: no penalty is imposed, even though guilt has been admitted or proved (CP(S)A, s. 246).
- *Admonition*: a warning by the court; follows conviction (CP(S)A, s. 246(1)).
- *Deferral of sentence*: technically no disposal; follows conviction; no time restriction 'to be of good behaviour'; may involve supervision (CP(S)A, s. 202).
- *Compensation order*: financial amends to a victim (CP(S)A, ss. 249–253).
- *Fines*: 'means' must be taken into account (CP(S)A, s. 211(7)).
- *Fine supervision and fines inquiry*: by social work available to courts (CP(S)A, s. 217).
- *Supervised attendance orders*: 10–100 hours supervised unpaid work; no consent required (CP(S)A, ss. 235–237).
- *Supervision and treatment orders*: treatment and social work supervision up to three years

for an accused who is unfit to plead (CP(S)A, s. 57).

- *Probation order*: standard, with conditions (including community service) intensive supervision from 6 months to 3 years; follows conviction but made 'instead of sentencing'; consent required (CP(S)A, s. 228).
- *Community service orders*: between 80 and 300 hours supervised unpaid work; consent required (CP(S)A, s. 238).
- *Community reparation orders*: between 10 and 100 hours supervised unpaid work for anti-social behaviour; no consent required (CP(S)A, s. 245).
- *Restriction of liberty orders*: restriction of movement including electronic monitoring up to 12 hours in any one day; supervised by social work; no consent required (CP(S)A, s. 245).
- *Drug treatment and testing orders*: treatment and supervision normally imposed by specialized drug courts; consent is required (CP(S)A, s. 234).

Bill Whyte

RELATED ENTRIES

Scotland: criminal justice social work; Scotland: youth justice.

Key texts and sources

McIvor, G. and McNeill, F. (2007) 'Probation in Scotland: past, present and future', in L. Gelsthorpe and R. Morgan (eds) *Handbook of Probation*. Cullompton: Willan Publishing.
For Scottish courts, see http://www.scotcourts.gov.uk/.
For the Crown Office and Procurator Fiscal Service, see http://www.crownoffice.gov.uk/.

SECTION 90 AND 91 OFFENDERS

Young offenders aged 10–17 inclusive, convicted under the Powers of the Criminal Courts (Sentencing) Act 2000 of murder (s. 90) or other grave crimes (s. 91).

Violent and murderous crimes by children and young people tend to be exceptional within the general trend of juvenile crime, reflected in the separate legislation set up to deal with them. Initially these youngsters are the responsibility of the Youth Offending Service, but many serve long sentences and, when they reach 18 years, supervision will normally be assumed by the Probation Service. Offender managers, thus, need to be cognizant of the legislative provisions through which these young people have reached them; their typical custodial trajectory; significant research findings about their backgrounds; and the implications of these findings for their sentence management.

Sometimes these young offenders are described as 'Section 53s': for nearly 70 years they were sentenced under s. 53 of the Children and Young Persons Act 1933. While the wording of ss. 90, 91 and 92 of the 2000 Act is different from the corresponding sections of the 1933 Act, the effect is precisely the same.

Detention under s. 90 (formerly s. 53(i)) is the *only* available sentence when a 10–17-year-old is convicted of murder. The two 11-year-olds convicted of the murder of toddler, James Bulger, in 1993 are well-known examples of this. Under this provision, young people are detained 'during Her Majesty's pleasure' for an indeterminate period, but given a tariff date, which is the earliest point at which they may be *considered* for release on life licence.

Under s. 91, a determinate custodial sentence is passed on those convicted of (usually violent) offences punishable, in the case of an adult, with imprisonment for 14+ years. Examples of these offences are manslaughter, rape and arson, though a net-widening effect has occurred in recent years with courts sometimes invoking s. 91 for lesser offences such as burglary to circumvent the maximum two-year detention and training order.

Under s. 92 of the 2000 Act, all s. 90/91 offenders are detained 'in such place and such conditions as the Secretary of State may direct'. Those under 15 years, and others deemed to be particularly vulnerable, are usually held in local authority secure children's homes, and those aged 15–17 years in juvenile young offender institutions (YOIs). At 18 years, if still in custody, they transfer to a young adult YOI and, at 21, to an adult prison.

Boswell (1996) found that 72 per cent of the s. 90/91 population had experienced one or more forms of emotional, physical, sexual or organized abuse, and 57 per cent had experienced significant loss of family or others close to them. Similar findings have emerged from other research into violent populations (Widom and Maxfield 2001). This prevalence should prompt offender managers to ask relevant questions and ensure their supervisees receive appropriate intervention, with the accompanying aim of reducing their risk of reoffending.

Gwyneth Boswell

RELATED ENTRIES

Criminal careers; Criminal Justice Act 2003; Criminology; Extended sentencing; Risk assessment and risk management; Young offenders; Youth Justice Board (for England and Wales).

Key texts and sources

Boswell, G. (1996) *Young and Dangerous: The Backgrounds and Careers of Section 53 Offenders.* Aldershot: Avebury.

NACRO (2002) *Children who Commit Grave Crimes.* London: NACRO.

Widom, C. and Maxfield, M. (2001) 'An update on the cycle of violence', *National Institute of Justice Research in Brief*, February: 1–8 (available online at http://www.ncjrs.gov/pdffiles1/nij/184894.pdf).

See NACRO's website (www.nacro.org.uk) and the Youth Justice Board's website (www.youth-justice-board.gov.uk).

SELF-HARM

Self-harm involves deliberately inflicting pain and/or injury to one's own body without suicidal intent.

Self-harm and suicide can be related but are different. Probation and prison staff work with vulnerable individuals and need to understand how to reduce these particular risks of harm. The Howard League estimates that over 21,000 people a year self-harm in custody. OASys recognizes self-harm as an area for assessment in every case.

Self-harm may be distressing and difficult to comprehend. It may be an effective coping strategy for dealing with overwhelming feelings of despair, loss, low self-esteem and powerlessness. Those who self-harm are usually managing quite deep feelings of pain, loss, hurt, low self-esteem, self-loathing or anxiety.

Self-harm is more common than we may think, and understandings of this are culture specific. Body-piercing, tattoos, binge-drinking, fast driving, over- and/or under-eating and excessive risk-taking can all be seen as forms of self harm; cutting, burning, self-mutilation and the insertion of foreign bodies may differ only in that they are more direct, less culturally acceptable and can be seen as more directly or immediately harmful.

How are suicide and self-harm related? While in most cases of self-harm suicidal intent would not appear to be present, self-injury is a statistical predictor of an increased likelihood of suicide, and the feelings that lead to self-harm may reach a level which leads to suicidal intent. Self-harm should not be seen as either 'attention seeking' or something 'to be stopped'. Self-injury may be a survival strategy to prevent something more damaging or final; it may help avert suicidal feelings; and it can represent risk minimization and self-restraint for a person at a particular time.

Criminal justice staff should categorize risk of harm to self as low, medium or lethal/potentially lethal, then consider whether the actual behaviour is direct or indirect. Regular self-harming behaviours, in the same way as regular low-level offending, may be problematic but not present a high risk of harm. Harm minimization and healthcare may be the priority. It may be useful to consider what factors make a person vulnerable to the behaviour, what impact the current environment or sentence is having on his or her risk, what situational triggers are present and what protective factors and agents can be put in place to reduce risk.

Who is most at risk? Key factors in those who seriously self-harm include a sense of powerlessness, helplessness and isolation. Without meaningful support to address underlying problems, attempts to control self-harm may escalate it and could lead to suicidal intent. Those suffering from depression (coping with acute drug, alcohol and mental health problems and unable to express or have their feelings recognized) are at increased risk.

Institutional or organizational cultures can validate self-destructive behaviours and reinforce self-harm as a way of communicating distress. Hostility between staff and service users or the withdrawal of positive support can increase risk factors.

The following worker skills are therefore required:

- Listen and take seriously.
- Enable the person to define problems as he or she sees them.
- Encourage consideration of alternative strategies.
- Facilitate empowerment and ownership.
- Promote confidence, self-esteem.
- Focus on strengths and coping strategies.

Staff therefore need:

- support;
- supervision;
- boundaries;
- mentoring;
- training;
- stress management; and
- personal insight.

Francis Cowe

RELATED ENTRIES

Offender Assessment System (OASys); Suicide.

Key texts and sources

Babiker, G. and Arnold, L. (1997) *The Language of Injury – Comprehending Self Mutilation.* Leicester: BPS.

A pocket guide for staff (*The ACCT Approach: Caring for People at Risk in Prison*) is available online at http://www.hmprisonservice.gov.uk/adviceandsupport/prison_life/selfharm.

See also http://www.mind.org.uk/Information/Booklets/Understanding/Understanding+self-harm.htm and http://www.prisonreformtrust.org.uk.

SENIOR PROBATION OFFICERS

The first-line manager grade in the National Probation Service. A senior probation officer is usually a qualified and experienced probation officer employed by a probation board to manage and account for the work of a team of offender managers.

Most offender management is carried out by teams of probation officers and probation service officers – usually between 5 and 15 staff – under the management of a senior probation officer (SPO). SPOs are usually (though not necessarily) qualified and experienced probation officers. Their duties include the organization and allocation of work within their team and the supervision and annual appraisal of staff. They are expected to make sure that their team is aware of service policies and procedures and that these are properly implemented. They are responsible for ensuring that the work of their team contributes to national and local service objectives, usually translating these into team and individual measures of achievement. Their accountability for the performance of their team is to higher management.

Management, as understood today, came late to the Probation Service. In 1909, a Home Office departmental committee argued against an internal management structure in the service, believing it would interfere with the close relationship between the magistrates' courts and their probation officers. Case committees of local magistrates were established to oversee the work of the probation officers. However, by the 1930s, the rapid expansion of the service had led to the appointment of principal probation officers (chief officers) and SPOs, the latter having organizational and supervisory responsibility for groups of probation officers. The role of the SPO was at first akin to that of a senior practitioner, providing casework supervision to main-grade officers but also retaining a caseload. Enabling staff to do their job as well as possible and promoting their professional development were seen as the principal objectives of the role. SPOs enjoyed a degree of autonomy in deciding how their team should operate.

The introduction of management by objectives, performance targets and central control (see Managerialism) has given SPOs responsibility for monitoring and assessing the work of their staff, to ensure that the standards set by the service are met. However, they retain their supervisory and developmental role, which has expanded with the increase in the numbers of probation service officers. SPOs now have much less autonomy but they continue to play a significant part in liaison with local organizations, as well as with courts. Unpaid work units and approved premises are managed by SPOs, as are prison probation teams. In most areas, there are opportunities for SPOs to contribute to discussions on policy development, representing their teams as well as themselves, and to undertake some specialist roles in training or policy implementation.

Kathy Ferguson

RELATED ENTRIES

Accountability; Chief officers; Managerialism; Probation officers; Probation service officers.

Key texts and sources

Fellowes, B. (1992) 'Management and empowerment: the paradox of professional practice', in R. Statham and P. Whitehead (eds) *Managing the Probation Service Issues for the 1990s*. Harlow: Longman.

McWilliams, W. (1992) 'The rise and development of management thought in the English probation system', in R. Statham and P. Whitehead (eds) *Managing the Probation Service Issues for the 1990s*. Harlow: Longman.

SENTENCE PLAN

A document setting out the content and arrangements for managing an offender during a custodial or community sentence.

The practice of having a clear plan of what is to be undertaken while supervising an offender has been central to probation culture for many decades. Before the implementation of OASys and the Offender Management Model, the process of assessment led to the development of a 'supervision plan' that was reviewed quarterly.

Sentence planning, as a term, had its origin in the prison system, and probation staff are accustomed to contributing to prisoners' sentence plans, either through correspondence or by attending 'sentence planning boards'.

One of the key duties of an offender manager now is to prepare a sentence plan, as part of the case record, whether a custodial or a community sentence. The offender manager then has to take the necessary steps for its implementation and to ensure the plan is reviewed and amended as necessary at regular intervals.

In the fourth section of OASys the assessment data are used to generate the sentence plan. The plan will incorporate the risk management plan if the offender is assessed as posing a medium, high or very high risk of harm to specific people or to the public. The plan will encompass all the elements of the sentence, including the punitive interventions, interventions to support 'protective factors', interventions to reduce 'barrier factors', personal change programmes, and restrictive interventions, and, if the sentence is a custodial one, the plan will contain interventions promoting resettlement.

The plan will reflect the intensity of supervision that is required and will match the offender to the appropriate tier of the Offender Management Model. This will inform the level of resource used to deliver the aims of the sentence plan. The basic structure of the tiers is as follows:

- *Tier 1*: punishment only.
- *Tier 2*: punishment and help.
- *Tier 3*: punishment, help and change.
- *Tier 4*: punishment, help, change and control.

Tier 4 includes multi-agency public protection arrangement (MAPPA) level 3 cases and prolific and priority offenders, and attracts most resources.

The offender manager is responsible for the sequencing of interventions throughout the sentence. This has to be paced in a way that enables the offender to gain maximum benefit from the various activities. It also has to be logical in terms of the motivational and pre-course work necessary before participating in, for example, accredited programmes.

In prisons, the pre-existing sentence planning procedures have been integrated into the offender management process, following pathfinder work in the north west of England in 2005. The main adjustment is that it is now frequently the responsibility of a community-based offender manager to initiate and complete the sentence plan. Offender supervisors in prison, and other prison staff with knowledge of the offender, are required to contribute to the process. Offender managers are also responsible for attending and chairing the sentence plan reviews that take place in prison.

David Hancock

RELATED ENTRIES

Assessment; Interventions; Offender Assessment System (OASys); Offender management; Risk assessment and risk management.

Key texts and sources

Home Office (2006) *Offender Management for Custodial Sentences* (PC 09/2006). London: Home Office.
NOMS (2006) *The Offender Management Model.* London: Home Office.

SENTENCING GUIDELINES COUNCIL

An independent statutory body to provide authoritative guidance on sentencing.

The Halliday Report established the need for a Sentencing Guidelines Council (SGC). Ostensibly, the justification was to ensure consistency of sentencing – an issue that was causing increasing public comment. However, the idea was also a recognition that new sentencing proposals might lead to an unintended rapid growth in the size of the prison population. This was seen as undesirable both in terms of reducing reoffending and in being beyond the budget the Treasury would authorize.

The Criminal Justice Act 2003 enacted the new sentences and established the SGC. The Act introduced wide statutory purposes of sentencing, and the interpretation of these across the variety of individual situations where offences are committed to arrive at a consistent punishment was another reason for an authoritative SGC.

The council is chaired by the Lord Chief Justice who sits with seven judicial members and four non-judicial. They represent policing, criminal prosecution, criminal defence and the interests of victims. In addition, the chair of the Sentencing Advisory Panel is a member of the SGC, and there is a representative of the National Offender Management Service, who is not a member but who can attend meetings and speak.

The SGC aims to:

- give authoritative advice on sentencing;
- give a strong lead on the approach to allocation and sentencing issues; and
- enable sentencers to make decisions based on effectiveness of sentencing and the most effective use of resources.

The Sentencing Advisory Panel is another independent body, comprising judges, academics, criminal justice practitioners and representatives of the public. The panel advises the SGC on sentencing guidance. The SGC reviews that advice, formulates draft guidelines and publishes them for public consultation. It then revises the draft and publishes guidelines.

In December 2004 guidance was issued concerning seriousness, the new sentences of the 2003 Act and the reduction in sentence for a guilty plea. Guidance on manslaughter by reason of provocation was published in 2005, and in 2006 guidelines covered robbery, breach of a protective order and domestic violence.

Writing in 2004, Michael Tonry predicted that the type of SGC enacted in 2003 would fail. First, he noted that councils composed primarily of judges invariably fail to produce meaningful guidelines. Secondly, he perceived that the Act fell short of Halliday's requirement for the production of comprehensive guidelines. Thirdly, he thought the new scheme, with roles for several separate bodies, was too complex.

Writing in February 2007, in the light of a prison overcrowding crisis, John Halliday commented that his recommendation for the production of comprehensive guidelines had not been implemented. He said that he had anticipated that the relationship between guidelines and their expected effect on the prison population would be a matter for an open discussion with government. He went on to note that neither government nor the SGC appeared to be seeking a mature dialogue of this kind. That would require strong leadership and imagination on both sides and, he argued, it would be mutually beneficial were it established.

David Hancock

RELATED ENTRIES

Criminal Justice Act 2003; Halliday Report; Punishment (aims and justifications).

Key texts and sources

Halliday, J. (2007) 'Our judges have had enough messages from ministers', *Guardian*, 6 February.

Tonry, M. (2004) *Punishment and Politics*. Cullompton: Willan Publishing.

The SGC website is at **www.sentencing-guidelines. gov.uk**.

SERIOUS FURTHER OFFENCES

A serious further offence (SFO) is one of a number of defined offences committed by an offender currently or recently under supervision. The specific types of offences are defined in policy. An SFO will result in an organizational investigation, following a standard format.

When an offender currently or recently under supervision commits a serious offence, this is a matter of great concern to the offender manager, his or her line manager and the entire organization. Such offences will usually have a direct victim who has been seriously harmed, and the SFO investigation process is a structured way of finding out if anything could have been done to avoid this. Outcomes of investigations may include policy changes, training inputs and, in rare cases, disciplinary action.

SFO investigations are led by a senior manager. The investigation begins with the correct and timely identification of an allegation. This is often following the first hearing in court. However, it is not unusual for SFOs to be brought to the immediate attention of offender managers via inter-agency work with the police, stemming from multi-agency public protection arrangements (MAPPAs).

Offender managers must advise their line manager immediately of the SFO. A copy of the current local policy for SFO investigations should be sought and followed. The most recent probation circular on SFOs should also be accessed via EPIC (a resource bank for probation staff) because the policy and procedures are subject to regular changes.

Case records will be reviewed and, depending on the case, may be required by the line manager or senior investigating manager immediately. Modern case-record systems allow access to files electronically from the outset, and copies may be made. Evidence from files can very quickly enter the wider criminal justice domain, and area policy and practice on this are variable.

At each stage of the SFO, other people will also be informed. These will include the regional offender manager (ROM) and the regional manager of the National Probation Directorate (NPD). The latter has a review and dissemination of learning role. The ROM is informed because the probation board is accountable to him or her for public protection and reducing reoffending. The National Offender Management Service (NOMS) Public Protection Unit will also be informed at each stage. This provides reports to ministers and, ultimately, the Home Secretary and, although these are usually reports which do not identify individual cases, in some very serious circumstances they will do so.

The probation board chair will be informed and kept up to date at each stage of the process. At the conclusion of the investigation the board (or a committee of the board) will consider the final report in a meeting that is not open to the public. Progress in implementing any recommendations will be reported to the board subsequently.

The Home Secretary has the power to order an independent review of a case by HM Inspectorate of Probation. The recommendations from such reviews lead to policy development and practice change, and the current SFO procedure is informed by the HMIP report (2006), *An independent Review of a Serious Further Offence Case: Damien Hanson and Elliot White*.

There is inevitably fall-out from SFO incident, but the gains are that investigations inform and improve practice. Although employers will have to deal with negligence appropriately if it emerges from an investigation, the procedure is not intended to encourage or support a 'blame culture'. On the contrary, it is there to clarify, explore and learn from the operation of process and systems.

Jo Mead

RELATED ENTRIES

Accountability; HM Inspectorate of Probation; Multi-agency public protection arrangements (MAPPAs); Public protection; Risk of harm; Supervision of offenders.

Key texts and sources

HMIP (2006) *An Independent Review of a Serious Further Offence Case: Damien Hanson and Elliot White* (available online at **http://www.inspectorates.homeoffice.gov.uk/hmiprobation/inspect_reports/serious-further-offences/**).

Home Office (2006) PC 08/2006 (available online at **http://www.probation.homeoffice.gov.uk/files/pdf/PC08%202006.pdf**).

Home Office (2006) PC 41/2006 (available online at **http://www.probation.homeoffice.gov.uk/files/pdf/PC41%202006.pdf**).

SEX OFFENDER TREATMENT PROGRAMMES (SOTPs)

Accredited programmes designed to increase personal responsibility, to address the consequences of sexual offending, to increase victim empathy, challenge cognitive distortions and develop individual strategies to reduce the risk of reoffending.

Accredited programmes for sex offenders in groups have been shown to be an effective way of challenging cognitive distortions, denial and minimization. All facilitators undertake the same training and are subject to a treatment manager and audit according to rigorous standards. In a prison setting, facilitators may be derived from three principal disciplines – prison officers, probation staff and psychology staff. In the community, programmes are largely delivered by probation staff, and this may include some involvement by forensic psychologists.

The assessment process is critical in order to match the offender to the programme that is likely to be most effective according to the individual offending profile. This is achieved by the use of a variety of actuarial tools and assessment instruments, including Thornton's Risk Matrix 2000, OASys, the Hare Psychopathy Checklist Revised (PCL-R to assess for personality disorders), penile plethysmographic assessment (to establish sexual preference), psychometric tests and semi-structured interviews.

Programmes delivered in prisons

Core SOTP

This programme consists of 85 sessions over 26 weeks. The assessment criteria are that offenders have an IQ of 80 or above, are not in complete denial of the offence and accept enough responsibility for their behaviour in order to be able to discuss it in a group setting. The programme aims to increase the offender's responsibility for his offending behaviour and for his life in general. It attempts to elicit excuses and address distorted beliefs and perceptions. The Core SOTP seeks a greater understanding of the victim's suffering and challenges offenders who misinterpret the victim's reactions. The programme aims to reduce the risk of reoffending by increasing awareness of recurrent patterns of events, feelings, thoughts and behaviours which led to the offence, and by ascertaining how these factors can be controlled in the future. Motivational interviewing is included and the consequences of offending are analysed. The Core programme contains 20 discussion-based blocks that are divided as follows:

1. Lifestyles, relationships, attitudes, emotions and sexual interests that contribute towards sexual offending.
2. Enhancing an understanding of victim empathy – seeing the offence from the victim's perspective.
3. Relapse prevention – developing plans and strategies to avoid reoffending.

A reassessment exercise is completed some six weeks following the completion of the programme.

Adapted SOTP

This comprises approximately 70 sessions over 26 weeks. The target group for this programme are offenders whose IQ is lower than 80. Offenders whose first language is not English and who may have difficulties in understanding the material presented in the Core programme may also be offered a place on an Adapted programme. Facilitators deliver the programme in a style that is responsive to the individual to ensure that learning disabilities or communication difficulties do not hamper the process.

Rolling SOTP

This has between 45 and 60 sessions, usually over 26 weeks. The Rolling programme is designed for sex offenders assessed as low risk of reoffending and/or those who have completed the Core or Extended programme but have ongoing treatment needs. The programme addresses the same issues as the Core SOTP, and one challenge for facilitators is managing the dynamics of a continually changing group.

Extended SOTP

This has 74 sessions and 26 weeks' duration. This programme is reserved for those sex offenders who have completed the Core SOTP but are assessed as having continuing high deviance and further treatment needs. Individual therapy may be used to address sexual fantasy and arousal.

Better lives booster

This comprises 35 sessions, often of 12 weeks' duration. It is a motivational programme aimed at sex offenders who have successfully completed the Core SOTP at an earlier stage in their sentence and is used to assist in the preparation for re-categorization to an open prison and/or release into the community. With the introduction of more indeterminate sentences for public protection via the Criminal Justice Act 2003, it is envisaged that the use of this programme will increase.

Programme reports

All programme facilitators are required to produce a written report that reflects the progress made by the offender.

Post-programme reviews

A formal review of the programme is convened within six months of completion of all SOTP courses (within three months for the Better Lives Booster). This is an interactive review that involves the offender, the facilitator, the offender manager and a family member (or other support) whom the offender wishes to invite. This may be a critical meeting and will often identify issues that should be addressed either during the remainder of the custodial element of the sentence or when the offender is released on licence.

Programmes in the community

Community – Sex Offender Group Programme (C-SOGP)

A 50-hour modular programme, delivered via a three-year community order. The aims are to increase self-responsibility and to reduce minimization by challenging distorted thinking, identifying maladaptive relationship styles and core beliefs, learning new skills to improve self-management and to control deviant fantasies, developing victim empathy, relapse prevention skills and new lifestyle goals.

Thames Valley – Sex Offender Group Programme (TV-SOGP)

The 160 blocks of this programme are split into five core components:

1. Foundation block (60 hours aimed at low-deviance offenders).
2. Victim empathy (16 hours).
3. Life skills (40 hours).
4. Relapse prevention (44 hours).
5. Partner programme (36 hours intended for female partners in an ongoing relationship with the offender).

High-deviance offenders are required to complete all 160 blocks.

N-SOGP

This comprises two components for low risk/deviance and high risk/deviance, respectively. The core programme of at least 144 hours is aimed at high-risk/deviance offenders and followed by 36 hours' relapse prevention. For low-risk/deviance offenders, individually prepared work will be completed, usually followed by relapse prevention.

Ann Snowden

RELATED ENTRIES

Accredited programmes; Assessment instruments and systems; Motivation; Public protection; Sex offenders; Treatment manager.

Key texts and sources

National Probation Directorate (2002) *The Treatment and Management of Sexual Offenders in Custody and in the Community.* London: National Probation Directorate.

Pearson, F., Lipton, D., Cleland, C. and Yee, D. (2002) 'The effects of behavioural/cognitive-behavioural programmes on recidivism', *Crime and Delinquency*, 48: 476–96.

Perkins, D. (1991) 'Clinical work with sex offenders in secure settings', in C. Hollin and L. Howells (eds) *Clinical Approaches to Sex Offenders and their Victims.* Chichester: Wiley.

SEX OFFENDERS

The engagement in sexual activity by penetration, touching, viewing or causing others to engage in sexual activity or exploitation, where there is an absence of consent between the offender and victim. In this context consent is taken to include whether the victim had the capacity to consent, whether by age, the use of coercion or mental disorder.

The term 'sex offender' covers a wide range of behaviour, and professionals should rely on an analysis of each individual case rather than generic terms. For example, the clinical definition of a paedophile is someone who has a recurring pattern of sexual arousal to pre-pubescent children (i.e. below the age of 12–13). Therefore not all child sex offenders by this definition would be clinically assessed as paedophiles.

The public and, indeed, criminal justice professionals, are most anxious when faced with cases of offenders who have a history of stranger abduction and sexual assault of a child without prior grooming behaviour. Inevitably, it is also these cases that attract high media attention. However, stranger abduction and sexual murder are extremely rare. A recent report (Beech *et al.* 2006) states that 'estimates would suggest that there are around 200 men within the prison system in the UK identified as having committed a murder with an apparent or admitted sexual motivation'.

Grubin (1998) states that 'the majority of child molesters sexually assault children they know. Most studies find this to be the case at least three quarters of the time, with up to 80 per cent of offences taking place in either the home of the offender or the home of the victim.' Kelly *et al.* (1991) surveyed over 1,200 children who reported experiences of sexual abuse and found (after excluding indecent exposure offences) that 13 per cent of their abusers were relatives (parents, siblings, uncles/aunts, cousins or grandparents); 68 per cent someone known to them (family friend, other adult or peer); and 18 per cent a stranger.

This reflects the heterogeneity of the sexual offender population. Traditionally, sex-offending behaviour has been classed by victim type (boy/girl/adult); intra-familial or extra-familial; and by type of activity (contact vs. non-contact offending). However, caution is required in assessing risk based on previous victim type as there is a subgroup of offenders who offend against both boys and girls, and others who offend against both children and adult victims.

This heterogeneity is also found in reconviction rates. While average reconviction rates have been found to be in the region of 13–17 per cent, offenders against boys tend to reconvict at a higher rate and have more victims, as do extra-familial and non-contact offenders. A meta-analysis of studies involving 23,393 offenders over a four to five year follow-up period found that 13.4 per cent of sexual offenders recidivated with a sexual offence, with 18.9 per cent for rapists and 12.7 per cent for child molesters (Hanson and Bussiere 1998). However, these rates are an underestimation since many sexual offences are never reported. Longer follow-up periods considerably increase these rates, with 35–45 per cent reconvicting after 15–25 years. It should be noted that there are variations in the time intervals between recidivism since rapists were found to recidivate soon after release compared with those who offend against children. This has consequences for the intensity of supervision for each sex offender.

The supervision of sex offenders will be dependent on risk assessment using OASys,

together with specific sex-offender risk tools, including Risk Matrix 2000 (for static risk factors) and Structured Assessment of Risk and Need (SARN) (for dynamic stable and acute risk factors) These tools provide a weighting for the presence of known risk factors, such as sexual deviance, criminal lifestyle, intimacy deficits, poor emotional self-regulation and general self-management (e.g. problem recognition and solving; impulsivity, etc.). In England and Wales the assessment is made by combining risk of reconviction (using static factors) with level of deviance (using dynamic factors) and risk of harm (using OASys). Practitioners should be aware that dynamic and acute risk factors can change, so that regular monitoring and review are required.

All sex offenders who are required as part of their sentence to notify the police of their address (commonly referred to as the sex offender register) will be subject to monitoring by multi-agency public protection arrangements (MAPPAs). This requires risk assessment to be undertaken and risk management plans to be developed in each case. The level of risk will determine the number of agencies involved in this process, and the frequency of reviews.

A thorough review of sexual offences resulted in Part 1 of the Sexual Offences Act 2003, while Part 2 of the Act details the additional powers available to the courts in respect of prohibitive orders, such as the sexual offence prevention order, the disqualification order, etc. In sentencing for serious sex offences, courts will consider 'the degree of harm to the victim, the level of culpability of the offender and the level of risk posed by the offender to society' (as outlined in *Milberry & others* in the Court of Appeal [2003] 2 Cr App R (s) 31). The Criminal Justice Act 2003 introduced a new sentence of indeterminate public protection for serious sexual offences, in which detention is necessary beyond the determinate period in order to protect the public from serious harm. The intention is that the offender will not be released from custody until there is evidence that his or her risk has been reduced.

David Middleton

RELATED ENTRIES

Assessment instruments and systems; Criminal Justice Act 2003; Extended sentencing; Multiagency public protection arrangements (MAPPAs); Public protection; Risk assessment and risk management; Risk of harm; Sex offender treatment programmes (SOTPs).

Key texts and sources

Beech, A.R., Oliver, C., Fisher, D. and Beckett, R. (2006) *Step 4: The Sex Offender Treatment Programme in Prison: Addressing the Offending Behaviour of Rapists and Sexual Murderers.* London: HM Prison Service.

Grubin, D. (1998) *Sex Offending against children: Understanding the Risk. Police Research Series Paper* 99. London: Home Office (available online at **http://www.homeoffice.gov.uk/rds/prgpdfs/fprs99.pdf**).

Hanson, R.K. and Bussiere, M.T. (1998) 'Predicting relapse: a meta-analysis of sexual offender recidivism studies', *Journal of Consulting and Clinical Psychology,* 66: 348–62.

Kelly, L., Regan, L. and Burton, S. (1991) *An Exploratory Study of the Prevalence of Sexual Abuse in a Sample of 16–21 Year Olds.* London: Child Abuse Studies Unit, Polytechnic of North London.

Ward, T., Polaschek, D.L.L. and Beech, A.R. (2006) *Theories of Sexual Offending.* Chichester: Wiley.

Guidance to courts on sentencing may be found at **http://www.sentencing-guidelines.gov.uk/**.

SOCIAL CAPITAL

Social capital is a resource that stems from the bulk of social interactions, networks and network opportunities that people or communities have within an environment of trust and reciprocity, and informed by specific norms and values. A relatively new concept in understanding crime and responses to it, it is a recognizable descendant of probation's earlier recognition of the value of community development.

Social capital is a multifaceted and contested concept. Definitions typically involve the notion of 'social networks, the reciprocities that arise from them, and the value of these for achieving mutual goals'. It is common to distinguish *bonding, bridging* and *linking* social capital. Bonding social capital resides in friendship relationships and peer groups that provide a sense of belonging. Bridging social capital is about creating links with people outside our immediate circles, broadening opportunities and horizons. (Bonding social capital is good for 'getting by' but bridging networks are crucial for 'getting ahead'.) Linking social capital is about access to influential others and power structures.

There are different perspectives on the relationships between social capital and crime. Putnam's (2000) notion of social capital as a community asset, which has heavily influenced New Labour's social policy, emphasizes civic engagement and norms of reciprocity and trust to maintain community cohesion and social order – social capital as the 'glue' of society. This perspective sees an association between high social capital and lower crime rates, while communities with low levels of social capital (characterized by anonymity, limited neighbourliness and low levels of civic participation) face increased risks of crime and disorder.

For the Probation Service, a focus on social capital as a 'glue' would involve paying attention to issues of community cohesion. Work with offenders and 'at risk' people would emphasize integration into mainstream society. However, this approach risks introducing into the debate a strong normative element, linking it inevitably to political ideology. Social capital might be used to provide subtle ways of regulating communities to achieve harmony and integration.

Other perspectives (e.g. Bourdieu 1986; Coleman 1997) see social capital as a *private good* – an asset that individuals possess as a result of participating in a set of social relationships or a group. From a social justice and social inclusion perspective, embedded in ideologies of democratic empowerment and change that are sensitive to rights and civil liberties, social capital is seen as a *social resource*, giving access to opportunities, education and the labour market and leading to collective efficacy. Within this, 'risk pathways' and offending are linked to notions of 'static' or 'dynamic' social capital. These types of social capital play a key part in people's lives –

not only in terms of their well-being but also in the creation of new opportunities, choice and power. Static social capital draws on bonded networks, based upon their immediate locale, and are characterized by a strong sense of belonging, though distant from the wider community. Young offenders or those 'at risk' are typified by their static social capital (i.e. strong bonds to a limited group, a protective and narrow radius of trust, a restricted sense of belonging and a less optimistic and often fatalistic outlook on life). Static social capital might be the context within which to take risks (e.g. commit crime), but paradoxically it restricts the capacity to take risks associated with 'moving on' or to negotiate the risks associated with normal life transitions.

For probation, a focus on social capital as a resource and as the social context within which people negotiate everyday life would involve paying attention to locale, peers, networks and the social resources to which people have access. Work with 'at risk' people would need to strengthen resilience by enabling them to enhance 'dynamic' and bridging social capital.

Recognition of the importance of social capital prompts searching questions about contemporary probation practice and the risk that it is distancing itself from the community. This prompts consideration of the character and significance of community service (unpaid work), as well as the consequences of probation staff being 'further' from the communities they serve. At least arguably, the focus on individual offending has diminished recognition of the value of strengthening contacts with families, volunteers and formal and informal partnerships – all networks that potentially support desistance.

Thilo Boeck

RELATED ENTRIES

Citizenship; Community; Desistance; Partnerships; Poverty; Social exclusion.

Key texts and sources

Baron, S., Field, J. and Schuller, T. (2001) *Social Capital: Critical Perspectives*. Oxford: Oxford University Press.

Boeck, T., Fleming, J. and Kemshall, H. (2006) *Social Capital and Young People* (available online at http://www.dmu.ac.uk/Images/ESRC%20practitioners%20leaflet%20final%20-%20pdf_tcm2-40394.pdf).

Bourdieu, P. (1986) 'The forms of capital', in J. Richardson (ed.) *Handbook of Theory and Research for the Sociology of Education*. New York, NY: Greenwood Press.

Coleman, J.S. (1997) 'Social capital in the creation of human capital', in F. Ackerman *et al.* (eds) *Human Well-being and Economic Goals*. Washington, DC: Island Press.

Field, J. (2003) *Social Capital*. London: Routledge.

Halpern, D. (2005) *Social Capital*. Cambridge: Polity Press.

Putnam, R. (2000) *Bowling Alone – the Collapse and Revival of American Community*. New York, NY: Simon & Schuster.

SOCIAL EXCLUSION

The condition that has come to be called social exclusion will be found in any society where one social class or group has been able to expand its power and influence, to increase its prosperity or to impose its culture, at the expense of another.

It is a mark of a civilized and healthy society that its political and social system will enable the minority of 'outsiders' to assert their interests against those of the more powerful 'insiders'; that they will be respected for doing so; and that those in relatively privileged positions will have some sense of responsibility towards those who are less fortunate.

The features and processes which are associated with social exclusion have been analysed in different ways at different times, by Karl Marx, among others. By the middle of the twentieth century, the hope was that the divisions would be reduced and eventually eliminated by the welfare state and through the post-war political consensus. In the event, new divisions appeared and came increasingly to be associated with criminality. All agreed that the problem was related to such features as poverty, poor education, social and racial prejudice, dysfunctional families, single parenthood and difficulties with mental health. Sociological studies during the 1960s (for example, by David Downes and Paul Rock) focused on the nature and causes of 'deviance', while criminologists distinguished between 'left' and 'right' realism – those on the left favouring social and economic solutions, those on the right arguing for law enforcement and punishment. In the 1990s, Charles Murray and others argued that the problems were an actual consequence of the welfare state and its encouragement for people to become dependent on state benefits.

The Labour government that came into office in 1997 described the problem as follows: 'Social exclusion happens when people or places suffer from a series of problems such as unemployment, discrimination, poor skills, low incomes, poor housing, high crime, ill health, and family breakdown. When such problems combine, they can create a vicious cycle.'

The government created a Social Exclusion Unit, originally in the Cabinet Office but later transferred to the Department for Communities and Local Government, which produced a series of policy action team reports during the government's first five years. The Cabinet Office also developed the idea of 'social capital', which it defined as 'networks together with shared norms, values and understandings that facilitate co-operation within or among groups'. The main features were 'citizenship, neighbourliness, trust and shared values, community involvement, volunteering, social networks, and civil political participation'.

The government introduced a range of policies, the aims of which were essentially to reduce the number of children growing up in poverty, to improve people's access to paid work, to reduce the number who relied on benefits and to regenerate deprived neighbourhoods. Examples included Sure Start, the Connexions Service, the New Deal for Communities, improvements in housing, a programme known as 'Together We Can' and a range of measures to promote social cohesion and racial equality. Many of these relied on contributions from the voluntary and community sector, which came to have an increasingly significant role in the provision of public services. The policies were in many ways a continuation of policies traditionally favoured by the political left, but they often carried penalties for those who failed to take advantage of benefits or opportunities once they have been offered.

The government continued to recognize the strong correlation between social exclusion and criminality. Its policies focused both on efforts to prevent criminality and the temptation to offend in the first place, and on the need to reduce reoffending when a person had already been convicted and had served a prison or community sentence. The Social Exclusion Unit produced an important report (*Reducing Re-offending by Ex-prisoners*) in 2002, and the National Offender Management Service (NOMS) issued the *Reducing Re-offending National Action Plan* in 2004. Regional plans followed. Programmes that could be seen as related to civil renewal included 'Reducing Re-offending Alliances', 'Community Payback' and 'Making Good'.

Concepts such as 'social exclusion' and the related ideas of community and social responsibility can be interpreted in different ways. They can be interpreted openly, in the spirit of a liberal, tolerant and compassionate society, or restrictively, as a way of demanding social conformity and of insisting on compliance with norms and expectations as a condition of social acceptance. Failure to comply then brings punishment and leads to further exclusion. The balance that a government, society or community finds between the two sets of attitudes and approaches will change over time, but the balance is one of the features that defines its character.

There were inevitable tensions between the government's policies to reduce social exclusion and its policies for criminal justice. The latter had the intention and effect of continually expanding the scope of the criminal law and the number of people who were brought within it; of extending the degree of control the state could exercise over the lives of those who had been convicted; and of increasing the penalties to be imposed on those who failed to comply with their conditions. Policies such as these, together with the stigma that is attached to a criminal conviction, inevitably increase the social exclusion of those who are affected by them.

It is difficult to tell how the government's policies on social exclusion will develop in future, the extent to which the present or a future government will remain committed to them or the nature of their connection with policies on criminal justice and the treatment of offenders.

David Faulkner

RELATED ENTRIES

Citizenship; Community; Community justice; Diversity; Poverty; Punishment (aims and justifications); Punishment as communication; Reintegration; Social capital.

Key texts and sources

Catholic Bishops' Conference in England and Wales (2004) *A Place of Redemption – a Catholic Approach to Punishment and Prisons.* London: Burns & Oates.

Downes, D. and Rock, P. (2003) *Understanding Deviance* (4th edn). Oxford: Oxford University Press.

Faulkner, D. and Flaxington, F. (2004) 'NOMS and civil renewal', *Vista*, 9: 90–9.

Hills, J., Le Grand, J. and Piachaud, D. (eds) (2001) *Understanding Social Exclusion.* Oxford: Oxford University Press.

The report, *Reducing Re-offending by Ex-prisoners*, can be found at **www.socialexclusion.gov.uk/publications.asp?did=64**. The *Reducing Re-offending National Action Plan* can be found at **www.probation.homeoffice.gov.uk/files/pdf/NOMS%20National%20Action%20Plan.pdf**.

SOCIAL WORK

> 'The social work profession promotes social change, problem solving in human relationships and the empowerment and liberation of people to enhance well-being. Utilising theories of human behaviour and social systems, social work intervenes at the points where people interact with their environments. Principles of human rights and social justice are fundamental to social work' (British Association of Social Workers 2001).

The origins of probation practice are in what has been called social casework, with the ethos of 'advise, assist and befriend'. Foren and Bailey (1968) differentiated between the *formal* authority and the *personal* authority of probation officers (POs). They saw POs using breach proceedings sparingly as other alternatives were tried first. The therapeutic relationship (the essence of helping the offender) enabled the PO to strengthen the client's ego and to maintain contact. The main thing was that, to challenge the offending behaviour of the client, there had to be a relationship between the PO and offender, so that the PO could work therapeutically from a position of trust. It was possible for there to be a shared higher aim between them. This is more useful than ensuring contact – a somewhat superficial notion of compliance.

National Standards for the supervision of offenders were introduced in 1992. Supervision was described as 'challenging and skilful, requiring professional social work in the field of criminal justice'. Three years later the second version dropped this, talking instead of supervision as 'providing punishment and a disciplined programme for offenders'. Departing from the standards was not to be at the discretion of the PO but, rather, by the line manager. The PO had been given the task to provide punishment – the only agency in criminal justice with this mandate.

POs were trained in social work departments until the then Home Secretary, Michael Howard, removed this requirement in 1995. When a new training qualification was proposed by the incoming Labour government, it was most concerned that this should not be taught within existing social work departments. Was this because it would not be seen as being sufficiently tough on offenders? What is it about social work that it is now deemed to be unsuitable?

All the elements of the definition of social work (given at the beginning of this entry), adopted by the British Association of Social Workers (BASW) and the International Association of Schools of Social Work, will lead to public protection. There is nothing in this definition that is incompatible with working with offenders, both to protect the public and to challenge offending behaviour.

We are now faced with a probation crisis of confidence. The superficial nature of probation supervision is patently failing to protect the public, and the government is signalling its intention to rely on the voluntary sector. One day the centrality of knowing, understanding and working constructively with the offender will have to be reintroduced and social work with clients reinvented.

Anthony Goodman

RELATED ENTRIES

National Standards; Probation; Probation training.

Key texts and sources

BASW (2001) *Definition of Social Work* (available online at **http://www.basw.co.uk/articles.php?articleId=2&page=2**).

Foren, R. and Bailey, R. (1968) *Authority in Social Casework*. Oxford: Pergamon Press.

SOLUTION-FOCUSED WORK

Working in a solution-focused way directs attention to the offender's abilities and strengths rather than his or her assumed deficits and weaknesses. It is more than a set of therapeutic techniques; it is a way of thinking about people. It is very much strengths based.

Solution-focused work emphasizes that people *have* problems rather than that they *are* problems, and it recognizes that problems happen to people in the social environment in which they operate. Solution-focused work sees people as temporarily unable to find a way around a problem (and this may include a problem with the way in which they function in society). It also seeks to enhance those resources that people already use in order to help them function even better.

In some work with offenders, it may be stretching credulity to suggest that they are temporarily unable to find a way around the problems of behaving anti-socially, as they may have been doing it repeatedly and for a very long time. However, nobody is all bad behaviours, and taking a solution-focused perspective reminds us to value the skills and resources offenders already have, even if they need to adapt those for living more prosocially. It also reminds us to look always for the possibilities of change.

Solution-focused work concentrates on the following:

- How the client will know that change has taken place.
- What the client wants to change.
- What the central issue is which the client wants to change rather than what is the underlying cause of the problems.

- Times and places where the problems did not occur in order to build on these exceptions; in other words, if you can do it/not do it once, you can do it/not do it again.
- How we can use the skills and qualities of the client.
- How the client and the worker can collaborate in the change process. (adapted from O'Connell 1998).

Solution-focused therapy is a form of brief therapy, and practitioners need to be properly trained in order to practise it. However, it is possible to borrow a few useful concepts and techniques for work with offenders. Although solution-focused therapy is usually used in one-to-one and couples work, the concepts and techniques below can also be used in groupwork.

Solution-focused and optimistic language

Solution-focused language is always concentrated on the solution rather than the problems. For instance:

> *Offender:* I really need some help with my drinking problem.
>
> *Worker:* Tell me about your problem. How much do you drink each day?

Or (more solution focused):

> *Offender:* I really need some help with my drinking problem.
>
> *Worker:* What would you like to change? How will you know that things are improving?

The latter question encourages the client to develop a sense that change is possible and to focus on where he or she will be after that change rather than encouraging him or her to focus on his or her problems.

Trotter (2004) identifies that worker optimism has a positive impact on client outcomes. In the subtleties of language we can often convey an optimistic message. Compare these two examples:

> *Offender:* I have so many problems I feel completely overwhelmed.
>
> *Worker:* I can see it is really difficult for you at the moment. Shall we try and deal with one thing at a time? What is your biggest problem?

Or (more solution focused):

> *Offender:* I have so many problems I feel completely overwhelmed.
>
> *Worker:* I can see it is really difficult for you at the moment. What I often find most helpful is to break it down and deal with one thing at a time. Often if you can deal with one or two things some of the others fall into place. What would you like us to work on sorting out first?

In the latter case the worker has said essentially the same thing but, by using terms such as 'what I find most helpful' and 'what would you like us to work on sorting out' (not 'what is your biggest problem'), the worker is conveying the idea that the problems *can* be tackled and *can* be solved.

It is important, however, not to overdo it. The reality is often that clients' lives are very difficult and change is very challenging, and being overly optimistic and unrealistic is going to sound to the client as if the worker is minimizing his or her problems and is out of touch with reality.

Solution-focused techniques

The 'miracle question'

The miracle question is a key intervention usually used by solution-focused therapists in the first session. It concentrates on finding out what the client would like to be right, not what the client thinks is wrong.

The practitioner asks the client what the situation would be like if a miracle occurred (or a magic wand was waved) and everything was alright. This is often a useful first step in helping the client to imagine a different and better future and subsequently to work towards it.

Exceptions

Another useful technique borrowed from solution-focused therapy is concentrating on exceptions to the norm. This recognizes that, often, clients have had a brief taste of solutions but did not recognize them or acknowledge them. In this case, the worker asks the client about times when the problem did not exist (however briefly) and helps him or her to gather information from this experience that the client can use to find further solutions to the problem.

Scaling

A third technique from solution-focused therapy is scaling. Scaling is a useful way of getting a sense of how seriously the client views the problem, for setting goals and for monitoring progress. The worker asks the client to place the problem on a scale from 0 (terrible) to 10 (resolved). The worker's response to scaling shifts it from problem focus to solution focus.

Sally Cherry

RELATED ENTRIES

Cognitive-behavioural; Groupwork; Motivation; Motivational interviewing; Prosocial modelling.

Key texts and sources

Cherry, S. (2005) *Transforming Behaviour: Pro-social Modelling in Action.* Cullompton: Willan Publishing (ch. 2).

Hudson O'Hanlon, W. and Weiner-Davis, M. (1989) *In Search of Solution.* London: Norton.

O'Connell, B. (1998) *Solution-focused Therapy.* London: Sage.

Trotter, C. (2004) *Helping Abused Children and their Families: Towards an Evidence Based Treatment Model.* London: Sage.

STAFF SUPERVISION

> Supporting, guiding, monitoring and holding staff to account through a review process usually based on a series of regular meetings with the line manager. From the Latin *super* ('above') and *videre* ('to see'), meaning oversight, holding to account, maintaining order and a process of assurance.

Staff supervision has come a long way in recent years. In the past there were many justifiable criticisms of unstructured monthly sessions – annual staff reports loosely called appraisals, which drew as much on personal anecdote and potential prejudice as on evidence. Over the past decade practice has improved, along with a more business-orientated and performance-based approach.

Annual objectives are set, mirroring the performance objectives set for the probation area, against which the individual staff member's work is regularly measured. Staff are explicitly expected to be able to demonstrate that they are meeting their objectives, keeping to timescales, producing quality work and achieving compliance with National Standards.

Probation areas strive to achieve a consistent and evidenced measure of staff performance and training, and to attend to the development needs of the agency.

Staff supervision is usually planned to take place monthly. It can be less or more frequent depending on the experience of the member of staff. It is generally outlined by a contract of supervision, agreed terms of reference and a set of personal objectives, the purpose of which is to complement annual appraisals and staff performance management. These may be set down in a performance appraisal development review/record (PADR) or a local equivalent. Annual performance-related pay or incremental progression through pay points may be determined by this.

Supervision is undertaken within a line management relationship covering accountability, support and professional development. The staff member's capacity to undertake the work is assessed; progress against goals is measured; assurance is provided that standards of work are maintained; development needs are identified and actioned; and support is provided and good work acknowledged.

How good outcomes are achieved, as well as *what* outcomes are achieved, is equally important:

- *How*: throughout the organization, staff must be able to demonstrate the ability to motivate people to develop and grow, to offer consistent prosocial models of behaviour and have an ability to set and maintain boundaries.
- *What*: staff need to have excellent administrative, motivational and prosocial skills to undertake today's work, as well as the forensic knowledge and approach that have always been a part of the work.

Managers, too, need to model this. Supervisory relationships with staff, as with offenders, should be characterized by warm, empathic, clear and fair interactions. Supervisors have a pivotal role, through supervision, to enable staff to demonstrate performance. They should identify strengths and areas for improvement, and ensure that staff have development and competency opportunities identified and offered to them. As the professionalism and performance of probation come under greater scrutiny, supervision as a form of quality assurance becomes more important.

Centrally, a national agenda focusing on being a more representative organization is being promoted. 'Accelerate' is a positive action personal development programme, and the 'Living Leadership' initiative combines prosocial training with performance management development. Details of both are available on the National Offender Management Service (NOMS) website.

Karen MacLeod

RELATED ENTRIES

Accountability; Chief officers; National Standards; Performance management; Senior probation officers.

Key texts and sources

Bailey, R., Knight, C. and Williams, B. (2007) 'The Probation Service as part of NOMS in England and Wales: fit for purpose?', in L. Gelsthorpe and R. Morgan (eds) *Handbook of Probation*. Cullompton: Willan Publishing.

Gast, L. and Taylor, P. (1998) *Influence and Integrity: A Practice Book for Pro-social Modelling*. Birmingham: Midlands Probation Training Consortium.

NPD/NOMS human resources work is currently under development to produce a nationally agreed staff appraisal system (due to report by mid-2007). Once finalized, details will be found on the NOMS website (**www.noms.homeoffice.gov.uk**). Further details on human resources, diversity, support services and disability information can also be found on this website.

SUICIDE

> Suicide is an intentional act of self-destruction committed by someone who knows what he or she is doing and who knows the probable consequences of the act (Aldridge 1998).

Suicide is complex and statistics alone can mask the individual and social factors involved. Men in the community are four times more likely than women to kill themselves; women in prison are forty times more likely to commit suicide than women in the community. A disproportionate amount of suicides are by young men, and those in custodial, post-release or residential settings are at particular risk. Almost one third of custodial suicides occur within the first week of someone arriving, and one in seven occurs within two days of admission. OASys recognizes suicide as an area for assessment in every case.

Custody

Prison Service Order 2700 explicitly recognizes a duty of care for inmates, and current research commends to custodial establishments:

- reception/induction screening for risk of suicide and self-harm;
- strategies for moving prisoners at risk;
- improving communication about those at risk;
- staff understanding of self-injury and suicide;
- improved cell design; and
- listening schemes.

Scottish Prison Service guidance could form the basis of a nine-point action plan appropriate to any custodial, semi-custodial or community agency:

1. A proactive action and care strategy.
2. Management and policy commitment.
3. Investment in staff training and awareness.

4. A pro-rehabilitation culture.
5. Countering boredom and increasing offender activities.
6. Prisoner 'buddy' or 'self-help' schemes.
7. Strategy as ongoing and reviewed.
8. Every death is explored.
9. Continual improvement.

Hostels and community supervision

Rates of suicide among those on post-release supervision or licence are estimated to be seven times higher than that in the general population. Wilson (2005) suggests that the majority of these deaths occur quite soon after release. Between 1998 and 2002, some 87 people died in approved premises alone. PC 02/2004 may be seen as an attempt to counter this.

Before people kill themselves, many will have had contact with a service or helping agency. Many use medication received from their GP or over-the-counter medication. Isolation and lack of meaningful contact – whether on remand, immediately post-sentence or post-release – are areas that practitioners could address. *Continuity and quality of supervision and support may reduce risk.* Uncertainty and loss of hope are factors. Those involved in release decisions, licence conditions and the supervision of offenders should pay attention to planned, purposeful and supportive communication and resettlement strategies. Transition points in a sentence appear as risk factors.

Too much emphasis on controlling, directive and technical relationships may detract attention from listening and engaging with issues around drugs or alcohol misuse, relationships, accommodation, finance, health, social readjustment and isolation.

Francis Cowe

RELATED ENTRIES

Approved premises; Prisons and Probation Ombudsman; Self-harm.

Key texts and sources

Aldridge, D. (1998) *Suicide: The Tragedy of Hopelessness.* London: Jessica Kingsley.

HM Prison Service (2002) *Prison Service Order* 2700. London: HMSO.

Home Office (2004) *Death of Approved Premises Residents* (PC 02/2004). London: Home Office.

Wilson, S. (2005) *Death at the Hands of the State.* London: Howard League for Penal Reform.

See also http://www.howardleague.org/index.php?id=suicideprevention.

SUPERVISION OF OFFENDERS

Supervision: oversight, holding to account, maintaining order, a process of assurance (from the Latin *super* ('above') and *videre* ('to see')). Supervisor: person who manages or supervises. Supervision is both the description of the relationship which develops and the process within which it takes place. The quality of the 'supervisory relationship' is a critical success (or failure) factor. The relationship should be characterized by warm, empathetic, clear and fair interactions.

There are two major experiences of supervision in probation and offender management: staff supervision and supervision of offenders. Both have been reviewed and revised as the service has modernized to take account of evidence-led practice and human resources developments. This entry considers the supervision of offenders.

Offender supervision takes place in a compulsory framework under sentence by the court, either as a community order or the portion of a custodial sentence that is served on licence in the community. The Criminal Justice Act 2003 reformed the sentencing framework and established the nature and framework for the community sentence and custodial sentences.

The community order can run for up to three years. There is no minimum duration, but some of the requirements have a minimum number of hours that must be imposed.

The requirements in a community order may be combined subject to their being compatible, suitable for the offender, not compromising the offender's religious beliefs or times of work and education, and subject to the overall package being commensurate with the seriousness of the offending. The Sentencing Guidelines Council has advised that, in low seriousness cases, 'in most cases only one requirement will be appropriate, and the length may be curtailed if additional requirements are necessary'.

The supervision requirement corresponds with the former community rehabilitation order (probation) and obliges the offender to attend regular appointments with the responsible agency to promote rehabilitation. Work will be undertaken to change attitudes and behaviour, and this may include, for example, monitoring and reviewing patterns of behaviour, increasing motivation to achieve law-abiding goals, practical support, etc.

The context of supervision has changed in many respects over recent years (effective practice, multi-agency public protection arrangements (MAPPAs)). The Probation Service has had to demonstrate credibility, show that it can hold offenders to account; and counteract the populist view that community sentences are a 'let off'. The Probation Service is measured on its effectiveness (i.e. its ability to reduce reoffending, its ability to hold offenders to complete their sentences successfully and its swift action in relation to infringements of orders). It is a cornerstone of the Probation Service that it can work with offenders to change their anti-social behaviour, and the central plank of this approach is supervision.

National Standards, mandated under the powers of the Criminal Justice and Court Services Act 2000, dictate the minimum standard in relation to the content, frequency and quality of supervision. Supervision is both the description of the relationship (between the offender and the supervisor) and the process within which that relationship develops.

Supervision is the implementation of the sentence plan by the offender manager, who works with offender supervisors, case administrators and other key providers in an offender management unit. Effective supervisory relationships are characterized by warm, empathetic interactions where authority is used within a firm but fair relationship. Being 'scared straight' is ineffective in reducing reoffending. Research added impetus to the 'what works' proponents to adopt motivational interviewing and relapse prevention techniques. Interventions to change behaviour and to help offenders learn the cognitive and behavioural skills to change their lives also emerged from these developments.

In the National Offender Management Model, supervision is modelled on four tiers of intervention: punish, help, change, control. At tier 1, punishment is the only requirement: this is usually unpaid work. At tier 2, an element of punishment is combined with help. At tier 3, punishment, help and change are needed. Often this would involve an accredited programme and a supervision requirement. At tier 4, offenders have three or more requirements in an order or the equivalent on licence. Alternatively, they might be assessed as so likely to reoffend (such as a designated prolific and other priority offender) or cause serious harm that they need to work with staff or have oversight almost daily. If an offender poses a risk of serious harm requiring control as well as help, change and punishment interventions, clearly he or she will attract intensive work and a high resource requirement.

Throughout the process of supervision attention is paid to reducing reoffending, protecting the public (public protection) and specific victims, making reparation and rehabilitating the offender. The offender should experience the '4 Cs': consistency of prosocial messages; continuity of treatment and relationship; the commitment of staff; and consolidation of learned new skills and attitudes. For many staff across prison and probation, the introduction of the National Offender Management Model has been welcomed. The more person-centred approach has resonated with staff values and it is experienced as being more rewarding. Within the model there is the opportunity for the offender to form a continuous relationship with his or her offender manager from the beginning, at the pre-sentence stage, right through the sentence in the community or prison to the end, at successful completion. This is a far cry from the days of resource management when probation had different teams engaged in discrete interventions and it was not unusual for offenders to have worked with half a dozen or more staff. Good supervision requires commitment from staff (who are not just going through the motions), consistency of message and continuity of relationship so that change can be consolidated: indeed, the 4 Cs of the model.

The supervision process starts with a thorough assessment of the risk of the offender causing serious harm to the public or known victims and the risk of reoffending. Criminogenic needs are assessed using the national offender assessment system, OASys. Known and potential victims must first of all be protected and protective factors to prevent reoffending put in place. The offender's views and needs are canvassed in the Self-assessment Questionnaire and incorporated into the risk management and sentence plan. In devising the plan, offenders' individual needs have to be taken account of: what is manageable for them, their diversity needs, learning style, barriers to be overcome (e.g. access, childcare, isolation – being a sole female or black member of a group – work commitments, illiteracy, etc.).

ASPIRE is the shorthand used in the National Offender Management Model for the end-to-end process of sentence management: assessing (using OASys), sentence planning, implementing, reviewing and evaluating.

The structure is developed for undertaking quality supervision in the offender management model. However, none of it can take place unless there is a professional, respectful, prosocial and anti-discriminatory environment where offenders are encouraged and held to account. A strong background in motivational interviewing is vital.

Supervision can be undertaken by either the offender manager or the offender supervisor, or indeed a key worker. What is essential to the process is that the supervisee, the offender, is as equal a participant as possible in the process. It is him or her, after all, who will have to change, learn new skills, internalize control and new behaviours and practise those changed behaviours consistently in a law-abiding future life. To do that, all staff working with the offender take on a shared agenda (as a project) to motivate, support, assess, challenge, encourage, plan, review and evaluate – from the beginning to the end of the sentence.

Good supervision in the criminal justice system is based on:

- understanding diversity;
- assessing need and dangerousness;
- planning and sequencing interventions;
- overcoming barriers to change;
- motivating, supporting and implementing;
- enforcement;
- managing risk dynamically; and
- regular reviewing of progress and evaluating the effectiveness of supervision.

The supervision requirement is now embedded in the Criminal Justice Act 2003, and is administrated through the concept of sentence planning and sentence management. The umbrella of offender management as a process more rigorously describes the set of interactions with which the offender is supported through change. Central to this is the role played by a consistent offender manager who has an overall professional responsibility for the sentence.

Karen MacLeod

RELATED ENTRIES

ASPIRE; Assessment; Assessment instruments and systems; Community order; Community penalties; Criminal Justice Act 2003; Diversity; Enforcement; Interventions; Offender Assessment System (OASys); Offender management; Probation; Rehabilitation.

Key texts and sources

Andrews, D.A., Zinger, I., Hodge, R.D., Bonta, J., Gendreau, P. and Cullen, F.T. (1990) 'Does correctional treatment work?', *Criminology*, 28: 208–16.
Burnett, R., Baker, K. and Roberts, C. (2007) 'Assessment, supervision and intervention: fundamental practice in probation', in L. Gelsthorpe and R. Morgan (eds) *Handbook of Probation*. Cullompton: Willan Publishing.

Dowden, C. and Andrews, D. (2004) 'The impor-tance of staff practice in delivering effective correctional treatment: a meta-analytic review of core correctional practice', *International Journal of Offender Therapy and Comparative Criminology*, 48: 203–14.

Fuller, C. and Taylor, P. (2003) *Toolkit of Motivational Skills*. London: National Probation Directorate.

Gast, L. and Taylor, P. (1998) *Influence and Integrity: A Practice Book for Pro-social Modelling*. Birmingham: Midlands Probation Training Consortium.

Mair, G. and Canton, R. (2007) 'Sentencing, commu-nity penalties and the role of the Probation Service', in L. Gelsthorpe and R. Morgan (eds) *Handbook of Probation*. Cullompton: Willan Publishing.

Marlatt, G. and Gordon, J. (eds) *Relapse Prevention: Maintenance Strategies in the Treatment of Addictive Behaviors*. New York, NY: Guilford Press.

Miller, W.R. and Rollnick, S. (1991) *Motivational Interviewing*. NY: Guilford Press.

Miller, W.R. and Rollnick, S. (2002) *Motivational Interviewing*. NY: Guilford Press.

NOMS (2006) *The NOMS Offender Management Model*. London: Home Office.

Queries about offender management and the super-vision of offenders can be emailed to **omqueries@noms.gov.uk**. The *Reducing Re-offending National Action Plan* can be found at **www.probation.homeoffice.gov.uk/files/pdf/ NOMS%20National%20Action%20Plan.pdf**.

SUPPORTING PEOPLE

> A government programme established to improve the provision of housing support services to vulnerable people, and to help them live independently in the community.

The Supporting People programme began in April 2003. Support is available to people from all sectors of the community, including those who:

- have served a prison sentence;
- are homeless;
- suffer with mental or physical ill-health;
- have substance misuse problems;
- are vulnerable through age;
- are at risk of domestic violence; and
- are at risk of reoffending.

A Supporting People grant is allocated to each local authority whose commissioning body directs the services. The commissioning body is an equal partnership between the Probation Service, health service and the local authority. Before April 2003 the Probation Service paid for supported housing through the Probation Accommodation Grants Scheme. This money was then transferred to the Supporting People budget. The Probation Service became an equal partner in Supporting People planning groups, such as the Core Strategy Development Group and the commissioning body. This provided all probation services with the opportunity to influence their local Supporting People five-year strategy on offender housing-related support needs and the type of services needed to sup-port them. Local probation areas can not only influence the overall direction of Supporting People but can also maintain an oversight of existing offender-linked services and can encourage the development of new services to meet offender need. It further provides an opportunity to work in partnership with home-lessness teams and housing providers and to promote the need for stable accommodation for offenders to reduce reoffending and increase public protection.

The Supporting People programme can complement the work of offender managers and help people to live independently in the com-munity. If the support is delivered to people in their own homes, this is called 'floating support'. This would be appropriate, for example, for an offender who is setting up home for the first time, or someone with mental health or sub-stance misuse problems who finds it difficult to manage a tenancy. Floating support could pre-vent rent arrears accruing by ensuring housing benefit claims are made correctly, and could offer crisis intervention to negotiate and pre-vent eviction.

Support may also be delivered in specialist accommodation, such as a homeless hostel, a women's refuge or defined offender/alcohol/ substance misuse (drugs) provision. An offender leaving prison may need supported accommodation initially before moving to inde-pendent accommodation (see Reintegration;

Resettlement). Likewise, an offender in the community could move initially to supported accommodation specific to his or her needs and later move to a tenancy, with floating support, to help make the transition to independent living.

Housing-related support services can include the following:

- Setting up and maintaining a home or tenancy.
- Managing benefit claims.
- Developing domestic/life skills.
- Mediation in neighbour disputes.
- Finding alternative accommodation if needed.
- Providing housing advocacy.
- Advising on repairs and home improvements.
- Establishing personal safety and security.
- Supervising and monitoring health and well-being.
- Establishing social contacts and activities.
- Gaining access to other services.

Services are provided by local authorities, registered social landlords and the voluntary and private sector through contracts with the Supporting People administering authorities. All services are reviewed every three years to ensure that they provide value for money, a qualitative service and are strategically relevant. Stakeholders and service users should be consulted during the review process. Virtually all offender services are defined as 'short term', which means the work should be completed within a two year maximum and there is no cost to the individual or referring agency.

The government has committed itself to reducing reoffending, and this is outlined in the *Reducing Re-offending National Action Plan.* This plan views 'appropriate and accessible accommodation as the foundation for successful rehabilitation and reducing the risk of harm to others'. Research has shown that prisoners who return to their community homeless are up to twice as likely to reoffend within two years, compared with people returning to stable accommodation. Probation areas that have embraced the Supporting People programme, that have provided evidence of offender need and secured supported accommodation and floating support services appropriate to that need will be contributing to the aims of the national action plan. This will have a significant impact on crime reduction and public protection in each area.

Una Mulrenan

RELATED ENTRIES

Criminogenic needs; Domestic violence; Interventions; Public protection; Rehabilitation; Resettlement.

Key texts and sources

Taylor, R. (2004) *'Supporting People' – Guidance for the National Offender Management Service.* London: Home Office (available online at **www.probation.homeoffice.gov.uk/files/pdf/ Commissioning%20Guidance%206.pdf**).

Each local authority is likely to have a website with a section devoted to its Supporting People programme. See also **www.spkweb.org** under 'Subjects/client groups/offenders and ex-offenders'.

T

TEAMWORK

> Teamwork involves people working together to accomplish more than they could alone.

Most definitions of a team and the concept of teamwork that arises from it suggest that, when people work together effectively, they produce a quantity and quality of work that is higher than each would produce individually. A wide-ranging theoretical debate exists about what constitutes not only teamwork but also a team. For example, Payne (2000) suggests that the terms 'team' and 'teamwork' represent *aspirations* towards co-operation, collaboration and co-ordination that might or might not exist in practice, depending on the stage of the staff group and its development. So a newly formed work group might feel less like a team than one whose members have been working together for several years.

Research into successful team behaviour suggests that their effectiveness is in part dependent upon the *balance* of specific team roles – governed more by personal attributes and preferences than by skills, knowledge and job task – and team members' ability to transfer between them. Belbin (1993) identified these roles as follows:

- *Shapers*: high achievers, demonstrating drive and creativity but can be abrasive and prone to fall out with people.
- *Co-ordinators*: good team managers able to bring out the best in people but less likely to be creative themselves.
- *Plants*: contribute original and creative thinking to a team but can be poor at following their ideas through and careless with detail.
- *Monitor evaluators*: bring an objective approach to decision-making but can be crit-

ical and ready to find fault in the behaviour of others.
- *Implementers*: practical, organized, responsible and hard working but can be somewhat inflexible and thrown by sudden changes.
- *Resource investigators*: keep the team in touch with the world outside the team but quickly lose interest in projects, preferring to work on new ideas.
- *Team workers*: bring friendliness, sensitivity and caring to the team although tend to be indecisive in 'crunch' situations.
- *Completer-finishers*: excellent attention to detail and task completion but inclined to worry unduly, which can create problems for them personally.
- *Specialists*: have particular knowledge or expertise to share with the team but less willing to undertake general tasks.

No one role is 'better' than another – it is the mix and balance of roles and team members' ability to transfer between them which contribute to overall team effectiveness. A work group or team in which members can exploit the strengths and ease the weaknesses of teamwork is likely to generate 'added value' in terms of individual job satisfaction and overall team achievement.

Team role theory offers just one of many perspectives on teamwork and team dynamics. Others include Tuckman's (1965) stages of group formation (forming–storming–norming–performing), Adair's (1973) work on balancing the needs of the task with that of the group and individuals, and the identification by Quinn *et al.* (2000: 60–1) of factors that make up a good team player. What is missing from many of these is the way power – both formal and informal – is distributed within a team and the tensions this can produce between team members.

Power in teams, as with organizations, is likely to reflect the distribution of power within society: those with more have the ability to influence or control people, events, processes or resources to a greater extent than those with less. Being part of a dominant team culture – most often white, middle class, able bodied and heterosexual – means having control over its terminology, language, humour and dress code, and having an inherent understanding of 'the way things are done'. Good teamwork recognizes these processes and attempts to share power and its rewards, and to use this constructively in the team environment.

Theoretical nuances aside, probation staff have traditionally belonged to a primary work group known as a team – for example, field team, court team, groupwork team – and have been managed by a team senior probation officer. Within these teams members have worked towards a common goal or purpose, having particular (but not necessarily the same) experience and expertise and having accountability for their work. Teamwork has consisted of members meeting together to communicate, allocate work, collaborate on cases, plan and take decisions about future actions.

The strengths of teamwork are as follows:

- Contributing to professional development – formally through co-working challenging cases and informally through discussion of shared experiences.
- Discussing new ideas, including what will and will not work in relation to offender management.
- Developing a collective response to promoting equality, celebrating and supporting diversity, challenging inappropriate behaviour and promoting anti-discriminatory practice.
- Increasing people's motivation and building confidence as certain types of practices are seen to work.
- Working together to identify and manage the stresses of the job.

The weaknesses of teamwork include the following:

- Potential for time to be wasted in unproductive meetings and discussions.

- Conflict – about an assumed 'common purpose'; about the different roles and how they relate to each other; about a lack of resources; about workload distribution; and about team leadership.
- The development of a team culture that is negative, oppressive and unwelcoming.

The National Offender Management Service (NOMS) Offender Management Model introduces a new concept of teamwork – one in which an offender management team consisting of a variety of people from different organizations and professional backgrounds will work together to implement a single sentence plan for an individual offender. There will therefore be particular challenges and opportunities in inter-agency work (for example, multi-agency public protection arrangements (MAPPAs)). While key aspects of teamwork – for example, communication – will continue to be central to the work, it will be the offender manager rather than the team senior who will be at the hub of each team. He or she will work closely with key workers delivering interventions, an offender supervisor responsible for implementing the plan and a case administrator keeping everything on track.

Tina Eadie

RELATED ENTRIES

Accountability; Diversity; Inter-agency work; Interventions; Multi-agency public protection arrangements (MAPPAs); Offender management; Partnerships; Senior probation officers.

Key texts and sources

Adair, J. (1973) *Action-centred Leadership*. London: McGraw-Hill.
Belbin, M. (1993) *Team Roles at Work*. London: Butterworths.
Payne, M. (1990) *Working in Teams*. Basingstoke: Macmillan Education.
Payne, M. (2000) *Teamwork in Multiprofessional Care*. Basingstoke: Macmillan.
Quinn, R.E., Faerman, S.R., Thompson, M.P. and McGrath, M.P. (2000) *Becoming a Master Manager* (2nd edn). Chichester: Wiley.
Tuckman, B.W. (1965) 'Development in small groups', *Psychological Bulletin*, 63: 384–99.

THERAPEUTIC COMMUNITY

A term applied to treatment settings that are characterized by an open culture of debate and inquiry; a focus on the here and now relationships between people; non-hierarchical relationships between staff and participants; and an openness by all to learning from the experience of living and working together in groups.

The origin of the term 'therapeutic community' has two roots. In the UK it was developed after their Second World War experience by London psychiatrists, Maxwell Jones and Tom Main, at the Henderson and Cassel Hospitals.

Independently of this, in California in 1958, Charles Dederich, a recovering alcoholic dissatisfied with some limitations of Alcoholics Anonymous, founded an organization called Synanon, where ex-alcoholics and ex-drug addicts could live together and help one another to stay 'clean'.

From these roots, Kennard (1998) has identified four broad and distinct ways in which the term therapeutic community is now used. First, the therapeutic community approach is used for the transformation of large asylum-type institutions into more active, humane, caring places where the human rights and dignity of residents are recognized and respected. Secondly, the term is used for small establishments in the mental health, social services or prison systems that use the therapeutic community principles, and usually work with problems of personality disorder or social maladjustment. Thirdly, there are the 'concept houses', usually concerned with the rehabilitation of drug addicts or offenders. Phoenix House and the Ley Community are examples in the UK. Fourthly, the term is applied to communities that offer an alternative to mental hospital treatment. They arise from the anti-psychiatry movement and are very varied.

Therapeutic communities have an informal and communal atmosphere. This reflects the principle of 'communalism' described by Rapoport (1960) as one of four general attributes of therapeutic communities. The others are the centrality of meetings in the therapeutic programme, sharing the work of running the community and the therapeutic role of all the community members. Meetings are the principal therapeutic method (see Groupwork). They are used to share information, build cohesion, make transparent the decision-making process and provide a forum for personal 'feedback'. This process of giving 'feedback' is used to exert pressure on individuals whose attitude or behaviour is disturbing to others.

In the UK prison system, Grendon Underwood was designed to function as a collection of wings each run as a separate therapeutic community. Smaller therapeutic communities have been set up at Wormwood Scrubs, Gartree and Barlinnie. For a time in the 1980s at least one approved probation hostel (approved premises) sought to implement a therapeutic community regime. In his latter years, Maxwell Jones did much to demonstrate how his original ideas of therapeutic community could be implemented in the setting of community psychiatry.

David Hancock

RELATED ENTRIES

Approved premises; Drugs; Groupwork; Personality disorder.

Key texts and sources

Kennard, D. (1998) *An introduction to Therapeutic Communities.* London: Jessica Kingsley.

Rapoport, R.N. (1960) *Community as Doctor.* London: Tavistock.

The Association of Therapeutic Communities (ATC) (**www.therapeuticcommunities.org**) is the main UK organization supporting the development of therapeutic communities.

TRACKING

> The use of satellite technology to monitor exclusion orders and offenders' movements. Tested in England through a pilot project, but not yet fully operational.

Satellite tracking is the latest and most technologically advanced form of electronic monitoring. It allows the location and movements of an offender to be determined, rather than simply enforcing a static curfew. This is achieved by using GPS (global positioning system) satellites and analysing data based on signals from at least three of the 23 that orbit the earth.

Managing such systems can be undertaken in several different ways. In 'passive mode', data relating to movements are constantly transmitted but stored until they can be analysed at a control centre. In 'active mode' systems, the data on movement are transmitted constantly and are monitored in real time. This is extremely expensive and has led to the development of hybrid systems, which monitor continuously but do not switch to active mode unless the wearer leaves his or her designated area or enters an exclusion zone.

This ability to monitor exclusion zones has been seen as particularly useful in relation to some kinds of sex offenders, in domestic violence or stalking cases and in other high-risk situations. It is not without practical difficulties and some dangers, however. Exclusion zones have to be carefully drawn and understood and, unless response to breaches is swift and effective, their use may lead to a false sense of security.

In England and Wales, the Home Office piloted the use of satellite tracking technology in three areas (Greater Manchester, West Midlands and Hampshire) from September 2004 until June 2006. The aim was two-fold – to monitor compliance with exclusion orders and to monitor the whereabouts of a range of offenders. The original aim was to monitor almost 500 offenders, but the actual numbers tracked were considerably lower. Practical issues included a loss of signal and mapping problems.

A wide range of GPS programmes are under way in North America, Europe and elsewhere but most are small-scale projects, designed to test feasibility and acceptability to both sentencers and politicians. The only significant published research to date has been in Florida, the first state to use GPS technology and by far the biggest user, with over 1,000 new cases each year from 2001. In a wide-ranging comparison of basic (radio frequency) tagging and GPS systems, it concluded that both worked well in reducing risks to public safety. However, it also found that basic monitoring was just as effective and over four times cheaper than the more advanced system. The University of Birmingham is undertaking research on the English GPS experiment. Publication is expected in 2007.

Dick Whitfield

RELATED ENTRIES

Curfews; Domestic violence; Electronic monitoring; Sex offenders.

Key texts and sources

Nellis, M. and Lilly, J.R. (2004) 'GPS tracking – what America and England can learn from each other', *Journal of Offender Monitoring*: 5–24 (a useful introduction to the subject).
Padgett, K., Bales, W. and Blomberg, T. (2006) 'Under surveillance', *Journal of Criminology and Public Policy*, 61–91 (contains the Florida research).

TRANSGENDER

> 'Transgender', 'transsexual' and 'transvestite' are a few of the labels used to describe individuals who do not fit conventional boundaries in terms of their gender identity. Although 'trans' is often aligned with lesbian, gay and bisexual in 'LGBT', it is quite different from sexual orientation. Trans people may be heterosexual, homosexual, bisexual or asexual.

Transsexual individuals (also known as transmen or transwomen) have physical characteristics of one sex but a very strong sense of being of the opposite gender. This 'gender dysphoria' can only be resolved by transitioning – living in the gender with which they identify (for them their true gender) rather than as the sex they were born. Transmen and women will usually undergo hormone treatment and surgery to align their physical characteristics as closely as possible with their true gender.

Transvestites/cross-dressers identify as their birth sex but have a need temporarily to adopt the opposite gender role, typically by cross-dressing. Some dictionaries describe this as being for sexual gratification – but this is misleading.

Intersex describes a number of conditions where the individual has indeterminate genitalia. Intersex individuals are usually assigned to the sex of the most dominant sexual characteristic – which may not be how they eventually identify (in which case they may 'transition' to their true gender). They may, alternatively, identify as neither male nor female. Transgender can either be used as an umbrella term for the above or to describe someone who lives in the opposite gender but does not want to undergo surgery.

The Gender Recognition Act (GRA) 2004 enables individuals to gain legal recognition in their 'acquired gender' (as the Act puts it). This applies to those who have been diagnosed as having or having had 'gender dysphoria' and who have lived in their acquired gender for a minimum of two years and intend to live in that role permanently (surgery is not a prerequisite). Once they have been granted recognition, they can apply for a new birth certificate and marry in their acquired gender. They also have some legal protection in respect of privacy regarding their gender history.

This means that if anyone learns, in the course of his or her duties, that someone has applied for a gender recognition certificate (GRC) or has been granted a GRC, it is a criminal offence, punishable by a fine of up to £5,000, to disclose that information (or the gender history of someone with a GRC) to anyone else. This is a 'strict liability' offence and there is no pleading 'reasonableness'. There are some exceptions to the restriction, which include proceedings before a court. Probation staff who

deal with transsexual/transgendered individuals are advised to obtain advice on the implications of Section 22 of the GRA.

Helen Dale

RELATED ENTRIES

Gender; Heterosexism; Lesbians and Gay Men in Probation (LAGIP).

Key texts and sources

See key texts and sources at related entries.

TREATMENT MANAGER

The treatment manager has a vital role in ensuring that an accredited programme is delivered effectively in the way the programme designer intended. The main role is to maintain treatment integrity, ensuring tutors' adherence to the programme manual and helping them to balance this with responsivity to those undertaking the programme.

A treatment manager is appointed for each team of tutors delivering an accredited programme. They contribute to the initial selection of tutors and have the following principal responsibilities:

- Maintaining the integrity of the offender selection procedure by ensuring the risk/needs profile is accurate and the offender is allocated to the most appropriate programme.
- Ensuring the pre- and post-programme psychometric testing of offenders is completed.
- Maintaining treatment integrity by video monitoring. The treatment manager views programme tapes, as well as checking session registers and session review forms completed by the tutors.
- Supervision of staff. The aims of supervision are to ensure good-quality programme delivery by providing guidance to tutors and developing their skills. Video monitoring is used as the basis for tutor feedback in supervision. Equality and diversity issues are

addressed in supervision, as is responsivity. The supervisor is responsive to the differing needs of the tutors, modelling the responsivity expected of the tutors.

- Contributing to the assessment of tutor competence by scoring performance, feeding back and assessing the use of feedback.
- Ensuring good-quality post-programme reports by quality-assuring and countersigning the tutors' reports on offenders. The reports are used as the basis for post-programme review meetings, which the treatment manager attends when they are likely to be complex.
- Facilitating the change control process by maintaining a log and implementing nationally agreed changes. Treatment managers report programme and treatment integrity issues to the programme manager.

Staff of various grades (for example, psychologist, senior probation officer, senior practitioner, probation officer or probation service officer) can undertake the treatment manager role. A treatment manager must have passed the tutor assessment centre and completed all tutor training available for the programme to be managed.

A treatment manager can be appointed following one year's experience as a tutor, having delivered the programme at least four times and having achieved an average score of 3.5 on video/audio-monitoring forms. Once appointed, the person must attend treatment manager training within nine months of taking up the role. This involves an information day, supervision skills training and video-monitoring training. After that, the treatment manager is expected to attend regional support days.

A mentor, who is an experienced treatment manager, must be provided for new treatment managers while they are managing their first two programmes. The treatment manager should deliver at least 50 per cent of one programme per year to retain his or her skills as a tutor. Regional training consortia have a role in the training, accreditation and development of accredited programmes staff, including treatment managers.

Heather Jasper

RELATED ENTRIES

Accredited programmes; Accredited programmes in common use; Assessment; Diversity; Effective practice; Regional training consortia; Responsivity; Sex offender treatment programmes (SOTPs); Staff supervision.

Key texts and sources

Home Office (2002) *Treatment Manager Strategy* (PC 57/2002). London: Home Office.

TRIANGLE OF OFFENDER NEEDS

A diagram that shows a range of possible criminogenic factors useful to practitioners in considering a sentence plan.

Over the years, several commentators have sought to codify the range of differing issues that need to be considered in the process of working with offenders to reduce the likelihood of reoffending. One of the most satisfactory models is shown in Figure 9. Colin Roberts first set it out in 2002 and, since its inception, it has become a well respected icon of probation practice. A valuable feature of the model is the way the different factors are positioned, those relating mostly to the individual offender being at or near the apex of the triangle, and those relating mostly to the accessibility of community resources being at or near the base.

David Hancock

Key texts and sources

See key texts and sources at related entries.

RELATED ENTRIES

Assessment instruments and systems; Criminogenic needs; Offender Assessment System (OASys); Partnerships.

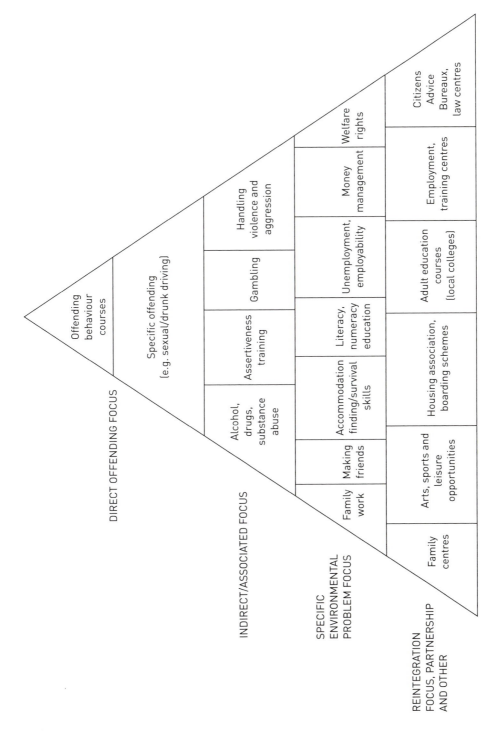

Figure 9 Triangle of offender needs
Reproduced by kind permission of Colin Roberts

U

UNITED NATIONS

A collaborative international body comprising representatives of the governments of all nations for the pursuit of peace, justice and development.

The United Nations (UN) adopted the Universal Declaration of Human Rights in 1948. It was the first global instrument to define fundamental human rights and to promote their protection. Although the declaration is not binding and lacks enforcement systems, it has served as a model and as a standard for other UN and regional initiatives. Its influence is very powerful and it established some enduring standards for criminal justice and sentencing. Five of the basic rights set out in the universal declaration are as follows:

- Freedom from torture or cruel, inhuman or degrading treatment or punishment.
- Freedom from arbitrary arrest or detention.
- The right to a fair and public trial.
- The right to be presumed innocent in criminal charges.
- Protection from retrospective criminal law.

In the European context, the later European Convention on Human Rights is more practically relevant since it has been incorporated into the legislation of many European countries, including the UK, and it has become enforceable by both national and European courts.

In 1985 the UN passed a resolution restricting the use of custodial sentences for juveniles to cases of serious violent crime or persistence in committing other serious offences. The resolution included 'Standard Minimum Rules for the Administration of Juvenile Justice', known as the Beijing Rules. They are not enforceable, but they are certainly influential in providing a clear standard of international expectations.

Similar status is attached to the 'UN Standard Minimum Rules for Non-custodial Measures'. These apply to adults, were approved in 1990 and are known as the Tokyo Rules. They represent a detailed international agreement about promoting the use of community sentences. They are non-binding but set a recognized standard. The rules promote greater community involvement in the management of criminal justice, and they argue for an increased use of community penalties as part of a movement towards the 'depenalization' and decriminalization of offenders.

David Hancock

RELATED ENTRIES

Community; Conférence permanente Européenne de la Probation (CEP); Council of Europe; Human rights; Probation in Africa; Probation in Europe; Probation in the USA and Canada; Punishment (aims and justifications).

Key texts and sources

Kurki, L. (2001) 'International standards for sentencing and punishment', in M. Tonry and R.S. Frase (eds) *Sentencing and Sanctions in Western Countries*. New York, NY: Oxford University Press.

Ville, R., Zvekic, U. and Klaus, J. (1997) *Promoting Probation Internationally*. Rome and London: United Nations Interregional Crime and Justice Research Institute.

The Beijing Rules (UN Doc A/40/53 (1985)) are available online at **www.unhchr.ch/htl/menu3/b/h_comp48.htm**. The Tokyo Rules (UN Doc A/45/49 (1990)) are available online at **www.unhchr.ch/htl/menu3/b/h_comp46.htm**. See also the United Nations Interregional Crime and Justice Research Institute's website (**www.unicri.it/**).

UNPAID WORK

One of the 12 possible requirements that can be included in a community order. It requires the offender to provide unpaid work for the benefit of needy individuals, groups or the community as a whole.

The unpaid work requirement replaced the sentence of community punishment in April 2005 when the Criminal Justice Act 2003 was implemented. The statutory purposes of this sentence are punishment, reparation and rehabilitation. In making this requirement the court must be satisfied that the offender is suitable to perform work, and the number of hours to be worked must be specified within the range of 40–300. The recommended guideline for courts states that 40–80 hours is appropriate for low-seriousness offending, 80–150 hours for medium seriousness and 150–300 hours where the level of seriousness is high. The unpaid work should normally be completed within 12 months.

National Standards require the offender manager to complete a post-sentence assessment interview within five days of an unpaid work requirement being made. In this the offender manager is responsible for the completion of the risk of harm assessment, for collecting relevant information to match the offender to work, informing initial work allocation. This meeting also feeds into the pre-placement work sessions in which all aspects of the sentence (including rules, enforcement procedure and health and safety instruction) are provided. Within this session more detailed assessments with regard to Skills for Life and the opportunities and expectations of vocational skills learning can be delivered.

Offenders are expected to commence work within 10 days of the requirement being made and are expected to complete a minimum of 6 hours per week until all the hours are worked.

Elements of unpaid work

All offenders undertaking unpaid work projects or placements must have an OASys risk of harm screening and, if necessary, a risk of harm assessment, completed before allocation to a worksite. Risk must be reviewed using data from all the staff involved. Medium and high-risk offenders must only be placed with suitably qualified supervisors, and particular care must be exercised when placing sex offenders.

Schemes must be organized to maximize inclusion. Work sessions must be arranged so as not to prevent the offender being readily available to seek or take up employment if unemployed. Unpaid work should not conflict with an offender's entitlement to benefit or disrupt education or training activities. It must take account of religious and cultural requirements. The views of lone women or black and minority ethnic offenders (diversity) must be sought and taken into account when deciding on a work placement.

Work must be available at weekends and evenings. Placements must be available to meet the needs of disabled offenders, and each scheme needs to provide a wide range of placements to accommodate individual offender needs. Special arrangements apply to 16 and 17-year-olds to comply with the Children's Act 2004.

Offenders on unpaid work may be credited with an allowance for completing basic literacy or other work necessary to enable them to gain maximum benefit from the sentence. Training and literacy work has been shown to reduce reoffending. The allowance, which must not exceed 20 per cent of prescribed hours, can also provide time to build on learning undertaken through the unpaid work activity itself and should support offenders getting qualifications through vocational skills learning. Work placements should facilitate this.

Offenders and staff must work in situations that have been appropriately assessed in terms of health and safety. Offenders need to receive appropriate health and safety instruction within the scheme.

Placements need to be of good quality and have to be reviewed against quality standards on a minimum six-monthly basis. Unpaid work must not replace paid employment. Effective practice research provides significant evidence that certain features of work projects improve the rehabilitative effect of unpaid work. Work that is experienced as useful and rewarding, work that offenders can see would not have been done without them or where they can see that they are able to help others who need that help increases the likelihood of compliance and reduces the likelihood of reoffending. Further, the opportunity to develop employment-related skills and to learn from positive relationships with staff has an additional positive impact.

All staff need to be trained in the principles of prosocial modelling. This needs to be monitored and quality assured. Schemes in which staff are positive in demonstrating good behaviour are seen to be more effective. Practical examples include the following:

- Being respectful and addressing everyone by name.
- Listening and observing as well as showing and telling.
- Being consistent and impartial.
- Being open and responsive in relation to offender concerns and questions.
- Sharing in the activity.
- Praising work that is done to the best of each person's ability.
- Facilitating contact with beneficiaries.
- Ensuring positive comments from beneficiaries are fed back to offenders.

Evidence suggests that offenders respond best to a clear, consistent application of the rules. Good-quality information leaflets that set out expectations must be provided. Offenders need to be given a record of the hours worked on each occasion. Commencing orders promptly and being able to work regularly are factors that assist in securing compliance.

History and development

Throughout its 30-year history, unpaid work has proved itself a uniquely attractive sentence and one that is robust enough to adapt to what have often been major changes. The current National Probation Service (NPS) manual quotes from the 1991 edition of Jarvis's *Probation Officer's Manual*, commenting that the sentiments expressed are still recognizable today:

> The sentence has proved to have a certain attraction in the wider community through its visibility … Its attraction is that it can be seen as embodying a number of different approaches to sentencing … It is cost effective in comparison with other sentences. It contains elements of work discipline and through such work tangible achievements can be observed. The fact that the work is unpaid and compulsory … can be seen … to have a punitive element. It also symbolises the reparative element in sentencing, the offender paying back to the community by his/her work and such work being targeted on identifiable community needs. There are links with voluntary service organisations in its delivery. And finally there is a rehabilitative element when it has a beneficial effect on the offender's personal and social functioning.

Community service was introduced as a court sentence in the 1970s and remained largely unchanged until the 1990s when many probation areas began to model their community service provisions on effective practice principles that drew upon earlier research by Gill McIvor. This was formalized with a range of pilot schemes based on these 'effective practice principles', which led to the introduction of enhanced community punishment in 2003. (The Criminal Justice and Court Services Act 2000 had renamed community service as community punishment.)

Enhanced community punishment aimed to maximize the rehabilitative elements of the sentence (such as skills learning, problem-solving and prosocial modelling) while retaining its rigour as a punitive sentence. The main elements were as follows:

- *Integrated case management*: a systematic approach to offender management and sentence planning, based on OASys.
- *Placement quality standards*: ensuring that all placements and projects met a minimum standard.
- *Prosocial modelling*: to ensure that the attitudes and behaviour of staff, particularly those of supervisors, provided offenders with positive role models.
- *Problem-solving at work*: supervisors were encouraged to model logical problem-solving to offenders in planning and completing

activities on a worksite. Offenders were provided with a learning log that could be used to support formal accreditation.

- *Guided skills learning*: introduced accredited qualifications for the work done as part of the sentence, an aid to improving employability.

The Criminal Justice Act 2003 introduced unpaid work as one of the 12 requirements of the community order. While enhanced community punishment had enjoyed provisional accreditation from the Correctional Services Accreditation Panel in 2003, this was allowed to lapse in 2005, and the unpaid work scheme regulations relaxed some of the procedures and requirements that had existed earlier.

Community Payback was introduced in 2005. This is a national strategy for making unpaid work more visible in local communities and for encouraging neighbourhoods to become more directly involved in the scheme by nominating work projects and placements.

The year 2005 also saw the introduction of the National Offender Management Model into the unpaid work scheme. The separation of offender management and the intervention of unpaid work proved a challenge, since the structuring of the Enhanced Community Punishment Scheme had stressed the integration of the two into a holistic model.

Alan Goode

RELATED ENTRIES

Assessment; Community order; Compliance; Criminal Justice Act 2003; Diversity; Offender management; Prosocial modelling; Punishment (aims and justifications); Punishment as communication; Reconviction; Rehabilitation; Reparation; Risk assessment and risk management.

Key texts and sources

McIvor, G. (2004) 'Reparative and restorative approaches', in A. Bottoms *et al.* (eds) *Alternatives to Prison: Options for an Insecure Society.* Cullompton: Willan Publishing.

National Probation Service (2006) *A Manual on the Delivery of Unpaid Work.* London: Home Office.

Worrall, A. and Hoy, C. (2005) *Punishment in the Community.* Cullompton: Willan Publishing (particularly ch. 7).

V

VICTIM AWARENESS

Understanding the impact of crime on the specific victim or, more generally, on potential victims.

The concept of victim awareness is one aspect of the increased interest in and concern for victims of crime. Offenders, and also the staff working with them, are encouraged to understand the impact of the offence on the victim and also to develop a more general understanding of the potential impact of criminal activity and anti-social behaviour on potential victims and the wider public.

OASys requires an assessment of the extent to which the offender recognizes the impact of the offence on the victim and the community. Similarly, when setting objectives for the supervision of offenders, staff are asked to consider whether work is necessary to improve their attitude to victims.

Staff working with offenders use a variety of techniques to increase victim awareness. At the pre-sentence report stage, report authors may discuss the impact of the offence on the victim using information contained in victim impact statements or police documents to test and challenge the offender's attitudes and understanding.

Work intended to increase victim awareness forms part of both individual and group supervision of offenders. It may involve using information gained directly from the victim (for example, as part of the victim contact process) and, in some schemes, may involve direct communication between the victim and offender by letter or face to face, perhaps in a process of mediation. However, much work intended to raise victim awareness and increase empathy is of a more general nature. For example, individuals discuss their own experience of being victims and consider how they were affected before making the link with their own offending. Fictional scenarios can be used to generate discussion about the consequences of crime for victims and to explore victims' needs for such things as retribution or reparation. Some organizations and campaigning groups produce videos or websites that contain moving accounts of the impact of offending on real people, which can be used in direct work with offenders.

Victim awareness is an important aspect of the supervision and management of offenders for a number of reasons. Encouraging offenders to think more about the impact of their behaviour on others could be argued to be a good thing in itself. One consequence of paying proper attention to victim issues is that a more detailed assessment of an individual's offending history and risk factors can be compiled.

It is also often assumed that offenders who become more aware of the consequences of offending for their victims will become more remorseful and less likely to offend. However, the empirical basis for this assumption is not clear, with some studies failing to establish a link between remorse and reconviction.

Jane Dominey

RELATED ENTRIES

Mediation; Pre-sentence report (PSR); Reparation; Restorative justice; Victim contact; Victims.

Key texts and sources

Bagaric, M. and Amarasekara, K. (2001) 'Feeling sorry? Tell someone who cares: the irrelevance of remorse in sentencing', *Howard Journal of Criminal Justice*, 40: 364–76.

Dominey, J. (2002) 'Addressing victim issues in pre-sentence reports', in B. Williams (ed.) *Reparation and Victim-focused Social Work*. London: Jessica Kingsley.

VICTIM CONTACT

Probation work to consult and notify victims about the release arrangements of offenders serving 12 months or more for a sexual or violent offence. This was extended to the victims of mentally disordered offenders in 2005.

Traditionally, the work of the Probation Service was focused on offenders but, in the 1970s, attitudes began to change, and the Probation Service was responsible for founding the first Victim Support Scheme in Bristol, which was registered as a charity in 1979. In 1990 the Home Office published a 'Victim's Charter' and, for the first time, a requirement was placed upon probation services to have contact with victims, specifically the families of victims in lifer cases. In 1996 a second Victim's Charter was published extending the contact to all victims of violent and sexual crime where the offender was sentenced to four years' imprisonment and over.

In 2000, a thematic inspection report noted that few policy statements from probation areas 'emphasised the different approach to work with victims that was required as compared with direct work with offenders'. Victim contact work was extended through the Criminal Justice and Court Services Act 2000. Section 69 of the Act put victims' rights into statute for the first time. Probation has a duty to contact victims of sexual or violent offences where the offender is sentenced to one year's imprisonment or more, to ascertain whether they want to be kept informed of any conditions the offender may be subject to on release, and whether they want to make any representations concerning such conditions. Guidance for implementation was provided in PC 62/2001.

Face-to-face contact should be offered within 56 working days of sentence. The Probation Service is then required, if the victim wishes, to provide information about the conditions of release, which relate to the victim and his or her family.

The responsibility for victims was initially regarded with some scepticism by probation staff who traditionally focused on direct work with offenders. Concerns were raised about sharing information with service users and about confidentiality. This is particularly an issue where victim information contributes to the decisions of the Parole Board. In a significant number of cases victims request that their views remain confidential. Guidance in Prison Service Order 6000 (ch. 5) sets out the process for making decisions about the disclosure of information to the offender. Where possible, a summary is provided which the offender can see. In exceptional cases the information is withheld, and the prisoner is made aware of the reasons for this. As a last resort, victim information can be withdrawn.

Concerns about limiting information provided to the Parole Board or potentially putting a victim at risk have led to the development of 'special victim advocates' who can protect victims' interests as well as avoid any conflict of interest for the prisoner's legal representative. Practice varies between prisons and remains problematic.

Victims cannot be told the establishment where the offender is serving his or her sentence, although they do have the right to be informed of any change in categorization or other significant event, such as temporary release. Information is limited to the month of release and not the actual date, and only the general area of release. Victim views frequently result in requests for additional licence conditions, the two most common being non-contact and geographical exclusions.

Although feedback is limited to some local satisfaction surveys and a Mori telephone poll conducted in 2004, it does appear that the information provided by victim contact staff is generally welcomed. Victims prefer to be contacted sooner rather than later and find the victim contact officers knowledgeable and supportive. A significant number of victims would like access to more information about an offender's progress through the system and increased contact. Care needs to be taken to reduce any confusion between probation victim contact and the charity Victim Support.

The 2003 thematic inspection report, *Valuing the Victim*, recognized the complexity of the victim contact role. Because initial contact is often within weeks of the Crown Court sentence, many victims remain distressed, traumatized or afraid. It is not possible to talk to a victim without hearing about his or her experiences as a witness in court or the power that a sex offender continues to exert upon his victim. Ideally, victim contact officers should have built up local networks for referring victims on to other agencies – for example, for counselling, treatment for post-traumatic stress and claiming criminal injury compensation.

As the Probation Service has prioritized protection of the public, victim information has become increasingly important in the risk assessment and management of offenders. Information can be provided about the original offence that was not revealed in court or witness statements – for example, when attempted murder is plea bargained down to GBH or ABH, when offences are left to lie on file in the public interest or when harassment is continued to be orchestrated from prison. Recent local risk guidelines in one probation area identify 16 points during a sentence when consultation between case managers and victim contact staff should take place.

Section 32 of the Domestic Violence, Crime and Victims Act 2004 instituted a new victims' code of practice, published in March 2006.

It is gratifying to see the role of this relatively new probation initiative being recognized as making a significant contribution to the criminal justice system and enabling victims of crime to survive and move on from their experiences.

Ann Gerty

RELATED ENTRIES

Licence; Parole Board; Risk assessment and risk management; Victim awareness.

Key texts and sources

HMIP (2003) *Valuing the Victim*. London: Home Office.

Home Office (2001) *Further Guidance: Working with Victims of Serious Crime* (PC 62/2001). London: Home Office.

Home Office (2005) *Victims of Mentally Disordered Offenders* (PC 42/2005). London: Home Office.

Williams, B. and Goodman, H. (2007) 'Working for and with victims of crime', in L. Gelsthorpe and R. Morgan (eds) *Handbook of Probation*. Cullompton: Willan Publishing.

The Home Office *Code of Practice for Victims of Crime, 2006* is available online at **www.homeoffice.gov.uk/documents/victims-code-of-practice**.

VICTIMS

Victims of crime are the people injured, harmed or killed by offenders. The word 'victim' is rarely used in criminal courts, however – victims are more commonly referred to as injured parties. In some contexts, the term is also taken to cover the survivors of murder and manslaughter victims.

Until recently, victims of crime were neglected by the criminal justice system in general – and by the Probation Service in particular. This has changed in relation to probation in the period since 1990, when the 'Victim's Charter' was first published, giving criminal justice agencies specific responsibilities. The charter was the origin of the victim contact service provided by probation staff, but it also reflected a wider change in attitudes which led to important changes in agencies' responses to victims. In the probation context, working with victims was new and, for many staff, threatening: some felt that they had trained to work with offenders and saw no need for change. For this reason, among others, change, when it came, was slow. However, the pace was forced by successive governments, responding to public opinion: a stronger Victim's Charter was published in 1996, and victim contact arrangements were extended and then put on a statutory basis. In 2006 the charter was replaced by a 'code of conduct' with the force of law, backed up by a commissioner responsible for enforcing it.

One of the problems with the Victim's Charter was that it was never well known. Even the second version, which contained detailed requirements (including the victim contact service), was lengthy and poorly presented. Despite tens of thousands of copies being distributed, few victims of crime used it. Similarly, the Probation Service continues to be seen as a service for offenders, although it has been working with victims since the early 1990s. The code of conduct takes a different approach from that of the charter: rather than treating victims of crime as consumers of a service and trying to inform them of their rights, the code instead sets out the minimum requirements of the criminal justice agencies which come into contact with them. It remains to be seen whether this approach will prove to be more effective.

Victim contact is not the only way in which probation work impinges on victims. The authors of pre-sentence reports are required to demonstrate 'victim awareness' by considering the impact of offences upon victims, although in many cases they have little information on which to base such an assessment. The supervision of offenders also involves victims' issues: people under supervision are encouraged to consider the effects of their offending behaviour upon their victims, and many groupwork programmes include specific sessions which formalize this. When serious offenders are considered for early release on licence, probation reports should address victims' concerns and safety.

Research has identified a range of needs expressed by victims. These include being promptly provided with correct information, being treated with respect and sensitivity, in some cases being paid compensation and, in a minority of cases, receiving support. The criminal justice system makes a poor job of meeting these needs, but huge efforts have been made to change this, and practice is certainly improving. The need for support is largely met by voluntary agencies, but the statutory agencies which come into contact with victims can all take steps to improve their practice – as the code of conduct requires them to do. Some groups or individuals may find victim services less relevant or accessible – for example, victims from black and minority ethnic groups may believe that victim support services are predominantly geared up for white victims and be reluctant to seek support from them.

Victims are individuals, and their differences should be recognized. The real impact of offences on people differs. For example, since women as victims of domestic violence have often suffered numerous assaults before they report this abuse, their experience of victimization is quite different from that of (say) a young man assaulted outside a pub. Again, victims of racially aggravated crime are less likely to report offences and, if they do, they are less likely to report the incident as racially aggravated. Victims of 'hate crime' not only suffer the actual incident but they also experience the assault(s) as a cumulative process over time, associated with – and a threat to – their identity and affecting their whole 'community'.

For these and other reasons, it is impossible to predict how people will react to becoming victims of crime, particularly if they have other difficult issues to deal with. The victims of apparently minor offences can find these very hard to deal with. On the other hand, some people cope with serious offences in a matter-of-fact way. A great deal appears to depend upon the support networks people have in place. The great majority of those offered help by agencies such as Victim Support decline the offer of a visit from a volunteer, but some of those who do take it up remain in contact for months or even years.

One thing that victims tend to find helpful is reassurance about their reaction to victimization: it can be enormously helpful to be told that others react in similar ways and that there is nothing abnormal about their own responses. Common reactions to victimization include emotional and physical changes. Some people experience a profound loss of trust in others, exaggerated vigilance and fear. Depending upon the type of offence, some victims also describe disturbing feelings of rage. Victimization can also lead to denial, shock, humiliation and shame. Initially, there may be nightmares and heightened startle reactions. Child victims sometimes temporarily regress developmentally.

People working with victims need to be aware of the symptoms of post-traumatic stress, because people experiencing this may require professional help. It is an extreme form of many of the normal reactions described above, but it also involves abnormal reactions, such as withdrawal from social life and avoiding situations which might remind the victim of the offence, intrusive thoughts and dreams, emotional turbulence and intense and long-lasting pain. Intrusive thoughts or 'flashbacks' are the most easily recognized warning sign: people who find they cannot concentrate on the here and now because of their response to victimization often find this terrifying.

While it is often assumed that victims are likely to be vengeful, in many cases they are not. They often agree to meet 'their' offender to discuss the offence and how to put matters right, and research shows that, in many cases, they do so partly in order to help the offender (as well as to give him or her a 'piece of their mind'). Restorative justice also offers some hope of meeting many of the needs discussed above: victims are more likely to be kept informed, provided with timely information, compensated and dealt with respectfully through restorative justice than through conventional criminal justice.

Brian Williams

RELATED ENTRIES

Reparation; Restorative justice; Victim awareness; Victim contact.

Key texts and sources

Dignan, J. (2005) *Understanding Victims and Restorative Justice.* Maidenhead: Open University Press.

Williams, B. (2005) *Victims of Crime and Community Justice.* London: Jessica Kingsley.

Williams, B. and Goodman, H. (2007) 'Working for and with victims of crime', in L. Gelsthorpe and R. Morgan (eds) *Handbook of Probation.* Cullompton: Willan Publishing.

The victim section at **http://www.cjsonline.gov.uk/victim/index.html** contains useful information and links. See also **http://www.victimsupport.org.uk/**.

VIOLENT OFFENDERS

Offences against the person are considered to be the most serious offences, yet effective interventions with violent offenders are relatively underdeveloped. Eagerness to denounce such behaviour can distort understanding and lead to irrelevant or even counterproductive responses.

In any policy discussion that tries to distinguish between those who deserve the weightiest punishments and those who might be candidates for non-custodial measures, violent offenders are always on the 'wrong' side of the divide. Community sentences may be argued to be suitable for many offenders, but violent offenders, by contrast, are rhetorically consigned to custody. Violent offenders, together with sex offenders, were the explicit exception to the principle in the Criminal Justice Act 1991 that punishment should be proportionate to the offence committed, punishment beyond desert being permitted where this was necessary on grounds of public protection. Many of the specified offences that would, on a second conviction, attract a life sentence (under the Crime Sentences Act 1997) were offences of violence, and the extended sentencing provisions of the Criminal Justice Act 2003 have a particular focus on violent offenders.

Only sexual offenders (a particular category of violent offender?) are denounced with equal vehemence and, for sex offenders, there is often a suggestion of psychopathology – with the associated implication that sex offenders may not be fully responsible for their behaviour. By contrast, violent offending is much less likely to be understood in this way, and there are relatively fewer ideas about effective intervention. As Matza (1969) showed, however, the zeal to denounce and deplore can distort an understanding of crime and, through misunderstanding the phenomenon, can lead to ill-considered responses.

In some ways, hostility towards violent offenders is unsurprising. Violent offenders are likely to be prominent in any surveys of fear of crime. The effects on victims of violence, after all, can be profound, enduring and indeed life-changing. At the same time, we are perhaps somewhat selective in our sensibilities. No 'violent offenders' can match in scale (or cruelty) the death, pain and suffering inflicted by some states on their own citizens or by some countries against others in warfare. Dangerous drivers, employers who fail to take proper care of the health and safety of staff, those responsible for pollution of many kinds and manufacturers who jeopardize the safety of their customers or the general public to maximize their profits are not usually considered as violent offenders, despite the enormous harm they can cause.

There are many approaches to an understanding of violent offenders, seeking to explain a disposition to violence or perhaps a reduced inhibition from recourse to violence. There are biological theories that try to identify biogenetic propensities to violence and psychological theories of several varieties which (for example) posit influences on development that incline people to violent offending. Sociological understandings are likely to insist that manifestations of violence may reflect and contribute to structural differences in power – for example, domestic violence, racist offending and other modes of hate crime both reflect and sustain structural disadvantage and oppression. There are, of course, women

offenders who commit offences of violence – and who may be all the more liable to heavy punishment because of the 'double deviance' of both violence and behaviour contrary to expected gender norms. Yet male offenders are heavily over-represented, and being 'hard', standing up for yourself, your family and your mates is one culturally approved way of 'doing masculinity'. As with many questions about human conduct, we need an account that does justice to all these factors (see the discussion in Drugs of the value of biopsychosocial approaches).

A conventional distinction is made between 'instrumental' violence and 'hostile' or 'expressive' violence. Instrumental violence is purposeful: violence deployed as a means to an end – for example, violence (or its threat) during robbery – while expressive or 'hostile' violence is an expression of rage, violence for its own sake. This distinction underlies one of the criteria that determines suitability for accredited programmes. CALM (see Accredited programmes in common use), for instance, is said not to be suitable for perpetrators of instrumental violence.

This distinction, like many such dichotomies, may be oversimplified. For example, in very many cases of robbery, the paradigm case of instrumental violence, the thrill of the offence, seems quite as significant a part of the motivation as the profit. A recent study identifies 'five main motives for street robbery: "good times/partying", "keeping up appearances/flash cash", "buzz/excitement", "anger/desire to fight", and "informal justice/righting wrongs"' (Bennett, et al. 2006: 8). Expressions of rage and hatred, moreover, often have a 'payoff' for the perpetrator. If there is a distinction to be made here, expressive and instrumental may perhaps be better seen as ends of a continuum.

David Farrington (this volume – Criminal careers) comments instructively on the consideration that violent offenders are not 'specialists': 'the versatility of offenders means that it does not make much sense to have specific programmes for violent offenders. Since criminal career research shows that violent offenders are essentially frequent offenders, programmes to prevent violent offending should target frequent or chronic offenders.'

At the same time, there does seem to be a subgroup of offenders who repeatedly commit violent (as well as other) offences, some of whom seem destined to rehearse transactions that frequently result in violence. A dated but instructive study by Hans Toch (1972) shows how such people react to situations – and indeed *create* situations – as if acting out a script in which violence is the outcome. Certainly, probation officers will recognize offenders who believe that violence 'just happened', with no appreciation of build-up or of ways in which things could have been managed differently. Indeed, some violent offenders are poor in self-assertion, and the consequent frustrations can lead to an 'explosion' of rage. If this is correct, then some responses to violence could be irrelevant or even counterproductive.

While policy generalizes about 'violent offenders', in truth violent crime is diverse in origin, motivation, seriousness and impact. The work of Toch and others has been valuable in demonstrating how contexts and interactions can produce violence, rather than this being simply a property of a few violent people. It would be comfortable to think that there is an identifiable group of violent offenders who can be identified and incapacitated. As with many offences, however, violent offending turns out to be a phenomenon that is more intimately associated with the way in which society is ordered and with our routine activities than it is comfortable for us to acknowledge.

Rob Canton

RELATED ENTRIES

Accredited programmes; Accredited programmes in common use; Criminal careers; Criminal Justice Act 1991; Criminology; Extended sentencing; Gender; Masculinity and offending; Multi-agency public protection arrangements (MAPPAs).

Key texts and sources

Bennett, T., Brookman, F. and Wright, R. (2006) *A Qualitative Study of the Role of Violence in Street Crime* (available online at **http://www.crimereduction.gov.uk/violentstreet/violentstreet007.htm**).

Levi, M. with Maguire, M. (2002) 'Violent crime', in M. Maguire *et al.* (eds) *The Oxford Handbook of Criminology* (3rd edn). Oxford: Oxford University Press.

Matza, D. (1969) *Becoming Deviant.* Englewood Cliffs, NJ: Prentice Hall.

Toch, H. (1972) *Violent Men.* Harmondsworth: Penguin Books.

VOLUNTEERS

People who work with offenders in an unpaid capacity.

The history of volunteers in criminal justice is a long and honourable one. The Society of Voluntary Associates (now simply SOVA) was the first voluntary sector organization to have, as its *raison d'être*, the recruitment, training and deployment of volunteers in criminal justice. Formed in 1975 by volunteers working with the (then) Inner London Probation and Aftercare Service, SOVA sought from the start to have volunteers recognized as needing good selection and training, appropriate tasks, support and supervision. The organization holds that no volunteer should be used to replace any paid member of staff. These basic tenets of good practice with volunteers have not changed.

Any criminal justice body exploring the use of volunteers must examine a number of things. Are there clear benefits to offenders from using volunteers? Are there clear expectations of those volunteers? Are volunteers to be given appropriate training? Are volunteers to be allowed access to appropriate information about the person with whom they will work? Above all, does the organization know what it wants volunteers to do, and can it provide sufficient work? It is SOVA's experience that, where these questions are not satisfactorily answered, any volunteer scheme will fail.

Volunteers are now working at all points of the system. This ranges from bail support (remand services) and unpaid work through imprisonment and resettlement. More frequently, and with substantial government encouragement, volunteers are deemed 'mentors' and have a clear guidance role with offenders.

A recent and highly desirable development is the advent of 'peer mentors'. This describes offenders, often prisoners, who are trained to support their fellows. SOVA is engaged in this, as are many others. Probably the best known example would be Samaritan-trained 'listeners' in prisons.

The value of using volunteers to work with offenders is substantial. They provide stability in lives which have often had none; they provide one-to-one support not possible from professional staff; and, although their reporting lines are clear, they do not represent 'authority' in the same way that paid staff do. They bring a considerable range of skills and abilities not always present in specialist professional staff. These can include language skills, practical skills, basic skills support and many others. Another key strength that volunteers bring is the ability to give additional dedicated and valuable time to assist offenders with a particular area of need.

Notwithstanding this value it remains true that there is some resistance from individual professionals to utilize this resource. There are a number of reasons for this. There is still a pervasive mythology that volunteers are not reliable. This is not SOVA's experience, but does point to the importance of the selection and training process. Equally, volunteers do undoubtedly take time to manage and support. Hard-pressed professionals can find this a task too far. Finally,

volunteers, albeit donating their time, do have financial implications for those using them in terms of travel costs and so on.

There is, on occasion, some suspicion of the motives of volunteers wishing to work with offenders. Research, however, suggests a wide and legitimate range of motivation, from:

- 'To give something to the community';
- 'My retail business is local to the prison. I was in awe of this mysterious institution and wanted to venture inside …';
- 'To see whether my interest in becoming a probation officer was well founded'; to
- 'As an ex-offender who has made good in life I would like to be able to say "Stop, there is another way"'.

With the coming of the National Offender Management Service (NOMS) and its declared aim of providing a 'seamless service' to offenders, volunteers may have an even more important role to play. They are people who can form a 'bridge' between custody and the community, visiting offenders in prison and subsequently supporting their resettlement in the community. This has always been considered desirable, and is sometimes achieved, but funding arrangements between the Prison and Probation Services have often been a barrier to this.

If we are serious about preventing reoffending, we must provide a way for offenders to resettle in their communities in a positive way. Volunteers come from the community, represent the community, and can have an exceptional role to play in achieving that resettlement.

Gill Henson

RELATED ENTRIES

Community; Reintegration; Social exclusion.

Key texts and sources

Information about SOVA and its projects throughout England and Wales can be found at www.sova.org.uk.

WELSH

The native language of Wales, enjoying equal status with English in the courts and other public services.

The Welsh language is in daily use in all parts of Wales, both in the private domains of family life and in the public realms of government, commerce and the courts. After two centuries of accelerating decline, the last quarter of a century has witnessed a stabilization, and subsequent growth in use, of the language. This expansion has been concentrated among young people. It is important to distinguish between *absolute* and *relative* numbers of Welsh speakers. In absolute terms, the largest number of Welsh speakers is almost certainly in Greater London, with some 50,000 Welsh speakers. In Wales, the largest numbers are also found in the urban concentrations of Swansea and Cardiff. In relative terms, however, the highest proportions of Welsh speakers are to be found in the rural areas of north and west Wales. In Gwynedd, 76 per cent of the population are Welsh speakers. In Monmouth, the proportion falls to 13 per cent.

Welsh language considerations are particularly important for the Probation Service for three main reasons. First, there is a clear entitlement to use Welsh in court proceedings. The Welsh Courts Act 1942 established the first set of statutory rights in this area, confirmed and expanded in the Welsh Language Acts of 1967 and 1993. Where cases are, in whole or part, heard through the medium of Welsh, the Probation Service needs to operate effectively in that context. Court-based rights include the provision of documentation in Welsh, with individual defendants having the right, for example, to have pre-sentence reports provided in Welsh.

Secondly, the Probation Service operates in a general context of a strengthening of Welsh linguistic rights. The Welsh Language Board, established statutorily in 1993, requires public bodies to prepare and implement Welsh language schemes which show how they will treat Welsh and English languages on the basis of equality. Since 1993 the climate of opinion has shifted, so that many schemes go beyond formal and neutral equality to enhance, promote and facilitate the use of Welsh. These obligations extend to public organizations based outside Wales but that operate in its borders. The Welsh language scheme of Her Majesty's Courts Service, which came into existence in April 2005, is a good example of direct probation relevance.

Thirdly, direct probation practice still rests on an ability to understand the lives of individuals and to apply those insights both to the sentencing process and any subsequent intervention. Traditionally, Welsh has been a language of 'domains', spoken more at home and within the family than in dealings with public bodies. Individual users of the Probation Service are likely to have to disclose and discuss matters, often of a very private nature. How much more difficult that process becomes when such information has to be provided in a language other than that in which it would ordinarily be conveyed. Effective practice at the individual level, therefore, just as much as organizational matters, depends on the provision of a service in the language of user choice, wherever such individuals live.

Mark Drakeford

RELATED ENTRIES

RELATED ENTRIES

Effective practice; Interpreting and translation.

Key texts and sources

The best single source is the Welsh Language Board (**http://www.bwrdd-yr-iaith.org.uk/**). The Care Council for Wales also publishes relevant information (**http://www.ccwales.org.uk/**).

WOMEN OFFENDERS

Fewer than 20 per cent of all known offenders are women; they constitute 15 per cent of all offenders given community orders and 6 per cent of the prison population.

Gender is the strongest single predictor of criminalization. Some 80 per cent of all known (recorded) offenders are men and 94 per cent of the prison population is male. Crimes committed by women are overwhelmingly non-violent (predominantly theft and handling stolen goods, though drug-related crime has increased), despite media attention on the small number of young women identified as being more anti-social, drunken and violent than in the past.

Because so few women commit crime, it is sometimes argued that women offenders are also *abnormal women*. Traditional theories of female offending have been contradictory: women criminals are 'more masculine' than 'normal' women; women criminals are governed by their (female) hormones; women criminals are 'undersocialized' and emotionally needy; and women criminals are 'oversocialized' into being manipulative and devious. Although all these explanations may apply in individual cases, there is no evidence to support these ideas as general theories of female offending. Contemporary writers argue that many women who commit crimes do so out of poverty. They have histories of abuse, institutional care, homelessness and drugs or alcohol misuse. Some women commit crimes out of greed or for excitement, as do some men, but these are

relatively few. Women who commit violent crimes often do so after years of physical or emotional abuse.

At first sight it may appear that women offenders are treated more leniently by the police and the courts than male offenders. They are more likely than men to be cautioned, given discharges or placed under supervision. On the other hand, they are less likely than men to be fined, sentenced to unpaid work or sent to prison. There is little evidence to support the claim that women are systematically dealt with more severely than men. However, this does not rule out the possibility that individual women may receive unusually harsh treatment for reasons that may be considered discriminatory. While women who fulfil stereotypically feminine roles as good wives, mothers and daughters may receive lenient sentences, unmarried or divorced women, women with children in care and black and Asian women appear to get heavier sentences. They seem to get punished for who they are rather than for what they have done. Some 29 per cent of women in prison are from minority ethnic groups – far in excess of their proportion in the general population. Some of these women are drugs couriers who will be subject to deportation when they finish their sentence, but many black women in prison were born in the UK and commit the same offences as white women.

Research suggests that the greater use of custody for women over the past decade has not been driven by an increase in the seriousness of women's offending but by a more severe sentencing response. When the Criminal Justice Act 1991 was first implemented, there was some optimism that just deserts for women would actually result in less punishment (because women commit less serious offences and have fewer previous convictions than men) and better provision (because access to community orders had to be anti-discriminatory according to s. 95 of the Act). But later amendments and a wilful misinterpretation of 'equal opportunities' rhetoric led to a rapid expansion of the female prison population, with a larger proportion of women than men being imprisoned on first conviction.

The largest proportionate growth in community penalties for women has been in unpaid work orders, which have increased by 85 per cent in the past decade. Nevertheless, the absolute numbers remain small, and women experience a number of problems when undertaking unpaid work (such as childcare, inappropriate work, insufficient female supervisors and sexual harassment).

Community rehabilitation (formerly probation) orders remained the most popular community sentence for women, though their increase has been less marked, suggesting some ambivalence about their contemporary role, especially when the use of accredited offending behaviour programmes is involved. There are now a number of accredited programmes, based on cognitive-behavioural approaches, that can be used with either men or women and that may be adapted to all-women groups. However, programmes designed specifically for women have had greater difficulty in obtaining accreditation because they do not always meet the criteria for 'what works'.

Policymakers talk about 'adapting' programmes and assessment instruments for use by women and concede that women have different responsivity needs, so that programmes may require changes to examples, exercises and delivery style. From this perspective, women present only a minor challenge to the delivery of programmes. However, a more radical criticism of cognitive-behavioural programmes is that, at a fundamental level, they fail to contextualize women's offending within their often long-term victimization, and they insist that women have more rational choices in their lives than, in reality, they do. A number of writers have argued that such programmes are not part of the process of the 'empowerment' of women but, rather, of their 'responsibilization'. Instead of empowering women to make genuine choices, it is argued, cognitive-behavioural programmes hold women responsible for their own rehabilitation but in conditions not of their own choosing.

The case for promoting greater use of community orders for women as alternatives to custody is unassailable. Women commit fewer crimes than men, their criminal careers are shorter and they serve shorter (though equally disruptive) prison sentences. Their reconviction rates are lower than those of men *regardless of the sentence they receive*. All this indicates that both the economic and social costs of imprisoning women are difficult to justify in the majority of cases.

Anne Worrall

RELATED ENTRIES

Accredited programmes; Diversity; Gender; Reconviction; Responsivity.

Key texts and sources

Carlen, P. (ed.) (2002) *Women and Punishment: The Struggle for Justice.* Cullompton: Willan Publishing.

Carlen, P. and Worrall, A. (2004) *Analysing Women's Imprisonment.* Cullompton: Willan Publishing.

Gelsthorpe, L. and McIvor, G. (2007) 'Difference and diversity in probation', in L. Gelsthorpe and R. Morgan (eds) *Handbook of Probation.* Cullompton: Willan Publishing.

Home Office (2004) *Statistics on Women and the Criminal Justice System, 2003* (available online at **www.homeoffice.gov.uk/rds/pdfs2/s95women03.pdf**).

McIvor, G. (ed.) (2004) *Women Who Offend: Research Highlights in Social Work.* London: Jessica Kingsley.

Y

YOUNG OFFENDERS

> Variously defined, the term 'young offenders' sometimes refers to people under the age of 18, but in the adult system may refer to those under 21.

'Young offender' is a somewhat confusing term in that it is used to refer to different groups. To those in youth justice, young offenders are those under 18; to others working in the adult system, young offender is a term often used to describe individuals under the age of 21; and in the prison estate the term refers to offenders between the ages of 18 and 21. This confusion, in some ways, may relate to confused definitions around what we mean by youth in a wider context, which Muncie observes is an 'ill defined and variable period of the life-span between infancy and adulthood' (2004: 314) and one which has changed throughout history. Indeed, if we as a society are unsure about what we mean by the term youth, then it is understandable that there is also some element of confusion around what we mean by the term young offender in the context of the criminal justice system and, indeed, how we work with them effectively.

However, for our purposes we can make a distinction regarding what is meant by young offender in the context of youth justice. This distinction rests on the way in which the child is defined in both national and international law and also in how the criminal justice system is configured to respond to children in trouble. In the criminal justice system there are different agency responsibilities for those under and over 18 years of age. Those between 10 (the age of criminal responsibility in England and Wales) and 18 are supervised by youth offending teams,

and those between 18 and 21 are supervised by the Probation Service. Prior to 1998, the Probation Service was responsible for supervising offenders from the age of 16 (and, at an earlier period, sometimes people as young as 12 or 13.) However, s. 39 of the Crime and Disorder Act 1998 established multi-agency youth offending teams which assumed responsibility for supervising all offenders under the age of 18.

This Act, which has been described as the most radical overhaul of the youth justice system in the last 50 years, effectively removed the supervision of 16–18-years-olds from the control of the Probation Service. Thus, the newly formed youth offending teams took statutory responsibility for all offenders under the age of 18 – a group which can arguably be most appropriately described as *child offenders* as all individuals under the age of 18 are defined as children by the United Nations' definition of a child. This distinction also acknowledges that, as these individuals are legally children, they require different considerations from those that would normally apply to adult offenders.

Prior to the Crime and Disorder Act 1998 there was a raft of legislation which set up, and subsequently developed, a different system for dealing with child offenders. A particularly significant piece of legislation was the Children Act 1908 which set up separate child (or juvenile) courts. This represented a major step in separating the systems for dealing with child offenders from the systems in place to deal with adults. Prior to this, child offenders were dealt with in the same way as adult offenders, with no special provision.

A distinct system of juvenile justice subsequently evolved to deal with children and young people who offend. This includes a different court of summary jurisdiction (the Youth Court, formerly the Juvenile Court) and a different range of sentencing powers. These include specific custodial sentences, served in a different part of the prison estate, and a range of different community penalties, supervised by specialist youth offending teams. There are also distinct pre-court disposals for young people in the form of reprimands and final warnings.

Arguably the Children Act 1908 represented the first real step in acknowledging the need to consider welfare when dealing with children who offend. This welfare clause has never been removed from statute. Therefore an acknowledgement that criminal justice responses to child offenders should be mindful of the welfare needs of the child has been of central importance in the process of developing a separate system for dealing with child offenders. This has been reflected in legislation in the UK and also more recently in the United Nations Convention on the Rights of the Child (s. 40). This particular section required the establishment of a distinct youth justice system specifically for children and also required that the welfare of children caught up in these systems must be the paramount consideration (Article 3).

Here lies a crucial distinction: when dealing with child offenders there is the necessity to consider the welfare needs of the young person as well as justice requirements. These two, often competing, priorities have, to differing degrees, shaped changes in youth justice policy and practice over the last century, with the prioritization of either welfare or justice reflecting broader shifts in political and social discourse. For example, Goldson and Muncie (2006) have argued that, at present, punitive and retributive discourses are in ascendancy in England and Wales – an assertion that appears to have some grounding in the rising child prison population (at present the highest in western Europe as a percentage of population).

Joe Yates

RELATED ENTRIES

Scotland: youth justice; Youth Justice Board (for England and Wales); Youth offending teams.

Key texts and sources

Goldson, B. and Muncie, J. (eds) (2006) *Youth Crime and Justice.* London: Sage.
Morgan, R. and Newburn, T. (2007) 'Youth justice', in L. Gelsthorpe and R. Morgan (eds) *Handbook of Probation.* Cullompton: Willan Publishing.
Muncie, J. (2004) *Youth and Crime: A Critical Introduction* (2nd edn). London: Sage.
Pitts, J. and Bateman, T. (eds) (2005) *The Russell House Companion to Youth Justice.* London: Russell House.
The Youth Justice Board website is a useful resource (**http://www.yjb.gov.uk/en-gb/**). See also the National Association for Youth Justice website (**http://www.nayj.org.uk/**).

YOUTH JUSTICE BOARD (FOR ENGLAND AND WALES)

A non-departmental public body that oversees the youth justice system in England and Wales.

The Youth Justice Board (YJB) works to prevent offending and reoffending by children and young people under the age of 18. It also seeks to ensure that custody for them is safe, secure and addresses the causes of their offending behaviour. The organization was established on 30 September 1998 under s. 41 of the Crime and Disorder Act 1998 to see through the changes stipulated by the Act and to focus on preventing reoffending.

The YJB is a non-departmental public body, sponsored by the Home Office and accountable to the Home Secretary. There are 12 board members, who are appointed by the Home Secretary, and these include people who have extensive recent experience of the youth justice system. They are supported by the YJB's central London office, nine regional offices and an office in Wales, so that work throughout England and Wales can focus on local needs and circumstances.

The YJB is responsible for the following:

- Advising the Home Secretary on the operation of, and standards for, the youth justice system (based on research and data collection).
- Monitoring the operation and performance of the youth justice system and the provision of youth justice services (see below).
- Setting national standards for the provision of youth justice and custodial accommodation.
- Purchasing places for, and placing, children and young people remanded or sentenced to custody by the courts.
- Identifying and promoting effective practice (through the research programme and performance monitoring and improvement work).
- Making grants to local authorities or other bodies to support the development of effective practice (amounting to £43 million in 2006–7).
- Commissioning research and publishing information on the operation of the youth justice system.

The Chief Executive ensures that the YJB has a clear aim and targets that are approved by ministers. The senior management team helps the YJB meet its corporate targets by agreeing corporate priorities, reviewing budgets and monitoring expenditure, and identifying and managing risk. The senior management team also considers and communicates corporate issues and reviews data on the performance of the YJB and the youth justice system. The senior management team is expected to provide leadership based on the YJB's corporate values of leadership, partnership, teamwork, openness, respect and trust.

The work of the YJB focuses on researching, creating, funding and monitoring programmes that aim to tackle the specific risk factors known to be associated with the likelihood of a young person offending or reoffending. These programmes are delivered by youth offending teams (YOTs) and the secure estate for children and young people.

The YJB then sets performance indicators for YOTs and the secure estate in its corporate plan, and monitors performance against them every year (performance management), identifying and sharing effective practice and offering support.

Performance data are collected quarterly, and performance is monitored through quality assurance and support visits by YJB staff. These indicators measure those areas of service delivery associated with practice likely to reduce offending.

The YJB also commissions research that evaluates the practices and policies of the youth justice system. The findings are used to develop effective practice guidance and to ensure resources are used to their best effect. All research published is available from the publications section of the YJB website.

The YJB is seeking to develop a youth justice system in which more offenders are caught, held to account for their actions and stop offending; children and young people receive the support they need to lead crime-free lives; victims are better supported; and the public has more confidence.

Katherine Savage

RELATED ENTRIES

Effective practice; Scotland: youth justice; Young offenders; Youth offending teams.

Key texts and sources

Crime and Disorder Act 1998.

Audit Commission (1996) *Misspent Youth: Young People and Crime.* London: Audit Commission.

Morgan, R. and Newburn, T. (2007) 'Youth justice', in L. Gelsthorpe and R. Morgan (eds) *Handbook of Probation.* Cullompton: Willan Publishing.

YJB (2004) *National Standards for Youth Justice.* London: YJB.

YJB (2006) *Youth Justice Annual Statistics, 2005/06.* London: YJB.

www.yjb.gov.uk

YOUTH OFFENDING TEAMS

Teams of practitioners drawn from different agencies working within local authority boundaries to provide criminal justice services to young people.

There are 156 youth offending teams (YOTs) in England and Wales. They are based either on unitary authorities or on county boundaries. YOTs were established by the Crime and Disorder Act 1998, legislation that did much to strengthen inter-agency work. The Act also brought the Crime and Disorder Reduction Partnerships into being, of which the YOTs are a part. A manager who works within the framework set by an inter-agency management group runs the YOT. The YOT comprises a range of practitioners usually seconded from the following backgrounds:

- Local authority (criminal justice, children's services, youth and community) social workers.
- Local authority education officers.
- Police officers.
- Probation officers.
- Health (young people and substance misuse) professionals.
- Connexions and other professionals who can link young people to training and employment.

The YOT will also foster close working relationships with other statutory and voluntary organizations that can assist young people in relevant areas, such as housing, childcare and resettlement.

In addition to the practitioners outlined above, many YOTs recruit staff directly to work on time-limited projects that are funded by the Youth Justice Board (YJB). These are often focused on new initiatives in areas of greatest need in urban areas.

YOTs provide a full range of community-based services for young people who are at risk of being in trouble with the law and appearing before the youth court. By bringing together so many agencies that support the strengths of communities, the YOTs seek to engage and use the social capital of the neighbourhoods they serve.

They are involved in preventative schemes and pre-court work with the police in 'reprimand' and 'final warning' schemes. Where young people up to the age of 18 appear before the youth court, YOT members will be involved in preparing pre-sentence reports in appropriate cases. YOTs carry out the supervision of offenders in the community when such an order

is made, and they supervise young offenders in the community after periods in custody.

Cavadino and Dignan (2006), in contrasting the Scottish youth justice system (which is predominantly welfare based) with the YOTs in England and Wales, describe the 'neo-correctionalist' thinking that has predominated south of the border since 1998. They point to some key principles that have informed policy development:

- *Prevention of offending*: YOTs are encouraged to carry out preventative work, resources permitting. Recent legislation has created child curfews and child safety orders, both designed to keep children from offending.
- *Effective interventions*: there is a wide range of community sentences available to the youth court and implemented by YOTs. The Intensive Supervision and Surveillance Programme was introduced to respond to prolific offending, and there has been a rapid growth in the use of anti-social behaviour orders, encouraged as a response to nuisance behaviour which was not sufficiently regulated by the criminal law. Increasing intensity of supervision, combined with increased attention to enforcement, has inevitably led to more use of custody.
- An increased expectation that *young people will take responsibility for their own actions*.
- *Reparation*: there has been a move towards restorative justice in YOT practice. This was underlined by the use of the reparation order and then, in 2002, by the introduction of a referral order. This is a youth court order that refers the offender to a community panel on which a range of local people, including parents and victims, may sit. Through a non-judicial process, a 'youth offender contract' may emerge. The development was hailed as a significant measure for diverting offenders from court, but the achievements of the system have been generally disappointing.
- *Efficiency*: the 'Persistent Young Offender Pledge' was one of the key government promises when it came to office in 1997. It sought to reduce by half the time from arrest to sen-

tence for persistent young offenders. It reflected concern that the youth justice system was bogged down with processes and that delays at court were a major contribution to the ineffectiveness of intervention. Much progress has been made in this area, mainly by all agencies prioritizing these cases. The work of the YJB and YOTs has focused attention on youth offending and made practice more transparent and accountable. The YJB soon established systems for monitoring performance in the YOTs and comparing workloads, outcomes and costs.

The size of the Probation Service contribution to the YOT varies from area to area. Some areas were historically more active with young people at the time the YOTs were formed. Probation areas second probation officers to work in the YOTs, and they contribute their skills in assessing and managing offenders in the community. They also deliver specific programmes designed for young offenders. It is generally a welcomed secondment, and it will be interesting to see how the future of secondments works in practice as the Probation Service itself becomes more fragmented. Probation officers who stay in YOTs for long periods lose their capacity to represent contemporary probation practice, since this moves on so quickly. Probation boards contribute cash to the central overheads of the YOT for offices, management and support services. The amount required may vary considerably from authority to authority, and boards have little room to influence the levy, which has to be shared by all the participating agencies.

The youth justice system has undergone both advances and reversals in recent years. The new arrangements provide a much more joined-up and imaginative range of opportunities for engaging with young people who offend, but the number of young people in custody has risen considerably. This perhaps reflects unintended consequences of a more complex system, as well as the popular call for harsher penalties. It was not long ago that several large urban areas were declaring with pride that they were 'custody-free areas' as far as young offenders were concerned. The concept seems completely unrealistic today.

In commenting on his resignation from the Chair of the YJB, Professor Morgan said in February 2007 that, in recent years, community initiatives had been stifled by the need to pay for youth custody. He described this as: 'the worst conceivable environment in which to improve someone's behaviour. Even if we greatly improve the regime or make them much tougher, starker, as some people plead for, the results would be miserable, i.e. most of these young people will come out and seriously re-offend.'

David Hancock

RELATED ENTRIES

Anti-social behaviour; Crime and Disorder Reduction Partnerships; Inter-agency work; Reparation; Resettlement; Restorative justice; Scotland: youth justice; Social capital; Young offenders; Youth Justice Board (for England and Wales).

Key texts and sources

Cavadino, M. and Dignan, J. (2006) *Penal Systems: A Comparative Approach.* London: Sage.

Morgan, R. and Newburn, T. (2007) 'Youth justice', in L. Gelsthorpe and R. Morgan (eds) *Handbook of Probation.* Cullompton: Willan Publishing.

There is much useful information on the YJB website (**www.yjb.gov.uk**).

Appendix I

ABBREVIATIONS

The following list includes not only abbreviations used in this Dictionary but also many others found in common use in probation and probation-related documentation.

AA	Adoption Act/Alcoholics Anonymous/appropriate adult
ABC	acceptable behaviour contract
ABH	actual bodily harm
ABPO/Abpo	Association of Black Probation Officers
abs. dis.	absolute discharge
ABSWAP	Association of Black Social Workers and Allied Professions
ACAS	Advisory Conciliation and Arbitration Service
ACC	Association of County Councils
ACE	assessment, case recording and evaluation
ACL	approved cost limit
ACO	assistant chief officer
ACOP	Association of Chief Officers of Probation (formerly CPC)
ACPC	Area Child Protection Committee
ACPO	assistant chief probation officer (now ACO)
ACR	automatic conditional release
AD	absolute discharge
ADC	Anti-discrimination Committee
adj.	adjourned
ADP	anti-discriminatory practice
ADSS	Association of Directors of Social Services
AEG	Alcohol Education Group
AEO	attachment of earnings order
AFI	area for improvement
AGM	annual general meeting
AIDS	acquired immune deficiency syndrome
AllER	All England Law Reports
AMA	Association of Metropolitan Authorities
AMP	Anger Management Programme

AO	administrative officer
AOABH	assault occasioning actual bodily harm
AOM	assistant office manager
AP	accredited programme/approved premises
APHBR	Approved Probation Hostel and Home and Bail Hostel Rules 1976
APT & C	administrative, professional, technical and clerical staff
AR	Adoption Rules
AR & E	anti-racism and equality
ARO	alcohol-related offending
ASBO	anti-social behaviour order
ASPBH	Association of Staff of Probation and Bail Hostels
ASPIRE	Assessment, Sentence Plan, Intervention, Review, Evaluate
ASRO	Addressing Substance-related Offending (programme)
AT	assistive technology
AUR	automatic unconditional release
AW	assistant warden
BA	Bail Act
BACS	Bank Automated Clearing System
BASW	British Association of Social Workers
BIO	bail information officer
BIS	Bail Information Scheme
BME	black and minority ethnic
BS	British Standard
BTEC	Business and Technology Education Council
BWF	Black Workers' Forum
BWSG	Black Workers' Support Group
CA	Children Act
CAA	Criminal Appeal Act
CABX	Citizens' Advice Bureaux
CACD	Court of Appeal Criminal Division
CAFCASS	Children and Family Court Advisory and Support Service
CARATS	Counselling, Assessment, Referral, Advice, Throughcare Service
CC	Citizen's Charter
CCCJS	Co-ordination of Computerization in the Criminal Justice System
CCETSW	Central Council for Education and Training in Social Work
CCLO	Crown Court liaison officer
CCP	Change Control Panel
CCT	compulsory competitive tendering
C Ct	Crown Court
CCU	Citizen's Charter Unit
C & D	crime and disorder
CDA	Crime and Disorder Act
CDP	Crime and Disorder Partnership
CDPA	Copyright Designs and Patents Act
CDRP	Crime and Disorder Reduction Partnership
CDT	community drug team

CDVP	Community Domestic Violence Programme
CEP	Conférence permanente européenne de la Probation
CESG	Communications-Electronics Security Group
CFP	Council for Family Proceedings
CI	circular instruction (prisons)
CIPFA	Chartered Institute of Public Finance and Accountancy
CJ	criminal justice
CJA	Criminal Justice Act
CJB	Criminal Justice Board
CJC	criminal justice community
CJCC	Criminal Justice Consultative Council
CJ & CSA	Criminal Justice and Court Services Act
CJIP	Criminal Justice Interventions Programme (now DIP)
CJIT	criminal justice information technology
CJIT	Criminal Justice Integrated Team
CJO	criminal justice organization
CJPO	Criminal Justice and Public Order (Act)
CJS	criminal justice system
CJX	criminal justice extranet
CLAN	centrally led action network
CLIO	Client Information and Office System
CLR	Criminal Law Reports
CM	case manager
Cm	Command (e.g. Command paper)
CMA	Computer Misuse Act
CMT	case management team
c-NOMIS	Computer National Offender Management Information System
CO	chief officer/clerical officer/combination order (now CPRO)/community order
conc.	concurrent (sentences)
con. dis.	conditional discharge
consec.	consecutive (sentences)
COSHH	Control of Substances Hazardous to Health
CP	community punishment
CPC	Central Probation Council
CPI	Criminal Procedure and Investigations (Act)
CP(I)A	Criminal Procedure (Insanity) Act
CP(IUP)A	Criminal Procedure (Insanity and Unfitness to Plead) Act
CPN	community psychiatric nurse
CPO	chief probation officer (now CO)/community punishment order
CPRO	community punishment and rehabilitation order
CPS	Crown Prosecution Service
CPU	Community Punishment Unit
CQSW	Certificate of Qualification in Social Work
CRAMS	Case Record Administration and Management System
CRE	Commission for Racial Equality
CRN	client reference number/common reference number
CRO	community rehabilitation order (replaces probation order)
CSA	Child Support Agency/community service assistant
CSAP	Correctional Services Accreditation Panel

CSB	Cognitive Skills Booster (programme)
CSM	cognitive skills management/community service manager
CSO	community service officer/community service order (replaced by CPO)
CSR	Correctional Services Review
CSS	Certificate in Social Service/community service supervisor
CVS	Council for Voluntary Service
CYPA	Children and Young Person Act

DA	district audit/district auditor
DAM	district administration manager
DAO	district administrative officer
DAT	drug action team
DCO	deputy chief officer
DCPO	deputy chief probation officer (replaced by DCO)
DCR	discretionary conditional release
DCWO	divorce court welfare officer
D & D	drunk and disorderly
DELIUS	delivering information to users
DfES	Department for Education and Skills
DIAL	Drivers Impaired by Alcohol (project)
DID	Drink Impaired Drivers (programme)
DIP	director of inmate programmes/drug intervention programme
DipPS	Diploma in Probation Studies
DipSW	Diploma in Social Work
DM	district manager
DOC	Directorate of Custody
DofE	Department of the Environment
DofEE	Department of Education and Employment
DOH	Department of Health
DPA	Data Protection Act
DPAS	Drug Prevention Advisory Service
DPMCA	Domestic Proceedings and Magistrates' Courts Act
DPP	Director of Public Prosecutions
DRR	drug rehabilitation requirement
DSE	display screen equipment
DSRG	Data Standards and Reporting Group
DSS	Department of Social Security
DTO	detention and training order/drug treatment order
DTTO	drug treatment and testing order
DV	domestic violence
DVMPA	Domestic Violence and Matrimonial Proceedings Act
DVU	Domestic Violence Unit
DWD	driving while disqualified

EASI	easily accessible service information
EAT	Employment Appeals Tribunal
EBS	employment and basic skills
EC	European Commission/European Community

ECP	enhanced community punishment
ECR	electronic case record
EDR	earliest date of release
E & E	Efficiency and Effectiveness (inspection)
EEM	European Excellence Model
EFQM	European Foundation for Quality Management
e-GIF	e-Government Interoperability Framework
e-GMF	e-Government Metadata Framework
e-GMS	e-Government Metadata Standard
EHO	environmental health officer
EIA	Electronic Interchange Agreement
EIIP	Electronic Information Interchange Policy
eOASys	Electronic Offender Assessment System
EPDB	Effective Practice Development Board
EPI	Effective Practice Initiative
EPTM	effective practice training manager
ERCG	early release on compassionate grounds
ERDF	European Regional Development Fund
ESF	European Social Fund
ESI	Effective Supervision Inspection
ESOL	English for speakers of other languages
ET	employment training
ETE	employment, training and education
ETS	enhanced thinking skills (replaced by GOP)
EV	external verifier
FAO	family assistance officer
FCBC	Family Court Business Committee
FCSC	Family Court Services Committee
FCWO	family court welfare officer
FD	Family Division (of High Court)
FDR	fast delivery report (previously PSR)
FMIS	financial management information systems
FOIA	Freedom of Information Act
FPCR	Family Proceedings Courts (Children Act) 1991 Rules
FPR	Family Proceedings Rules 1991
FTA	failed to appear/attend
GAL	guardian ad litem
GALRO	guardian ad litem and reporting officer
GBH	grievous bodily harm
GOP	general offending programme (formerly ETS)
GSI	government secure intranet
GSL	guided skills learning
GSX	government secure extranet
HALOW	Help and Advice Line for Offenders' Wives
HASWA	Health and Safety at Work Act

HDC	home detention curfew
HIV	human immuno-deficiency virus
HMIP	HM Inspectorate of Probation
HMP	Her Majesty's prison
HMSO	Her Majesty's Stationery Office (now OPSI)
HO	Home Office
HOC	Home Office circular
HOI	Home Office inspector
HOPB	Home Office probation bulletin
HORU	Home Office Research Unit
HOU	Homeless Offenders Unit
HR	human resources
HRA	Human Rights Act
H & S	health and safety
HSE	Health and Safety Executive
IAGSF	Information Age Government Security Framework
IAPS	interim accredited programme software
ICCP	Intensive Control and Change Programme
ICM	integrated case management
IDAP	Integrated Domestic Abuse Programme
IEC	International Electrotechnical Commission
IG	instruction to governors
IIP	Investors in People
ILMG	Information and Library Management Group
IMI	internal monitoring and inspection
IP	individual placement/Internet protocol
IS	information security/information services/information systems
ISAT	information systems and technology
ISO	International Standards Organization
ISP	Information Security Programme
ISSB	Information Systems Strategy Board
ISSP	Intensive Supervision and Surveillance Programme
ISSU	Information Systems Strategy Unit
ISU	Information Services Unit
IT	industrial tribunal/information technology/intermediate treatment
ITG	Information and Technology Group
ITTSI	Investigating, Targeting, Tailoring and Sequencing Interventions
IV	internal verifier
JCC	Joint Consultative Committee
JNC	Joint Negotiating Committee
JNCC	Joint Negotiating and Consultative Committee
JP	justice of the peace
JSA	Job Seekers Allowance
KPI	key performance indicator

LA	local authority
LAC	local authority circular
LACSAB	Local Authorities Conditions of Service Advisory Board
LAGIP	Lesbians and Gay Men in Probation (including bisexual and transgendered people)
LARRPs	local awards for recruitment and retention purposes
LCCS	local crime: community sentence
LCD	Lord Chancellor's Department
LCJB	Local Criminal Justice Board
LED	licence expiry date
LGA	Local Government Act/Local Government Association
LGMB	Local Government Management Board
LGR	Local Government Review
LRC	Local Review Committee
LSC	Learning and Skills Council
LSCB	Local Safeguarding Children Board
MAPPA	multi-agency public protection arrangements
MAPPP	multi-agency public protection panel
MARAC	multi-agency risk assessment conference
MCA	Magistrates' Courts Act
MDOs	mentally disordered offenders
MHA	Mental Health Act
MoPS	Manual of Protective Security
MPSO	money payment supervision order
NAAPS/Naaps	National Association of Asian Probation Staff
NACRO	National Association for the Care and Resettlement of Offenders
NAI	non-accidental injury
NALGO	National Association of Local Government Officers (replaced by UNISON)
NAPBH	National Association of Probation and Bail Hostels
NAPO/Napo	National Association of Probation Officers
NASPO	National Association of Senior Probation Officers (replaced by PMA)
NAVH	National Association of Voluntary Hotels
NAVSS	National Association of Victim Support Schemes
NCJB	National Criminal Justice Board
NCVO	National Council for Voluntary Organizations
NCVQ	National Council for Vocational Qualifications
NEC	National Executive Committee
NEO	no evidence offered
NESTS	National Estates Strategy
NFA	no fixed abode
NG	not guilty
NISW	National Institute for Social Work
NJC	National Joint Council
NNC	National Negotiating Council
NOAF	National Offender Accommodation Forum
NOM	national offender manager
NOMIS	National Offender Management Information System (use c-NOMIS)

NOMS	National Offender Management Service
NOTA	National Organization for the Treatment of Abusers
NPD	National Probation Directorate
NPRIE	National Probation Research and Information Exchange
NPS	National Probation Service of England and Wales
NPSIMS	National Probation Service Information Management Strategy
NPSISS	National Probation Service Information Systems Strategy
NS	National Standards
NSM	National Standards monitoring
NSPCC	National Society for the Prevention of Cruelty to Children
NTA	National Treatment Agency
NTO	National Training Organization
NUPE	National Union of Public Employees (replaced by UNISON)
NVQ	National Vocational Qualification
NWMT	National Workload Measurement Tool
OAF	Offender Accommodation Forum
OALG	Offender Accommodation Liaison Group
OASDG	Offender Accommodation Service Delivery Group
OASys	Offender Assessment System
OB	offending behaviour
OBG	Offending Behaviour Group
OCP	Organization Consulting Partnership
ODEAT	OASys Data Evaluation and Analysis Team
OGRS	Offender Group Reconviction Scale
OLASS	Offenders' Learning and Skills Service
OM	offender manager/office manager
OMU	Offender Management Unit
OPCS	Office of Population Census and Statistics
OPSI	Office for Public Sector Information
OSAP	Offender Substance Abuse Programme
OSMB	Operational Services Management Board
p.	page
PACE	Police and Criminal Evidence (Act)
PAGS	Probation Accommodation Grants Scheme
PAR	performance appraisal report
para.	paragraph
PBA	Probation Boards' Association (formerly ACOP)
PC	personal computer/ probation centre/probation circular
PCCA	Powers of Criminal Courts Act
PCCSA	Powers of Criminal Courts (Sentencing) Act
PCOJ	perverting the course of justice
PCR	Procedural Change Review
PD	Prison Department
PDA	practice development assessor
PDO	potentially dangerous offender
PDU	Practice Development Unit

PED	parole eligibility date
PFI	Private Finance Initiative
PHW	probation hostel worker
PI	Prison Department circular instruction
PICA	Public Interest Case Assessment
PID	project initiation document
PIP	Probation Inspection Programme
P & ITB	Performance and IT Board
PLC	Probation Liaison Committee
PMA	Probation Managers' Association
PMS	Protective Marking Scheme
PNC	Police National Computer
PO	parenting order/probation officer
POISE	Planned Office Information System Environment (Home Office network used by NPD)
POP	Prolific Offenders Project
PORTIG	Probation Officer Recruitment and Training Implementation Group
PPOs	prolific and other priority offenders (formerly POPOs)
PPT	Probation Programmes Team/Public Protection Team
PPU	Public Protection Unit
PPWS	pre-placement work session
PQS	Placement Quality Standards/Post-qualifying Studies
PR	Probation Rules/public relations
PRES	Pre-release Employment Scheme
PRET	Probation Research and Educational Trust
PRINCE	Projects in a Controlled Environment
PRINCE2	Projects in a Controlled Environment 2
PRP	performance-related pay
PSA	Petty Sessional Area
PSAI	post-sentence assessment interview
PSAW	Problem Solving at Work
PSD	Petty Sessional Division
PSIS	Policy Support and Information Services
PSM	prosocial modelling
PSO	probation service officer
PSR	pre-sentence report (replaced by SDR)
PSS	Probation Statistics System
PSU	Probation Studies Unit (Oxford)
PTU	Probation Training Unit
QAG	Quality Assurance Group
QAM	quality assurance manager (ECP)
Q & E	quality and effectiveness
r.	Rule
RAS	remote access solution
RDS	Research Development and Statistics Directorate
Regs	Regulations

REM	race and ethnic monitoring
RFC	request for change
RFS	request for service
RIC	remanded in custody
RIDDOR	Reporting of Injuries, Diseases and Dangerous Occurrences Regulations
RIPA	Regulation of Investigatory Powers Act
RMIS	Resource Management Information System
RO	referral order/reparation order
ROB	remanded on bail
ROG	Research Officers' Group
ROHS	risk of harm screening
ROM	regional offender manager
ROR	risk of reoffending
RRAP	Reducing Re-offending Action Plan
RSD	regional staff development
RTC	Regional Training Consortium
RWWM	regional 'what works' manager
s.	Section
SALSA	Strategic Applications Linked to the STEPS Architecture
SAO	senior admin officer
SAR	subject access request
SCA	supplementary credit approval
Sch. 1	Schedule 1 offence/offender
SCO	senior clerical officer
SCOOP	Society of Chief Officers of Probation
SDA	Service Delivery Agreement
SDR	standard delivery report (replaces PSR)
SED	sentence expiry date
SEU	Sentence Enforcement Unit
SI	Statutory Instrument
sine die	without a fixed date
SIR	social inquiry report (now SDR)
SLA	Service Level Agreement
SMART	Specific, Measurable, Achievable, Realistic, Time limited
SMIN	supporting management information needs
SNOP	Statement of National Objectives and Priorities
SO	standing order/supervision order
SOVA	Society of Voluntary Associations
SP	Supporting People
SPM	Supporting Performance Measure
SPO	senior probation officer
SRB	Single Regeneration Budget
SSD	Social Services Department
SSE	specific sentence enquiry
SSO	suspended sentence order
SSP	Statutory Sick Pay
SSR	specific sentence report (replaced by FDR)

SSSO	suspended sentence supervision order
STEP	SOVA Training and Employment Project
STEPS	Standard Technical Environment for the Probation Service
SWIP	Shared Working in Prisons
T(A)DA	take and drive away
TEC	Training and Enterprise Council
TF	Think First
TIC	taken into consideration
TIG	Trial Issues Group
TM	treatment manager
TPO	trainee probation officer
TR	temporary release
TSO	team support officer
TUPE	Transfer of Undertakings (Protection of Employment) Regulations
TURER	Trade Union Reform and Employment Rights (Act)
TWOC	take without owner's consent
UCB	unconditional bail
UNISON	Union representing APT & C and some other grades of staff
UPW	unpaid work
USI	unlawful sexual intercourse
VAC	voluntary aftercare
VAT	Value Added Tax
VCT	voluntary competitive tendering
VDUs	visual display units
VER	voluntary early retirement
VISOR	Violent and Sex Offender Register
VLO	victim liaison officer
VSBRM	Violence, Sexual, Burglary, Robbery, Motoring (serious offence categories)
VSS	Victim Support Services
WAGGIT	Women's Advisory Group on Gender Issues in Training
WAMP	weighted average measure of performance
WRVS	Women's Royal Voluntary Service
WW	'what works'
YIP	Youth Inclusion Programme
YOI	young offender institution
YOS	Youth Offending Service
YOT	young offender team
YTC	youth treatment centre
YWCA	Young Women's Christian Association
YWHP	Young Women's Housing Project

Appendix II
Probation timeline

Some major milestones in the 100-year history of probation, 1907–2007.

Date	Milestone	Relevant Dictionary entries
1907	The Probation of Offenders Act instituted probation as an agreement between the court and offender to which the offender must consent, in the place of a sentence or punishment	Probation; Probation officers
1912	The National Association of Probation Officers established	Napo
1930	The first training scheme for probation officers introduced by the Home Office	Probation training
1948	The Criminal Justice Act amended the 1907 Act and became the primary legislation for probation, incorporating the aims of welfare and rehabilitation	Probation values; Rehabilitation
1960	The Central Council of Probation Committees established	Central Council of Probation Committees (CCPC)
1967	The Criminal Justice Act formed the Probation and After-care Service through the amalgamation of probation with other statutory and voluntary bodies responsible for the supervision of offenders released from prison. Parole introduced	Parole Board; Reintegration; Resettlement
1972	The Criminal Justice Act introduced the community service order and other 'alternatives to custody', such as day training centres	Day centres; Groupwork; Unpaid work

▶

Date	Milestone	Relevant Dictionary entries
1982	The Criminal Justice Act simplified custodial regimes for young offenders, detention centres and youth custody centres, replacing the former detention centres, Borstals and young prisoner centres. The Act formalized additional requirements in probation orders. The Association of Chief Officers of Probation formed, replacing the Chief Officers' Conference and the Association of Deputy and Assistant Chief Probation Officers	Association of Chief Officers of Probation (ACOP); Borstal
1984	The *Statement of National Objectives and Priorities* published by the Home Office, reflecting the increasing central influence over probation services	Managerialism
1985	The Prosecution of Offences Act created the Crown Prosecution Service	Crown Prosecution Service (CPS)
1987	The Grimsey Report on the probation inspectorate published. The Home Office paper, *Tackling Offending – an Action Plan*, published	HM Inspectorate of Probation; Punishment in the community
1989	The first National Standards introduced	National Standards
1990	The first Victim's Charter and the beginning of probation's formal involvement with victims	Victim awareness; Victim contact; Victims
1991	The Criminal Justice Act (mostly implemented in October 1992) made probation a sentence and emphasized seriousness and proportionality in sentencing. It introduced curfew as a sentence and authorized electronic monitoring. Section 95 refers to a duty not to discriminate improperly. A period of financial cutbacks began with the introduction of cash limits	Anti-discriminatory practice; Criminal Justice Act 1991; Curfews; Electronic monitoring; Pre-sentence report (PSR)
1993	Stephen Lawrence murdered. Key performance targets defined for the first time	Hate crime; Macpherson Report; Performance management; Racially motivated offenders
1995	The National Standards revised. The ending of the recruitment and training of probation officers for four years	Enforcement; Probation training

Date	Milestone	Relevant Dictionary entries
1997	The 'what works' initiative and accredited programmes launched. The Crime (Sentences) Act removed the requirement of consent to most community penalties. It developed preventive sentencing measures and mandatory sentences	Accredited programmes; ASPIRE; Cognitive-behavioural; Correctional Services Accreditation Panel; Criminogenic needs; Effective practice; Evaluation; Reconviction; Research; Responsivity; Risk principle
1998	The Diploma in Probation Studies established. The Crime and Disorder Act and the Human Rights Act implemented. The Teesside judgement on staffing	Anti-social behaviour; Community justice; Community safety; Council of Europe; Crime and Disorder Reduction Partnerships; Crime prevention; Drug treatment and testing orders (DTTOs); Human rights; Multi-agency public protection arrangements (MAPPAs); Probation officers; Probation service officers; Regional training consortia; Youth Justice Board (for England and Wales); Youth offending teams
1999	The development of OASys began, building on earlier assessment instruments	Actuarialism; Assessment instruments and systems; Offender Assessment System (OASys)
2000	The Criminal Justice and Court Services Act implemented, establishing the National Probation Service and CAFCASS in April 2001. The NPS set 'enforcement, rehabilitation and public protection' as its watchwords. The Act changed the names of the former probation order, community service order and combination order. MAPPAs set on a statutory basis. Zahid Mubarek murdered	Children and Family Court Advisory Support Service (CAFCASS); Community penalties; Compliance; Dangerousness; Enforcement; Mubarek Inquiry; Multi-agency public protection arrangements (MAPPAs); National Probation Service for England and Wales; Public protection; Rehabilitation; Risk of harm
2001	The probation boards and their national association formed. The Halliday Report on sentencing and the principles of punishment published	Halliday Report; Probation boards; Probation Boards' Association (PBA); Punishment (aims and justifications)
2003	The Criminal Justice Act implemented the Halliday Report proposals. (The main sentencing proposals were implemented in April 2005.) The Act set out the statutory purposes of punishment. The Carter Report published in December. This led to the formation of the National Offender Management Service the following year, the separation of offender management and interventions, and the introduction of contestability. *The Heart of the Dance* NPS diversity strategy published	Carter Report; Community order; Contestability; Criminal Justice Act 2003; Dangerousness; Diversity; Extended sentencing; Interventions; National Offender Management Service (NOMS); Offender management; Prison; Privatization; Public protection; Reparation

▶

Date	Milestone	Relevant Dictionary entries
2005	The National Standards revised to meet the needs of the new sentences. Unpaid work replaced enhanced community punishment	National Standards; Unpaid work
2006	Offender management introduced into prisons, and the separation of offender management and interventions effected in most probation areas. Legislation introduced into Parliament to support the Carter Report principles	Probation trusts; Regional offender managers (ROMs)
2007	Ministry of Justice created and assumed responsibility for NOMS	Ministry of Justice

Appendix III

CONCEPT MAPS

In this appendix is a set of concept maps. These complement the list of entries in the thematic index, setting out related entries in the form of a diagram. Related entries are placed adjacent to one another and/or are connected by lines on the diagram. Although the main purpose is to suggest linked topics in the Dictonary, the exercise of compiling the map shows organizational and conceptual connections as well.

It is important to remember that there is no one way of drawing maps like these. It would be possible to 'map' different domains – or to map these quite differently.

Many readers will want to improve upon these maps by constructing their own versions. The exercise often raises useful and suggestive questions about which topics are connected, and why some lines have been drawn and other possible connections have not been drawn.

Court and sentencing

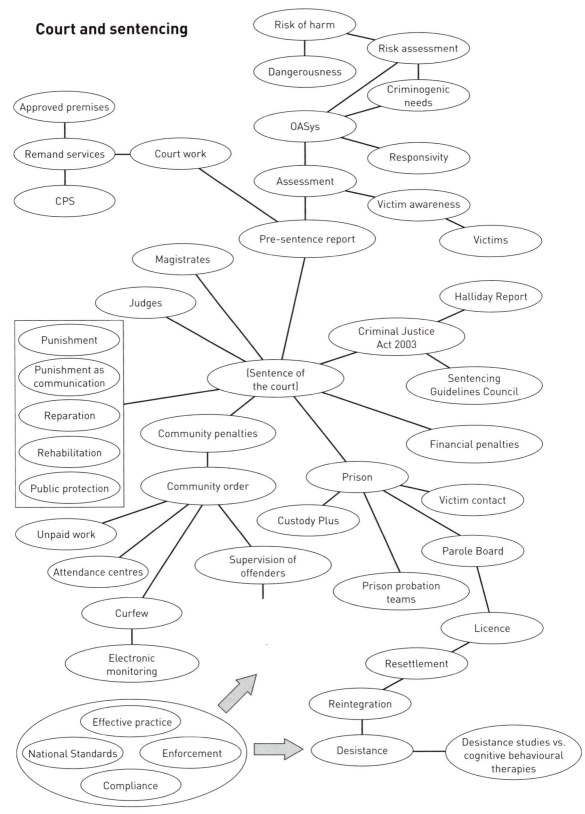

Practice

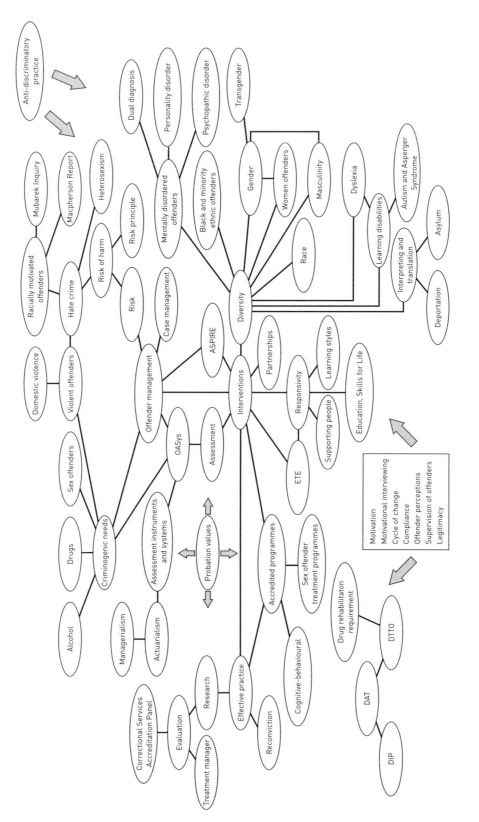

Organisation

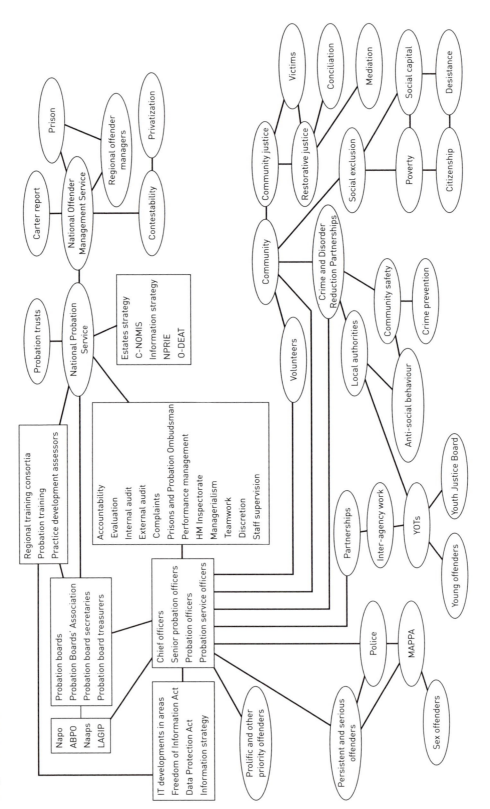

Policy

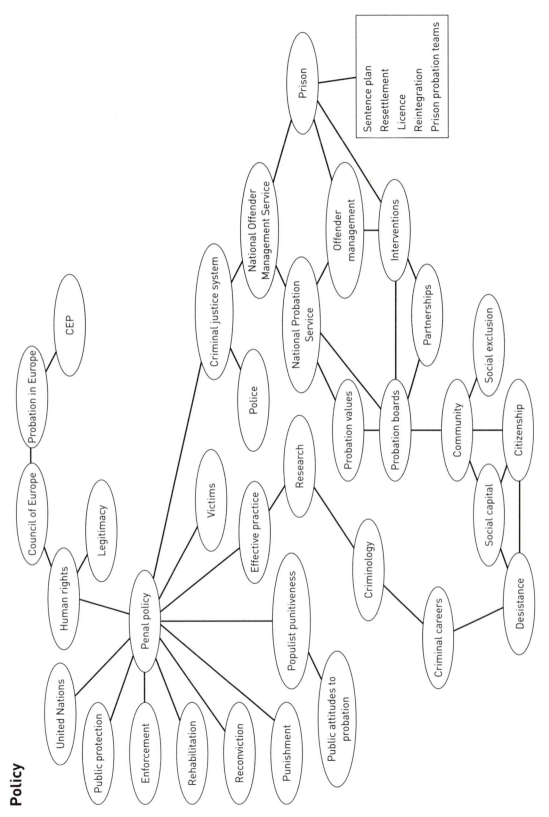

References

Adair, J. (1973) *Action-centred Leadership*. London: McGraw-Hill.

Alagappa, M. (1995) 'Anatomy of legitimacy', in M. Alagappa (ed.) *Political Legitimacy in South East Asia: The Quest for Moral Authority*. Stanford, CA: Stanford University Press.

Aldridge, D. (1998) *Suicide: The Tragedy of Hopelessness*. London: Jessica Kingsley.

Allen, R. and Hough, M. (2007) 'Community penalties, sentencers, the media and public opinion', in L. Gelsthorpe and R. Morgan (eds) *Handbook of Probation*. Cullompton: Willan Publishing.

Andrews, D. (1995) 'The psychology of criminal conduct and effective treatment', in J. McGuire (ed.) *What Works: Reducing Reoffending. Guidelines from Research and Practice*. Chichester: Wiley.

Andrews, D.A. and Bonta, J. (1998) *The Psychology of Criminal Conduct* (2nd edn). Cincinnati, OH: Anderson Publishing.

Andrews, D.A. and Bonta, J. (2003) *The Psychology of Criminal Conduct* (3rd edn). Cincinnati, OH: Anderson Publishing.

Andrews, D.A., Zinger, I., Hodge, R.D., Bonta, J., Gendreau, P. and Cullen, F.T. (1990) 'Does correctional treatment work?', *Criminology*, 28: 208–16.

Annison, J. (2006) 'Style over substance: a review of the evidence base for the use of learning styles in probation', *Criminology and Criminal Justice*, 6: 239–57.

Arnott, H. and Creighton, S. (2006) *Parole Board Hearings – Law and Practice*. London: Legal Action Group.

Ashworth, A. (1992) *Sentencing and Criminal Justice*. London: Weidenfeld & Nicholson.

Ashworth, A. (2005) *Sentencing and Criminal Justice*. London: Butterworths.

Aubrey, R. and Hough, M. (1997) *Assessing Offenders' Needs: Assessment Scales for the Probation Service. Home Office Research Study* 166. London: Home Office.

Audit Commission (1996) *Misspent Youth: Young People and Crime*. London: Audit Commission.

Audit Commission (2002) *Changing Habits: The Commissioning and Management of Community Drug Treatment Services for Adults*. London: Audit Commission.

Audit Commission (2004) *Drug Misuse 2004: Reducing the Local Impact*. London: Audit Commission.

Audit Commission (2006) *Competition and Contestability in Local Public Services: Research Proposal and Interim Report*. London: Audit Commission.

Aye Maung, N. and Hammond, N. (2000) *Risk of Re-offending and Needs Assessment: The User's Perspective. Home Office Research Study* 211. London: Home Office.

Babiker, G. and Arnold, L. (1997) *The Language of Injury – Comprehending Self Mutilation*. Leicester: BPS.

Bagaric, M. and Amarasekara, K. (2001) 'Feeling sorry? Tell someone who cares: the irrelevance of remorse in sentencing', *Howard Journal of Criminal Justice*, 40: 364–76.

Bailey, R. (1995) 'Helping offenders as an element in justice', in D. Ward and M. Lacey (eds) *Probation: Working for Justice*. London: Whiting & Birch.

Bailey, R., Knight, C. and Williams, B. (2007) 'The Probation Service as part of NOMS in England and Wales: fit for purpose?', in L. Gelsthorpe and R. Morgan (eds) *Handbook of Probation*. Cullompton: Willan Publishing.

Baker, K. (2004) 'Is ASSET really an asset? Assessment of young offenders in practice', in R. Burnett and C. Roberts (eds) *What Works in Probation and Youth Justice: Developing Evidence-based Practice*. Cullompton: Willan Publishing.

Barker, R. (2001) *Legitimating Identities: The Self-presentation of Rulers and Subjects*. Cambridge: Cambridge University Press.

Baron, S., Field, J. and Schuller, T. (2001) *Social Capital: Critical Perspectives*. Oxford: Oxford University Press.

Basic Skills Agency (1998) *Influences on Adult Basic Skills*. London: BSA.

BASW (2001) *Definition of Social Work* (available online at **http://www.basw.co.uk/articles.php?articleId=2&page=2**).

Baumol, W. and Willig, R. (1986) 'Contestability: Developments since the book', *Oxford Economic Papers*. Oxford University Press, 38: 9–36.

Beaumont, B. and Mistry, T. (1996) 'Doing a good job under duress', *Probation Journal*, 43: 200–4.

Beck, U. (1992) *Risk Society: Towards a New Modernity*. London: Sage.

Beech, A.R., Oliver, C., Fisher, D. and Beckett, R. (2006) *Step 4: The Sex Offender Treatment Programme in Prison: Addressing the Offending Behaviour of Rapists and Sexual Murderers*. London: HM Prison Service.

Beetham, D. (1991) *The Legitimation of Power*. London: Macmillan.

Belbin, M. (1993) *Team Roles at Work*. London: Butterworths.

Bennett, T., Brookman, F. and Wright, R. (2006) *A Qualitative Study of the Role of Violence in Street Crime* (available online at **http://www.crimereduction.gov.uk/violentstreet/violentstreet007.htm**).

Bhui, H. (2006) 'Anti-racist practice in NOMS: reconciling managerialist and professional realities', *Howard Journal*, 45: 171–90.

Blair, R. J. R. (2003) 'Neurobiological basis of psychopathy', *British Journal Psychiatry*, 182, 5–7.

Blom-Cooper, Sir L. and Morris, T. (2004) *With Malice Aforethought: A Study of the Crime and Punishment for Homicide*. Oxford: Hart Publishing.

Bobbitt, P. (2002) *The Shield of Achilles*. London: Penguin Books.

Bochel, D. (1976) *Probation and After-care: Its Development in England and Wales*. Edinburgh: Scottish Academic Press.

Boeck, T., Fleming, J. and Kemshall, H. (2006) *Social Capital and Young People* (available online at **http://www.dmu.ac.uk/Images/ESRC%20practitioners%20leaflet%20final%20-%20pdf_tcm2-40394.pdf**).

Boswell, G. (1996) *Young and Dangerous: The Backgrounds and Careers of Section 53 Offenders*. Aldershot: Avebury.

Boswell, G. and Wedge, P. (2002) *Imprisoned Fathers and their Children*. London: Jessica Kingsley.

Bottoms, A.E. (1977) 'Reflections on the renaissance of dangerousness', *Howard Journal*, 16: 70–96.

Bottoms, A.E. (1979) 'The Advisory Council and the suspended sentence', *Criminal Law Review*, 437–46.

Bottoms, A.E. (1995) 'The philosophy and politics of punishment and sentencing', in C.M.V. Clarkson and R. Morgan (eds) *The Politics of Sentencing Reform*. Oxford: Clarendon Press.

Bottoms, A.E. (2001) 'Compliance and community penalties', in A.E. Bottoms *et al.* (eds) *Community Penalties: Changes and Challenges*. Cullompton: Willan Publishing.

Bottoms, A.E. (2004) 'Empirical research relevant to sentencing frameworks', in A.E. Bottoms *et al.* (eds) *Alternatives to Prison*. Cullompton: Willan Publishing.

Bottoms, A.E., Gelsthorpe, L. and Rex, S. (eds) (2001) *Community Penalties: Change and Challenges*. Cullompton: Willan Publishing.

Bourdieu, P. (1986) 'The forms of capital', in J. Richardson (ed.) *Handbook of Theory and Research for the Sociology of Education*. New York, NY: Greenwood Press.

Boutellier, H. (2000) *Crime and Morality: The Significance of Criminal Justice in Post-modern Culture*. Dordrecht: Kluwer Academic.

Bowling, B. and Phillips, C. (2002) *Racism, Crime and Justice*. London: Longman.

Bracken, D. (2005) 'Developments and trends in Canadian probation', *Vista*, 10: 99–108.

Braithwaite, J. (1989) *Crime, Shame and Reintegration*. Cambridge: Cambridge University Press.

Bridges, A. (1998) *Increasing the Employability of Offenders: An Inquiry into Probation Service Effectiveness. Probation Studies Unit Report* 5. Oxford: University of Oxford Centre for Criminological Research.

Brody, S. (1976) *The Effectiveness of Sentencing. Home Office Research Study* 35. London: HMSO.

Brown, A. and Caddick, B. (eds) (1993) *Groupwork with Offenders*. London: Whiting & Birch.

Brownlee, I. (1998) *Community Punishment: A Critical Introduction*. London: Longman.

Burnett, R. (1996) *Fitting Supervision to Offenders: Assessment and Allocation Decisions in the Probation Service. Home Office Research Study* 153. London: Home Office.

Burnett, R., Baker, K. and Roberts, C. (2007) 'Assessment, supervision and intervention: fundamental practice in probation', in L. Gelsthorpe and R. Morgan (eds) *Handbook of Probation*. Cullompton: Willan Publishing.

Burney, E. (2005) *Making People Behave: Anti-social Behaviour, Politics and Policy*. Cullompton: Willan Publishing.

Bushway, S.D., Piquero, A., Broidy, L., Cauffman, E. and Mazerole, P. (2001) 'An empirical framework for studying desistance as a process', *Criminology*, 39: 496–515.

Calverley, A., Cole, B., Kaur, G., Lewis, S., Raynor, P., Sadeghi, S., Smith, D., Vanstone, M. and Wardak, A. (2004) *Black and Asian Offenders on Probation. Home Office Research Study* 277 (available online at **http://www.homeoffice.gov.uk/rds/pdfs04/hors277.pdf**).

Canton, R. (2007) 'Probation and the tragedy of punishment', *Howard Journal* (forthcoming).

Canton, R. and Eadie, T. (2005) 'From enforcement to compliance: implications for supervising officers', *Vista*, 9: 152–8.

Carlen, P. (1983) *Women's Imprisonment*. London: Routledge.

Carlen, P. (2002a) 'Women's imprisonment: models of reform and change', *Probation Journal*, 49: 76–87.

Carlen, P. (ed.) (2002b) *Women and Punishment: The Struggle for Justice*. Cullompton: Willan Publishing.

Carlen, P. and Worrall, A. (2004) *Analysing Women's Imprisonment*. Cullompton: Willan Publishing.

Carter, P. (2003) *Managing Offenders, Reducing Crime: A New Approach*. London: Home Office.

Catholic Bishops' Conference in England and Wales (2004) *A Place of Redemption – a Catholic Approach to Punishment and Prisons*. London: Burns & Oates.

Cavadino, M. and Dignan, J. (2002) *The Penal System: An Introduction* (3rd edn). London: Sage.

Cavadino, M. and Dignan, J. (2006) *Penal Systems: A Comparative Approach*. London: Sage.

Cavadino, M. and Dignan, J. (2007) *The Penal System: An Introduction* (4th edn). London: Sage.

Chapman, T. and Hough, M. (1998) *Evidence Based Practice: A Guide to Effective Practice*. London: Home Office.

Cherry, S. (2005) *Transforming Behaviour: Pro-social Modelling in Action*. Cullompton: Willan Publishing.

Chigwada-Bailey, R. (1997) *Black Women's Experiences of Criminal Justice*. Winchester: Waterside Press.

Children and Family Court Advisory Support Service (2005) *Delivering Quality Services for Children: Transforming Services – Transforming the Organisation. Business Plan 2005/07*. London: CAFCASS.

Chouhan, K. (2002) 'Race issues in probation', in D. Ward *et al.* (eds) *Probation: Working for Justice*. Oxford: Oxford University Press.

Chui, E. and Nellis, M. (2004) *Moving Probation Forward: Theory, Policy and Practice*. London: Pearson Longman.

Clark, M.D. (2005) 'Motivational interviewing for probation staff: increasing the readiness to change', *Federal Probation*, 69: 22–8.

Clarke, D. (2006) 'Communities engaging with community service', *Criminal Justice Matters*, 64: 34–35.

Clear, T. (1999) *The Community Justice Ideal*. Boulder, CO: Westview Press.

Clear, T. and Rumgay, J. (1992) 'Divided by a common language: British and American probation cultures', *Federal Probation*, 56: 3–11.

Coffield, F., Moseley, D., Hall, E. and Ecclestone, K. (2004) *Should we be Using Learning Styles? What Research has to Say to Practice*. London: Learning and Skills Research Centre (available online at **http://www.lsrc.ac.uk/publications/index.asp**).

Cohen, S. (1980) *Folk Devils and Moral Panics* (2nd edn). London: Martin Robertson.

Coleman, J.S. (1997) 'Social capital in the creation of human capital', in F. Ackerman *et al.* (eds) *Human Well-being and Economic Goals*. Washington, DC: Island Press.

Commission on the Future of Multi-ethnic Britain (2000) *The Future of Multi-ethnic Britain: The Parekh Report*. London: Profile Books for the Runnymede Trust.

Coopers & Lybrand/JISC (1995) *Guidelines for Developing an Information Strategy* (available online at **www.webarchive.org.uk**).

Correctional Services Accreditation Panel (2005) *Annual Report, 2004–5*. London: CSAP.

Coyle, A. (2005) *Understanding Prisons*. Maidenhead: Open University Press.

Crawford, A. and Newburn, T. (2002) 'Recent developments in restorative justice for young people in England and Wales: community participation and representation', *British Journal of Criminology*, 42: 476–95.

Criminal Justice Review Group (2000) *Review of the Criminal Justice System in Northern Ireland* (available online at **http://www.nio.gov.uk/criminal-justice**).

Crow, I. (2001) *The Treatment and Rehabilitation of Offenders*. London: Sage.

Crown Prosecution Service *Conditional Cautioning* (available online at **http://www.cps.gov.uk/publications/others/conditionalcautioning04.html**) n.d..

Cuppleditch, L. and Evans, W. (2005) *Re-offending of Adults: Results from the 2002 Cohort. Home Office Statistical Bulletin* 2505 (available online at **http://www.homeoffice.gov.uk/rds/pdfs05/hosb2505.pdf**).

Davies, G. (2006) *Service User Consultation on the Impact of Drug Treatment and Testing Orders and DRRs across Dyfed-Powys*. Available from Dyfed-Powys DIP, St David's Park, Jobswell Road, Carmarthen SA31 3HB.

Department for Constitutional Affairs (2006) *Making Sense of Human Rights* (available online at **http://www.dca.gov.uk/peoples-rights/human-rights/pdf/hr-handbook-introduction.pdf**).

Department of Health (1999) *Drug Misuse and Dependence: Guidelines on Clinical Management* (available online at **http://www.dh.gov.uk/assetRoot/04/07/81/98/04078198.pdf**).

Department of Health (2001) *Treatment Choice in Psychological Therapies and Counselling: Evidence Based Clinical Practice Guidelines.* London: Department of Health.

Despicht, K. (1987) *Specificity in Probation Practice. Social Work Monograph.* Norwich: University of East Anglia.

DfEE (2001) *Skills for Life: The national strategy for improving adult literacy and numeracy skills.* London: DfEE.

DfES (2004) *Raising Standards: A Contextual Guide to Support.* London: DfES (available online at **http://www.dfes.gov.uk/readwriteplus/bank/LLDD.pdf**).

Dignan, J. (2002) 'Reparation orders', in B. Williams (ed.) *Reparation and Victim-focused Social Work. Research Highlights in Social Work* 42. London: Jessica Kingsley.

Dignan, J. (2005) *Understanding Victims and Restorative Justice.* Maidenhead: Open University Press.

Ditchfield, J. (1994) *Family Ties and Recidivism: Main Findings of the Literature. Home Office Research Bulletin* 36. London: HMSO.

Dominey, J. (2002) 'Addressing victim issues in pre-sentence reports', in B. Williams (ed.) *Reparation and Victim-focused Social Work.* London: Jessica Kingsley.

Dowden, C. and Andrews, D. (2004) 'The importance of staff practice in delivering effective correctional treatment: a meta-analytic review of core correctional practice', *International Journal of Offender Therapy and Comparative Criminology*, 48: 203–14.

Downes, D. and Rock, P. (2003) *Understanding Deviance* (4th edn). Oxford: Oxford University Press.

Drakeford, M., Haines, K., Cotton, B. and Octigan, M. (2001) *Pre-trial Services and the Future of Probation.* Cardiff: University of Wales Press.

Duff, A. and Garland, D. (eds) (1994) *A Reader on Punishment.* Oxford: Oxford University Press.

Duff, R.A. (2003) 'Probation, punishment and restorative justice', *Howard Journal of Criminal Justice*, 42: 180–197.

Durrance, P. and Williams, P. (2003) 'Broadening the agenda around what works for black and Asian offenders', *Probation Journal*, 50: 211–24.

Eadie, T. and Canton, R. (2002) 'Practising in a context of ambivalence: the challenge for youth justice workers', *Youth Justice*, 2: 14–26.

Farrall, S. (2002) *Rethinking What Works with Offenders.* Cullompton: Willan Publishing.

Farrall, S. and Calverley, A. (2006) *Understanding Desistance from Crime.* Maidenhead: Open University Press.

Farrall, S., Mawby, R.C. and Worrall, A. (2007) 'Prolific/persistent offenders and desistance', in L. Gelsthorpe and R. Morgan (eds) *Handbook of Probation.* Cullompton: Willan Publishing.

Farrant, F. and Levenson, J. (2002) *Barred Citizens.* London: Prison Reform Trust.

Farrington, D.P. (ed.) (2005) *Integrated Developmental and Life-course Theories of Offending.* New Brunswick, NJ: Transaction Books.

Farrington, D.P. and Welsh, B.C. (2007) *Saving Children from a Life of Crime: Early Risk Factors and Effective Interventions.* Oxford: Oxford University Press.

Farrington, D.P. *et al.* (2006) *Criminal Careers up to Age 50 and Life Success up to Age 48: New Findings from the Cambridge Study in Delinquent Development. Home Office Research Study* 299. London: Home Office (available online at **http://www.homeoffice.gov.uk/rds/pdfs06/hors299.pdf**).

Faulkner, D. (2004) *Civil Renewal, Diversity and Social Capital in a Multi-ethnic Britain.* London: Runnymede Perspectives.

Faulkner, D. (2006) *Crime, State and Citizen: A Field Full of Folk* (2nd edn). Chichester: Waterside Press.

Faulkner, D. and Flaxington, F. (2004) 'NOMS and civil renewal', *Vista*, 9: 90–9.

Feeley, M. and Simon, J. (1994) 'Actuarial justice: the emerging new criminal law', in D. Nelken (ed.) *The Futures of Criminology*. London: Sage.

Feinberg, J. (1970) 'The expressive function of punishment', in his *Doing and Deserving*. Princeton, NJ: Princeton University Press.

Fellowes, B. (1992) 'Management and empowerment: the paradox of professional practice', in R. Statham and P. Whitehead (eds) *Managing the Probation Service Issues for the 1990s*. Harlow: Longman.

Field, J. (2003) *Social Capital*. London: Routledge.

Fitzgerald, M. (1993) *Ethnic Minorities and the Criminal Justice System. Royal Commission on Criminal Justice Research Study* 20. London: HMSO.

Foren, R. and Bailey, R. (1968) *Authority in Social Casework*. Oxford: Pergamon Press.

France, A., Hine, J., Armstrong, D. and Camina, M. (2004) *The On Track Early Intervention and Prevention Programme: From Theory to Action*. London: Home Office.

Fuller, C. and Taylor, P. (2003) *Toolkit of Motivational Skills*. London: National Probation Directorate.

Gadd, B. (1996) 'Probation in Northern Ireland', in G. McIvor (ed.) *Working with Offenders*. London: Jessica Kingsley.

Garland, D. (1985) *Punishment and Welfare: A History of Penal Strategies*. Aldershot: Gower.

Garland, D. (1990) *Punishment and Modern Society*. Oxford: Oxford University Press.

Garland, D. (1997) 'Probation and the reconfiguration of crime control', in R. Burnett (ed.) *The Probation Service: Responding to Change. Proceedings of the Probation Studies Unit First Colloquium*. Oxford: University of Oxford Centre for Criminological Research.

Garland, D. (2001) *The Culture of Control*. Oxford: Oxford University Press.

Garside, R. and McMahon, W. (eds) (2006) *Does Criminal Justice Work? The 'Right for the Wrong Reasons' Debate* (available online at **http://www.crimeandsociety.org.uk/briefings/dcjw.html**).

Gast, L. and Taylor, P. (1998) *Influence and Integrity: A Practice Book for Pro-social Modelling*. Birmingham: Midlands Probation Training Consortium.

Gearty, C. (1998) 'No human rights please, we're capitalists', *Independent*, 13 December: 14.

Gelsthorpe, L. (2001) 'Accountability: difference and diversity in the delivery of community penalties', in A.E. Bottoms *et al.* (eds) *Community Penalties: Change and Challenges*. Cullompton: Willan Publishing.

Gelsthorpe, L. (2007) 'Probation values and human rights', in L. Gelsthorpe and R. Morgan (eds) *Handbook of Probation*. Cullompton: Willan Publishing.

Gelsthorpe, L. and McIvor, G. (2007) 'Difference and diversity in probation', in L. Gelsthorpe and R. Morgan (eds) *Handbook of Probation*. Cullompton: Willan Publishing.

Gelsthorpe, L. and Padfield, N. (eds) (2003) *Exercising Discretion: Decision-making in the Criminal Justice System and Beyond*. Cullompton: Willan Publishing.

Gill, A. (2004) 'Voicing the silent fear: south Asian women's experiences of domestic violence', *Howard Journal*, 43: 465–83.

Goldson, B. and Muncie, J. (eds) (2006) *Youth Crime and Justice*. London: Sage.

Graham, J. and Bowling, B. (1995) *Young People and Crime. Home Office Research Study* 145. London: HMSO.

Greatorex, P. and Falkowski, D. (2006) *Anti-social Behaviour Law*. Bristol: Jordan Publishing.

Grubin, D. (1998) *Sex Offending against Children: Understanding the Risk. Police Research Series Paper* 99. London: Home Office (available online at **http://www.homeoffice.gov.uk/rds/prgpdfs/fprs99.pdf**).

Hagan, J. and Peterson, R.D. (eds) (1995) *Crime and Inequality*. Stanford, CA: Stanford University Press.

Hagell, A. and Newburn, T. (1994) *Persistent Young Offenders*. London: Policy Studies Institute.

Haines, K. and Morgan, R. (2007) 'Services before trial and sentence: achievement, decline and potential', in L. Gelsthorpe and R. Morgan (eds) *Handbook of Probation*. Cullompton: Willan Publishing.

Haines, K. and Octigan, M. (1998) *Reducing Remands in Custody: The Probation Service and Remand Service*. London: ACOP.

Hall, N. (2005) *Hate Crime*. Cullompton: Willan Publishing.

Halliday, J. (2007) 'Our judges have had enough messages from ministers', *Guardian*, 6 February.

Halpern, D. (2005) *Social Capital*. Cambridge: Polity Press.

Hamai, K., Villé, R., Harris, R., Hough, M. and Zvekic, U. (1995) *Probation Round the World: A Comparative Study*. London: Routledge.

Hanson, R.K. and Bussiere, M.T. (1998) 'Predicting relapse: a meta-analysis of sexual offender recidivism studies', *Journal of Consulting and Clinical Psychology*, 66: 348–62.

Harding, J. (2000) 'A community justice dimension to effective probation practice', *Howard Journal*, 39: 132–49.

Harper, G. and Chitty, C. (2005) *The Impact of Corrections on Re-offending: A Review of 'What Works'. Home Office Research Study* 291. London: Home Office (available online at **http://www.homeoffice.gov.uk/rds/pdfs04/hors291.pdf**).

Hawkins, D.R. (2002) *Power vs. Force: The Hidden Determinants of Human Behavior*. Sedona, AZ: Veritas Publishing.

Hawkins, K. (ed.) (1992) *The Uses of Discretion*. Oxford: Clarendon Press.

Haxby, D. (1978) *Probation: A Changing Service*. London: Constable.

Heape, N. (1999) *A Developing Probation Service National Information Strategy*. London: Home Office (available online at **www.nationalarchives.gov.uk/ERO/records/ho415/1/cpd/probu/strategy.htm**).

Hearn, J. and Whitehead, A. (2006) 'Collateral damage: men's "domestic" violence to women seen through men's relations with men', *Probation Journal*, 51: 38–56.

Hearnden, I. and Millie, A. (2003) *Investigating Links between Probation Enforcement and Reconviction* (available online at **www.homeoffice.gov.uk/rds/pdfs2/rdsolr4103.pdf**).

Hearnden, I. and Millie, A. (2004) 'Does tougher enforcement lead to lower conviction?', *Probation Journal*, 51: 48–59.

Hedderman, C. (2007) 'Past, present and future sentences: what do we know about their effectiveness?', in L. Gelsthorpe and R. Morgan (eds) *Handbook of Probation*. Cullompton: Willan Publishing.

Hedderman, C. and Hough, M. (2004) 'Getting tough or being effective: what matters?', in G. Mair (ed.) *What Matters in Probation*. Cullompton: Willan Publishing.

Heidensohn, F. (2002) 'Gender and crime', in M. Maguire *et al.* (eds) *The Oxford Handbook of Criminology* (3rd edn). Oxford: Oxford University Press.

Hepburn, J.R. (2005) 'Recidivism among drug offenders following exposure to treatment', *Criminal Justice Policy Review*, 16: 237–59.

Hill, L. (2002) 'Working in the courts', in D. Ward *et al.* (eds) *Probation: Working for Justice* (2nd edn). Oxford: Oxford University Press.

Hills, J., Le Grand, J. and Piachaud, D. (eds) (2001) *Understanding Social Exclusion*. Oxford: Oxford University Press.

Hine, J. and Celnick, A. (2001) *A One Year Reconviction Study of Final Warnings*. London: Home Office (available online at **http://www.homeoffice.gov.uk/rds/pdfs/reconvictstudywarn.pdf**).

Hirschi, T. (1969) *Causes of Delinquency*. Berkeley, CA: University of California Press.

HM Chief Inspector of Constabulary, HM Chief Inspector of Probation, HM Chief Inspector the Crown Prosecution Service, HM Chief Inspector of the Magistrates' Court Service and

HM Chief Inspector of Prisons, Audit Commission. (2004) *Joint Inspection Report into Persistent and Prolific Offenders*. London: Home Office Communications Directorate.

HM Inspectorate of Prisons (2005) *Annual Report, 2003–4*. London: Home Office.

HM Inspectorate of Prisons (2006) *Annual Report, 2004–5*. London: Home Office.

HMIP (2000) *Towards Race Equality: A Thematic Inspection*. London: Home Office.

HMIP (2001) *Through the Prison Gate* (available online at **http://inspectorates.homeoffice.gov.uk/ hmiprisons/thematic-reports1/prison-gate**).

HMIP (2003) *Valuing the Victim*. London: Home Office.

HMIP (2004) *Towards Race Equality: Follow-up Inspection Report*. London: Home Office.

HMIP (2005a) *An Effective Supervision Inspection Programme Thematic Report: 'I'm not a Racist but…'* London: Home Office (available online at **http://www.ncblo.co.uk/documents_ download/HMIP%20I'm%20not%20really%20a%20racist%20but%20RMOs.pdf**).

HMIP (2005b) *Effective Supervision Thematic Element*. London: HMIP.

HMIP (2006) *An Independent Review of a Serious Further Offence Case: Damien Hanson and Elliot White* (available online at **http://www.inspectorates.homeoffice.gov.uk/hmiprobation/ inspect_reports/serious-further-offences/**).

HM Prison Service (2002) *Prison Service Order* 2700. London: HMSO.

HM Prison Service (2006) *Foreign National Prisoners Liable to Deportation. Prison Service Instruction* 6000. London: SPI 2006–28. HM Prison Service.

HM Prison Service (2006) *Immigration and Foreign Nationals in Prison. Prison Service Order* 4630. London: PSO 2006–261. HM Prison Service.

HMI Prisons and HMI Probation (2001) *Through the Prison Gate: A Joint Thematic Review*. London: Home Office.

Hollin, C.R. and Palmer, E.J. (eds) (2006) *Offending Behaviour Programmes: Development, Application, and Controversies*. Chichester: Wiley.

Hollin, C., Palmer, E., McGuire, J., Hounsome, J., Hatcher, R., Bilby, C. and Clark, C. (2004) *Pathfinder Programmes in the Probation Service: A Retrospective Analysis. Home Office Online Report* 66/04. London: Home Office.

Holt, P. (2000) *Case Management: Context for Supervision*. Leicester: De Montfort University (available online at **http://www.dmu.ac.uk/Images/Monograph%202_tcm2-35042.pdf**).

Home Office (1910) *Report of the Departmental Committee on the Probation of Offenders Act 190* (Cd 5001).

Home Office (1988) *Punishment, Custody and the Community* (Cm 424). London: HMSO.

Home Office (1990) *Crime, Justice and Protecting the Public* (Cm 965). London: HMSO.

Home Office (1998) *Tackling Drugs to Build a Better Britain: The Government's 10-year Strategy for Tackling Drug Misuse* (Cm 39450). London: HMSO.

Home Office (1999) *Diploma in Probation Studies*. London: Home Office.

Home Office (2000) Approved Premises Handbook, London: Home Office (available online at **http://www.probation.justice.gov.uk/files/pdf/Approved%20Prem.pdf**)

Home Office (2001) *The British Crime Survey*. London: Home Office.

Home Office (2001a) *Approved Premises Regulations 2001* (Statutory Instrument 2001 no. 850). London: HMSO.

Home Office (2001b) *Design Standards for Probation Service and Non-hostel Buildings*. London: Home Office.

Home Office (2001c) *Further Guidance: Working with Victims of Serious Crime* (PC 62/2001). London: Home Office.

Home Office (2001d) *Making Punishments Work: The Report of a Review of the Sentencing Framework for England and Wales* (the Halliday Review). London: Home Office Communications Directorate.

Home Office (2001e) *National Probation Service Management Statement and Financial Memorandum.* London: Home Office.

Home Office (2001f) *Probation Estate: Property Management and Legal Arrangements* (PC 56/2001). London: Home Office.

Home Office (2002a) *Approved Premises Handbook.* London: Home Office.

Home Office (2002b) *Better Quality Services Review.* London: Home Office/National Probation Service Training Consortia.

Home Office (2002c) *Justice for All* (Cm 5563). London: Home Office.

Home Office (2002d) *Treatment Manager Strategy* (PC 57/2002). London: Home Office.

Home Office (2002e) *Updated Drug Strategy, 2002.* London: Home Office.

Home Office (2003) *Prison Statistics for England and Wales 2001,* (CM5743) London: TSO.

Home Office (2003a) *Approved Premises Planning and Development Programme Framework.* London: Home Office.

Home Office (2003b) *MAPPA Guidance* (NPD/057/2003). London: Home Office.

Home Office (2004a) *Black and Asian Offenders on Probation. Research Study* 277. London: Home Office Research, Development and Statistics Directorate.

Home Office (2004b) *Confident Communities* (available online at **http://www.crimereduction. gov.uk/publications10.htm**).

Home Office (2004c) *Death of Approved Premises Residents* (PC 02/2004). London: Home Office.

Home Office (2004d) *Home Office RDS and YJB Standards for Impact Studies in Correctional Settings* (available online at **http://www.homeoffice.gov.uk/rds/pdfs04/ rds_correctional_standards.pdf**).

Home Office (2004e) *Reducing Crime – Changing Lives: The Government's Plans for Transforming the Management of Offenders.* London: Home Office.

Home Office (2004f) *Statistics on Women and the Criminal Justice System, 2003* (available online at **www.homeoffice.gov.uk/rds/pdfs2/s95women03.pdf**).

Home Office (2005a) *Criminal Justice Act 2003 – New Sentences and the New Report Framework* (PC 18/2005). London: Home Office.

Home Office (2005b) *Implementing Section 10 of the Children Act 2004* (PC 22/2005). London: Home Office.

Home Office (2005c) *National Guide for the New CJA Sentences for Public Protection.* London: Home Office.

Home Office (2005d) *National Standards 2005* (PC 15/2005). London: Home Office.

Home Office (2005e) *Public Protection Framework, Risk of Harm and MAPPA Thresholds* (PC 10/2005). London: Home Office.

Home Office (2005f) *Reducing Re-offending Delivery Plan.* London: Home Office.

Home Office (2005g) *Role Boundary Issues in the NPS* (PC 90/2005). London: Home Office.

Home Office (2005h) *Statutory Guidance on Implementing Section 11 of the Children Act 2004* (PC 63/2005). London: Home Office.

Home Office (2005i) *Victims of Mentally Disordered Offenders* (PC 42/2005). London: Home Office.

Home Office (2006a) *Changes to Admissions Policy for Approved Premises* (PC 26/2006) (available online at **www.probation.homeoffice.gov.uk/output/page31.asp**).

Home Office (2006b) *Drug Misuse Declared: Findings from the 2005/6 British Crime Survey. Home Office Statistical Bulletin.* London: Home Office.

Home Office (2006c) *Five Year Plan: Protecting the Public and Reducing Re-offending* (Cm 6717). London: HMSO.

Home Office (2006d) *Foreign National Prisoners* (PC 24/2006). London: Home Office.

Home Office (2006e) *Further Guidance on Prolific and Priority Offenders (PPOs)* (PC 30/2006) (available online at **www.homeoffice.gov.uk/output/page31.asp**).

Home Office (2006f) *Information Exchange between the IND, Prison Service and NPD Regarding Licences and Bail Hearings* (PC 37/2006). London: Home Office.

Home Office (2006g) *Offender Management for Custodial Sentences* (PC 09/2006). London: Home Office.

Home Office (2006h) PC 08/2006 (available online at **http://www.probation.homeoffice.gov.uk/ files/pdf/PC08%202006.pdf**).

Home Office (2006i) PC 41/2006 (available online at **http://www.probation.homeoffice.gov.uk/ files/pdf/PC41%202006.pdf**).

Home Office (2006j) *Public Value Partnerships*. London: Home Office.

Home Office (2006k) *Tackling Hate Crime: Homophobic Hate Crime* (available online at **http://www.crimereduction.gov.uk/ sexual028.pdf**).

Home Office *A Guide to the Criminal Justice System in England and Wales*. London: Home Office (available online at **http://www.homeoffice.gov.uk/rds/cjspub1.html**).

Home Office *Information on the Criminal Justice System*. *Digest* 4 (available online at **http://www.homeoffice.gov.uk/rds/digest41.html**).n.d.

Home Office *Justice and Prisons* (available online at **http://www.homeoffice.gov.uk/justice/ what-happens-at-court/sentencing/**).n.d.

Home Office *Restorative Justice* (available online at **http://www.homeoffice.gov.uk/crime-victims/ victims/restorative-justice/**).

Home Office/NOMS (2006) *Offender Management Model*. London: Home Office.

Hood, C. (1991) 'A public management for all seasons', *Public Administration*, 69: 3–19.

Hood, R. (1965) *Borstal Re-assessed*. London: Heinemann.

Hood, R. (1992) *Race and Sentencing*. Oxford: Clarendon Press.

Hood-Williams, J. (2001) 'Gender, masculinities and crime: from structures to psyches', *Theoretical Criminology*, 5: 37–60.

Hope, T. and Sparks, R. (eds) (2000) *Crime, Risk and Insecurity: Law and Order in Everyday Life and Political Discourse*. London: Routledge.

Hopkinson, J. and Rex, S. (2003) 'Essential skills in working with offenders', in W.H. Chui and M. Nellis (eds) *Moving Probation Forward*. Harlow: Pearson Education.

Hopley, K. (2002) 'National Standards: defining the service', in D. Ward *et al.* (eds) *Probation: Working for Justice* (2nd edn). Oxford: Oxford University Press.

Hough, M., Clancy, A., Turnbull, P.J. and McSweeney, T. (2003) *The Impact of Drug Treatment and Testing Orders on Offending: Two-year Reconviction Results*. *Findings* 184. London: Home Office.

House of Commons (2001) *The Implementation of the National Probation Service Information Systems Strategy*. *Report by the Comptroller and Auditor General*. London: HMSO.

House of Commons (2002) *Thirty-second Report: The Implementation of the National Probation Service Information Systems Strategy*. London: House of Commons.

Howard, J. and Shepherd, G. (1987) *Conciliation, Children and Divorce: A Family Systems Approach*. London: Batsford.

Howard, P. (2006) *The Offender Assessment System: An Evaluation of the Second Pilot*. Home Office Research Findings 278. London: Home Office.

Howard, P., Clark, D. and Garnham, N. (2006a) *An evaluation of the Offender Assessment System (OASys) in Three Pilots, 1999–2001*. London: Home Office (available online at **http://www.noms.homeoffice.gov.uk/downloads/oasys-210606.pdf**).

Howard, P., Clark, D.A. and Garnham, N. (2006b) *The Offender Assessment System: An Evaluation of the Second Pilot*. RDS Findings 278. London: Home Office.

Hudson, B. (2003) *Justice in the Risk Society*. London: Sage.

Hudson, B. and Bramhall, G. (2005) 'Assessing the "other": constructions of "Asianness" in risk assessments by probation officers', *British Journal of Criminology*, 45: 721–40.

Hudson O'Hanlon, W. and Weiner-Davis, M. (1989) *In Search of Solution*. London: Norton.

Hughes, O. (2003) *Public Management and Administration* (3rd edn). Basingstoke: Macmillan.

Humphreys, C. and Thiara, R. (2003) 'Mental health and domestic violence: "I call it symptoms of abuse"', *British Journal of Social Work*, 33: 209–26.

Huxham, C. (ed.) (1996) *Creating Collaborative Advantage*. London: Sage.

James, A.L., James, A. and McNamee, S. (2003) 'Constructing children's welfare in family proceedings', *Family Law*, 33: 889–95.

Jamieson, J., McIvor, G. and Murray, C. (1999) *Understanding Offending among Young People*. Edinburgh: HMSO (available online at **http://www.scotland.gov.uk/cru/resfinds/swr37-00.htm**).

Johnstone, G. (ed.) (2003) *A Restorative Justice Reader*. Cullompton: Willan Publishing.

Johnstone, G. and Van Ness, H. (eds) (2006) *Handbook of Restorative Justice*. Cullompton: Willan Publishing.

Joint Council for the Welfare of Immigrants (2006) *Immigration, Nationality and Refugee Law Handbook*. London: Joint Council for Welfare of Immigrants.

Jones, T. and Newburn, T. (2005) 'Comparative criminal justice policy-making in the United Kingdom and the United States: the case of private prisons', *British Journal of Criminology*, 25: 58–80.

Karp, D. and Clear, T. (eds) (2002) *What is Community Justice?* London: Sage.

Kay, J. and Gast, L. (1998) *From Murmur to Murder*. Birmingham: Midlands Probation Training Consortium.

Keith, B. (2006) *Report of the Zahid Mubarek Inquiry*. London: Home Office.

Kelly, L., Regan, L. and Burton, S. (1991) *An Exploratory Study of the Prevalence of Sexual Abuse in a Sample of 16–21 Year Olds*. London: Child Abuse Studies Unit, Polytechnic of North London.

Kemshall, H. (2003) *Understanding Risk in Criminal Justice*. Buckingham: Open University Press.

Kemshall, H. and Canton, R. (2002) *The Effective Management of Programme Attrition* (available online at **http://www.dmu.ac.uk/faculties/hls/research/commcrimjustice/commcrimjus.jsp**).

Kemshall, H., Canton, R. and Bailey, R. (2004) 'Dimensions of difference', in A. Bottoms *et al.* (eds) *Alternatives to Imprisonment: Options for an Insecure Society*. Cullompton: Willan Publishing.

Kemshall, H., Dominey, J., Knight, V., with Bailey, R. and Price, A. (2004) *Offender Perception Data Project*. Leicester: De Montfort University.

Kemshall, H., Mackenzie, G., Wood, J., Bailey, R. and Yates, J. (2005) *Strengthening Multi-agency Public Protection Arrangements (MAPPAs). Report* 45. London: Home Office Research, Development and Statistics Directorate (available online at **http://www.homeoffice.gov.uk/rds/pdfs05/dpr45.pdf**).

Kemshall, H. and Wood, J. (2007) 'High-risk offenders and public protection', in L. Gelsthorpe and R. Morgan (eds) *Handbook of Probation*. Cullompton: Willan Publishing.

Kennard, D. (1998) *An Introduction to Therapeutic Communities*. London: Jessica Kingsley.

Kennedy, S. (2001) 'Treatment responsivity: reducing recidivism by enhancing treatment effectiveness', in L. Motiuk and R. Serin (eds) *Compendium 2000 on Effective Correctional Programming*. Ottawa: Correctional Services Canada (available online at **http://www.csc-scc.gc.ca/text/rsrch/compendium/2000/chap_5_e.shtml**).

Knight, C. (2002) 'Training for a modern service', in D. Ward *et al.* (eds) *Probation: Working for Justice*. Oxford: Oxford University Press.

Kurki, L. (2001) 'International standards for sentencing and punishment', in M. Tonry and R.S. Frase (eds) *Sentencing and Sanctions in Western Countries*. New York, NY: Oxford University Press.

Levi, M. with Maguire, M. (2002) 'Violent crime', in M. Maguire *et al.* (eds) *The Oxford Handbook of Criminology* (3rd edn). Oxford: Oxford University Press.

Lewis, S. (2005) 'Rehabilitation: headline or footnote in the new penal policy?', *Probation Journal*, 52: 119–35.

Lewis, S., Raynor, P., Smith, D. and Wardak, A. (eds) (2006) *Race and Probation*. Cullompton: Willan Publishing.

Liebmann, M. (ed.) (2000) *Mediation in Context*. London: Jessica Kingsley.

Lockyer, A. and Stone, F. (eds) (1998) *Juvenile Justice in Scotland: Twenty Five Years of the Welfare Approach*. Edinburgh: T. & T. Clark.

Mackie, A., Raine, J., Burrows, J., Hopkins, M. and Dunstan, E. (2003) *Clearing the Debts: The Enforcement of Financial Penalties in Magistrates' Courts. Home Office Online Report* 09/03. London: Home Office.

Macpherson, Sir W. (1999) *Report of an Inquiry by Sir William Macpherson of Cluny Advised by Tom Cook, the Right Reverend Dr John Sentamu, Dr Richard Stone, Presented to Parliament by the Secretary of State for the Home Department by Command of Her Majesty* (the Stephen Lawrence Inquiry) (Cm 4262-I). London: HMSO.

Maguire, M. (1992) 'Parole', in E. Stockdale and S. Casale (eds) *Criminal Justice Under Stress*. London: Blackstone Press.

Maguire, M. (2004) 'The Crime Reduction Programme: reflections on the vision and the reality', *Criminal Justice*, 4: 213–38.

Maguire, M. (2007) 'The resettlement of ex-prisoners', in L. Gelsthorpe and R. Morgan (eds) *Handbook of Probation*. Cullompton: Willan Publishing.

Maguire, M., Morgan, R. and Reiner, R. (eds) (2002) *The Oxford Handbook of Criminology* (3rd edn). Oxford: Oxford University Press.

Maguire, M. and Raynor, P. (2006) 'How the resettlement of prisoners promotes desistance from crime – or does it?', *Criminology and Criminal Justice*, 6: 19–38.

Mair, G. (1988) *Probation Day Centres. HORS* 100. London: HMSO.

Mair, G. (2004a) 'What works – a view from the chiefs', in G. Mair (ed.) *What Matters in Probation*. Cullompton: Willan Publishing.

Mair, G. (ed.) (2004b) *What Matters in Probation*. Cullompton: Willan Publishing.

Mair, G. (2005) 'Electronic monitoring in England and Wales: evidence-based or not?', *Criminal Justice*, 5: 257–78.

Mair, G. and Canton, R. (2007) 'Sentencing, community penalties and the role of the Probation Service', in L. Gelsthorpe and R. Morgan (eds) *Handbook of Probation*. Cullompton: Willan Publishing.

Mair, G., Lloyd, C. and Hough, M. (1997) 'The limitations of reconviction rates', in G. Mair (ed.) *Evaluating the Effectiveness of Community Penalties*. Aldershot: Avebury.

Mantle, G. (2004) 'Social work and child-centred family court mediation', *British Journal of Social Work*, 34: 1161–72.

Mantle, G., Fox, D. and Dhami, M. (2005) 'Restorative justice and three individual theories of crime', *Internet Journal of Criminology* (available online at **www.internetjournalofcriminology.com**).

Mantle, G., Moules, T. and Johnson, K. (2006) 'Whose wishes and feelings? Children's autonomy and parental influence in family court enquiries', *British Journal of Social Work*.

Marlatt, G. and Gordon, J. (eds) *Relapse Prevention: Maintenance Strategies in the Treatment of Addictive Behaviors*. New York, NY: Guilford Press.

Marshall, T.F. (1999) *Restorative Justice: An Overview*. London: Home Office Research, Development and Statistics Directorate (available online at **http://www.homeoffice.gov.uk/rds/pdfs/occ-resjus.pdf**).

Martinson, R. (1974) 'What works? Questions and answers about prison reform', *The Public Interest*, 35: 22–54.

Maruna, S. (2001) *Making Good: How Ex-convicts Reform and Rebuild their Lives*. Washington, DC: American Psychological Association.

Maruna, S. and Farrall, S. (2004) 'Desistance-focused criminal justice policy research: introduction to a special issue on desistance from crime and public policy', *Howard Journal of Criminal Justice*, 43: 358–67.

Maruna, S. and Immarigeon, R. (eds) (2004) *After Crime and Punishment: Pathways to Offender Re-integration*. Cullompton: Willan Publishing.

Maruna, S. and Ward, T. (2006) *Rehabilitation. Key Ideas in Criminology Series*. London: Routledge.

Maslow, A.H. (1954) *Motivation and Personality*. New York, NY: Harper & Bros (available online in Davidmann, M. 'Motivation: summary' at **http://www.solbaram.org/articles/motvtnsu.html**).

Mason, J. and Murphy, G. (2002) 'People with intellectual disabilities on probation: an initial study', *Journal of Community and Applied Social Psychology*, 12: 44–55.

Mattessich, P.W., Murray-Close, M. and Monsey, B.R. (2001) *Collaboration: What Makes it Work* (2nd edn). Saint Paul, MN: Amherst H. Wilder Foundation.

Matthews, R. (ed.) (1999) *Imprisonment*. Dartmouth: Ashgate.

Matthews, R. and Pitts, J. (2001) *Crime, Disorder and Community Safety*. London: Routledge.

Matza, D. (1969) *Becoming Deviant*. Englewood Cliffs, NJ: Prentice Hall.

May, C. (1999) *Explaining Reconviction Following a Community Sentence: The Role of Social Factors. Home Office Research Study* 192. London: Home Office.

McDermitt, M.J. and Garofalo, J. (2004) 'When advocacy for domestic violence victims backfires', *Violence Against Women*, 10: 1245–66.

McDonald, C. and Gray, M. (2006) 'Pursuing good practice? The limits of evidence based practice', *Journal of Social Work*, 6: 7–20.

McGhee, J., Mellon, M. and Whyte, B. (eds) (2004) *Addressing Deeds: Working with Young People who Offend*. London: NCH.

McGuire, J. (2004) *Understanding Psychology and Crime: Perspectives on Theory and Action*. Maidenhead: Open University Press/McGraw-Hill Education.

McGuire, J. (ed.) (1995) *What Works*. Chichester: Wiley.

McGuire, J. *Cognitive-behavioural Approaches – an Introduction to Theory and Research* (2000) (available online at **http://inspectorates.homeoffice.gov.uk/hmiprobation/docs/cogbeh1.pdf**).

McGuire, J. and Priestley, P. (1985) *Offending Behaviour: Skills and Stratagems for Going Straight*. London: Batsford.

McIvor, G. (1992) *Sentenced to Serve*. Aldershot: Gower.

McIvor, G. (2004a) 'Reparative and restorative approaches', in A. Bottoms *et al.* (eds) *Alternatives to Prison: Options for an Insecure Society*. Cullompton: Willan Publishing.

McIvor, G. (2004b) *Reconviction following Drug Treatment and Testing Orders*. Edinburgh: Scottish Executive.

McIvor, G. (ed.) (2004c) *Women Who Offend: Research Highlights in Social Work*. London: Jessica Kingsley.

McIvor, G. and McNeill, F. (2007) 'Probation in Scotland: past, present and future', in L. Gelsthorpe and R. Morgan (eds) *Handbook of Probation*. Cullompton: Willan Publishing.

McKnight, J. (2005) *NOMS – the Vision, the Blueprint and an Alternative: Napo's Response*. London: Napo (available online at **www.napo2.org.uk**).

McLaughlin, K., Osborne, S. and Ferlie, E. (eds) (2002) *New Public Management: Current Trends and Future Prospects*. London: Routledge.

McLoughlin, D., Leather, C. and Stringer, P. (2002) *The Dyslexic Adult: Interventions and Outcomes*. London: Whurr.

McNeill, F. (2004) 'Desistance, rehabilitation and correctionalism', *Howard Journal of Criminal Justice*, 43: 420–36.

McNeill, F. (2006) 'A desistance paradigm for offender management', *Criminology and Criminal Justice*, 6: 32–64.

McNeill, F. and Whyte, B. (2007) *Reducing Reoffending: Social Work and Community Justice in Scotland*. Cullompton: Willan Publishing.

McWilliams, W. (1983) 'The mission to the English Police Courts – 1876–1936', *Howard Journal*, 22: 129–47.

McWilliams, W. (1985) 'The mission transformed: professionalisation of probation between the wars', *Howard Journal*, 24: 257–74.

McWilliams, W. (1986) 'The English probation system and the diagnostic ideal', *Howard Journal*, 25: 41–60.

McWilliams, W. (1987) 'Probation, pragmatism and policy', *Howard Journal*, 26: 97–121.

McWilliams, W. (1992) 'The rise and development of management thought in the English probation system', in R. Statham and P. Whitehead (eds) *Managing the Probation Service Issues for the 1990s*. Harlow: Longman.

Merrington, S. (2002) 'Assessment tools in probation', in R. Burnett and C. Roberts (eds) *What Works in Probation and Youth Justice: Developing Evidence-based Practice*. Cullompton: Willan Publishing.

Merrington, S. and Hine, J. (2001) *A Handbook for Evaluating Probation Work with Offenders*. London: Home Office (available online at **http://inspectorates.homeoffice.gov.uk/hmiprobation/docs/whole.pdf**).

Merrington, S. and Stanley, S. (2005) 'Some thoughts on recent research on pathfinder programmes in the Probation Service', *Probation Journal*, 52: 289–92.

Merrington, S. and Stanley, S. (2007) 'Effectiveness: who counts what?', in L. Gelsthorpe and R. Morgan (eds) *Handbook of Probation*. Cullompton: Willan Publishing.

Messerschmidt, J. (1993) *Masculinities and Crime: Critique and Reconceptualization of Theory*. Lanham, MD: Rowman & Littlefield.

Messerschmidt, J. (2006) 'Masculinities and crime: beyond a dualist criminology', in C.M. Renzetti *et al.* (eds) *Rethinking Gender, Crime and Justice: Feminist Readings*. Los Angeles, CA: Roxbury.

Miller, W.R. and Rollnick, S. (1994) 'Variations in the effectiveness in the treatment of patients with substance use disorders: an empirical review', *Addiction*, 89: 688–97.

Miller, W.R. and Rollnick, S. (2002) *Motivational Interviewing*. New York, NY: Guilford Press.

Moffitt, T. (1993) 'Adolescence-Limited and Life-Course-Persistent Antisocial Behavior: A Developmental Taxonomy', *Psychological Review*, 100(4): 674–701.

Mooney, J. and Young, J. (2000) 'Policing ethnic minorities: stop and search in north London', in A. Marlow and B. Loveday (eds) *After Macpherson: Policing after the Stephen Lawrence Inquiry*. London: Russell House Press.

Moore, R. (2003) 'The use of financial penalties and the amounts imposed: the need for a new approach', *Criminal Law Review*, 13–27.

Moore, R., Gray, E., Roberts, C., Taylor, E. and Merrington, S. (2006) *Managing Persistent and Serious Offenders in the Community: Intensive Community Programmes in Theory and Practice*. Cullompton: Willan Publishing.

Morgan, R. (2007) 'Probation, governance and accountability', in L. Gelsthorpe and R. Morgan (eds) *Handbook of Probation*. Cullompton: Willan Publishing.

Morgan, R. and Newburn, T. (2007) 'Youth justice', in L. Gelsthorpe and R. Morgan (eds) *Handbook of Probation*. Cullompton: Willan Publishing.

Morris, T. (1994) 'Crime and penal policy', in D. Kavanagh and A. Seldon (eds) *The Major Effect*. London: Macmillan.

Moss, K. and Prins, H. (2006) 'Severe personality (psychopathic) disorder: a review', *Medicine, Science and the Law*, 46: 190–207.

Muncie, J. (2004) *Youth and Crime: A Critical Introduction* (2nd edn). London: Sage.

Muncie, J., Hughes, G. and McLaughlin, E. (eds) (2002) *Youth Justice: Critical Readings*. London: Sage.

Murray, J. and Farrington, D. (2005) 'Parental imprisonment: effect on boys' anti-social behaviour and delinquency through the life course', *Journal of Child Psychology and Psychiatry*, 46: 1269–78.

NACRO (2002) *Children who Commit Grave Crimes*. London: NACRO.

Nash, M. (2003) 'Pre-trial investigation', in W.H. Chui and M. Nellis (eds) *Moving Probation Forward: Evidence, Arguments and Practice*. Harlow: Pearson Education.

National Association of Probation and Bail Hostels (2005) *Issues for Women Offenders in Approved Premises*. (Occasional Paper 3) London: National Association of Probation and Bail Hostels.

National Audit Office (2002) *Collection of Fines and other Financial Penalties in the Criminal Justice System*. London: HMSO.

National Audit Office (2006) *The Electronic Monitoring of Adult Offenders*. London: National Audit Office (available online at **http://www.nao.org.uk/publications/nao_reports/05-06/0506800.pdf**).

National Autistic Society (2005) *Autism: A Guide for Criminal Justice Professionals*. London: National Autistic Society (available online at **www.autism.org.uk/cjp**).

National Probation Directorate (2002a) *The Heart of the Dance*. London: Home Office.

National Probation Directorate (2002b) *The Treatment and Management of Sexual Offenders in Custody and in the Community*. London: National Probation Directorate.

National Probation Directorate (2004a) *Approved Premises – Resource Review*. London: Home Office.

National Probation Directorate (2004b) *Approved Premises and Offender Housing Strategy for Higher Risk Offenders*. London: Home Office.

National Probation Directorate (2005) *Interventions: A Guide to Interventions in the National Probation Service* (NPD/010/2005) (available on line at **http://www.probation. homeoffice.gov.uk**).

National Probation Service (2002a) *The National Probation Service Information Management Strategy*. London: Home Office.

National Probation Service (2002b) *Managing Information. NPS Briefing* 05. London: Home Office.

National Probation Service (2005a) *National Guide for the New Criminal Justice Act 2003 Sentences for Public Protection* (edition 1, version 1). London: Home Office.

National Probation Service (2005b) *National Standards 2005* (available online at **http://www. probation.homeoffice.gov.uk/files/pdf/NPS%20National%20Standard%202005.pdf**).

National Probation Service (2006a) *A Manual on the Delivery of Unpaid Work*. London: Home Office.

National Probation Service (2006b) *Learning and Skills for Offenders* (A1749). London: Home Office.

Nellis, M. (2000) 'Creating community justice', in S. Ballintyne *et al.* (eds) *Secure Foundations: Key Issues in Crime Reduction and Community Safety*. London: Institute for Public Policy Research.

Nellis, M. (2001) 'The new probation training in England and Wales: realising the potential', *Social Work Education*, 20(4): 415–32.

Nellis, M. (2002) 'Community justice, time and the new National Probation Service', *Howard Journal of Criminal Justice*, 41: 59–86.

Nellis, M. (2003) 'Probation training and the community justice curriculum', *British Journal of Social Work*, 33: 943–59.

Nellis, M. (2004) '"Into the field of corrections": the end of English probation in the early 21st century', *Cambrian Law Review*, 35: 115–33 (available online at **http://www.aber.ac.uk/clr/**).

Nellis, M. (2005) 'Electronic monitoring, satellite tracking and the new punitiveness in England and Wales', in J. Pratt *et al.* (eds) *The New Punitiveness*. Cullompton: Willan Publishing.

Nellis, M. (2007) 'Humanising justice: the English Probation Service up to 1972', in L. Gelsthorpe and R. Morgan (eds) *Handbook of Probation*. Cullompton: Willan Publishing.

Nellis, M. and Gelsthorpe, L. (2003) 'Human rights and the probation values debate', in W.H. Chui and M. Nellis (eds) *Moving Probation Forward: Evidence, Arguments and Practice*. Harlow: Pearson Education.

Nellis, M. and Lilly, J.R. (2004) 'GPS tracking – what America and England can learn from each other', *Journal of Offender Monitoring*, 17: 5–24.

Newburn, T. (ed.) (2003) *Handbook of Policing*. Cullompton: Willan Publishing.

NOMS (2005) *NOMS Change Programme: Strategic Business Case*. London: Home Office.

NOMS (2006) *The NOMS Offender Management Model*. London: Home Office.

NOMS Property Service (2005) *Probation Estate Annual Report, 2004/05*. London: Home Office.

Norrie, K. (2005) *Children's Hearings in Scotland*. Edinburgh: W. Green.

O'Connell, B. (1998) *Solution-focused Therapy*. London: Sage.

Oldfield, M. (2002) *From Welfare to Risk: Discourse, Power and Politics in the Probation Service. Issues in Crime and Community Justice Monograph* 1. London: Napo.

O'Mahony, D. and Chapman, T. (2007) 'Probation, the state and community – delivering probation services in Northern Ireland', in L. Gelsthorpe and R. Morgan (eds) *Handbook of Probation*. Cullompton: Willan Publishing.

O'Malley, P. (1992) 'Risk, power and crime prevention', *Economy and Society*, 21: 252–75.

Padfield, N. (ed.) (2007) *Whom to Release? Parole, Fairness and Criminal Justice*. Cullompton: Willan Publishing.

Padgett, K., Bales, W. and Blomberg, T. (2006) 'Under surveillance', *Journal of Criminology and Public Policy*, 5: 61–91.

Pannick, D. (1987) *Judges*. Oxford: Oxford University Press.

Parekh, B. (2000) *Rethinking Multiculturalism – Cultural Diversity and Political Theory*. Basingstoke: Palgrave.

Parker, T. (1991) *Life after Life*. London: Pan.

Paterson, F. and Tombs, J. (1998) *Social Work and Criminal Justice. Volume 1. The Policy Context*. Edinburgh: HMSO.

Pawson, R. and Tilley, N. (1997) *Realistic Evaluation*. London: Sage.

Payne, M. (1990) *Working in Teams*. Basingstoke: Macmillan Education.

Payne, M. (2000) *Teamwork in Multiprofessional Care*. Basingstoke: Macmillan.

Pearson, F. *et al.* (2002) 'The effects of behavioural/cognitive-behavioural programmes on recidivism', *Crime and Delinquency*, 48: 476–96.

Perkins, D. (1991) 'Clinical work with sex offenders in secure settings', in C. Hollin and L. Howells (eds) *Clinical Approaches to Sex Offenders and their Victims*. Chichester: Wiley.

Piquero, A.R., Farrington, D.P. and Blumstein, A. (2007) *Key Issues in Criminal Career Research: New Analyses of the Cambridge Study in Delinquent Development*. Cambridge: Cambridge University Press.

Pitts, J. and Bateman, T. (eds) (2005) *The Russell House Companion to Youth Justice*. London: Russell House.

Plant, M. and Cameron, D. (eds) (2000) *The Alcohol Report*. London: Free Association Press.

Please, K. (2002) 'Crime reduction', in M. Maguire *et al.* (eds) *The Oxford Handbook of Criminology*. Oxford: Oxford University Press.

Power Inquiry (2006) *Power to the People* (the report of the Power Inquiry) (available online at **www.powerinquiry.org/report**).

Prime, J., White, S., Liriano, S. and Patel, K. (2001) *Criminal Careers of those Born between 1953 and 1978 in England and Wales*. Home Office Statistical Bulletin 4/01 (available online at **http://www.homeoffice.gov.uk/rds/pdfs/hosb401.pdf**).

Prins, H. (1999) *Will They Do it Again? Risk Assessment and Management in Criminal Justice and Psychiatry*. London: Routledge.

Prins, H. (2005a) 'Mental disorder and violent crime: a problematic relationship', *Probation Journal*, 52: 33357.

Prins, H. (2005b) *Offenders, Deviants or Patients?* (3rd edn). London: Routledge.

Prins, H. (2006) 'The law and mental disorder: an uneasy relationship', in K. Moss and M. Stephens (eds) *Crime Reduction and the Law*. London: Routledge.

Prior, D. (2005) 'Civil renewal and community safety: virtuous policy spiral or dynamic of exclusion?', *Social Policy and Society*, 4: 357–67.

Prison Reform Trust (2004) *England and Wales: Europe's Lifer Capital* (available online at **http://www.prisonreformtrust.org.uk/subsection.asp?id=352**).

Prison Reform Trust (2006) *Bromley Briefings: Prison Fact File* (available online at **http://www.ws3.prisonreform.web.baigent.net/uploads/documents/factfile1807lo.pdf**).

Prochaska, J.O. and DiClemente, C.C. (1982) 'Transtheoretical therapy: toward a more integrative model of change', *Psychotherapy: Theory, Research and Practice*, 19: 276–88.

Prochaska, J.O. and DiClemente, C.C. (1992) 'In search of how people change: applications to addictive behaviours', *American Psychologist*, September: 1102–14.

Prochaska, J.O. and DiClemente, C.C. (1994) *The Transtheoretical Approach: Crossing Traditional Boundaries of Therapy*. Malabar, FL: Krieger Publishing.

Putnam, R. (2000) *Bowling Alone – the Collapse and Revival of American Community*. New York, NY: Simon & Schuster.

Quinn, R.E., Faerman, S.R., Thompson, M.P. and McGrath, M.P. (2000) *Becoming a Master Manager* (2nd edn). Chichester: Wiley.

Rack, J. (2005) *The Incidence of Hidden Disabilities in the Prison Population*. London: The Dyslexia Institute (available online at http://www.dyslexia-inst.org.uk/pdffiles/Hidden%20 Disabilities%20Prison.pdf).

Radzinowicz, L. and Hood, R. (1990) *The Emergence of Penal Policy in Victorian and Edwardian England*. Oxford: Oxford University Press.

Rapoport, R.N. (1960) *Community as Doctor*. London: Tavistock.

Rassool, G.H. (2001) *Dual Diagnosis: Substance Misuse and Psychiatric Disorders.* Oxford: Blackwell Science.

Raynor, P. (2003a) 'Evidence-based probation and its critics', *Probation Journal*, 50: 334–45.

Raynor, P. (2003b) 'Research in probation: from "nothing works" to "what works"', in W.H. Chui and M. Nellis (eds) *Moving Probation Forward: Evidence, Arguments and Practice.* Harlow: Pearson.

Raynor, P. (2004) 'Rehabilitative and reintegrative approaches', in A. Bottoms *et al.* (eds) *Alternatives to Prison.* Cullompton: Willan Publishing.

Raynor, P. (2006) 'The Probation Service in England and Wales: modernised or dehumanised', *Criminal Justice Matters*, 65: 26–7.

Raynor, P., Kynch, J., Roberts, R. and Merrington, M. (2000) *Risk and Need Assessment in Probation Services: An Evaluation. Home Office Research Study* 211. London: Home Office.

Raynor, P., Roberts, C., Kynch, K. and Merrington, S. (2000) *Risk and Need Assessment in Probation Services: An Evaluation. Home Office Research Study* 211. London: Home Office.

Raynor, P. and Robinson, G. (2005) *Rehabilitation, Crime and Justice.* Basingstoke: Palgrave Macmillan.

Raynor, P. and Vanstone, M. (2002) *Understanding Community Penalties: Probation, Policy and Social Change.* Buckingham: Open University Press.

Raynor, P. and Vanstone, M. (2007) 'Towards a correctional service', in L. Gelsthorpe and R. Morgan (eds) *Handbook of Probation.* Cullompton: Willan Publishing.

Reid, G. and Kirk, J. (2001) *Dyslexia in Adults: Education and Employment.* Chichester: Wiley.

Reiss, A.J. (1971) *The Police and the Public.* New Haven, CT: Yale University Press.

Rex, S. (1999) 'Desistance from offending: experiences of probation', *Howard Journal of Criminal Justice*, 38: 366–83.

Rex, S. (2005) *Reforming Community Penalties.* Cullompton: Willan Publishing.

Rex, S. and Matravers, A. (eds) (1998) *Pro-social Modelling and Legitimacy.* Cambridge: Institute of Criminology, University of Cambridge.

Rex, S. and Tonry, M. (eds) (2002) *Reform and Punishment: The Future of Sentencing.* Cullompton: Willan Publishing.

Risk Management Authority (2005) *Risk Assessment Tools Evaluation Directory (RATED)* (available online at **www.RMAscotland.gov.uk**).

Roberts, C. (2004) 'Offending behaviour programmes: emerging evidence and implications for practice', in R. Burnett and C. Roberts (eds) *What Works in Probation and Youth Justice.* Cullompton: Willan Publishing.

Roberts, J. and Hough, J.M. (eds) (2002) *Changing Attitudes to Punishment: Public Opinion, Crime and Justice.* Cullompton: Willan Publishing.

Roberts, J. and Hough, J.M. (2005) *Understanding Public Attitudes to Criminal Justice.* Maidenhead: Open University Press.

Roberts, J. and Smith, M. (2004) 'Custody Plus, Custody Minus', in M. Tonry (ed.) *Confronting Crime: Crime Control Policy under New Labour.* Cullompton: Willan Publishing.

Robinson, G. (2003a) 'Implementing OASys: lessons from research into LSI-R and ACE', *Probation Journal*, 50: 30–40.

Robinson, G. (2003b) 'Risk and risk assessment', in W.H. Chui and M. Nellis (eds) *Moving Probation Forward: Evidence, Arguments and Practice.* London: Pearson Longman.

Robinson, G. (2005) 'What works in offender management', *Howard Journal*, 44: 307–18.

Robinson, G. and McNeill, F. (2004) 'Purposes matter: the ends of probation', in G. Mair (ed.) *What Matters in Probation.* Cullompton: Willan Publishing.

Rumgay, J. (2004) 'The barking dog? Partnership and effective practice', in G. Mair (ed.) *What Matters in Probation.* Cullompton: Willan Publishing.

Rumgay, J. (2007) 'Partnerships in probation', in L. Gelsthorpe and R. Morgan (eds) *Handbook of Probation*. Cullompton: Willan Publishing.

Sampson, R.J. and Laub, J.H. (1993) *Crime in the Making: Pathways and Turning Points through Life*. London: Harvard University Press.

Sanglin-Grant, S. (2003) *Divided by the Same Language?* London: Runnymede Trust.

Scott, P. (1977) 'Assessing dangerousness in criminals', *British Journal of Psychiatry*, 131: 127–42.

Scottish Executive (2006) *Reducing Reoffending: National Strategy for the Management of Offenders*. Edinburgh: Scottish Executive.

SED (1966) *Social Work in the Community*. Edinburgh: HMSO.

Shapland, J., Atkinson, A., Atkinson, H., Chapman, B., Colledge, E., Dignan, J., Howes, M., Johnstone, J., Robinson, G. and Sorsby, A. (2006) *Restorative Justice in Practice – Findings from the Second Phase of the Evaluation of Three Schemes. Findings* 274. London: Home Office (available online at **http://www.homeoffice.gov.uk/rds/pdfs06/r274.pdf**).

Singh, G. and Heer, G. (2004) *Recruitment, Retention and Progression: The Asian Experience within the National Probation Service* (available on request from **gurdev.singh@nottinghamshire.probation.gsi.gov.uk**).

Smith, D. (2005) 'Probation and Social Work', *British Journal of Social Work*, 35: 621–37.

Smith, D. and Stewart, J. (1997) 'Probation and social exclusion', *Social Policy and Administration*, 31: 96–115.

Smith, D. and Vanstone, M. (2002) 'Probation and social justice', *British Journal of Social Work*, 32: 815–30.

Social Exclusion Unit (2002) *Reducing Re-offending by Ex-prisoners*. London: Office of the Deputy Prime Minister (available online at **http://www.socialexclusionunit.gov.uk/downloaddoc.asp?id=64**).

Solanki, A., Bateman, T., Boswell, G. and Hill, E. (2006) *Research into the Use of Anti-social Behaviour Orders for Young People*. London: Youth Justice Board.

Soothill, K., Peelo, M. and Taylor, C. (2002) *Making Sense of Criminology*. Cambridge: Polity Press.

Spalek, B. (2006) *Crime Victims: Theory, Policy and Practice*. Basingstoke: Palgrave Macmillan.

Sparks, J.R. and Bottoms, A.E. (1995) 'Legitimacy and order in prisons', *British Journal of Sociology*, 46: 45–62.

Spencer, J. and Deakin, J. (2004) 'Community reintegration: for whom?', in G. Mair (ed.) *What Matters in Probation*. Cullompton: Willan Publishing.

Stanko, E.A. (2001) 'The day to count: reflections on a methodology to raise awareness about the impact of domestic violence in the UK', *Criminal Justice*, 1: 215–26.

Stone, N. (1999) *A Companion Guide to Enforcement* (3rd edn). Ilkley: Owen Wells.

Stone, N. (2001) *A Companion Guide to Sentencing*. Crayford: Shaw & Sons.

Sutton, C. (1999) *Social Work, Community Work and Psychology*. Leicester: British Psychological Society.

Sutton, C. and Herbert, M. (1992) *Mental Health: A Client Support Resource Pack*. NFER/Nelson.

Szasz, T. (1984) *Myth of Mental Illness*. New York: Harper Colophon.

Taylor, P. and Gunn, J. (1999) 'Homicides by people with mental illness', *British Journal of Psychiatry*, Jan 174: 564–5.

Taylor, R. (2004) *'Supporting People' – Guidance for the National Offender Management Service*. London: Home Office (available online at **www.probation.homeoffice.gov.uk/files/pdf/Commissioning%20Guidance%206.pdf**).

Taylor, R. *et al.* (2004) *Blackstone's Guide to the Criminal Justice Act 2003*. Oxford: Blackstone Press.

Thompson, N. (2006) *Anti-discriminatory Practice* (4th edn). Basingstoke: Palgrave Macmillan.

Tilley, N. (ed.) (2006) *Handbook of Crime Prevention and Community Safety*. Cullompton: Willan Publishing.

Toch, H. (1972) *Violent Men*. Harmondsworth: Penguin Books.

Together Academy *Reparation Orders* (available online at **http://www.together.gov.uk/article.asp?c=169&displayCat=no&aid=1250**).n.d.

Tonry, M. (2001) 'Symbol, substance and severity in western penal policies', *Punishment and Society*, 3: 517–36.

Tonry, M. (2004) *Punishment and Politics*. Cullompton: Willan Publishing.

Tonry, T. and Farrington, D. (1995) *Building a Safer Society*. Chicago, IL: University of Chicago Press.

Travis, A. (2006) 'Offenders' anger control classes help make some more dangerous', *Guardian*, 24 April: 4.

Trotter, C. (1999) *Working with Involuntary Clients*. London: Sage.

Trotter, C. (2004) *Helping Abused Children and their Families: Towards an Evidence Based Treatment Model*. London: Sage.

Tuckman, B.W. (1965) 'Development in small groups', *Psychological Bulletin*, 63: 384–99.

Turnbull, P.J., McSweeney, T., Webster, R., Edmunds, M. and Hough, M. (2000) *Drug Treatment and Testing Orders: Evaluation Report*. Home Office Research Study 212. London: HMSO.

Tyler, A. (1995) *Street Drugs*. London: Hodder & Stoughton.

Tyler, T. (2003) 'Procedural justice, legitimacy and the effective rule of law', in M. Tonry (ed.) *Crime and Justice: A Review of Research. Volume 30*. Chicago, IL: University of Chicago Press.

Underdown, A. (1998) *Strategies for Effective Offender Supervision: Report of the HMIP What Works Project*. London: Home Office.

van Kalmthout, A. and Derks, J. (eds) (2000) *Probation and Probation Services – a European Perspective*. Nijmegen: Wolf Legal Publishers.

van Kalmthout, A., Roberts, J. and Vinding, S. (eds) (2003) *Probation and Probation Services in the EU Accession Countries*. Nijmegen: Wolf Legal Publishers.

Vanstone, M. (1985) 'Moving away from help? Policy and practice in probation day centres', *Howard Journal*, 24: 20–8.

Vanstone, M. (1993) 'A "missed opportunity" reassessed: the influence of the day training centre experiment on the criminal justice system and probation practice', *British Journal of Social Work*, 23: 213–29.

Vanstone, M. (2000) 'Cognitive-behavioural work with offenders in the UK: a history of influential endeavour', *Howard Journal*, 39: 171–83.

Vanstone, M. (2003) 'A history of the use of groups in probation work. Part One. From "clubbing the unclubbables" to therapeutic intervention', *Howard Journal*, 42: 69–86.

Vanstone, M. (2004) 'Mission control: the origins of a humanitarian service', *Probation Journal*, 51(1): 34–47.

Vanstone, M. (2004a) 'A history of the use of groups in probation work. Part two. From negotiated treatment to evidence-based practice in an accountable service', *Howard Journal*, 43: 180–202.

Vanstone, M. (2004b) *Supervising Offenders in the Community: A History of Probation Theory and Practice*. Aldershot: Ashgate.

Ville, R., Zvekic, U. and Klaus, J. (1997) *Promoting Probation Internationally*. Rome and London: United Nations Interregional Crime and Justice Research Institute.

von Hirsch, A. (1993) *Censure and Sanctions*. Oxford: Oxford University Press.

von Hirsch, A. and Roberts, J. (2004) 'Legislating sentencing principles: the provisions of the Criminal Justice Act 2003 relating to sentencing purposes and the role of previous convictions', *Criminal Law Review*, 639–52.

Wahidin, A. and Cain, M. (eds) (2006) *Ageing, Crime and Society*. Cullompton: Willan Publishing.

Walker, N. (ed.) (1996) *Dangerous People*. Oxford: Blackstone Press.

Walklate, S. (2004) *Gender, Crime and Criminal Justice* (2nd edn). Cullompton: Willan Publishing.

Walters, J. (2003) 'Trends and issues in probation in Europe.' Paper delivered to the PACCOA conference, Hobart, Tasmania, 1 September (available online at **http://www.paccoa.com.au/**).

Ward, T., Polaschek, D.L.L. and Beech, A.R. (2006) *Theories of Sexual Offending*. Chichester: Wiley.

Watkins, T., Lewellen, A. and Barrett, M. (2001) *Dual Diagnosis: An Integrated Approach to Treatment*. London: Sage.

Weber, M. (1968) *Economy and Society: An Outline of Interpretative Sociology* (ed. G. Roth and C. Wittich). New York, NY: Bedminster Press.

Whitehead, P. and Statham, R. (2006) *The History of Probation: Politics, Power and Cultural Change, 1876–2005*. Crayford: Shaw & Sons.

Whitehead, P. and Thompson, J. (2004) *Knowledge and the Probation Service: Raising Standards for Trainees, Assessors and Practitioners*. Chichester: Wiley.

Whitfield, D. (2001) *Introduction to the Probation Service*. Winchester: Waterside Press.

Widom, C. and Maxfield, M. (2001) 'An update on the cycle of violence', *National Institute of Justice Research in Brief*, February: 1–8 (available online at **http://www.ncjrs.gov/pdffiles1/ nij/184894.pdf**).

Wilcox, A. and Hoyle, C. (2004) *The National Evaluation of the Youth Justice Board's Restorative Justice Projects*. London: Youth Justice Board (available online at **http://www.yjb.gov.uk/ Publications/**).

Williams, B. (2005) *Victims of Crime and Community Justice*. London: Jessica Kingsley.

Williams, B. and Goodman, H. (2007) 'Working for and with victims of crime', in L. Gelsthorpe and R. Morgan (eds) *Handbook of Probation*. Cullompton: Willan Publishing.

Willis, A. (1986) 'Help and control in probation: an empirical assessment of probation practice', in J. Pointing (ed.) *Alternatives to Custody*. Oxford: Blackwell.

Wilson, S. (2005) *Death at the Hands of the State*. London: Howard League for Penal Reform.

Worrall, A. and Hoy, C. (2005) *Punishment in the Community: Managing Offenders, making choices* (2nd edn). Cullompton: Willan Publishing.

Youth Justice Board (1999) *National Standards for Youth Justice*. London: YJB.

Youth Justice Board (2004) *National Standards for Youth Justice*. London: YJB.

Youth Justice Board (2006) *Youth Justice Annual Statistics, 2005/06*. London: YJB.

Zamble, E. and Quinsey, V.L. (1999) *The Criminal Recidivism Process*. Cambridge: Cambridge University Press.

Index

Note: Words represented in **bold** indicate main Dictionary entries. Words represented in ***bold italics*** do not necessarily appear elsewhere in the Dictionary but provide cross-references to main entries.

'Accelerate' 303
Accommodation *see* **Supporting People**
see also approved premises
    funding 199, 307
    inter-agency work 143
    OASys 185
accountability 1–2
    discretion and 94
    internal audit 144
    partnerships 100
    staff supervision 302–3
    targets and 1
accreditation panel – *see* **Correctional Services Accreditation Panel**
accredited programmes 2–4 *see also* Correctional Services Accreditation Panel; groupwork
    achievements and problems 3
    attrition 23–4
    audits 63
    Criminal Justice Act 2003 3
    criteria for 63
    development of 2–3
    effectiveness 258
    evaluation 122
    future of 3–4
    groupwork 131–2
    implementation failure 114–15
    learning disabilities 150
    learning styles 151
    motivation and 167
    OASys 184
    programme requirement 51
    research results 114–15
    responsivity 270–1
    in Scotland 281
    staff supervision 313–14
    supported desistance 91–2
    targets 3
    treatment model 113
    women offenders 330

accredited programmes in common use 4–6 *see also* sex offender treatment programmes (SOTPs)
    groupwork 131–2
ACE (Assessment and Case Evaluation System) 18, 277
Action Plans
    accommodation and 308
    development of 202, 248, 298
    inter-agency work 114
    introduction of 298
    Probation Circular 49/2005 248
    recommendations of 248
    responsibility for 176
actuarialism 6–7, 16, 17, 274 *see also* OASys (Offender Assessment System)
    criticisms of 205
addressing substance related offending (ASRO) 5 *see* **Accredited Programmes in common use**
ADHD (attention deficit and hyperactivity disorder) 110
Adult Literacy Inspectorate 111
African probation 228–30
Aftercare – *see* **resettlement**
age of consent 164
age–crime relationship 68–9, 90, 130, 195
aggravating factors 70, 79, 249
aggression replacement training (ART) 5 *see* **Accredited programmes in common use**
alcohol 7–9
    alcohol requirement 52
    alcoholism 8–9, 311
    drink impaired drivers (DIDs) 5, 131
    dual diagnosis 107–8
    electronic monitoring (EM) 116
    missionaries 65
    OASys 185
    offender substance abuse programme (OSAP) 5
    treatment 8–9, 180
alternative dispute resolution (ADR) *see* **mediation**
alternatives to custody 52, 113 *see* **Community**

penalties; Punishment in the community
anamnestic assessment 16
Anger management 5, 325 *see* Accredited
    Programmes in common use
anti-discriminatory practice 9–11
    criminogenic needs 75–6
    to diversity 96
    groupwork 131
anti-poverty measures 210–11
anti-social behaviour 11–12 *see also* prosocial
    modelling
    anti-social behaviour orders 11–12
    breach of 23
    criminal careers and 68
Anti-social Behaviour Act 2003 11, 80
anti-social personality disorder 108, 206
Anti-terrorism, Crime and Security Act 2001 134
appraisal see staff supervision
approved premises 12–14
    bail hostels 264
    Criminal Justice Act 2003 148
    Criminal Justice and Court Services Act 2000 12
    deaths 219
    estate strategies 121–2
    privatization 219–20
    residence requirement 51–2
    suicide 304
    types of offender 148
arbitration 162
area child protection committees (ACPCs) 37
arson 73
Asian communities 174
Asian offenders
    criminogenic needs 76
    women offenders 329
Asperger syndrome 24–5
ASPIRE 14–15, 33, 188–9, 191
assessment 16 *see also* risk assessment
    alcohol problems 8
    ASPIRE 14
    child protection 192–3
    specialist 186–7
Assessment, Care in Custody and Teamwork
    (ACCT) plans 193
assessment instruments and systems 17–19 *see also*
    assessment
    inaccuracies in 7, 274–5, 277–8
    new developments 142
    sex offenders 293, 294
    types of 277
    women offenders 330
ASSET 18
Association of Black Probation Officers (ABPO)
    19–20

Association of Chief Officers of Probation (ACOP)
    20–1, 36, 224
    Management Information Strategy 140
asylum 21–2, 89
attendance centres 22–3
Attorney General 72, 80
attrition 23–4
    accredited programmes 23–4
    criminal justice system 23
Audit Commission 62, 125 *see* External Audit
Auditing Practices Board (APB) 125
audits *see* external audit; internal audit
Australia, restorative justice 163
autism 24–5
awards *see* Butler Trust

bail / bail information see remand services
basic skills see education skills for life
behavioural change *see* cognitive-behavioural; cycle
    of change; motivational interviewing
behaviourism 45
Better Lives 295
bifurcation 26–7
black and minority ethnic (BME) offenders 27–9
    criminogenic needs 76
    policy development 19
    research 96
    women offenders 329
Borstal 17, 29–30
Breach see enforcement; compliance
British Crime Survey (BCS) 23, 98, 103, 246
Bulger case 286
burglary 68, 73
Butler Trust 30–1

C-NOMIS 43–5, 176, 177, 190
CAFCASS *see* Children and Family Court Advisory
    Support Service (CAFCASS)
CALM (controlling anger and learning to manage it)
    5, 325 *see* Accredited Programmes in
    Common Use
Cambridge Study in Delinquent Development 68
Canada probation 2, 232–3
    restorative justice 163, 272
*CARAT (Counselling, Advice, Referral, Assessment
    and Through Care)* services 106, 217
    Workers *see* Prison Probation teams
care/control 168
Carlisle Committee 1990 26
Carter Report (2004) 32–3
    Butler Trust and 30–1
    case management 33
    contestability 32, 61
    financial penalties 127

offender management 188
persistent offenders 204
recommendations of 175–6
responses to 173
seamless sentences 155
case management 33–4
case managers 33, 192
core elements 192
National Probation Service Information Systems
  Strategy (NPSISS) 140
offender/supervisor relationship 167, 194
punish, help, change and control 190
case records 34–5
C-NOMIS 43–5
data protection 86
diversity 146
interim case record 142
Catalyst think-tank 219
'catch and convict' 55
cautions 73, 265, 273
gender and 130
Central After-care Association 29
Central Council of Probation Committees (CCPC)
  21, **35–6**, 224
Central Probation Council 36
change, cycle of 83–4
Chicago School 77
chief officers 36–7
accountability 1, 144, 179, 227
Association of Chief Officers of Probation
  (ACOP) 20–1
Criminal Justice and Court Services Act 2000 224
local safeguarding children boards (LSCBs) 37
responsibilities of 226
status of 224
child abuse 98
child curfews 80
child protection 37–9
framework for assessment 192–3
home visits 138
local safeguarding children boards (LSCBs) 37–8,
  198
priority of 193
Children Act 1908 331–2
Children Act 1989 37 *see* CAFCASS
Children Act 2004 37–8, 317
children and families of offenders 39–40
conciliation 59–60
criminal careers 68–9
family group conferences 50, 272, 273
home visits 138
mediation 163
**Children and Family Court Advisory Support
  Service (CAFCASS) 40–1**, 65, 163, 172

Children and Young Persons Act 1933 286
Children (Scotland) Act 1995 282
Children's hearings see **Youth Justice in Scotland**
children's homes 286
Church of England Temperance Society (CETS) 36
circuit judges 149
citizenship 42–3, 51
civil renewal 42
co-morbidity **107–8** *see* **dual diagnosis**
cognitive-behavioural 45–7 *see also* accredited
  programmes in common use; prosocial
  modelling
vs. desistance studies 92–3
domestic violence 99
effectiveness 63, 113
enforcement and 120
motivation and 167
OASys 185
outcomes 46–7
solution-focused work 300–2
women offenders 330
combination orders 53 *see* **community penalties;
  community order; supervision of offenders;
  unpaid work**
Commission on the Future of Multi-ethnic Britain
  (CFMEB) 95
Commissioning see **contestability; Carter Report;
  NOMS; offender management**
Communications Officers Group 178
communicative theories 251–3
community 47–9 *see also* community justice; crime
  and disorder reduction partnership;
  reintegration; social capital; social exclusion
  community domestic violence programme 5–6 *see*
    Accredited Programmes in Common Use
  Crime and Disorder Act 1998 47
  definitions 47–8, 53
  desistance and 91–2
  home visits 138
  social capital 48
  terminology 254
community justice 43, **49–51**, 241
community orders 51–2
community penalties and 72
Criminal Justice Act 2003 51
duration of 305
learning disabilities 150
requirements 51–2, 220, 305
Community Payback 147, 181, 319
community penalties 52–4
community orders and 72
compliance 56–9, 65
Criminal Justice Act 1991 53
history of 52–3

public opinion 246
  as punishment 253–4
  suitability for 185–6
community punishment and rehabilitation orders
    23, 51 *see* unpaid work; community
    penalties; community order
community punishment order see unpaid work
community rehabilitation centres 87
community rehabilitation orders 23, 52, 87, 330 *see*
    supervision of offenders; community
    penalties; community order
community safety 54–5, 143 *see also* crime and
    disorder reduction partnerships
Community Safety Partnerships 66, 180
community service orders 52 *see* unpaid work
  in Africa 229
  in Europe 231
  in Scotland 286
Community – Sex offender Group Programme
    (C-SOGP) 295
compensation orders 127, 246, 285
competition *see* contestability
complaints 55–6, 80
  Prisons and Probation Ombudsman 218–19
Completion see attrition
compliance 56–9
  enforcement and 57, 120–1
  legitimacy and 57, 152–4
  in North America 233
  offender/supervisor relationship 167, 194
concept maps 347–51
conciliation 59–60, 136, 162–3
Concilliation and Arbitration Service (ACAS) 136
conditional cautions 265
Conférence Permanente Européenne de la Probation
    see (CEP) 60–1, 117, 230
Constitutional Affairs 165
contestability 32, 61–2, 74, 176
  in Carter Report 61–2
  evaluation of 62, 198
  investment in 62
  Napo response 173
  PBA view 224–5
continuity 190
control theories 78, 90
Coopers & Lybrand 140, 141
correctional agencies 73
Correctional Services Accreditation Panel 2, 4,
    62–4, 131
Council of Europe 60, 64–5, 166, 230
counselling styles *see* motivational interviewing
Court of Appeal 149
court work 65–6
  adjournment times 213

deportation 88–9
  history of 65
  judges 149
  numbers of reports 201
  review process 65
  standard delivery reports 65 *see also* pre-sentence
    reports (PSRs)
CRAMS 140, 142 *see* C-NOMIS
Crime and Disorder Act 1998 see crime and disorder
    reduction partnerships; DTTO; YOTs
  anti-social behaviour 11
  community 47
  community safety partnerships 66
  crime and disorder reduction partnerships 66
  drug treatment and testing orders (DTTOs) 106
  extended sentencing 125
  local authorities 157
  partnerships 34
  racially motivated offences 134
  reparation orders 272
  Youth Justice Board (YJB) 332
  youth offending teams (YOTs) 143, 331, 334
crime and disorder reduction partnerships 66–7
  community representatives 47, 48
  Correctional Services Accreditation Panel 62–3
  Crime and Disorder Act 1998 66
  DATs and 100
  effective practice and 114
  funding 2
  hate crime 134
  initiatives 73
  local authorities 66, 143, 157
  members of 66, 199
  prolific and other priority offenders (PPOs) 204,
    242
  research 266
  responsibilities of 199
  responsibility for 165
  social crime prevention 54
  targets 3
crime prevention 67–8
  community safety 54–5
  framework for 67
  inter-agency work 143
  key risk factors 69
  situational 67
Crime (Sentences) Act 1997 196, 324
criminal careers 68–70, 185, 325
Criminal Courts Act 1973 12
Criminal Courts (Sentencing) Act 2000 22, 286–7
Criminal Justice Act 1948 12
Criminal Justice Act 1967 124, 196
Criminal Justice Act 1991 70–1 *see also* Halliday
    Report

community penalties 53
financial penalties 127
HMI Probation 136
National Standards 182
Parole Board 196
previous convictions 70
probation as penalty 220
proportionality 70, 253
PSRs 213
risk of serious harm 276
violent offenders 324–5
women offenders 329
Criminal Justice Act 2003 71–2
accredited programmes 3
approved premises 148
community orders 51
community rehabilitation centres 87
custody provisions 81–2
dangerousness 72
drug treatment and testing orders (DTTOs) 106
extended sentencing 125
hate crime 134
indeterminate sentences 72, 197
lifers 196
MAPPAs (multi-agency public protection arrangements) 170
persistent offenders 204
preventative sentences 85
previous convictions 71
proportionality 71
PSRs 213
reparation 251, 265
risk of serious harm 85, 248
seamless sentences 155
sentencing framework 81–2
Sentencing Guidelines Council (SGC) 290–1
seriousness 71, 291
sex offenders 293
supervision of offenders 306
suspended sentences 71
unpaid work 147, 317
Criminal Justice and Court Services Act 2000 see
  National Probation Service; Probation
  Boards; CAFCASS
approved premises 12
CAFCASS 40
chief probation officers 224
creation of 179
HMI Probation 136
inter-agency work 143
MAPPAs (multi-agency public protection arrangements) 170
Probation board secretaries 226
probation board treasurers 226

probation boards 222, 223–4
risk of serious harm 276
supervision 305
victim contact 321
criminal justice boards 72–3, 222
Criminal Justice Information Technology 178
criminal justice interventions teams (CJITs) 106
Criminal Justice Reform 121, 165
criminal justice system 73–4
attrition 23
chivalry hypothesis 130
CJITs (criminal justice interventions teams) 106
collaboration 121
crime prevention and 67
joint inspectorates 137
Ministry of Justice 165–6
Criminal Procedures (Scotland) Act 1995 283, 284
Criminal Records Bureau 118–19
criminal responsibility, defences to 164
criminogenic needs 74–6
interventions and 146–7
most common 117
needs principle 113, 147
OASys 185–6
triangle of offender needs 314–15
criminology 76–9
crisis intervention see solution-focused approaches
critical few 171
Crown Court 65, 73, 149 see Judges
Crown Office and Procurator Fiscal Service 285
Crown Prosecution Service (CPS) 73, 79–80
culpability 71
cultural discrimination 9
curfews 80–1 see also electronic monitoring (EM)
breach of 23
curfew orders 53
exclusion zones 312
numbers of 80
responsibility for 147–8
in Scotland 286
tracking 312
current offender, terminology 119
Custody Minus 81–2 see Custody Plus, Intermittent
  Custody and Custody Minus
Custody Plus 81–2
postponments 71, 133
resettlement 269
terminology 119
custody provisions 81–2
cycle of change 58, 83–4, 167

dangerousness 85–6 see also risk of serious harm
Criminal Justice Act 2003 72

dangerous and severe personality disorder 206 *see* personality disorder
  extended sentencing 72, 124, 125
  variables 85
  sentencing; MAPPAS (multi-agency public protection arrangements); public protection; risk assessment and management; risk of harm; sexual offenders; violent offenders.
data protection 35
Data Protection Act 1998 86–7, 129
Day Centres 87–8
Day Training Centres – see **Day Centres**
Debt see **poverty**
Department for Education and Skills (DfES) 118
Department of Communities and Local Government 54
deportation 88–9
desistance 90–2
  main life events 69
  motivation and 167
  offender/supervisor relationship 167, 194
  theories of 69, 90–1
desistance studies 92–3
determinate-sentence prisoners 196
deterrence 250 *see* **punishment: aims and justifications**
deviance theories 77, 78, 90
DipPS (Diploma in Probation Studies) see **probation training; Practice Development Assessor; Regional Training Consortia**
Director of Probation 179
discharge without punishment 70
disclosure of personal information 86, 118–19, 321
discretion 73, **94**, 121, 182
discretionary conditional release (DCR) cases 197
discrimination *see* **anti-discriminatory practice; racism**
district judges see **magistrates**
diversion see **mentally disordered offenders**
diversity 95–7
  anti-discriminatory practice and 10
  criminogenic needs and 75–6
  criminology and 78
  in Europe 231
  fairness and 28
  inspection programme 137
  interpreting and translation 144–6
  legitimacy and 154
  motivation and 167
  National Standards 182
  risk principle 277–8
  victims 323
domestic violence 97–9
  CAFCASS 41

child protection 38
community domestic violence programme 5–6
conciliation 59
integrated domestic abuse programme (IDAP) 6, 131
victims 323
Domestic Violence, Crime and Victims Act 2004 322
double jeopardy 71
drink impaired drivers (DIDs) 5, 131
Drink Impaired Drivers Programme (DIDs) see **Accredited Programmes in Common Use**
drug action teams (DATs) 99–101 *see also* Drugs Intervention Programme (DIP)
  accountability 100
  chief probation officers 180
  inter-agency work 143
  members of 100, 106
  partnerships 66
  responsibilities of 99
drug rehabilitation requirement (DRR) 101–2
  completion rates 107, 180
  introduction of 51
drug treatment and testing orders (DTTOs) 106–7
  completion rates 180
  introduction of 51
  management of 192
  replaced by drug rehabilitation requirement 101
  in Scotland 286
drugs 102–5
  addressing substance related offending (ASRO) 5
  drug courts 107
  dual diagnosis 107–8
  key group tests 180
  OASys 185
  Offender Substance Abuse Programme 131
  offender substance abuse programme (OSAP) 5
  therapeutic communities 311
Drugs Intervention Programme (DIP) 99, **105–6**, 193
dual diagnosis 107–8, 164
dyslexia 108–9, 110
dyspraxia 110

early release see **licence**
education, skills for life 110–12 *see also* Employment, Training and Education (ETE)
  benefits from 117–18
  inter-agency work 148
  targets 117, 180
effective practice 112–15 *see also* cognitive-behavioural; Correctional Services Accreditation Panel
  accredited programmes 2, 4, 113
  attrition 23–4

diversity and 75
Effective Supervision Inspection Programme 136
evaluation 122–4, 267
'Every case is a project' 190
National Standards 182
principles of 113, 147
reconviction rates 257–8
research and 114–15, 266
responsibility for 136
in Scotland 281
teamwork 309–10
electronic monitoring (EM) 115–17
compliance 116
debates and issues 53
expansion of 80
providers 170
tracking 312
Employment, Training and Education (ETE)
117–19
basic skills 110–12, 117
employment levels 211
inter-agency work 118, 148
end-to-end management see offender management;
resettlement
enforcement 120–1
compliance and 56–9, 121
court work 65
financial penalties 128
inspection programme 137
inter-agency work 199
licence and 155
Enhanced Community Punishment programmes 3,
63, 147, 243, 318–19 see also unpaid work
'Enhanced Thinking Skills' 4 see Accredited
Programmes in common use
equal opportunities 10, 147
ESOL (English for speakers of another language) 112
estate strategies 121–2
Europe
Convention on Human Rights 64, 316
Ministry of Justice 165
penal policy 230
Prison Rules 64
European Court of Human Rights 64, 138
European Excellence Model see evaluation
European Foundation for Quality Management
(EFQM) 160
European probation 60–1, 64, 116, 230–2
evaluation 122–4
research and 266
evidence-based practice see effective practice
extended sentencing 72, 85, 124–5, 196
external audit 125–6

fairness 28, 153
families of offenders see children and families of
offenders; Children and Family Court
Advisory Support Service (CAFCASS)
Family Court see CAFCASS
Family Court Welfare Service (FCWS) 40
fast delivery reports (FDRs) 213–14
fear of crime 54, 72, 130, 325
Feltham Young Offender Institution 169
feminism
criminology 78, 96–7
domestic violence 98–9
financial penalties 127–8
poverty and 210
in Scotland 285
forced marriages 97
4 Cs 190, 305–6
France 165
Freedom of Information Act 2000 86, 128–9

gay men
domestic violence 98
heterosexism 135–6
masculinity and 161–2
staff association 154–5
gender 130–1 see also masculinity; women offenders
anti-discriminatory practice 96–7
criminology 78
offending rates and 130, 329
risk principle 277
suicide and 303
transgender 312–13
Gender Recognition Act 2004 313
gene for crime 77
General Offending programmes 3
German Ministry of Justice 165
groupwork 131–2
day centres 87
teamwork 309–10
therapeutic communities 311
guilty pleas 291

Halliday Report 2001 133–4
generic community sentences 51, 133
prison population 291
proportionality 71, 133
short prison terms 81
Hanson and White case 137, 248, 276, 292
Hare Psychopathy Checklist 294
hate crime 134–5, 257, 323
Criminal Justice Act 2003 134
HDC (Home Detention Curfew) see prison
probation programmes; curfew;
electronic monitoring

hearsay evidence 71
heterosexism 134, **135–6**, 161–2
high court judges 149, 284–5
High Court of Justiciary 284
higher risk offenders 13, 85, 124–5
HIV 105
HM Inspectorate of Probation 136–7
  case records 35
HM Inspectorate of Probation (*continued*)
  *An Independent Review of a Serious Further
    Offence* 292
  public protection 248
  racially motivated offenders 96
  rights of 1
  Towards Race Equality 28
  Valuing the Victim 322
Home Office
  Confident Communities 48
  Crime, Justice and Protecting the Public 70
  Criminal Justice - the Way Ahead 204
  Every Child Matters 6
  Justice for All 82, 133
  Penal Policy in a Changing Society 30
  Public Value Partnerships 61, 62, 176
  Reducing Crime: Changing Lives 175, 176
  Research Development and Statistics Directorate
    177, 178
  responsibilities of 165
  Restructuring Probation to Reduce Reoffending
    237
  Statement of National Objectives and Priorities
    181–2
  Tackling Drugs Together 99
home visits 138
homophobia see **heterosexism**
honour crimes 97
hostels see **approved premises; supporting role**
human rights 138–9
  European Convention 64, 316
  types of 139
  Universal Declaration of Human Rights 316
Human Rights Act 1998 42, 64, 138–9

immigration 21–2, 89
Immigration Act 1971 88
Incapacitation see **punishment: aims and
    justifications**
indeterminate sentences 85, 155, 196, 197 *see also*
    lifers
  Criminal Justice Act 2003 72, 197
Information and Library Management Group 177
Information Commissioner 86
information exchange 177–9

information sharing *see* inter-agency work:
    information sharing
information strategy 140–1
information technology developments in areas
    44–5, **141–2**
institutional racism 10, 157–8, 170 *see* **Macpherson;
    race and racism**
integrated domestic abuse programme (IDAP) 6 *see*
    Accredited Programmes in Common Use
Intensive Supervision and Surveillance Programme
    334
inter-agency work 142–4 *see also* drug action teams
    (DATs); MAPPAs (multi-agency public
    protection arrangements); partnerships
  hierarchy of models 193
  information sharing 6, 38, 39, 44, 143
  offender management as seen by other agencies
    192–3
  Probation Circular 52/2004 39
  teamwork 309–10
interactionist theories of desistance 91
intermittent custody 71, **81–2** *see* **Custody Plus,
    Intermittent Custody and Custody Minus**
internal audit 126, **144–5**
International Criminal Victimization Survey 246
interpreters 145–6
intersex 313
interventions 146–8
  case management 33–4
  effectiveness 258
  evaluation 122–4
  minimum intervention approach 201
  responsivity 270–1
  'wrap around' services 192

Jobcentre Plus 170
Joint Prison/Probation Services Accreditation Panel
    2
judges 149
  judicial independence 166
  review process 101
  in Scotland 284–5
jury trials 71, 73
just deserts model 70, 201 *see* **punishment: aims and
    justifications**
justice model see **punishment: aims and
    justifications**
juveniles see **young offenders**

Keith Report (2006) 96
Key Performance Indicators see **performance
    management**
Kilbrandon Committee (1964) 283
Knowledge management see **information strategy**

labelling 77
LAGIP (lesbians and gay men in probation) 134–5,
   154–5
Lawrence, Stephen 134 *see* **Macpherson Report
   (1999)**
Learning and Skills Council (LSC) 118, 148
learning disabilities 150–1 *see also* autism; dyslexia
   in prison population 110
   sex offender treatment programmes (SOTPs) 295
learning styles 151–2
   motivation and 167
   prosocial modelling 244
   responsivity 270
legitimacy 152–4
   compliance and 57, 152
lesbians
   domestic violence 98
   heterosexism 135–6
   staff association 154–5
LGBT (lesbians, gay men, bisexuals and transgender)
   see **heterosexism; transgender; LAGIP**
   people 135–6
licence 155
   breach of 81, 155
   extended sentencing 125
   home visits 138
   resettlement 268–9
   suicide 304
   victim awareness 323
lifers 156
   Criminal Justice Act 2003 196
   oral hearings 196
   recalls 196
   release 196
literacy deficits 110–11
'Living Leadership' 303
local authorities 157
   community safety 54
   crime and disorder reduction partnerships 66,
      143
   duty to co-operate 170
   estate strategies 121
   Supporting People 307
local safeguarding children boards (LSCBs) 37–8,
   198
Lombroso, Cesare 76–7
Lord Advocate 285
Lord Chancellor 72, 165
Lord Chief Justice 290
LSI-R (Level of Service Inventory-Revised) 18

Macpherson Report (1999) 158–9
   institutional racism 10, 158

magistrates 65, 73, 101, **159**
male victims, domestic violence 98
Management of Offenders (Scotland) Act 2005 282
managerialism 160–1
   case management 34
   human rights and 139
   probation values and 240
   training and 236
manslaughter, provocation and 291
**MAPPAs (multi-agency public protection
   arrangements)** 170–1
   child protection 38
   community representatives 143
   intensive interventions 275
   priority of 193
   Probation Circular 10/2005 247–8
   public protection cases 247
   reasons for 192
   reintegration 263
   resettlement 268–9
   sex offenders 293
   statutory requirements 198
   teamwork 309–10
Marx, K. 298
masculinity 78, 98, **161–2**
maturational reform theories 90
mediation 41, **162–3**, 272 *see also* conciliation
   in Europe 230–1
Mental Health Act 1959 245
Mental Health Act 1983 163, 206
mentally disordered offenders 163–5 *see also* dual
   diagnosis
   Care Programme Approach 193
   drug use 104
   mental health requirement 52
   personality disorder and 206
   risk principle 277
   self-harm 287–8
   therapeutic communities 311
   victim contact 321–2
mentors 327
meta-analysis see **effective practice; evaluation;
   research**
minimum wage 211
Ministry of Justice 165–6
minority groups *see* **diversity**
miracle questions 301
miscarriages of justice 74
Misuse of Drugs Act 1971 104
mitigating factors 28, 70, 79, 109, 164
money payment supervision orders see **financial
   penalties**

monitoring 122 *see* evaluation; supervision
Morrison Report 1962 35
motivation 166–8 *see also* desistance
   compliance and 57–8
   cycle of change **83–4**
   hate crime 135–6
   importance of 192
   offender/supervisor relationship 167, 194
   responsivity 270–1
   review process 101
motivational interviewing 58, **168–9**, 300–2
Mubarek Inquiry 44, **169–70**
murder *see also* lifers
   gender and 97
   homicidal seriousness 71
   mentally disordered offenders 164
   sex offenders and 293
   trial for 73
   young offenders 286–7

N-SOGP 296
Naaps (National Association of Asian Probation
   Staff) **173–5**
Napo 172–3
   anti-discriminatory practice 240
   probation service officers 235
National Association of Probation Officers 172
National Asylum Support Service (NASS) 22
National Audit Office (NAO) 125, 141 *see* **External
   audit**
National Criminal Justice Board 72
National Drug Strategy 99 *see also* Drugs
   Intervention Programme (DIP)
National Objectives and Standards (Scotland)
   280–1
National Offender Management Information System
   (NOMIS) 141
National Probation Directorate
   Data Standards Unit 178
   effective practice 136
   estate strategies 122
   The Heart of the Dance 96
   Interventions Unit 3
   local governance and 224
   *Management Statement and Financial
     Memorandum* 228
   Performance and Planning Unit 178
   role of 179, 180
   serious further offences (SFOs) 292
**National Probation Research and Information
   Exchange (NPRIE) 177–9**
**National Probation Service for England and Wales
   179–81**
   accountability 1

   complaints 55–6, 218–19
   effectiveness 52
   estate strategies 122
   information strategy 140–1
   public protection priority 247
   reforms 203
   resource allocation 277
   targets 179–80, 247
National Probation Service Information Systems
   Strategy (NPSISS) 140
National Probation Service Service Information
   Management Strategy (NPSIMS) 141
National Standards 181–2
   case records 35
   enforcement 120
   home visits 138
   introduction of 201
   PSRs 213
   recalls 120–1
   serious offenders 79
   supervision 299
National Treatment Agency (NTA) 99, 180 *see* **Drug
   Intervention Programme**
   Models of Care 105
needs principle 113, 147 *see also* criminogenic needs
neo-correctionalist model 201, 334
new penology *see* **actuarial justice**
new public management (NPM) 160
New Zealand, restorative justice 163, 272
NOMIS (National Offender Management
   Information System) 141
**NOMS (National Offender Management Service)
   175–7** *see also* offender management
   aims of 175, 215
   creativity 259
   establishment of 32, 175
   future of 224
   information strategy 140, 141
   Napo response 173
   Public Protection Unit 246–7, 292
   Reducing Re-offending National Action Plan 23,
     118, 248, 298, 308
   teamwork 310
non-custodial disposals 52
North American probation 232–3
Northern Ireland
   electronic monitoring (EM) 116
   probation board 225–6
   restorative justice 273
'nothing works' 266

**O-DEAT (OASYS Data Evaluation and Analysis
   Team) 16, 183–4**

OASys (Offender Assessment System) 184–7
  C-NOMIS and 44
  criminogenic needs 147
  literacy deficits 111
  number of records 16, 176
  Probation Circular 48/2005 248
  risk management plan 247–8
  self-harm 287
  sentence plans 186, 289
  sex offenders 294
  suicide 303
  User Group 177
  validation 18, 183
  victim awareness 320
offender/ex-offender, terminology 119
Offender Learning and Skills Service (OLASS) 118
offender management 188–91 *see also* offender
      management as seen by other agencies;
      Offender Management Model
  deportation 89
  evaluation 176
  induction 111
  information strategy 141
  interventions and 146
  Offender Management Inspection Programme
      136
  offender managers 235, 289, 290
  terminology 188, 192
offender management as seen by other agencies
      192–3
Offender Management Bill 2007 203, 238
Offender Management Model see offender manage-
      ment
  alternatives to 192
  core elements 192
  evaluation 176
  impact of 191
  IT systems 176
  offender journey 188–90
  priority of 193
  tiering 190, 289–90, 305
offender perceptions 75, 194–5
offender substance abuse programme (OSAP) 5 *see*
      Accredited Programmes in Common Use
Offenders' Learning and Skills Service (OLASS) 148
OGRS (Offender Group Reconviction Scale) 17, 258,
      277 *see* assessment instruments
older offenders 156, 195
'One-to-One' programme 3, 5 *see* Accredited
      programmes in common use
oral hearings 196–7
oral reports 213

paedophiles 292–3
Parole Board 196–7
parsimony principle 250
partnerships 197–200 *see also* crime and disorder
      reduction partnerships
  accountability 100
  case management and 33–4
  contestability 61
  Crime and Disorder Act 1998 34
  desistance 91
  drug rehabilitation requirement (DRR) 101–2
  'Public Value Partnerships' 61, 62, 176
  teamwork 309–10
Pathfinders 2, 191, 266, 267 *see* evaluation
pathways to reducing re-offending 39, 75, 269
penal policy 200–1
  bifurcation 26–7
  citizenship 43
  in Europe 230
  populist punitiveness 208–9
  public attitudes and 1
performance management 201–3 *see also* National
      Standards
  criminal justice boards 72
  Data Standards and Reporting Group 177
  holistic framework for assessing quality 203
  inspection and 136
  managerialism 160–1
  performance bonus 1, 179–80, 202
  Performance Improvement Programme 136
persistent offenders 69, 204–5
personal discrimination 9
personal reduction in substance misuse (PRISM) 5
      see Accredited Programmes in Common Use
personality disorder 205–7 *see also* mentally
      disordered offenders; psychopathy
  assessment instruments and systems 294
  dual diagnosis 107–8, 164
PFI (public-private partnership) strategy 122
planning stage 14
Plato 7
police 207–8
  arrest-referral services 106
  cautions 130
  collaboration with 181, 207–8
  discretion 73
  diversity and 96
  institutional racism 10, 158, 170
  inter-agency work 143
  legitimacy 152–3
Police Reform Act 2002 100
populist punitiveness 27, 208–10
poverty 210–11, 298

power, legitimacy and 152–3
practice development assessors (PDAs) 211–12
pre-sentence reports (PSRs) 212–15
   black and minority ethnic (BME) offenders 28
   categories of cases 79
   complaints 218–19
   literacy deficits 111
   OASys 184
   Probation Circular 18/2005 187, 213
   risk assessment 214, 278
   role of 70, 74
   template 187
   victim awareness 323
'prevent and deter' 54–5
preventative sentences 85
Prevention of Crime Act 1908 29
preventive detention 124, 242
previous convictions 70, 71
principal probation officers 36–7
prison 215–17 *see also* prison probation teams
   accredited programmes 217–18
   aims and justification 250
   Assessment, Care in Custody and Teamwork
      (ACCT) plans 193
   child population 332
   complaints 218–19
   costs of 176, 215
   duty of care 303–4
   learning disabilities 110
   legitimacy and 153
   older offenders 195
   personality disorders 206
   population increase 215, 216, 253, 254, 269–70,
      291
     privatization 219
   public/private pay 219
   resettlement units 269
   therapeutic communities 311
   wages 195
   women offenders 329
   young offenders 331
prison probation teams 217–18
Prisons and Probation Ombudsman 56, 218–19
private law cases 41
private prisons 176
privatization 4, 219–20
probation 220–2
   definitions of 220
   history of 220
   offender management and 221
   as penalty 220
   terminology 220, 221
Probation Board for Northern Ireland (PBNI)
   225–6

probation board secretaries 226–7
probation board treasurers 227–8
probation boards 222–3
   accountability 1, 144
   budgets 62
   complaints 55–6
   estate strategies 122
   local safeguarding children boards (LSCBs) 37
   partnership budgets 62, 199–200
   regional training consortia 260
   replacement for 237
   serious further offences (SFOs) 292
   youth offending teams (YOTs) 335
Probation Boards' Association (PBA) 36, 223–5,
   237–8
Probation Circular 32/2000, regional training
   consortia 260
Probation Circular 62/2001, victim contact 321
Probation Circular 02/2004, suicide 304
Probation Circular 52/2004, information sharing 39
Probation Circular 10/2005, MAPPAs 247–8
Probation Circular 18/2005, PSRs 187, 213
Probation Circular 41/2005, regional training
   consortia 260
Probation Circular 48/2005, OASys 248
Probation Circular 49/2005, Action Plans 248
Probation Circular 59/2005, research 267
Probation Circular 63/2005, Children Act 2004 38
Probation Circular 24/2006, immigration 89
Probation Circular 37/2006, asylum 89
probation committees 35, 224
probation in Africa 228–30
probation in Canada 2, 232–3
   restorative justice 163, 272
Probation Circulars see National Probation Service
Probation Committees see Central Council of
   Probation Committees
probation in Europe 60–1, 64, 116, 230–2
probation in Northern Ireland 116, 225–6, 273
Probation of Offenders Act 1907 221
Probation of Offenders (Scotland) Act 1931 280
probation officers 233–4 *see also* probation service
   officers; senior probation officers (SPOs)
   advise, assist and befriend 234, 299
   Asian staff 174
   continuing professional development 260
   legitimacy 153–4
   Napo and 172–3
   offender/supervisor relationship 91–2, 167, 194,
      299, 305–6 *see also* prosocial modelling
   staff supervision 302–3
   values 95
   youth offending teams (YOTs) 335
Probation Officer's Manual (Jarvis) 318

Probation Ombudsman see **Prison and Probation Ombudsman**
probation orders 52–3, 220, 253
  in Scotland 286
Probation Rules 1926 36
Probation Rules 1937 36
Probation Service see **National Probation Service for England and Wales**
probation service officers 234–5
probation training 235–7
  continuing professional development 236–7, 302
  diversity 96
  practice development assessors (PDAs) 211–12
  public protection 248
  Probation Studies 233
  qualifications 172, 235–6
  regional training consortia 260–1
  responsibility for 136
  responsivity 271
  social work 300
probation trusts 203, 237–8
probation unions *see* **Association of Black Probation Officers (ABPO); Napo**
probation values 239–41
  diversity 95
  human rights and 139
  practice guide 173
PROBIS 140
procurators fiscal 285
programme integrity see **accredited programmes; effective practice; interventions; research**
Programme Reducing Individual Substance Misuse see **Drug rehabilitation requirement**
prohibition 7
Project Quality Assurance Board 177
prolific and other priority offenders (PPOs) 241–3
  approved premises 148
  community justice and 50–1
  definitions of 204
  Drugs Intervention Programme (DIP) 106
    Intensive Supervision and Surveillance Programme 334
  national strategy 208
  PPO strategy 54–5, 180
  priority of 193
  prolific offender projects 207–8
  responsibility for 199
prosocial modelling 243–4
  civic participation and 91–2
  court work 65
  examples of 318
  motivation and 167
  solution-focused work 300–2

psychology *see* **cognitive-behavioural**
psychopathy/psychopathic disorder 244–5 *see also* **mentally disordered offenders; personality disorder**
public attitudes to probation 245–6 *see also* **punishment in the community**
  criminal justice boards and 72–3
  inter-agency work 143
  penal policy and 1
  populist punitiveness 208–9
public protection 246–9 *see also* **community safety; dangerousness; risk of serious harm**
  action plans 248
  approved premises 13
  dangerousness **85**
  employment and 118
  extended sentencing 196
  failure of 300
  indeterminate sentences 196, 197
  inter-agency work 143
  licence and 155
  lifers 156
  OASys 186
  priority of 193
  protective sentencing 125
  Public Protection Unit 246–7
  targets 247
punishment, aims and justifications 249–51
  Criminal Justice Act 1991 70–1
  financial penalties 128
  public attitudes to probation 245–6
  rehabilitative punishment 262
  reparation 265
punishment as communication 251–3
punishment in the community 253–4

quality assurance framework 123–4

racially motivated offenders 256–7 *see also* **Macpherson Report (1999); Mubarek Inquiry**
  Crime and Disorder Act 1998 134
  hate crime and 134
  probation officers and 96
  victims of 323
racism 255–6 *see also* **racially motivated offenders**
  Asian staff 174–5
  criminogenic needs 76
  elimination of 96
  institutional racism 10, 157–8, 170, 255–6
  pre-sentence reports (PSRs) 28
  racist incidents 157
rape 73
Raymond v. Honey (1983) 43

Reasoning and Rehabilitation see **accredited**
    programmes
Rebalancing Sentencing 188
recalls 29, 120–1, 197 *see* **enforcement; licence**
reconviction 257–9
    financial penalties 128
    OASys 185
    OGRS (Offender Group Reconviction Scale) 17
    predicting 17, 258
    prolific and other priority offenders (PPOs) 242
    rates of 81–2
    re-offending and 257–8
recorders 149
Reducing Re-offending National Action Plan
    accommodation and 308
    development of 202, 248, 298
    inter-agency work 114
    Probation Circular 49/2005 248
    Reducing Re-offending Delivery Plan 39
    responsibility for 176
reductivism 249–50
referral orders 23, 272, 334
refugees 21
regional offender managers (ROMS) 257–60
    partnerships 199, 259–60
    performance management 203
    regional reducing re-offending delivery plans 269
    role of 176, 223, 259–60
    serious further offences (SFOs) 291
regional reducing re-offending delivery plans 269
regional staff development units 260
regional training consortia 260–1, 314
rehabilitation 261–2
    aims and justification 250
    criminogenic needs **74–6**, 147
    Halliday Report 133
    licence and 155
    'nothing works' 266
    'rehabilitate and resettle' 55
    prolific and other priority offenders (PPOs) 242
Rehabilitation of Offenders Act 1974 263
reintegration 262–3
    community and 49
    community rehabilitation orders 87
    long-term change and 167–8
    resettlement 268–70
reintegrative shaming 272
relationships 185
release on licence 74
remand services 65, 73, 80, **263–4**
reparation 265 *see also* restorative justice
    breach of orders 23
    community boards 50
    Crime and Disorder Act 1998 272

Criminal Justice Act 2003 251, 265
    in Scotland 286
reprimands 73
requirements see **community order**
research 266–8 *see also* effective practice; O-DEAT
    (OASYS Data Evaluation and Analysis Team)
    critical success factors 147
    developmental theories 69
    empirical methods 17
    evaluation 122–4
    evaluation as 122–3
    NPRIE 177–9
    offender perceptions 194
    quality assurance framework 123–4
    researchers 123
Research Officer Group 178
resettlement 268–70
    licence and 155, 268–9
    Supporting People 307–8
responsivity 113, 244, **270–1**
responsivity principle 147
restorative justice 271–4 *see also* reparation
    aims and justification 251
    citizenship and 43
    human rights and 139
    mediation and 163
    restorative justice model 201
    victim needs 324
    youth justice 334
retribution /retributivism 70–1, 133, 204, 249, 253
    see **punishment: aims and justifications**
revocation see **enforcement; licence; parole**
Rice case 137
risk assessment 274–5 *see also* actuarialism
    home visits 138
    inaccuracies in 274–5, 277–8
    inter-agency work 143
    models 17–18
    risk society 278–9
    types of cases 196
risk management 274–5
    home visits 138
    inter-agency work 143
    levels of 170–1
    risk management plans 247–8, 275
    risk principle 277–8
Risk Matrix 2000 293, 294
risk minimization 6
risk of harm 276–7
    categories of 247
    inspection programme 137
risk of serious harm *see also* dangerousness; public
    protection
    Criminal Justice Act 1991 276

Criminal Justice Act 2003 85, 248
Criminal Justice and Court Services Act 2000 276
definitions of 276
levels of 186
MAPPA categories 170–1
OASys 186, 247–8
sentencing 248
'serious' 247
risk principle 113, 147, 277–8
risk society 6, 278–9
Roberts's triangle see triangle of offender needs
robbery 68, 73, 325
robbery, reduction strategy 73
ROTL (release on temporary licence) see prison
    probation teams

safeguarding children see child protection
Safer Cities Programme 143
scaling 302
Scotland
    Community Justice Authorities 282
    compensation orders 285
    drug treatment and testing orders (DTTOs) 107
    electronic monitoring (EM) 116
    National Strategy on Offender Management 282
    Prison Service guidance 303–4
    prosecutions 285
    restorative justice 273
    Risk Management Authority 275, 281
    Social Work (Scotland) Act 1968 280
Scotland, courts and sanctions 284–6
Scotland, criminal justice social work 280–2
Scotland, youth justice 282–4, 334
seamless sentences 155
Section 90/91 offenders 286–7
self-assessment 186
self-harm 65, 186, 287–8
senior probation officers (SPOs) 1, 288–9
sentence plans 289–90 *see* sentence management
see also criminogenic needs
    child protection 38
    lifers 156
    OASys 186, 289
    prolific and other priority offenders (PPOs) 242
    Self-assessment Questionnaire 306
    triangle of offender needs 314–15
sentencing *see also* Criminal Justice Act 1991;
    Criminal Justice Act 2003; Halliday Report
    2001
    bifurcation 27
    Criminal Justice Act 1991 70, 253
    Criminal Justice Act 2003 71, 81–2
    levels of 53

parsimony principle 250
populist punitiveness 208–9
proportionality 70–1, 133, 204, 249, 253, 277
risk of serious harm 248
unduly lenient sentences (ULS's) 79–80
Sentencing Advisory Panel 290–1
Sentencing Guidelines Council (SGC) 290–1
    aims of 72, 290
    community orders 51
    establishment of 133, 188, 290
    prison population regulation 32
    requirements 305
serious further offences (SFOs) 291–2
serious offenders 137, 204–5
    Criminal Justice Act 2003 71, 291
sex offender treatment programmes (SOTPs)
    294–6
    learning disabilities 150
sex offenders 292–4
    approved premises 13
    Community Sex-offender Groupwork Programme
      132
    dangerousness 85
    extended sentencing 124–5
    licence 155
    MAPPA categories 170
    reconviction 257, 293
    sentencing 70–1, 133, 248
    victim contact 321–2
Sexual Offences Act 2003 293
shoplifting 68
Skills for Life *see* education, skills for life
Smith and West case 197
social capital 296–7
    poverty and 210–11
    reintegration 263
social exclusion 297–9
    community safety 55
Social Exclusion Unit 269, 298
social inclusion see social exclusion
social inquiry reports (SIRs) 212–13 *see* pre-
    sentence report
social justice 10, 42
social learning theory see **cognitive behavioural**
social services, duty to co-operate 170
social work 299–300
    advise, assist and befriend 234, 299
    in North America 233
    in Scotland 280–1
    values and 240
Social Work (Scotland) Act 1968 280
Society of Voluntary Associates (SOVA) 326–7
sociological perspectives 77–8

solution-focused work 300–2
South African Development Community 228–30
special victim advocates 321
Spousal Abuse Risk Assessment (SARA) 6
staff supervision 1, 302–3, 313–14, 318
standard delivery reports (SDRs) 65, 214
Statement of National Objectives and Priorities /
  Statements of Local Objectives and Priorities
  (SNOP / SLOP) see **National Standards**
stereotypes 9
'Straight Thinking on Probation' (STOP) 2
strain theories 77
Street Crime Initiative 73
street robbery 325
structural discrimination 9
Structured Assessment of Risk and Need (SARN)
  293
substance abuse 5, 83
substances see alcohol; drugs
suicide 303–4
  Assessment, Care in Custody and Teamwork
    (ACCT) plans 193
  complaints 219
  gender and 303
  as offence 164
  self-harm and 287
summary offences 73
supervision of offenders 304–7
  breach of orders 23, 52
  importance of 189
  numbers of offenders 49, 201
  offender perceptions 194
  offender/supervisor relationship 91–2, 167, 194,
    234, 299, 305–6 *see also* prosocial modelling
  optimistic language 301
  personality disorder 206–7
  responsibility for 306
  risk principle 277–8
  in Scotland 285–6
  sentence plans *see* sentence plans
  solution-focused techniques 301–2
  suicide 304
  supervision plan 167–8, 199–200, 289
  supervision requirement 52
Supporting People 307–8
  inspection programme 137
  inter-agency work 143
surveillance see electronic monitoring; MAPPA;
  tracking
suspended sentences 52, 53, 71 *see* **Custody Plus,**
  Intermittent Custody and Custody Minus

tagging 115–16
tariff dates 156
targets see performance management
task-centred see solution-focused
teamwork 309–10
Thames Valley – Sex Offender Group Programme
  295
theft 73
therapeutic communities 206, 311
'Think First' programme 3, 4–5, 168 *see* Accredited
  programmes in common use
Throughcare see resettlement; sentence plan
tiers see offender management; MAPPA
tracking 312
training *see* probation training
transgender 134–5, 312–13
translation 145–6
transsexual see transgender
transvestite see transgender
Treasury Counsel 80
treatment managers 313–14
triangle of offender needs 314–15

unduly lenient sentences (ULS's) 79–80
unemployment, crime and 117
United Nations 316
  child definition 331
  Convention on Refugees 21
  Convention on the Rights of the Child 229, 332
unpaid work 317–19
  community punishment orders 51
  Criminal Justice Act 2003 147, 317
  number of hours 147
  public opinion 246
  as punishment 254
  reparation 265
  in Scotland 285
  social capital and 297
  women offenders 330
USA probation 232–3
  community justice 50
  restorative justice 272
  tracking 312

victim awareness 320–1
victim contact 155, 321–2
  Probation Circular 62/2001 321
victims 322–4 *see also* restorative justice
  conciliation 59–60
  empowering 67
  human rights and 139
  reparation 265

special victim advocates 321
Victim's Charter 321, 322, 323
Victim Support 323
violent offenders 324–6
  accredited programmes 69, 325
  dangerousness 85
  extended sentencing 124–5
  licence 155
  Male Violence Programme 132
  MAPPA categories 170
  masculinity and 162
  mentally disordered offenders 164
  persistent offenders 326
  prevention 69
  sentencing 248
  sentencing proportionality 133
  theories of 325
  victim contact 321–2
  women offenders 329
  young offenders 286–7
voice verification 115
volunteers 326–7
  accredited programmes 4
  budgets for 199
  in Europe 231

weekend imprisonment 81
welfare model 201
welfare of children see **child protection; children and**
  families of offenders
welfare reports 41
Welsh Courts Act 1942 328
Welsh language 328–9
'What Works' *see* effective practice
Williams case 137
women offenders 329–30
  acquisitive crime programme 5
  anti-discriminatory practice 96–7
  compared with men 130
  criminology 78
  diversity 96–7
  lifers 156
  older offenders 195
  risk principle 277
  violent offenders 325
  Women's Programme 132

women victims
  black and ethnic minorities 98
  community domestic violence programme 5–6
  domestic violence 38, 97–8, 130
Women's Acquisitive Crime Programme see
  Accredited Programmes in Common Use
Women's Aid 97
Woolf, Lord Chief Justice 165
'Working Together to Safeguard Children' 37, 38

young offenders 331–2
  anti-social behaviour orders 11
  attendance centres 22–3
  criminal careers and 68–9
  in custody 335
  family group conferences 50, 273
  licence 155
  masculinity and 162
  maturational reform theories 90
  in North America 232–3
  persistent offenders 204
  Persistent Young Offender Pledge 73, 334–5
  prevent and deter 242
  referral orders 272, 334
  reparation orders 265
  risk factors 69
  in Scotland 282–4, 334
  section 90 and 91 286–7
  self-assessment 18
  unpaid work 317
  young offender institutions 286
Youth Inclusion Programme 6
youth justice see YOT, Youth Court, YJB
Youth Justice and Criminal Evidence Act 1999 272
Youth Justice Board (YJB) 332–3
  accountability 332, 335
  assessment instruments and systems 18
  attendance centres 23
Youth Offending Service 286
youth offending teams (YOTs) 333–5
  Crime and Disorder Act 1998 143, 331, 334
  duty to co-operate 170
  establishment of 331, 333–4
  inspection programme 136–7
  management of 157
  prevent and deter 242
  specialist skills 198–9